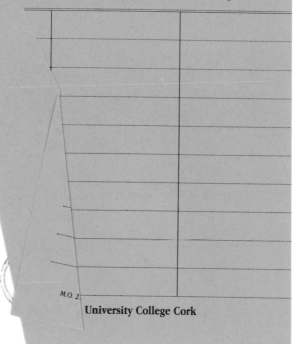

Quality of Life Research

Quality of Life Research

A CRITICAL INTRODUCTION

Mark Rapley

SAGE Publications
London • Thousand Oaks • New Delhi

First published 2003

SAGE Publications Ltd
6 Bonhill Street
London EC2A 4PU

SAGE Publications Inc
2455 Teller Road
Thousand Oaks, California 91320

SAGE Publications India Pvt Ltd
B-42, Panchsheel Enclave
Post Box 4109
New Delhi, 100 017

British Library Cataloguing in Publication data

A catalogue record for this book is
available from the British Library

ISBN 0 7619 5456 2
ISBN 0 7619 5457 0 (pbk)

Library of Congress Control Number: 2002107101

Typeset and designed by GCS, Leighton Buzzard, Beds.
Printed in Great Britain by Athenaeum Press, Gateshead.

CONTENTS

LIST OF FIGURES AND TABLES

Figures

Tables

A P O L O G I A

Let us begin by seeing the assessment of quality of life in practice. In the extracts below, transcribed from recordings of the administration of Schalock and Keith's (1996) *Quality of Life Questionnaire*, we see how the moment-by-moment interaction of quality of life assessors and assessees produces scores on a standardized QOL measure.[1] Each question has three response options, scored 1, 2 and 3.

Extract 1

Interviewer	D'you feel out of place out an' about in social situations?
Anne	No
Interviewer	Anne? Never?
Anne	No
Interviewer	Sometimes?
Anne	No
Interviewer	Or usually?
Anne	Sometimes I do
Interviewer	Yeah? OK, we'll put a two down for that one then

Extract 2

Interviewer	Oh right, OK then, right then, so Arthur would say that your life brings out the best in you?
Arthur	Brings out the best in you
Interviewer	Or treats you like everyone else?
Arthur	Anybody else
Interviewer	Or doesn't give you a chance?
Arthur	Uh er treats yer uh uh all alright
Interviewer	The same as everyone else? You the middle one?
Arthur	Yeers.

These sorts of exchanges, typical of the administration of *any* quality of life questionnaire (Houtkoop-Steenstra, 2000), suggest that assessment of quality of life – whatever the designers of questionnaires, or the writers of survey manuals, say – is, *in practice*, far from straightforward.

If we are to get a firm grip on quality of life research, and become informed practitioners, we need to be aware of both the positive findings, persuasive theories and impressive-looking measures, and also of the practical and theoretical difficulties inherent in the ideas, concepts and assessment methods of the area. This book introduces – and offers a critical reflection upon – social scientific research on QOL, outlining those persuasive theories, impressive measures and positive findings, but also warning against uncritical acceptance. The intention is to equip students with an understanding of the main approaches to quality of life research, and the conceptual-analytic tools needed to become discerning 'consumers' of the literature. Much of this book is designed to *show*, as well as *tell*, how such a critical engagement might proceed. To support the development of a critical stance, each chapter ends with study questions.

We take as a guide Michel Foucault's (1985: 8) observation on the purpose of knowledge:

> What would be the value of the passion for knowledge if it resulted only in a certain knowingness ... and not, in one way or another ... in the knower's straying afield from himself ... the question of knowing if one can think differently than one thinks, and perceive differently than one sees, is absolutely necessary if one is to go on thinking and reflecting at all.

We'll put a two down for that one then.

Note

1. Data are drawn from Rapley and Antaki (1996). Transcription is simplified.

PREFACE

quality *n.* 1. a characteristic, property or attribute. 2. high grade; superior.
of *prep.* A particle indicating 5, a relation of identity.
life *n.* 1. Condition which distinguishes animals and plants from inorganic
objects and dead organisms … 5, course or mode of existence.
(Macquarie Dictionary, 1992)

In 1990 the leading ethnographer of the lives of people with intellectual disabilities,[1] Robert Edgerton, suggested that the term 'Quality of Life' was the 'shibboleth of the 1990s' (1990: 149). The term 'shibboleth' implies not only the importance of the concept, but also the contentious nature of the field and the potential upshot of QOL research. In public life, and the social sciences, the notion of QOL has come – since the 1960s – to be a routinely invoked concept. The term appears in the discussion of everything from the relative 'liveability' of towns, cities and nations to the aims and effects of social policy, from the relative benefits of differing models of human service provision to the individualized outcomes of a vast number of medical and psychotherapeutic practices.

This is not to suggest that questions about what constitutes a life of quality, or what the characteristics, properties or attributes of such a life might be, only began in the 1960s. As Socrates famously noted, the unexamined life is one unworthy of living (Plato, 1903). Much of Western philosophy and literature since can be read as an extended response to his questions about life's quality and qualities. While some might dismiss such endeavours as frippery produced in 'a playground for philosophical speculation' (Veenhoven, 1997), the upshot of such questioning has always been practical and serious – both historically and in the present. The Nazi conceptualization of a life of quality entailed the idea of 'life unworthy of life' – an idea that warranted the 'euthanasia' of people with intellectual disabilities, the chronically ill, and the inmates of mental hospitals by German doctors and psychiatrists in the 1930s and 1940s (Gilbert, 1986: 239). Currently, the idea that it is possible to *quantify* the *quality* of a life – to establish numerical parameters for the relative value of lives with particular qualities – is a warrant for the selective abortion of particular foetuses (Kuhse and Singer, 1985), the provision (or not) of life-sustaining medical interventions (Nord, 1999) and, in some jurisdictions, 'physician-assisted suicide' for those whose quality of life is 'pointless and empty' (Sheldon, 2000: 1174).

It is in the contemporary social sciences that the most sustained efforts have been made to define, describe and understand quality of life. In their 1996 literature review Antaki and Rapley (1996a) identified over 2,500 journal articles specifying 'quality of life' as a keyword in the preceding three years. Hughes *et al.*'s (1995) survey identified 44 separate definitions between 1970 and 1993. Cummins (1997a: 1–2) noted 'well in excess of 100 definitions and models ... some are clearly representative of others while some are cast in such vague or inclusive terminology that their heuristic value approaches zero'. The electronic archives of the *British Medical Journal* identify 702 articles with 'quality of life' in their titles between 1994 and 2001. Muldoon *et al.* (1998: 542) state that 'over 1000 new articles a year are indexed under "quality of life"'. Entering 'quality of life' into Google returned no fewer than 'about' 3, 410, 000 webpages! QOL is, evidently, a concept of powerful – if not pervasive – resonance in contemporary life. Yet the very popularity of the concept (and use as a 'lay' rather than 'technical' term) has resulted in a fragmented literature. The literature is, furthermore, a site of considerable controversy over issues ranging from the adequacy of QOL as a scientific construct, to the meaningfulness of QOL measurement and the social policy relevance of QOL measures.

To add to the confusion the various social scientific literatures conduct their own QOL debates in isolation from each other, and sub-areas within each field show little appreciation of work in adjacent specialisms. In the developing field of health-related QOL (HRQOL) separate, and condition-specific, measures of HRQOL exist for almost every problem for which there is a medical specialty. Multiple QOL measures exist for kidney disease and end-stage renal failure specifically (Cagney *et al.*, 2000; Wu *et al.*, 2001; Martin and Thompson, 2001); for acne (Klassen *et al.*, 2000; Martin *et al.*, 2001); for head and neck cancer (Hammerlid and Taft, 2001); for respiratory disease (De Vries *et al.*, 2000) – with a number of asthma-specific measures (Ehrs *et al.*, 2001); for epilepsy (Ergene *et al.*, 2001); for vertigo (Prieto *et al.*, 1999); and for genital herpes (Spencer *et al.*, 1999). There are even QOL measures to assess the QOL of parents whose children have problems – for instance toddlers with motor disorders (Hendriks *et al.*, 2000).

Given such fragmented – often contradictory – literatures there is, says leading QOL researcher Bob Cummins, no hope of a comprehensive overview. He suggests that 'the literature is now too vast for any individual researcher to fully assimilate' (1997b: 118). Hence this book is selective. QOL is placed in its historical and cultural context; concepts underpinning QOL as a global construct are outlined; definitional controversies and commonalities across disciplines are discussed; and an introduction to key evaluative methods and tools – purpose, potential and limitations – across a range of sites is provided. My approach to the identification of exemplary studies – or, as it lacks the connotation of excellence, *illustrative* studies – is guided by Silverman's (1997) recommendation that *aesthetic criteria* be accorded a central place in the evaluation of social scientific research.

[...]volumes have been written about how theoretical or political positions (either implicit or explicit) shape the research task ... Such positions have relatively little to do with many researchers' sense of what constitutes a 'worthwhile' research problem, 'interesting data' or a 'compelling' analysis ... I believe that the most important impulse has more to do with our tacit sense of the sort of appearance or shape of a worthwhile piece of research. In that sense research is informed by an aesthetic. (Silverman, 1997: 239)

Accordingly I discuss pieces of research that offer what ethno-methodologists would describe as *perspicuous instances*. That is, work discussed has been selected by virtue of its capacity to illustrate with clarity, simplicity and economy (cf. Wittgenstein, 1961) major conceptual and methodological issues in QOL research. Each chapter concludes with suggestions for further reading, and a list of questions for further study. The Resources section (Appendix 3 page 249) lists sites providing starting points for further research, journals to consult and texts which provide more detailed guidance on various research approaches.

The book is divided into two parts: In Part 1, Chapters 1–3 offer a critical overview of key philosophical, conceptual and methodological issues. These chapters draw widely on QOL literatures across disciplines and population groups. Chapter 4 offers a review of methodological issues in quantitative and qualitative QOL research, with a discussion of the strengths and weaknesses of the principal methodological tools. The promises and pitfalls of these methods are illustrated with reference to specific QOL instruments and research approaches. Part 2 illustrates the application of the principles, concepts and methodologies discussed in Part 1. These chapters demonstrate work at a range of levels – from the analysis of social policy to service outcome research – with reference to population groups where QOL research is most developed. These chapters offer 'worked examples' of QOL research, and illustrate the diversity of approaches to the topic. The aim is, after Wittgenstein, a 'showing' rather than a 'telling'. The areas covered highlight controversial issues identified in Part 1. Thus, discussion of the adequacy of QOL as a scientific construct in Chapter 2 is picked up in Chapter 5 by an illustration of how the work of Foucauldian thinkers offers a deeper appreciation of the relationship between social scientific studies of QOL and their cultural context. Chapter 6 unpacks the ethical debate in Chapter 3 by a detailed analysis of HRQOL research. The discussion of conceptual issues in the development of generic versus population-specific QOL measures in Chapter 4 is illustrated in Chapter 7 by empirical work on these topics. Chapter 8 analyses recent developments in the psychological literature and Chapter 9 offers a recapitulation of the main themes and a response to criticisms of the philosophy, theory and practice of QOL research in the literature. Directions for research are identified.

Note

1. I use the term 'intellectual disability (-ies)' to refer to people also known as people with learning difficulties (UK) and people with mental retardation (USA).

ACKNOWLEDGMENTS

I am grateful to Charles Antaki, Steve Beyer, Bob Cummins, Hanneke Houtkoop-Steenstra, Ken Keith, John Lobley, Alec McHoul, Jim Ridgway and Bob Schalock for their analytic perspicuity, friendship, advice, discussions, disagreements and generous practical assistance. Susan Hansen has made it all possible.

I thank Bob Cummins, Mike Salvaris, Robert Schalock, the American Association on Mental Retardation and the World Health Organization for permission to reproduce copyright material.

Note

This book draws on some of my earlier work and extends analyses previously published. Chapter 3 draws on Rapley, M. (2001) Policing Happiness, in Newnes, C., Holmes, G. and Dunn, C. (eds) *This is Madness Too*. Ross-on-Wye, PCCS Books and McHoul, A. and Rapley, M. (2002) "Should we make a start then?": A strange case of a (delayed) client-initiated psychological assessment, *Research on Language and Social Interaction*, 35, 1: 73–91. Chapter 4 draws upon Antaki, C. and Rapley, M. (1996). Questions and answers to psychological assessment schedules: hidden troubles in 'Quality of Life' interviews, *Journal of Intellectual Disability Research*, 40, 5: 421–37; Rapley, M., Ridgway, J. and Beyer, S. (1998) Staff:staff and staff:client reliability of the Schalock and Keith (1993) Quality of Life Questionnaire, *Journal of Intellectual Disability Research*, 42, 1: 37–43. Chapter 5 extends Rapley, M. and Ridgway J. (1998). Quality of Life talk: the corporatisation of intellectual disability. *Disability and Society*, 13, 3: 451–71. Chapter 9 develops Antaki, C. and Rapley, M. (1996). "Quality of Life" talk: The liberal paradox of psychological testing. *Discourse and Society*, 7, 3: 293–316 (by the kind permission of Sage Publications Ltd 1996).

This book is for Ella and Tom.

PART ONE – THEORY

Introduction – Where Has QOL Come From?

> My nominee for the key issue in the study of language and the brain during the first century of the third millennium is a concept that is slippery, burning, neglected, and crucial. That concept is definition and measurment of quality of life. (LaPointe, 2001: 135)

> The quality of life construct has a complex composition, so it is perhaps not surprising that there is neither an agreed definition nor a standard form of measurement. (Cummins, 1997a: 6)

This chapter offers a historical overview of the development of the concept of 'quality of life' in both public life and as an object of study in the social and human sciences. Drawing extensively on the work of Kenneth Land, Heinz-Herbert Noll and Michael Salvaris, I outline the development of the QOL construct, from being a social scientific index of the relative well-being of whole populations (a measure of the state of states) to being a measurable aspect of individual subjective experience (an index of the state of persons). The intention is not to produce a 'Whig' history[1], but to examine the relations between ideas of what QOL might be across what are usually termed 'levels of analysis': that is as a property of both individual persons *and* human collectivities.

QOL as the State of States

It is important to begin by placing the idea of quality of life (or QOL) into historical context. To do so we must suspend both our ordinary or commonsense understandings of what the term 'quality of life' means, and also formal operational definitions of the idea in the social scientific literatures (see Kendall and Wickham, 1999: chapter 1). For, as Mike Salvaris (2000: 4) suggests in his account of the social indicators movement in Australia:

> Political economists from Hobbes to Marx have observed that 'the most powerful instrument of political authority is the power to give names and to enforce definitions' (Chorover, 1979); and in western society since the Industrial Revolution, there has been no more potent idea to be defined (and thus harnessed) than the idea of progress. This idea, with its connotations of destiny and inevitability, has become almost 'the meta

narrative of history' (McLintock, 1992) – legitimating political power, elevating those who define and interpret it, and providing a unifying theme for the policies of nations.

Writing in 1996, Veenhoven suggested:

> 'In the first half of this century, quality-of-life in nations was largely measured by the material level of living. The higher that level in a country, the better the life of its citizens was presumed to be ... quality-of-life was measured by GNP related measures, currently by 'real' GDP per head ... Yet in the 1960's, the opinion climate changed ... This gave rise to a call for broader indicators of quality-of-life, which materialized into the so called 'Social Indicator' movement. (Veenhoven, 1996: 1)

While accurate in terms of its chronology, such an account – falling as it does into historicist fallacy – shows just how 'slippery' the notion of QOL can be. Clearly, if in the first half of the twentieth century it was the GNP, or 'the material level of living', that was gauged, then it was not 'quality of life' that was being measured. What Veenhoven's account suggests then is that it is possible – as indeed he himself points out later in his paper – to (re)define (or 'give a name to' as Chorover put it) almost *any* social statistic or collection of social statistics as 'QOL'.

Cummins attributes the coining of the term quality of life in its 'modern form' as a characteristic of persons *as well as* an indication of national prosperity, to a 1964 speech by President Johnson in which he is reported to have stated that *progress* on social goals 'cannot be measured by the size of our bank balance. They can only be measured by the quality of the lives our people lead' (Cummins, 1997b: 117). Similarly Noll (2000) suggests that: 'as early as in 1964 former U.S. President Lyndon Johnson stated: "the great society is concerned not with how much, but with how good – not with the quantity of goods but with the quality of their lives"'. The idea of quality of life as a measurable indicator of the 'great society's' achievements has, since its inception, been inseparable from the notion of progress. With an elegant symmetry, in the social sciences, as in political economy, 'the most powerful instrument of [political] authority is the power to give names and to enforce definitions'.

The development of a 'modern', or *individualized*, notion of QOL was neither immediate nor inevitable. Noll (2000) points to the development of two contrary conceptualizations of quality of life, one being a Scandinavian view based in the works of writers such as Drenowski (1974), Erikson and Uusitalo (1987) and Erikson (1993), centred on notions of the 'good society' and of social well-being as a welfare issue. In this work welfare is conceived of as based in access to resources by which people can control and direct their 'level of living' and, in the provision of which, public policy may have leverage. Erikson and Uusitalo (1987: 189) specify the resources citizens require in order to secure their own welfare:

'resources are defined in terms of money, property, knowledge, psychic and physical energy, social relations, security and so on'. In consequence Scandinavian thinking focuses exclusively on *objective indicators* of the level of living, or quality of life, of society as a whole.

However, as Noll notes, what he terms 'the American quality of life' approach commands more of a consensus in the 'Western' world. In this model, quality of life research – or welfare measurement – is primarily based in the assessment of *subjective indicators* at the level of individual citizens. Noll (2000) suggests of the 'American' model that

> in the tradition of the utilitarian philosophy and 'mental health research' ... this approach ultimately defines welfare as subjective well-being. The most important indicators of subjective well-being used, actually, are measures of satisfaction and happiness.

So where has the idea of 'quality of life' come from? Along with Cummins, Veenhoven and Noll, Land (2000) locates the beginnings of QOL in the 'social indicators movement' of the 1960s. The impetus, it is claimed, was the joint efforts of a NASA and the American Academy of Arts and Sciences project to predict the societal effects of the space race (Land, 1983; Noll and Zapf, 1994). Noll (2000) describes the origin of the movement thus:

> [...] social indicators research was created in the United States in the mid-1960s ... The project came to the conclusion that there was almost a complete lack not only of adequate data but also of concepts and the methodology for this purpose. Presumably it was Raymond Bauer, the director of the project, who also invented the term and concept of 'social indicators' [Bauer, 1966: 1]. In his definition, social indicators were 'statistics, statistical series, and all other forms of evidence that enable us to assess where we stand and are going with respect to our values and goals'.

Land (2000) points out that what came to be called the 'social indicators movement' by 1969 had much earlier progenitors. Carley (1981) has suggested that large scale formalization of interest in measures of the state of states was part of a broader trend towards the organization of national social, economic and demographic information that began in Western societies during the Enlightenment. This trend was consolidated through the seventeenth and eighteenth centuries and accelerated dramatically over the course of the twentieth century. Such a view resonates with Foucault's work (1973, 1977, 1978) on the rise of governmentality, surveillance and the individual subject in the emerging nation states over the same period. It is regrettable that while much current societal-level QOL work appreciates its own political relevance (for example, Veenhoven (1996) considers that his proposed measure of 'Happy Life Expectancy'

(HLE) would have 'political appeal'), most leading QOL researchers are dismissive of poststructuralist readings of the development of social indicators and their transformation into devices of individual surveillance (Cummins, 2001a).

Early in the development of such indicators Land (1975) points to the activities of the Chicago school in the 1930s and 1940s, specifically the work of Ogburn on the theory and measurement of social change and his responsibility for the production, in 1933, of *Recent Social Trends in the United States*. Noll (2000) identifies the work of Drenowski at the United Nations on systems of social indicators in the 1950s as an early contribution to the project of improving the 'measurement of the level of living by identifying components of welfare and by constructing respective indicators' (Noll, 2000). By 1969 the future direction of health economic uses of social indicators had been anticipated, as had one of the key individual-level uses of the notion of quality of life. Gudex (1990) identifies the publication by Klarman *et al.* (1968) of a cost-effectiveness analysis of chronic renal disease treatment as the beginning of the QALY (quality adjusted life year) movement in medicine (of which more in Chapter 6).

At the societal level, in 1969 the US Department of Health, Education, and Welfare document *Toward a Social Report* identified health and illness; income and poverty; the physical environment; public order and safety; social mobility; learning, science and art; and participation and alienation as key social indicators (USDHEW, 1969). The definition of a 'social indicator' in this document is attributed by Land (2000) to the economist Olson – namely a 'statistic of direct normative interest which facilitates concise, comprehensive and balanced judgements about the condition of major aspects of a society' (USDHEW, 1969: 97). In all cases, Land argues, Olson viewed such indicators as direct measures of welfare which afforded the conclusion that, if changes occurred in the right direction, all else being equal, things have improved, or that people could be understood to be 'better off'.

Both Noll and Land attribute the rapid international diffusion of social indicators work to the social and political climate of the 1960s and 1970s. Noll (2000) suggests that while this was a period of prosperity, it was also a period when questioning of economic growth as the major goal of public policy and the primary indicator of social progress began. This questioning has, more recently, again become a pressing political issue with the development of anti-globalization protest movements. Noll argues that, during this period: 'there was increasing doubt whether more should ever equal better … The concept of "quality of life" was born as an alternative to the more and more questionable concept of the affluent society and became the new, but also much more complex and multidimensional goal of societal development' (Noll, 2000). Land's (2000) description of the flurry of activity at this time – which depended on widespread acceptance of active government shaping societal structures and processes for the greater good – captures the period well. Land writes of the intellectual enthusiasm for social indicators in the United States that:

> In the early 1970s, this led to numerous developments, including the establishing in 1972, with National Science Foundation support, of the Social Science Research Council Center for Coordination of Research on Social Indicators in Washington, D.C., the publication of several major efforts to define and develop a methodology for the measurement of indicators of subjective well-being (Campbell and Converse 1972; Andrews and Withey 1976; Campbell, Converse, and Rodgers 1976); the commencement of a federal government series of comprehensive social indicators ... the initiation of several continuing data series based on periodic sample surveys of the national population ... the publication in 1974 of the first volume of the international journal *Social Indicators Research*; and the spread of social indicators/social reporting to numerous other nations and international agencies, such as the United States Nations [sic] and the Organization for Economic Cooperation and Development. (Land, 2000)

Land (2000) describes the social indicators movement in the USA as 'faltering' in the 1980s. These developments were much less marked in Europe, despite the rise of similar, right-wing conservative/neoliberal political ideologies and comparable economic difficulties. For example, while they vary considerably in their coverage, European countries routinely report social indicators at a national level. Of the EU member states, the Dutch biennial *Social and Cultural Report* (first published in 1974), the United Kingdom's annual *Social Trends* (first published in 1970), and France's triennial *Données Sociales* (first published in 1973) have now been in publication for over a quarter of a century (Habich and Noll, 1994).

This high level of activity, despite a hiatus in the USA in the 1980s, has continued. International agencies such as the World Bank (e.g. World Bank, 2000) and other nations (e.g. the Australian Bureau of Statistics' *Social Trends* which commenced in 1994) have joined in the publication of indicators of the social well-being of nations – in addition to the well-established measures provided by the OECD (OECD, 1982) and the United Nations' *Human Development Index* (United Nations, 1995). One can, argues Noll (2000), 'interpret the rise of social indicators research above all as an answer to the increased demands for information made by an active social policy and by the challenge to operationalize and to quantify its core formula: the concept of quality of life'. Veenhoven (1996: 1) has put it similarly: 'one of the main aims of social indicator research is to develop a comprehensive measure of quality-of-life in nations that is analogous to GNP in economic indicator research'. His HLE, as we have seen, is commended by its author not only on the grounds of its scientific merit, or its accuracy of measurement, but because it 'is likely to have political appeal'.

The role of social indicators in informing politics is also clear to writers like Zapf (1977), who suggests that they may contribute to 'enlighten[ing] us in some way about structures and processes, goals and achievements, values and opinions' (Zapf, 1977: 236). Social indicators thus offer, in Noll's (2000) words,

> standards for the level of modernization of a society and [a] register [of] progress in modernization ... [T]he primary function is not the direct guidance and efficiency control of political decisions, but broad social enlightenment and the provision of an information base which supports politics ... The primary function ... is the measurement of the level and distribution of welfare in a society, whereby welfare development can be understood as a specific dimension of the comprehensive process of modernization.

Or, as Salvaris (2000) might have it, 'progress' – with a capital P.

While Land characterizes the 1980s as a low point in social indicators research, it was during this time of 'conservative ideology' with its celebration of the market, the responsibility of individuals and the importance of 'small government', that interest in the idea of quality of life as a construct at the individual level began. Coinciding with the idea that 'there is no such thing as society, only individuals and their families' said to be at the centre of Margaret Thatcher's politics, the 1980s saw the popularity of 'total quality management', 'continuous quality improvement' and 'managing for quality' (Schalock, 1994: 275). In this environment, the notion that quality of life was a property of individual persons became an 'idea whose time had come' (Hatton, 1995: 25). Cummins (1997b: 117–18, my emphasis) notes the intertwining of scientific and popular interest in the individualized notion of QOL:

> New interest in individual, personal values, began to emerge. Spitzer (1987) states that only four papers had QOL in their titles between 1966–1970, while this applied to 33 papers over the next five years ... This exponential rate of increase has been maintained to the present time where the term has become a *political and media catch-word*. The literature is now too vast for any individual researcher to fully assimilate.

Similarly, in their analysis of social policy for people with disabilities, Rapley and Ridgway (1998: 451) noted that:

> No less than in other areas of contemporary society, the powerful rhetoric in ... the late 1980's and early 1990's is that of 'quality'. As the concepts of competition and market economics, borrowed from commerce and

industry, have been applied to human services, so too have they been accompanied in managerial and political rhetoric by their closely associated claims of increased consumer control, enhancement of choice and quality improvement. In addition to these rhetorical claims, human services have also increasingly borrowed the rhetorical tools of corporate culture. In addition to the discourse of consumerism, human services have also begun to deploy a corporate discourse which frames their activities in terms of 'total quality management', 'performance indicators', 'business plans' and 'mission statements'.

Chapter 5 offers a detailed analysis of these developments. However, it is clear that what Cummins terms the 'modern' form of QOL has strayed a long way from the initial, and limited, conceptualization of quality of life as an index of the well-being of populations. The idea of QOL has become much more than a social policy analogue for the GDP – and is now tightly enmeshed with a set of other, and explicitly ideological, knowledges and unashamedly 'American' political and commercial projects. QOL has become not just a concept that ties together a variety of social indicators to offer an index of the success of public policy, but an integral part of the *marketing* of public policy. Land (2000) is undeniably correct when he points out that, in the 1990s, the 'widespread political, popular, and theoretical appeal of the "quality-of-life" (QOL) concept' became 'vividly apparent'. The 'QOL concept' that emerged in the 1990s, Land claims, not only offers 'a goal of social and economic policy' but also

encompasses all (or at least many) domains of life and subsumes, in addition to individual material and immaterial well-being, such collective values as freedom, justice, and the guarantee of natural conditions of life for present and future generations. The political use of the QOL notion is paralleled in the private sector by the widespread use and popularity of numerous rankings – based on weighted scales of multiple domains of well-being – of the "best" places to live, work, do business, play, etc., be they cities, states, regions, or nations. The theoretical appeal of the QOL concept as an integrating notion in the social sciences and related disciplines is, in part, due to the perceived importance of measuring individuals' subjective assessments of their satisfaction with various life domains and with life-as-a-whole .... QOL bridges the discipline of marketing research and strategic business policy with social indicators. Marketing is an importance social force – with far-reaching direct and indirect impacts on the prevailing QOL in a society – through consumer satisfaction (Samli 1987; Sirgy and Samli 1996) and its impact on satisfaction with life-as-a-whole. The intersection of marketing research with social indicators through the QOL concept led to the organization in the mid-1990s of the International Society for Quality-of-Life Studies.

QOL has become an *increasingly* slippery or complex construct over the course of its use. It is now widely used to describe everything from the state of nations' bank balances to the happiness of individuals with the contents of theirs. QOL describes outcomes of political projects, as well as how pleasant (or otherwise) it is to live in Brisbane, Berlin or Beijing. QOL describes the judgments of individuals about their happiness with their sexual relationships, club memberships and domestic arrangements, and also what will be exponentially improved (or so the marketing people claim) by the purchase of this or that washing powder, package holiday or new home. QOL simultaneously indexes the levels of crime, home ownership and participation of women in government in the nation state, and signifies the 'output' of unconscious brain states.

Varieties of Social Indicators

When the quality of life is approached as a population, or societal-level concern, two broad approaches, which, after Noll (2000), will be termed 'Scandinavian' and 'American', can be distinguished. These approaches may be separated by their position in relation to Campbell's (1972) dictum that 'quality of life must be in the eye of the beholder', that is, the relative importance of 'objective' and 'subjective' indicators of social well-being. Early American work focused on 'objective' indicators: health, poverty, unemployment rates and the like which 'represent social facts independently of personal evaluations' in contrast to 'subjective' indicators which rely upon and 'emphasize the individual perception and evaluation of social conditions' (Noll, 2000). A selection of frequently used objective and subjective social indicators is shown in Table 1.1.

It is only subsequently that the contemporary focus on 'the eye of the beholder' has become a central component of ideas about what QOL is. It is not only at the population level that debate still continues: for example, controversy continues in the mental health and intellectual disability literatures about the relative merits of either side of the objective–subjective QOL distinction, in the search for an appropriate indices of service quality at the individual level (Hatton, 1998; Cummins, 2001a).

To return to the population level, in his overview Noll offers a clear account of the two positions – and the conceptual difficulties inherent in both. He writes that:

> Using objective indicators starts from the assumption that living conditions can be judged as being favorable or unfavorable by comparing real conditions with normative criteria like values or goals. An important precondition, however, is that there is political consensus first about the dimensions that are relevant for welfare, second a consensus about good and bad conditions and third about the direction in which society should

Table 1.1 Objective and subjective social indicators

Frequently used objective social indicators (represent social data independently of individual evaluations)

Life expectancy
Crime rate
Unemployment rate
Gross Domestic Product
Poverty rate
School attendance
Working hours per week
Perinatal mortality rate
Suicide rate

Subjective social indicators (individuals' appraisal and evaluation of social conditions)

Sense of community
Material possessions
Sense of safety
Happiness
Satisfaction with 'life as a whole'
Relationships with family
Job satisfaction
Sex life
Perception of distributional justice
Class identification
Hobbies and club membership

Source: Items drawn from Cummins (1996b); Hagerty *et al.* (2001) and Noll (2000).

move. This is of course sometimes, but not always the case. Probably there is consensus that we would consider a reduction of unemployment or crime and an increase of the average income or educational level as an improvement and progress. We could perhaps be less sure, when it comes to indicators like the age of retirement; and it might indeed be debatable whether a reduction of income inequality should in general be regarded as social progress, given the fact that there is a trade-off between distributional justice and efficiency concerning economic growth ... Using subjective social indicators is, instead, based on the premise that welfare ... is perceived by individual citizens and can be judged best by them ... This position, too, is not undisputed and has caused a deep controversy about the principles of welfare measurement. Particularly Scandinavian welfare researchers criticized this subjective quality of life approach and the use of subjective indicators. One of their concerns 'with an approach based on people's own assessment of their degree of satisfaction is that it is partly determined by their level of aspiration' (Erikson 1993: 77). Looking at how satisfied people are, from this point of view is criticized as 'measuring how well they are adapted to their present conditions'. According to R. Erikson (Erikson 1993: 78) – one of the most prominent proponents of Scandinavian welfare research – people's opinions and preferences should go into the democratic political process through their activities as citizens, but not through survey questions and opinion polls. (Noll, 2000)

Land (2000) expands Noll's dichotomy of objective and subjective indicators to distinguish three types of social indicators: criterion indicators, descriptive social indicators and life satisfaction and/or happiness indicators. More recently Veenhoven (1996) has proposed 'comprehensive' social indicators or 'summary welfare indices' (Noll, 2000), which combine aspects of each of these approaches. In Veenhoven's case, the Happy Life Expectancy (HLE) index of quality of life in nations represents an arithmetic product of a happiness indicator[2] and a criterion indicator (life expectancy), of which more below.

Criterion indicators

Given the declared commitment of social indicators research to 'enlighten-ment' (Zapf, 1977) many indicators are intended to be directly related to social and economic policy-making considerations. This linkage may be seen in MacRae's (1985: 5) definition of criterion indicators as 'measures of those variables that are to be included in a broadly policy-relevant system of public statistics'. Such social indicators, Land (2000) suggests, may be otherwise characterized as '"target" or "output" or "outcome" or "end-value" variables, toward changes in which some public policy (program, project) is directed'. That is, they offer criteria (Ferriss, 1988) against which the success of policy initiatives may be gauged. In the summary of their *World Development Report 2000/2001* the World Bank (2000) offers a clear example of the use of such indicators on an international basis:

At the start of a new century, poverty remains a global problem of huge proportions. Of the world's 6 billion people, 2.8 billion live on less than $2 a day and 1.2 billion on less than $1 a day. Eight out of 100 infants do not live to see their 5th birthday. Nine of 100 boys and 14 of 100 girls who reach school age do not attend school. Poverty is also evident in poor people's lack of political power and voice and in their vulnerability to ill health, economic dislocation, personal violence and natural disasters.

Criterion indicators (income, life expectancy, school attendance) are also termed *normative welfare indicators* (Land, 1983: 4). As Noll (2000) has pointed out, while broad agreement may exist within and possibly even across societies about *some* of these indicators, what counts as a 'normative' indicator of welfare is likely to be culturally (even subculturally) relative, and determined by political and ideological considerations. For example, while it appears that the World Bank considers school attendance by both boys and girls of school age an unambiguous criterion indicator of (high) social welfare, there are societies – such strict Islamic states – where the presence of girls in classrooms would be considered an unambiguous social evil. Equally, the selection of criterion indicators is a matter of local choice and relative weighting. In sub-Saharan Africa, south-east Asia and Latin America, attending school is a lesser social priority than economic production: for societies where school-age children are essential contributors to the workforce, such a criterion reveals an unmistakably ethnocentric set of values.

Descriptive social indicators

Descriptive social indicators are 'indexes of the state of society and changes taking place therein' (Land, 2000). This approach 'focus[es] on social measurements and analyses designed to improve our under-standing of what the main features of society are, how they interrelate, and how these features and their relationships change'. Although these indicators appear to have much in common with criterion indicators, and indeed this category may show considerable overlap with, or even include policy or criterion indicators, unlike criterion indicators descriptive social indicators

> may be more or less directly (causally) related to the well-being goals of public policies or programs ... For instance, in the area of health, descriptive indicators might include preventive indicators such as the percent of the population that does not smoke cigarettes, as well as criterion indicators such as the number of days of activity limitations in the past month or an index of self-reported satisfaction with health. (Land, 2000)

Land (1983) has also suggested that these indicators have the flexibility of *varying degrees of abstraction*. That is, descriptive social indicators may be based on minimal data series that need little statistical manipulation (such as age-specific death rates) to more involved indices (such as years of life-expectancy at age x for men, years of disability-free life expectancy at age y for smokers). These indicators also offer the benefit of being capable of presentation as demographic- or time-budget-based systems of social accounts (Juster and Land, 1981).

Life satisfaction and/or happiness indicators

Again grounded in a decidedly Western notion – that the ultimate purpose of human experience is 'happiness' and, hence, the ultimate measure of social good must be the degree of such a state individuals have achieved – is work on so-called 'subjective' social indicators. These indicators developed from Campbell and Converse's (1972) highly influential *The Human Meaning of Social Change*.

The conceptual key to this work is acceptance of the position that measurement of individual psychological states (values, attitudes, beliefs and aspirations) in the population at large is essential to understand both social change and QOL. This position is flatly rejected by Scandinavian researchers on the grounds that the measurement of individuals' low aspiration/high adaptation is fruitless as an index of social well-being. Others, such as Rapley (2001), have pointed out the absence of a clear theoretical link between any specific policy and any particular individual avowal of happiness – and any persuasive mechanism by which such a connection might operate.

Furthermore 'social indicators' like satisfaction, happiness and life fulfilment are not truly 'social' at all in the sense that the unemployment rate, suicide rate, average life expectancy and high-school participation rate are meaningful demographic averages for a particular *society*. These indicators are only 'social' in the sense that they are collections of individuals' avowals of particular personal judgments, usually of 'contentment', 'satisfaction' or 'happiness' with *x*. As such, these indicators are of a very different kind to the criterion or descriptive social indicators discussed above. Whereas one can sensibly say that Mr Smith is out-of-work and unhappy about it, or that Jodie quit school in year 10 because she couldn't see the point of staying on, it makes no sense at all to say that Mr Smith's unemployment rate is one hundred per cent or that Jodie's high school participation rate is zero per cent.

Despite this, two major studies in the 1970s and a summary collection in the mid-1980s (Andrews and Withey 1976; Campbell *et al.*, 1976; Andrews, 1986), which examined levels of individuals' satisfaction both with the quality of life as a whole[3] and also a host of 'domains' of their lives – from the specific (house, job, family) to the global (life-as-a-whole) – have given rise to an immense literature. The idea that individual appraisals of quality of life are not just essential to understanding the quality of life of nations (the 'American' position), but may even be considered a moral imperative (Shea, 1976) commands considerable currency.

This literature itself diverges according to whether QOL is conceptualized as a *singular entity* or as a *multi-dimensional construct*, made up of a potentially limitless number of 'domains'. For example, Cummins (1996b) identified 173 domains in an analysis of 32 studies. Veenhoven (1996: 22) suggests that 'the most commonly used item is the question: 'Taking all together, how happy would you say you are? Very happy, fairly happy, not too happy, or not at all happy?' Cummins (1997b) suggests that Andrews and Withey's (1976) question 'How do you feel about your life as a whole?', is widely used as QOL index. Given the plethora of multiple-domain life satisfaction measures subsequently developed, Cummins (1996) reports comparative meta-analysis of eleven large-scale studies in which a sufficiently close relationship between scores on single-item measures and the aggregate scores of multiple-domain measures was obtained to prompt the question as to whether the latter are, as summary indicators, essentially redundant.

The current state of social indicators and population well-being research

Much work continues on the development of measures of individual well-being (the Australian Centre on Quality of Life directory includes 447 QOL measures). *Soi-disant* QOL literature also focuses on relative prosperity, GDP, unemployment rates, political democracy and so on. This is one of the major difficulties caused by the overdetermination of the notion. For example, studies addressing population health, social capital or inequalities in health (Cattell, 2001; Forbes and Wainwright, 2001; Navarro and Shi, 2001; OECD, 2001) deal in matters (such as psychological distress, well-being, poor physical health) which are also clearly within the purview of *other* literatures which claim to deal with QOL *qua* QOL (for example, Veenhoven, 1996). The comprehensive absence of rigour of thought and expression in the field (Wolfensberger, 1994) is illustrated by the OECD report *The Well-being of Nations: The Role of Human and Social Capital* (OECD, 2001).

The OECD is a clear instance of the conflation of the notion of well-being across levels of analysis: of nations and individuals respectively. The Executive Summary states that: 'human and social capital are related both to overall well-being and to economic growth ... our social objective is not simply to increase economic growth; it is also to improve well-being' (OECD, 2001: 1) and, later (2001: 4), that:

> Research links social capital, and access to such capital, with improved health – for example, one study shows that social connectedness is associated with a reduced risk of Alzheimer's disease; greater well-being according to self-reported survey measures ... [and] ... improved government – regions or states with higher levels of trust and engagement [social capital] tend to have better quality government.

Here, we see the use of 'well-being' as a construct analogous to economic growth (the notion of 'overall well-being' clearly being a measure applicable to whole populations). A couple of pages later 'well-being' is deployed as a construct that applies both to individual physical health outcomes (reduced risk of Alzheimer's disease) *and* to 'self-reported survey measures' of individual 'well-being'.

Equally, many studies describe themselves as addressing 'population health' with instruments described by their authors as 'quality of life measures'. For example Kind *et al.* (1998) report a study of the population health of the United Kingdom using the EuroQOL EQ-5D, described by its authors as offering 'a new facility for the measurement of health-related quality of life' (EuroQOL Group, 1990: 199). Kind *et al.* (1998: 736) describe their study as 'part of a wider study of practical ways of measuring health related quality of life'. However, while the EuroQOL EQ-5D claims to measure 'HRQOL', it defines QOL in terms of a three-point rating of one's 'health state today' on each of five individual-level dimensions – self-care, mobility, usual activities (study, work, housework, family or leisure), pain or discomfort and anxiety or depression. In the area of 'usual activities', for example, the choices are 'I have no problems with performing my usual activities'; 'I have some problems with performing my usual activities'; and 'I am unable to perform my usual activities'. Secondly the measure asks respondents to 'say how good or bad your own health is today' on a 0 ('worst imaginable health state') – 100 ('best imaginable health state') visual analogue scale.

In the Kind *et al.* (1998) study the average state of health recorded was 82.5, and 'a moderate problem on at least one dimension was reported by 42% of respondents' (1998: 737). Kind *et al* suggest that – as a consequence of their sampling strategy – 'the results may well underestimate the health related quality of life of the general population' (1998: 739). Thus a self-proclaimed measure of 'HRQOL' focuses on individuals' views about their health but makes no mention of the concept of quality of life *qua* quality of life. The measure does not ask respondents how they feel about being 'unable to perform my usual activities'. Yet the results are said both to have 'obvious potential' in gaining the 'patient's point of view in monitoring medical care outcomes' while also offering to account for general population level QOL outcomes (Kind *et al.*, 1998: 740).

The literature also contains numerous papers which elide individuals' health status, political movements and QOL. For example Rogers-Clark (1998: 6, my emphasis) states that 'the Women's Health movement is linked inextricably with the broader Women's movement. Feminism has two goals: to *actively improve women's quality of life*; and to remove those fundamental patriarchal ideologies within contemporary society which lead to the oppression of women.' This is very clearly to place the issue of quality of life into a socio-political frame. The current state of women's QOL, for Rogers-Clarke at least, is held to be lower than it might as a result of the dominance of 'fundamental patriarchal ideologies'. This conceptualizes QOL as a structural phenomenon – rather than construing quality of life as an aggregate of individual judgments by specific women. Farlinger (1996: 109, my emphasis) argues that the 'description of the *quality of life* today for women begins with information on indicators such as income, population, refugees, percent women in political office or boardrooms ... The key to effective policies is to measure the cause and effects of environmental degradation and find ways to provide feedback to the decision-makers and ourselves to change behavior.' Here, QOL is not an interior aspect of many individual psyches but a global attribute of a collectivity of women which may be estimated by a variety of *specific indicators* (income, refugees, women in boardrooms, etc.) rather than inferred from the continuing hegemony of 'patriarchal ideologies'.

Frey and Al-Roumi (1999: 73) ask 'why do some countries have a high quality of life?' and offer the following answer: 'One important explanation is that political democracy fosters life quality.' Proponents of this perspective argue that 'political democracy acts to center the public agenda on state actions that enhance life quality.' That Western political democracies such as the USA and the UK show reasonably high levels of happiness on most surveys (see Cummins, 2001b; Veenhoven, 1991, 1996) and at the same time low, and decreasing, levels of active participation by their citizens in the democratic process suggests that the mechanism may be less straight-forward.

Veenhoven's work attempts to link the happiness of population groups with social arrangements and political economy. Davis (1984) has shown the responsiveness of people's judgments of their 'happiness-with-life-as-a-whole' to changes in respondents' financial status as opposed to current income level. The connection of subjective well-being to income levels has been a problem since Easterlin's (1973) demonstration that, while the association of happiness with income within countries is not strong, income differences between nations predict national differences in happiness. Veenhoven (1997: 12) states that 'the richer the country, the happier its inhabitants', but qualifies Easterlin's (1973) analysis by noting that 'correlations between personal happiness and personal income are strong in poor countries and weak in rich nations' and concludes that this finding 'does not fit the theory that happiness derives from social comparison', an essential theorem of work that defines QOL as an individualized, subjective state.

While not invoking the construct of QOL, much work examines population level variables as determinants of the 'mood' of countries. Hogenraad and Grosbois (1997) describe (in the key QOL journal *Social Indicators Research*) the determinants of (what we may gloss as) a lowering of the quality of Belgian life – in their terms the level of 'threat' to the security and continued existence of the Belgian nation. Such an analysis allows us to see, in negative as it were, the factors considered conducive to an absence of threat. It is suggested that, based on 91 expert historians rating the threat severity for each year, and an analysis of objective economic, social and political indicators, a constellation of individual and population-wide factors produce 'threat'. They state that, on the basis of indicators of threat or fear, such as 'crime, unemployment, apprehension at starting a family, buying a car, or starting a new business, etc … The present threat index … for Belgium is found to depend on a 5-variable subset composed of: suicide, unemployment, and balance of trade, for the positive associations; and GNP and car registrations, for the negative associations' (Hogenraad and Grosbois, 1997: 221). The quality of Belgian life it would seem, then, is best enhanced by a thriving new-car market and a high GDP. The 'mood' that Belgian life is under threat, it appears, again is primarily determined by similarly macro-level phenomena (unemployment, the balance of trade). The one unequivocally individual-level indicator of threat (suicide) is, one would have thought, more likely to be an outcome of high levels of threat, rather than a predictor of it.

More Recent Developments

Veenhoven (1996: 5–6) identifies the many issues raised by the idea of measuring the quality of life of nations very clearly when he states:

> The most fundamental problem with … QOL-indicators is that they involve criteria of a different order. They do not distinguish between means and ends, nor between societal input and societal output … If we are not clear about what we mean with QOL, we will never have sensible measures of it … A first thing then is to distinguish between the quality of nations and the quality-of-life *in* nations.

In order to facilitate such a distinction Veenhoven (1996) proposes a new index: the HLE.

Happy life expectancy

Veenhoven attempts to bridge the conceptual gap in levels of measurement between genuinely social social indicators of the quality of life (GDP, unemployment rates, etc.), with individual level indicators by suggesting that 'happiness' be considered the best indicator of individuals' satisfaction. Veenhoven identifies a range of problems with measures of quality of life in nations such as the United Nation's *Human Development Index* (1995) and Estes's (1984) *Index of Social Progress*. Extant indices show arbitrary selection and relative weighting of indicators, culture-bound indicator selection, opacity of meaning of aggregate scores and confusion of means and ends. For example, a long life is what is termed an end value – valued for itself – whereas an affluent life may offer a means to that end. Veenhoven (1996: 5) also points out the concerns raised by Salvaris (2000). That is, he questions the manner in which some of the indexes [of national quality of life] are in fact more specific and equate quality-of-life more or less with 'modernity'. They measure in fact the degree to which characteristics of the dominant Western society are present in a nation ... [I]t is misleading to call that 'quality-of-life'. Modernization should not be equated with the good life.

Veenhoven's proposal, then, is to (re)conceptualize QOL as the 'flourishing' or 'thriving' of lived existence. He draws an analogy between persons, fauna and flora to argue that:

the flourishing of plants or animals in a given ecological environment is usually measured by their functioning as apparent in growth, adequacy of behavior and absence of disease ... Can the flourishing of humans in a social environment be measured by the same criteria? To some extent yes. Human thriving also manifests physically, particularly in good health and a long life. Therefore we can induce the quality-of-life in a nation from the *health* of its citizens ... Unlike plants and animals, humans can reflect on themselves and their situation. Their suit to society is therefore also reflected in their judgments. As such we can also infer quality-of-life in a nation from the citizen's *appraisals* of life. (Veenhoven, 1996: 12, emphases in the original)

Such a conception has the merit of placing the lived experience of persons, and their appraisals of the quality of that experience, into a social context; of noting that the issue can be construed as a matter of the 'goodness of fit' between persons and their environment (cf. Zautra and Goodhart, 1979); and also of noting that (impoverished) quality of life may be evident in both 'behavioural manifestations of malaise' (Veenhoven, 1996: 17) and subjective complaints of misery.

Veenhoven (1996) suggests that while international data on un-happiness are unsuitable for computational purposes, ratings of subjective happiness across nations are sufficiently comparable to permit league tables of happy life expectancy. HLE is the product of subtracting (nation-specific) expected years in bad health from expected years of life and multiplying standard life expectancy by average happiness on a scale from 1 to 0. Or:

$$\text{HLE} = \text{Standard life expectancy} \times 0 - 1 \text{ Happiness}$$

Thus if life expectancy in country y is 50 years, with an average happiness score of 0.5, the product of $50 \times 0.5 = 25$, thus the HLE of country y is 25 years. This figure 'characterizes most of the poor nations in the present day world' whereas for 'the most livable nations' the HLE is 64 years (1996: 29). High HLE values mean that 'citizens live both long and happily' while low values suggest that 'the life of the average citizen is short and miserable.

Medium values of happy life expectancy in a country can mean three things: 1) both moderate length-of-life and moderate appreciation-of-life, 2) long but unhappy life, and 3) short but happy life' (1996: 30).

There are two conceptual and practical difficulties here. Firstly a long miserable life and a short happy one are, while numerically identical, diametrically opposite in terms of 'quality'. Secondly, the statistic describes the experience not of persons, but of a conceptual abstraction – the 'Average Citizen'. Veenhoven reports that, in a 1990 survey of 48 countries, on average, HLE in Northern Ireland (56.49) and Norway (57.16) were almost identical. That the average Norwegian citizen was unlikely to have their life expectancy, happy or otherwise, suddenly shortened by random sectarian shootings or car bombings – as were the citizens of Northern Ireland – cannot be captured by the HLE, which, it is claimed, is a 'comprehensive' indicator of the quality of life in a nation (1996: 28). Equally, while average Australian HLE in 1990 was 59.49 – putting Australia in fifth place after Switzerland, Sweden, the Netherlands and Iceland – the use of an average figure disguises the fact that, for Australia's Indigenous peoples, life expectancy (whether happy or not) has been barely 40 years since the 1950s.

Such concerns have led some workers to argue that for social indicators of well-being or quality of life to be locally meaningful, they need to be locally identified and defined. These developments are now considered.

Social indicators of the quality of life: a locally-based movement

There are now well-established sets of social indicators at the international and national levels. Chapter 2 considers the relation between *definitions* of QOL and *measures* of the construct in more detail, but for now it is important to recognize that debate about the utility of population level indices concerns issues of the meaning of measures of well-being that are deeply *practical* as well as *conceptual*. For example, Redefining Progress has suggested what they describe as a more accurate measure of progress, the *Genuine Progress Indicator* (GPI).

Cobb *et al.* (2000: 1) suggest this measure:

> starts with the same accounting framework as the GDP, but then makes some crucial distinctions: It adds in the economic contributions of household and volunteer work, but subtracts factors such as crime, pollution, and family breakdown: as such the GPI attempts to capture a more holistic picture of the *sustainable* life quality of nations, or 'genuine progress in people's quality of life'.[4]

Redefining Progress acts as an international clearing house for locally-based community indicators projects (Cobb *et al.*, 2000; Eckersley, 1998). Measures such as the GPI are a response to what Salvaris (2000: 4) has called 'a growing concern about the influence of economic output indicators, most notably the Gross Domestic Product (GDP)[5] as proxy measurements of human progress'. Salvaris and other critics of the GDP point out that it is both misleading (it is a poor measure of the actual condition of the economy and the society) and also that it is overly powerful (that is, the GDP is too influential in shaping our everyday understanding of progress and well-being). Salvaris (2000: 5) argues that:

> measuring the market value of economic production tells us very little about the broader health of the community or the environment, and nothing about the social costs of what has been produced in the economy, or about its usefulness or sustainability.

This account greatly broadens the scope of what is usually meant by the term 'social indicator'. Such concerns raise serious questions about notions like 'modernity' and 'progress' as indices of life quality complementary to those of Veenhoven (1996), but from a rather different perspective. In Box 1.1 some of the other future challenges for social indicators research, adapted from Noll, are identified.

Box 1.1 Future directions for social indicators research

1. *Reconsidering the concepts of welfare and the quality of life.* In a world of rapidly changing social contexts and problems, such as the crisis of the welfare state and global ecological problems, the usefulness of concepts – like modernization, individual welfare, subjective well-being, social capital and quality of life – needs to be reconsidered for the observation of social development at the beginning of the twenty-first century.

2. *Construction of summary welfare indices.* In the light of increasing economic and political integration in Europe, for example, and in the context of the problems of globalization and late capitalism, there is a need for internationally comparable summary indices synthesizing the various dimensions of welfare into one single measure. Examples of new summary welfare indices are the Genuine Progress Indicator (GPI).

3. *Development of local initiatives.* At the same time as developing international indices, much work will need to focus on the development of locally relevant, community-owned indices of social well-being. The National Citizenship Project and the 'Quality of life in Newcastle' projects in Australia and 'Sustainable Seattle' in the US offer models of this approach (Salvaris, 2000).

In addition to the development of indicators like the GPI, concerns about the *ethical positions* implicit in measures of life quality have spurred locally-based projects across the world in an effort to develop indicators of the quality of life of local communities, which are locally meaningful and based on explicit philosophical positions. These developments are discussed in Chapter 2. However, before we move on to these 'grassroots' indicators of the quality of life, we must consider quality of life as an individual-level construct.

QOL as a State of Persons

That there is now a 'modern form' of understanding of QOL could be taken to imply that understandings based on non-individualized notions of QOL were pre-modern, archaic or ignorant of up-to-date ideas. Yet collectivist and relational understandings of the concept continue to thrive and the appeal to modernity to warrant ideas itself has a dubious history (Chorover, 1979; Salvaris, 2000).

Brock (1993) has pointed out that theorizing the good life at the individual level has been the site of considerable historical disagreement and contestation. He distinguishes three broad approaches to QOL in terms of theories of the 'good life'. *Hedonist theory* holds that the ultimate good is to have certain kinds of conscious experiences – happiness, pleasure, satisfaction – that typically accompany pursuit of desires. *Preference satisfaction theory* (closely related to the currently influential *multiple discrepancy theory* (Michalos, 1985)) holds that the good life consists in the satisfaction of desires and preferences, with what is good being understood as people getting what they want and prefer with a minimal number of unsatisfied wants (discrepancies) equating to a better good. *Ideal theory* suggests that at least part of the good life is to do with neither conscious enjoyment nor the satisfaction of preferences, but instead consists in the satisfaction of specific normative ideals (cf. Cummins, 2000a). Megone (1990), in contrast, draws upon Aristotle to suggest that the good life consists in man's fulfilment of the *purpose of being human*, namely leading an active *rational* life. Sadly this line of reasoning seems to have been something of a cul-de-sac in the social scientific literatures, but see McHoul and Rapley (2001a) for a discussion of the philosophical implications.

As the above suggests, the observation that the link between objective conditions and subjective well-being is sometimes paradoxical at the national level is also influential at the individual level. Hence the position that subjective *and* objective states should be monitored in the 'American' social indicators literature and in endeavours derived therefrom: for example, Noll (2000) states that 'in our own German approach individual welfare or quality of life is therefore defined as "good living conditions which go together with positive subjective well-being'". Land (2000) suggests that subjective well-being may both show 'traitlike' and 'statelike' characteristics. There is, according to Land, a consensus that subjective well-being demonstrates both reactivity to situations and events – a state alterable by circumstances – while at the same time being 'a durable psychological condition that differs among individuals and contributes to stability over time and consistency across situations' or a trait, a more or less fixed aspect of how particular individuals view their world (Stones *et al.*, 1995; Veenhoven, 1994, 1998; Ahuvia and Friedman, 1998). This synthetic view has recently been strongly contested by Cummins (1995, 1997b, 1998b, 2001b).

Subjective well-being, QOL and biological determinism

So up-to-date is Cummins' view that he has recently proposed (2001a, 2001b; 2001c; Cummins *et al.*, in press) that QOL is a 'hard-wired', homeostatically controlled, brain state. Subjective well-being is: 'a dispositional brain system that acts to keep each individual's well being within a narrow positive range' (2001a: 5) held constant at approximately 75 per cent of scale maximum (or 75%SM) on whatever quality of life, satisfaction or happiness scale it is measured.

This view is representative of the dominant form of theorizing within Western psychology and affiliated disciplines (or the psy-complex as Rose (1999) has called them), which seeks to locate the source of all of human experience within biology. Such views are a part of a broader trajectory in Western thought, which has gathered pace since the 1970s, and which has increasingly sought to replace phenomenological, social or sociological understandings of human experience and the quality of life (as much of the social indicators research discussed above may be understood) with individualized biological and/or cognitive accounts. Increasingly accounts dispense with the notion of the *person* as an explanatory 'variable': instead the focus is on putative intra-personal componentry, described in terms of computer metaphors (Button *et al.*, 1997), and often held to be the 'output' of genetically determined brain mechanisms. What may once have been viewed as transcendental human experience (joy), or existential crisis (depression), are no longer understood as states of being-in-the-world experienced by persons, but rather are respecified, as if we were discussing a faulty central heating system, as the 'consequences of homeostatic failure' (Cummins *et al.*, in press). The influential work of Cummins and colleagues on the homeostatic hypothesis is discussed in detail in Chapter 8.

In Summary

The concept of quality of life has travelled from being a shorthand term encompassing the political aims of the 'Great Society', through a period of intense social scientific formalism at both individual and population levels, back to its original status as an all-pervasive 'political and media catchword' (Cummins, 1997b). In the process the concept has developed a double life: the term 'quality of life' has come to index, simultaneously, collections of a bewildering array of 'indicators' of the quality of living conditions within the nation state, and also the 'output' of automatic brain states. Like psychology, the discipline from which the most influential formulations of QOL as an individual attribute have come, the idea has a short history, but a very long past. Again like psychology, QOL is an idea which clearly has a robust future, even if the contours of that future are both politically contentious and, presently, opaque. Quite what QOL actually *means* is the focus of Chapter 2.

Notes

1. 'Whig histories' attempt to account for how it is that past events have caused current ones. The use of history in this book owes more to Foucault, whose recommendations for the use of history entail analysis of the conditions of possibility of particular discourses, and the diagnosis of the present, as research goals.
2. Veenhoven's Happiness Index (Veenhoven, 1984) has two questions: To what extent do you regard yourself as a happy person? How satisfied are you with your present life? Both are scored on four-point scales. Psychometrics are reported by Debats (1996).
3. Andrews and Withey's (1976) measure is the single question 'How do you feel about your life as a whole?' with responses measured on a Likert scale anchored on 'delighted' ('satisfaction') and 'terrible' ('dissatisfaction'). Cummins (1996b) describes the measure as 'one of the few empirical benchmarks for life quality'. Campbell *et al.* (1976) asked respondents to rate satisfaction with health, social and family connections, material wealth/well-being and work/productive activity on a five-point scale.
4. The calculation of the GPI begins with the personal consumption component of the Gross Domestic Product (GDP), including capital investment, government spending and net exports and factors in social, environmental and economic phenomena that diminish or enhance people's quality of life, but that are not typically measured in monetary terms or included in economic analyses. For example, while the GDP simply counts money changing hands, the GPI factors in hidden environmental costs such as pollution and depletion of natural resources (Cobb *et al.*, 2000: 1).
5. The GDP is a summary measure of the total value of all goods and services traded in an economy.

Study Questions

- Should modernization be equated with the good life?
- What might be the *mechanisms* which link large-scale social indicators, social policy and individual claims of happiness?
- What are the key indicators of life quality in the community where I live?
- Should social policy be influenced by measures of the happiness of citizens?
- How do *aggregate* measures of well-being and the lived experience of *individual persons* relate to one another?

Suggestions for Further Reading

Gullone, E. and Cummins, R. A. (eds) (2002) *The Universality of Subjective Well-Being Indicators*. Dordrecht, Kluwer.

Salvaris, M. (2000) *Community and Social Indicators: How citizens can measure progress. An overview of social and community indicator projects in Australia and internationally*. Hawthorn, Victoria, Institute for Social Research, Swinburne University of Technology.

Veenhoven, R. (1996) Happy Life Expectancy: a comprehensive measure of quality-of-life in nations. *Social Indicators Research*, 39: 1–58.

CHAPTER 2

A Life of Quality – Just What Does QOL Mean?

The term 'quality of life' is great in speeches, but when it is given the stature of a research concept, it becomes an uncertain tool unless it is controlled by a precise definition and rigorous discipline in thought and word. (Wolfensberger, 1994: 318)

Preamble

In her review of the clinical psychological and psychiatric literatures Boyle (2002) described the conceptual and practical difficulties caused by professional or technical uses of 'multi-referential lay constructs' – terms like 'depression' or 'anxiety' – which have widespread circulation in everyday language, and are also employed in the social scientific literatures with a (notionally) tightly limited 'professional' meaning. As Brown (2000: 352) notes: 'quality of life is already a well-worn term within society. Everything from clothes to condoms tends to be marketed from this perspective – a perspective where quality of life equates to pleasure.' The difficulty that the overdetermination of meaning of such terms causes in the attempt to use them scientifically is spelled out by Watson. He argues that:

> Ordinary or lay usages of technical terms, and the mundane conceptions of society that they routinely convey, both continue to operate in the technical or professional ... usage. They operate in the background through the shaping or moulding of the professional usage, despite ... attempts to redefine those ordinary meanings of such terms ... the ordinary language meanings of such terms ... can not be wished away or redefined by fiat. Thus [we] can not proceed like the Queen of Hearts in *Alice in Wonderland*, [we] can not command a word to mean whatever [we] want it to mean. (Watson, 2000: 4)

This is a critical point for social scientific research that wishes to engage with a notion such as 'quality of life' which is already imprecise in ordinary usage. Taking our cue from Watson, consider for a moment Alice's further adventures. In *Through the Looking Glass* Alice meets the Red and the White Queens – who have a remarkable set of attributes including the White Queen's ability to remember both backwards and forwards. More pertinent is the Red Queen's response to Alice's attempt to correct her answer to the Queen's inquiry about the cause of lightning: '"It's too late to correct it," said the Red Queen: "when you've once said a thing, that fixes it, and you must take the consequences"' (Carroll, 1982: 186). The QOL literature is, it would seem, unevenly distributed across these two positions. On one hand, with the Red Queen, many appear to believe that 'once you've said a thing' – having operationally defined what QOL is – that 'that fixes it'. On the other, with Alice and Rod Watson, another stream of work is less certain about what sort of a 'thing' quality of life might be, 'scientifically', and questions whether it makes any sense to regard QOL as a social scientific *thing* at all. This 'side' is, in consequence, deeply sceptical about the possibility of 'fixing it' technically. Which side of this binary one adopts does – as the Red Queen implies – make a major difference.

Defining Quality of Life

Happiness; life-satisfaction; well-being; self-actualization; freedom from want; objective functioning; 'a state of complete physical, mental and social well-being not merely the absence of disease' (WHO, 1997: 1); balance, equilibrium or 'true bliss' (Kant, 1978: 185); prosperity; fulfilment; low unemployment; psychological well-being; high GDP; the good life; enjoyment; democratic liberalism; the examined life (*pace* Socrates); a full and meaningful existence (cf. Sheldon, 2000). Not only are all of these terms used in the literature in discussions of what constitutes (a) 'quality of life' but it is difficult if not impossible to reconcile them. It is difficult to better the contention of Cummins *et al.* (in press) that:

> Among the most inconsistently used terms within the human sciences is that of 'quality of life'. Indeed, the words 'quality of life' are used with such abandon that readers must delve into the text to ascertain the intended meaning. Other terms such as 'happiness' and 'well-being' are likewise afflicted.

As we have seen in Chapter 1, when talking about QOL, the literatures invoke matters ranging from objective estimations of the life circumstances of individuals, to those individuals' 'subjective' estimations of their appreciation of those circumstances; from macroeconomic indicators, the 'amounts' of other abstract quanta such as 'human' and 'social capital' (OECD, 2001; Putnam, 1995, 2002) such economies 'possess', to individual happiness with material circumstances. QOL is linked to specific political systems, with some effectively defined *as* quality of life or as an index of it (neoliberal economic policies and democracy being the usual 'variables' related to 'high' QOL, possibly because most QOL research emanates from countries which can afford the of luxury contemplating it – see Frey and Al-Roumi, 1999; Mattes and Christie, 1997).

Some studies evaluate quality of life retrospectively – and at the remove of centuries (although the White Queen would be unimpressed by such a feat). While acknowledging that 'attempts to evaluate the quality of life in historical perspective have been hindered by the absence of data on the perceptions that people held about their well-being', Ostroot and Snyder (1996: 109) nevertheless report a study of the QOL of the people of Aix-en-Provence since 1695. Similarly, Jordan (2001) reports on the QOL of Ireland in the nineteenth century through an analysis of the writings of William Bence Jones, a resident landlord of the time. This project represents a follow-up of his earlier work on quality of life in the context of Irish emigration in the nineteenth century via Irish bootmaker John O'Neill's autobiography, *Fifty Years Experience of an Irish Shoemaker in London* (Jordan, 1999).

There are, further, legion 'indicators', 'components' or 'domains' of *both* societies' *and* individuals' quality of life. Chapter 4 considers this, primarily quantitative, approach in more detail, but for now, the state of the field may be judged by the title of another of Cummins's (1996) papers: 'The domains of life satisfaction: An attempt to order chaos'. The multiplicity of domains identified range from the commonsensical and widely applicable – the availability of decent accommodation and social relationships (Cummins, 1997b) to the highly idiosyncratic – the presence of car parking near the oncology department (Coates *et al.*, 1983). In addition to 'indicators', the literature contains a multiplicity of investigations of the 'effects' of a bewildering variety of activities and states of being-in-the-world upon QOL, variously defined. Thus we read reports on 'the effect of swimming with dolphins on human well-being and anxiety' with 'human well-being' described as 'how "positive" participants felt at that moment' (Webb and Drummond, 2001: 82). A more unusual study of 'human well-being' investigated the 'association between religion, religiosity and well-being' (Anson and Anson, 2001: 83) using *death* as the index of 'well-being' – or rather of its absence. Turning this logic on its head, there also exists a myriad of studies examining the effects of QOL *itself* (again variously defined) on other states of the world: for instance Hagerty *et al.*, (2000) study of the relationship between QOL and the outcomes of elections. Hagerty *et al.* (2000: 347) claim their work shows that QOL, as measured by 'GDP per capita, food availability, inflation, crime rates, divorce rate, and percent of females in the labor force … is the best predictor of voters' behavior' and that 'changes in QOL … significantly affect election outcomes'.

How QOL is defined (or 'fixed') is highly heterogenous across the social scientific literatures. QOL is frequently used as a synonym for the absence of post-operative complications and/or physical robustness in medical settings, as an index of the quantity and quality of staff attention in psychiatric settings and as a shorthand term for community connectedness in intellectual disability settings. In intellectual disability research the definition of QOL has been said to be 'researcher specific' (Lansdesman, 1986) or, as the Queen of Hearts would have it, the term 'means what I want it to mean'.

This chapter addresses two major ongoing theoretical debates. Firstly, what is the relative merit and status of 'objective' and 'subjective' measures of QOL? Secondly, can there be a universal definition of QOL or do definitions of QOL – and the measures derived therefrom – require calibration against the specific life circumstances of populations under study?

Definitions of QOL

In citing definitional diversity as one of the key problems of QOL research, I am recapitulating the commonest observation in reviews of the various QOL literatures. Across the social sciences literature reviews – be they focused on issues of methodology (e.g. Haase *et al.*, 1999), surveys of the QOL measures available in a particular sub-field (e.g. Cagney *et al.*, 2000; Hagerty *et al.*, 2001) or providing brief educational updates for particular professions (Higginson and Carr, 2001) – all concur in their identification of huge variability in the definition of QOL. It is routinely observed that not only do particular studies frequently lack a formal definition of QOL, but also that widely used measures of QOL fail to relate to an explicit theory of QOL and fail to show how QOL 'outputs' are related to 'inputs' in the shape of either public policy (Hagerty *et al.*, 2001), or more local circumstances (Rapley, 2001). Cagney *et al.'s* (2000: 327) account of a review of measures used in the area of end-stage renal disease is typical of the issues:

> From 436 citations, 78 articles were eligible for final review, and of those, 47 articles contained evidence of reliability or validity testing. Within this set, there were 113 uses of 53 different instruments: 82% were generic and 18% were disease specific. Only 32% defined quality of life ... Testing was completed for test-retest reliability (20%), inter-rater reliability (13%), internal consistency (22%), content validity (24%), construct validity (41%), criterion validity (55%), and responsiveness (59%). Few articles measuring quality of life in ESRD defined quality-of-life domains or adequately described instrument development and testing ... Standardized reporting and more rigorous testing could help researchers make informed choices about instruments that would best serve their own and their patients' needs.

In an era in which medicine is increasingly said to be 'evidence-based', the quality of research on QOL (at least in the area of renal disease) is at best mixed and at worst unacceptably poor. It is not only in empirical work that problems are apparent: Haase *et al.* (1999: 125) argue that 'theoretical work on health-related quality of life (HRQL) is not well developed and is often derived from a "shopping list" of concepts that lack clear identification of the theory or assumptions underlying their selection'.

The corollary of atheoretical index development and definitional heterogeneity is that the various phenomena which are taken to be contributory to QOL are equally diverse, be QOL conceptualized as either an individual-level or a population-level construct. Hence, while perhaps a majority of formal definitions in the social science literatures would agree that QOL is a multidimensional construct, neither the number nor the variety of dimensions is yet agreed despite the fact that in some areas – such as intellectual disability – a 'consensus' has been announced (Cummins, 1997a; Felce and Perry, 1996a; IASSID, 2001). This definitional diversity, and the difficulties flowing from it, is one of the problems clearly identified by writers such as Hatton (1998), Taylor (1994) and Rapley (2001) who are cautious about the use of QOL as an individual-level outcome variable: this work will be discussed in more detail in the next chapter.

Quality of Life Defined as a Population-level Construct

That what QOL might 'be' at population level is as heterogenous as it is at an individual level is shown in the diversity of indicators in the literature. Again, there is broad agreement both that quality of life is a *multi-dimensional* construct, and that QOL can be can be related to *normative expectations* about the qualities which citizens' lives may reasonably be anticipated to show (levels of access to income, for example). Precisely *which* dimensions of the lives of individuals or collectivities are selected as indicators of quality of life varies according to different authorities. Such variability occurs for theoretical and practical reasons, and often for a mixture of both. As we saw in Chapter 1, two broad camps exist with regard to the role of *objective* and *subjective* indicators in QOL assessment at both the population and the individual level.

Objective and subjective indicators of QOL

Cummins (1997a: 7) suggests that the separate measurement of objective and subjective components, or 'axes', of quality of life is essential. He states that 'the contemporary literature is quite consistent in its determination that, while both of these axes form a part of the QOL construct, they generally have a very poor relationship to one another. For example, physical health and perceived health are poorly correlated.'

Noll (2000) suggests that the possible combinations of circumstances and personal appraisals of them can be conceptualized as a 2 × 2 matrix (see Figure 2.1). He terms good living conditions and positive well-being

Categories of individual welfare

Objective Living Conditions	Subjective Well-Being	
	Good	Bad
Good	WELL-BEING	DISSONANCE
Bad	ADAPTION	DEPRIVATION

Figure 2.1 Dimensions of objective and subjective well-being (*Source:* Zapf 1984: 25).

'Well-Being' and bad living conditions with a negative evaluation of them 'Deprivation'. 'Dissonance', he suggests, refers to the 'inconsistent combination of good living conditions and dissatisfaction, and is sometimes also called the 'dissatisfaction dilemma' (clearly implying the value judgment that those who are fortunate should be happy with their lot).

'Adaptation' refers to what many researchers see as the problematic combination of bad living conditions and high levels of satisfaction, sometimes known as the 'satisfaction paradox' or 'disability paradox'. The existence of persons in this quadrant is simultaneously the driving force behind the contention that objective and subjective evaluations of QOL *must* be separately measured, the reason why 'Scandinavian' researchers ignore subjectivity altogether and instead measure only 'objective' circumstances (see Hatton, 1998), and the cause of considerable anger among disability researchers who note that only the able-bodied would *necessarily* expect people with disabilities to have an inferior quality of life (Koch, 2001).

The case is still open. Cogent and internally coherent arguments can be made for both 'Scandinavian' and 'American' positions on the objective versus the subjective in defining 'quality of life' and the indicators which are, in consequence, seen as appropriate as indices of the good life. Fundamentally, 'American' inspired researchers and government agencies accord an important role to individuals' assessments of their happiness in the assessment of population well-being, whereas 'Scandinavian' researchers rule out individual happiness when measuring the quality of national life. Again as we saw earlier, researchers such as Veenhoven (1990, 1996, 1997), Noll (2000) and Berger-Schmitt and Jankowitsch (1999) argue for the importance of measuring both objective and subjective quality of life, and in practice, most national governmental agencies which collect data on national well-being include both objective and subjective indicators in their systems of social statistics.

National well-being as a multidimensional concept

That the idea of quality of life is now deeply embedded in the ways that Western countries think themselves (Rose, 1992) is illustrated by the Australian Bureau of Statistics's (ABS) (2001) introduction to its new series of social indicators *Measuring Wellbeing*. The ABS states that 'a major driving force in human activity is the desire for optimal health, for better living conditions and *improved quality of life*. Individuals seek to achieve this for themselves, for their family, and for the communities of which they are a part' (ABS, 2001: 3, my emphasis). Having suggested that improving one's quality of life is a major motivator of human activity, and identified measuring well-being (apparently an interchangeable term with quality of life) as essential to governmental monitoring of the effectiveness of social policy, the ABS then enters the caveat that, when it comes to defining what it means by the term quality of life (or well-being), the 'first step in producing meaningful statistics is to map the conceptual territory that is to be measured. In the case of measuring well-being, this is a large task' (ABS, 2001: 6). However, undaunted, the ABS offers the following definition of well-being/quality of life:

> From birth to death, life enmeshes individuals within a dynamic culture consisting of the natural environment (light, heat, air, land, water, minerals, flora, fauna), the human made environment (material objects, buildings, roads, machinery, appliances, technology), social arrangements (families, social networks, associations, institutions, economies), and human consciousness (knowledge, beliefs, understanding, skills, traditions). Wellbeing depends on all the factors that interact within this culture and can be seen as a state of health or sufficiency in all aspects of life. Measuring wellbeing therefore involves mapping the whole of life, and considering each life event or social context that has the potential to affect the *quality of individual lives*, or the cohesion of society. At the individual level, this can include the physical, emotional, psychological and spiritual aspects of life. At a broader level, the social, material and natural environments surrounding each individual, through interdependency, become part of the wellbeing equation. (ABS, 2001: 6, my emphasis)

While this definition is commendably inclusive and comprehensive, it suggests that measuring well-being/quality of life, or 'mapping the whole of life' is simultaneously both a necessity and an impossibility (Morreim, 1992). Consequently, the ABS explicitly recognizes that 'measuring wellbeing involves making *value judgements* about what aspects of life are important to wellbeing and what social issues are most pressing' (ABS, 2001: 6, my emphasis).

The approach adopted by the ABS is to take the early OCED social indicators as a base set, and to recognize that the development of a system

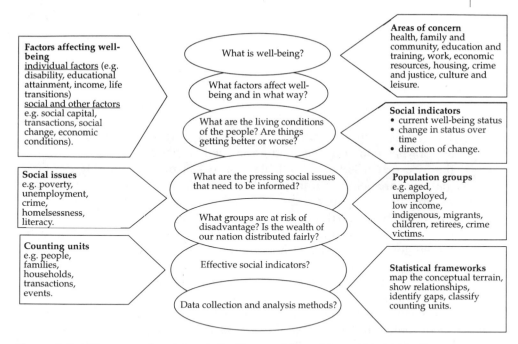

Figure 2.2 ABS system of social statistics (*Source:* Adapted from ABS, 2001: 5).

of social statistics designed to inform national policy-making *necessarily* has to involve 'making a range of pragmatic decisions about what phenomena will provide the greatest insight into these issues, how these phenomena can be measured accurately, and how the resulting measures can be combined, constructed and presented to be informative and accessible' (ABS, 2001: 6). The conceptual model adopted by the ABS is shown in Figure 2.2.

As shown, the Australian system is informed by issues of *theory and methodology* (what is well-being?), by a series of *value judgments* (which policy matters are in 'pressing need' of being informed?) – reflecting the Australian context, the inclusion of matters pertaining to Indigenous Australians in the model – and by a 'range of *pragmatic decisions*' about the available statistical base which can be used to represent, if not the whole of life, then at least Australian national well-being as accurately and completely as possible within the constraints operative (for example, government funding for census-taking).

The ABS explicitly recognizes that there probably can never be a single measure of well-being that will be approved of by all parties interested in the quality of people's lives. Rather, some indicators can, at least in affluent Western nations, be considered 'fundamental' to the measurement of the well-being of national communities (mortality rates, inequality measures and unemployment rates are cited). However, the ABS (2001: 6) also makes the crucially important point that at any one time the range of social indicators ... will be a subset of all possible wellbeing indicators, influenced by the preoccupations and concerns of contemporary culture. The focus of social statistics will also be constrained by what social conditions can be appropriately influenced by policy and intervention.

This point cannot be stressed too strongly. Writers such as Cummins are not persuaded of this, and an influential body of work is critical of the idea that it is both inevitable and in fact probably highly desirable that what are held to count as 'well-being indicators' should be 'influenced by the pre-occupations and concerns of contemporary culture'. Yet decisions about 'what social conditions can be appropriately influenced by policy and intervention' (and, thus, what aspects of QOL should be targets for assessment and intervention) cannot but be historically and culturally contingent. In the 1970s levels of employment in state-owned industries such as coalmining and car manufacturing were identified by countries such as the UK and Australia as appropriate for policy intervention, whereas domestic violence against women was not. By the 1980s the relative positions of these 'social conditions' had been entirely reversed.

The ABS suggests that its definition of QOL has been driven by *pragmatic* as well as by *theoretical* considerations. This is not, necessarily, a 'bad thing' but demonstrates that what the concept of 'quality of life' 'means' is dependent upon the purposes to which any given operational-ization of the concept is to be put. The important point, and here the ABS is exemplary, is that such practical considerations need to be *transparent*. The ABS (2001: 7) states that:

The ABS has given primacy to objective measures of wellbeing, largely for the pragmatic reasons that such information is most useful to government agencies concerned with the delivery of services, and is more readily interpreted. However, subjective measures can provide an important supplement to objective measures, and for this reason are provided by the ABS within specific areas of concern.

The ABS review of readily available statistics, analysis of contemporary 'preoccupations and concerns' and an appraisal of the 'social conditions [which] can be appropriately influenced by policy' has led to the identification of eight major areas of concern – shown in Table 2.1. To all intents and purposes then, the act of *identifying these areas defines quality of life* in the Australian national context.

The ABS is also exemplary in its clarity about its methods and its limitations, and in the clear links it establishes between the areas of concern, measurement units adopted and the policy relevance of the social indicators selected. In Box 2.1 the social and political questions relating to

Table 2.1 Australian system of social indicators

Aspects of life contributing to well-being	Areas of concern
Support and nurture through family and community.	Family and community
Freedom from disability and illnesss.	Health
Realization of personal potential through education.	Education and training
Satisfying and rewarding work both economic and non-economic.	Work
Command over economic resources, enabling consumption.	Economic resources
Shelter, security and privacy, through housing.	Housing
Personal safety and protection from crime.	Crime and justice
Time for and access to cultural and leisure activities.	Culture and leisure

Source: Australian Bureau of Statistics (2001: 7).

Box 2.1 Linkages between areas of concern and social policy in the Australian Bureau of Statistics Framework, *Measuring Wellbeing*

How population relates to well-being
A population can be described in terms of the well-being of its members and the resources needed to sustain and enhance their well-being. Changes in the size, composition or geographic distribution of a population are important because they present a large number of issues concerned with meeting economic and social needs. Population numbers also put pressure on the environment in ways that may not be sustainable over the longer term and potentially threaten living standards. Predicting changes in population size, composition and distribution can help in developing strategies to meet changing needs and to enhance people's well-being.

What are some key social issues relating to population?

• Ensuring that political representation and government expenditures are fairly distributed.
• Whether or not continued population growth is sustainable.
• The need to adapt to changes resulting from the ageing of the population.
• Whether the annual number and mix of migrants coming to or leaving Australia is ideal.
• Whether or not pro-birth policies should be adopted.
• Identifying communities with greatest needs for resources.
• Improving outcomes for the Indigenous population and other disadvantaged groups.

Source: Australian Bureau of Statistics (2001: 28).

the quality of life for the population as a whole that can be informed by social reporting are clearly identified.

Global quality of life

What quality of life for populations means on a global scale can be distilled from the social indicators identified by major international organizations. In *World Development Indicators*, the World Bank (1997a) identifies indicators of sustainable development as People, Environment, Economy, States and Markets and Global Linkages. In the report, *Expanding the Measure of Wealth: Indicators of Environmentally Sustainable Development* (World Bank, 1997b), it is suggested that, because poor environmental performance is, in the long-term, unsustainable and, in the short-term, deleteriously affects the health and well-being of populations, the items listed in Table 2.2 are key performance indicators of environmental life quality at a national level. The World Bank effectively defines high QOL at a population level as, at least in part, determined by patterns of land use

Table 2.2 The World Bank's 1997 World Development Indicators (WDI) – environment section

- *Land use and deforestation* Land area; rural population density; cropland, permanent pasture and other land as a percentage of total land area; total forest area; annual deforestation.
- *Protected areas and biodiversity* nationally protected area; total number and threatened species of mammals, birds and higher plants.
- *Freshwater use* Per capita freshwater resources; annual freshwater withdrawals; freshwater withdrawals by agriculture, industry and domestic use; percentage of rural and urban population with access to safe water.
- *Energy use* production and use of commercial energy; annual and per capita use of commercial energy; use of traditional fuels; growth rate and per capita production of electricity.
- *Energy efficiency, dependency and emissions* Real GDP per unit of energy use; net energy import as a percentage of commercial energy use; total carbon dioxide emissions per capita and per unit of real GDP.
- *Urbanization* Urban population; urban population as a percentage of total population; average annual growth rate of urban population; population in urban agglomerations of a million or more; population in the largest city as a percentage of total population; percentage of urban population with access to sanitation.
- *Traffic and congestion* Number of vehicles per 1,000 people; number of vehicles per kilometre of road; road traffic volumes in million vehicle-kilometres; number of people killed or injured per 1,000 vehicles.
- *Air pollution* Emissions and ambient concentrations of suspended particulate matter and sulphur dioxide.
- *Government commitment* Status of country environmental profile; national conservation strategy; biodiversity profile; compliance with Convention on International Trade in Endangered Species of Wild Flora and Fauna; participation in climate change, ozone layer, chlorofluorocarbon control and law of the sea treaties.

Source: World Bank (1997b: 107).

and extent of deforestation; the existence of protected areas and the protection of biodiversity; proportion of the population with access to usable fresh water; levels of urbanization including the percentage of the urban population who have access to sanitation; extent of air pollution; and demonstrable environmentally-friendly policies.

Likewise the European System of Social Indicators (EUSI) project (Berger-Schmitt and Noll, 2000) has been based on an inventory of the goals and objectives of the European Union and an analysis of the social indicators literature. EUSI has identified six major goal dimensions of European societal development which, with *quality of life* identified as the 'overarching objective' (Berger-Schmitt and Noll, 2000: 42) form the core of EUSI. Berger-Schmitt and Noll (2000) state that the goal dimensions were selected as directly relevant to the concepts of *quality of life*, social cohesion and sustainability. They argue that, at the European level, QOL incorporates two 'goal dimensions': the improvement of objective living conditions such as working conditions, state of health or standard of living and the enhancement of subjective well-being, as assessed by measures of happiness or satisfaction.

While the goal dimensions addressed by the concepts of *social cohesion* and *strengthening social connections and ties* are described as separate from QOL, many of the measures identified would, under other definitions, be construed as domains of life quality. Thus 'social cohesion' is described as having, as 'goal dimensions', the reduction of social disparities, social inequalities and social exclusion as may be indicated by regional disparities in the distribution of welfare within a society and equal opportunities. The third goal dimension, strengthening social connections and ties – elsewhere referred to (for example, OECD, 2001; Putnam, 1995) as 'social capital' – or the social relations within a society (informal networks, associations and organizations as well as formal societal institutions) are seen as key components.

Two other EUSI goal dimensions draw on the concept of sustainability as described in the World Bank's (1997a) 'four capital approach'. According to this approach, sustainability requires the preservation of the societal capital (physical capital, social capital, human capital, natural capital) in order to secure acceptable living conditions for future generations. The two subsidiary goal dimensions are: preservation of human capital, with indicators focusing on 'the processes and measures that affect people's skills, education and health', and the preservation of natural capital, with social indicators of the 'processes and measures that improve or deteriorate the base of natural resources' being identified as indices.

EUSI is, according to Berger-Schmitt and Noll (2000), structured by both these goal dimensions and a subset of life domains. Within each life domain up to eight goal dimensions are operationalized in terms of domain-specific measurement dimensions, subdimensions and indicators. The life domains identified as a subset of the broader scale social indicators are specified

Table 2.3 Indices of national well-being in the European System of Social Indicators: life domains, measurement dimensions, subdimensions and indicators

Life Domain: Population

Measurement Dimension: Population Size
Resident Population
Population Growth
   Crude Birth Rate
   Crude Death Rate
   Rate of Natural Population Increase
   Rate of Population Increase
Population Structure
Structure of Population by Age and Sex
   Population Aged Less than 15 Years
   Population Aged 15–24 Years
   Population Aged 25–64 Years
   Population Aged 65–79 Years
   Population Aged 80 Years and Older
Sex Ratio of Population
Dependency Structures
   Age Dependency Ratio
   Burden of Child Population
   Burden of Inactive Population
   Burden of Population in Education and Training
   Burden of Retired Population
Structure of Population by Marital Status
   Single Persons
   Married Persons
   Divorced Persons
   Widowed Persons

Measurement Dimension: Population Density and Agglomeration
Population Density
   Population Density
Agglomeration of Population
   Population of Large Cities
   Population of Small Municipalities

Measurement Dimension: Migration and Foreign Population
Internal Migration
   Inter-municipal Migration Rate
   Interregional Migration Rate
Immigration
   Immigration Rate
   Share of Non-National ImmigrantsShare of EU Immigrants
   Share of European Non-EU Immigrants
   Share of Non-European Immigrants

continued over

Table 2.3 continued

Share of Children in Immigrants
Share of Youth in Immigrants
Share of Working Age Immigrants
Emigration
   Total Emigration Rate
   Share of National Emigrants
   Share of Children in Emigrants
   Share of Youth in Emigrants
   Share of Working Age Emigrants
Asylum Seekers
   Inflow of Asylum Seekers
   Share of Asylum Seekers from Europe
   Share of Asylum Seekers from Asia
   Share of Asylum Seekers from Africa
   Share of Asylum Seekers from Latin American and Caribbean Countries
   Recognition Rate of Asylum Applications
Foreign Population and Acquisition of Citizenship
   Percentage of Total Foreign Population
   Share of Foreign Population from EU Countries
   Share of Foreign Population from European Non-EU Countries
   Share of Foreign Population from Non-European Countries
   Share of Children in Foreign Population
   Share of Youth in Foreign Population
   Share of Working Age People in Foreign Population
   Acquisition of Citizenship

---

under the headings of: Population; Households and Families; Housing; Transport; Leisure, Media and Culture; Social and Political Participation and Integration; Education and Vocational Training; Labour Market and Working Conditions; Income, Standard of Living, and Consumption Patterns; Health; Environment; Social Security; Public Safety and Crime; Total Life Situation. Within each of these areas, as noted, further sub-indices are identified: for the life domain of 'Population' a further three measurement dimensions are identified (Population Size, Population Density and Agglomeration, Migration and Foreign Population), with multiple subdimensions and indicators – as shown in Table 2.3.

Assessing the quality of QOL indices

Hagerty *et al*. (2001) have reported a comprehensive survey, conducted on behalf of the International Society for Quality of Life Studies (ISQOLS), of population level QOL indices. Table 2.4 shows the major areas of life satisfaction/quality of life identified in a selection of measures designed to

Table 2.4 Domains of QOL measured by selected indices of population well-being

COMQOL (Cummins, 1997)	Index of Economic Well-Being	American Demographics Index	Johnston's QOL Index (Johnston's 1988)	UN Human Development Index (UNHDP, 1990)	Index of Social Health (Fordham Institute, 1999)	Virginia QOL Survey (Virginia Tech, 1998)	Index of Social Progress (e.g. Estes, 1997)	Swedish ULF
Relationship with family and friends (weight = 100)		Divorce rate	Family stability		Child abuse	Satisfaction with family life		Social contacts
Emotional well-being (weight = 98)					Teenage suicide	Happiness		
Material well-being (weight = 77)	GDP, housing, capital stock, capital investment, poverty rate	Income and employment, consumer expectations, productivity	Earnings and income, housing	PPP/capita	Average weekly earnings, access to affordable housing		Economic	Material living standards, housing, transport, leisure
Health (weight = 67)			Health	Longevity	Infant mortality, health insurance coverage, out-of-pocket health costs for >65	Satisfaction with health and health care	Health status	Health

Work and productive activity (weight = 61)	Employment	Employment, education		Unemployment, high school dropouts	Satisfaction with work and employment, satisfaction with education	Education	Employment, working environment
Feeding part of one's local community (weight = 27)	Number of endangered species	Poverty, equality	Literacy	Poverty rate >65, gap between rich and poor	Satisfaction with environment	Women status, political participation, cultural diversity, demographic	Social mobility, participation
Personal safety Crime rate (weight = 27)	Crime rate	Public safety		Homicides, alcohol-related traffic fatalities	Satisfaction with law enforcement	Defence effort, geography	Victimization
Subjective QOL					Good place to live, go to school, go to college, get job		

Source: Adapted from Hagerty et al. (2001).

inform national policy. As is apparent, the variation across measures is not only huge, but also suggests that a clear consensual theoretical specification of QOL as a population level construct, and the relation between such things as school attendance and the reports of individual citizens about their personal happiness, is yet unattained.

The difficulty of linking various phenomena to QOL as an end-state is a pervasive problem. Hagerty *et al.* (2001) note that 'most of the indexes [*sic*] reviewed failed to specify any well-established theory behind the index. By theory, we mean the "nomological net" of concepts and causal paths that specify how QOL is related to exogenous and endogenous variables.' In consequence they suggest a systems theory structural model of QOL in an attempt to define both the meaning and the mechanisms of production of quality of life (see Figure 2.3).

In the 'input' column are 'exogenous environmental variables affecting citizens' QOL'. Many of these items are familiar social indicators of QOL conceptualized as a population-level construct: socio-economic status, extent of freedom, income inequality. However, while Hagerty *et al.* (2001) note that aspects of these indicators are, at least in principle, amenable to alteration by public policy, it is of some concern that 'personality' is conceived of as an 'input variable'. Such a 'variable' may be better placed in the second column, where *throughput* variables, described as 'the *individual's response* to this environment (e.g., education achieved, marriage choice)' are itemized. It is somewhat naïve to see such matters (which are again measurable as 'objective social indicators') as being exclusively individual 'variables' which 'reflect the *individual's choice* in response to the environment and to public policy'. Such a view fails to take account of the fact that access to meaningful 'individual choice' about such things as 'consumption' or even 'marriage' is not a 'variable' normally distributed across populations, the QOL of which this model attempts to describe. QOL 'output' is disaggregated in the third column into Cummins's (1996b) domains which subsequently feed into the three higher order outputs suggested by Veenhoven (1999): happiness (or SWB), personal survival and contribution to the human heritage, described as 'the result of input and throughput'. Yet while this model may be equally comprehensible to biologists and public policy-makers, as Hagerty *et al.* (2001) contend, it is still far from explicit *how*, precisely, the model is supposed to *work*. How 'personality' determines 'marriage and children', which in turn results in happiness with 'family and friends' and, ultimately, 'SWB output' is unspecified.

Local quality of life indicators

Salvaris's (2000) review of social indicators offers a rather different perspective on the definition of QOL. Hagerty *et al.* (2001: 2–6) identify the users of reliable and valid QOL indexes as 'public policymakers'. The members of this category are identified as:

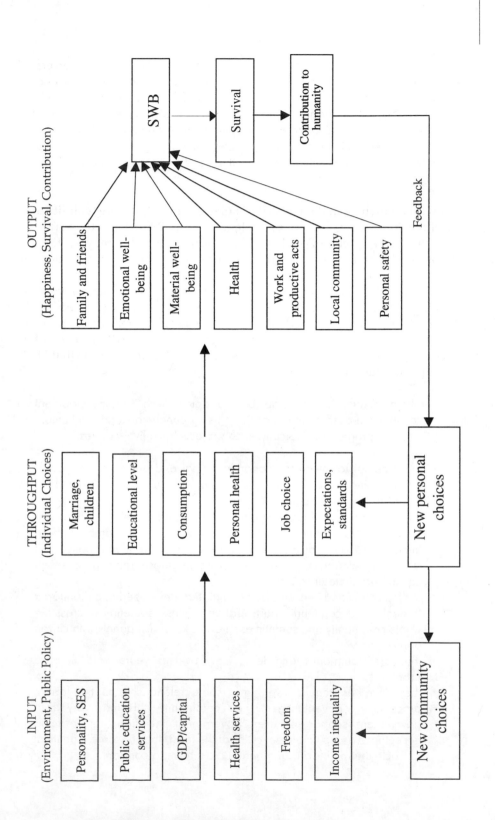

Figure 2.3 Systems theory structure of quality of life concepts and causes (*Source:* Hagerty *et al.* 2001).

physicians and counsellors helping individuals in need ... social workers helping families in need ... town governments developing policies and programs that can help enhance community QOL ... state bodies developing policies and programs that can assist residents of the entire state or province ... national agencies developing policies and programs that can assist citizens of that country ... international agencies developing policies and programs that can assist the world's citizens and the planet at large.

However, nowhere in their 14 criteria (see Chapter 4) for the 'validity and usefulness of such QOL indexes' (Hagerty *et al.*, 2001: 1) do they suggest that the end-recipients of public policy – ordinary people – may legitimately be entitled to a view of what constitutes the 'validity' of indicators of social well-being.

Salvaris (2000) instead views social indicators as a *social movement*. Asking if social indicators are to be a 'technocratic panacea' (Salvaris, 2000: 7) or whether they might contribute to enhancing the democratic process, he argues that locally-developed indicators of QOL allow *citizens* rather than academics, politicians or administrators to decide what it is that QOL means. He suggests that:

For three decades now, there has been a rapid growth in the development of community based planning projects using benchmarks and indicators to measure progress ... Typically, such projects have five features:

- they attempt to integrate economic, social and environmental goals around some overall vision of progress or well being, some 'path to the future' for that particular community;
- they set concrete goals or 'benchmarks' and develop appropriate 'indicators' to monitor progress in achieving them; some of these benchmarks and indicators are expressed in conventional policy and statistical categories; others (for example, those relating to social capital) are quite unconventional;
- the indicators and benchmarks are initiated, developed and monitored through some community participation process, sometimes across the whole community and sometimes through specialist panels with citizen participation;
- they are commonly long term (i.e., over 5 years) and iterative processes;
- they have, or acquire over time, some relationship to the formal processes of governance in their community; this may vary from government support or even government initiation, to *de facto* acceptance as legitimate policy, or at the least, they become a political obstacle that politicians and bureaucrats have to confront.

Describing the development of community social indicators across the Western world (in the USA, Canada, Norway, Australia and Ireland) as a 'social movement', Salvaris sketches the origin of the movement in the convergence of three separate phenomena; first, the general recognition that 'broad social and economic problems need community-wide solutions' (Salvaris, 2000: 2); second, 'a sense of actual or likely decline in economic and social well-being, and a desire to find integrated community wide solutions'; and third, challenging studies (such as Frey and Al-Roumi, 1999) that suggest democracy unproblematically increases QOL he argues that:

> The second factor is a democratic problem. Democracy, community and citizenship have been perceived as weakening institutions ... as a product of many factors: the size and complexity of government and society; globalisation and a perceived loss of autonomy in national policy; lack of trust in the main political parties; and the effects of a decade or more of government cuts in social and community infrastructure ... public alienation from political processes, growing social inequality, a decline in social trust and civic participation, more corporate and commercially oriented models of governments that have brought fundamental changes in the language and culture of democracy. Perhaps the most conspicuous example of the latter is the gradual transformation of citizens into 'customers' (Saul, 1997). There is no single solution to compound problems like these, but there is some agreement on the most obvious remedies. (Salvaris, 2000: 3)

Perhaps the most striking of the remedies Salvaris identifies is the proposal that genuinely *meaningful* – as opposed to 'valid' in Hagerty *et al.*'s (2001) sense – social indicators of QOL should be developed by community consultation processes, for local purposes. Also essential is: an emphasis on social inclusion; a 'community health' approach to defining life quality rather than a focus on 'improved "customer service"'; the development of social trust and stronger communities via more meaningful and cooperative governance; and the creation of 'more open and democratic processes and forums, for resolving conflicting interests, creating greater accountability and extending opportunities for citizen participation in governance' (Salvaris, 2000: 3). Assuming that the *meaning* of quality of life is a local and political matter – rather than a universal, abstract and apolitical or academic one – may enhance the quality of people's lives.

Such projects have been established at all levels from the nation-state to local communities. National-level projects, such as the Canadian Policy Research Networks (CPRN) project, has convened a citizen-based consultancy to identify national quality of life indicators. The CPRN project (*Asking Citizens What Matters for Quality of Life*) starts from the premise that:

> While there is much activity on quality of life indicators in Canada, there is no initiative underway ... that seeks input from citizens. CPRN is seeking to fill that void. It is leading and working with a Steering Committee representing a broad cross-section of organizations interested in developing a set of national indicators to track Canada's progress in quality of life, through a citizen engagement process. (CPRN, cited in Salvaris, 2000: 23)

Salvaris also describes social indicators/QOL projects in Australia. Local government-based projects in NSW, Australia also ask *citizens* rather than 'public policymakers' or academic researchers 'what matters for quality of life'. In the Sutherland Shire, in south Sydney, NSW (with a population of over 200,000 people) the Shire (the local government unit) produces a 'State of the Shire' report which monitors well-being in 12 'life spheres' drawn from a 1996 'Community Priorities' survey. Indicators of well-being in Sutherland Shire – or 'what matters for quality of life' – are measures of: community safety; community issues; decision-making; economy; education; environment; health; housing; land use; leisure; neighbourhoods; and transport.

Similarly, *Measuring the Quality of Life in Newcastle* also links community development to the articulation of locally-meaningful indices of QOL. This project has adopted 27 key social indicators developed by a community-based working group as 'local indicators' of life quality for the project. As such, what quality of life *means* in Newcastle, NSW *is the range of measures adopted by the community as indicators of the quality of life*. In Newcastle QOL means: 'clean beaches; quality of community space; air quality; appropriate educational opportunities for all; unemployment levels; appropriate transport networks; conservation of local native plants and animals; resource consumption; availability of appropriate housing for all; community participation in decision making; social support networks; perception of safety; income levels; and the diversity of employment and industry sectors' (Australia Institute and City of Newcastle, 2000, as cited in Salvaris, 2000).

Salvaris (2000: 41) describes a 'framework for national well-being indicators' as shown in Table 2.5. This collection of indicators thus represents an operational definition of what QOL actually *means* at a local population level in nation-states. Again we see that the 'health and well-being' of individuals is identified as a key indicator (in aggregate) of the well-being of collectivities.

Thus *national well-being* may be defined as populations being offered what 'enlightened societies provide for their citizens' (Edgerton, 1996: 88). That

Table 2.5 A framework for national well-being indicators

1. Individual health and well-being
2. Good work opportunities
3. A fair society
4. A secure and crime-free society
5. A productive and responsible economy
6. Good government and laws
7. A healthy, sustainable environment
8. Healthy communities and active citizens
9. A vigorous cultural life
10. Good international relations

Source: Salvaris (2000).

is, the quality of life of the nation-state may be judged by the extent to which individual members are healthy and active citizens; individuals have 'good work opportunities'; social relations are characterized by 'fairness', security and freedom from crime in a context of good government and legislation; where the economy is not merely productive but also 'responsible'; where the environment and human communities are healthy, sustainable and offer vigorous cultural life; and where the nation-state enjoys 'good international relations'.

Such indicators clearly share much with those described by the United Nations, the EUSI, the ABS and the World Bank. Table 2.6 shows Australia's relative standing in relation to the OECD on a range of such indicators, broken down, as for example the EUSI project does, into a series of sub-indicators. Once more, one may infer an operational definition of high life quality from such specifications. A high quality of life is indicated by: earnings growth; the absence of poverty and unemployment; decent housing; health spending and life expectancy; an educated population; high levels of cultural participation and low rates of crime; equity in social opportunities; and the absence of political corruption in the broader context of responsible environmental management.

One of the difficulties with such large-scale indices as developed by the OECD, the World Bank or the ABS is that not only may they – owing to their aggregate form – unintendedly mask very real differences between population subgroups but they may be distant from the concerns of individual citizens or local communities. Community social indicator projects are then a response to such forced abstraction. But, while Bruce and Sheila in Newcastle may feel that the cleanliness of the local beach is a key determinant of their QOL, this perception may not be universally shared.

In response to such concerns, the development of notions of QOL as an individual-level construct has occurred. Here again, we encounter a

Table 2.6 Social health in OECD countries: Australia

Field Indicator	Australia		
	Actual	Rank (total)	% best practice
Income			
1 Real GDP per head (US$000)	19.6	14 (23)	52
2 Population below income poverty line (%)	13	15 (17)	46
3 Real earning growth by employee p.a. 1980–92	0.5	12 (19)	28
Work			
4 Total unemployment rate (%)	8.5	13 (21)	73
5 Long-term unemployment (12 months+)	2.6	10 (20)	83
6 Labour market participation %	51	7 (23)	69
Housing			
7 Home ownership rate %	70	2 (12)	93
8 Proportion of public and supported housing %	5.7	10 (12)	11
Health			
9 Life expectancy at birth (yrs)	78	5 (23)	75
10 Spending on public health (% GDP)	5.8	14 (23)	48
11 Life satisfaction/happiness (index/100)	76.7	7 (23)	96
Education			
12 Fulltime students per 100 ppl aged 5–29 yrs	55	19 (21)	19
13 Public education spending (% GDP)	5.6	11 (23)	41
14 Population with higher education (%)	24.3	7 (18)	42
Culture			
15 Ownership of TV per 1,000 ppl	641	3 (23)	71
16 Telephone lines per 1,000 ppl	510	11 (23)	46
17 Daily newspapers copies per 1,000 ppl	257	13 (22)	39
Social stress			
18 Suicides per 100,000 ppl	19	7 (18)	66
19 Prisoners per 100,000 ppl (excludes USA)	120	19 (19)	0
20 Intentional homicides by men per 1,000 ppl	2.5	18 (23)	83
Equity/democracy			
21 Income inequality (top 20% by bottom 20%)	9.6	17 (18)	1
22 Women in Parliament	24	4 (23)	47
23 Central gov. spend social security (% total CGS)	1.0	11 (17)	12
24 Comply with UN human rights conventions %	91	16 (22)	6
25 Perceived corruption (Transparency Internat.)	8.7	10 (23)	76
26 Development aid (ODA) ($ per cap. donor country)	62	13 (20)	13
Environment			
27 Energy use (000 kg oil equiv. per head)	5.3	18 (23)	42
28 Environment pollution (CO_2 emissions kg p. cap)	16.2	21 (23)	28
29 Protected areas as total land area	8.7	14 (23)	25

Indicator sources: OECD, World Bank, UN and country data.
Source: Salvaris (2000). Reproduced with permission.

tension between the proponents of universalist and individualist approaches, between those who believe that quality of life is a phenomenon that is shared universally by all persons, with definable and empirically measurable domains, and those who believe that the quality of a person's life is best understood not as a quantum of individual 'mind stuff', but rather as a 'sensitizing concept' (Taylor, 1994) which can help to alert us to the things that matter in life to particular persons. There are those who seek to 'map the world' in its entirety, and those who focus on specific, and maybe ungeneralizable, appreciations of small parts of it. It is to quality of life defined as an individual, subjective, experience that we now turn.

Quality of Life as an Individual-level Construct

> To me, quality of life means to feel good and to have what is needed to cope with your life in the best way possible. (Robert Groulx, President, People First of Montreal, quoted in Groulx et al., 2000: 23)

Chapter 1 discussed the development of the idea that QOL is not merely a matter of the 'quality of the lives which ... people lead' at an aggregate population level. Recently the idea has developed that it also makes sense to conceive of QOL as an aspect of individual subjectivity, a psychological quantum expressing the satisfaction of particular people with their individual lives. A major effort has been expended on trying to arrive at a formally specified, *operational definition* of the construct. The effort, then, has been to refine unsuitably vague 'lay' notions of the good life – such as Robert Groulx's – and to replace them with formal, technical, definitions and criteria.

There are two broad approaches to this: firstly, attempts to specify generic definitions of QOL that apply to humanity as a whole and, secondly, attempts to specify locally relevant QOL constructs such as 'health-related QOL' or 'disease-specific QOL'. Such definitions vary in their specificity and levels of theoretical sophistication.

Universal QOL Definitions

Many population-level systems of social indicators can be read as specifying a definition of QOL, as it were, by default. Collections of statistics are held together not by an explicitly stated *theory* of the good life, but by a set of commonsense understandings that these various indicators make up a set of diagnostic social facts against which the goodness, or quality, of life is judged. Thus, at least in Western countries, while high levels of unemployment do not need to be explicitly defended as indicators of a (poor) quality of living in a particular society, other statistics, for example income inequality, as the work of Salvaris (2000) suggests, increasingly do.

At the individual level efforts centre on a formal operational definition of what QOL *is as such*. The question – while it sounds quite straight forward – can be asked and answered in a multiplicity of ways, and the particular ways that the social sciences go about answering such questions, by attempting to specify formal definitions of the phenomenon and operational criteria for inferring the construct, are only one, and not necessarily the best, way to go about such enquiries. To ask 'what is quality of life?' is *not* to ask the same sort of a question as asking 'what is a planet?' or 'what is electricity?' It is, in principle, not possible to say Groulx's 'definition' of QOL, 'to feel good and to have what is needed to cope with your life in the best way possible' is wrong, or that it is misguided or erroneous. This subtle but crucial point is overlooked by many writers in the social sciences who routinely claim that it is *other* researchers who have got it wrong, that what quality of life *really* is, is the way they themselves happen to define it.

There are now a small number of candidate definitions available in the literature which appear to receive wide – but not unanimous – endorsement. A range of these definitions is presented below, with brief observations about some of the difficulties each entails. All specify that QOL is an *individual psychological* perception of the *material reality* of aspects of the world. The WHOQOL Group (1993: 1) defines QOL as:

> an individual's perception of their position in life in the context of the culture and value systems in which they live and in relation to their goals, expectations values and concerns ... incorporating in a complex way the person's physical health, psychological state, level of independence, social relationships, personal beliefs and their relationship to salient features of the environment ... Quality of life refers to a subjective evaluation which is embedded in a cultural, social and environmental context ... quality of life cannot simply be equated with the terms 'health status', 'life satisfaction', 'mental state', or 'well-being'. Rather it is a multidimensional concept.

This definition of QOL benefits from comprehensiveness and efforts to relate the idea to cultural, social and environmental contexts and to local value systems. It is, however, unclear how QOL – as an 'individual's perception of their position in life' or 'a subjective evaluation' – cannot be 'simply equated with a mental state'. A similar definition appealing to cultural relativity is provided by Goode (1994a: 148):

> QOL is experienced when a person's basic needs are met and when he or she has the opportunity to pursue and achieve goals in major life settings ... The QOL of an individual is intrinsically related to the QOL of other

persons in his or her environment ... the QOL of a person reflects the cultural heritage of the person and those who surround him or her.

Efforts at universality and comprehensiveness cause problems in and of themselves. If one were to ask a Yolgnu lawman from Arnhem Land, Australia and a Los Angeles movie star for their 'subjective evaluations' of the QOL, what confidence might we have that these estimations had anything in common? Could we be confident that the 'thing' being 'subjectively evaluated' was the *same* thing in both cases? The very 'multidimensionality' built into the WHOQOL's definition and the cultural relativism central to Goode's almost certainly guarantees that whatever 'QOL' is for a Yolgnu lawman, it is not at all the same thing as it is for Harrison Ford.

A similar set of concerns arises, but for the opposite reasons, with another candidate definition. Woodill *et al.* (1994: 67) define QOL as:

The degree to which a person enjoys the important possibilities of his or her life ... This definition can be simplified to – 'How good is your life for you?'

In avoiding specificity about the component domains of QOL Woodill *et al.* (1994) dodge the difficulties caused by the WHO's specificity. The fact that the relationship between an Inuit hunter and 'salient features of the environment' is utterly different from that obtaining between a New York lawyer and her environment is accommodated, but at the price of a definition of QOL that is far from universal. As each individual has different 'important possibilities' in their life, and the extent to which they 'enjoy' them is likely to be variable, the concept becomes so individually-specific as to be of little use for comparing the QOL of different population groups. Such definitions then result in a formal operationalization of the construct that remains not only completely culturally relative but also individually specific.

Similarly problematic is the definitional preamble advanced by Schalock and Parmenter (2000: 4) in the consensus document on QOL produced for the International Association for the Scientific Study of Intellectual Disability. They write that:

It is necessary to understand the semantic meaning of the quality of life concept, and its use throughout the world to appreciate fully its importance and relevance to persons. In reference to its meaning, 'quality' makes us think of the excellence or exquisite standard associated with human characteristics and positive values such as happiness, success, wealth, health, and satisfaction; whereas, 'of life' indicates that the concept concerns the very essence or essential aspects of human existence.

This account again fails the test of universality at the same time as endeavouring to address it. Quite what the 'essence' of human existence is has bedevilled philosophy since Plato (as Schalock and Parmenter acknowledge) and there is, as yet, no sign of a 'consensus' on the question. Similarly, to claim that 'values such as happiness, success, wealth, health, and satisfaction' are universally 'positive' is simply to be blinded by ethnocentrism. Health, wealth and the pursuit of happiness may be the essence of the American dream, but to assert that this is true of humanity as a whole is intellectual and cultural imperialism. Later it is observed that:

> Quality of life encompasses the basic conditions of life such as adequate food, shelter, and safety plus life enrichers such as inclusive social, leisure, and community activities. These enrichers are based on the individual's values, beliefs, needs and interests. (Schalock and Parmenter, 2000: 7)

Again attempts at universality become immediately enmeshed in Western middle-class values. That is 'life enrichers' have every possibility of being one thing in Ulan Bator and quite another in San Diego. The taken-for-grantedness of the specification of 'life enrichers' such as 'leisure' neglects the fact that the very *idea* of 'leisure' is, in and of itself, an almost entirely modern Western concept which has little, if any, meaning – in the Western Anglophone sense of sufficient spare time and disposable income to engage in non-productive activities – if one is a rag picker living in Calcutta or an Indonesian pieceworker manufacturing 'leisure' goods like Nike trainers for Western consumers.

However, IASSID feel confident that, while a universal definition of QOL may be unavailable, in practice such a specification is possible by defining instead a set of 'conceptualization principles'. This is to attempt a definition of quality of life as an individual-level concept by the back door. It is suggested that quality of life:

1. Is composed of those same factors and relationships for people with intellectual disabilities that are important to those without disabilities.
2. Is experienced when a person's needs are met and when one has the opportunity to pursue life enrichment in major life settings.
3. Has both subjective and objective components; but it is primarily the perception of the individual that reflects the quality of life he/she experiences.
4. Is based on individual needs, choices, and control.
5. Is a multidimensional construct influenced by personal and environ-mental factors such as intimate relationships, family life, friendships, work, neighborhood, city or town of residence, housing, education,

health, standard of living, and the state of one's nation. (Schalock and Parmenter, 2000: 7)

The 'conceptualization principles' here are close to the earlier definition by the WHOQOL Group (1993) and have been developed from Felce and Perry (1993: 13) who define QOL, as a universal material/psychological phenomenon, as follows:

> Quality of life is defined as an overall general well-being which comprises objective descriptors and subjective evaluations of physical, material, social and emotional well-being together with the extent of personal development and purposeful activity all weighted by a personal set of values.

This definition has been produced as a schematic model by Felce and Perry (1996) and is shown in diagrammatic form in Figure 2.4.

The model draws together the suggestions of the IASSID group and makes several key claims. It is suggested that 'quality of life' is the same for people whether or not they are intellectually disabled (that is QOL is the same for all of humanity); that for all people QOL is more than just the meeting of basic needs, it is derived from 'life enrichment' and the individual perception thereof. This point, it must be noted, veers into tautology: QOL is … what the individual perceives the quality of their life to be. Equally explicit is the idea that, in arriving at such a circular perception, QOL is based on 'needs, choices, and control', presumably over such things as the 'opportunity to pursue life enrichment in major life settings'. Again the culture-bound nature of such a *soi-disant* 'international' conclusion is noticeable. The final aspect of the international consensus view, 'principle 5', that quality of life 'is influenced by personal and environmental factors such as intimate relationships, family life, friendships, work, neighborhood, city or town of residence, housing, education, health, standard of living, and the state of one's nation' is in some tension with the earlier 'principle 3'. Recall that quality of life 'is primarily the perception of the individual'. If influenced by known and knowable multidimensional factors how is the perception individual? If individual, how do we know what factors influence this particular person's particular perceptions of their quality of life?

At the individual level, however, perhaps the most influential definition of quality of life is offered by Cummins (1997a: 6) who defines quality of life thus:

> Quality of life is both objective and subjective, each axis being the aggregate of seven domains: material well-being, health, productivity, intimacy, safety, community and emotional well-being. Objective domains comprise culturally relevant measures of objective well-being. Subjective

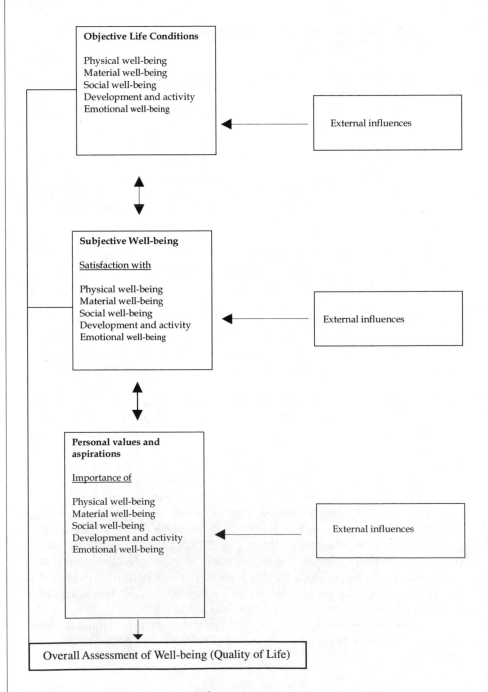

Figure 2.4 A model of quality of life.

Source: Felce and Perry (1996). Reproduced with the permission of the AAMR.

domains comprise domain satisfaction weighted by their importance to the individual.

This definition has the advantages of individual weighting of the importance of the various domains, the identification of the subjective domains via a careful review of the literature and the identification of objective domains that are 'culturally important'. Whether these domains are as likely to be important to non-Anglophone, or 'non-Western', populations is an open question. The studies of the perceptions of Aboriginal Australians in Melbourne, discussed at the end of this chapter, suggests that this is an area requiring further study.

Definitions of health-related quality of life

Many sub-areas of QOL research have developed specialty-specific definitions of QOL. Perhaps the best example is in medicine, where many definitions of 'health-related quality of life' have been advanced. Here again the ongoing debate regarding objective versus subjective descriptions of the meaning of quality of life surfaces. For example Wiklund *et al.* (1986) identify the three major components of QOL in clinical medical settings as: functional capacity, subjective perceptions, and symptoms and their consequences. Rather more broadly, Testa and Nackley (1994: 537) suggest that QOL means a range of both *objective* circumstances and *subjective perceptions* of them. They describe:

a set of domains related to the physical, functional, psychological, and social health of the individual. When used in this context it is often referred to as 'health-related quality of life'... Health-related quality of life involves the five broad dimensions of opportunity, health perceptions, functional status, morbidity or impairment, and mortality.

Walker (1992: 265) suggests that QOL is best defined as a more centrally subjective response to a range of strictly limited, and medically-related, circumstances. For Walker, QOL means:

a broad range of physical and psychological characteristics and limitations which describe an individual's ability to function and derive satisfaction from so doing ... health related quality of life is probably the key term and this is defined as the level of well-being and satisfaction associated with an individual's life and how this is affected by disease, accidents and treatment.

Finally Carr *et al.* (2001: 1240) suggest that quality of life is *purely* a matter of subjectively experienced health-related discrepancies. That is

quality of life … is those aspects of an individual's subjective experience
that relate both directly and indirectly to health, disease, disability and
impairment … health related quality of life is the gap between our
expectations of health and our experience of it.

Cummins (1997b: 124) provides a scathing critique of all such HRQOL
definitions. The key problem in these specifications of QOL, he argues, is
'confusion as to what might constitute a reasonable set of dependent
variables to measure medical outcome, and quality of life … variables
are referenced either to what is "normal" or to pathology, and … [QOL]
… is defined through medically related measurement'. Further, Cummins
(1997b) points out that the idea that people may be medically or physically
compromised and yet enjoy a quality of life equal to, or higher than, that of
the non-disabled general population is not countenanced in such
definitions (we will return to this point briefly below). In summary,
Cummins (1997b: 125) argues that:

health-referenced QOL definitions impose an overly restricted view of the
construct. They tend to produce self-fulfilling prophesies by concentrating
on the negative aspects of disease and injury. In contrast, broader
approaches to measurement allow for a much more positive view …
Using broader forms of measurement, people with a physical disability, an
intellectual disability, or people who have survived an organ transplantation can register a level of subjective well-being as high, or higher, than
the normal range for the population.

These are serious and sensible objections, but they overlook the key
consideration of the *variation* that there may be in the *purpose* of QOL
measurement across settings and levels of analysis. Such objections also
implicitly assume that there is a singular and universally meaningful
definition of the concept. As we saw earlier the ABS (2001), for example,
explicitly recognizes that what counts as QOL for its particular purposes
must be driven by the purposes to which such data are intended to be put.
In medical settings it is reasonable that if one is interested in how patients'
QOL is influenced by medical procedures, that one's definition of QOL is
driven by those factors of most local importance. 'Using broader forms of
measurement' may well produce different results, but there is no point
using measurement tools or technologies which are not directly relevant to
the questions one wishes to ask. It is, as the 'social indicators movement'
has shown us, often the case that locally-derived indicators of QOL are,
inherently, more meaningful. That is, the fact that many ordinary people
do not appear to find academic accounts of QOL meaningful is the issue to
which we now turn.

The Forced Abstraction of the Meaning of QOL

In this section the idea of HRQOL is used to illustrate a wider problem in the measurement of QOL as an individual-level construct. As we saw earlier, workers dealing with population-level social indicators such as Salvaris (2000) have argued strongly that whatever it is that QOL means, its meaning should be defined locally by those to whom it is immediately meaningful. This section looks at the issue at the level of the individual conceptualization of quality of life.

While Cummins (1997b) insists that the use of terms such as 'health-related quality of life' are conceptually incoherent in and of themselves, workers such as Mozes et al. (1999) have used survey techniques to evaluate the divergence between 'lay' and professional understandings of 'health-related quality of life'. Specifically they asked: 'what are the relations between the domains included in the operational definition of HRQL tools and global health ratings' (Mozes et al., 1999: 269). With a representative Israeli sample multiple linear regression was used to examine the relationship between the SF-36 global rating of health-related quality of life[1], socio-economic status, presence of disease and each of the domains of the SF-36. Only 52 per cent of the variance of the global rating score was explainable by the regression model, with the SF-36 general health domain explaining 38.5 per cent of the variance. With another 7.0 per cent of the variance accounted for by the physical functioning domain, other domains of the SF-36, socio-economic variables and disease contributed minimally to the total explained variance of the global ratings of HRQL. Mozes et al. (1999) conclude: 'There is a considerable difference between the operational definition of the research community of HRQL and the public perception of this term.' Complicating matters further is work that suggests that there may be considerable divergence between the research community and many population groups in their understandings even of the composite *terms* of ideas such as 'health-related quality of life'.

In their analysis of problems in theoretical HRQL work Haase et al. (1999) identify the uncritical adoption of 'function-based' understandings of HRQL in the medical literatures. Function-based models of HRQL derive their focus 'predominantly from a biomedical perspective, emphasizing maintenance of functional abilities by management of clinical concerns, toxicity of treatments and functioning across several domains' (Haase et al., 1999: 125). 'Meaning-based approaches', by contrast, develop a focus on 'the patterns and experience of illness from a subjective and holistic perspective. Meanings are derived from patients' understanding of the situation and their autonomy, beliefs, choices and relationships with others' (Haase et al., 1999: 125). Advocating a 'meaning-based' approach to understanding what HRQOL means to young people with cancer, they argue that this technique can identify intervention approaches that are 'important, appropriate and acceptable to the child/adolescent and family' (Haase *et al.*, 1999: 125). Tellingly, they describe the divergence in outcomes that are likely if the a priori assumptions inherent in most function-based (HR)QOL under-standings drive the development and interpretation of measures of HRQL. Drawing on an earlier study by Haase and Rostad (1994) Haase *et al.* (1999: 125, my emphasis) point out that:

> when a child's or adolescent's social function is assessed from the function-based perspective by instrument items asking about the ability to be involved in a social activity, *involvement in the activity is assumed to be positive*. Thus, when items asking if an adolescent can attend school or visit friends are answered 'never' or 'rarely', a decreased quality of life in the social dimension is assumed. Missing from the items is the *meaning* that staying at home has for the adolescent. Remaining at home and being unable to see friends may indicate decreased HRQL for many adolescents with cancer. However ... at least some adolescents and families view the time at home positively, as an opportunity to be together, strengthen family ties and focus on friendships that endure in spite of isolation.

The problems engendered by a priori assumptions about the *meaning* of broad notions like health and activity are also shown by ethnographic work by Thompson and Gifford (2000). They report a detailed 22-month ethnographic study of 'the lived experiences of diabetes and lay meanings of risk' (2000: 1457) among Aborigines living in Melbourne, Australia. Much epidemiological work in the dominant medical research/population health paradigm fails to acknowledge that 'health' is not best understood as a purely individual outcome of 'healthy lifestyles'. Thompson and Gifford (2000: 1458) point out that:

> when Melbourne Aborigines talk about trying to manage their diabetes, it is not only their sugar that is out of balance, it is their whole life. And when they talk about stabilizing their sugar, these discourses are often woven into wider narratives about individual and community struggles to maintain a sense of coherence, control and stability over present life circumstances and the future. Achieving a 'balance' in life requires the maintenance of meaningful connections to family, the land, the past and future, all of which are important for health and well being. For Aborigines, like many indigenous people throughout the world, health and identity are linked closely to land and culture.

This suggests that the very idea of 'health' as understood in 'Western' medicine (and of course presupposed and operationalized by all HRQOL-specific measures and the 'health' domains of generic QOL measures) not only is not the same 'thing' for the Aboriginal community, but can hardly be said to bear even a family resemblance. In Aboriginal terms the notions of 'health', 'balance' and community 'well-being' ('QOL'?) are not just elided but are inseparable. They are not 'variables' that can sensibly be described as quanta possessed by individuals in the here-and-now: rather the well-being of individuals *today* is part and parcel of the social trajectory of Aboriginal people as a whole in the space-time continuum that links the dreaming to the future.

Using participant observation, informal interviews, focus group discussions and in-depth interviews with senior members of the Aboriginal community, Thompson and Gifford (2000) developed an understanding of Indigenous Australians' notions of health, disease and well-being which, while focused on diabetes, have a much wider ramification. Drawing on the theoretical framework in Narrative Theory (Garro, 1992; Garro, 1994a, b; Good, 1994) they suggest that this approach was 'particularly powerful in informing the data analysis for two reasons. First, a narrative style of communication is the dominant mode of talk within the Aboriginal community, and thus an appropriate way to both collect information for this study and to interpret the results' (Thompson and Gifford, 2000: 1461). In total 52 Aborigines, both with and without diabetes took part in 38 in-depth interviews, two focus group discussions and two small group discussions, with all interviews and focus group discussions being tape-recorded, transcribed and analysed using content and thematic analysis (Bernard, 1994; Patton, 1990). By adopting such an approach it is thus possible to avoid the unsettling experience described by Mozes *et al.* (1999) of finding that the meaningfulness of the constructs with which you are working are opaque to the population you wish to study.

Furthermore, if the quality of people's lives is understood in their terms, it is possible to be much more specific about the costs and benefits of efforts to improve circumstances which deleteriously affect life quality. The understandings so afforded may be paradoxical, or as ethnomethodologists would have it 'intuitively non-apparent'. Thompson and Gifford (2000: 1458) suggest that:

> understandings and experiences ... of illness cannot be separated from people's experiences of unstable, unpredictable and disempowered realities of everyday life, as it is lived through recollections of past, experiences of present and concerns about the future ... Current epidemiological models that focus on individual level [risk] factors not only ... fail to take into consideration the wider social and political contexts of risk and well-being, but, paradoxically, some of the key factors epidemiologists have identified as 'risk' are, in many cases, factors of connection and protection when seen from the Aborigines' perspective. Indeed, some of the public health interventions that rely heavily on

individual risk factor modification, from an Aboriginal point of view, can clearly be considered to be risky, not only to their diabetes but also to their more general health and well-being.

What we see here then – but from a perspective notionally removed from QOL research *qua* QOL research – is an echo of the concerns raised by writers such as Taylor (1994) and Rapley and Ridgway (1998) – discussed in Chapter 3. That is, in construing 'health' (or QOL) as an essentialized, individualized possession or attribute, interventions designed to further the public good, the quality of services or the well-being of individuals may not only misrepresent what such notions mean in local terms, but may also serve to promote the misallocation of resources and/or to actually damage or put at risk the connectedness of persons to important social structures.

Although their discussion of the upshot of their research is placed in the context of both epidemiology in general, and health-promotion around indigenous diabetes in particular, the conclusions that Thompson and Gifford (2000: 1468–9) come to are pertinent much more broadly. They argue that:

> interventions may actually act to sever the connections that tie the individual to the wider social fabric and that is central to the promotion of health. Aborigines view diabetes as a major health issue but they are clear that it needs to be addressed within the wider political, economic and social context of their daily life; connections to kin, land and community are core to their individual identities, sense of meaning and coherence in life. They articulate that interventions must not focus only on improving health in the objective sense, but also, and perhaps more importantly, begin by cementing and strengthening the ties that bind. Our study has shown how it is vital to begin any epidemiological study by first understanding the meanings of risk and protection from the point of view of those affected.

If we take 'health' in the quote above in the Aboriginal sense then the conclusions reached are pertinent to QOL research in the social sciences *as a whole*. Arguably it is vital to begin any QOL study by first understanding the meanings of the concept from the point of view of those affected. It is this issue, the question of 'whose (quality) of life is it anyway?', that Chapter 3 considers.

In Summary

While specifications of what quality of life means at the individual level are numerous, a consensus in the social scientific literatures seems to be coalescing around an operational definition similar to that advanced by Bob Cummins (above) – at least when QOL is considered as a universal construct. This is not to suggest that these definitions are without problems: far from it. And, further, this is also not to say that QOL continues (and no doubt will continue) to be defined in very local terms, for highly specific local purposes, at many sites of social scientific research. Likewise, at the population level, what QOL means continues to be immensely varied: with indices ranging from governments' adherence to CITES to the cleanliness of local beaches. Again, this is not – in and of itself – a 'bad thing', and indeed there is reason to believe that what Salvaris has called the 'social indicators movement' may well offer a mechanism for the active enhancement of the quality of life (however it is defined) for communities at a very local level.

We have also seen that controversy continues (for both population and individual-level conceptualizations of QOL) about objective and subjective aspects of QOL definition and measurement. It is widely agreed in the literature that, however defined, 'objective' estimations of QOL and 'subjective' estimates of personal well-being not only do not covary neatly, but may be contradictory. This routinely confirmed empirical finding has long been recognized in both folk-wisdom – proverbs like 'money can't buy you happiness' – and popular culture: as the Beatles sang, 'Can't buy me love' (Lennon and McCartney, 1967). Here the issue comes down to an *aesthetic choice* by the individual researcher. The moot question is not 'which account is correct?', but rather, 'which argument do I find most compelling?'

Note

1. The SF-36 (Ware and Sherbourne, 1992) is an extremely widely used measure of HRQOL. It has 36 items tapping eight health concepts: physical functioning, bodily pain, role limitations due to physical health problems, role limitations due to personal or emotional problems, general mental health, social functioning, energy/fatigue, and general health perceptions. It also includes a single item that provides an indication of perceived change in health. The RAND 36-Item Health Survey 1.0 includes the same items but has a slightly different scoring algorithm. Psychometric reliability and validity studies are numerous: see for example Hays *et al.* (1993) and McHorney *et al.* (1993).

Study Questions

- How would I define *my* quality of life?
- What social indicators of well-being, or quality of life, are relevant in the local community where I live?
- Is the 'Scandinavian' or the 'American' approach to quality of life more compelling as far as I am concerned, and why?

- Is quality of life a universally definable concept, or should it be defined locally on an as-needs basis?

Suggestions for Further Reading

ABS (2001) *Measuring Wellbeing: Frameworks for Australian Social Statistics*. Canberra: AGPS.

Felce, D. and Perry, J. (1995) Quality of life: its definition and measurement, *Research in Developmental Disabilities*, 16, 1: 51–74.

Organization for Economic Cooperation and Development (2001) *The Wellbeing of Nations: The Role of Human and Social Capital*. Paris: OECD.

Salvaris, M. (2000) *Community and Social Indicators: How Citizens Can Measure Progress. An Overview of Social and Community Indicator Projects in Australia and Internationally*. Victoria: Institute for Social Research, Swinburne University of Technology.

Veenhoven, R. (1997) Advances in the understanding of happiness, *Revue Québécoise de Psychologie*, 18: 267–93.

CHAPTER 3

Whose Quality of Life Is It Anyway?

The development of QOL research has raised many ethical and philosophical questions. This chapter outlines the key philosophical questions in QOL research and then discusses practice issues at the interface of philosophical debate and research design/methodology. The notions of 'mainstream' and 'emancipatory' (Oliver, 1996) research paradigms will be compared and their purposes and procedures contrasted. Questions that must be addressed in any QOL research project are identified: Who is QOL research for? To what purposes may QOL research findings be put? What are the ethical obligations of researchers designing and reporting QOL studies? Is research on QOL which compromises well-being justifiable? In what way can/do the perspectives of research *participants* inform the selection of research methods and tools? What are the ethical implications of developments such as QALYs? A checklist of questions to consider in the development of a QOL research project is presented.

Conceptual and Philosophical Issues

QOL is now widely deployed as a shorthand term for the collective well-being of human groups and also as a summary description of the particulars of individual lives. Although the use of large-scale systems of social indicators necessarily presupposes a host of value judgments, and hence ethical, moral and, essentially, political positions (some of which, such as the positive valuation of widespread school participation, the presence of women in the workforce or democratic political systems have been highlighted earlier), it is QOL understood as an aspect of individual subjectivity that throws these issues into sharpest relief. This chapter discusses the major ethical and conceptual issues arising with specific reference to QOL research at the individual level.

    QOL has become a driving force in service design, delivery and outcome evaluation across medicine and social care. The quality of life of 'patients'/ 'service users' is now routinely advocated as a measure of the 'quality' and 'value for money' of services. QOL is even advocated as *the* yardstick by which decisions about the (dis)continuation of not just service programmes or intervention techniques, but also individual lives, should be judged. Statements such as Blunden's (1988: 117) have begun to appear with increasing frequency:

> The quality of life of the developmentally disabled persons who live in community residences must feature prominently in any discussion of service quality ... community services should lead to a demonstrable improvement in the quality of residents' lives.

Such statements are not always framed as expectations of the outcomes of well-designed services. Rather, the assessment of QOL is increasingly presented as a *moral imperative* if human service practice is to be ethically sound. Thus:

> Several instruments are now available which allow people with cognitive impairments to record their subjective QOL. It is recommended that such measurement be regarded as an essential ethical requirement whenever issues of intervention, education or service delivery are under consideration. (Cummins, 1997b: 24)

There seems to be no reason why this should not be a 'good thing'. It is, surely, right that people's QOL should be an important consideration in the design of services, or that the relative contribution to the enhancement of QOL offered by different techniques should inform decisions about funding or treatment. There are, however, some very serious conceptual and ethical difficulties entailed in the use of the idea of QOL like this. The first is that of objectivity.

The problem of objectivity

The great majority of QOL studies take it for granted that the first task (at either individual or societal levels) is to *operationally define* the construct. As Chapter 2 showed, there are myriad definitions of QOL, and as many problems with them. This work is predicated upon a priori acceptance of the conjecture that QOL is an hypothetical construct (like gravity, diabetes or intelligence) which may, via strict and objective criteria, permit measurement and quantification. That is, it is presumed *in advance* that there is a single 'thing' in the world, called 'quality of life', of which it may sensibly be said that different people, communities or nations have in greater or lesser quantities (cf. Feyerabend, 1974). This approach underpins the development of *all* scales, questionnaires and indices which offer numerical values for 'QOL' states, and reaches its most extreme expression in the development of measures of quality- and disability-adjusted life years (QALYs and DALYs), which explicitly value the quality of years of life, and then express that value in terms of single number between 0 and 1. What all of these approaches share in, then, is their adherence to a theoretical (and hence methodological) position which suggests that – in principle – *all* states of being in the world are amenable to objective operational definition, and meaningful description in numerical terms.

But this approach has been subject to serious questioning. While we have become used to making sense of statements like 'Hugh is so bright, he has an IQ of 145', we tend to forget that describing aspects of persons, their experiences and their capacities in this way is a remarkably recent development (Rose, 1999). The wry humour of Douglas Adams's (1979) observation that 'the meaning of life is 42' works *precisely because* it is, in terms of our everyday sense making, nonsensical.

Similarly, while the QOL literatures may be full of statements which describe statistical aggregates of persons' happiness in such terms – for example, Cummins *et al.*'s (in press) notion that life satisfaction is best described as '75 ± 2.5%SM'– which seem, in *those contexts*, discursively unproblematic, one wonders how the researchers would take to describing their *own* satisfaction with the world in such terms. 'My QOL today is 73.75' is, of course, an outlandish formulation. That is, such numerical presentations and formally specified operational definitions may give a *spurious* impression of objectivity and of neutral scientific knowledge. The very real problems that such appearances can mask are well illustrated by thinking about an example offered by Deutscher (1973) in a discussion of the way in which *the same* 'objective' terms (and even *identical* specific numerical values) may describe very different subjective experiences. Deutscher (1973: 191) notes that:

> when an American truck driver complains to the waitress at the diner about his 'warm' beer and 'cold' soup, the 'warm' liquid may have a temperature of 50°, while the 'cold' one is 75° ... The standard for the same objects may well vary from culture to culture, from nation to nation, from region to region and, for that matter, within any given social unit – between classes, age groups, sexes, or what have you; what is 'cold' soup for an adult may be too 'hot' to give a child.

Most older British readers would probably experience the American truckie's 'warm' beer as being much too 'cold', while Australian readers would no doubt sympathize with his predicament. However, even noting this, a series of other problems are *caused by* the attempted translation of lived experiences into formally specified, operationally defined constructs. It is important to remember that, as Megone (1990), puts it: '"the quality of life" is a grandiose term. The ordinary man ... does not often talk in terms of the quality of his life, nor is the quality of life, more generally, a common topic of conversation'. And, similarly, it is important to remember that 'quality of life' is in no way the same sort of an 'object' or 'thing' as a bowl of soup or a glass of Budweiser, about which genuinely independent, objective judgments (of temperature or quantity) can be made.

The confusion of the naming of hypothetical constructs – such as 'intelligence', 'QOL' or 'schizophrenia' – with the naming of *things in the world*, reification, is an ever present problem in the social sciences (Pilgrim and Bentall, 1999). As Megone (1990) point outs, the consequence of efforts to transform 'grandiose' vernacular terms into formal, theoretical, concepts can be substantial. Megone (1990: 29, my emphasis) notes that:

> even if there is some fairly standard idea of what quality of life concerns, might it be that any attempt to produce a more refined notion for the purpose of measurement, employing theoretical devices, inevitably distorts from the original? ... The notion of quality of life is employed by theorists to address certain problems on the basis that those actually facing the problems see this as a relevant factor. But if the theorist ... solves the problem in terms of a distorted theoretical account of the factor, distorted because the theoretical refinements slant the notion in a certain way – if this is the case, then ... the theorist has *not solved the original problem*.

The existence of theoretical models of QOL which command consensus in the field may thus *appear* to offer an answer to questions such as 'what is QOL', but there is room for doubt about whether they have done so without a distorted, and distorting, account. As Hatton has observed, 'most systems for assessing quality of life also provide methods for summarizing and standardizing the experience of individuals to produce quality of life "scores" which can then be compared' (Hatton, 1998: 105), or, in other words, most systems for assessing QOL have *built into them* a set of theoretical refinements which 'distort' or 'slant the notion in a certain way' – not least transforming verbal reports into arbitrary numerical scores.

   As such then, theoretical models or operational definitions of QOL – and the measurement tools which are derived from them – cannot be seen in the same terms as theoretical models or technical measures of gravity, evolution or climate. As McHoul and Rapley (2001) have noted, neutron stars, capybaras and the wind are not members of the same class as persons' accounts of the quality of their life, if for no other reason than that they are incapable of theorizing themselves. Unlike constructs such as QOL, in the case of phenomena like the wind scientists are not tempted to confuse statements about the *amount* of a property exhibited by a phenomenon and the phenomenon *itself*. This is why we hear statements on the weather forecast like 'cyclone Eliza is travelling at 200 kilometres per hour' not 'cyclone Eliza *is* 200 kilometres per hour'.

   Even apparently objective scores on QOL scales are products not only of a complex set of interactions (between researchers and participants) but also of a prior set of *value judgments* about what is to *count* as QOL, which domains should be measured and the manner of the measuring. At the population level this point is perhaps more readily appreciated, as agencies such as the ABS (2001) are, as we have seen, explicit about the *pragmatic* factors influencing the selection of indicators which they use to define QOL. Quantitative individual-level research is much less explicit about the politics of operational definition, domain specification and item selection, but is no less affected by these influences than population-level QOL research. Inasmuch as quality of life is not a 'thing', so too such objective scores, however impressive they appear and however convoluted their statistical manipulation, are also not the 'thing' itself. The quality of life is, emphatically, not 42.

The problem of subjectivity

What Melbourne Aborigines define as 'health' is at considerable variance from the operational definitions of public health researchers and social epidemiologists (Chapter 2). Conversely, what constitutes 'health' from an Aboriginal perspective includes many aspects of QOL specified in many of the formal definitions of the term considered in Chapter 2. As we saw in the Apologia, achieving precise measurement of individuals' views employing standardized measures may be a hit-and-miss affair (Antaki and Rapley, 1996a, 1996b; Rapley and Antaki 1996; Antaki et al., 2000). With his usual clarity, Cummins (1997b: 121–2) puts the issue well:

> but what of the subjective axis? Here the situation is not so clear. If a respondent to a QOL scale does not regard one or more of the domains as having much relevance to their personal situation, then it does not matter how satisfied or dissatisfied they are with domains that contribute little to the individual's life. If, on the other hand, a respondent regards strong links with their family and friends as integral to their life quality, then their level of satisfaction with such a domain is of paramount relevance.

This is a critical issue: the relative importance of various aspects of life may differ at any given moment for each of us, and the relative importance of specific matters may change over a lifetime. Of course if two people give different weightings to questionnaire domains, their scores are *not* directly comparable: the domains of QOL mean different things to them. If weightings change over time, the scores the person has recorded at the two time points are *not* comparable: what QOL means has changed.

These worries presuppose that any given set of domains identified by the questionnaire designer is itself genuinely representative of QOL for each and every respondent. For Melbourne Aborigines it seems that *any* standardized measure of HRQOL is unlikely to capture their subjective view of *either construct*. Interviews with adults with mild intellectual disabilities reported by Rapley *et al.* (1998) suggested that enforced sterilization; the denial of adulthood; the absence of autonomy; stigma, belittlement and rejection; and an awareness that these were the results of being identified as an 'intellectually disabled person' were inseparable from the subjective 'quality' of their lives. But items tapping these issues appear on no QOL questionnaire yet designed. Furthermore, when people complete such questionnaires, like Anne and Arthur in the Apologia – quite *whose* (subjective) QOL judgment is represented via a summary score assigned by the interviewer ('we'll put a two down for that one then') is a troubling issue (Antaki and Rapley, 1996a; Antaki *et al.*, 2000).

A second major problem in this area, and particularly troublesome in the HRQOL and medical QOL literatures, has been identified by a number of writers including Cummins (1997b) and Koch (2001). Koch (2001: 454–5) points out that *all* studies seeking prospective judgments about future health states (for example time trade-off and standard gamble studies – discussed in detail in Chapter 6) implicitly rely on five axioms (see Box 3.1)

Box 3.1 Axioms underpinning studies of future health state preferences

Axiom 1 A person without a chronic physical deficit can accurately compare healthy and restricted states.

Axiom 1a Healthy persons have sufficient knowledge and experience to make judgments about life quality and satisfaction in the context of physical limit or disability.

Axiom 2 A healthy person can accurately predict what he or she would want in extremes.

Axiom 3 Individuals have a core personality whose perspective and judgments are constant whatever the physical or social context.

Axiom 4 In public and personal health planning what is important is solely the degree to which an individual's physical condition deviates negatively from the norm.

Axiom 5 The discrete individual is always the sole and best judge of appropriate treatment or non-treatment at any moment.

Source: Koch (2001)

Each of these presuppositions is conceptually problematic and Koch (2001) offers detailed empirical work to suggest that Axioms 1 to 3 cannot be sustained. It appears that 'healthy' people (those 'without a chronic physical deficit') find it very difficult to make comparisons between unimpaired and impaired states that reflect the views of people who are already impaired, and a major reason for this is that 'healthy people' have very little idea at all what the experience of disablement is actually like. Such circumstances have led writers such as Oliver (1996) not only to suggest that 'mainstream' social scientific research is oppressive of people with disabilities, but also to demand that the research community adopt 'emancipatory' procedures or, in brief, a stance of cooperation and inclusivity – rather than one of distanced 'expertise'.

Further, all studies which ask for responses to hypothetical scenarios about future health states implicitly adopt a psychological model of the person (Axiom 3) which has come under sustained critical attack and, some would argue, is no longer tenable (see Antaki *et al.*, 1996; Edwards, 1997; McHoul and Rapley, 2001; Coulter, 1999). In consequence, accurate predictions – of future wishes when *in extremis* – can be neither expected nor relied upon. Axioms 4 and 5 are, of course, ethico-political questions through and through and not strictly speaking social scientific matters at all. The fact that a vast body of social scientific work is, however, predicated upon precisely these axioms again demonstrates that the field is not as untainted by moral, or value, judgments as is often suggested by research methods textbooks.

The problem of population-specificity

We have seen, in Chapter 2, a preview of the issue of universal vs. population- or condition-specific definitions of QOL and its measurement, an issue closely related to the controversy over objective vs. subjective indicators of QOL. The issue revolves around the purpose to which QOL measurement is to be put, and whether such measurement is understood and intended as a component of grand theory building or is intended to assist in the development of localized understandings of QOL for local purposes (for example, in human service evaluation studies). *If the primary purpose is grand theory building, then there are good reasons for not supporting the development of definitions of QOL that are specific to groups like people with intellectual disabilities or the elderly, or for targeted patient populations – kidney disease, acne, vertigo and so on. Rosen (1986: 366–7) drew attention to the consequences of such group-specific definitions. While his specific concern was with people with intellectual disabilities, the point he makes applies generally. He noted that, were

> the existence of mental retardation, with its concomitant limitation in cognitive and social functioning [held to be] relevant as a factor determining quality of life requirements … the definition of quality of life would need to be defined differently for people with mental retardation who are functioning at different developmental levels … one might be forced into the distasteful position that individuals with more severe levels of mental retardation are entitled to less of a quality of life than those who are less severely retarded.

Rosen's worries again reflect the importance of value, or aesthetic, judgments in the field. As he noted, the logic of holding 'limitation in cognitive and social functioning relevant' *demands* that the corresponding

QOL entitlement for such persons be considered lower than for others. The problems which arise in the translation of such a priori ethical considerations into formal QOL instruments is illustrated by Cummins (1997b: 123), who notes that:

> a view that is limited to a population sub-group can restrict the view of what might constitute a high life quality for its members. Such definitions are shaped by the deficits of the groups to which they refer and, as a consequence, have been down-graded to reflect the assumption of a lower life quality than normal. Such assumptions, however, are likely to be invalid. The huge literature on positive and negative affect ... is consistent in its appreciation that each is independent of the other, such that people with serious disabilities may nevertheless describe themselves as happy, enthusiastic and excited about life.

While Cummins hints at the politics of QOL measurement in the context of his primarily methodological concern, Taylor and Bogdan (1990: 27) draw attention directly to the ethics of the QOL research programme as a whole. They note that:

> we seldom make enquiries into the QOL of people who are not disabled or disadvantaged in some way ... we usually examine QOL only when we know or suspect that people are suffering ... herein lie[s] ... the danger of studying the QOL of people with mental retardation.

Such studies also raise the ethical question of whether, and to what extent, individuals with intellectual disabilities should 'influence the selection of quality of life criteria for themselves' (Rosen, 1986: 365). To date it would seem that the research community is guilty of adopting precisely the approach that Edgerton (1990) cautioned against – namely that of 'imposing' QOL variables onto almost all respondent groups, regardless of their level of intellectual competence.

'Emancipatory' versus 'mainstream' QOL research

The issue of imposed definitions of QOL is the issue at the heart of the major criticism of writers such as Finkelstein (1993), Oliver (1996) and Duckett and Fryer (1998) of the oppressive and disempowering agenda of the 'mainstream' research 'establishment' in its relations to and with disabled people (Clements *et al.*, 1999).

The 'danger' Taylor and Bogdan (1990) draw attention to, then, is the conduct of research which does not *consult with* the people whose lives are examined, but rather treats persons as *objects of study*. Such work – 'mainstream' social scientific research – overlooks or denies Chorover's (1979) point that the power to give names (to things such as 'QOL') is exactly that: the exercise of *power*. The argument is that if QOL research is to actually be of *use* to people who *are* disabled or disadvantaged in some way, it must be explicitly 'emancipatory'. That is, to be ethically acceptable, research must be *consciously* designed, conducted and reported not only in collaboration with people who are disadvantaged, but also in a manner which respects *their* expertise on the lived experience of disablement (Goodley and Rapley, 2001). A key requirement of emancipatory research is that the results of such inquiries are not only communicated to academic peers, but also – and indeed primarily – reported back to research participants in a form that makes sense in their terms. From an emancipatory perspective research practices should always be *explicitly* politicized (as opposed to the perspective of 'mainstream' work which, in its silence on politics, itself makes a political statement) with a firm commitment to research which contributes to freeing people with disabilities from the oppression of 'normal' society.

This perspective is a major challenge to much social scientific research. While there are technical-methodological problems in operationalizing QOL differently for different groups, the pursuit of a universally applicable definition of the construct (what Cummins (1997b: 136) describes as a 'total quality of life construct') the individualized approach to its measurement is challenged here on the grounds of the politics/ethics of research into which the approach is embedded. Such a challenge reconceptualizes many of the problems already discussed in Chapter 2 as essentially *local* matters. That is, many in the disability movement (the hearing impaired for example), regard issues such as 'cultural relativity' as applying not only to gross differences between ethnic or national groups, but also as operative between the hearing and the deaf within any given society.

The 'mainstream' approach is strongly criticized not only for conceptual incoherence, but also as politically and ethically problematic, by *camouflaging* inequality (Emerson and Hatton, 1994; Hatton, 1998). If QOL is defined carefully enough it can appear that 'gross differences in objective life quality' have no bearing *at all* on people's happiness, and hence divert attention away from these matters (Hatton, 1998; Rapley, 2001). Ager and Hatton (1999: 337) put the position well:

> having argued for the value of addressing the subjective experience of individuals, it seems somewhat strange to assert the necessity of reliance upon methods underpinned by conventional psychometric theory, rather than encourage, for example, the use of more discursive analysis of individuals' accounts of their life experience ... insistence upon 'subjective' data may ... inappropriately distract attention away from the unambiguous significance of 'objective' indicators of experience. Cummins (1997) dangerously equates objective life circumstances with 'material' circumstances ... ignoring the many objective experiences which reflect differential access to power and opportunity and material resources.

The worry that concerns such as this are merely 'sensationalist' or 'postmodern' objections (Cummins, 2001a: 8) is tempered by recalling that Veenhoven (1996) specifically commended the likely 'political appeal' of the HLE. Such objections are not simply a matter for concern at the level of national social indicators (see also Reicher, 2001). The very idea of the *quality* of a life is shot through with political and ethical considerations and clear-cut personal implications.

The ethics of operational definition and scale design

If we are designing an individual-level psychometric QOL measure, *choosing* not to include an item on forced sterilization or other belittling treatment (despite the fact that many people with intellectual disabilities will have experienced this) ensures that, *even should an assessor wish to*, it is impossible for this aspect of QOL to be measured. That the circumstances of marginalized social groups entail very specific circumstances (such as having staff in authority over one) that can, sensibly, be linked to how good life might be, would seem to be an argument for the inclusion of these matters, not their exclusion, from attempts to gauge QOL.

To build a grand theory of QOL, it is of course essential to have a universally applicable unitary operational definition (if at the expense of individualized meaning). However, if one wishes to know about how this particular population group feel about their QOL, it would appear more coherent to follow, at the individual level, the 'emancipatory' paradigm, and to develop measures or indices in consultation with those directly affected. The results of adopting this approach are previewed below, and further described in Chapter 4.

Other objections to the QOL research programme

There is then reason to be cautious about using the idea of quality of life as a formal social scientific term. Taylor (1994) draws a helpful distinction between the notion of quality of life, as deployed in lay discourse, and 'quality of life' as a scientific construct, which he suggests be known as 'QOL' in order to differentiate the two ideas. Taylor (1994) suggests that the two uses are distinct in terms of both their *pragmatic use* and *phenomenological reference*, and, further, have a different *ontological* status. He proposes three key distinctions. Firstly that 'quality of life is a useful sensitizing concept whereas QOL is a reification'; secondly that 'quality of life' means something while QOL 'seems to mean everything' and, thirdly, that 'quality of life is lived and experienced while QOL is superimposed on that experience' (Taylor, 1994: 260–3). Wolfensberger has suggested that QOL is a 'Kraft cheese term', and should be abandoned in scientific discourse and replaced by a research programme in which efforts at 'total' definitions are discontinued and 'the fractioning of QOL into more clear cut components with different names' (Wolfensberger, 1994: 318) is substituted.

From a feminist perspective Eckermann has argued that existing QOL research is implicitly politicized. While the addition of QOL measures to the range of indicators traditionally used to assess health and well-being offers a richer understanding of health outcomes, most measures remain undifferentiated by *gender* and are, thus, not only insensitive to the 'subtle effects of gender socialization on health and well-being', but also disregard the particular experience of women (Eckerman, 2000: 29). Again, we see a call for the further *fractioning* – rather than 'totalizing' – of the concept. All of these objections may, in summary, be held to pivot on the central question: 'Whose quality of life is it anyway?' That is, who should define what QOL actually is?

The Views of 'Patients'

Whether notions like QOL are viable as 'technical' constructs has been questioned by a number of writers. There may, also, be serious differences between 'lay' and 'technical' views of matters such as what HRQOL 'is'. Much of the literature (at both individual and population levels) may then be characterized by its inadequate attention to the views of everyday people – be they described as 'patients' or otherwise – about the lay usage of the notion.

In their study of people with chronic obstructive pulmonary disease Leidy and Haase (1999: 70) conducted in-depth interviews with a small group of twelve people about the 'quality' of their lives. They summarize informants' views by noting that:

> participants ... were engaged in the challenge of preserving their personal integrity as they faced increasing limitations in their ability to perform day-to-day activities ... Personal integrity represents a sense of satisfying wholeness that encompasses the integration, totality, and collective of intra-personal and inter-personal characteristics, including one's physical appearance and functioning, skills, roles, knowledge, memories, environment, family, and friends. It is a sense of one's individuality and wholeness as a human being. Two characteristics are central to a sense of personal integrity: effectiveness, or 'being able,' and connectedness, or 'being with,' each of which are expressed through daily activity and challenged through limitations in physical capacity.

What Leidy and Haase (1999) suggest is that 'personal integrity', or the quality of a life, is not a one-off judgment but a *process* of engagement with lived experience. Similarly, in their analysis of the quality of life of people coping with kidney dialysis, Martin and Thompson (2001: 57, my emphasis) suggest that: 'the crucial issue in obtaining an optimal quality of life is the *process of adaptation* and acceptance of chronic illness'. The difficulty of formal, psychometric QOL measurement, is that quality of life is assessed in cross-sectional, or one-off, snapshots via the completion of questionnaires and, hence, cannot capture an adaptation *process* (Wenzel, 2001). Perhaps the most troubling aspect of such a divorcing of measurement from the process of a lived life is seen in efforts to fix, numerically, the value of particular forms of life or health states. It is to the ethics of such attempts – in the shape of quality- and disability-adjusted life years – that we now turn.

Quality of Life and the Value of Life

It is a widely accepted view that the state of one's health may (dramatically) affect an assessment of the quality of one's life, of whether life is worth living or not, despite empirical evidence to challenge this view (further discussed in Chapter 6). If we concede that some people have lives so appalling they are not worth living, 'it becomes hard to deny the existence of a grey area where a life may be worth living but is less worth living than normal. Then we may say that the condition that makes that life less worth living than normal is its low "quality of life"' (Aksoy, 2000: 19; Glover, 1977). Such judgments are problematic even as subjective, personal and private ones made by terminally ill people and their physicians – as the case of Jack Kervorkian ('Doctor Death') shows. Such subjective judgments – that death is preferable to a 'low quality of life' – are, however, routinely made (as we shall see in more detail in Chapter 6) by doctors in the Netherlands on behalf of, and without necessarily consulting, their intellectually disabled 'patients'.

Cubbon (1991) argues that, given limited health care resources, even in affluent Western societies, there is no principled way of allocating resources that produces a win: win outcome. Because resource allocation – or 'rationing' – has to occur, decision-makers need a mechanism whereby they can choose between patients, and it is unfortunate but inevitable therefore that some groups of people will be *knowingly deprived*. Statistics like Quality Adjusted Life Years (QALYs) are no worse and no better than any other alternative: they have a transparent calculation protocol and there is no option that leaves *everyone* better off. Ends justify means.

There are serious ethical dilemmas here, and the development of QALYs has always been predicated upon the notion that transparent, explicit, public statements about the quality of particular lives, expressed in a common, numerical form offers one way out of the difficulties of variation in subjective, personal opinion. However, as Aksoy (2000: 21) points out:

to consider (extreme) suffering as something worse than death is a consideration based upon supposition since no one knows what kind of experience dying is, nor how it feels to have one's life terminated (not merely threatened) by another ... The idea that the quality of someone's life could be judged 'worse than being dead' has always met with criticism. It could be argued that the opportunity for choice from among a reasonable array of life plans is an important and independent component of quality of life, but, whether being dead can be counted one such life plan is rather open to dispute. It is possible to compare the quality of two lives, or of a single person's life under two conditions, but it is not possible to make the QOL comparison needed here, because one of the alternatives to be compared is non-existence. If a person no longer exists, there is no life that could possibly have any quality so as to enter into a comparison with the quality of life sustained by treatment.

It also seems to be the case that, although people may rate the *hypothetical* outcomes (of road accidents for example), as being as bad, or even as worse than death, when people experience these events they tend not regard their lives as valueless or as having a negative value (Koch, 2000; Jones-Lee *et al.*, 1985; Loomes and McKenzie, 1990). These studies also show that doctors regularly and reliably rate hypothetical health states more negatively, and often as little better than death, than do their patients. Given that such evaluations are widely accepted in the medical literatures as guiding doctors' decision-making about treatment, and also given that techniques such as QALYs are *designedly* independent of patients' views, again we see the problems in asking the question, whose quality of life is it anyway?

Against 'realist' justifications for QALYs (Cubbon, 1991) Harris (1991: 186) has argued that 'each person has an equal claim upon the health resources of the world and in particular those of his/her own society: that no individual or group or type of individual has a more valuable life or a greater claim to life-saving resources than any other. This is part of the claim that all people are entitled to treatment as equals.' Bridging the gap between earlier discussions of social indicators of the quality of life in nation-states (Chapter 1) and the apparently esoteric and medically specific nature of QALYs (Chapter 6), Harris locates the argument against QALYs firmly in terms of the broader questions of the political economy of health. In a neat twist on one of the prevailing tropes of the 'enterprise culture' (Rose, 1992 – see Chapter 5), the idea of 'mutual obligation' between citizen and state, Harris (1991: 187) writes that:

> any nation state's claim to the allegiance of its citizens is contingent upon it being willing and able to protect the lives and liberties of its citizens. In the absence of plausible threats of foreign domination, the greatest threat to the life and liberty of citizens of most democracies comes from threats to health. A society that says that particular citizens, whether individually

identifiable in advance or not, will not be so protected has effectively declared such individuals to be outlaws – outside the protection of the State – and forfeited its claim to their allegiance.

Singer *et al.* (1995) argue, in contrast, that spending taxpayers' money on publicly provided health care entails a fiscal responsibility to get value for money. If resources are limited we cannot save every life that might be saved: is it then unfair to give a lower priority to saving the lives of those with incurable conditions that significantly reduce their quality of life? Harris (1995) argues that this does indeed place people in double jeopardy and is inherently unfair. Respecting persons *as such* means adhering to the *equality principle* that each individual is valued as an individual, as one, and as no more – or less – than one, whatever their life expectancy or present or predicted quality of life.

Thus, while all QOL judgments may be held to violate the equality principle, that is to violate the principled viewing of all persons as sharing in *equality of life*, QALYs can also be held to shift the question from asking 'is this treatment beneficial for this patient?' to 'is the patients' life of benefit to them?' (Ramsey, 1978; Harris, 1987). One of the most basic problems with the QALY approach, then, is the focus on quality of life in terms of abstract *life years*, rather than in terms of the *daily lives of persons*. QALYs shift our focus onto QOL as an abstract, technological concept – life years – rather than the experience of actual living, breathing people. The consequences of such technologies are, of course, shouldered by living, breathing people. It is the unintended consequences of QOL measurement that occupy the final part of this chapter.

Can QOL Assessment Negatively Affect Quality of Life?

The presumption in most of the literature is that QOL assessment is a 'good thing'. Although many caveats are entered about the present limitations of particular measures or approaches, in general terms, and from whichever tradition the work is drawn, QOL assessment tends to be framed as making a positive contribution. Thus QOL assessment assists service providers to evaluate how well services are performing (Schalock, 1997; Anderson and Lewis, 2000); it offers patients a chance to have their say (Rapley and Beyer, 1996; Costantini *et al.*, 2000); QOL assessment permits the 'rational' allocation of scarce resources (Sprangers *et al.*, 2000); it adds information not routinely available from the usual medical focus on symptomatic change (Carr and Higginson, 2001); and it offers a means to direct research funding (Fayers and Bjordal, 2001) among many other benefits. But what if assessing QOL were actually detrimental to the well-being and quality of life of those who participate in the exercise?

The medical literature recognizes that QOL measurement may raise ethical issues related to negative outcomes. Ravenscroft and Bell (2000) found that, whereas in over half of the intensive care units they surveyed 'perceived quality of life' was one of the most common reasons for terminating patients' life support, in over half staff agreed that end-of-life decisions were made on the basis of 'arbitrary quality of life (QOL) judgements' (Ravenscroft and Bell, 2000: 437). The conclusions drawn about medical termination of life included the observation that 'an obvious area for attention is the absence of accurate assessment of premorbid health and QOL, and more comprehensive audit of outcome' (Ravenscroft and Bell, 2000: 439). While on the face of it this may seem an eminently reasonable suggestion, in response to their article, Woodrow (2001) suggests – to the contrary – that 'the comment that belated or absent measurement of Quality of Life is "clearly inadequate" ignores the contentious nature of measuring Quality of Life. Another recent review [Aksoy, 2000] concludes that: "quality of life cannot be measured either accurately or reliably, and so should not be used as a criterion for health care services"'(Woodrow, 2001: 205).

Higginson and Carr (2001: 1297–8) put the theoretical issues clearly:

> the breadth of quality of life as a concept means that problems might be identified that are outside the usual remit of medical care. This raises a number of ethical concerns. Firstly the act of measuring quality of life in a clinical setting may generate the expectation that the clinician will be able to influence it ... In situations where this is not possible, patients may be seen to be harmed by the process of measurement. Secondly, some ... have opposed the clinical measurement of quality of life on the grounds that it represents the 'overmedicalisation' of life and clinical interference in aspects of patients' lives that should not be the concern of the clinician.

Another close ethnomethodological look at the administration of the *Quality of Life Questionnaire* (Schalock and Keith, 1996) illustrates the issues.[1] Whereas the bulk of the literature presents QOL as *scores* (of individuals, patient groups, service systems or nation-states) ethnomethodological approaches, and other qualitative methods, try to gain access to what happens in the *process* of score generation which quantitative methods present as a problematic (but basically uninteresting) procedural issue. In other words, the focus now is on trying to understand *how* it is that scores are arrived at when QOL is actually assessed in practice.

A number of papers in the medical literature have noted that the forms of QOL assessment derived by academics and researchers are often perceived by patients as puzzling or irrelevant to the issues *they* feel are pertinent to QOL (Carr and Higginson, 2001; Bowling, 1995; Coates *et al.*, 1983). Similarly, Lauritzen and Sachs (2001) have noted how the practices of routine health surveillance, monitoring and reporting *in and of themselves* introduce unpleasant and possibly aversive threats into patients' lives.

In the two examples[2] below the people whose QOL is being assessed show *their* appreciation of the exercise in similar terms. That is, what is assumed by the bulk of the literature to be a positive, or at least benign, activity (the assessment of their QOL) may be received by the recipients of such monitoring not as a useful and empowering exercise, but rather as a very real and immediate threat to their well-being.

In the first extract we enter at a point five minutes into the session where Mike (the interviewer) and Bob (the 'intellectually disabled' interviewee) are engaged in the preliminaries to the assessment proper over a cup of tea, discussing Bob's holiday plans. This extract is, necessarily, quite long and illustrates, I hope, at least one of the benefits of qualitative approaches – namely that really interesting data about the quality of people's lives are available in the fine-grained detail of interaction, not only in quantitative summaries of those interactions.

Extract 1: From McHoul and Rapley (2000b)

```
93 M:      how long will you go for (..)
94 B:      just a wee:k=
95 M:      =°huh° (1.0) and who you gonna go with
96         (2.0)
97 B:      °Henry° (..) Ste:ven: ('t) (1.0) the other
98         Steven (.) Rod >(no– no)< Steven Pallister (..)
99         you wouldn't know 'im  ⌈°would you°=
100 M:                             ⌊no::
101 M:     =°no° is he staff? (..)
102 B:     eh?
103 M:     is he staff?=
104 B:     =no: (.) °err° res:ident
...
129        (7.0) ((2 knocks and    ⌈pouring  sound))
130 B:                             ⌊(sings)) °Sa:nta  Claus
131        is comin' to town (.) Sa:nta Claus is co:ming
132        to town .h San:ta Claus is co:::ming: to:::
133        tow::n:°
134        ((stirring sound)) (16.0)
135 B:     there y'are
136 M:     thank you
...
144 B:     hhh (do you know more) than the residents
145        there?
146 M:     erm?
147 B:     (at the County Castle)
```

```
148 M:    I think so              ⌈yeah (..) I know quite a lot of them
149 B:                            ⌊((slurping  noise))  eh?
150 M:    I know quite a lot of them (.) there's not many
151       people left there now though
152 B:    no: (.) °er° .h >most of< um:: died didn't
153       they?
154 M:    hmm died or moved out (..) °hm?° did you used
155       to (..) °hhh° be at the Castle
156 B:    yeh=
157 M:    =°yeh°
158 B:    I didn't like it much
159 M:    no:?
160 B:    .hhh I'd sooner be 'ere
161 M:    yeah (.) how long have you been here Bob
162 B:    since from nineteen eighty nine
163 M:    (right) that's about >(so)< for five years now
164       (..)
165 B:    yeah
166 M:    yeah (1.0) and you wouldn't wanna go back
167 B:    <no> ((throaty syllable)) °y' can: sti–° (..)
168       you know what you can do: with it?
169 M:    what's that then
170 B:    .hh stick it up °where° the monkeys keep their
171       nuts
```

McHoul and Rapley (2002b) offer an extended analysis of this conversation. However, for present purposes it is important to note not so much the mundane nature of this chat, but rather the very careful design of Bob's contributions to it. The *topics* of these preliminaries to the actual QOL assessment, which may be thought to be off the point or irrelevant, repay close attention. While, with the possible exception of his singing (though as the interview was conducted two days before Christmas this is moot), these matters are ubiquitous topics for chat (places of origin, one's holidays, one's job, persons possibly known in common). However, it is also the case (and this time including the singing) that they *display* a deep and insightful knowledge (on Bob's part) of the kind of encounter this is. Namely, Mike is a psychologist, there to perform an assessment of his happiness and well-being. More precisely, Bob shows Mike (and us, the overhearing analysts) that he is conscious, should he be found wanting in the QOL department, that his place of residence could be altered – and, on his own estimation (see lines 170–1), for the worse.

Accordingly, and even before the official questioning starts, it is incumbent on Bob to *display* that he is extremely happy. Thus we discover that he takes overseas holidays, he sings and so forth. Thus Bob is not only *telling* Mike, in answers to the official questions to come, that he is happy or that his QOL is acceptable to him. In addition to this, he *shows* this appreciation of his life circumstances by *doing* having a great quality of life, or at least being content with his lot.

That Bob is not anomalous in this is also shown in the second extract, again taken from the opening moments of the administration of the *QOL.Q*. Arthur makes *his* understanding of the questioning to come explicit. In line 3 (arrowed) Arthur's question about the 'hardness' of the questions he is to be asked suggests that, for him too, this is not just a cosy chat about his happiness or 'quality of his life', but instead may include ''ard' questions: to wit this is another *test*.

Extract 2: Code: CA/KK/CD (From Rapley and Antaki, 1996)

```
1    I      erm (…) and I'd ↑like you to ↑answer some questio::ns to tell
2           me how you feel about the ⌈(unintell)
3 →  AR                              ⌊they're not 'ard ones are they (.)
4    I      not very ⌈hard
5    AR           ⌊ n o : o
6    I      no (.) and ↑if you don't understand ↓them Arthur you can just
            tell me (.)
7    AR     yeus
8    I      and I'll I'll say them differently (.)
9    AR     ym
...
17   I      so there's no ↓hurry    ⌈ (..) °do you have any° ↓ques↑tions?
            (.)
18                                  ⌊(paper shuffling)
19   I      to ↓ask ↑me?
20   AR     ye: ↑e:r↓:::s
21   I      what would you like to ↓ask me
22 → AR     I ↑like being I like being er (..) in 'ere (.)
23   I      you ↑like  ⌈being  =
24 → AR                ⌊(living) in 'ere like I like living in 'ere
```

That the reassurances offered by the interviewer are not heard by Arthur as such, and that he understands that his 'results' may be used by other people to inform decisions affecting the quality of his life, is made clear in lines 22 and 24. Rather than 'asking a question' as invited by his interviewer (in lines 17–21), Arthur uses the opportunity to make it clear, at the start of the interview, that he is happy living where he is. Adopting a more direct approach to matters than Bob, Arthur leaves no room for uncertainty on the interviewer's part. He repeats 'I like living in 'ere' three times. Why might this be? It is, I think, hard to avoid reading this exchange as other than a worried Arthur taking pains to state his understanding of the encounter. He knows, that is, that the answers he provides to a set of test questions are highly consequential. He is aware that his continued residence in his house is on the line. He fears that the likely upshot of a 'poor' performance is being relocated. 'I like living in 'ere', then, may be heard as conveying that his 'quality of life' interview *scares* him. Unfortunately, however, 'do you like living here' does not feature as a specified item on the questionnaire schedule, so this particular datum – despite its apparent importance to the quality of Arthur's life – must be disregarded in calculating his QOL score.

Table 3.1 Some ethical questions to consider when developing and designing a QOL study

- Whose quality of life is it anyway?
- Who is/are the expert(s) on QOL in the population I wish to study: academics or the people themselves?
- What is the relationship between the theoretical/operational definition of QOL used by the measures that I am going to employ and the everyday understandings of QOL of the people to whom I am going to administer them?
- What *are* the everyday understandings of QOL of the people I am working with?
- What procedures or methods might I adopt that would assist me to find out?
- Whose quality of life is it anyway?
- If everyday understandings are different from those proposed by the measure I intend to use, what are the ethical issues here?
- What *direct* and *specific* benefits to my research participants will flow from this quality of life project?
- If I cannot specify such direct benefits, in advance, what are the ethical implications of this failure?
- Is my proposed research 'mainstream' or 'emancipatory'? If 'mainstream' how could it be redesigned to give a genuine voice to my participants?
- what harm (physical, emotional, psychological) might my study of the quality of their lives cause to my participants?
- What indirect benefits may accrue to participants/the wider research community from my quality of life study?
- Whose quality of life is it anyway?

In Summary

There are serious ethical, conceptual and philosophical difficulties inherent in the study and assessment of QOL (see Table 3.1). At an individual level not only may QOL judgments be employed to make literally life-threatening decisions, they may also, in the gathering of data to inform them, be seen to do immediate harm (albeit of a less physically serious nature) to the people whose 'life quality' is supposedly 'objectively' being measured. That such harm may be caused to research participants is, in many jurisdictions (including the university where I work), sufficient for Human Research Ethics Committees to refuse a research permit.

From a wider perspective, attention has been drawn to the capacity for QOL research to offer an appearance of 'scientific' legitimacy to fundamentally ethically problematic practices in medicine (for example selective abortion, the allocation of resources to particular groups at the expense of others and (in)voluntary euthanasia) and in the operation of national economies on the basis of what some see as deeply flawed indices. Such concerns have included the recognition that, historically, not only have 'mainstream' research practices silenced disadvantaged people, but also that notions of 'lives worth living' have slipped into ideas such as 'lives unworthy of life'.

In this respect, writers cautioning against the use of QOL research have pointed to the active collaboration of medical, psychological and psychiatric professionals with both Nazi and Fascist regimes in the 'solution' of the problems such 'useless mouths' posed to the well-being, or quality of life, of the nation-state. Such concerns resonate with contemporary alarm about the creeping 'medicalization' and 'surveillance' of ever-wider areas of people's lives in the guise of concern for their well-being raised by writers such as Hatton (1998), Higginson and Carr (2001) and Taylor (1994). Such concerns also raise difficult questions about the ethics of employing as research tools measures which are based not on the views of the people to whom they are applied, but rather upon *researchers'* ideas about what quality of life is.

In the light of the ethical concerns raised in this chapter, Chapter 4 turns to examine research approaches that draw upon both 'mainstream' and 'emancipatory' thinking. Work which has focused upon the identification and the demarcation – or 'fractioning' – of domains of QOL is discussed. Workers in this stream of the quantitative tradition, such as Cummins, believe that it is possible to develop a formal operational definition of QOL which contributes both to theory building and that also offers individual persons, policy-makers, service providers and the research community a widely applicable and socially relevant measurement tool. Workers in the qualitative area have, traditionally, been more interested in the approach described by Ager and Hatton (1999): that of using a 'more discursive analysis of individuals' accounts of their life experience' to understand – in a manner which is attentive to the criticisms of writers such as Koch (2001) and Oliver (1996) – the quality of peoples' lives as they themselves experience it and, in so doing, contributing to the development of 'emancipatory' research practices.

Notes

1. The *QOL.Q* is a 40-item questionnaire which measures both objective circumstances and subjective perceptions of satisfaction with life in terms of four factors: Satisfaction; Competence/Productivity; Social Belonging and Empowerment/Independence. The other leading intellectual disability QOL

measure is the *ComQOL-ID-5* (Cummins, 1997a), a psychometrically more complex instrument which also measures objective circumstances and subjective perceptions of satisfaction in seven areas (Material Well-being, Health, Productivity, Intimacy, Safety, Place in Community and Emotional Well-being) but provides for the subjective weighting of objective factors by their level of importance to the individual. Broadly speaking the *QOL.Q* can be said to measure how happy people are in normalization-congruent service settings, whereas the *ComQOL-ID* provides for a direct comparison of (aspects of) life satisfaction between people with an intellectual disability and the normal population. Psychometrics for the QOL.Q are provided by Rapley and Lobley (1995); Rapley *et al.* (1998) and Schalock and Keith (1993). Psychometric studies of the *ComQOL-ID* can be found in Cummins (1997).

2. Extracts are transcriptions of audiotaped interviews. Transcription conventions for extract 1 are those developed by Gail Jefferson and are designed to capture the most important prosodic aspects of speech. Other extracts employ a simplified transcription. Appendix 1 shows Jeffersonian transcription conventions.

Study Questions

- Whose quality of life is it anyway?
- Is it ethically acceptable to employ predictions of future quality of life as a guide to end-of-life, or beginning-of-life, decision-making?
- What would the quality of my life be if I had Down syndrome/Alzheimer's disease/dialysis-dependent kidney disease?
- Is there such a thing as a life not worth living?

Suggestions for Further Reading

Clements, J., Rapley, M. and Cummins, R.A. (1999) On, to, for or with? Vulnerable people and the practices of the research community, *Behavioural and Cognitive Psychotherapy*, 27, 2: 103–16.

Hatton, C. (1998) Whose quality of life is it anyway? Some problems with the emerging quality of life consensus, *Mental Retardation*, 36: 104–15.

Kuhse, H. and Singer, P. (1985) *Should the Baby Live?* Oxford: Oxford University Press.

Ramsey, P. (1978) *Ethics at the Edges of Life*. New Haven, CT: Yale University Press.

CHAPTER 4

Quantitative and Qualitative Approaches

> Some, then, believe that [QOL] can only be assessed by asking the person directly (where possible); others doubt that such subjectivity is to be trusted, and prefer observable measures. Crudely: one school will want to ask how happy you are; the other will want to ask you or your guardians whether you have a job, a key to your house, and fresh linen every week, and will calculate your happiness from that. (Antaki and Rapley, 1996a)

Introduction – What is QOL Research for?

This chapter offers an overview of the major quantitative and qualitative approaches to QOL research. As is suggested by the quote from Antaki and Rapley (1996a) at the head of this chapter, and as we have seen elsewhere in Part 1, much, if not a majority, of QOL research is *not* primarily driven by a disinterested academic curiosity, but rather is functional or pragmatic. That is, across the social sciences, QOL research is conducted for a range of purposes, as Table 4.1 shows.

It is a basic principle in all social scientific work that the purposes of the research, and the specific research questions, should determine the methodology employed to seek answers. Another way to approach this is to remember that, as Edwards *et al.* (1995) put it, 'method is theory in disguise'. The adequacy of any research study is thus, to a greater or lesser extent, (pre)determined by the ability of the methodology adopted to provide sensible answers to the questions asked – and as we have already seen in Chapter 3, there are many QOL researchers (Hatton, 1998; Taylor, 1996; Wolfensberger, 1994; Rapley, 2001) who have raised serious questions about the ability of many of the research practices in the field to provide intellectually coherent answers to questions like 'what is quality of life?' Indeed, the final chapter of this book pursues this particular question – and its implications – in greater detail.

If we look at Table 4.1 it is apparent that there is a multiplicity of research questions, from disciplines as diverse as economics and health economics, nursing, epidemiology, medicine, disability studies, sociology and psychology, that can be brought together under the banner of 'QOL research'. In many cases, the methods by which answers are sought to the questions posed will often be determined by the dominant, or traditional, approach to research within the disciplinary field of study concerned. In most cases,

Table 4.1 Purposes of QOL research advanced in the literature

- Large-scale evaluation of effects of social policy (Baldwin et al., 1990).
- To set a 'national agenda' for human services (Goode, 1994a).
- To assist in the 'process which defines some individuals in society as deserving and others as undeserving ... who should live, and who will therefore die' (Baldwin et al., 1990a: 3).
- Political activism (Rogers-Clarke, 1996; Farlinger, 1996; Brown, 2000).
- Developing a more sophisticated understanding of the historical development of particular societies (Jordan, 1998, 2001).
- Developing a more sophisticated understanding of contemporary societies and social problems (Navarro and Shi, 2001).
- Promotion of human rights and equitable distribution of resources (OECD, 2001).
- Comparative evaluation of different models of human service provision or therapeutic methods (Emerson and Hatton, 1994; Bonicatto et al., 2001).
- To direct research, training and service development funding to specific 'needy' areas (Sprangers et al., 2000).
- To guide macro-level decisions about resource allocation (Fayers and Bjordal, 2001).
- Clinical governance (Carr et al., 2001).
- Clinical audit and systematic review of quality of medical care (Higginson, 1993) and residential services (Keith and Schalock, 2000).
- To provide 'the ultimate criterion of the effectiveness of social care delivery' (Perry and Felce, 1995: 1).
- Staff training in medical and nursing settings (Maguire et al., 1996).
- To direct professional focus onto 'patient-related' rather than technical aspects of health care (Higginson and Carr, 2001).
- To intervene in staff value systems to promote choice, independence and lifestyle of service recipients (Brown, 1997).
- To provide a common language for service providers (Schalock and Keith, 2000).
- To assist staff in human services to provide a more individually-centred service (Butterworth et al., 1997).
- To screen for patients' 'hidden problems' in medical settings (Higginson and Carr, 2001).
- Provision of an opportunity for 'consumers' to provide feedback on matters of concern to them (Bryant et al., 2001).
- To enable ideologically progressive coalitions between professionals and service users (Schalock et al., 2000; Schalock, 1997).
- Refinement of theoretical models of quality of life and development of more sensitive measurement approaches (Cummins, 1995; 1997b).
- Development of clearer understandings of the meaning of the term 'quality of life' and its relation to cultural theories of 'being human' (Rose, 1992; Rapley and Ridgway, 1998; McHoul and Rapley, 2001).

the approach will be primarily *quantitative*: that is 'amounts' of QOL will in some manner be measured. Increasingly, however, *qualitative* approaches to a number of these questions are being put forward.

Research questions can also be distinguished in terms of their *level of analysis* (Schalock, 1996): thus QOL research concerned with the large-scale evaluation of social policy (Baldwin *et al.*, 1990), to set a 'national agenda' for human services (Goode, 1994a), to contribute to developing a more sophisticated understanding of contemporary societies and social problems (Navarro and Shi, 2001) or which aims to inform the promotion of human rights and equitable distribution of resources (OECD, 2001) is clearly operating at a societal, or *macro*, level of analysis. Studies that look at matters such as clinical governance, audit and the systematic review of the quality of medical care (Carr *et al.*, 2001; Higginson, 1993) or the effectiveness of social care residential services (Perry and Felce, 1995) may be described as operating at an intermediate, or *meso*, level of analysis. At the *micro*, or individual, level of analysis, QOL research can be concerned with assisting staff in human services to provide a more individual-centred service (Butterworth *et al.*, 1997), screening for patients' 'hidden problems' (Higginson and Carr, 2001) and offering 'consumers' of various medical or social care services the opportunity to provide feedback on matters of concern to them (Bryant *et al.*, 2001). Some studies – for example those refining theoretical models of QOL and developing measurement approaches (Cummins *et al.*, 1997, 1997a) – may span levels of analysis.

As is also evident from Table 4.1, there are other questions that do not fall neatly into these 'levels of analysis'. For example, work which seeks to develop a more sophisticated understanding of the historical development of life quality in particular societies (Jordan, 1998, 2001) and work that tries to understand how the very idea of 'QOL research' has come to be possible in the first place (Rose, 1992; Rapley and Ridgway, 1998, McHoul and Rapley, 2001) cannot be fitted into such a conceptualization. Such work may rather be described as 'metatheoretical' or philosophical and draws more naturally on techniques from disciplines such philosophy, history or cultural studies.

While there are good reasons for regarding the qualitative–quantitative dichotomy as in many ways misleading, it serves present purposes. In particular this difference serves to keep in focus two of the issues raised in Chapter 3 – 'whose quality of life is it anyway?' and the closely related question – 'to whom do QOL research results belong?' It is primarily in qualitative work that the ethics of method have been explicitly debated, and particularly the question of whether research in general, and QOL research in particular, is in the best interests of the people who researchers often refer to as 'subjects', and without whose cooperation research could not be conducted. In response to such questions, a considerable body of qualitative QOL research is, more or less explicitly, allied to the 'emancipatory' research paradigm (Oliver, 1996) which adopts as one of its goals advocacy on behalf of particular groups. Such a stance shows up very clearly a major difference between qualitative and quantitative approaches – broadly speaking – in that whereas quantitative research methods operate on the assumption that research should be characterized by objectivity, neutrality and an apolitical position, many, but not all, qualitative approaches hold that such notions cannot stand up to scrutiny (see, for example, Edwards *et al.*, 1995).

As such many qualitative researchers hold that 'subjective' factors influence everything from the choice of research questions to the preference for one 'objective' operational definition over another – not to mention which studies eventually get published (see for example Schrecker *et al*'s., 2001, discussion of 'mental illness prevention' research). 'Neutrality' is simply not an accurate description of how the 'hard' sciences, let alone the social s ciences, work, particularly given the tendency for 'awkward' statistics to be unreported or explained away – even in studies of the QOL of patients taking part in randomized controlled trials of cardiovascular and oncology treatments listed in the prestigious Cochrane Register (Sanders *et al.*, 1998) – or for favourable statistical results to be selectively reported (McNamee and Horton, 1996) (see Potter 1996, especially Chapter 1, for a discussion of social studies of science) and that claims of an apolitical stance are simply to take a political stand with the status quo by refusing to question it (Barnes *et al.*, 1999; Finkelstein, 1993; Goodley, 1996).

On account of these *political* differences about epistemology proponents of qualitative and quantitative approaches to QOL research are frequently dismissive of each other's contribution. Many quantitative researchers mistakenly conflate *quantification* with *empirical analysis*. In this Chapter I outline major qualitative and quantitative approaches to QOL and demonstrate empirically rigorous work using a range of qualitative approaches drawn from ethnomethodology, conversation analysis and discourse analysis.[1] As space precludes more than an overview of the key issues, a range of texts which detail the nuts and bolts of specific approaches (for instance guides to particular quantitative statistical methods such as factor analysis and introductory level texts in qualitative areas such as conversation analysis) is included in the *Resources* section at the end of the book.

The aim of the chapter then is to offer an overview of the costs and benefits of various approaches, and to illustrate the methodological and conceptual issues with discussions of empirical work in the literature. Conversation analytic work on the administration of structured QOL interviews (Antaki and Rapley, 1996a, 1996b; Rapley and Antaki, 1996) illustrates the use of interview methods. Work on the QOL perceptions of adults with intellectual disabilities (Alderson, 2001) expands on this issue and also demonstrates the design and conduct of studies using discourse analytic methodology in QOL research.

Quantitative approaches are discussed via a description of two widely used psychometric measures of QOL and with reference to issues of rater and inter-rater reliability, particularly reliability in situations of proxy response. Again, these conceptual and methodological issues are illustrated with a discussion of empirical data bearing on the questions in the literature, and by the description and analysis of model studies approaching these questions.

Quantitative Approaches to QOL Research

Cummins (1996: 303) suggests that 'there are two basic approaches to the definition and measurement of subjective quality of life ... One regards the construct as a single, unitary entity, while the other considers it to be composed of discrete domains.' As we have seen in Chapters 1 and 2, this has prompted a considerable body of work attempting to specify the QOL of nation-states as an *aggregate*, or sum, of quanta of various material circumstances and/or reports of citizens' levels of satisfaction with their circumstances or their happiness as a whole. Similarly, at the individual level, there is an immense number of quantitative measures of QOL which vary in both their degree of generality/specificity, and in terms of the explicitness of the link between the items they measure and their theoretical base.

What quantitative approaches share is an insistence that the theoretical model of QOL adopted and the research design which follows from it must be congruent; that item selection in questionnaire design should be guided by empirical studies; that any QOL measure should demonstrate psychometric reliability and validity; and that studies of QOL should *triangulate* the construct with other theoretically congruent measures or relevant supplementary variables. As is evident from Table 4.2, however, much quantitative research – at least as reported in the medical literature – fails to meet even these basic criteria of statistical and study design adequacy.

The relation of theoretical models of QOL to research design is illustrated in this chapter by an overview of instruments designed to measure the QOL of nations, and a discussion of two key quantitative instruments for the measurement of individual quality of life. Cummins's ComQol and the World Health Organization's WHOQOL (Appendix 2) are examined here. ComQol was selected as it is an exemplary individual-level measure that theorizes QOL as a *universal* construct, and the WHOQOL was selected as it represents an exemplary health-related QOL instrument developed and promulgated by a major international agency. Field studies using both of these measures are discussed in Chapter 7, which also considers the triangulation of QOL with other measures.

In the first half of this chapter, issues of the reliability of QOL measures are addressed in *quantitative terms*, via a discussion of studies examining the inter-rater reliability of persons and their proxies on psychometric measures. The questionable reliability and validity of individual measures is also illustrated in the second part of this chapter by the use of *qualitative* research methods.

Measures to assess the QOL of nations

The approach adopted by the ABS is an exemplary illustration of the

Table 4.2 Most common flaws in QOL research studies in the medical literature

- Trials involving QOL measurement are not comparative.
- Sample size is not justified and is either too small to have statistical power, or too large, leading to statistical significance in the absence of clinical relevance.
- The QOL measure used is idiosyncratic, not validated and/or has not had its responsiveness assessed.
- No follow-up data on patients is provided.
- No description is provided of sample attrition and/or of the handling of missing data.
- Presentation of QOL results is flawed – for example, graphs are presented with no values given or standard deviations of scores in different domains of quality of life are omitted.
- Confidence intervals and/or effect sizes for differences between conditions are not presented.
- Levels of significance adopted do not take account of the number of comparisons performed, leading to false positive results.
- The clinical relevance of statistical changes in measured QOL are not discussed.

Source: Chassany et al. (1999).

explicit specification of the relationship between the theory of QOL adopted and the design of (a set of) measures to quantify it. The ABS (2001: 6) states that:

> individual wellbeing can be measured using people's subjective evalua-
> tion of themselves, based on their feelings, or by collating any number of
> observable attributes that reflect on their wellbeing. In some ways,
> wellbeing might best be assessed subjectively, as it is strongly associated
> with notions of happiness and life satisfaction. Thus personal wellbeing
> might be measured in terms of how happy or satisfied people are with their
> life or with aspects of their life (their job, health, etc.). While such measures
> can be difficult to interpret, subjective measures, as with other statistics,
> can be aggregated and monitored over time, and, in theory, provide a
> picture of the nation's view as to whether living conditions are getting
> better or worse.

This clear theoretical statement (based as it is in a recognizably 'American' conceptualization of QOL) thus underpins the selection by the ABS of the 'areas of concern' (Family and Community, Health, Education and Training, Work, Economic Resources, Housing, Crime and Justice, Culture and Leisure) that they specify as measures of the QOL in Australia. Unfortunately, as we saw in Chapter 2, not all such measures derive their indices so directly (if at all) from an explicit theory of quality of life.

However, in their review of 22 indexes proposed as measures of well-being for national policy formulation and evaluation, Hagerty et al. suggest that 'only recently have we had the resources and the science to begin measuring the "good life" and how it arises' (2001: 1) and suggest 14 criteria (Table 4.3) for evaluating such indices.

As reinventing the wheel serves little purpose, it is sufficient to note here that, for quantitative studies at population levels, meeting these standards should be considered the necessary and sufficient criteria for the use of *any* quantitative measure in QOL research. It is also clear that, with slight modifications, these criteria can also be held to apply to measures of the QOL of individuals – as is shown in Table 4.4.

However, it is important to recognize that while many of these criteria for the 'validity and usefulness of such QOL indexes to public policy' are eminently reasonable, others are problematic. Firstly, it must be noticed that these criteria mix those that can sensibly apply at the population level (for example, Criterion 3: 'The index should be based on time series to allow periodic monitoring and control') with those that are equally clearly only applicable to persons (Veenhoven, 1996) (for example, Criterion 14: 'The subjective dimension of each domain has both a cognitive and an affective component. They are measured by questions concerning "satisfaction"'. It is difficult to imagine that the economy of Bolivia has either a cognitive or an affective component, even though individual Bolivians may well get emotional about the GDP. Secondly, the existence of a real, universally meaningful, QOL construct 'out there' to be measured, is presumed, regardless of social and cultural differences around the globe (as is clearly implied by notions such as a construct needing to encompass

Table 4.3 Necessary and sufficient criteria for measures of the quality of life of nations

---

1. The index must have a clear practical purpose.
2. The index should help public policy-makers develop and assess programmes at all levels of aggregation.
3. The index should be based on time series to allow periodic monitoring and control.
4. The index should be grounded in well-established theory.
5. The components of the index should be reliable, valid and sensitive.
6. The index should be reported as a single number, but can be broken down into components.
7. The domains in aggregate must encompass the totality of life experience.
8. Each domain must encompass a substantial but discrete portion of the QOL construct.
9. Each domain must have the potential to be measured in both objective and subjective dimensions.
10. Each domain within a generic QOL instrument must have relevance for most people.
11. If a specific domain is proposed for a non-generic instrument, it must be demonstrated to contribute unique variance to the QOL construct beyond the generic domains for the target group.
12. Domains must be potentially neutral, positive or negative in their contribution to the QOL construct.
13. Domains must differ from the dimensions of personality, cognitive processes and affect in that they cannot be measured objectively.
14. The subjective dimension of each domain has both a cognitive and an affective component. They are measured by questions concerning 'satisfaction'.

Source: Hagerty *et al.* (2001: 1–11).

Table 4.4 Necessary qualities of individual-level QOL measures

Issue	Sub-type	Questions
Validity	Face	Does the measure cover issues that are clearly relevant to its users, for example, 'patients', professionals and carers?
	Construct	Does the measure show theoretically congruent relationships with other measures of the construct? For example, if a QOL measure is based on a theory of QOL that suggests work is an important domain, do scores on the measure correlate with respondents' employment status?
	Discrimination	Does the measure discriminate between groups in a manner consistent with the theory underlying it?
	Content	Does the measure contain domains/items that are pertinent to the study population?
Reliability	Test-retest	Do repeat administrations of the measure produce comparable results, all else being equal?
	Inter-rater	Do separate raters arrive at the same QOL judgments?
	Internal consistency	High levels of internal consistency imply reliability but also a degree of item redundancy.
Appropriateness		Is the measure well-validated?
		Is the format and content of the measure appropriate to the intended study group? Are the items well-phrased and conceptually clear? For example, if a measure is to be used with persons with an intellectual disability, is the level of complexity of the items appropriate?
		Is the measure both sufficiently brief, and sufficiently comprehensive, to avoid respondent fatigue and to capture all necessary information?
		Has the measure been used in the current setting before and with what results?
		If the measure is a translation or from another culture, what steps have been taken to ensure local comparability?
Sensitivity		Is the measure sufficiently sensitive to detect changes that are meaningful in relation to the study?
		For example, do changes in service/treatment practice which would be expected to produce changes in QOL scores actually do so?
Interpretabilty		Does the manual for the measure provide comprehensive data on reliability, validity and other trials of its use?
		Are comparative and/or normative data available?
		Can the results of the measure be readily translated into implications for individual treatment, service practice or policy development?

Source: Adapted from Higginson and Carr (2001).

'the totality of life experience', Criterion 7). Studies critical of this idea are discussed in the second part of this chapter.

Two measures: the WHOQOL-BREF and the comprehensive quality of life scales (ComQOL)

As we saw in Chapter 2 (p. 50), the WHOQOL Group (1993) defines QOL as a multidimensional concept and has developed the WHOQOL such that the structure of the instrument reflects both their theoretical definition of QOL and also 'the issues that a group of scientific experts as well as lay people in each of the field centers felt were important to quality of life' (WHO, 1997: 3). The WHOQOL-100 measures six domains of quality of life, with 24 facets (see Table 4.5). Each facet is measured by the use of four items scored on a five-point scale. A study examining the validity of the WHOQOL-100 with people diagnosed with 'depression' (Skevington and Wright, 2001) is discussed in Chapter 7.

The WHOQOL-BREF consists of 26 questions, comprising one item from each of the 24 facets (or dimensions) of QOL as operationalized in the 100-item scale, with the addition of two single items to measure 'overall quality of life' and 'general health'. Items chosen were selected on the basis of their correlation with facet total scores (WHOQOL Group, 1998).

The six domains of QOL identified in the WHOQOL-100 are cut down to four in the short form, as the WHOQOL Group state that 'recent analysis of available data, using structural equation modelling, has shown a four domain solution to be more appropriate' (WHOQOL Group, 1996: 7). The four-factor solution reported by the WHOQOL Group (1998), and which represents the theoretical structure of the BREF instrument, explains 58 per cent of the total variance of scores on the measure, but Hagerty *et al.* (2001) note that even in this reduced factor structure there are a high number of complex loadings (that is, items load onto more than one factor). They suggest that 'using the authors' criterion for facet inclusion as a loading >.3, Factor 1 ('health') contains eight facets and one that cross-loaded (7/8 non-complex facets), Factor 2 comprises (5/9), Factor 3 comprises (3/8), and Factor 4 comprises (2/6). It seems clear that only the first factor can be asserted with confidence' (Hagerty *et al.*, 2001: 18). These authors also raise questions about the comparability of the WHOQOL Group's reported confirmatory four-factor model and their prior principal components analysis. For example, they note that two of the 'psychological' items, 'positive feelings' and 'negative feelings', load onto single factors, but that these factors are *different*. Similarly, they point out that the 'bodily image and appearance' item loads, statistically, onto the 'social relationships' domain in the preliminary analyses, but is included in the 'psychological' domain in the confirmatory model.

In their summary of the adequacy of the WHOQOL instruments against the 14 criteria they propose, Hagerty *et al.*, (2001) are highly critical. While

Table 4.5 WHOQOL-BREF domains

Domain	Facets incorporated within domains
1. Physical health	Activities of daily living Dependence on medicinal substances and medical aids Energy and fatigue Mobility Pain and discomfort Sleep and rest Work capacity
2. Psychological/bodily image and appearance	Negative feelings Positive feelings Self-esteem Spirituality/religion/personal beliefs Thinking, learning, memory and concentration
3. Social relationships	Personal relationships Social support Sexual activity
4. Environment	Financial resources Freedom, physical safety and security Health and social care: accessibility and quality Home environment Opportunities for acquiring new information and skills Participation in and opportunities for recreation/leisure activities Physical environment (pollution/noise/traffic/climate) Transport

Source: World Health Organization (1996).

the WHO instruments are exemplary in their specification of an operational definition of QOL, it appears that this, in and of itself, is far from adequate as a guide to subsequent instrument development. It appears that item selection has been guided by other factors in addition to the existing empirical literature and, indeed, the statistical analyses the WHO conducted as part of instrument field trials. The theoretical model of QOL derived from the (common-sense) views of 'experts and lay people' appears at least as powerful a determinant of item facet placement as the powerful statistical techniques applied to the data. It is instructive that a scientific instrument developed by an international organization as well resourced and respected as the WHO should be described as follows. Hagerty *et al.*, (2001) state of the entire WHOQOL project that:

this exercise has been flawed in that: (a) the authors did not use their vast array of data to deduce domains, but rather adopted the six domains they proposed at the outset; (b) the processes of data reduction to arrive at the 24 facets are opaque as far as published material is concerned, and evidence is now available to cast doubt on the adequacy of assumed facet content; and (c) three of the four domains forming the WHOQOL-100 and BREF contain considerable cross-loading facets ... the weakest of the four domains is social relationships, and yet there is a high level of agreement within the QOL literature that this domain is preeminent in its contribution to the life quality of most people ... In summary, at this stage of its development, the WHOQOL cannot be recommended as a scale to measure overall QOL. (Hagerty et al., 2001: 19–20)

Cummins's comprehensive quality of life scales (ComQOL)

These parallel scales were developed by Cummins and his colleagues at Deakin University. Work on their development is described in Cummins (1995, 1996, 1997a). As we have seen in Chapter 2, Cummins defines QOL as both objective and subjective, with QOL the aggregate of seven domains: Material well-being, Health, Productivity, Intimacy, Safety, Community and Emotional well-being. Accordingly, the ComQOL scales (parallel forms exist, for example, for people with and without intellectual disabilities) include measures of the seven domains specified in Cummins's definition. Cummins (1996) reports a detailed semantic and psychometric analysis of over 170 proposed QOL domains in the literature which, he suggests, can be reduced to the seven domains he operationalizes as his definition and measure of QOL. Cummins (1996: 307–8) notes that the seven domains of ComQOL capture 83 per cent of the reported domain descriptions cited in the 32 studies analysed.

Each domain of the ComQOL scales has three objective and two subjective measures. The three objective measures for each domain are summed, and the domain sums, when aggregated, provide a unitary measure of objective well-being. One of the subjective measures of each domain is a satisfaction measure (a seven-point item measured on a 'delightful/terrible' scale), and an importance measure (presented as a five-point item). The product of the satisfaction multiplied by the importance score for each domain provides a measure of the subjective QOL represented by the domain, and the seven products sum to obtain a single measure of subjective well-being. The conceptual structure of ComQOL is presented in Table 4.6.

Cummins admits that the ComQOL is not based on a single theory of QOL (Hagerty et al., 2001). Instead he offers a range of theoretical arguments and selected empirical observations in support of his position. For example, his justification of the use of satisfaction × importance scores as indices of QOL is explicitly based on the work of Andrews and Withey (1976). However, extensive and solid psychometric studies of the ComQOL scales have been reported. In terms of internal consistency, for example, Cummins (1997a:

Table 4.6 Conceptual framework for the ComQOL

The instrument is based on the following propositions:

- Quality of life (QOL) can be described in both objective (O) and subjective (S) terms.
- Each objective (OQOL) and subjective (SQOL) axis is composed of seven domains:
    1. Material well-being
    2. Health
    3. Productivity
    4. Intimacy
    5. Safety
    6. Place in community
    7. Emotional well-being
- The measurement of each OQOL domain is achieved by obtaining an aggregate score based on the measurement of three objective indices relevant to that domain. For example, 'material well-being' is measured by an aggregate score of income, type of accommodation and personal possessions.
- The measurement of each SQOL domain is achieved by obtaining a satisfaction score of that domain which is weighted by the perceived importance of the domain for the individual. Thus SQOL = Σ (Domain satisfaction $\times$ Domain importance).

Source: Cummins (1997: 8–9).

45–8) reports Cronbach alphas for the ComQOL of $\alpha = 0.54$ for the sum of the objective measures, $\alpha = 0.65$ to 0.69 for the sum of importance measures, and $\alpha = 0.73$ to 0.81 for the sum of satisfaction measures. Test/retest reliability correlations are reported at 0.60 for the sum of importance and 0.36 for the sum of satisfaction measures. In terms of convergent validity, the ComQOL also performs well. For example, the ComQOL subjective health sub-scale correlates with the MOS Short Form 36 (SF-36) Physical Functioning scale at $r = 0.45$ and with the SF-36 Mental Health scale at $r = 0.60$ (Cummins, 1997a: 50).

It is also a helpful feature that a range of parallel forms exist to measure the QOL of, for example, people with intellectual disabilities using items directly comparable to those in the general adult form of the ComQOL. As Cummins (1998) notes, measures such as Schalock and Keith's (1993) QOL.Q, and the immensity of disease-specific QOL measures, have been designed for specific population sub-groups such as people with intellectual disabilities, people with acne or children and, strictly, cannot be used to make comparisons with the general adult population. Cummins (1997a: 6) notes that 'this is an important limitation since it means that the QOL experienced by such groups cannot be norm-referenced back to the general population'. As yet, the ComQOL has not been as widely used as its psychometric properties deserve. It is possible that this is due to both the length of the scale and to the complex pre-testing procedure involved in the intellectual disability parallel form.

Inter-rater reliability and proxy responses in QOL measurement

In the assessment of the adequacy of any quantitative measure, it is a canonical requirement that the instrument should produce the same results when applied to the same item by separate raters. If two people use the same ruler to measure the same piece of wood and one returns a measurement of six centimetres and the other nine centimetres, all else being equal, one would have grounds for concern about the precision of the measuring device. Such a measure would not have a high level of inter-rater reliability. The same requirement holds for all psychometric measures, including those of QOL.

In the area of much individual-level QOL research, however, matters are complicated by the fact that researchers often want to collect information about the QOL of people who find it difficult to provide accounts of their views: for example people with severe intellectual disabilities, people with dementing conditions, children or other 'patient' groups who are believed to be unreliable reporters on how they 'really' feel – for example, people in receipt of psychiatric services. In these cases the question becomes one of assessing the level of agreement between 'patients' and proxies answering on their behalf – carers, doctors, nursing staff and the like.

In general the literature suggests that when QOL is defined in objective terms, that is in terms of matters that can be readily observed by others (for example memberships of clubs and societies in the *QOL.Q* (Schalock and Keith, 1996) and the *ComQOL-ID* (Cummins, 1997a)) or the presence/absence of physical problems (for example the *Children's Quality of Life Questionnaire – TACQOL* (Vogels *et al.*, 1998)), agreement both between independent raters and also between professionals or carers as proxies and people themselves tends to be reasonably high. The literature is also clear that when QOL is defined either in subjective terms, or when subjective aspects of lived experience are included as domains of a composite measure, the picture is much less rosy. It seems to be the case that a task that Lovett (1993: 3) termed 'guessing at another's comfort' is indeed a problematic exercise.

For example, Sawyer *et al.* (1999) report a study comparing child/patient and parent ratings of HRQOL for adolescents undergoing treatment for cancer. Seventy adolescents (aged 10 to 18 years) and their parents completed what are described as 'standard' HRQOL question-naires. Participants completed the Child Health Questionnaire (Landgraf *et al.*, 1996),[2] the Functional Status II(R) Questionnaire (Stein and Jessop, 1990, 1991),[3] and the Impact-on-Family Scale (Stein and Riessman, 1980).[4] In general, the study found that there was good agreement between parent and adolescent HRQOL reports. However, parents of adolescents receiving active treatment for cancer reported that their child's illness was having a greater impact on their child's physical functioning, social and school activities than was reported by the adolescents themselves. Adolescents reported significantly higher scores for themselves than their parents did on the Child Health Questionnaire Role/Social-Physical and Self-Esteem scales. Sawyer *et al.* (1999: 43) concluded that:

> despite generally good agreement between parent and adolescent reports … it cannot be assumed that reports from parents are always an accurate reflection of the views of the adolescents. Studies examining the influence of independent factors on adolescents' HRQL must take into account differences in reports from these 2 informants and the possibility that key independent variables have differing relationships with the various domains which comprise adolescents' HRQL.

Similarly, Shaw *et al.* (2000) examined the agreement between proxies and older people with 'objective' issues of continence management. Their study examined the concordance of proxy responses and index respondents (women aged 65 years and older with neck of femur fractures) on issues around continence five days following surgery. Index respondents nominated a proxy respondent who was interviewed using the same schedule. Responses were compared using percentage agreement and Cohen's Kappa statistic. For questions relating to functional ability, Shaw *et al.* (2000) found that proxy responses were more reliable for personal care activities than for activities of daily living. They suggest that this result may be a consequence of instrumental activities questions being more ambiguous and open to individual interpretation. Interestingly, the study found that the more distant the relationship, and the lower the level of contact between staff and index respondents, the better the agreement found. However, proxy responses were found to be systematically biased, with their responses suggesting an *overestimation* of functional incapacity. Good concordance was found for questions directly addressing urinary and faecal incontinence, but fell for more detailed questions concerning the timing and frequency of incontinence. Shaw *et al.* (2000) attribute this higher level of disagreement to the use for these questions of graded response options rather than simple yes/no responses.

As with elderly people, in services for people with intellectual disabilities, proxy responses have often been employed to gauge QOL. The manuals for both of the most extensively psychometrically validated intellectual disability QOL measures, the QOL.Q (Schalock *et al.*, 1990; Schalock and Keith, 1996) and the ComQOL-ID (Cummins, 1997a), acknowledge that it may be necessary for staff members, or other significant persons, to act as proxy respondents, to complete the questionnaire 'as if they were the person'. Equally, both questionnaires recognize that this procedure is fraught with difficulty. However, if the vicarious – or proxy – feedback of more severely impaired service users is to be employed in service evaluation studies, then it is important that some measure of the success of staff members as proxy respondents be demonstrated. 'Success' in this context has usually been conceived of as the level of agreement between two independent members of staff; in other words staff–staff reliability.

Success in this respect is, however, an index of only limited utility. It is quite conceivable that staff responses may be highly reliable, yet also at considerable variance from the 'true' opinion of the service user. Clearly with non-verbal individuals there is no possibility of estimating the existence or extent of such possible discrepancies. However, the extent to which a measure supports consensual understandings of items across staff and participant groups can be estimated. In this sense success can also be construed as the extent to which staff and verbal participants agree on responses to items. The assumption underlying this procedure is that if staff members can assess, reasonably accurately, the QOL judgments of *verbal* individuals, then this ability will also hold true for *non-verbal* participants. The inferential step here is a large one. However, it seems reasonable to suggest that if a measure can be shown to elicit at least minimally acceptable levels of staff–participant concordance, then the confidence which can be placed in staff–staff reliability coefficients for non-verbal individuals would be correspondingly raised. Low correlations between the ratings of staff and verbal participants would suggest that evaluative judgments based on proxy respondents must be considered as deeply suspect.

Cummins (1997a) noted that proxy response data for the ComQOL-ID are very unreliable. A study reported by Reiter and Bendov (1996) likewise reported low correlations between staff and participant ratings on the QOL.Q (coefficients of between 0.26 and 0.31 for the Satisfaction, Competence/Productivity and Social Belonging/Community Integration factors) and a very low correlation coefficient ($r = 0.07$) between staff and service users on the Empowerment/Independence factor, with staff members consistently rating the quality of residents' lives more favourably than the residents themselves.

Rapley *et al.* (1998) report a similar study to those of Reiter and Bendov (1996) and Shaw *et al.* (2000) designed to assess the ability of the QOL.Q to support proxy responding. In the Rapley *et al.* (1998) reliability studies 13 pairs took part in the staff–client study and for the staff–staff study two members of staff completed the QOL.Q for 33 supported housing participants and a further 33 service users living in an institution, giving a total sample size of 66. For the staff–participant reliability study the QOL.Q was completed as a structured interview in the person's home.

Analysis of the data was conducted in three stages. Because of the small sample size for the staff–participant reliability study non-parametric statistics were used. Firstly Pearson Product Moment correlation coefficients between staff members' scores were computed and, secondly, relationships between individual proxy respondents and 'their' participants' scores were calculated. Thirdly, with the larger sample, the relation-

Table 4.7 Staff–staff reliability for the QOL.Q ($n = 63$)

Factor		Respondent	
Satisfaction	Staff 2	p value	r^2
Staff 1	0.877	0.001	0.76
Competence			
Staff 1	0.825	0.001	0.68
Empowerment			
Staff 1	0.881	0.001	0.77
Social Belonging			
Staff 1	0.829	0.001	0.68
QOL.Q total			
Staff 1	0.886	0.001	0.78

Source: Rapley et al. (1998).

ship between the proxy responses and participants' scores was analysed using t-tests for related samples.

The results showed that staff–staff reliability coefficients were comparable to those obtained by Schalock et al. (1990). Percentage predictive variance (r^2) values are high. Table 4.7 shows the correlation coefficients found, and their associated p values. As is apparent all correlation values are high, with significance being achieved at $p < 0.01$.

For the staff–participant reliability study staff–staff reliability coefficients for the proxy respondents, coefficients obtaining between participants' scores and the mean proxy response (the value Schalock et al. (1990) recommend be reported) and staff–participant reliability coefficients are shown in Table 4.8.

As can be seen in Table 4.8, with the exception of the Empowerment factor, the QOL.Q achieves a respectable level of staff–participant agreement. For the Empowerment factor the results suggest that staff and participants show a statistically non-significant, but serious, level of disagreement with each other. Staff proxies' scores, while being positively correlated, are also not closely related. Inspection of raw data revealed that the disagreement was accounted for by a pattern of disagreement in the context of a general staff overestimation of scores. In 9 of the 13 cases both staff members' scores on Empowerment were higher than those of participants. In general, staff–staff agreement appeared to be moderately stronger than staff–participant agreement.

Rapley et al. (1998) point out that, if proxy's scores are to be used to estimate participant's scores, two criteria must be satisfied. The first criterion is that *score reliability* is high; the second criterion is that the *mean scores* obtained from the two measures are *roughly equal*. Clearly, one could have perfect reliability, yet at the same time find that staff estimates of participant QOL are far higher than the participant's own estimates. Table

Table 4.8 Staff–participant and staff–staff reliability for the QOL.Q (n = 13)

Factor	Participant (r)	p	Staff 2 (r)	p
Respondent				
Satisfaction				
Staff 1	0.733	0.004	0.905	0.001
Staff 2	0.820	0.001		
Mean staff	0.765	0.002		
Competence				
Staff 1	0.651	0.016	0.962	0.001
Staff 2	0.648	0.016		
Mean staff	0.653	0.015		
Empowerment				
Staff 1	−0.268	0.343	0.159	0.603
Staff 2	−0.361	0.224		
Mean staff	−0.428	0.144		
Social Belonging				
Staff 1	0.694	0.008	0.746	0.003
Staff 2	0.628	0.022		
Mean staff	0.710	0.007		
QOL.Q total				
Staff 1	0.820	0.001	0.901	0.001
Staff 2	0.785	0.001		
Mean staff	0.823	0.001		

Source: Rapley *et al.* (1998).

Table 4.9 Comparison of staff and participant mean scores by factor and total QOL.Q score (n = 13, df =12)

Factor	Staff mean	Participant mean	t-value	1-tailed p
Satisfaction	22.6	23.7	−1.75	0.05
Competence/ Productivity	13.2	14.1	−0.78	0.22
Empowerment/ Independence	25.0	23.5	1.38	0.09
Social Belonging/ Comm. Integ.	22.1	19.4	3.53	0.01
QOL.Q total	82.1	80.8	0.83	0.21

Source: Rapley *et al.* (1998).

4.9 shows mean scores from staff and participants on each factor of the QOL.Q and the results of paired-sample t-tests, comparing staff mean vs. participant mean scores.

The inter-rater reliability data reported above suggested a worrying level of disagreement between staff and participants on the Empowerment factor. Data on mean scores suggest further causes for concern. As Table 4.9 shows, marginally significant differences in staff and participants' mean scores on the Empowerment factor were obtained. These results suggest that staff and participants' scores are also likely to show statistically significant differences on other factors. Inspection of the raw data for Social Belonging scores again showed a pattern of staff overestimations of participant scores in 11 out of 13 cases. Satisfaction results showed the opposite pattern, however. Here staff overestimated participant's scores in only four instances.

Staff–staff correlation coefficients seem to be consistently positive and statistically significant across the studies. Similarly, a cursory examination of the staff–participant reliability coefficients, with the exception of the extremely poor result for the Empowerment factor, would seem to suggest that staff proxies can make reasonably accurate judgments on behalf of participants. Reliability for the other factors is acceptable. The correlations suggest that for these factors, the measure elicits relatively accurate perceptions of participants' own QOL judgments by staff that know them well. Further analysis indicates, however, that this appearance of agreement is deceptive. In and of themselves, the marginal correlation result for the Competence factor and the poor agreement between staff and participants' scores on the Empowerment factor, replicating the Reiter and Bendov (1996) result, are cause for concern, particularly given staff overestimation of participant's judgments. Such a view is strengthened by the differences obtained in the analysis of mean scores on the Satisfaction and, particularly, on the Social Belonging factors. Here, although apparently in agreement and with highly correlated scores, staff and participants show statistically significant differences in mean scores, and very different patterns of response to items.

These results add weight to the view expressed in the literature that the use of proxy responses to QOL measures is highly problematic (Cummins, 1996). Proxy administration must always raise the possibility of respondent bias (in human services, often in favour of positive outcomes). In this study, values for items pertaining to staff performance, or to circumstances over which staff may exercise some control, are likely to be inflated by staff proxy respondents. Items addressing more general satisfaction with life circumstances appear less at risk of such a bias, but here are at risk of staff underestimation. Indeed, Rapley et al. (1998) were moved to speculate whether staff might not be prone to 'gild the lily', to inflate some QOL scores and not others. Box 4.1 summarizes the key issues in the use of proxy response in QOL research.

Box 4.1 Summary of key points relating to proxy respondents and quality of life assessments

General factors	Factors related to the person	Factors related to the proxy
Agreement depends on the concreteness, visibility and importance of the aspects of quality of life under consideration.	People may not complete quality of life measures in ways that accurately reflect their feelings. For example, people may seek to answer questions in ways that present themselves favourably. This may be related to findings of lesser agreement between respondents and proxies.	The lay caregivers' experience of caring, the amount of time they spend with the person and their own distress may influence their assessment of the person's quality of life.
Agreement is better for concrete, observable aspects and less good for more subjective domains, such as emotional health.	Proxies have a better chance of accurately reflecting quality of life if people are open with them about their problems and feelings.	Lower quality of life scores have been associated with increases in the burden on the caregiver, time spent together, the carer's distress and with the carer having a lower quality of life.
Agreement may improve over time, but evidence is contradictory.	Agreement between respondents and proxies seems to be greater when quality of life is either very good or very poor.	Extent of agreement may be influenced by the relationship between the patient and proxy, although the evidence for this is limited.
	Although people with severe and profound intellectual disabilities may not be able to complete self-report measures, people with mild and moderate intellectual impairment can and do respond validly.	The psychometric properties of the measure are important: if the measure is unreliable, then high agreement cannot be expected.
		Health professionals may project their own feelings of hopelessness and distress onto the people when assessing their quality of life.

Source: Adapted from Addington-Hall and Kalra (2001).

In summary

Quantitative approaches have produced an extraordinary number of definitions and measures of QOL. Studies of the QOL of an immense diversity of population groups have been conducted, and published accounts run into the tens of thousands. At the level of the nation-state a number of statistical series have been established which appear to be theoretically grounded and methodologically sound. However, the quality of much of the individual-level research published, and the psychometric adequacy of many of the measures employed, are deeply questionable. Of current individual QOL measures, Cummins's ComQOL is probably the most robust generic measure and clearly has much potential. However, many questions still remain open: the issue of proxy response still awaits resolution, and inventive approaches to matters such as this will occupy the field for a considerable time to come. It is also the case, however, that many researchers view what Edgerton (1990) called the 'American passion' for quantification with considerable scepticism. It is to qualitative studies of QOL that we now turn.

Qualitative Approaches

> Exact sciences give correct answers to certain aspects of life problems, but very incomplete answers. It is important of course to count and measure what is countable and measurable, but the most precious values in human life are aspirations which laboratory experiments cannot yet reproduce. (Dubos, 1959: 279)

Interest in qualitative research methods has increased greatly in the last few years. Even disciplines which have modelled themselves upon the 'hard' sciences, such as psychology, have recognized that even the 'hard' sciences can be understood as 'socially constructed' (Potter, 1996); that there are issues about ownership of 'expertise' in what QOL 'is'; and that traditional measurement technologies may not only have hidden troubles, but also may misrepresent informants. However, qualitative research is not homogenous, and writers such as Silverman (1998) have identified the dangerous contribution much qualitative work also makes to romanticizing the idea of persons as beings with 'deep interiors' (Gergen, 1992: 208). As Silverman points out, much of this variety of qualitative work, which claims to document the 'authentic personal experience' of individuals, is not only neglectful of the locally produced nature of social order and subjectivity, but also relies on romanticized notions which allow researchers to retain their version of what is 'really' going on. Of course, what this variety of qualitative work thus manages to do is not only to rely on the sort of a priori assumptions about 'reality' which it criticizes quantitative work for, but also slips in the privileged position of the analyst through the back door (see proponents of 'critical realist' qualitative methods such as Parker, 1998).

Having said this, much qualitative work has started from a recognition expressed by Westerhof *et al.*'s (2001: 179) study of the QOL of older persons. They note that 'existing studies on subjective well-being and successful aging ... appear to focus too narrowly on life satisfaction at the expense of other personally meaningful dimensions of life judgments'. That is, much qualitative work adopts an 'emic' approach – attempting to understand QOL from the perspective of research informants. These approaches ask questions flowing from such a recognition: rather than asking 'etic' (or analyst's) questions such as 'is the QOL of Italians higher than the QOL of Australians' (Verri *et al.*, 1999), these studies will ask questions like 'how do Italians understand "quality of life"?' This type of study is taking an 'emic' approach, offering the perspective of participants an equal footing with the theoretical, epistemological and methodological 'expertise' of the researcher. Wallcraft and Michaelson (2001) put this position well (at the risk of incurring Silverman's disapproval) when they describe research participants as 'experts by experience'. Put simply, most qualitative work in the traditions discussed here would seek to pass what Potter calls the 'dead psychologist test', that is examine social interaction – for example discussions of the quality of life – that would have occurred *anyway*, even if the psychologist who wished to study it was no longer with us.

Epistemology, conversation and discourse analysis

Ethnomethodologically-inspired qualitative work starts from Sacks' (1992) insight that, in coming to understand a culture, one may assume that cultures show *order at all points*. Secondly, *that descriptions of activities, persons and their qualities* may be 'correct' in infinite ways. Schegloff (in Sacks, 1992: xlvi) describes the Sacksian position clearly:

> Sacks points out that [sampling] depends on the sort of order one takes it that the social world exhibits. An alternative to the possibility that order manifests itself at an aggregate level and is statistical in character is what he terms the 'order at all points' view. This view understands order not to be present only at aggregate levels and therefore subject to an overall differential distribution, but to be present in detail on a case by case, environment by environment basis. A culture is not then to be found only by aggregating all of its venues; it is substantially present in each of its venues.

Much qualitative work in conversation analysis, discourse analysis and discursive psychology follows Sacks' lead more or less closely (and without necessarily citing Sacks) in assuming that, in the examination of *fragments* of a culture (for example, how people talk about the quality of their lives), that which operates *across a culture as a whole* will come clearly into view. As such, quantitative concerns about sample sizes, representative sampling and so on do not assume importance in this work. Secondly, Sacks shows us that when we talk about matters of human experience there are, in principle, multiple 'correct' descriptors. Hence while it may be 'important …to count and measure what is countable and measurable' much – though by no means all – qualitative work takes a *relativist* position towards the sort of 'exact' truth statements sought by quantitative methodologies (Edwards *et al.*, 1995; Edwards and Potter, 2001).

The third distinguishing feature of most qualitative work (with the notable exceptions of Content Analysis and much Grounded Theory (Glaser and Strauss, 1967) – see Willig, 2001; Richardson, 1996) is the insistence on the presentation of data for *the reader* to inspect (rather than just the end results in the form of p values and so on) to allow the reader to interrogate the adequacy of the analysis. The fourth and final core difference between quantitative and qualitative work is the criteria that are employed to gauge the quality of studies and the analyses they report. Unlike the lists of 14 criteria by which to assess psychometric measures we encountered earlier (Hagerty *et al.*, 2001), or publicly agreed standards for alpha values, inter-rater reliability coefficients and the like, the quality of qualitative work is judged against criteria of analytic rigour, fidelity to previous empirically-documented instances and aesthetic power (see Peräkylä, 1997). That is, unlike quantitative studies, the merit of qualitative work is judged in terms of the *persuasiveness of the argument* presented, rather than simply taking a suitably low probability value as making, and simultaneously closing, the case.

Interviews

Interviews (structured or semi-structured) with individual respondents, or in the form of group interviews (often known as 'focus groups' – see Puchta and Potter, 1999 and Puchta and Potter, forthcoming), are increasingly popular across the social sciences. This section considers the use that can be made of such methods and some of the difficulties with their use.

Alderson (2001) describes an exploratory study based on interviews with 40 adults who have congenital conditions for which prenatal tests are routinely conducted. In the published study, she reports detailed interview data from conversations with five adults with Down syndrome. Her study has been selected for inclusion here as an example of interview-based discourse analytic work for four reasons.

- Firstly, the study *directly addresses serious and important questions about the use of the QOL concept* – in this case the use of medical technologies to inform, literally, life and death decisions.

- Secondly, the study *questions everyday commonsense* – rather than respecifying it in academic terms. In this case, the study problematizes the view that prenatal testing is a 'good thing', and that the lives of people with Down syndrome are, inevitably, lives of lesser quality.
- Thirdly, the study problem is expressed with clarity, the implications of the research are placed in academic and applied contexts, and the *study design and methods of analysis are closely, explicitly and directly tied to the research questions* asked.
- Fourthly, the study explicitly recognizes the *limitations and difficulties* (both ethical and methodological) of the research approach adopted.

Alderson (2001) starts with the identification of the key research issue. That is, the taken-for-granted upshot of a positive amniocentesis result (for Down syndrome in this case) is the recommendation of selective abortion, on the assumption that affected foetuses will have a low quality of life. Alderson's study follows from the recognition that this *assumption* is exactly that, an *assumption*. The research question thus becomes, simply, 'how good is the evidence that Down syndrome inevitably leads to a low quality of life?' Alderson (2001: 627) states:

> Routine prenatal screening is based on the assumption that it is reasonable for prospective parents to choose to prevent a life with Down's Syndrome. This paper questions whether Down's Syndrome necessarily involves the costs, limitations and suffering which are assumed in the prenatal literature, and examines the lack of evidence about the value and quality of life with Down's Syndrome. Tensions between the aims of prenatal screening policies to support women's personal choices, prevent distress, and reduce the suffering and costs of disability, versus the inadvertent effects of screening which can undermine these aims, are considered.

The study is also exemplary in its clear specification of the procedural and ethical problems in conducting research in this area. Alderson (2001) notes that asking people questions about whether their parents had wanted them, or perhaps had been tempted to abort them, may be very distressing. She says (2001: 630), openly, that:

> I felt anxious about asking people, in effect: 'What are your views about the value and quality of your life? Do you feel your life is worth living? Did/do your parents want you and what might they have decided if prenatal tests had been available to them before you were born?' These sensitive questions were not asked directly, although several interviewees, including one with Down's syndrome, raised the later ones. Most of the 40 interviewees talked openly about screening, but those with Down's syndrome and spina bifida were most likely to express or imply distress about this topic, so that direct questions were more limited with them.

It is important, then, to recognize that despite the fact that 'official' questions on a structured interview schedule (or probes in a semi-structured protocol) do not *explicitly* ask 'did your parents want you?' interviewees are very likely to understand what they are, 'in effect', being asked. As we saw in Chapter 3, while some think that people with an intellectual disability are incapable of validly responding to interviews or questionnaires (Heal and Sigelman, 1990), Alderson's respondents, like Bob and Arthur, demonstrate to the contrary that they are well aware of the underlying agenda.

Alderson goes on to show how, by the use of semi-structured interviews – rather than, say, a fixed response questionnaire – the methodology of the study was directly driven by the aim of the research:

> [T]hrough enquiring about their everyday and past lives, and their hopes and concerns, we aimed to create a picture with each person of their positive and negative experiences, of the value and quality of their life to them, and of potential lives with their condition. (Alderson, 2001: 630–1)

This sort of study produces very different data to that derived from quantitative work. Rather than 'thin', quantified scores that represent, for example, a person's level of happiness with their sexual relationships with a single number, qualitative studies produce large quantities of transcribed interview material, at varying levels of orthographic sophistication. Thus while conversation analytic studies routinely use the Jeffersonian notation (Appendix 1) with details of pitch changes, pauses timed in tenths of seconds and phonetic orthography, many variants of discourse analysis (such as Alderson's study) employ a simple verbatim transcription. Alderson (2001: 631) describes her discourse analytic/thematic analysis approach to her data:

> I analysed transcripts by hand, and reread them for the overt themes, reported here in the order they were discussed during interviews, and for underlying themes: quality and value of life, costs, dependence, contributions to family and society, discrimination, replies which fitted mainly the medical or social model of disability.

As is evident, the discourse analytic approach here blends emic and etic concerns. Alderson attends to the views reported by her respondents in their terms, but at the same time is attentive to the way in which the things people say can *also* be understood in analysts' terms, here in terms of the extent to which they 'fit' academic theories, or models, of disability. Alderson's study offers material such as the extract reproduced below as her *primary data*. In this sort of work, then, the regular encountering of descriptions is considered sufficient (under the rubric of 'order at all points') to make limited, and non-statistical, claims about the generality of people's experience. The data fragment below, from a section of an interview dealing with recreational activities (here drama), with two informants with Down syndrome is preceded by a brief analytic observation. The extract illustrates clearly how what participants say at interview directly informs the analysis offered.

In their current play, *Mongol Boy*, a Victorian industrialist rejected his son who had Down's Syndrome and who joined a circus of freaks. Peter and Philip distinguished between the denigratory language in the play and their own views, raising a main theme of all 40 interviews: discrimination against disabled people.

Int: So do you like that kind of drama, that you're really involved in?
Peter: Oh yes, it's amazing.
Philip: It is very important, and when you learn to say the part you can. But it's not very nice to say this, and I'm not a very rude person, but I think that a learning disability part – I don't want to be rude –.
Int: You seem to me to be a very polite person.
Philip: I don't like to take the mickey of people because I know they've got rights, they're a human being like us you see, but they are 'freaks' very small people and it's wrong to take the mickey out of them … and make them upset because they've got rights as well.
Int: Yes, very important.
Philip: It is important.
Int: Yes, and do you think – with people with learning difficulties – that other people think enough about your rights?
Philip: Some people don't understand. They want us to keep quiet. Because they think, you've got a learning disability – like when I came out [of the house], somebody pushed me, just out here, pushed me and didn't apologise and I didn't like that at all.
Int: Did they push you by accident or on purpose?
Philip: I think they did it on purpose. They're very strange people.
Peter: And that happened at [names another place] –.
Philip: Yes, I know Peter, and it happened here too, a man and a woman tried to push me.
Int: And what did you do?
Philip: Well, the point is this, we are not allowed to talk to strange people.

(Alderson, 2001: 632)

On the basis of five such interviews, during which her informants discussed topics as diverse as discrimination, relationships, education, employment, leisure interests, hopes and their views on prenatal screening, Alderson draws telling conclusions, both about people with Down syndrome and also about the quality of the lives which these people reported. She states (Alderson, 2001: 627) that:

> they [the data] show how some people with Down's Syndrome live creative, rewarding and fairly independent lives, and are not inevitably non-contributing dependents. Like the other 35 interviewees, they illustrate the importance of social supports, and their problems with excluding attitudes and barriers. Much more social research with people who have congenital conditions is required, if prenatal screening policies and counselling are to be evidence based.

Alderson's study thus illustrates how qualitative work can shed important light upon the use of practices that rely on 'taken-for-granted' beliefs about the QOL of people with congenital disorders. Qualitative methods of study can also be brought to bear on quantitative approaches to measuring quality of life. As we have seen, increasing use is made of questionnaire-driven interview schedules in an effort to find out what people feel about the quality of their lives 'in their own words'. However, there are reasons for being cautious about interpreting the results of quantitative assessment instruments – even if they meet public criteria for *psychometric* validity and reliability. In the quantitative tradition it is crucial (so crucial, indeed, that it is usually simply assumed to be the case) that scores on such instruments represent records of *authentic answers* to *clear questions*. However, both the traditional forms of publication of quantitative work (which usually offer – at best – aggregate statistical data) and inattention to the interactional dynamics at work in interviews may disguise inauthenticity and unclarity. Work that illustrates these problems, using the methods of conversation analysis, is discussed below.

Conversation analysis

Assessing somebody's QOL using a standardized questionnaire requires that both interviewer and interviewee manage an interaction in order to record the respondent's views. This will necessarily be done in a series of turns at talk, where the precise placement of an utterance crucially affects its meaning. Information on the sequential positioning of utterances – and the subtleties of interaction – is, however, lost when talk is analysed in terms of numerical scores, by quasi-qualitative methods such as content analysis (see, for example, Atkinson, 1988), or when it is subjected to a pre-given categorization scheme (as was, influentially, done to the talk of people with intellectual disabilities by Sigelman et al., 1981). The principled avoidance of the pre-categorization of talk is a foundational principle of conversation analysis (CA). Conversation analysis is a theoretically-driven approach to social interaction, with a firm base in sociology and pragmatics (Atkinson and Heritage, 1984; Boden and Zimmerman 1991; Sacks, 1992; Silverman, 1998) and a growing influence in psychology (Edwards, 1995; Edwards and Potter, 2001). The use of CA illuminates the fine-grained interplay between speakers in interaction that is lost in grounded theory, content analysis and 'critical realist' discourse analysis. CA, then, offers the most sensitive possible tool to gain access to what is going on in QOL assessment interviews.

In other words, CA offers a method of analysis which pays attention not only to the content of what is said in QOL interviews, but also to the exact delivery of what is said, which has crucial effects on meaning. The techniques of CA have accumulated into a comprehensive vocabulary applicable to a wide range of social phenomena, including interaction in institutional settings (see, for example, Drew and Heritage, 1992; Hester and Francis, 2001; ten Have, 2001).

The 'reliability' and 'validity' of QOL assessment

Antaki and Rapley (1996a) used conversation analysis to examine the validity and reliability of standardized QOL measurement. They argued that, even though they may demonstrate acceptable validity and reliability in *psychometric* terms, QOL questionnaires may actually *distort* interviewees' 'own words' by severely underestimating the degree to which questions and answers are determined by the dynamics of QOL interviews. As such, their study examines the working out in practice of the theoretical concerns expressed by Megone (1990), Hatton (1998) and Mulkay *et al.* (1987) discussed in Chapter 3. That is, by using CA, the study actually *showed* in practice the theoretical concerns raised by these writers about the 'slanting' or 'distortion' that the 'theoretical refinement' of the notion of QOL into a psychometric schedule may cause.

Typical administration of the Schalock and Keith (1996) QOL Questionnaire involved two sorts of distortions. Firstly, there were distortions of the *questions* brought about by the need to paraphrase complex items, and the inevitable use of pre-questions and response listing. Secondly, and, perhaps more disturbingly, Antaki and Rapley (1996a) documented systematic distortions of *answers* brought about by interviewers' pursuit of answers and non-take-up of interviewees' matters. As space is limited, only a brief overview of their study is possible here; discussion focuses on the distortions caused by the question/answer format of the questionnaire and the transformations of respondents' answers brought about by interviewers' pursuing what appears to be their own QOL agenda rather than that of their interviewees.

Transformations of questions

The administration of face-to-face questionnaires very often requires, in practice, that items be paraphrased in order for respondents to grasp their meaning. Houtkoop-Steenstra's extensive work (2000) shows that this feature of interview interaction applies broadly, regardless of the cognitive skills of interviewees and *regardless* of the instructions to interviewers printed on formal measures that they use the *exact* wording of standardized questions. The QOL.Q manual is, then, unusual in that it specifically states that it is 'okay to paraphrase an item to improve understanding' (Schalock and Keith, 1996: 13). This causes severe problems – and not only in the case of items with obviously difficult words or expressions (for example Q. 19 asks about 'the benefits you receive at the workplace' and Q. 28 asks 'Do you have a guardian or conservator'). Serious difficulties regularly arise with apparently simple questions such as Question 9 – 'How successful do you think you are, compared to others?' Extract 1 shows a typical administration of this item.

Extract 1: Code: CA/MR/WM

```
 1   Int.    ↑how successful (.) d'you think you are (.) compared to
 2           other ↓people (.) ↑yeh? (..)
 3   Will    ↑m
 4   Int.    ↑more successful than average (.) a↑bout as successful
 5           as average (.) or ↓less successful (..)
 6   Will    °(syll)° (..)
 7   Int.    gi' me one of them
 8   Will    ↑yeh
 9   Int.    ↑which ↓one (...) >↑d'you think you do< ↑better at things
10           than the    ┌(public) (syll syll)
11   Will                └↑better (..) better ↓now
12   Int.    ↑yeh? (.)
13   Will    yes
```

In Extract 1 and the extracts that follow, 'Int.' is the psychologist conducting the QOL assessment. In Extract 1, Will is the respondent whose quality of life is being assessed. Will's first utterances where an answer might be expected are noncommittal (at line 3) and inaudible (line 6). When the interviewer asks explicitly for a choice among the alternatives (at line 7) Will offers an illegitimate reply – 'yeh': he does not specify which of the three alternatives he wishes to endorse. The interviewer paraphrases the original question 'how successful do you think you are, compared to others?' which now becomes 'd'you think you do better at things than the public?' Whether or not the candidate answer offered at line 11 – 'I do better (than the public) now' – is a legitimate response is arguable. In any case, the interviewer accepts it, and an official score (3) is recorded.

Extract 2 again shows the manner in which official QOL scores are generated by *changing the official question*. Thus the item 'do you feel that your job or other daily activities is worthwhile and relevant to you or other people?' becomes, by line 9, 'd'you think what you do is good?'

Extract 2: Code MT/I/JW

```
 1   Int.     d'you feel your job or other (.) daily activities-
 2   Anne     yes=
 3   Int.     =worth whi↑ well ↑wait till I finish (.) yeah? d'you think it's
 4            ↑worth↓while an'↑ and ↓relevant to you or (.)   ⌈ other
 5            people
 6   Anne                                                    ⌊yeah (.)
 7            ·other people
 8            (3.00)
 9   Int.     d'you think what you do is (..) good Anne? (.) d'you think
10            it's worth ↑do↓ing
11            (...)
12   Anne     .hh yes
13   Int.     (..) definitely?
14   Anne     yes
15   Int.     yeah? (..) ok (..)
```

The problem for us here, of course, is that the indexical 'what you do' and 'it' of the official QOL item are now undefined. There is no secure basis for supposing it is the 'job or other daily activities' of the official item that Anne's response refers to, and the twin official criteria of relevance to 'yourself or others' have disappeared. However, again, in line 15, we hear the interviewer accepting Anne's answer – that 'what she does' is 'good' and recording an official QOL score of 3. QOL.Q items always have three alternative answers. Item 1, for example, asks:

Overall, would you say that life: Brings out the best in you? (Score = 3) Treats you like everybody else? (Score = 2) Doesn't give you a chance? (Score = 1).

The serial listing of the alternatives provides for interviewees to offer candidate answers *before* the full set of alternatives has been presented, and this causes more trouble. The list structure of the interviewer's turn requires that the interviewee delays their answer, but the fact that each alternative is *in itself* a well-formed question prompts an immediate answer. Extract 3 shows how the *questionnaire format* produces three quite different 'answers' to a question:

Extract 3: Code: CA/KK/TH

```
 1    Int.     °right° (..) .hh d'you ever feel ↑lonely John?
 2    John     yeah (.) ↑very ↓lonely
 3    Int.     do you?
 4    John     hmm
 5    Int.     d'you feel lonely every ↓day?
 6    John     yeah
 7    Int.     (..) or (..) once a week?
 8    John     once a week
 9    Int.     (...)°right° (..) 'kay? (..) or ↑once a ↓month
10    John     ↑once a ↓month
11    Int.     (..)°↑once a ↓month°
12    (3 secs)
```

John, it appears, feels lonely every day (QOL score = 1), once a week (QOL score = 2) and once a month (QOL score = 3). It appears, by virtue of the interviewer's recycle of 'once a month' and the long silence following in lines 11–12, that he accepts this last utterance as John's official answer and gives him the highest possible QOL score.

What counts as the interviewee's answer?

We can see that the 'official' QOL questions are prone to serious distortion. Interactional dynamics also caused distortions in what counts as an 'official' answer to the questions asked. Antaki and Rapley (1996a) identified two sources of significant trouble in this respect: (1) the interviewer's pursuit of an *alternative* to apparently acceptable candidate answers; and (2) the ignoring of respondents' material, even though it often appeared designed to be informative about the respondent's quality of life.

Pursuing the 'right' answer

Antaki and Rapley (1996a) identified three reasons for interviewers to pursue a 'right' answer: the three-part listing structure of the scale seen above; the use by respondents of 'non-official' vocabulary; and the interviewer's own perceptions of what the respondent 'really' felt or believed. Extract 4 shows again how the three-part list structure of QOL questions *prompts changes* in what interviewees say about their quality of life. A legitimate candidate answer, at what the interviewer treats as the wrong place, has significant results:

Extract 4: Code MT/I/JW

```
 1    Int.     D'you ↑feel out of ↓place (..) >out an' about in<
 2             ↓social situ↓ations?
```

```
 3   Anne    ⌐No
 4   Int.    ⌊Anne? (.) Never?
 5   Anne    No
 6   Int.    Sometimes?
 7   Anne    ↓°No°
 8   Int.    Or usually?
 9   Anne    ↑Some↓times I ↑do
10   Int.    Yeah? (..) OK, we'll ↑put a two down for that one then
11           (sniff)
```

Anne's reply 'No' at line 3 seems unambiguous. The need for the interviewer to offer all three official alternatives (which occur at lines 4, 6 and 8) evidently implies to Anne that her original answer (repeated in lines 5 and 7) requires change or correction. By line 9, Anne has got the point: she says 'sometimes I do'. While this is a *clear change* from her emphatic 'no' in lines 3, 5 and 7 it is *this* response that is recorded as her official QOL score.

Interviewer's expectations
Interviewer's expectations were also identified by Antaki and Rapley (1996a) as contributing to distortions of answers. It seems that interviewer's expectations of what was actually the right answer – what the respondent *really* thought – could interfere with QOL assessment. A good example of this is seen in Extract 5.

Extract 5: Code HB/I/TT

```
 1   Int.    okay (.) overall would you say ↑that (.) ↓life brings ↑out (.)
 2           the ↓best in you
 3   Bob     ↑yes
 4   Int.    treats you like everybody ↓else=
 5   Bob     ↑yes:
 6   Int.    or doesn't give you a chance
 7   Bob     eh:?
 8           (1 sec)
 9   Int.    what >do you think ↓that< (.) life (.) brings out the best in
10           ↓you (..)   ⌐or (syll syll)
11   Bob                ⌊yeah the ↑best yeah yeah
12   Int.    right (..) so that's ↓your (.) your answer ↑yeah ⌐life>br< life
13   Bob                                                   ⌊↓yes yes
14   Int.    brings out the best in you does it?
15   Bob     (what's to do) with yer ↑lip:
16   Int.    ↓yeah I: I ↑cut it (.) shaving
17   Bob     (syll syll syll syll syll)
18   Int.    okay (.) so of those ↑three (.) you think ↓life brings out the
19           best it doesn't (.) treat ↓you like everyone ↓else an ↑it (.) it
```

```
20              ↓doesn't (.) not give you a chance
21    Bob       (hhh)=
22    Int.      yeah?
23              (2 sec)
24    Bob       °°(doesn't) give me a ↑chance°° .h          ⌈hh ((sniff))
25    Int.                                                  ⌊okay (1sec)
26              al↑right (..)
```

Bob gives a well designed answer in line 11: the answer shows an agreement token ('yeah'), a legitimate, 'official', response alternative delivered with an appropriate intonation contour ('the best') and two further agreement tokens in confirmation. Bob has previously (in lines 3 and 5) indicated that he has understood the options on offer, and in line 7 successfully sought a recycle of the third option from the interviewer. Despite this, the interviewer does not accept his selection of the official answer 'life brings out the best in me' as his QOL judgment. At lines 25–6 Bob's official QOL score is not recorded as the '3' he initially selected, but rather as a '1'.

Antaki and Rapley (1996a) concluded that the very serious interactional difficulties observed in their study (difficulties which were confirmed in a series of subsequent analyses) prevented easy reduction of these QOL assessment interviews to a quantitative score. Such a conclusion, they argued, means that these observations on the administration of a typical QOL questionnaire raise tricky questions about the whole enterprise of trying to find out people how feel about the quality of their lives. They suggested that:

> it is important to be clear that although there is one particular instrument of contemporary interest under examination … the argument generalises to *any* attempt to evaluate *any* psychological state of mind that requires the respondent to fit deeply-held beliefs or feelings (life satisfaction judgements, interpersonal evaluations or personal motivations) into pre-organised question and answer categories. Such avowals of belief and feeling are, we have seen, not independent of the particular question, the sequential run of questions and previous answers, and interpersonal and institutional context in which those questions are asked. (Antaki and Rapley, 1996a; my emphasis)

A Synthesis?

A major concern of this chapter has been to stress the necessity of explicit links between the way QOL is theorized and the methods chosen to study the concept. In the quantitative tradition this means that QOL measures must be based on an adequately theorized, a priori specification (or operational definition), of the model of QOL adopted, demonstrate psychometric reliability and validity, and show that they are sensitive to the circumstances in which people find themselves. In the qualitative tradition, the issues are more centrally concerned with clarity about the theoretical underpinnings of the analytic methods used and the purpose of proposed studies (not that this isn't also true for quantitative work). In either tradition the adoption of research designs and methods should be critically informed by a deep understanding of the research tradition within which the work is conducted. Where the traditions diverge perhaps most clearly is in their stance towards emic and etic perspectives in research – although, as we have seen in the second half of this chapter, it is entirely feasible to conduct studies which attend to both perspectives. It is of course also the case that it is possible – again as we have seen above – to employ qualitative methodologies to ask searching questions about the adequacy of quantitative work.

Notes

1. A discourse can be understood as an 'organized' way of speaking of (some aspect of) experience. Potter and Wetherell (1987) describe discourses as 'interpretative repertoires': constellations of grammatically and semantically coherent terms which collectively provide particular interpretations or descriptions of the 'way the world is'. A clear and problematic example is the use of medical discourse (with its talk of 'signs', 'symptoms' and 'illness') to describe psychological distress. From a Foucauldian perspective, a 'discourse' also includes those *practices* which, together with texts, establish, for example, subject positions. From a Foucauldian perspective, the example of medical discourse would also include analysis of the manner in which such practices as the establishment of 'mental health clinics' and 'psychiatric hospitals' staffed by people described as 'doctors' and 'psychiatric nurses', the prescription and consumption of 'antidepressants' and the appearance of 'problem pages' in magazines work to constitute persons as 'patients'.

2. The CHQ-PF-50 consists of 50 items assessing 14 aspects of functioning, including physical functioning, mental health, school and social limitations arising from their illness, family functioning and the impact of their physical and psycho-social health on their parents. Two summary scales, the Physical Summary Scale and the Psychosocial Summary Scale, are also scored. Psychometric data on the validity and reliability of this measure is available in Landgraf *et al.* (1996).

3. The Functional Status II(R) Questionnaire (FSQ) (Stein and Jessop, 1990, 1991) uses 14 items which rate the interference a child's illness causes in daily functioning, covering areas such as sleeping, eating, communication, energy and mood. Higher scores indicate better functional health status.

4. The Impact-on-Family Scale (Stein and Riessman, 1980) is a 24-item scale rating the impact of child illness on family functioning in four areas (changes in economic status of a family; quality of interaction with persons outside the immediate household; interactions between family members; subjective

distress for the child's caretaker). Validity and reliability is discussed by Stein and Riessman (1980).

Study Questions

- What are the losses and gains involved in representing the quality of a person's life as a numerical score?
- Who knows best about a person's quality of life?
- My QOL today is … ?
- How can qualitative studies of QOL assist in the development of quantitative approaches?

Suggestions for Further Reading

Berger-Schmitt, R. and Noll, H.-H. (2000). *Conceptual Framework and Structure of a European System of Social Indicators*, EuReporting Working Paper No. 9. Mannheim: Centre for Survey Research and Methodology. Available from: <http://www.gesis.org/en/social_monitoring/social_indicators/EU_Reporting/concept.htm>.

Edwards, D., Ashmore, M. and Potter, J. (1995) Death and furniture: the rhetoric, politics and theology of bottom-line arguments against relativism, *History of the Human Sciences*, 8, 2: 25–49.

McHoul, A. and Rapley, M. (eds) (2002) *How to Analyse Talk in Institutional Settings: A Casebook of Methods*. London and New York: Continuum International.

Puchta, C. and Potter, J. (forthcoming) *Focus Group Practice: Moderating Interaction in Market Research Focus Groups*. London: Sage.

Richardson, J. T. E. (1996) *Handbook of Qualitative Research Methods for Psychology and the Social Sciences*. Leicester: BPS Books.

Silverman, D. (1998) *Harvey Sacks: Social Science and Conversation Analysis*. Cambridge: Polity Press.

Willig, C. (2001) *Introducing Qualitative Research in Psychology: Adventures in Theory and Method*. Buckingham: Open University Press.

Yates, S., Taylor, S. and Wetherell, M. (2001) *Discourse as Data: A Guide for Analysis*. London: Sage.

PART TWO – PRACTICE

In Part 1, I identified some of the key conceptual, procedural and ethical concerns in contemporary QOL research. These chapters sought to place QOL research into its historical and cultural context, and to offer an account of both the prevailing consensus views and of the critical voices in the field. While we saw some brief examples of current research in these chapters, in Part 2 the focus is on the direct practical application of the ideas we have encountered so far. It is, of course, difficult to separate out theory and practice, or method, and this differentiation is – as has been seen – hard to sustain in practice. However, what the following chapters do is to *show* at greater length what QOL research actually looks like. The breadth of the field, and the space available, means that these chapters will not discuss the details of specific research procedures (statistical techniques like factor analysis, multidimensional scaling or logistic regression) or offer a detailed analysis and description of the variety of possible approaches to research (for example, questionnaire surveys, ethnographic work or action research). Where these matters arise methods texts that offer detailed guidance on the specific issues are identified. Rather the intention here is to offer an introductory overview, a flavour of some of the variety of research approaches in the field, and to identify important concerns that need to be addressed in the design and conduct of a range of QOL research projects.

Chapter 5 offers a worked example of an archaeological approach, based on the work of Michel Foucault, to develop an understanding of quality of life as a cultural object. Chapter 6 offers an overview of the use of the notion of quality of life to develop numerical indicators of life quality (QALYs and DALYs) in medicine, health economics and epidemiology. Chapter 7 considers the use of quality of life as an organizing construct in service evaluation research looking at the quality of services for people with mental health problems and intellectual disabilities. In Chapter 8, a worked example of the critical analysis of the literature in contemporary psychology is presented. Chapter 9, the final chapter, attempts to draw together the major themes of the book, and offers some tentative conclusions about where we go from here.

Throughout Part 2, it is *essential* to remember that while one particular population group ('schizophrenics', for example) may be the stated focus of the study under discussion, *all* of the work discussed here has been selected in order to illustrate *generally applicable* issues and problems. Throughout Part 2, key points about the conduct of quality of life research apply regardless of people's measured IQ or their possession (or otherwise) of a medical or psychiatric diagnosis.

CHAPTER 5

Researching QOL as Cultural Object

Chapters 1–4 outlined some of the key philosophical questions in QOL research, and some of the theoretical and methodological tensions between quantitative and qualitative research approaches. This chapter takes up these issues and offers a 'worked example' of the use of a qualitative approach to the study of QOL as a social phenomenon, at the level of the cultural production of 'quality of life' as both a meaningful device in lay discourse, and also as a legitimate object of social scientific study.

The concepts of 'quality', 'quality of life' and their variants are closely related in public discourse. They are discursive objects which have become, since the early 1980s, routinely deployed in all forms of public talk – from the promises of the advertisers of consumer products (*Build with Dale Alcock for quality lifestyles!!* being an entirely unremarkable property developer's advertisement in my local paper recently) to being the stated policy objectives of governments across the world (for example, enhancing 'quality of life' being a key objective of the British government's *Health of the Nation* White Paper and also that of the Health Department of Victoria, Australia).

The chapter introduces the key epistemological and methodological positions of Foucauldian thinkers (Rose, 1999; Kendall and Wickham, 1999), the work of discursive psychologists (Edwards and Potter, 1992; Potter, 1996) and a range of other critical theorists in what may be broadly be described as the postmodern, or social constructionist, tradition (Fairclough, 2001). The analytic tools these approaches provide are outlined. It is beyond the scope of this book to address these issues in detail, so here a qualitative analysis of the social production of 'QOL' as the necessary outcome of government policy is described to illustrate the methods and the relevance of the case study methodology to the conceptual issues raised in Part 1 (for example, the historical contingency of social scientific interest in QOL) is detailed. Kendall and Wickham (1999) provide a detailed introduction to the use of Foucault's methods of *archaeological* and *genealogical* inquiry. McHoul and Rapley (2002) offer an introductory level text describing, and showing through worked examples, the use of applied conversation analysis, discursive psychology and critical discourse analysis.

Quality of Life in Popular Culture – the Contribution of Foucauldian Thought

Rose (1992) offers what, on the surface, appears to be an insubstantial account of a small ad he began to notice appearing in the *The Guardian*, a British 'quality' daily newspaper, in 1989. Rose (1992: 141, my emphasis) writes that:

> it was for a private organization called 'Self-Helpline' and offered a range of telephone numbers for people to ring for answers to some apparently troubling questions. There were 'Emotional problems', from 'Dealing with infidelity' to 'Overcoming shyness'. There were 'Parenthood problems', from 'My child won't sleep' to 'I feel like hitting my baby'. There were 'Work problems', such as 'Am I in the right job' or 'Becoming a supervisor'. And there were 'Sexual problems' from 'Impotence' to 'Better orgasms'. For the cost of a telephone call, callers could obtain 'self-help step by step answers to dealing with your problems and improving the *quality of your life*'.

Rose notes that it may be thought that the ad is trivial, and its preoccupations far removed from something as 'weighty' as 'enterprise culture' (Rose, 1992: 141), in much the same way that the claims of Australian house builders to be able to 'improve the quality of your lifestyle' are apparently far removed from the concerns about quality of life discussed in earlier chapters. However, what Rose demonstrates is that such advertisements resonate with much broader and deeper presuppositions concerning what it means to be human *at all* in contemporary Western societies. That is to say the 'enterprise culture' – a phenomenon precisely coterminous with what Schalock (1994: 266) describes as the 'quality revolution' – and the 'forms of political reason' that promote it 'accord a vital *political* value to a certain image of the self.' Such a value, as Rose notes, is far from being any longer, if it ever truly was, a pet project of the political right, but rather has become the dominant political mentality of the 'West' and is increasingly so in what were once 'Eastern bloc' countries. It is, in the terms of an earlier chapter, a peculiarly 'American' – as opposed to 'Scandinavian' – view of self and the relation between self and society.

Rose argues that the extraordinarily potent view of the individual as the 'enterprising self', which now dominates 'Western' political mentality, furnishes the conditions of possibility for Self-Helpline, Dale Alcock and a raft of other 'experts of subjectivity' to proffer their services in the improvement of the citizen's quality of life. Such a view of the self, suggests Rose (1992: 141–2):

> resonates with basic presuppositions concerning the contemporary self

that are widely distributed in our present, presuppositions that are embodied in the very language that we use to make persons thinkable, and in our ideal conceptions of what people should be ... The self is to be a subjective being, it is to aspire to autonomy, it is to strive for personal fulfilment in its earthly life, it is to interpret its reality and destiny as matters of individual responsibility, it is to find meaning in existence by shaping its life through acts of choice ... The guidance of selves is no longer dependent upon the authority of religion or traditional morality; it has been allocated to 'experts of subjectivity' who transfigure existential questions about the purpose of life and the meaning of suffering into technical questions about the most effective ways of managing malfunction and improving 'quality of life'.

The critical point that Foucauldian scholarship then makes is that these are *ways* of *thinking* about selves, they are ways of *judging* those selves and, importantly, they prescribe ways of *acting* upon those selves – but that they could always have been (indeed historically have been) – otherwise. As such, while Cummins *et al.*'s (in press) 'homeostatic model of subjective well-being' discussed in Chapters 2 and 8 may appear on the surface to be nothing but the dispassionate description of empirical particulars forced upon us by the ineluctable progress of science, a Foucauldian position notes that this is *but one way* of thinking selves, and, moreover, one which is dependent not upon 'objective science' in its own presuppositions, but rather upon the *prior* acceptance of a particular cultural, political under-standing of the nature of personhood and the correct ways of investigating such a condition (see also Feyerabend, 1974).

That is to say the model, as but one example, *takes for granted* that the proper object of its enquiry and explanation is the *individual* self, which is a subjective being, aspiring to autonomy, striving for personal fulfilment (a promotion at work, or a satisfying meal perhaps proffering such an outcome), interpreting reality in terms of individual responsibility and finding meaning in existence (and, it must be said, satisfaction with the quality of its earthly life) by shaping its life through acts of choice.

Further, such scholarship recognizes that these *new* ways of thinking selves are not only historically, but also culturally, contingent. That is, whereas in the West since the Enlightenment the development of advanced liberal democracies has seen the transformation of the populace from 'subjects with duties and obligations' to 'individuals with rights and freedoms' (Rose, 1992: 142) it is also the case that contemporary thinkings of the self, or notions of personhood, vary enormously across cultures. As we will see in the 'worked example' below, it is only very recently indeed that such a way of thinking selves has been extended to some marginal groups – such as people with an intellectual disability – even in modern Western societies. It is also the case that such a way of thinking furnishes the criteria by which selves are currently judged to be competent members of a shared social and moral order: the 'mad' for example, are at root identifiable as such by their failure to enact self-hood in these terms (see Coulter, 1979).

The use of Foucauldian methods (though see Kendall and Wickham's caution about such a term) is, then, an exercise in the careful description of the 'order of things' (Foucault, 1970) which is aware that causal explanations must be partial (in both senses of the term) and that, rather than engaging in contestable *causal* accounts, it is necessary to recognize that the production of the present – quite as much as any historical event – is dependent upon a host of *contingencies*. That is, the present is as historically adventitious (Sacks, 1992) as the past. The course of events, or of any particular event (the emergence of quality of life as an organizing notion in the social sciences), is then seen not as the necessary outcome of a chain of causes (a Marxist view), but rather as one possible result of a complex set of relations between a range of other events. In other words, as Gavin Kendall and Gary Wickham (1999: 4) say, the

> use of history is not a turn to teleology, that is it does not involve assumptions of progress (or regress). This is why we say it involves histories that never stop: they cannot be said to stop because they cannot be said to be going anywhere ... Foucauldian histories are histories of the present not because understanding an ideal or complete present is the spur to investigation ... Foucauldians are not seeking to find out how the present has emerged from the past. Rather the point is to use history as a way of diagnosing the present.

Kendell and Wickham would, therefore, probably throw up (their hands in horror) at the shades of Whig historicism in the account of the emergence and development of the idea of 'quality of life' presented in Chapter 1.

Drawing upon the work of Foucault and Rose, the remainder of this chapter offers a worked example, to show how QOL – as a cultural object – may be researched, and to demonstrate how such an analysis offers us a view of the conditions of possibility of the present. The example considers, in detail, the case of the public pronouncements of government and professionals about social policy for people with intellectual disabilities in the United Kingdom between the late 1960s and the early 1990s. However, the specificity of the case materials is of little consequence: what matters here is the method of analysis. As such, even if one knows little of the detail of the subject matter, what is important is to *see* how (any) official texts can be used to develop an understanding of the practical uses of ideas like quality of life in forming both persons and social practices towards them.

As elsewhere in the social sciences the notion of 'quality of life' has recently become a key device in the intellectual disability research community. Historical study of the rhetoric of government and academia in the United Kingdom suggests that the idea of QOL has come to be intimately bound up with broader discourses of managerialism and corporatism in contemporary Western societies. That is, rather than being the ideologically pure and scientifically untroubled notion the research community, implicitly, claims it to be, QOL discourse can be understood as *mutually constructed* by government and 'psy-complex' practices.

As we saw earlier, notions of 'quality' and 'customer satisfaction' have come, since the mid-1980s, to occupy a central position in the discourse of commercial, professional and public life. A couple of clear examples of the changes in language occurring during this period are the transformation, by what was then British Rail, of people who were once 'passengers' into 'customers' and the similar transformation, in universities, of both those who give and those who attend lectures. Universities now tend to speak of themselves as having 'consumers' of 'educational services' rather than 'students' and, with appropriate symmetry, lecturers are now often construed not as scholars, but as 'content providers'.

'Ideas' such as quality of life are, then, much more than useful professional shorthand (Antaki, 1994; Potter, 1996). Such ideas do not act, neutrally, to describe established realities, but rather actively shape the social world (Potter and Wetherell, 1987; Potter, 1996), and in consequence, the place of people (with or without intellectual disabilities) within it. Antaki suggests that the function of such discursive objects, in talk, be it ministerial rhetoric, service providers' 'mission statements' or planners' 'strategic visions' is to 'do some work on the setting up or knocking down of social realities' (Antaki, 1994: 120). This suggests that an understanding of the rhetorical use of such notions as QOL by government and service providers is of considerable importance. The inspection of the 'talk' of government, in the shape of ministerial speeches or policy documents, the pronouncements of the academic or of the applied research community – the 'psy-complex' in Rose's (1986) analysis – may show the nature of the social realities to which their authors are committed, and which they wish to be accepted as 'true' in society as a whole.

The Psy-complex and the Social Regulation of (Dis)order

Greig (1993: 5) noted the widespread acceptance of what he termed the 'language' of normalization[1] by UK health authorities and direct service providers over the course of the 1980s. This acceptance may be construed as a function of the ready subsumability of its consumerist themes within another – corporatist – discourse, specifically that of a government committed to 'consumer choice'. For example, the Personal Social Services Research Unit (1987: 4) noted that :

various labels for describing aspects of consumerism in Care in the Community can be used. Involvement, participation, self-determination, choice, opportunities, power and control are all components of user involvement.

The 'labels' for 'consumerism' identified here closely approximate to versions of normalization (Wolfensberger, 1972) which describe a set of desirable service 'accomplishments'. However, by simply replacing the term 'consumerism' with 'normalization', the PSSRU's analysis of factors influencing government social policy may be translated into a typical statement of the aims and objectives – or in currently popular managerialist rhetoric the 'mission statement' or 'vision' – of all community-based (and probably many institutional) service providers across the human services. It thus seems clear that other discursive forces, in addition to normalization, may be implicated in the development of both community care and of the notion of 'quality of life' as a 'master construct'. The widespread deployment of the corporatist discursive themes of 'quality' and 'consumerism' has been precisely contemporaneous with the wholesale adoption of the 'language of normalization' (Greig, 1993) in human services.

Sociological and archaeological (Foucault, 1978) work on the social management of 'mental disorder' and the development of what Rose (1999) termed the psy-complex – psychiatry, clinical psychology, social work, mental health nursing – has relevance here. Rose's (1986, 1999) analyses of the psy-complex, or 'all those disciplines concerned with troubles and disorders of conduct, emotion and thought and the conditions for mental health' (1986: 284), with their echoes of the 'military-industrial complex', make explicit the reciprocal, indeed symbiotic, relationship between government and the regulators and researchers of mental order and disorder. Following Foucault, Rose's analyses point to the increasing 'psychologization' of society at large, and the contingent development of a broad societal focus upon individual subjectivity as the locus of well-being, (mental) health and quality of life.

Miller (1986) argues that the development of the psy-complex has greatly broadened the range of available mechanisms and locations, or sites, for the social regulation of disorder. Part of this process has been achieved by the placing of responsibility for order upon the self: as we saw in the introduction to this chapter, even 'quality' daily newspapers are now sites for the advertisements of 'experts of subjectivity' touting for business. A consequence of this, in terms of the regulatory machinery of 'liberal' societies, is that 'as far as possible individuals remain a part of society [and] become responsible for maximising their potential contribution to society' (Miller, 1986: 32) by, if possible, 'helping them selves' (see Miller and McHoul (1998) for an extended analysis of these developments). In the present context, this responsibility has also come to be construed, very recently, as also applying to persons with intellectual disabilities, but with an additional gloss that allows for assistance with the regulation of order by the self, by the provision in Western societies of intellectual disability services in the community. Such services, provided by the psy-complex on behalf of government, have – and this is, arguably, no coincidence – in the last thirty years increasingly come to stress the importance of the development of social and behavioural competence on the part of 'clients' as a key service goal (Evans *et al.*, 1987; Emerson and Hatton, 1994). Miller's (1986) conceptualization of both the development and the current nature of Western liberal societies, the relation of the individual to the state in such societies, and the role of members of the psy-complex within them, illuminates clearly the progression in the declared, rhetorical, objectives of government vis-à-vis people with intellectual disabilities. This analysis sheds light upon the development of the indices selected as appropriate outcome measures of service practice, by academic psychologists or other members of the psy-complex, warranted by government to evaluate the efficacy of these systems.

As a topic for the attention of the psy-complex the 'lifestyle', or quality of the life, of people with intellectual disabilities is very recent. While Schalock (1996) has suggested that QOL has always been a concern of the psy-complex, it is only since the 1980s that the style of life that intellectually disabled people may be thought as having, has become explicitly constructed in rhetoric as an object of interest (Antaki and Rapley, 1996a). This rhetoric reflects dramatic changes in prevailing social constructions of persons with intellectual disabilities. The development of political rhetoric and the publicly avowed construction of intellectual disability which has advanced with it have legitimated a new social construction of intellectual disability and, consequently, of the role of human services. It can be argued that it is this new social construction of intellectual disability, mutually constructed by government and the psy-complex, which has facilitated and legitimated not only a new set of public policies concerning people with intellectual disabilities – 'community care' – but which, in keeping with the 'sponsoring' corporatist/managerialist discourse, has also put in place the conditions of possibility for the emergence of talk about the quality of life of people with intellectual disabilities to develop into an organizing construct in human service/psy-complex practice.

Thus, in the light of discursive psychology's observations on the 'work' of discourse, in particular of rhetoric (see Antaki, 1994; Billig, 1991; Edwards and Potter, 2001; Potter and Wetherell, 1987), and the analyses offered by Miller and Rose of the role of the psy-complex/government partnership in the regulation of order, an analysis of the rhetoric constructing intellectual disability and QOL is warranted. The rhetoric of government defines the nature of the 'social realities' that academia and the psy-complex are empowered to regulate, and acts as legitimation of action on the part of those authorized to dispose of resources on its part. Thus inspection of the rhetoric of government and its agents, and the discourses they deploy, may then demonstrate the social construction of, among other things, social identities such as 'persons with an intellectual disability' and the rights, obligations and expectations of the 'lifestyle' or 'quality of life' to be associated with such identities.

Lifestyles and Intellectual Disability in 'Community Care' Policy: The Uses of QOL

The 'standard history' of the development of community care policy (which, in brief, appeals to developments in conscience and science as warrants for 'progress') can be contrasted with an analysis of the rhetoric of the executive and of the psy-complex. The aim of the analysis is to examine the nature of the 'social realities' (Antaki, 1994) – and the policy positions they buttress or necessitate – constructed by the rhetoric of official texts, and to argue that not only is community care comprehensible in terms of the coherence of the rhetorical and political commitments of the dominant political mentality of the 'enterprising self', but also that QOL (as a discursive object) has a parentage considerably less ideologically and scientifically 'pure' than the social scientific literatures would imply.

Collins (1992: 7) identifies the first usage of the term 'community care' in an official government publication in the *Report of the Royal Commission on the Law Relating to Mental Illness and Mental Deficiency* (1957). However, the formal adoption of community care as explicit social policy did not occur until after the executive's response to the Ely scandal (DHSS, 1969)[2] and the subsequent policy guidance in the command paper *Better Services for the Mentally Handicapped* (DHSS, 1971). The *Report of the Committee of Enquiry into Mental Handicap Nursing and Care* (DHSS, 1979) offered an explicit model of 'care' clearly influenced by what has subsequently become known as the 'ordinary life' perspective. The report suggested a range of service developments flowing from a 'belief in the primacy of a 'normal' lifestyle' (DHSS, 1979: 22) which aimed towards: 'a decent and dignified life for mentally handicapped people' (DHSS, 1979: 139). In Wales, official thinking was further advanced. The *All-Wales Strategy for the Development of Services for Mentally Handicapped People* (AWS) (Welsh Office, 1983) was explicitly based upon statements of respect for the individuality of people with intellectual disabilities; for example the Strategy review document published in 1991 reiterated the 1983 principle that people with intellectual disabilities have a right to 'ordinary patterns of life within the community' and the clear recognition that people with intellectual disabilities 'can expect … additional help from the communities in which they live … to develop their maximum potential' (Welsh Office, 1991: para. 38).

Statements in the AWS about the 'rights' of people with intellectual disabilities, and the description of people with intellectual disabilities as capable of development, is a very different discourse to that of the 1980

DHSS policy review *Mental Handicap: Progress, Problems and Priorities* (DHSS, 1980). The rhetoric of the AWS made two debts clear. The use of the term 'ordinary' to describe life styles acknowledged the King's Fund Centre's (1980) position paper *An Ordinary Life* which had laid out a detailed framework for community-based services to complement the strategic vision of the Jay Report. The employment of the term 'ordinary' in the King's Fund document itself represented a masterstroke of rhetorical understatement in response to those – for example government – who claimed the continuing necessity for 'extra-ordinary', or special, facilities such as mental handicap institutions at the time (DHSS, 1980).

In order for this 'ordinary' model of care to be more widely acceptable, however, a number of rhetorical accommodations, and a new public social construction of the nature of intellectual disability, were required. Such a construction began to emerge in the Second Report of the House of Commons Select Committee on Social Services, *Community Care: With Special Reference to Adult Mentally Ill and Mentally Handicapped People* (HMSO, 1985), which concluded that, with sufficient financial and human resources, local authorities – rather than hospitals or other health service providers – could and would provide an adequate lifestyle for people with intellectual disabilities. Further, in a subtle but significant shift in terminology, what may now – in managerialist discourse – be termed the 'client group' was referred to as 'mentally handicapped people' rather than '*the* mentally handicapped'. The Committee recommended that 'new residential services for all but a small minority of mentally handicapped adults be in the form of ordinary housing within the wider community' (HMSO, 1985, Vol. 1: cxvii). Shortly afterwards, in a major review of policy in the field the Griffiths Report (1988) laid out, explicitly, the central corporatist/managerialist, market economic tropes of 'cost-effectiveness' and 'value for money' that were to become central to government policy. In keeping with the government's consumerist rhetoric Griffiths (1998: para. 3.4) suggested that:

> There is value in a multiplicity of provision, not least from the consumers' point of view, because of the widening of choice, flexibility, innovation and competition it should stimulate. The proposals are therefore aimed at stimulating the further development of the 'mixed economy' of care.

It should be noted here that Griffiths, the expert appointed by government to advise on future policy directions, explicitly refers to people with intellectual disabilities as 'consumers'. Community-based care is constructed as offering 'consumers' the advantages of the (multiplicity of the market) in the provision of a 'mixed economy' care. In the subsequent NHS and Community Care Act 1990 corporatist notions of value for money, cost-effectiveness and quality monitoring were cemented into a nascent 'contracting culture' with the establishment – in another borrowing from the discourse of commercial banking – of organizational units called National Health Service 'Trusts' (see Collins, 1992, 1993 for a detailed discussion). Contemporaneous with the Act a range of other key changes in the social construction of intellectual disability invoked by the rhetoric of the executive and members of the psy-complex are evident.

'Quality of Life' – Core Theme in the Corporate Discourse

The sharpness of the shifts in social policy and the public social construction of people with intellectual disabilities offered by government can be gauged by comparing the rhetoric of the so-called *MENCAP Speech* by Stephen Dorrell, the then Minister of Health, in June 1991 (DOH, 1991) and the *Local Authority Circular (92)15* (LAC (92) 15) (DOH, 1992) with the social constructions of persons with an intellectual disability invoked in the earlier policy guidance and Acts of Parliament briefly discussed above.

Although no longer sustaining the eugenic theory that intellectual disability was caused by inherited degeneracy or wilful moral degradation legislated by the Mental Deficiency Act 1913 , the rhetoric of government in the period prior to the NHS and Community Care Act 1990 routinely invoked a social construction of people with intellectual disabilities as a homogenous group – 'the mentally handicapped', a group which required 'nursing and care'. Before *Caring for People* (the White Paper which preceded that Act), people with intellectual disabilities were constructed in official texts not as individuals with rights, not even as 'people', but rather what would now be termed – again in the discourse of commerce – as a 'client' group, a client group, furthermore, which was not composed of individual 'service users', but rather could be constructed as a group noun describing a 'condition' which, as we will see below, could pose 'problems', upon which there could be 'progress' and for which government could set 'priorities'. While *Caring for People* represented a major change in the direction of social policy, perhaps more striking was the appropriation of the theme of 'care' into the lexicon of the corporate/managerial discourse: government now, like the manufacturers of washing powder, the international airlines and the providers of telephones, claimed to be 'caring'.

In the earlier White Paper *Mental Handicap: Progress, Problems and Priorities* (DHSS, 1980) implementation of the 1971 policy guidance had been reviewed. Consistent with its title was the policy that there was a strong case for 'special units … for certain groups … [some] … may need to live permanently in such units' (DHSS, 1980: 34). The White Paper made it clear that 'current Department policy is that some require long-term health care whilst others require long-term placement' (DHSS, 1980: 18). The assumption underpinning government policy was made explicit: it is 'taken for granted that there are some mentally handicapped people who need hospital care and a distinct group of others who need local authority or other similar residential care' (DHSS, 1980: 22). The construction here is not the now familiar, indeed formulaic, 'people with an intellectual disability' but consists in references to 'certain groups' or a similarly vague 'some mentally handicapped people' and 'others'.

In contrast, Stephen Dorrell's so-called MENCAP speech[3] of 25 June 1991 (DOH, 1991) not only displayed a reflexive awareness of its own rhetoric in the explicit use of the new term 'learning disability' rather than the previously officially preferred 'mental handicap', but also explicitly deploys the corporatist/managerialist discourse referred to above as offering a candidate organizing principle in service provision – with a particular emphasis laid on 'quality'. The speech explicitly allows for the notion of 'quality of life' as an outcome of service practice, in effect a formal governmental endorsement of the idea. Furthermore Dorrell legitimates, by virtue of the stress laid on the theme of consumerism, a view of service users as customers, as 'citizens', and in so doing offers formal validation of the explicit deployment of the themes of the corporatist discourse in the rhetoric of the psy-complex.

As we have seen, Rose (1992) suggests that the thinking of persons in terms of the 'enterprising self', which now dominates 'Western' political mentality, furnishes a version of self as subjective being, aspiring to independence and seeking fulfilment though individual responsibility and acts of choice. Seeking approval for governments' new policy goals, in the MENCAP speech government-as-corporation deploys a rhetorical emphasis on the newness and modernity of its products. Thus Dorrell urges that 'individuals', rather than 'the mentally handicapped' or 'mentally handicapped people', should 'not be offered predetermined sets of services because of ill-considered or outdated notions' (DOH, 1991: para. 6). However, in the context of social care, the managerialist, corporate discourse does not make sense without 'customers': it is necessary therefore to transform 'the mentally handicapped' from a homogenous population who require 'care' *en masse*, into one affording recognition to 'individuals' – people who are capable of being consumers; people who can, or can be assisted to, choose between 'packages of care' or 'accept it as their mission' (DOH, 1991: para. 47) to work together with providers to plan and implement services. On this reading the Minister's assertion that changes in terminology 'reflect ... the values which inform our thinking' is absolutely consistent: it is the values of the enterprise culture that demand that 'the mentally handicapped' become here, rhetorically at least, '*citizens* ... full members of our society* ... ' (DOH, 1991: 1–2, my emphasis).

The MENCAP speech exemplifies the deployment of the theme of 'quality', indeed of 'quality of life', as the central component in the broader corporate discourse. Often invoked alongside the consumerist rhetoric, appeals to subjectivity and the individualized pursuit of 'the good life' are frequent, both as goals for individuals and as 'service principles' (DOH,

1991, para. 5). Services are to offer, with a (knowing) nod to the 'language of normalization' (Greig, 1993), 'appropriate support and opportunities founded on the *right values* and service principles' (DOH, 1991: para. 5, emphasis added). This support is to be offered to 'individuals' with 'respect and dignity'. Addressing 'individual' 'social care needs', with an explicit recognition of the 'ordinary life model' (DOH, 1991: para. 17), is to be the statutory responsibility of local authorities who are to 'contract' with a range of 'care providers' that are 'outward looking and closely associated with the general community' (DOH, 1991: para. 19).

Like the MENCAP speech, the subsequent policy paper *Social Care for Adults with Learning Disabilities (Mental Handicap)* (LAC (92) 15) (DOH, 1992), is explicit in the construction of intellectual disability it offers. The new 'citizens' of the MENCAP speech, 'people with learning disabilities', are no longer permanently deficient invalids who require nursing and other specialist care in hospital settings or special units. Unlike the 1980 position, which held that some would always need the special facilities of hospitals, the Circular constructs a radically different social reality. Here, rather than identifying a population group that requires extraordinary attention to a permanent, unchanging condition, the Circular suggests that, 'with appropriate support and opportunities ... [they] ... are capable of considerable personal development and of making a positive contribution to society. Few, if any, need to live in hospitals' (DOH, 1992: 1). These 'individuals' then are no longer people incapable of subjective being, of aspiring to independence, of making acts of choice.

Social Care for Adults with Learning Disabilities (Mental Handicap) (DOH, 1992) exemplifies the deployment of the managerial discourse, and specifically the 'quality' theme, in government rhetoric. *Social Care for Adults with Learning Disabilities (Mental Handicap)* gives specific guidance to local authorities on the provision of services to adults with learning disabilities: throughout the client group is referred to as 'people with learning disabilities', with the use of the parenthetical term 'mental handicap' of its title discouraged. The policy advice spells out the requirement for 'social' rather than 'hospital' or 'health' care, and instructs local authority social services departments in matters to be addressed when 'designing and developing care management and quality assurance arrangements' (DOH, 1992: 1). Having introduced the notion of the 'care package', it is of note that 'care' is no longer something offered as part of an ongoing and intimate personal relationship between people: rather it is now a something that, like any other 'product' or commodity, may be 'packaged' and which needs also to be 'contracted' and 'managed'. Furthermore the 'quality' of the product is apparently sufficiently unpredictable that (formalized) 'quality assurance' mechanisms need to be 'designed'.

The discourse invoked here is that of the corporation. We see the key device of 'quality' and the failure to refer to the objects of attention as a homogenized population group, 'the learning disabled', are not discussed. Rather, people formerly referred to as '*the* mentally handicapped' are now consumers, consumers who may have a grievance: the rhetoric of consumer choice and empowerment is invoked. 'The personal preferences of the individual' are to guide service planning and 'people should be helped to express their views and preferences ... sometimes people with learning disabilities ... will be dissatisfied with the services offered' (DOH, 1992:2). *Social Care for Adults with Learning Disabilities (Mental Handicap)* is explicit in its references to 'meeting the social needs of people ... within a mixed economy of care' (DOH, 1992: 2). Our newly disgruntled consumers, it appears, are no longer are in need of nursing.

In the light of Rose's and Miller's analyses of the endeavour to maintain people as contributory members of the society of which they are a part, the annex to *Social Care for Adults with Learning Disabilities (Mental Handicap)* is telling. In a subsection considering employment, the document appeals not only to subjectivity and intersubjectivity as sites for the regulation of conduct but also to the national interest in self-regulated conduct. The Circular (DOH, 1992: 9–10) suggests that:

> Participation in a paid job will help them to achieve a greater social independence and self-assurance. If they go out to work and pay their own way in the world, they are likely to see themselves as more valued members of the community making a contribution to that community ... it is important that the country makes the best use of the skills and potential contribution from all its citizens.

The implications of this are far reaching. Here full 'citizenship', with its rights and obligations, is held out to people who only just over a decade earlier had been described in governmental policy advice as a homogenous, and problematic, client group in need of better nursing care. These newly minted 'enterprising selves', it is suggested, will too come to find their subjectivity enhanced by producing and consuming; they will gain autonomy – 'independence and self-assurance' – and they will come, via the intersubjective ratification of their fellow citizens, to self-fulfilment, to see themselves as 'valued members of the community'.

The Welsh Office's review of the All-Wales Strategy (AWS) (Welsh Office, 1991) replicates the construction of intellectual-disability-as-enterprising-self seen in the MENCAP speech. The AWS review deploys the themes of quality and consumerism as way stations for the explicit invocation of the notion of 'quality of life' as an organizing construct within the corporatist/managerialist framework of service provision which the text constructs. Again invoking intersubjectivity as the site of concern, the document (Welsh Office, 1991: para. 2) claims that the All-Wales Strategy:

> enable[s] people ... to live fulfilled lives, as independently as possible, in their own homes in the wider community, with care and support tailored to their needs as individuals ... the Strategy has demonstrated that ... local services can provide improved quality, more choice for individuals, and greater responsiveness to their needs ... people ... are experiencing greater independence and have more control over their lives.

In the same way that university students have been transformed into 'customers', here people with intellectual disabilities are transformed from a homogenized population to become 'individuals' who happen to be users of services. As 'users' or 'consumers'/'customers' of services, they have preferences ('choices') and can be expected to express them in their search for 'fulfilled lives'. The adoption, by service providers, of such a consumerist approach is what allows 'individual' enterprising selves to acquire Rose's (1992) 'autonomy' – here, 'independence' and 'control'. One of the roles of services thus becomes not just the provision of social care but also to 'assist service users to find their voice in individual and local planning ... to ensure that their needs and wishes are properly identified' (Welsh Office, 1991: 17). Most radically, perhaps, while newly enfranchised as citizens in England, in Wales people with intellectual disabilities are called upon to become the 'partners' of government. The Welsh Office (1991: 33) argues that:

> the contribution which users, carers, the voluntary and private sectors can and should make to planning ... needs careful management to ensure that each partner ... can make a valuable contribution.

The term 'partner', with its echoes of the world of commerce, and the identification of people with intellectual disabilities as 'valuable' contributors to a 'managed' planning process, positions them as not just the recipients of the care of the state, but as the *colleagues* of both state and the voluntary and private sectors.

The theme of 'quality' is routinely invoked, and equally routinely linked to the notions of 'care', 'responsiveness' to 'individuals' and fiscal rectitude. Thus 'the new framework set out in the *Caring for People* White paper provides the right basis for social services authorities to work ... to develop quality care' (Welsh Office, 1991: para. 20). Further, in paragraph 31, the document states that:

> The Secretary of State places great importance on improving monitoring and evaluation to ensure that services are of high quality and provide consistent value for money ... he proposes to establish mechanisms better to assure quality and assess value for money ... to implement ... practices that are responsive to the wishes and needs of individuals.

At a first reading it is entirely plausible that the Minister might be referring here to library services, the fire brigade or even to the state of the sewers. That is to say, this construction of the role of government in the provision of 'services' is not immediately identifiable as referring to the particular and specific needs of a particularly vulnerable group of people. What we have here is the state-as-corporation describing its governing political mentality. With an appeal to modernity as warrant, the implication is that neither 'value for money' nor 'quality care' was available under the 'old' framework: a framework incapable of 'quality' not just because it had inadequate measures in place to 'assure quality' but on account of the fact that it was unresponsive to the 'wishes and needs of individuals'.

It was not just government that adopted this new rhetoric in the 1980s and 1990s: the psy-complex too adopted the now linked 'languages' (Greig, 1993) – or discourses – of normalization and corporatism. Thus *Services for People with Learning Disabilities and Challenging Behaviour or Mental Health Needs* (DOH, 1993) – the report of an expert panel of academics and service providers convened by government – not only promotes 'the supported ordinary housing model' of care (DOH, 1993: 12) but also stresses the fact that 'successful services' are 'individualised' (DOH, 1993: 9). In 'successful' services the report claims, 'packages of care are constructed' on the basis of 'thoroughly knowing and understanding the individual' (DOH, 1993: 9).

Furthermore, in direct advice to 'commissioners' of services (another term making explicit the link between markets and the development of so-called 'social care'), the report stresses that 'value for money cannot be judged solely on the basis of costs ... commissioners ... should attend to the general *quality of life* as measured by, for example, the widely used "five service accomplishments" as well as by user satisfaction' (DOH, 1993: 19, my emphasis). In assessing value for money, 'service purchasers' are advised to 'attend to the general *quality of life* in addition to the specific treatment of challenging behaviour.' (DOH, 1993: 28, my emphasis). The regular measurement of the quality of life of service users is promoted as an example of 'good practice' (DOH, 1993: 22). It is noted that many services deploy the rhetoric of normalization while showing widely different standards of performance. Therefore commissioners are said to need to be able to: 'distinguish good outcomes from window-dressing' (DOH, 1993: 20). Again we note that the term 'window-dressing' is another a borrowing from the discourse of commerce, in this case retailing.

The rhetoric of these texts invokes a discourse recognizable as that dissected by academic theoreticians of 'quality of life'. The person with an intellectual disability is constructed as an 'enterprising self', as an individual with subjective wishes and preferences. The response of the state is no longer the direct control of deviance – a dispenser of institutional nursing care to the 'mentally handicapped' – but rather is to function as the 'caring' chair in the boardroom deliberations of a range of 'partners'. There is a range of individualized demands – 'wishes and needs' – which it is the function of services to negotiate meeting. Human services are positioned as the 'providers' (retailers?) of a range of aids (and accessories) that may be 'purchased' with a view to achieving a 'fulfilled' life. The individual 'service user' is an impaired consumer – almost a confused shopper – with the rights of citizenship, but also the concomitant personal responsibility to consume and to contribute.

In adopting these positions it should be noted that the rhetoric of government not only makes regular reference to the notion of 'quality', but also that the construct of 'quality of life' is explicitly used. Not only is 'quality of life' deployed as an *aspect of individual subjectivity*, it is also construed as an *outcome of service practice*. In the MENCAP speech it is what 'mental handicap nurses' in 'large mental handicap hospitals' have historically provided (DOH, 1991: para. 15). A high quality of life is what well-considered and up-to-date policy, by treating people with 'respect and dignity' (DOH, 1991: para. 6) – as individualized 'consumers' – offers as its latest product. In the All-Wales Strategy review (Welsh Office, 1991) 'quality of life' is invoked by the claims that the AWS has provided people with 'a fulfilled life', an outcome of services responsive to individual wishes and needs. In *Services for People with Learning Disabilities and Challenging Behaviour or Mental Health Needs* 'quality of life' is one of the 'good' outcomes which 'successful services' will deliver.

In these documents what has become an individualized outcome of service activity – a high 'quality of life' – is, in keeping with the idea that 'the customer is always right', to be assessed by assisting people to 'find their voice' (Welsh Office, 1991), to report on their own satisfaction with life. Such an idea is also expressed in the House of Commons Select Committee on the Social Services Seventh Report. The report, on 'quality', explicitly suggests that 'inspection units be *required* to take account of the views of service users' in assessing the quality of service provision (Social Services Committee, 1990: para. 106, my emphasis). Clearly, then, if this is the discursive position of government, the most appropriate index for the psy-complex to select in the process of 'monitoring and evaluation to ensure that services are of high quality and provide consistent value for money' (Welsh Office, 1991) is the quality of life achieved by people with intellectual disabilities and reported on by themselves.

In Summary

Rather than being ideologically pure developments of normalization, notions of 'consumerism', 'quality' and 'quality of life' are, rather, intimately bound up in the powerful discourse of corporatism and managerialism which, although pervading most strongly the rhetoric of the right, is, as Rose (1992) notes, the dominant political mentality of the present. As such, we have seen here how, over the course of the twenty years after 1980, a group of people previously 'thought' as a degenerate moral threat have been transformed into candidate enterprising selves.

That is, in the texts analysed in this chapter, people with an intellectual disability have moved from being represented as a homogenous population group in need of the care of others, into *individual* selves or subjective beings who can be understood as aspiring to autonomy and striving for personal fulfilment. The anonymous undifferentiated mass of 1980 – 'the mentally handicapped' – have become, by the 1990s, identifiable persons with individual responsibilities and duties, who may be expected to seek meaning in existence, be motivated by the search for satisfaction with earthly life and, most importantly, exercise such subjectivity by acts of choice. People with intellectual disabilities are, thus, recruited as 'enterprising selves'.

From this perspective it seems plausible that the notion of quality (of life) derives its legitimation as a site of social scientific study not so much from advances in science (as Hagerty *et al.* (2001) for example claim), but rather from its subsumability into projects of governmentality and the discourse of enterprise culture. The fact that the quality of life/QOL of service users has an 'intuitive' appeal as a template against which to test the 'success' of community services merely reflects this new way of thinking (intellectually disabled) selves. The resonance of this new thinking of people with intellectual disabilities as candidate enterprising selves with our everyday thinking of our selves in this way has doubtless assisted in the concept's ready assimilation into academic discourse. As has been noted, considerable rhetorical energy has been expended by government and the psy-complex in promoting the concept as a 'service quality' measure. Indeed the frequency and enthusiasm with which the social scientific literature endorses QOL as furnishing services with a means of comparing the 'number of satisfied customers' under different regimes, and rewarding these regimes appropriately, might be taken to suggest a widespread approval of this approach.

However, the analysis here would suggest that the contingencies for the adoption of the notion by the executive and its psy-complex partners may differ. The executive deploys a range of common tropes ('quality', 'consumerism', 'individual choice') as key elements of a superordinate discourse of commerce, managerialism and market economics – of 'enterprise culture'. Conversely, in the intellectual disability research community at least, the notion of QOL is understood as following from the normalization movement and as inheriting its social justice ideological commitments. Examination of a prototypical psy-complex QOL measure (Schalock and Keith's, 1996, *Quality of Life Questionnaire*) indeed reveals a strong welfarist commitment to the position of the individual inconsistent with, indeed on occasion subversive of, the hegemony of corporatized service provision and the managerialist rationale for its employment (Antaki and Rapley, 1996a; Antaki and Rapley, 1996b; Rapley and Antaki, 1996).

Notes

1. Normalization was a controversial theory of human service practice that captured the imagination of many service providers and planners from the mid-1970s onwards. In brief, normalization suggested that services should attempt to offer their 'clients' a life as close to the 'normal' as was possible. See Wolfensberger (1972) for an overview.
2. The 'Ely scandal' flowed from revelations in the newspaper *The News of the World* of appalling living conditions and abusive treatment of residents at a hospital for people with intellectual disabilities (then a so-called 'subnormality' hospital) in Ely, a suburb of Cardiff, Wales.
3. MENCAP is the major British charity, or NGO (non-governmental organization) which provides services for people with intellectual disabilities and their families, runs public education campaigns and lobbies government over the direction of social policy.

Study Questions

- How are other 'marginalized' groups – such as elderly people, homeless people or people described as 'mentally ill' – currently thought with respect to the 'enterprise culture' in the West?
- How are people with intellectual disabilities, the 'mentally ill' and elderly people thought of in non-Western cultures?
- In what other sites has 'quality', or enterprise culture talk, risen to prominence over the past twenty years?
- If possible at all, how can 'quality of life' be thought in non-Western cultures?

Suggestions for Further Reading

Foucault, M. (1977) *Discipline and Punish: The Birth of the Prison*. London: Allen Lane.
Kendall, G. and Wickham, G. (1999) *Using Foucault's Methods*. London: Sage.
Miller, T. and McHoul, A. (1998) *Popular Culture and Everyday Life*. London: Sage.
Rose, N. (1999) *Governing the Soul: The Shaping of the Private Self, 2nd edn*. London: Free Association Books.

CHAPTER 6

QOL in Health and Social Care Research

QOL research in medical settings focuses most clearly on issues of the objective operationalization and quantification of the construct. A second (though not necessarily secondary) key concern has been the ethically difficult development of QALYs and DALYs, and more recently, a focus on the related concept of 'customer satisfaction' with health/social care provision as an adjunct variable to concern with QOL. This chapter draws on the work of key critical thinkers such as Nord to review methodological approaches used in the development of QOL indices, such as QALYs and HRQOL measures, routinely used in health and social care settings.

Health-related QOL

Some authorities (most notably Cummins) are deeply sceptical of notions such as 'HRQOL' and the use of condition- or disease-specific measures. Much of this debate is a consequence of two different endeavours talking past each other. Cummins's work attempts to specify QOL as a global construct, whereas QOL research in the vast majority of medical settings revolves around pragmatic concerns. Usually, these are efforts to evaluate whether *this* procedure, for *these* patients, with *this* condition, produces an identifiable increase in QOL (in whatever way, locally, for this particular condition, it is defined).

QOL work in this area has contributed to the development of what, in the UK, may be a new approach to medicine. In view of Rose's (1992) conception of the rights and duties of 'entrepreneurial selves' in postmodernity, this 'new' approach is understandable as another instance of the increasing responsibility of persons to collaborate with the professions in the use of technologies of the self. However, in the policy document *The Expert Patient*, the British Department of Health (2001: 5) suggests that:

> an observation often made by doctors, nurses and other health professionals ... is 'my patient understands their disease better than I do.' This knowledge and experience held by the patient has for too long been an untapped resource. It is something that could greatly benefit the quality of patients' care and ultimately their quality of life ... today's patients with chronic diseases need not be mere recipients of care. They can become key decision-makers in the treatment process ... Self-management

programmes can be specifically designed to reduce the severity of symptoms and improve confidence, resourcefulness and self-efficacy.

Such an approach may, by reducing the severity of symptoms and improving 'confidence, resourcefulness and self-efficacy', be understood as contributing directly to improving patients' health-related quality of life (HRQOL).

What is HRQOL?

The US Centers for Disease Control and Prevention offer a definition of HRQOL that would probably command a consensus. HRQOL encompasses those aspects of overall QOL that can be clearly shown to affect health – be it physical or mental health (CDC, 2000). As with the concept of QOL itself, HRQOL is conceptualized as being both an individual- and a population-level construct. The CDC (2000: 6) contends that for individuals, HRQOL 'includes physical and mental health perceptions and their correlates, including health risks and conditions, functional status, social support, and socioeconomic status … On the community level, HRQOL includes resources, conditions, policies, and practices that influence a population's health perceptions and functional status.'

Why measure HRQOL?

Many Western governments claim the intent to 'increase quality of life' (DOH, 2001). Their agencies state that their 'mission' is 'to promote health and *quality of life* by preventing, and controlling disease, injury and disability' (CDC, 2000, my emphasis). Accordingly, it is necessary to adopt procedures to gauge success in these endeavours (see Petersen and Lupton, (1996). The CDC (2000: 6) suggest that:

> measuring HRQOL can help determine the burden of preventable disease, injuries, and disabilities, and it can provide valuable new insights into the relationships between HRQOL and risk factors. Measuring HRQOL will help monitor progress in achieving the nation's health objectives. Analysis of HRQOL surveillance data can identify subgroups with relatively poor perceived health and help to guide interventions to improve their situations and avert more serious consequences.

Idler and Benyamini (1997) have suggested that self-assessed health status better predicts mortality and morbidity than many objective measures of health: thus there is considerable potential in assessing the HRQOL individuals. Essentially what QOL research seeks to do in the medical/health area, then, is to answer questions, at both individual and community levels, like 'what are the effects on patients' QOL of using procedure *x*?' 'What QOL benefits flow from adopting policy *y*?' 'What endpoints should be used for clinical trials or to evaluate the efficacy of therapeutic interventions?' and 'How should effectiveness be quantified for cost-effectiveness analysis (CEA)?'

At the community level HRQOL is assessed using a wide range of specific measures – such as the EuroQOL-5D (described below) – and by summary indices in the form of QALYs and DALYs. At the individual level a huge number of HRQOL measures supplement traditional outcome indicators such as mortality rates, tumour size or blood sugar control. More recently, medical literatures have adopted three broad approaches to the use of QOL as an 'endpoint'. Studies report physician or patient judgments of the patient's QOL (in terms of symptoms or functional status) and patient evaluations of health states (in terms of preferences, 'utilities' or values). Morreim (1992) distinguishes 'Consensus Quality of Life research' (CQL) – asking healthy people to answer hypothetical health questions known as 'time trade-offs' or to assign relative values to differential impairments in terms of their 'utility' impact on QOL – and Personal Quality of Life research (PQL), which evaluates individuals' own judgements about the QOL in terms of the effects of disease and therapeutic intervention.

Morreim (1992) notes that PQL is generally more helpful in the *individual practice of* medicine. As the task of medicine is to assist *individual* patients, it makes more sense to ask patients about their QOL than to seek the judgments of healthy citizens about hypothetical situations. Examples of both approaches are considered below. However, a moment of reflection and an overview of the current state of the art is in order.

The quality of QOL research in medical settings

In considering QOL in medical settings – where judgments of life quality have life-threatening consequences – we must remember that quality of life is not an object or thing but a *judgment of the value* of life circumstances. As such, it is crucial that treatment decisions involving relative valuations of the quality of a patient's life, and the decision-making tools which inform them, are based in ethically sound research conducted and reported to rigorous standards.

Van der Maas *et al.* (1996) estimate that, in the Netherlands, 43 per cent of all deaths involve 'end-of-life' decisions by doctors (the decision to withdraw or withhold treatment, the prescription of lethal doses of analgesics or the active killing of the patient) with higher rates for people with intellectual disabilities or psychiatric problems. Van Thiel *et al.*'s (1997) study of end-of-life decisions involving people with intellectual disabilities found that, while only two patients had actively asked to die, doctors felt that *their* estimation of the patient's suffering was sufficient to 'assist' the patient to die, in three cases by lethal injection. Van Thiel *et al.*

(1997: 90) note that 'all of them were incompetent and did not express their wishes about the decision ... deaths were reported as natural in all cases'. Groenewoud *et al.* (1996) surveyed nearly half of all Dutch psychiatrists: 37 per cent had received at least one request for assisted suicide, and twelve had complied. Groenewoud *et al.* (1996) estimate each psychiatrist conducts between two and five assisted suicides a year. They suggest:

> excluding those who had ever assisted ... 64 percent thought physician-assisted suicide because of a mental disorder could be acceptable, including 241 who said they could conceive of instances in which they themselves would be willing to assist.

Such findings put evaluations of the quality of a life firmly onto centre stage, even in specialisms like psychiatry which are distant from those where QOL judgments are a routine aspect of practice (oncology, intensive care or transplant surgery). That Dutch psychiatrists kill people they describe as 'mentally disordered' or 'incompetent' raises serious ethical questions about informed consent, about the criteria against which the quality of these lives were judged and found wanting, and the evidence base upon which these judgments were made.

Much HRQOL research – even that published in prestigious journals – fails on the counts above. Much is based in dubious ethical practices and research design (e.g. not consulting patients about their QOL) and/or is methodologically so flawed as to be worthless. In their study of the quality of QOL reporting in medicine, Gill and Feinstein (1994) found that only 15 per cent of investigators defined QOL, just over a third justified selection of the measure used, and a mere 13 per cent asked patients to assess their QOL. Sanders *et al.* (1998) found QOL reporting rose from 0.63 per cent of studies in 1980 to 4.2 per cent in 1997. While, by 1987, 8.2 per cent of cancer trials reported QOL data, Sanders *et al.* (1998: 1193) noted that the field was confounded by a bewildering array of measures and that:

> of the 67 studies sampled ... 48 used 62 different pre-existing instruments and a further 15 studies reported new measures, with few following the methods proposed [by the *Lancet*] for the development and testing of instruments ... it is implausible that some 40 different measures of generic or psychological well-being could be justified in 48 trials.

Even in RCTs (randomized controlled trials), then, the 'gold standard' of outcome studies, reporting of QOL research is, say Sanders *et al.* (1998: 1194), 'poor'. Not only were patients generally not consulted about their QOL (despite QOL being defined as the most important outcome variable in 23 of the 67 studies), but also 'in about 30 per cent of studies it remained unclear whether patients had contributed any information at all'. Citing

Slevin *et al.*'s, (1988) study, it is concluded: 'Clearly some investigators continue to believe that health professionals can make a valid assessment of their patients' QOL in spite of evidence to the contrary' (Sanders *et al.*, 1998: 1194). These assessments are most technically developed in the form of QALYs and DALYs.

What are QALYs and DALYs?

Nord (1992a, 1992b) notes that the QALY concept is central to the health status approach to QOL research. Quality adjusted life years (QALYs) are derived from the notion that the relative effectiveness of medical interventions, or the value of health care programmes, is a function of the significance of the health improvements delivered to patients: the longer patients survive to enjoy the benefits of medical/healthcare intervention and the greater the number of patients who are helped by a given system. Phillips and Thompson (1998: 1) suggest that:

> QALYs provide a common currency to assess the extent of the benefits gained from a variety of interventions in terms of health-related quality of life and survival for the patient. When combined with the costs of providing the interventions, cost-utility ratios result; these indicate the additional costs required to generate a year of perfect health (one QALY). Comparisons can be made between interventions, and priorities can be established based on those interventions that are relatively inexpensive (low cost per QALY) and those that are relatively expensive (high cost per QALY).

The QALY is a straightforward statistic. The QALY represents life expectancy adjusted for QOL. In health economic terms QALYs allow comparisons across medical interventions that differ in their effects on longevity and on different aspects of QOL. Years of life in different states of physical or mental dysfunction or various symptomatic states are assigned values on a scale of 1.0 (healthy) to 0.0 (dead). These values reflect the relative quality of the states and allow morbidity and mortality improvements to be combined into a single weighted measure – QALYs gained. Thus, for example, 10 years of life in perfect health = 10 QALYs; 15 years of life with a mildly compromised QOL (e.g. persistent back pain) may be rated at 0.8 relative to perfect health, with QALY value calculated as the product of the QOL rating of 0.8 multiplied by the years of life = (15 × 0.8) = 12 QALYs.

Alternatively, if one lives five years on medication with perfect health followed by seven years with lowered QOL from side effects, scoring 0.5, this intervention would return 8.5 QALYs ((5 × 1) + (7 × 0.5) = 8.5). The argument for QALYs is that it is possible by, assigning a numerical value to the lowered 'utility' of a life with medical problems, to arrive at an objective 'bottom line' judgment about whether intervention is 'worth it'. If the projected value of life after intervention is less than that which might be expected with untreated disease, treatment should be withheld.

Such calculations can compare different treatments. If John has kidney failure and renal transplant improves his health from 0.3 to 0.9 for one year, and renal dialysis extends Jane's life for five years in a 0.6 state, then by simple arithmetic renal dialysis has returned 3.6 QALYs gained ((0.9 – 0.3) + (5.0 × 0.6) = 3.6). The cost per QALY gained (the 'cost : utility ratio' or the 'cost-effectiveness ratio') may then be calculated. For example, an analysis of QALYs gained by kidney transplants may return a higher absolute number of QALYs, say 5.2 QALYs. However, if the cost of dialysis is $100 per QALY gained and the cost of kidney transplantation is $500 per QALY gained, dialysis has a much better cost : utility ratio than transplantation. More QOL is purchased for less outlay: dialysis produces 'more bang for your buck' allowing resource allocation choices producing maximal health for money spent (Hyder et al., 1998).

Such calculations may be expressed as cost-utility ratios using the formula.

$$\text{Cost-utility ratio} = \frac{\text{Cost of Intervention A} - \text{Cost of Intervention B}}{\text{No. of QALYs produced by Intervention A} - \text{No. of QALYs produced by Intervention B}}$$

Nord (1992a: 875) points out that 'when prioritising between them the standard health economist recommendation is to rank the programmes from the lowest cost per QALY value to the highest and to select from the top until available resources are exhausted'. However such statistics cannot tell us anything about the benefits – or 'utility' – to Jane's two toddlers of having a mum around for another five years in a health state of 0.6, as opposed to no mum in health state 0.0.

Calculating QALYs

Measuring QOL to compute QALYs primarily uses two methods, psychometric scales measuring HRQOL (e.g. WHOQOL (WHO, 1997), the CDC's HRQOL 14 or EuroQOL EQ5D (see Table 6.1)). Many studies employ psychometric measures as stand-alone instruments and report scale scores rather than QALYs. Joseph and Rao (1999) report a comparative study of the effects of leprosy on the QOL of people with and without the disease in Andhra Pradesh using the WHOQOL.[1] Alternatively, studies may opt for the direct assessment of the 'utility' of various health/ill-health states, a concept sometimes phrased in terms of 'health preferences'.

Use of psychometric QOL scales varies across studies. In some cases patients report on activities or symptoms in the recent past, providing an evaluation of their current health state, whereas in others they may make relative judgments about changes in their health status or future hypothetical health states. For the purposes of calculation present state is used. Such patient-reported facts do not necessarily indicate the relative importance to the patient of different aspects of health, nor place values on the effects of poor health on life activities. Such an approach also often relies on the expert judgment of researchers or health professionals to give the patient an overall QOL score ranging from 0.0 to 1.0, where 0.0 = death and 1.0 = perfect health, drawing on utility weights of values generated by general population surveys.

Tables 6.1 and 6.2 show health states from the EuroQOL-5D and a selection of average utility weights for various health states based on the ratings of over 3,000 people in the UK. A variety of health states are rated as progressively less desirable than perfect health, with the final state being ranked (with a minus value) as being worse than death. It should be noted that while such studies may be statistically representative of nations, they may also misrepresent the utilities assigned by patients themselves. For example, in a comparison of the utilities of members of the general public and patients with aneurysmal subarachnoid haemorrhage Polsky et al. (2001) found that pairwise comparisons of 243 of the EuroQol's 245 health states diverged, with 95 per cent of these differences being statistically significant. Polsky et al. (2001: 33) note that 'the general public rated states with the highest levels of function higher but states with worse levels of function lower, than did ... patients'. In such hypothetical tasks, the general public tend to overestimate the decrease in QOL associated with impaired health states.

The same approach was employed by Salkeld et al. (2000) who report a combined methodology using the EuroQOL-5D and a utility measure, a time trade-off task (TTO), to investigate the relationship between fear of falling, hip fracture and QOL in older women.

EQ-5D scores were calculated using the utility weights of values from the UK general population survey, and combined with the results of a preference task (rank-ordering four hypothetical hip-fracture scenarios) and the TTO to conclude that the preference weight for a 'bad' hip fracture was valued at 0.05, with a 'good' hip fracture valued at 0.31. Salkeld et al. (2000: 341) note that 'of the women surveyed, 80 per cent would rather be dead (utility = 0) than experience the loss of independence and QOL that results from a bad hip fracture and admission to a nursing home'. Phillips and Thompson (1998) report a comparative evaluation of two drugs for breast cancer, with health states describing patients' experience of the disease from pre-treatment to terminal illness scored by oncology nurses. Phillips and Thompson's (1998: 2) summary illustrates the extremely detailed cost-effectiveness analysis such procedures may offer:

Table 6.1 EuroQOL EQ-5D health states

Scores for the EuroQOL EQ-5D are a measure of individual functioning in five dimensions.

Mobility
1. No problems walking about.
2. Some problems walking about.
3. Confined to bed.

Pain/discomfort
1. No pain or discomfort.
2. Moderate pain or discomfort.
3. Extreme pain or discomfort.

Self-care
1. No problems with self-care.
2. Some problems washing or dressing.
3. Unable to wash or dress self.

Anxiety/depression
1. Not anxious or depressed.
2. Moderately anxious or depressed.
3. Extremely anxious or depressed.

Usual activities (work, study, housework, leisure activities)
1. No problems in performing usual activities.
2. Some problems in performing usual activities.
3. Unable to perform usual activities.

As each dimension has three levels – no problem, some problems and major problems – the EuroQOL returns a total of 243 possible health states, which with the addition of 'unconscious' and 'dead' produce a total of 245 possible health states.

Paclitaxel generates 0.5111 QALYs and docetaxel 0.6016 QALYs – a difference of 0.0905 QALYs, equivalent to an additional 33 days of perfect health (0.0905 × 365). The additional costs of docetaxel amount to £220 per patient, which means that it costs £2,431 (£220/0.0905) to generate an additional QALY by using docetaxel.

Table 6.3 illustrates the wide range of procedures for which this sort of analyses have been conducted. The table also shows the huge variation in terms of cost per QALY. Such analyses may allow for relative weightings of intervention importance to be derived; thus we can see that neurosurgical intervention for malignant intracranial tumours is, at 1990 British prices, 97 times more expensive per QALY gained than pacemaker implantation.

What such figures conceal, however, is the details of both the procedures and the recipients of the intervention. That is, 'intracranial tumours' covers a

Table 6.2 EQ-5D health state valuations

Health state	Description	Valuation
11111	No problems	1.000
11221	No problems walking about; no problems with self-care; some problems with performing usual activities; some pain or discomfort; not anxious or depressed	0.760
22222	Some problems walking about; some problems washing or dressing self; some problems with performing usual activities; moderate pain or discomfort; moderately anxious or depressed	0.516
12321	No problems walking about; some problems washing or dressing self; unable to perform usual activities; some pain or discomfort; not anxious or depressed	0.329
21123	Some problems walking about; no problems with self-care; no problems with performing usual activities; moderate pain or discomfort; extremely anxious or depressed	0.222
23322	Some problems walking about, unable to wash or dress self, unable to perform usual activities, moderate pain or discomfort, moderately anxious or depressed	0.079
33332	Confined to bed; unable to wash or dress self; unable to perform usual activities; extreme pain or discomfort; moderately anxious or depressed	−0.429

Source: Phillips and Thompson (1998).

very wide range of conditions of differing severity. Secondly, it may be argued (see Cubbon, 1991) that life-saving brain surgery is more 'valuable' for a 35-year-old executive than it is for a 65-year-old pensioner.

Utility Measures

Utility measures can be employed to evaluate any health state – current health, previous health or, as in the Salkeld *et al.* (2000) study, *hypothetical* future states. Utility measures also allow for the evaluation of other outcomes, for example length of life. Using such measures allows respondents to evaluate the relative utility (or desirability) of various health states rather than simply reporting on their present symptoms or current functional status. Thus answers are influenced by the preferences and

Table 6.3 Relative costs of a variety of medical health care and health promotion activities and interventions

Intervention	£/QALY at 1990 prices
Cholesterol testing and diet therapy (all adults aged 40–69)	220
Neurosurgical intervention for head injury	240
GP advice to stop smoking	270
Neurosurgical intervention for subarachnoid haemorrhage	490
Antihypertensive treatment to prevent stroke (ages 45–64)	940
Pacemaker implantation	1,100
Hip replacement	1,180
Valve replacement for aortic stenosis	1,410
Cholesterol testing and treatment (all adults aged 40–69)	1,480
Kidney transplantation	4,710
Breast cancer screening	5,780
Heart transplantation	7,840
Home haemodialysis	17,260
Hospital haemodialysis	21,970
Neurosurgical intervention for malignant intracranial tumours	107,780

Source: Adapted from Phillips and Thompson (1998).

goals of individual respondents as well as their preparedness to take risks. Responses require respondents to make an explicit trade-off on their relative preferences for particular health states (again usually rated from 1.0 = perfect health to 0.0 = death).

Assessment of health utilities most commonly uses one or more of three techniques: direct rating scales, time trade-off (TTO) and standard gamble (SG). Using a direct rating scale respondents are presented with a description of a health state and asked to rate it on a 0 to 1 (or 0 = bad as death to 100 = good as perfect health) scale. For example Salkeld *et al.* (2000: 345) used ratings of four health states described as:

Full health – Anne
Anne is a similar age to you. She lives in her own home and cares for herself. Anne is active in her local community and is out and about with friends quite a bit. She swims regularly and enjoys visiting her children each weekend. Anne walks without any aids and can manage her 12 steps at home without any problems. She enjoys shopping and cooking for herself. Anne does not need any help with the housework and derives pleasure and relaxation from gardening.

Fear of falling – Mary
Mary is a similar age to you. She lives alone in her own home and cares for herself. Mary is involved in community fundraising and enjoys playing bridge. Mary recently had a fall. She did not break any bones but was

badly cut and bruised. She is scared of falling. Mary continues to walk without aids. She still looks after herself and does her own housework. Mary has been a bit depressed since her fall. She has returned to her bridge group but is anxious when she is outside the home because she is scared of falling again.

Good hip fracture – Jean
Jean is a similar age to you. She lives in her own home and cares for herself. Before her fall Jean was out and about quite a bit with her church group. She swam on a regular basis and occasionally looked after her grandchildren. Jean broke her hip when she fell. She is finding it difficult to do everything at home now that she walks with a stick. She needs help in shopping as she no longer drives or feels confident to shop alone. She can prepare only simple meals and is missing being able to bake for her friends. Jean can no longer manage the housework by herself. She misses her church activities but finds it too painful and tiring to be out for long periods. Jean experiences feelings of frustration and anger. Jean gets tearful thinking about all the things she can't do.

Bad hip fracture – Elizabeth
Elizabeth is a similar age to you. Until her recent fall, she lived in her own home and managed to care for herself. She was active in her local community. Elizabeth broke her hip when she fell. She is now unable to live alone as she requires a great deal of help to do most things. Elizabeth now lives in a nursing home near to her family but away from her friends. She is limited in where she can walk because of the frame and is unable to walk for long distances. She is unable to shower or dress without help from the nurse. She is unable to pursue her gardening or community work. Her leg aches sometimes at night. She has become anxious and is easily upset.

Having ranked and *directly rated* their 'preference' for these hypothetical scenarios a further time trade-off study was undertaken.

Time trade-off method

Time trade-off (TTO) studies use such hypothetical scenarios and offer respondents a forced choice between two states where outcomes are known with certainty (Dolan *et al.*, 1996). An example typical of a TTO study would offer respondents the following choices and establish the point at which they are, by increments, indifferent between them.

Imagine that you have chronic fatigue syndrome (CFS) and that you feel constantly tired, lethargic and have pain in your joints almost every day. You have some problems with shopping for yourself, lifting things and concentrating on work for more than an hour or so at a time. You have tried the most commonly prescribed medications, but they have not helped. Other than your CFS, you are in good health. You are 50 years old and can expect to live another 30 years.

An experimental drug is available that would totally eliminate your chronic fatigue syndrome and restore full health. However, this medication would decrease your life expectancy. If the medication decreased your life expectancy by five years you would have the following options. A. Live with CFS for 30 years B. Live in full health for 25 years Which option would you choose?

Patients are asked for the trade-off they are prepared to make in terms of years of life in full health for the benefit of the intervention (in this case the imaginary experimental drug). In Salkeld *et al.* (2000) the choice was between living in a state of less than full health for five or ten years (depending on the participants' age) and then dying, or living for a lesser period of time as 'Anne' (in full health) and then dying, with 'tradeable' time increments of six months or a year. The time in full health was varied until participants were indifferent between alternatives. The trade-off being asked for here was 'shorter periods of life in full health for longer periods of life with lower quality of life' (Salkeld *et al.*, 2000: 342). Given the choices above, a person may respond to the preference options as follows, with a tick (√) indicating their preferred choice:

1.	A. CFS for 30 years	√	B. full health for 25 years
2.	A. CFS for 30 years	√	B. full health for 22 years
3.	A. CFS for 30 years	√	B. full health for 21 years
4.	A. CFS for 30 years		B. full health for 20 years
5. √	A. CFS for 30 years		B. full health for 19 years
6. √	A. CFS for 30 years		B. full health for 18 years

The 'point of indifference' between options is at option 4. This set of preference choices returns the conclusion that 20 years in full health is just as good as 30 years with CFS, or a willingness to 'trade-off' ten years of life. Using the utility weight formula x/t (where x = years in full health and t = years with disease) then U – the utility weight – is $20/30 = 0.67$. This figure may be transformed into a QALY: thus living with CFS for 1 year yields 0.67 QALYs. The result can also be specified in terms of QALYs 'gained': living with CFS for 30 years yields $0.67 \times 30 = 20$ QALYs.

In Salkeld *et al.*'s study, extremely low mean utility weights assigned to the three non-full health options (fear of falling 'Mary' = 0.67; 'good' hip fracture 'Jean' = 0.31; 'bad' hip fracture 'Elizabeth' = 0.05) suggested that 'most women were prepared to trade off considerable length of life to avoid the reduction in quality of life that happens after a hip fracture' (Salkeld *et al.*, 2000: 343). Although Salkeld *et al.* compared the utility weights assigned by those women in their sample who had and had not actually suffered a hip fracture – and found no significant difference in weights – clearly there are issues to be addressed in this method. Firstly in real life, there can be no knowing of the two alternatives on offer with the 'certainty' that Dolan *et al.* (1996a, 1996b) indicate the TTO method requires. Secondly, the way that options get weighted clearly depends on the way they are described. As Table 6.1 shows, apparently fine-grained differences in EuroQOL health state descriptions produce quite divergent utility values. Other issues also arise – for example not only the questionable realism of many TTO 'choices' – but also the reliability and validity of measures such as the EuroQOL with very elderly people. Coast *et al.* (1997) assessed the validity and reliability of the EuroQOL in elderly people, focusing particularly on people's ability to self-complete the scale. They state:

> Ability to self-complete the EuroQOL was found to be strongly related to both increased age and reduced cognitive function ... This research points to the need for rigorous studies (such as randomized controlled trials) to assess the impact of the format of administration of the EuroQOL on the scores obtained. (Coast *et al.*, 1997: 1)

The third utility measure employs the standard gamble (SG) method. This method asks respondents to take a gamble, or to weigh the odds, in two alternative states of health to arrive at a utility judgment. To return to our earlier example, such a method might ask a person the following question.

> Imagine that you have chronic fatigue syndrome and that you feel constantly tired, lethargic and have pain in your joints almost every day. You have some problems with shopping for yourself, lifting things and concentrating on work for more than an hour or so at a time. You have tried the most commonly prescribed medications but they have not helped. An experimental drug is available that would totally eliminate your chronic fatigue syndrome and restore full health. Unfortunately it carries a small but serious risk of toxic side effects.
>
> Which would you prefer? 90 per cent chance of perfect health and 10 per cent chance of immediate death or 100 per cent chance of life with CFS.

Like the TTO method, the relative odds can be varied until the respondent is unable to express a clear preference for one state. Thus we could vary the odds such that the choice demanded was between an 85 per cent chance of perfect health and a 15 per cent chance of sudden death, or a 100 per cent chance of life with CFS; between a 95 per cent chance of perfect health and a 5 per cent chance of sudden death or a 100 per cent chance of life with CFS and so on. When a respondent is indifferent between the two options (say at the 90 per cent chance of perfect health and 10 per cent chance of immediate death or 100 per cent chance of life with CFS stage) the utility weight is calculable from the following formula:

$$U(CFS) = 0.90 \times U(\text{Perfect Health}) + 0.10 \times U(\text{Death})$$
$$U(CFS) = 0.90 \times (1.0) + 0.10 \times (0) \text{ thus } U(CFS) = 0.90$$

An alternative approach to using the standard gamble method may pose a question in terms of anticipated life expectancy. For example:

> you have been diagnosed with prostate cancer. This reduces your life expectancy to ten years compared to a healthy person your age. A surgical treatment is available. If this treatment is successful, it would increase your life expectancy to be the same as a healthy person your age – 30 years. However, this surgery involves a risk of death. What risk of death would you accept?

If a respondent was willing to accept a 25 per cent risk of death, this can be respecified as saying that a life expectancy of ten years and a 25 per cent chance of death within two weeks in exchange for a 75 per cent chance of life expectancy of 10 years become equivalently attractive options. As the standard utility of expectable life is $U(30 \text{ yrs}) = 1.0$ and that of death is $U(0 \text{ yrs}) = 0.0$, then the utility weight is simply derived from the relative odds accepted. That is $U(10 \text{ yrs}) = 0.75 \times U(30 \text{ yrs}) + 0.05 \times U(0 \text{ yrs}) = 1.00 \times U(10 \text{ yrs})$. Accordingly: $((0.75 \times 1.0) + (0.05 \times 0.0) = U(10 \text{ yrs}) = 0.75))$.

Such studies allow for the relative costing of medical procedures in terms of cost per QALY and, in principle, for the differential weighting of forms of health care provision into 'league tables'. Another key use for utility weight analyses is the investigation of the weights assigned not by patients, but by *their doctors*. While their study addressed doctors' HIV utilities, as Owens *et al.* (1997: 77) point out:

> understanding of quality of life (QOL) with human immunodeficiency virus (HIV) is important because the merits of prevention and treatment alternatives may depend substantially on how these interventions affect QOL. Physicians' views about QOL are important, because they influence the therapeutic options that physicians consider or offer, the recommendations that physicians make, and because they are important for the analysis of certain policy questions.

Owens *et al.*'s study assessed physicians' utilities of health states for HIV with hepatitis B as a comparison. The TTO method returned median utilities of 0.833 for asymptomatic HIV, 0.417 for symptomatic HIV and 0.167 for AIDS. Each two-way comparison was statistically significant at the 0.01 level. Median utilities for asymptomatic hepatitis B, mildly symptomatic hepatitis B, and severely symptomatic hepatitis B were 0.917, 0.667 and 0.167. Again each comparison was statistically significant. With one year in full health equal to one QALY, then living for one year with asymptomatic HIV equals 0.833 QALYs. One year with symptomatic HIV equals 0.417 QALYs (just under 60 per cent less 'valuable' than a year in full health) and one year with full AIDS (or severely symptomatic hepatitis B) is worth 0.167 QALY, or, in other words, this is a year of life that has only slightly more 'utility' than death.

Owens *et al.* (1997) show that, although *doctors* varied substantially in their ratings of health states, they assessed the utility of life with HIV, including asymptomatic infection, as so severely reduced as, in the case of AIDS itself, to be barely distinguishable from being dead. This finding is in tension with Tsevat *et al.* (1999) who found that when *patients* with HIV were asked to 'trade off' life years for a return to 'full health', they were reluctant to do so: not only did patients often report an *improved* QOL *after* infection, but they clearly differ from the physicians surveyed by Owens *et al.* (1997) in the 'utility' they assign to life with HIV.

That utility perceptions may shape treatment decisions is shown by Patil *et al.*'s (2001) study of the preference values of physicians with regard to hepatitis C (HCV) and the use of antiviral therapy treatment. Patil *et al.* (2001) note that while most people with hepatitis C are asymptomatic, infection can lead to cirrhosis, cancer and death. As such, doctors making treatment decisions, and their patients, have to balance (trade off) the potential costs of HCV treatment – medication side effects and the cost of therapy – against potential future benefits. The most frequently used medications cause a number of unpleasant side effects and the cost of treatment is high. On the other hand a good response to medication is associated with undetectable viral load, improved liver function, and gains in health-related QOL.

Patil *et al.* (2001) also note that 'physicians' perspectives on HCV and its treatment may influence the advice that they give about treatment appropriateness. Patil *et al.* (2001) used an alternative methodology for measuring utilities, a visual analogue scale anchored on 0 per cent = death and 100 per cent = life without hepatitis C. Participants rated vignette descriptions of health states (see Table 6.4), derived from 'findings of our previous study of symptoms in patients with HCV and on a consensus of a group of hepatologists' (Patil *et al.*, 2001). With visual analogue scales (as in the EuroQOL 5D) participants simply draw a line on the scale to indicate their preference value. Participants also nominated the threshold sustained viral response rate to medication that they believed would be necessary for them to make a recommendation to their patients that they commence treatment.

Patil *et al.* (2001) report that 'physicians felt that hepatitis C causes a dramatic reduction in health status'. Utility values decreased rapidly as the severity of symptomatology increased (with the correlation statistically significant at the 0.001 level). Median preference value for Health State 1 ('No Symptoms, No Cirrhosis') was 88 per cent (or 0.88 QALY), or asymptomatic HCV infection was rated as a 12 per cent reduction in life

Table 6.4 Descriptions of Hepatitis C health states and treatment side effects from the Patil *et al.* (2001) study

Health state 1	Hepatitis C with no symptoms, no cirrhosis	No physical symptoms May transmit to sexual partner May develop cirrhosis
Health state 2	Hepatitis C with mild symptoms, no cirrhosis	Sometimes do not feel rested Tire more easily than usual May transmit to sexual partner May develop cirrhosis
Health state 3	Hepatitis C with moderate symptoms, no cirrhosis	Frequently do not feel rested Tire easily Limited in physical activities May transmit to sexual partner May develop cirrhosis
Health state 4	Hepatitis C with mild symptoms, cirrhosis	Sometimes do not feel rested Tire more easily than usual May transmit to sexual partner Have cirrhosis May get liver cancer May get liver failure
Health state 5	Hepatitis C with severe symptoms, cirrhosis	Sleep is disturbed Usually feel tired Limited in physical activities including work Little interest in sex Have cirrhosis May get liver cancer May need liver transplant
Treatment side effects	Side effects of treatment for hepatitis C appetite	Needle sticks three times a week Pills twice daily Flu-like symptoms Fever, chills, nausea, headache, poor Tend to improve after the first two weeks Tiredness, difficulty sleeping irritability, difficulty concentrating Chance of other life threatening medical problems that go away after treatment is completed such as low blood count, hair loss and depression

quality as compared to life without. The median preference value for the most severe health state (Health State 5 'Severe Symptoms, Cirrhosis' was only 18 per cent (utility = 0.18 QALY) representing a decrement in QOL of 82 per cent compared to life without HCV.

The median preference value for life with the side effects therapy was 47 per cent (utility = 0.47) indicating that treatment side effects themselves were assigned a preference value suggesting that QOL was less than half as good on antiviral treatment as compared to life without HCV. In terms of level of therapeutic response necessary to recommend treatment, a median of a 60 per cent sustained response rate was obtained (in contrast to the 30 per cent response rate offered by current antiviral therapy). Patil *et al.* (2001) report no significant correlations between preference values for hepatitis C health states, ratings of side effects of therapy and treatment thresholds.

As they recognize, Patil *et al.*'s (2001) findings offer an interesting parallel to those of Owen *et al.* (1997). The parallels suggest that the two different methodologies (time trade-off and visual analogue scale) obtain sufficiently similar results to offer support to each other, a finding echoed by Hakim and Pathak's (1999) study of the comparability of rating scales, standard gamble and discrete choice conjoint modelling methods. The use of a visual analogue scale does, however, have considerable advantages in terms of its simplicity of administration (Nord, 1991), although Selai and Trimble (1997) have noted that a number of patient groups may have considerable difficulties with the technique.

As did Owen *et al.* (1997), Patil *et al.* (2001) report a very wide range for physicians' preference ratings of treatment side effects, suggesting that while doctors' beliefs about the impact of side effects vary substantially they are, overall, negative. The absence of a correlation between ratings of treatment side effects and thresholds for recommending treatment suggests either inadequate knowledge of the disease among primary care doctors or the operation of preconceived notions about the disease and its treatment. This finding is, again, in keeping with the literature which suggests that both doctors' health state preferences and the disability weights they assign to particular conditions, may differ substantially from their patients (Costantini *et al.*, 2000; Rothwell *et al.*, 1997), and are considerably less positive (AbouZahr and Vaughan, 2000).

Noting that Treadwell *et al.* (2000) showed that HCV patients preferred to expedite their periods of poor health and higher utilities for therapy, even with side effects, than for life with delayed treatment, Patil *et al.* (2001) suggest that, in their study, 'in contrast, the physicians…had a relatively high threshold for recommending treatment, which would lead them to postpone therapy in the majority of cases'. Patil *et al.* (2001) suggest that one of the ways in which utility analysis may be of benefit is in facilitating doctor–patient decision-making on the basis of mutually understood utility preferences.

DALYs and Their Difficulties

Brown (2001: 769) suggests, based on the WHO's 'World Health Report 2001' that:

> psychiatric and neurological disorders account for nearly a third of the world's disability, measured in years lived with a disability. The burden is currently greatest in the industrialised countries, mainly because their populations are older, but as life expectancy in developing nations rises, these countries too are expected to see mental health problems become more prevalent. By 2020, depressive disorders are expected to be the second biggest cause of disease burden worldwide. (WHO, 2001)

This view is based on the DALY, or disability adjusted life year, a statistic representing 'years lived with a disability' or, alternatively, the 'burden of disease'. As was noted in Chapter 1, such estimates are contrary to Cummins's (2001b) view that absolute levels of international subjective well-being have been unchanged over the last twenty or so years. Data in the *World Health Report 2001*, which also notes that 'in Australia … depression is ranked as the fourth most common cause of the total disease burden, and is the most common cause of disability' (WHO, 2001: 88), are consistent with work by Lewis and Wilkinson (1993) which suggests that profound, persistent unhappiness and anxiety was reported by 22 per cent of respondents in 1977 and 31 per cent in 1986, or James's (1997) analysis of dramatically increased suicide rates in Western countries over the last 50 years.

Arnesen and Nord (1999: 1423) note that the aim of the DALY is ambitious: they cite the International Burden of Disease Network (1998, cited in Arnesen and Nord, 1999: 1423) as suggesting that, while 'the burden of disease has yet to entirely replace traditional approaches to the assessment of health needs as an influence on political decision making', this development is clearly anticipated by the project. The concept of the DALY is complementary to the QALY and is designed to assist with the identification of health problems and their relative magnitude, the recognition of disease patterns, the prioritization of health problems and to inform allocation of health care resources (AbouZahr and Vaughan, 2000; Murray, 1994; Murray and Acharya, 1997). In the World Health Report (e.g. WHO, 2000, 2001), the primary summary measure of population health used is otherwise known as Disability-Adjusted Life Expectancy, or DALE. DALEs are described by Sadana *et al.* (n.d.: 3) as:

> measures [of] the equivalent number of years of life expected to be lived in full health, or healthy life expectancy … As a summary measure of population health, DALE combines information on the impact of premature death and of disability and other non-fatal health outcomes.

DALYs have also been described as a 'health gap measure that quantifies loss of health for a population against a normative standard, and are not intended to be a measure of total well-being' (Salomon *et al.*, 2001: 268). Murray and Lopez (1997, cited in AbouZahr and Vaughan, 2000: 656) suggest that the development of the DALY was driven by the fact that:

> given the current state of health measurement, most analyses must ultimately fall back on measures of mortality, morbidity and disability. Analyses of outcomes, determinants, resources and even intervention effectiveness in reproductive health require clear and unambiguous specificity to facilitate meaningful measurement.

DALYs are thus intended to offer 'clear and unambiguous specificity to facilitate meaningful measurement'. As QALYs represent numerically the years of healthy life lived, so DALYs are a measure of the number of years of healthy life lost. DALYs, like QALYs, multiply the number of years lived by a quantification of the quality of those years and, whereas we have seen that QALYs employ what are termed 'utility' weights of health states (for example, recall that the utility weight of a 'bad' hip fracture was = 0.05 in the Salkeld *et al.*, 2000 study), DALYs use 'disability weights' to summarize the 'burden of disease'. Disability weights are assigned according to the classification of diseases, injuries and their sequelæ in the International Classification of Diseases (ICD-9) ((WHO, 1975) into 107 causes of death and 483 disabling sequelæ of illness or injury. Determination of disability weights is achieved by a process which begins with premature mortality deaths being assigned to a disease category and grouped by age, sex and demographic region based on death records where these are available. Standard protocols for DALY calculation specify that each state of ill health is assigned a disability weight by 'expert judgment' on the familiar scale from death to perfect health on a metric from 1.0 to 0.0 where death records are unavailable (Murray and Lopez, 1996). Years of healthy life lost are estimated on the basis of the difference between actual ages of death and the ideal standard life expectancy (in the 1993 exercise, 82.5 years for women and 80 years for men).

In the case of specific disabilities, incidence by age, sex and demographic region are derived from official records where available, or from the opinions of experts where not. Years lived with a disability are obtained by multiplying the expected duration of the disability (to remission or death) by a disability weight which supposedly reflects the average severity of the disability 'burden' when compared to full health or death. Having defined seven disability classes the Global Burden of Disease (GBD) project then assigned a weighting, based on expert consensus, to each of the 483 disabling conditions using person trade-off methods (on which more follows). When these assessments were being made expert panels were 'asked to evaluate the average individual with the condition described taking into account the average social response or milieu' (AbouZahr and Vaughan, 2000: 656). Quite what 'the average individual' who is HIV positive could possibly be is difficult to imagine (are they male or female? young or old? gay, straight or bisexual? perhaps they are the arithmetic mean of these categories – an androgynous, middle-aged person with serious sexual identity issues?), and the notion that there might be such a thing as an 'average social response or milieu' for, say, HIV, which manages to take the mean response of societies across sub-Saharan Africa, the Asia/Pacific and the former socialist economies of the Eastern Bloc, actually is, in practice, unimaginable.

Such reliance on a priori categorization is (almost) guaranteed to produce such difficulties. In this context, it is of note that in their study of the QOL of people with HIV/AIDS in Dublin (using the SEIQoL-DW[2], Hickey et al. (1996) found that the higher order categorization 'people with HIV/AIDS' (precisely the variety of umbrella disease categorization employed in the ICD-9, and hence the global burden of disease project in the assignment of disability weights) was entirely inadequate to capture the variability in the commonalities that *sub-groups* of the diagnostic group 'people with HIV/AIDS' showed in their estimations of the domain weights of various QOL domains. For example, gay people with HIV/AIDS and injecting drug users with HIV/AIDS nominated different issues as having a major impact on their QOL and, similarly, those with asymptomatic HIV identified comparable issues both to those in the study with 'full-blown' AIDS and HIV negative controls. Similar problems of misleading patient groupings, and the questionable reliance on average population scores, are identified by Fayers and Bjordal (2001) in their critique of Sprangers et al. (2000) on the QOL of people with chronic medical conditions. Fayers and Bjordal (2001: 978) note that:

> the investigators group the disorders with abandon; they combine thyroid-gland impairments with diabetes, to form a 'disease cluster' of endocrinological disorders, and multiple sclerosis, a debilitating illness with no prospect of recovery, together with migraine … for some diseases, population surveys will commonly be characterised by many cases of low severity, which may make average HRQL values seem close to those of the normal population, even though for a common disease the small proportion of severely ill patients could represent a large number of individuals who urgently need attention.

Despite these difficulties DALYs are, like QALYs, straightforward to compute. DALYs are calculated by multiplying the disability weighting for the specific condition by the number of years lived in that health state and added to the number of years lost due to the disease. The initial calculation of unweighted DALYs lost due to a particular disease in a specific population group is then found by employing the formula:

Years lost due to premature death = Expected standard lifetime – Age at death + Time lived with a disability = Duration of disability × Severity weighting

With future burdens discounted at 3 per cent per annum and differential weightings that value the quality of years lived in childhood and old age less, we can see, in Arnesen and Nord's (1999: 1423) example, that:

If the utility of deafness is 0.67, the disability weight of deafness is $1 - 0.67 = 0.33$.

Disregarding age weighting and discounting, and assuming life expectancy of 80 years, a deaf man living 50 years represents $0.67 × 50 = 33.5$ QALYs gained and $0.33 × 50 + 30 × 1 = 46.5$ DALYs lost.

By employing DALYs it is possible to identify – as the WHO has for depression – global patterns in the prevalence and 'burden' of various diseases. Table 6.5 illustrates the comparative rankings that may then be afforded by the methodology, in this case the differential burden of disease in the area of reproductive health 'carried' in various parts of the world by men and women.

Among the many objections to DALYs identified by Arnesen and Nord (1999) the foremost is perhaps the most difficult: they state that: 'While the idea of expressing burden of disease in a single index is tempting, any attempt to summarise information about quality of life and length of life in one number is bound to run into conceptual and methodological problems' – the same objection made by Edgerton (1996) and Taylor (1994) to expressing the concept of QOL itself in numerical terms. Arnesen and Nord (1999) identify a range of conceptual problems in the DALY. They suggest that the DALY procedures of discounting future health gains and losses and of age weighting not only discourage preventive medicine, but also discriminate against children, old people and future generations – with the estimates of life expectancy selected tending to discriminate against women. The expert panels' approach to the assignment of disability weights ensures that the weights assigned reflect the prior values, beliefs and expectancies of a skewed sample, who may or may not view, say, deafness in the same way that deaf people do or assign the same 'utility' to it. As Rothwell et al. (1997: 1582) put it, not only do doctors demonstrate that they do not understand which aspects of health actually matter to their patients but also that 'doctors are not good at estimating the overall quality of life of their patients'.

As such, age weighting and discounting measures central to the DALY procedure reflect not the *utility of life to individuals*, but rather the *societal usefulness of people's years of life*. Arnesen and Nord (1999) argue that 'the DALY approach implicitly attaches lower value to life extending

Table 6.5 Total DALYs lost due to reproductive ill-health in women and men of reproductive age as a percentage of total DALYs lost in the 15–44 year age group, 1990

	Total DALYs lost (%)									
	STDs excluding HIV		HIV		Maternal conditions	Reproductive cancers		Total		
	Female	Male	Female	Male		Female	Male	Female	Male	
Established marked economics	2.36	0.10	0.99	4.08	2.09	3.18	0.02	8.62	4.20	
Former socialist economies	3.52	0.30	0.03	0.09	6.25	2.83	0.03	12.63	0.41	
Sub-Saharan Africa	6.31	1.79	8.38	6.29	24.45	0.54	0.02	39.69	8.54	
India	6.58	2.49	0.20	0.43	19.19	1.42	0.01	27.40	2.93	
China	0.21	0.05	0.00	0.01	6.91	0.99	0.01	8.12	0.06	
Asia/Pacific	7.00	2.05	0.14	0.24	14.55	1.66	0.01	23.36	2.30	
Middle East	1.47	0.32	0.03	0.18	18.70	0.97	0.02	21.17	0.51	
Latin America/Caribbean	3.97	0.60	1.06	3.63	9.64	2.14	0.02	16.80	4.25	
World	4.23	1.09	1.78	2.02	14.47	1.42	0.01	21.90	3.12	

Source: AbouZahr and Vaughan (2000).

programmes for disabled people than to corresponding programmes for people without disability'. They illustrate the discriminatory possibilities of the DALY by offering a comparative quantification of the differential value (quality?) attached to one year of life for people with and without disabilities. Arnesen and Nord (1999: 1424) note that:

> disability weightings in use [Murray, 1996] tell us that the value of one year for 1000 people without disabilities on average is set equivalent to the value of one year for 9524 people with quadriplegia, 4202 people with dementia, 2660 blind people, 1686 people with Down's syndrome without cardiac malformation, 1499 deaf people, 1236 infertile people, and 1025 underweight or overweight people (2 SD from mean weight : height ratio)

Both AbouZahr and Vaughan (2000) and Arnesen and Nord (1999) are concerned with the very specific problems caused by the methodology used by the expert panels to assess disability weights such as these. The procedure used (an amended version of the time trade-off method) was the person trade-off technique (Murray, 1996). In the DALY protocol, the expert panels answered two person trade-off questions, and consistency between the two answers was then forced. The first question (Person trade-off 1 below) demands an abstract judgment about the relative value of the lives of people with and without disabilities, while the second asks experts to rate the value of cures for different chronic conditions in relation to therapeutic activities that may extend life. Arnesen and Nord (1999: 1424) explain the issue here clearly: 'How many people cured of blindness does the respondent consider equal to prolonging the lives of 1000 people? If the response is 5000, the corresponding disability weight of blindness is 1000 : 5000 = 0.2.'

Calculating a disability weight from the first person trade-off is a rather chilling exercise. The question asked is:

Person trade-off 1
You are a decision maker who has enough money to buy only one of two mutually exclusive health interventions. If you purchase intervention A, you will extend the life of 1000 healthy [non-disabled] individuals for exactly one year, at which point they will all die. If you do not purchase intervention A, they will all die today. The alternative use of your scarce resources is intervention B, with which you can extend the life of n individuals with a particular disabling condition [blindness, deafness, Down syndrome] for one year. If you do not buy intervention B, they will all die today; if you do buy intervention B, they will die at the end of exactly one year.

The expert's task is to provide the n in question: how many disabled people's lives are worth the same as 1,000 'healthy' people's? The question presupposes that the answer will *have* to be more than 1,000 and the transformation of this hypothetical number to a disability weight is straightforward. As Murray and Lopez (1996) note: 'If the participant judges that 1000 healthy people would have an equal claim on the resources as 8000 people with some severe disability, the weight assigned to that particular disability is equal to 1 minus 1000 divided by 8000, or 0.875' (cited in Arnesen and Nord, 1999: 1424). Perhaps a more serious methodological concern is forced consistency between the two weightings. In methodological terms, it is important that two judgments should reflect the same valuation of the same health state. However, while *methodologically* coherent, this procedure raises many of the same *conceptual* incoherencies as the necessity of forced choice responses to individual items on psychometric QOL measures discussed in Chapter 4. Again Arnesen and Nord (1999: 1424) describe the difficulties engendered by the entirely sensible (in methodological terms) requirement that the two person trade-off valuations are equivalent:

> to see how this works, consider the case of blindness. Assume that a panellist, on ethical grounds, responds that extending the life of 1000 sighted people and 1000 blind people is equivalent. The resulting disability weighting for blindness is zero. Assume that in the second question the panellist answers that relieving 5000 people of blindness is as valuable as prolonging the lives of 1000 people. This gives a disability weighting of 0.2. The valuation so far has yielded two different disability weightings for the same health state. The panellist is now asked to reconsider these responses and choose a new pair of answers to produce the same disability weighting. The panellist might end up by selecting PTO1 = 1100 and PTO2 = 11 000, which together yield a disability weighting of 0.09. This weighting, however, does not correspond to any actual preference of the respondent: it is basically an artefact, generated by the requirement for consistency between questions that address different issues.

Such issues raise serious doubts about the validity of the disability weights calculation protocol. Indeed, so serious are the concerns raised that the continued use of the metric has been subject to critical review (Murray *et al.*, 1999) by the WHO. It would seem that these procedures must be considered extremely carefully: it is to such a review that we now turn.

Difficulties with the QALY and DALY Approach: Dying and Disability

Cummins (1997b: 126) describes the QALY as a 'bizarre notion based on invalid psychometric assumptions' and, in particular, is scathing of the standard use of hypothetical scenarios. He suggests that:

the QALY methodology is complete nonsense in that it implies any relationship with subjective QOL. No one can validly respond to such hypothetical situations... So how does all of this fit with the idea that people can validly report on the vicarious experience of disability? Of course it does not fit at all. The only people who can report on this experience are people who have the particular form of disability under discussion.

Nord (1999) argues that the key weakness of the QALY is that researchers ask healthy people to imagine they are ill and then ask them to describe their position on the allocation of medical resources. As we have seen, Polsky *et al.* (2001) suggest we should be very sceptical about accepting the preferences of the general public about the relative utility of various health states as representative of the views of patients. Nord (1999, 1992a) argues instead that we should be asking those with illnesses or disabilities the difficult questions about health resource allocation. A closely allied criticism of the approach is that both the measures themselves, and the procedures whereby they are arrived at, are highly technical for non-specialists and are not transparent to ordinary people. Work by Mulkay *et al.* (1987), Morris and Durand (1989) and Nord (1991) suggests that expressing QOL in terms of numbers is highly problematic: to most people such numbers have little meaning as they have no experience with them in everyday life.

In consideration of the views of 'ordinary people', Koch (2001) reports an intriguing study addressing precisely the points raised above. The notion that people *can* predict their evaluations of future health states is, clearly, central to the entire QALY programme. We have seen that there are reasons to be cautious about the use of hypothetical scenarios especially when we consider the artificial nature of the scenarios that people are asked to judge (Nord, 1999) as well as the artefactual nature of the choices experts (and patients) may be asked to make (Arensen and Nord, 1999), not to mention the dramatically different evaluations that asking 'experts' about their 'patients'' lives, and 'patients' about their own lives produce (Cummins, 1997b; Goodinson and Singleton, 1989; Ferrans, 1990). Indeed, in their study of terminally ill patients using the EORTC QOL Questionnaire,[3] Sahlberg-Blom *et al.* (2001: 550, my emphasis) report that, 'despite having an *assessed* lower quality of life in many dimensions than people in general ... patients experienced happiness and satisfaction during their last month of life'.

Koch's (2001) study, in an imaginative twist, takes Cummins's and Nord's point and does precisely what they suggest. Koch surveyed persons with acquired disabilities on a range of QOL issues and found, for example, that *after* disablement 'whatever the quantity of time spent with family, friends, and on spiritual matters the quality of the experience in each area was richer and more meaningful' (Koch, 2001: 459). As he notes, such a finding echoes Young and McNicoll's (1998) whose study of the perceived QOL of people with ALS (motor neuron disease) found that participants reported both a richer spiritual life and stronger interpersonal ties than before diagnosis.

Koch concludes that:

> the experience of disability forces changes in perception and values depending on a range of accommodations. These are based on the presence or absence of social and familial support as well as the specific nature of the physical restriction. If support exists – in the home, work place, and the greater community – people may decide to continue with a restricted life for far longer than might have earlier been anticipated. If however support is absent, and life becomes restricted ... life quality diminished as a result ... Prospective health planning instruments axiomatically assume individuals can predict accurately the choices they would make in the event of a physically limiting condition ... that among study respondents was extremely rare ... That most respondents report a strong life quality, despite their moderate to severe physical limitations, apparently speaks not to a 'disability paradox' ... but to a process of social and familial adaptation whose benefits were clearly unanticipated by respondents prior to injury or diagnosis.

Such findings are both immensely encouraging and simultaneously rather depressing: they raise very serious questions about assigning 'disability weights' to disease states, and must call into question the idea that it is possible to make, sensibly, statements like 'the utility of tetraplegia is 0.13'. Again we see that, when the 'patients' whose QOL researchers and practitioners attempt to fix numerically are *themselves* asked about it, QOL is better understood as a *process* phenomenon: not as a once-and-for-all metric.

The 'medical model' underpinning QALYs and DALYs uses 'the pathogenesis and natural history of disease as the conceptual framework for assessing morbidity and mortality and for interpreting the effects of various interventions' (Hyder *et al.*, 1998, cited by Koch, 2001: 455). The use of medicalized, or pathologized, conceptions of QOL (the absence of symptoms; the ability to score better than 'dead' or 'unconscious' on the EuroQOL; ideas like the QALY and the DALY) has been criticized on both empirical and theoretical grounds (for example, Cummins, 1997b; Koch, 1994; Kuczewski, 1999; Nord, 1992a, 1999; Young *et al.*, 1994). Koch notes that it is a perspective 'held in particular contempt by writers advancing a "disabilities perspective" who argue, with Chamie (1995), that physical differences are not illnesses and should not be treated as such' (Koch, 2001: 455). In closing this chapter, then, it would seem that many would agree with Aksoy's (2000: 22) evaluation of QOL measurement in medical settings when he argues that 'it is not possible to measure the QOL of an individual either accurately or reliably. It is, therefore, our duty to respect individuals' lives and try to improve their condition as much as possible'.

In Summary

QALYs and DALYs attempt to standardise the QOL provided by different interventions, to arrive at cost : benefit ratios for medical practices, and to express the 'burden of disease' in a 'common currency'. These approaches are taken very seriously by influential global organizations – such as the World Bank and the WHO. However, when doctors, patients and the general public rate different (ill) health states, using techniques such as TTO studies, they routinely return – sometimes grossly – divergent views about the utility or quality of life. Many people with conditions that doctors regard as so near to death as not to be worth arguing about regularly report that the quality of their life *after* diagnosis or disablement is higher than previously. Despite the serious conceptual, methodological and practical difficulties entailed, the future of this technology seems to be assured: the pressing question is, then, how to tame it.

Notes

1. The WHOQOL 100 Scale consists of six domains measuring QOL in the areas of physical, psychological, independence, social relationships, environment and spiritual well-being. As the title suggests the scale contains 100 items divided unevenly between the domains. Psychometric properties are reported by the WHOQOL Group (1998).
2. The SEIQOL (McGee et al., 1991; O'Boyle et al., 1993) rates subjective QOL in medical contexts using a complex scale and multiplies scores derived from 'best possible – worst possible' visual analogue scales by personally estimated weights on five descriptors of QOL selected by respondents.
3. The EORTC QLQ-30 (Aaronsson et al., 1993) consists of 30 questions covering physical functioning (5), role functioning (2), cognitive functioning (2), emotional functioning (4), social functioning (2), general quality of life (2), fatigue (3), nausea and vomiting (2), pain (2), and six single items (short of breath, trouble sleeping, lack of appetite, constipation, diarrhoea and financial problems).

Study Questions

- How might one know, with enough certainty to meaningfully evaluate its 'utility', what it is like to be rendered paraplegic?
- How well do concepts like Disability Adjusted Life Years reflect the views of people with disabilities about their lives?

- How do decisions about the 'quality of life' of patients actually get made in particular health care settings?
- What criteria should we employ to judge what is an 'acceptable' or 'unacceptable' quality of life?

Suggestions for Further Reading

Baldwin, S., Godfrey, C. and Propper, C. (eds) (1990) *Quality of Life: Perspectives and Policies*. London: Routledge.

Koch, T. (2001) Future states: the axioms underlying prospective, future-oriented, health planning instruments, *Social Science and Medicine*, 52: 453–65.

Nord, E. (1999) *Cost-value Analysis in Health Care*. Cambridge: Cambridge University Press.

Nord, E. (1992a) An alternative to QALYs: the saved young life equivalent, *British Medical Journal*, 305: 875–8.

CHAPTER 7

QOL research with special populations

It has been suggested that QOL offers the 'ultimate criterion for the assessment of the effectiveness of social care delivery' (Perry and Felce, 1995: 1). This chapter examines applied QOL research with 'special' populations as this research illustrates with particular clarity many of the methodological issues involved in the use of structured questionnaires. The questionable theoretical coherence of using individually measured QOL as an outcome measure of the quality of care or service practices, the relationship between etic and emic constructions of what constitutes 'quality of life', and the theoretical place of particular life circumstances/ social arrangements in the conceptualization of QOL are examined.

Applied QOL Research

Heal and Sigelman (1990: 174–5) suggest that:

> there are compelling philosophical reasons for providing mentally retarded consumers with opportunities to tell us how they perceive their lives and how they would like their lives to change ... developing any reliable and valid quality-of-life measure requires considerable effort ... [an] effort that promises to result in a fuller understanding of the lives of developmentally disabled citizens.

However, Emerson and Hatton (1994) suggest that, for this group and for people with mental health problems, the literature has, instead, focused on objective indices such as community participation, engagement in activity or skill levels. Reliance has been placed upon 'measurable "objective" indices which, by consensus are thought to be associated with a better quality of life ... such factors as physical health, access to health care, quality of housing ... employment status and disposable income' (Emerson and Hatton, 1994: 11). The relation of these variables to subjective assessments of life satisfaction or QOL is generally accepted as being weak. Where QOL has been employed as a variable in its own right, one of the major methodological difficulties in applied work has been the tendency for researchers to design their own scales, often with an unstated theoretical base, rather than conducting validation work on pre-existing scales. Cummins and co-workers suggested that, of over eighty such scales they had identified by 1994, none reached minimally acceptable standards

of psychometric validation (Cummins *et al.*, 1994). Perhaps in consequence, in their review of the British applied research, Emerson and
Hatton (1994: 12–13) noted that:

> given the generally acknowledged importance of listening to the views of
> the consumers of our services and the weak relationship between
> 'objective' indicators of quality of life and expressed life satisfaction, it is
> somewhat surprising that such a low proportion of studies have sought to
> elicit the views of service users.

It is not only British work that has failed to solicit the views of service
consumers. In his review of American ethnographic research, Edgerton
(1990: 153) suggested that while many studies have offered a rich picture of
people's vocational, residential and recreational patterns, they have failed
to give an adequate picture of:

> the actual quality of those lives, the life events that have had the greatest
> impact on these lives, or the feelings of the people themselves about their
> lives ... in short we know all too little about ... their satisfaction with those
> lives.

Edgerton advocates research based in ethnographic naturalism. Such an
approach is often described as 'emic', or grounded in the perspective of the
respondent, as opposed to 'etic' work which privileges the perspective of
the analyst. Emic approaches offer the opportunity, often through
prolonged contact with participants, 'to make inferences about
individuals' satisfaction with the quality of their lives that we believe are
both reliable and valid' (Edgerton, 1990: 155). As Edgerton suggests, this
approach – drawn as it is from the traditions of ethnomethodology rather
than 'positivistic behavioral science' (Edgerton, 1990: 154) – removes some
of the dilemmas inherent in positivist research on QOL, for example of
psychometric validity and reliability, discussed in Chapter 4, and is also
attentive to the ethics of 'emancipatory research' discussed in Chapter 3.

Studies in this tradition have suggested that people with intellectual
disabilities have a number of concerns about support services which have
a bearing on *their* judgments of the quality of their lives. Cattermole *et al.*
(1988), for example, found that people were deeply dissatisfied with the
independence they were allowed in the home environment. Bowd (1989)
observed that criteria employed by adults with mental retardation to
evaluate their quality of life differed from those of professionals. Sands *et
al.* (1991) found that, while levels of satisfaction with services were high
over all, services tended to enculturate a 'sense of dependency and
compliance' (Sands *et al.*, 1991: 313) and interviewees reported considerable dissatisfaction with the range of opportunities and choices
offered. Rapley *et al.* (1998) reported that many Australian adults with

intellectual disabilities are keenly aware of stigmatization and prejudice from 'normal' community members.

However, this work, while offering richly textured accounts of quality of life from the perspective of the individual participant, is difficult to use as a method for evaluating service quality. Such work is extremely time-consuming, is essentially open-ended and, by virtue of its attempted fidelity to the views of particular individuals, does not offer the sort of data that is readily amenable to aggregation and quantification. In consequence, there have been two major efforts to devise formal, psychometric QOL measures as evaluation tools in services for people with an intellectual disability. Cummins's work on the ComQOL has been discussed in Chapter 4. Here the focus is on the other widely used and researched measure, the Schalock and Keith (1996) *Quality of Life Questionnaire* (see Cummins, 1997c, for an overview and evaluation of scales used in applied intellectual disability research).

Population-Specific Measures – the Work of Schalock and Keith

Schalock and Keith have developed a conceptual model of QOL which is attentive to the issues discussed in Chapters 2 and 3. The Schalock and Keith model of QOL recognizes the multifactorial nature of the construct, its individually specific, yet culturally homogenous, domains of reference; and acknowledges that the experience of intellectual disability is essential to QOL judgments and, further, recognizes the interactive – indeed socially constructed – nature of the concept. From this explicit theoretical position they have developed a measurement instrument as an operationalization of their conceptual model in the form of the *Quality of Life Questionnaire* (QOL.Q; Schalock and Keith, 1996).

Schalock and Keith disagree with Cummins about whether QOL should be operationalized using a generic or population-specific conceptualization. Schalock and Keith's operationalization of 'quality of life' is such that four assumptions are reflected explicitly. They assume that (1) QOL is a unitary construct in the sense that there are no differences between the needs of people with mental retardation and those without for, for example 'affiliation, a sense of worthiness, decision making and choices'; that (2) QOL is the product of the interactions of self with others; that (3) QOL is an outcome of the meeting of basic needs and the discharge of basic responsibilities in community settings; and that (4) the QOL experienced by any individual is a subjective phenomenon determined by their perception of their situation rather than how the individual is seen by others (Schalock *et al.*, 1990: ii–iii).

Schalock *et al.* (1990) and Schalock and Keith (1996) report the development and psychometric validation of the QOL.Q, a 40-item measure which, with an American standardization population, reliably discriminated between respondents across a range of living and work environments, for example between residents of independent apartments and group homes (Schalock and Keith, 1996). The standardization manual suggests that factor analysis shows that items load reliably onto four factors – Satisfaction, Competence/Productivity, Empowerment/Independence and Social Belonging/Community Integration, a structure replicated by Rapley and Lobley (1995) in Britain. These factors were designed to reflect the core domains of life quality identified by the work of Andrews and Withey (1976), Campbell *et al.* (1976), Flanagan (1978) and others discussed above. Items tap each of the five domains of life quality identified in the integrative model of QOL offered by Felce and Perry (1996a) which was discussed in Chapter 2, and address explicitly at least four of the seven components identified by Cummins's (1997a) comprehensive definition of QOL and the dimensions identified in his 1998 review.

The theoretical approach Schalock and Keith adopt recognizes that subjective evaluations of life quality are individually calibrated. However, for the purposes of measurement, the QOL.Q assumes that the importance of the core domains of QOL is sufficiently comparable across individuals to allow the specification of a range of items which are treated as being of equivalent importance. While this approach can be criticized for blurring the individual-specific comparative weightings of QOL domains (an essential component of Cummins's ComQOL), it does allow for higher-order comparisons between studies or units of service.

Unlike the ComQOL-ID which separates the measurement of satisfaction with objective circumstances from the estimation of their importance, Schalock and Keith (1990, 1996) treat satisfaction as a component part of QOL judgments. However, acknowledging that basic human needs hold across cognitive levels, Schalock and Keith reflect Cummins's insistence that QOL is a universal construct, despite their divergent assumption that, while the construct may have a higher-order generality, the detail of the items which reflect QOL domains is influenced by individuals' immediate circumstances. Accordingly, Schalock and Keith (1996) argue that, if we are to describe the utility of services well, it is essential to address those issues in the lives of people with intellectual disabilities which are pertinent purely to this group.

Population-Specific QOL Measures as Service Evaluation Tools

The following section of the chapter describes in detail three small-scale service evaluation studies conducted in services for people with intellectual disabilities in Britain and Australia. These studies were designed to do three things. Firstly, they were to *triangulate* the life experience of service users afforded by the service in question: to gather data on a range of experiences which the services claimed to be supporting or providing in order to arrive at a synthesis of converging data about people's lives. Secondly, they were to evaluate the *utility* of using a well-validated and psychometrically-sound quality of life questionnaire (the QOL.Q) as an outcome measure in service evaluation practice. (Does it add useful information? Is it feasible as a measure given the characteristics of the population? Does the measure return acceptable levels of data? Is the data set compromised by unacceptable levels of missing data? Does the QOL data tell us something we didn't know on the basis of established measures? Is QOL an 'ultimate criterion'?) Thirdly, the studies were designed to answer questions about the measure at a *conceptual/theoretical level*. (Does the measure show appropriate statistical relationships to other measures – that is does it show convergent validity? Does the measure demonstrate sensitivity to change in quality of life over time? Is the measure contaminated by confounding variables?)

The studies described are small in scale. However, their inclusion here is designed to demonstrate that it is both sensible and feasible to conduct such limited analyses. Such studies, by the use of appropriate statistical procedures (for example a stringent alpha criterion, the employment of non-parametric statistics, and the use of less frequently employed indices such as measures of effect size), can provide results in which reasonable confidence can be placed in terms of their *indicative* use. That is to say, if studies such as those discussed below return data which provide unsatisfactory answers to the questions identified above, then we can be reasonably certain that either the quality of life measure in question is of little use or that larger-scale studies are unwarranted.

Britain – the Rapley and Beyer (1996, 1998) Studies

Rapley and Beyer (1996) report the use of the QOL.Q[1] in the evaluation of a small community residential service. The study suggested that, in common with much of the literature, the experience of adults with intellectual disabilities in community-based services could be characterized as being one of 'isolation and disengagement' (Rapley and Beyer, 1996: 31). Contacts with other people in community settings were sparse and primarily functional, with staff contact with service users in the domestic setting generally occurring at a low level, particularly in the area of assistance giving. Measured QOL entered into theoretically appropriate, and statistically significant, relationships with objective measures of community integration; for example, 'the extent to which people had and met friends was correlated with higher QOL.Q scores' (Rapley and Beyer, 1996: 38). Rapley and Beyer (1996) concluded that, in view of the consistent relationships between measured QOL and established service quality criteria, the addition of QOL measurement to 'traditional' evaluative indices such as adaptive behaviour, engagement and community participation was a potentially useful development.

Emerson and Hatton (1994, 1996) have pointed out that the results of many longitudinal studies of service quality have been confounded by the effect of differing ability levels of service users on outcome variables such as social integration or engagement, or by the employment of different informants, in different settings, in the measurement of outcomes. To be useful service evaluation instruments, therefore, QOL measures need to be sensitive to changes in service users' experience over time that is not attributable to gross changes in residential setting and consequent differential staffing expectations or values. Furthermore, such instruments should be resistant to confounding by service users' adaptive behaviour levels. In order to examine the utility of the QOL.Q – and hence quality of life assessment more generally – as a service evaluation tool, the follow-up study reported by Rapley and Beyer (1998) took account of both of these potentially confounding variables, firstly by replicating the study reported by Rapley and Beyer (1996) in the same service after a two-year interval and, secondly, by statistically controlling for the effects of differing participant abilities on the outcome variables selected for study.

In order that the study could, meaningfully, be compared to the existing service evaluation literature, data were collected on service users' experience in the major outcome domains identified by Emerson and Hatton (1994, 1996) as the most frequently used in the international literature. As such, well validated measures of adaptive behaviour, involvement in domestic routines and contact with support staff, and participation in community life were used. Measures selected were thus representative of those used in the relevant literature and, also, represented life domains which could – on the basis of the theoretical model of quality of life informing the QOL measure used – be expected to enter into statistical relationships with quality of life scores.

The *adaptive behaviour* levels of service users were described using Part One of the AAMD Adaptive Behaviour Scale (ABS) (Nihira *et al.*, 1975).[2] *Involvement in routines and contact with staff* was measured by direct observation using the computerised Momentary Time Sampling[3] data collection system (Beasley *et al.*, 1993) loaded onto a hand-held Psion Organiser. Behaviour of staff and participants was observed and the behaviour exhibited by target participants was coded under four categories: Activity, Social Activity, Staff Contact and Problem Behaviour. Coding categories include behaviours which may readily be observed in the domestic setting. Owing to known problems of observer error and drift, on some occasions two observers attended each observation session to allow inter-observer coding reliability to be assessed. *Participation in community life* was assessed using the Social Networks Questionnaire[4], a slightly modified form of the Lifestyles Questionnaire employed in the evaluation of the All-Wales Strategy (Evans *et al.*, 1994).

As with the previous study, ABS data were analysed as raw scores. Data from direct observations were converted into percentage of observed points at which the target behaviour was observed employing the MTSTAB program (Stein and Mansell, 1992). As the study was part of a larger comparison of institutional and community-based services, inter-observer reliabilities were estimated across all settings. A 5.72 per cent reliability sample (23 hours reliability observations out of 402 hours total observations) was taken. Mean occurrence reliabilities across observers and settings by observation category were: Activity = 93.16 per cent; Social Activity = 96.11 per cent; Contact = 94.48 per cent; Problem Behaviour = 91.90 per cent. Total participant engagement was computed as a variant of the definition offered by Stein and Mansell (1992). Engagement was computed as the sum of the percentage time each participant's behaviour was coded as Leisure/Recreation, Personal/Selfcare, Chores/Electrical, Chores/Other, Clear Social Act and Unclear Social Act across sessions. In addition to client behaviours, Positive, Negative, Neutral and Assistance-giving staff contact were summed to provide an overall mean score of all participant activity and associated staff contact.

Data from the Social Networks Questionnaire were coded using a minimally revised version of the framework described by Evans *et al.* (1987). The summary variable of 'Community Participation' was computed as the sum of scores on all SNQ categories, offering a global index of the extent of participants' social networks and the level of integration opportunities afforded by community-based activity. Quality of Life was computed as total QOL.Q score.

Statistical procedures

At the 5 per cent level the non-parametric Wilcoxon signed-ranks test indicated that participants' ABS Total scores showed significant changes over the two years separating the studies ($z = -2.04$, $p = 0.02$). As a conservative procedure, and on the basis of the theoretical concerns outlined by Emerson and Hatton (1994, 1996), it was assumed that this change in scores represented a possible confound of the other outcome measures. Accordingly a repeated measures ANCOVA was computed to examine changes in scores on the three summary variables of Engagement, QOL and Social Integration. Individuals' total ABS score, as measured in the first and second studies, was used as a varying covariate to control for the influence of adaptive behaviour levels of participants. Because of the small sample size and concerns about violations of assumptions for parametric tests, non-parametric statistics were employed to examine changes in sub-items of the summary variables over time.

Results

Table 7.1 reports summary data for the main effects of the repeated measures analysis of variance. While only changes for the QOL main effect and sub-items of the QOL.Q and SNQ reached statistical significance, a number of theoretically appropriate and indicative changes in observed scores reached significance at the 0.05 level. For the RMANCOVA, the effect size (partial eta squared, η^2) was used as an index of the magnitude of the main effect. Green *et al.* (1997: 230) define η^2 for the factor interpreted as 'the proportion of the variance of the dependent variable related to the factor, holding constant (partialling out) the covariate. Traditionally an η^2 of .01, .06 and .14 represent small, medium and large effect sizes respectively.' In this analysis partial eta squared therefore represents an index of the size of the change in observed outcome measures (dependent variables) related to the passage of time (Time 1 and Time 2 representing the two levels of the time factor), with adaptive behaviour levels partialled out. Observed levels are adjusted for one-tailed tests of significance.

As Table 7.1 shows, when adaptive behaviour levels are controlled for, the QOL measure shows a significant difference in mean scores between T1 and T2. The Social Integration measure shows a marginally significant difference in mean scores between T1 and T2, but no significant difference in mean Engagement scores was observed. Partial eta squared values suggest that the effect size of both of the significant results is strong.

Table 7.1 Change in QOL.Q scores over time – repeated measures analysis of covariance

Variable	Sum of squares	d.f	Mean square	F	Prob.	η^2
Quality of Life						
QOL	659.14	1	659.14	17.55	0.01	0.66
Error	338.08	9	37.56			
Regression	220.18	1	220.18	5.86		
Social Integration						
Social Integration	28.31	1	28.31	5.13	0.03	0.50
Error	27.60	5	16.07			
Regression	12.40	1	12.40	2.25		
Engagement						
Engagement	19.43	1	19.43	0.00	0.47	0.00
Error	49688.97	9	5521.00			
Regression	39.07	1	39.07	0.01		

Source: Rapley and Beyer (1998).

As noted above, because of the very small sample sizes, Rapley and Beyer (1998) used non-parametric statistics for their univariate analyses. One-tailed Wilcoxon matched pairs signed-ranks tests were computed to examine the changes over time in component items of the summary variables. A conservative α level of 0.01 was set for these comparisons: z values and one-tailed p for comparisons are reported. Obtained scores for T2 exceed those for T1 for all statistically significant comparisons reported.

These results show that a number of small-scale changes appear to have occurred in the network in the two years separating the two evaluation studies. Although Adaptive Behaviour Scale scores increased, the possibility that this change is due to measurement error (Felce and Perry, 1996b) is strong. Although overall mean levels of Engagement did not differ significantly over time, the level of variation in scores decreased, suggesting that engagement was more evenly spread across service users in the network at the second round of data collection. The pattern of service users' engagement in a range of domestic activities also appeared to have changed: for example, at the second round of data collection levels of 'No activity' had decreased. A noticeable increase in community-based activity appeared to have occurred – for example average SNQ Total Scores rose from 24.71 to 28.77. These increases in purposeful domestic activity and community-based activity were accompanied by statistically significant changes in mean QOL on all but the Social Belonging subscale.

Rapley and Beyer (1998) drew *limited and tentative* conclusions from these studies. They noted that, while an AB comparison design can only provide an indicative result, the finding of increased service user ability levels was in contrast to many other UK studies which have reported a plateau effect after an initial, post-resettlement, increment (e.g. Lowe *et al.*, 1993; Emerson and Hatton, 1996). Noting that Felce and Perry (1996) suggested that small changes in ABS scores require corroborative observational data in order to be interpretable, they argued that the small increases in observed domestic activity possibly offered such corroboration.

Secondly, they concluded that – when the confounds were controlled – multivariate analyses suggested that measures of the social integration and the QOL showed small increases over two years. Possibly reflecting these small changes in domestic activity and community-based activity, mean QOL scores improved, suggesting that the instrument is sensitive to such change.

Thirdly they suggested that QOL measurement appeared to reflect the gains identified by the other measures, and thus may add to evaluative practice but that, alone, QOL was an insufficient index of service users' experience. In order to achieve a rich description of service quality, objective indices are required to describe the detail of the participation in ordinary communities afforded to people with intellectual disabilities by community-based services.

Australia – the Rapley and Hopgood (1997) Study

Thirty-four adults with intellectual disabilities in five supervised community based residences participated in this study. Two residences were located in suburbs of a large regional city; the remaining three were located in small country towns. The study was designed both to consolidate the findings of the Rapley and Beyer (1996, 1998) work and to test further ideas about factors contributing to the QOL of people with intellectual disabilities. As such the study sought to evaluate the contribution that place of residence (urban versus rural) might make to QOL, and to assess the relationship between participants' sense of belonging to their community and their QOL.

As in the Rapley and Beyer studies, ability levels of service users were measured using the AAMD Adaptive Behaviour Scale (Nihira *et al.*, 1975). Engagement in domestic activity was measured using of the Index of Participation in Domestic Life (Raynes *et al.*, 1989a)[5] and participation in community life was measured using the Index of Community Involvement (Form II) (Raynes *et al.*, 1989b).[6] Participants' sense of community was assessed by employing the Neighbourhood Sense of Community Index (NSCI) (Pretty *et al.*, 1994).[7]

Analysis

The study examined the relationship between measures of key outcomes identified in the literature and tested the ability of the measures to discriminate between residential settings and between urban and rural locations. All measures yielded individual data, and scores for individuals were averaged across settings and measures. Examination of the data revealed no missing data or outliers. Patterns of relationships between measures were examined with correlational analyses using the Pearson product-moment correlation coefficient. In order to explore variation between settings analyses of variance were employed.

Analysis of covariance, with ABS scores as covariate to control for confounding by ability levels (Emerson and Hatton, 1994), was not necessary as the correlation between ABS scores and the IPDL only achieved significance at the 0.05 level. A positive, but weak, relationship was observed between the ABS (Part 1) and QOL.Q total ($r = 0.3$) with a small percentage predictive variance in QOL scores by ability levels ($r^2 = 0.09$). ABS scores and other summary measures were not correlated.

Prior to ANOVA, Levene's test (Levene, 1960) for homogeneity of variance was conducted to check for violation of parametric testing assumptions. A conservative criterion of $\alpha = 0.05$ was set. In the case of violation of assumptions non-parametric Kruskall-Wallis or Wilcoxon tests were employed. Univariate ANOVAs were conducted to examine differences between residential settings and rural and urban locations. Post hoc comparisons (Bonferroni tests) were conducted. A stringent criterion alpha of 0.01 was set due to the large number of analyses planned.

Relationships between the measures: exploratory analysis

QOL.Q sub-scales showed moderate to high inter-correlations. As expected from the literature, engagement (IPDL) was related to both higher ability levels and to lower levels of problem behaviour, but only marginally. Main summary measures (apart from the NSCI) entered into theoretically appropriate relationships with QOL scores. A high correlation was obtained between the IPDL and the QOL.Q.

If staff activity were the central mediating factor in service users' activities shown in many studies, the ICI and the IPDL should be positively correlated. However, no correlation was observed. This result suggests that the influence of staff activity, a confound in other studies, does not appear to be unduly influencing results here, and that the measures are tapping clearly differentiable aspects of individual activity in community and domestic settings. Empowerment and Satisfaction correlate significantly with the IPDL and the ABS. A high correlation was found between the IPDL and Competence, with which the ICI displayed a weak relationship. NSCI scores were inversely related to Competence scores. These relationships indicate that opportunities for meaningful activity in both domestic and community environments are associated with higher QOL, but that (as the Competence sub-scale primarily measures job satisfaction) these opportunities are more readily available to service users who are involved in some form of employment and higher ability levels. A strong sense of community is, however, less likely to be reported by these participants.

Table 7.2 Relationships between summary measures and QOL.Q sub-scales

	IPDL	ICI	NSCI	ABS Part 1	QOL.Q
IPDL	–	–	–	–	–
ICI	0.11	–	–	–	–
NSCI	–0.19	0.22	–	–	–
ABS. Part 1	0.38*	–0.15	0.01	–	–
ABS. Part 2	–0.33*	0.06	0.27	0.35*	–0.27
QOL.Q	0.67**	0.35**	–0.17	0.30**	–
Competence	0.66**	0.35*	–0.35*	0.09	0.80**
Empowerment	0.48**	0.06	0.00	0.34*	0.67**
Satisfaction	0.55**	0.16	–0.02	0.40**	0.68**
Social Belonging	–0.19	0.27	0.17	–0.12	0.37**

* = $p < 0.05$
** = $p < 0.01$
All other values non-significant at $p < 0.05$
Source: Rapley and Hopgood (1997).

Table 7.3 One-way of analyses of variance by place of residence

Variable	d.f.	F	Probability
QOL.Q Total	4,33	3.986	0.010
Competence	4,33	13.779	0.001
Levene's test	4,29	11.599	0.001
Kruskall-Wallis χ^2	4	13.874	0.007
ICI	4,33	12.612	0.001
IPDL	4,33	6.443	0.001
Levene's test	4,29	5.573	0.002
Kruskall-Wallis χ^2	4	16.462	0.002
NSCI	4,33	10.529	0.001

Source: Rapley and Hopgood (1997).

Univariate analyses

Univariate analyses were conducted to examine differences in outcomes by participants' place (specific group home) and location (urban vs. rural) of residence. Where the assumption of homogeneity of variance was violated, a non-parametric Kruskall-Wallis test was employed for the residence comparisons and the Wilcoxon rank sum test for the dichotomous urban vs. rural comparison. The results of the analysis of the summary measures are reported in Table 7.3.

Results of ANOVAs and subsequent post hoc analyses suggest that there are significant differences by residence on all summary measures – though marginally for total QOL (p = 0.010) – and on the Competence sub-scale.

For QOL total score, urban residences scored significantly higher (mean = 86.36, s.d. = 6.68) than rural residences (mean = 73.75, s.d. = 6.33). Individuals in urban locations also scored significantly higher on the ICI (mean = 10.09, s.d. = 1.97) than their rural counterparts (mean = 7.91, s.d. = 1.31). Wilcoxon rank sum tests confirmed that levels of community activity were significantly different, at the 5 per cent level, across urban and rural locations (ICI; z = –2.0323, p < 0.0421). Similar results were also observed on the IPDL, with the urban residences (mean = 21.00, s.d. = 3.33) scoring significantly higher than rural residences (mean = 15.83, s.d. = 4.87). Results of ANOVA for the NSCI did not support the hypothesis that individuals living in small towns in rural areas would exhibit a greater sense of community.

Rapley and Hopgood (1997) argued that the expected heterogeneity of service outcomes was observed. The hypothesis that QOL would display theoretically congruent relationships with objective indicators of service quality was broadly supported. Appropriate relationships were found between independent objective indices and QOL. For example, both the IPDL and the ICI were related to higher QOL – that is, higher levels of domestic activity and community involvement were associated with higher overall quality of life scores.

Rapley and Hopgood (1997) noted that the addition of the QOL.Q to the objective indicators provided some valuable insights. Thus, activity measures suggested that service users were engaging in domestic activities, and in a limited range of community based activities. However, when QOL.Q Empowerment scores were analysed, there was little evidence to suggest that service users' choices about important life decisions, such as where to live and whom to live with, or apparently trivial ones – such as possessing a key to their own home – were being supported.

In summary

Measures such as the QOL.Q and ComQOL-ID offer indices of quality of life that are derived from a theoretical base and are attentive – as much as is possible with formal psychometric measures – to individuals' concerns. Whereas a strength of the QOL.Q is that it measures specific aspects of the lives of people with intellectual disabilities that differentiate their experience from the rest of the 'normal' population, the ComQOL-ID has the strength of direct comparability to the 'normal' population via the parallel form. Both appear to relate sensibly to established measures of service quality. However, it is going too far to suggest that QOL offers the 'ultimate criterion for the assessment of the effectiveness of social care delivery' (Perry and Felce, 1995) for while QOL measurement may relate to other indices, it does not replicate or reproduce them. If we wish to know about the extent of people's participation in community, direct measures of such variables are still required. What QOL measurement may offer is a sense not only of matters that are not captured by existing objective indices, but also of how people feel about, say, their levels of social interaction.

It is also the case, of course, that formal operationally-defined measures are necessarily 'etic': that is they are based in the views of researchers about what QOL is and which aspects of life matter. Even a measure such as ComQOL, which allows individual weighting of the importance of domains, does not allow respondents to provide their own domains, but requires them to use pre-given scales. As such, it is necessary to supplement formal psychometric scales with an 'emic' methodology based in the perspective of participants, if both an aggregate, quantitative account *and* a richly textured description of service quality is to be achieved. Chapter 4 has shown what such studies may look like.

QOL Research with Psychiatric Populations

While, as yet, not as well developed as the intellectual disability literature, much of the research reported to date with people with mental health problems recapitulates the issues, debates and confusions found there. As in the intellectual disability literature, QOL has usually been assessed through questionnaires or structured interviews focusing on the person's satisfaction with various life domains. The psychiatric literature also conflates distinct theoretical concepts such as 'satisfaction within a range of community residential alternatives' and 'quality of life' (Anderson and Lewis, 2000: 580), or 'quality of life' and 'social functioning'. In the study reported by Dickerson et al. (2000), for example, the QOLI (Lehman, 1988)[8] is described not as a measure of quality of life, but rather as a 'measure of social functioning'. This is also true of the relationship between 'symptoms' and QOL across this literature: for instance, Kaiser (2000: 92) notes that 'it is not surprising that a relationship is found between cognitive functioning and quality of life when the quality of life measures seem to be confounded to a considerable extent by psychiatric symptomatology'.

Such confounding is apparent in the way this literature – presupposing the validity of psychiatric classifications – accomplishes diagnosis employing criteria of impaired social functioning which demonstrate considerable overlap with the criteria then used, supposedly independently, to infer QOL. The scope for circularity is considerable. In their study of the 'determinants of quality of life at first presentation with schizophrenia' Browne et al. (2000: 173) note that 'at presentation, subjects already had a diminished QOL'. Presumably, if this is a first presentation for 'schizophrenia' – which is diagnosed on the basis of impaired social activity, interpersonal relationships and so on – both diagnosis and QOL must be being identified on the basis of the same set of presented 'indicators'. Either the study is 'double-dipping' or these researchers, by virtue of the issuing of a diagnosis of schizophrenia, *knew before it was assessed* that 'subjects already had a diminished QOL'.

In consequence the psychiatric literature shows, similar, though less heated, debates about whether population-specific QOL measures and research approaches such as interviews should take cognizance of the particular life circumstances of people described as 'mentally ill'. As in the intellectual disability literature, debate occurs about the relationship between objective and subjective indicators of QOL (Barry and Crosby, 1996; Prince and Gerber, 2001; Ruggieri et al., 2001; Skantze et al., 1992).

As in general medicine, we see not so much population-, but 'disorder'-specific measures beginning to proliferate. As there, these measures typically conflate 'disease' and 'QOL' by including symptom scales within measures described as assessing quality of life. For example, Wilkinson et al. (2000) report the development of the 30-item 'Self-report Quality of Life measure for people with Schizophrenia' (SQLS) which consists of three sub-scales – 'psychosocial', 'motivation and energy' and 'symptoms and side-effects'. Similarly, Heinrichs et al. (1984) describe 'The Quality of Life Scale: An instrument for rating the schizophrenia syndrome'. The effect of psychotropic medication on QOL is another favoured site for psychiatric research, but again much of this work is confounded by the equation of measures of, for example, the side effects of Risperidone with QOL per se (Franz et al., 1997; Priebe et al., 1999; Sharma, 1999). In summarizing this work, Kaiser (2000: 92) has made what by now should be a familiar comment: he notes 'whether or not subjective quality of life is related to cognitive deficits in schizophrenia … remains unclear and so far is only a hypothesis, although it is widespread as an advertising slogan for atypical antipsychotic medication'. Much of the work in this literature probably meets the criteria for advertising better than it does those for science.

Once more, the dissenting voices (those calling for an emic appreciation of the life circumstances of people with long-term mental health problems) appear to be in the minority. Furthermore, the psychiatric literature throws questions about the *purpose* of QOL research into particularly sharp relief. As we will see below, this literature has established conclusively that people with mental health problems score lower on QOL measures than do their 'healthy' peers; that people living in mental hospitals, by and large, report a lower QOL than people living in supported housing in the community; and that people with longstanding problems tend to have a lower QOL than those whose problems are relatively more recent. I am reminded that, as a psychology undergraduate, one of my lecturers was fond of telling us that the discipline was the 'science of the bloody obvious'.

Psychiatric Studies

Hermann et al. (2000) report a comparative study of patients with epilepsy and 'healthy' controls with three key aims: firstly to examine differences in self-reported psychiatric symptoms between patients with and without epilepsy; secondly, to assess the relationship between chronicity and co-morbid interictal psychiatric symptoms; and thirdly, to evaluate the impact of psychiatric symptoms on HRQOL. Using the Symptom Checklist-90-Revised[9] to assess psychiatric 'symptoms', participants with epilepsy also completed the Quality of Life in Epilepsy-89[10] to measure their HRQOL. Hermann et al. (2000) report that, compared to controls, epilepsy patients exhibited significantly higher (worse) scores on all but one of the 12 SCL-90-R scales. Increasing chronicity was associated with significantly higher scores across all SCL-90-R scales (indicating a worse state of affairs) and increased emotional-behavioural distress was associated with lower QOL scores across all 17 QOLIE-89 scales. Correlations between two SCL-90-R summary measures of emotional-behavioural distress (Global Severity Index, Positive Symptom Distress Index) and one specific scale

(Depression) with HRQOL were –0.54, –0.57, and –0.50 respectively, all significant at the $p < 0.01$ level. The authors conclude that interictal psychiatric symptoms are elevated among epilepsy patients compared with controls, and appear to be modestly associated with increasing chronicity of epilepsy. They suggest that 'this comorbid emotional-behavioural distress is specifically associated with a significantly poorer health-related quality of life, and suggests that quality-of-life research should devote greater attention to the potential impact of comorbid psychiatric distress' (Hermann *et al.*, 2000: 184).

Anderson and Lewis (2000) examined the association between resident characteristics, clinical factors, mental health service utilization and QOL for people living in an Intermediate care facility (ICF) and compared outcomes with QOL reported by people with 'psychiatric disorders' living in other residential settings in the literature. Information was collected from patients' notes, discussions with staff and semi-structured interviews; 100 people diagnosed with 'schizophrenia' completed the Quality of Life Interview – Brief Version (QOLI; Lehman, 1988), the Severity of Psychiatric Illness scale (SPI)[11] (Lyons *et al.*, 1997a; Lyons *et al.*, 1997b) the Barthel Activities of Daily Living Index (BAI)[12] (Blass, 1985) and the SF-12 (Ware *et al.*, 1998), a short form of the SF-36 discussed in Chapter 6.

Multivariate regression analyses suggested that higher levels of QOL were associated with reports that psychological problems did not interfere with work and activities, and with being rated as posing a lower level of danger to others. In other words, these variables were statistically significant predictors of a higher QOL score. A comparison of the QOL scores reported by ICF residents in Anderson and Lewis's (2000) study with other studies of the QOL of people with mental health problems (for example, Lehman *et al.*'s (1991) study of state hospitals) suggested that ICF residents reported significantly higher QOL scores than state hospital patients – but lower scores than community samples. Anderson and Lewis (2000: 580) suggest that their study:

> replicate[s] others in suggesting that persons living in state hospitals report a poorer quality of life than persons living in community residential alternatives (Lehman *et al.*, 1991). That residents of the ICF reported a lower quality of life as compared to other community facilities may be better understood within the role of the residential settings ... As Slaughter *et al.* (1991) suggest, variability in quality of life outcomes across treatment settings may be due to the interaction of other service components and housing services ... Future research needs to examine whether different types of service utilization, for example mental health service use, has an impact on life satisfaction in other residential settings and whether the intensity of service use or the receipt over time is associated with improved quality of life.

Here again we see the difficulty of specifying the necessary and sufficient conditions for 'service components' to have a direct bearing on the QOL experienced by their users. 'Improved quality of life' is conflated with 'intensity of [mental health] service use'. Interestingly Hansson *et al.* (2001) suggested that the level of experienced 'self-directedness' best predicts the QOL of psychiatric patients, which may explain the routinely found gradient in QOL reported by people in psychiatric services: with lowest levels for people detained in secure settings to highest in community-based services.

The confusion of measures of psychiatric 'symptoms' and 'quality of life' is illustrated by Skevington and Wright (2001) of the WHO Centre for the Study of Quality of Life at the University of Bath. In a study of the QOL of people receiving antidepressant medication in primary care, funded by Glaxo-Wellcome, they suggest that the 'study arises from the need for good quality of life (QOL) assessment and a new comprehensive generic QOL profile for cross-cultural use' (Skevington and Wright, 2001: 261). How the study of depressed primary care patients in Bath fosters the development of 'cross-cultural' QOL is unclear. Using the WHOQOL-100[13] and the Beck Depression Inventory, they report an AB design study of 106 patients with 'moderate depression' treated by their GPs. Participants completed both measures at the start of treatment and again six weeks later. Oddly, claiming to have measured depression and QOL at *six weeks*, Skevington and Wright then report that:

> depression decreased significantly over 2 months and 74% reported feeling better. WHOQOL-100 scores increased in 24 of the 25 facets, demonstrating that QOL improves significantly in the 8 weeks following the start of antidepressant treatment. It also shows the instrument's validity and sensitivity to changes in clinical condition. The UK WHOQOL-100 is confirmed as excellent to good. Antidepressants significantly and comprehensively improve QOL. (Skevington and Wright, 2001: 261)

These are very strong claims indeed.

However, there is a raft of difficulties with the study. Apart from the fact that 26 per cent of participants *did not* report feeling better, and 10.5 per cent reported feeling worse or 'very much worse', the patient group is anything but homogenous. We are told that 'patients needed to be at the beginning of a first episode of depression and suited to taking a course of antidepressants. Alternatively, they could be at the start of a new episode of depression and a new course of pharmacological treatment' (p. 261). So, we have two completely different types of patients: those who have *never* been depressed and *never* taken antidepressants, and those who have *repeatedly* experienced these circumstances. We are told that 69 per cent of participants had been depressed for under a year, but the mean duration of depression was 2 years 3 months (with a huge standard deviation of 4 years

4 months). An unspecified number had had 'up to 20 years recurrent illness' (p. 262). Even at a purely common-sense level, it would seem that there may be a difference in how new patients and those with '20 years of recurrent illness' might experience their misery and the quality of their lives. Furthermore, the sample was strongly skewed in a number of potentially important ways: 76 per cent were women, 35 per cent were unemployed and, although three-quarters were prescribed SSRIs (selective serotonin reuptake inhibitors), the other 25 per cent of participants took antidepressant medications which are completely pharmacologically distinct.

The statistics presented to substantiate the claims that the WHOQOL is 'excellent', and that 'antidepressants significantly and comprehensively improve QOL' simply cannot be trusted. Inadequate data is presented on drop-out rates, meaning that the reader has to work out that the attrition rate for the study was nearly *one-quarter* by inspecting the degrees of freedom of the t test results presented for the test-retest analysis of changes in BDI scores. However, the scores on the BDI prove inconvenient: after an average of 55 days of treatment, the 80 or so patients still in the study recorded a statistically significant 'improvement' from 'moderate to severe depression' to 'moderate depression'. As such a finding clearly cannot provide strong support for the authors' (preconceived?) views, the BDI scores are abandoned in favour of two unstated 'transition questions' which are said to be 'equivalent', despite the fact that their correlation with BDI changes scores is of the order of only 0.4 (p. 262). On the basis of this statistical manipulation – a facet analysis which shows *no relationship* between depression and QOL on nine of the WHOQOL facets, a maximum correlation between depression scores and one facet of QOL as measured by the WHOQOL of 0.58 (Positive feelings) and the very strong possibility that the large number of tests conducted has led to Type 1 errors – the authors feel able to claim, unequivocally, that antidepressants 'comprehensively improve QOL'.

In the light of the extremely strong and unequivocal claims that are made, both for the WHOQOL (see Hagerty *et al.*, 2001) and for antidepressant medication, Skevington and Wright (2001: 261) make the remarkable claim that:

> for psychometric testing it is unnecessary to control for antidepressant type, size of dose, length of treatment, level of compliance or incidence of comorbidity … it is sufficient to establish that scores of QOL are higher when people are well and lower when their health is worse.

Based on the study design reported, we cannot even know this with any certainty. If it doesn't matter what pills people take, if it doesn't matter what their problem is, if it doesn't even matter whether people actually take their pills or not, and if *we don't even bother to check*, then how can we claim that antidepressants have *anything to do with* QOL at all? If this is the rationale adopted, then this study does not *begin* to live up to the role it sets out for QOL research in psychiatry – namely that 'it is vital to the success of evidence-based medicine that the accuracy, reliability and validity of outcome measures are established' (p. 261). As it stands we cannot know what really happened to patients' depression or quality of life in this study, still less at *eight* weeks: what we can infer is that 25 per cent of patients had dropped out of the study by then. In passing, as Kaiser (2000) reminds us, eight weeks is the rule of thumb promoted by psychiatry and drug company advertising for the time that it takes 'antidepressants' to 'work'.

Somewhat more critically, Kemmler *et al.* (1997) report a study casting doubt on the rationale of the domains or 'facets' of life approach. Using a German version of the Lancashire QOL Profile,[14] the QOL of 48 'chronic schizophrenic outpatients with a long-term disease history' is reported. Correlations between general life satisfaction, satisfaction with specific life domains, psychological well-being and psychopathology were analysed using correlational and multiple linear regression analyses. Only social relations and health contributed significantly to the patients' general life satisfaction: the other domains (work, leisure, family relations and housing) failed to reach significance. Psychological well-being sub-scales (self-esteem, affective state) and 'psychopathology' were much more strongly related to general life satisfaction than the other life domains examined. What this study would seem to be telling us, then, is that people who meet current diagnostic criteria for schizophrenia are not terribly happy. Again, given that poor interpersonal relations is a key criterion indicator for such a diagnosis to be made, there would seem to be a high degree of redundancy in studies such as this.

Similarly, Taylor *et al.* (1998) analyse the differential impact of two types of community-based care ('intensive' and 'standard') on the QOL of 138 'people with psychosis' in London. Using the Lancashire Quality of Life Profile[14], Taylor and colleagues found that global QOL and the average of the domain-specific scores were stable over time. Weak improvements in the Living situation domain were noted in the 'intensive' sector. This improvement is accounted for by a large drop in in-patient admissions and increased social activity in the intensive sector. Over the entire study people reported poor objective QOL. Rather strangely, given that they document a 'large drop in in-patient admissions' and 'increased social activity', Taylor *et al.* (1998: 416) conclude that 'we failed to find an effect of intensive community care on QOL in people with psychosis. This may indicate an insensitivity to change in QOL measures, or that the intervention failed to produce the kind of changes in mental health and functioning which would be reflected in improved QOL.'

In contrast Simpson *et al.* (1989) report a comparative study of 'chronically mentally ill' patients in acute wards in a district general hospital, a hostel ward and group homes. They found that although 'severity of psychopathology corresponded to their placement' when analysis controlled for 'psychopathology', differences in quality of life were found between the three service settings – with residents in group homes and the hostel (as Anderson and Lewis, 2000 found) having a greater degree of similarity in QOL than those in the district general hospital. Precisely this profile was replicated in Shepherd *et al.*'s (1996) comparison of long-stay mental hospitals and community-based dispersed housing in outer London. Coid (1993: 611) has also noted that those who are involuntarily detained in mental hospitals have a 'poor quality of life'.

In Summary

Now clearly it is unfair to criticize those who have a direct interest in the provision of mental health services for assuming that these services must, of necessity, improve people's quality of life. It is probably unkind to note that it is unsurprising to discover that people diagnosed as 'severely mentally ill' are not very happy, that people incarcerated in mental hospitals report lower QOL than those in the community, or that 'psychopathology', impoverished social relations and low QOL are correlated. Equally it may be thought unnecessarily suspicious to be sceptical about reports produced by researchers funded by drug companies and affiliated to the World Health Organization, writing in psychiatric journals which depend on pharmaceutical advertising to stay in business, which find that the QOL measure developed by the WHO is 'excellent to good' and that 'antidepressants significantly and comprehensively improve QOL'. But the serious point here is that such assumptions and practices (and almost the entire psychiatric literature is predicated upon them), and the research studies which flow from them, show the wholesale adoption of an unthinking 'etic' procedural approach that 'tacitly treats common sense as both [its] resource and ... topic' (Silverman, 1998: 192). As Edwards (1997) has demonstrated, such an approach cannot but return incoherent results.

Notes

1. The QOL.Q is intended to be completed as a structured interview with service users with an intellectual disability. The QOL.Q presents respondents with a set of questions (such as 'how much fun and enjoyment do you get out of life?') which are answered by choosing between three alternatives (in this case 'not much/some/lots'). Answers are scored as 1, 2 or 3 and aggregated, higher scores indicating higher QOL. QOL.Q factors are: Satisfaction; Competence/ Productivity; Empowerment/Independence; and Social Belonging/Community Integration. Each factor has ten items, thus factor scores range from 10–30 and the total score is the sum of the factor scores. Psychometrics are reported by Rapley and Lobley (1995).

2. The ABS is a scale for the assessment of the activities-of-daily-living skills of people with intellectual disabilities. The ABS provides a criterion-referenced measure of individuals' effectiveness in coping with the natural and social demands of their environment. Part 1 is designed to evaluate an individual's skills and habits in ten behaviour domains considered important to the development of personal independence in daily living. Psychometrics are reported by Nihira *et al.* (1975) and Perry and Felce (1995).

3. MTS Activity codes provide for recording of engagement in activities such as 'Personal/Self-Care' (tasks such as grooming, washing and tooth-brushing) or 'Chores – electrical' (for example making toast). Staff Contact categories are coded as Positive, Negative, Neutral or Assistance completed using a 30-second momentary time sampling methodology. See Felce (1986) and Murphy (1987) for a detailed discussion of the use of direct observation as a research method.

4. The Social Networks Questionnaire measures three aspects of community life: the number of friends people had and the frequency of their meeting; the type and frequency of participation in social, sporting, recreational and any other activities outside of the home; and the degree to which these activities were specially organized for people with disabilities.

5. The IPDL measures the extent to which opportunities promoting individual independence and opportunities to participate in household maintenance are provided by intellectual disability services (Raynes *et al.*, 1989b). Each of 13 items is scored on a three-point rating scale; IPDL total score is the sum of item scores. The higher the total score the greater the indication of available opportunities for participation in domestic tasks. Raynes *et al.* (1989b) and Perry and Felce (1995) report psychometrics.

6. The ICI measures the extent of involvement in activities and use of facilities based in the local community (Raynes *et al.*, 1989a) and consists of 15 items. Raynes *et al.* (1989a) report psychometrics.

7. The NSCI consists of 12 items reflecting components of community membership, influence, integration and fulfilment of needs, and shared emotional connection. Pretty *et al.* (1994) report psychometric data.

8. The QOLI (Lehman, 1988, 1996) measures life circumstances and activities with indices of objective experiences and subjective feelings about these experiences. The short version contains 60 items. Objective items include Living Situation; Daily Activities and Functioning; Family; Social Relations; Work and School; Finances; Legal and Safety; and Health. Items are rated on dichotomous or ordinal scales with higher ratings indicating better functioning or more frequent behaviour except for the global ratings of health and general functioning. Sub-scale scores are the sums of items within each area that are rated on the same scale. The QOLI does not yield a total score. Psychometric properties are reported by Lehman *et al.*, (1986); Lehman *et al.*, (1982).

9. The SCL-90-R is a 90-item self-report inventory designed to reflect 'psychological symptom patterns' rated on a five-point scale of distress ranging from 'not at all distressed' to 'extremely distressed'. The SCL has nine symptom dimensions and three global distress scales. Symptom dimensions are: Psychoticism; Obsessive-compulsive; Paranoid ideation; Phobic anxiety; Hostility; Anxiety; Depression; Interpersonal sensitivity; and Somatization. The global distress scales are the Global Severity Index (the number of

symptoms reported with their intensity); Positive Symptom Distress Index (average level of distress reported for symptoms endorsed); and Positive Symptom Total (number of symptoms endorsed, regardless of the level of distress). For psychometrics see Derogatis (n.d.), Derogatis and Cleary (1977) and Derogatis *et al.* (1974).

10. The QOLIE-89 has 17 summary scales: Seizure worry; Medication effects; Health discouragement; Work/driving/social function; Language; Attention/ concentration; Memory; Overall QOL; Emotional well-being; Role limitations – emotional; Social isolation; Social support; Energy/fatigue; Physical; Role limitations – physical; and Pain. Psychometrics are described by Devinsky *et al.* (1995).

11. The SPI assesses clinical status on 21 dimensions. Dimensions include Risk behaviours; Complications to illness and Complications to treatment. Details are reported by Lyons *et al.* (1997a) and Lyons *et al.* (1997b).

12. The BAI (Blass, 1985) covers ten self-care activities: Bathing; Dressing; Grooming; Toileting; Transferring from bed to chair; Mobility; Stairs; Continence (bowel and bladder), and Feeding. Total score is the sum of the ten activities with a lower score indicating greater dependence. For psychometrics see Mahoney and Barthel (1965).

13. The WHOQOL series of measures are critically reviewed by Hagerty *et al.*, (2001). See Appendix 2 for the brief form, the WHOQOL-BREF.

14. The Lancashire QOL Profile (Oliver *et al.*, 1996) has nine domains with objective questions and a satisfaction question scored 1–7. Domains are Work; Leisure; Religion; Finance; Living situation; Legal and safety; Family relations; Social relations; and Health. The LQOL incorporates a double question on global life satisfaction, Cantril's Ladder as a visual-analogue scale for global well-being, positive and negative affect scales and a self-esteem scale. Psychometric details are reported in Missenden *et al.*, (1995-6) and Kaiser *et al.*, (1998).

Study Questions

- What are the pros and cons of adopting emic and etic perspectives on quality of life?
- Is the quality of life of people with intellectual disabilities or mental health problems best understood from 'their' (emic) perspective or from 'ours' (etic)?
- Is an enhanced quality of life an appropriate outcome to specify for recipients of human services?
- Can specific quality of life 'outcomes' be tied to human service interventions sufficiently closely to warrant the use of QOL measures as indices of 'success'?
- Which aspects of the life experience of people with intellectual disabilities or mental health problems are most important to the quality of their lives?

Suggestions for Further Reading

Brown, R. I. (ed.) (1997) *Quality of Life for People with Disabilities: Models, Research and Practice*, 2nd edn. Cheltenham: Stanley Thornes.

Lyons, J. S., Howard, K. I., O'Mahoney, M. T. and Lish, J. (1997) *The Measurement and Management of Clinical Outcomes in Mental Health*. New York: Wiley.

Rapley, M. (2001) Policing happiness, in C. Newnes, G. Holmes and C. Dunn (eds), *This Is Madness Too*. Ross-on Wye: PCCS Books.

Schalock, R. L. (ed.) (1997) *Quality of Life Volume II: Application to Persons with Disabilities*. Washington: American Association on Mental Retardation.

CHAPTER 8

Researching QOL as a Psychological Object

The idea that individual-level QOL is best understood as a psychological state has grown in popularity over recent years, but, as we have seen in Chapter 5, the historical development of this piece of contemporary cultural common sense is *itself* a topic that repays attention. Here, to complement that analysis, a critical review of the concept of QOL as a psychological object is offered. The purpose of this chapter is to *demonstrate* how a critical reading of the psychological quality of life literature may be conducted, taking as its analytic site Cummins's homeostatic theory of subjective well-being. This analysis is itself a part of an ongoing dialogue in the literature between Bob and myself (see Rapley and Ridgway, 1998; Cummins, 2001a) – and is a further contribution to that critical engagement. Indeed, without Bob's unfailingly generous assistance, this book would be much the poorer. Of course, this does not mean that we cannot disagree or question each other's point of view: indeed, it is an important measure of any contribution to the literature that it is taken seriously enough to be challenged.

As Rose has shown, we have come to think ourselves as, fundamentally, psychological beings. *Cogito ergo sum* has little competition as the slogan of the present. The very persuasiveness and apparent 'intuitive' sense of this way of thinking ourselves demands that we rethink this way of thinking (Foucault, 1970, 1978).

QOL as a Psychological Object

A body of work suggests that QOL is a psychological state representing a summary of estimations of the satisfactoriness of life in a limited number of areas or 'domains'. Campbell (1981) suggested psychological well-being could be conceptualized in terms of twelve domains of QOL: marriage, family life, friendships, general standard of living, work, neighbourhood, city/town of residence, housing, health, self, education, and national concerns. These factors compare favourably with those identified in Lehman's (1988) study of the QOL of the 'chronically mentally ill' (health, safety, religious concerns, living circumstances, family relationships, social relationships more generally, recreational activity, work and financial concerns). Keith (1990: 94) summarizes the literature thus:

it would be fair to say that Americans ... are concerned in rating the quality of their own lives with relationships, work, general material standard of living, opportunities for learning, the neighbourhoods/ communities/homes in which they live, health and safety, recreational/ social activities, and perception of self.

Cummins (1996b) has suggested that seven domains (Material well-being, Emotional well-being, Productivity, Intimacy, Safety, Community and Health) capture the 'totality' of the QOL construct. However, Cummins has recently advanced a theory of subjective well-being which radically recasts the concept. This theory – of the 'homeostatic control' of subjective well-being – is critically scrutinized in this chapter.

Subjective Well-being as Brain State

Cummins and his co-workers offer perhaps the comprehensive theory to date of QOL as a hard-wired, biologically determined brain state. That this work is widely seen as important may be gauged partly by the inclusion of key elements of Cummins's position into major recent theoretical statements by organizations such as ISQOLS (Hagerty *et al.*, 2001) and IASSID (2001), and also by the claims he and colleagues make themselves. In their conclusions to a chapter describing 'subjective well-being homeostasis' Cummins *et al.* (in press) make powerful claims for the 'revolutionary' importance of their view. They state that:

> the idea that it is normal and adaptive to view one's life positively is revolutionary ... such an idea fundamentally challenges the ideas of many influential psychologists and psychiatrists from the last century as to what constitutes desirable psychological functioning. Most essentially, the idea that the accurate perception of reality equates to optimal psychological functioning is clearly wrong.

In keeping with the use of worked examples to illustrate major issues in this book, a detailed account is offered here of Cummins's work, as a perspicuous instance of the individualistic psychological ('modern') stream of QOL research. The 'homeostatic' theory of subjective well-being is critically examined, as are some of the major difficulties with, and implications of, this way of understanding of what are, after all, people's verbal reports of how their life is.

A Critique of the Homeostatic Model

Cummins (2001b) has claimed 'remarkable stability in population life satisfaction'. His 1995 study held that life satisfaction could be defined as

75.0 ± 2.5 per cent of QOL scale maximum scores (%SM) and, using two standard deviations as a normative band, population means fall in the range 70–80%SM. Cummins (1998b) reported a similar analysis for 45 Western and non-Western nations. This study found a 'population standard' (Cummins, 2001) of 75 ± 2.5%SM for Western nations, while others reported lower levels of life satisfaction. Grand mean life satisfaction was 70 ± 5.0%SM. Cummins (2001) argues that both the Western and world ranges have an upper margin at 80%SM, while the world range falls beneath the Western normative margin of 70%SM to 60%SM.

Cummins (2001b) bases his argument that life satisfaction is homeostatically maintained largely on these data. He claims that:

> There are several reasons to posit such an idea. The first is based on the weight of empirical data that have been described. Despite very different circumstances of living, the World's populations have an average level of life satisfaction that varies by only about 20 percent. This is a strong indication that life satisfaction is not free to vary over its entire range. Second, it has long been speculated that animals like to feel good about themselves … and it is intuitive that humans benefit from having a positive outlook on life … So given these characteristics and the apparent benefits to the maintenance of life satisfaction … human selection has favoured this attribute … humans must also have evolved device(s) that allow the maintenance of life satisfaction.

Appeals to 'animals liking to feel good about themselves', evolutionary theory and the 'weight of empirical data' make a potent mix. However, the notion of an absolute range over which human life satisfaction may vary is *not* a given fact of nature – as its juxtaposition to evolution and the animal kingdom might imply. Such a joining is 'ontological gerrymandering' (Potter, 1996). We cannot ask animals if they 'feel good', and what contribution 'feeling good' might make to the individual reproductive success of specific animals – the fundamental criterion for the selection of characteristics in evolutionary theory – is nowhere addressed. Of course, if speculation about the evolutionary success of happy animals is not accepted, then there is no reason to countenance the idea that 'humans must also have evolved device(s) that allow the maintenance of life satisfaction within some range that is optimal for the survival of the population' (Cummins, 2001).

The idea of a fixed range over which 'a positive outlook' may fluctuate is a function of a pair of a priori decisions – firstly to regard 'feeling good about yourself' or 'life satisfaction' as a *thing* (to reify subjective experience), and secondly, to use the measurement technology of the physical sciences to quantify what has become an 'object'. It might also be thought that, if 'a positive outlook' can vary by 20 per cent depending on local conditions, a *contextual* understanding would be fruitful. This is not the case, however: Cummins *et al.* (in press) offer an extraordinarily detailed account – based on these speculations – which reduces 'having a positive outlook on life', later respecified as 'Subjective Well-Being output', to the automatic 'output' of the ghostly activities of the machine (Ryle, 1949).

Affective and Cognitive Components of Subjective Well-being

Cummins *et al.* (in press) argue that, since the seminal studies of Campbell *et al.* (1976), the view that personal (subjective) well-being is made up of affective and cognitive elements has been accepted. They refer to this phenomenon as *subjective well-being* (SWB).

In their analyses of six national samples Crooker and Near (1998) concluded that, in studies of subjective well-being, distinctions between cognitive and affective measures are *illusory*. However, Cummins *et al.* (in press) continue the dichotomization and use the term *happiness* to describe the affective component. For the putative cognitive element of SWB, it is suggested that personal evaluations of this dimension are generated via the computation of multiple internal comparisons. Net satisfaction is described as a positive linear function of the perceived differences between what one has versus (1) what one wants, (2) what others have, (3) the best one has had in the past, (4) what one expected to have in the past, (5) what one expects to have in the future, (6) what one deserves, and (7) what one needs. This yields a measurable state to provide a quantum of what Cummins *et al.* (in press) suggest should be called *life satisfaction*. The net satisfaction quantum thus derives from the meeting of what are termed 'multiple needs' (Cummins *et al.*, in press) on the basis of the assumption that the desire for satisfaction motivates people to act. Cummins *et al.* (in press) suggest that 'this applies to satisfaction with income, health, education, and other life facets, as well as with satisfaction with life as a whole' (Mallard *et al.*, 1997: 260). Other writers such as Veenhoven (1997: 29) are less sanguine, suggesting that, over and above 'sufficient food, housing and health care', what people 'need' is not the sort of thing which can be established *empirically*.

Having suggested that 'life satisfaction' is a 'linear function' of multiple comparisons, quite what arithmetic operations are then performed by the brain to produce a numerical value for SWB is not specified. We are not told if, across the hundreds of measures of SWB identified, SWB is (to be) treated as a simple additive product of separate affective and cognitive quanta, or whether their relationship is multiplicative, logarithmic or synergistic, nor the relative weights of each putative component. Similarly, it is not clear from the account how separate estimations of numerous different domains relate to numerical estimates of 'satisfaction' produced in response to single questions.

However, Cummins *et al.* (in press) go on to argue that, given its claimed ability to measure both cognitive and affective aspects of SWB, the ComQOL allows a measure of 'the aggregate of satisfaction across life domains [which] yields *Subjective Quality of Life* (SQOL)'. This is a little confusing given the earlier description of affective and cognitive evaluations of life as 'subjective well-being'. The ComQOL (Cummins, 1997a, 1997b) does, however, implicitly, answer the theoretical question about the arithmetic operations in the brain which produce well-being estimates: it is a simple procedure of adding up benefits on each domain, with domains weighted by importance, and then calculating an average. Whether the endorsement of this computational process is for psychological, physiological or neurological reasons, or just administrative convenience, is unclear. As Veenhoven (1997) has suggested, however, the mere fact of a correlation between sub-evaluations of domain benefit and overall ratings of happiness does not, and cannot, suggest that one causes the other.

A Normative Standard for Subjective Well-being

Cummins *et al.* (in press) state that: 'SQOL … can be described in terms of an empirical normative standard … Western population mean scores for SQOL predictably lie within the range 70 to 80 %SM' and claim that the measuring of such values reflects biologically based human universals (Cummins, 2001; Cummins *et al.*, in press). On the basis of meta analyses of general population surveys recalibrated to express scores as %SM, Cummins *et al.* (in press) claim that, when recoded in this manner, life satisfaction and SQOL scores consistently yield a mean of 75 and a standard deviation of 2.5. That is life satisfaction and subjective QOL scores across population samples usually fall into the 70–80%SM range as shown by Figure 8.1.

In other words, on average people around the world are 'normally' somewhere between three-quarters and 80 per cent satisfied with their life or, alternatively, the quality of their life is between 75 and 80 per cent (of what, one wonders?). Cummins (1995) suggests no study yet has returned an average value significantly above 80%SM. Further, even though the highest levels of life satisfaction are obtained from very wealthy people their values also average to around 80%SM (Cummins, 2000a). The findings of Groot and VandenBrink (2000) – who showed additional income made no difference to life satisfaction for people with minimum value of 80%SM – are cited to suggest a ceiling effect: that it is not physically possible to become happier than 80 per cent. Further evidence for biologically determined well-being is held to derive from the stability of these figures over time. On the basis of these data, and of a range of other studies, Cummins *et al.* (in press) argue that:

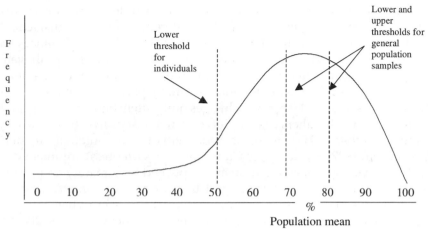

Percentage of scale maximum (%SM)

Figure 8.1 The normal distribution of subjective quality of life.
Source: Cummins *et al.* (in press).

These data, together with the predictable ranges of SQOL values, constitute converging evidence that SWB is not simply free to vary at the whim of personal circumstances, but is managed. This idea, that SWB is under active internal control, is termed SWB homeostasis.

The general idea of the proposed homeostatic system is that SWB is managed, for each individual, within a 'set-point-range' (Cummins, 2000b). That is, each person has an in-built 'set-point' for their normal level of SWB, as proposed by Headey and Wearing (1992), and their perceived SWB is normally held within a narrow range around this setting.

A Role for Circumstances?

While these data are (intendedly) described by proponents of a biological view as convincing evidence that 'SWB is not simply free to vary at the whim of personal circumstances', the correlation coefficients relied upon are quite *low* if a strong biological mechanism is determining people's verbal behaviour. The shared variance between the satisfaction reports of the highest coefficient cited – a value of 0.65 reported by Bowling (1996) – is a mere 42 per cent, or well under half. If this is hard evidence for biological control, what is influencing the other 58 per cent of the variance in happiness reports? While Cummins (2001b) claims that the life satisfaction of Western populations was stable between 1980 and 1990, Veenhoven cites Witt *et al.* (1979) to suggest that elderly Americans became happier between 1950 and 1970 and also points out that the Heady and Wearing (1992) study on which Cummins *et al.* (in press) draw to stake their 'satisfaction is determined by biology' claim, actually demonstrated that 'life events explained some 25 per cent of the differences in life satisfaction' (Veenhoven, 1997: 15) and that 63 per cent of national differences in happiness 'can be explained by variation in societal qualities' (Veenhoven, 1997: 19). Contra Cummins *et al.* (in press) Veenhoven claims that: 'happiness does not remain the same over time: particularly not over the length of a lifetime ... Happiness changes quite often; both absolutely and relatively towards others ... Happiness is not insensitive to change in living-conditions ... Happiness is not entirely an internal matter' (Veenhoven, 1997: 20). To accept Cummins *et al.*'s (in press) argument one has to believe that something dramatic happened to humanity as a whole between 1970 (when the data suggest that for at least some Americans happiness was changeable) and the decade 1980–1990 (when Western populations' levels of happiness suddenly became, after Cummins (2001b), fixed).

Life Events and Subjective Well-being

Cummins *et al.* (in press) allow a limited role for life events as temporary disruptions to biologically based well-being. If people experience an event which 'depresses their SWB below threshold', homeostatic control 'should improve their levels of SWB over time'. They cite data suggesting that people who have received bad medical news (Bloom *et al.* 1991) or have suffered spinal injuries (Bach and Tilton, 1994) report, later, that life satisfaction has returned to previous levels. They further suggest that the stability of SWB over time is restricted to two sorts of people, firstly those who score in the 'normal' range and experience no life events or, as they state, 'under maintenance conditions, where no threat to homeostasis can be recognized, there should be no systematic relationship between the objective circumstances of people's lives and their SWB'. This, of course, makes the measurement of SWB for almost any policy-relevant or service evaluation purpose, at any level, pointless. The second group are those who experience what is termed 'homeostatic defeat' due to some chronic condition, like extreme poverty, to which they cannot adapt (a position which blames individuals' biology rather than their circumstances for their misery).

As is shown in Figure 8.2, the influence of life events is modelled as dependent upon the 'strength of extrinsic conditions'. If these are strong, or 'if the strength of the agents exceeds the homeostatic threshold ... the extrinsic agents begin to wrest control of SWB away from the homeostatic system, causing SWB to rise or fall. As this occurs, the agencies and SQOL start to co-vary' (Cummins *et al.*, in press). Of course this position presupposes that 'the strength of the agents' is universally determinable (as of course is their composition) and independent of the values, appraisals and social mores of people whose brain systems are so violently taken control of.

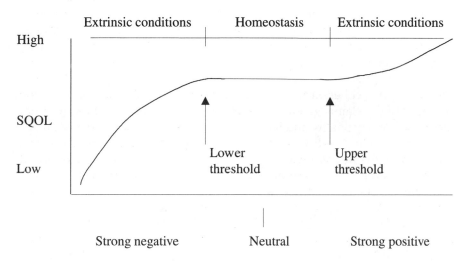

Figure 8.2 The relationship between subjective and objective quality of life.
Source: Cummins *et al.* (in press).

Personality and Subjective Well-being

Cummins *et al.* (in press) do allow for other putatively stable 'internal' brain systems to have a role in determining SWB, and here the 'affective' component of the two-factor model of SWB seems to come to the fore. These are the 'personality' factors of 'neuroticism' – which is described as 'the source of constitutional negative affectivity' – and 'extraversion' which is held to be 'the source of constitutional positive affectivity ... the natural opposing force to neuroticism'.

Despite a huge literature critical of the incoherence of the concept of 'personality', and the fact that the 'personality' literature is almost as internally fragmented and contradictory as the QOL literature itself, in a near perfect recapitulation of Kant's *Critique of Judgment* (see McHoul and Rapley, 2001),[1] Cummins *et al.* (in press) state that: 'It seems reasonable to suggest that it is the balance between these two personality dimensions that provides the set-point-range for SWB.' These 'dimensions' are then supported by a further set of proposed 'homeostatic variables' and mediated by what are called 'cognitive buffers'. On the basis of a review of some of this literature, Cummins *et al.* (in press) argue that:

> when the correlations are averaged across the five factors, the highest loading category is Self-esteem (.31) followed by SQOL and Ill-being,

both on .27. The lowest are Just World Beliefs (.14) and Motivation (.13).
... factors of neuroticism and extraversion, and to a lesser extent conscientiousness, have a robust relationship with subjective well-being
conceptualised either as SWB or SQOL. In addition, these three factors
also have a reliable influence on the two putative 'buffer' variables of self-
esteem and control.

The conceptual coherence of this account is questionable, as indeed is the
certainty of the claims given the psychometric marginality of many, if not
most, tests of personality and its putative 'components'. Indeed, just such a
caveat is later entered: Cummins *et al.* (in press) note that 'there are,
however, many different ways to measure self-esteem, and these different
instruments may yield very different results ... self-esteem scales are not
equivalent'. But to return to these claims: surely the initial claim that
Cummins *et al.* made was that SWB and SQOL are different 'things', and
that confusing one for the other is what the proposed model claimed to
avoid? Isn't, according to the proposed model, 'motivation' to satisfaction
the fundamental drive for the whole of human action and the SWB system
itself? If so, then why is 'motivation' one of the lowest loading variables?
What relationship do 'just world beliefs' have to anything under
consideration here: surely there is an immensity of cultural variability in
what constitutes a 'just world'? What clear theoretical bearing does
'conscientiousness' (not a component – until now – of the model) have on
satisfaction, whether conceptualized as SQOL, SWB or happiness? Is
'control' really a 'personality' variable or better understood as the *actual*
presence or absence of leverage over real-world events?

However, in keeping with the biological determinism of the model,
personality – rather than real-world events – is identified as the serious
contender for a role in the generation of the well-being reported by people.
Cummins *et al.* (in press) note that:

It seems that the strength of the relationship between personality and SWB
will be situationally variable and, apart from being dependent on the
nature of the measures employed, it will be determined by the degree of
challenge that objective circumstances bring to the homeostatic system.
... while it is clear personality and SWB are linked, no simple general
estimate of the strength of this linkage can be made. However, it is
possible that if samples were separated on the basis of their relative
degree of homeostatic threat, more consistent estimates would emerge.

It seems rather optimistic to imagine that one could ever establish a
universally agreed ranking of 'homeostatic threats', and hence this appeal
employs wishful thinking to buttress an unsupported position. It may
appear that the above view relegates personality (the nature of which
'thing', it is conceded, will vary according to the manner in which it is

measured) to the second rank after 'situational variability', 'objective circumstances' and the 'homeostatic system'.

However, Cummins *et al.* then make a series of startling claims. Following Switzky (1999: 70) they assert that 'personality [is] at the center of operations', that personality is the 'fulcrum around which all other psychological, educational, and self-regulatory processes rotate to energize behavior and performance' and that personality is the key determinant of evaluations of the strength of met and unmet needs. Furthermore, apparently, when people are asked to consider whether the support they have from family, friends and others is adequate (presumably their 'level of satisfaction with social support') the startling claim is now advanced that, rather than such a judgment being a rational (albeit probably automatic and unconscious) calculation of 'have–want' discrepancies, or the relativities of benefits received weighed against actual requirements, this is not a matter of (rational) judgment or computation at all. Instead it is claimed that the 'evidence for a genetic link appears to be strongest in relation to perceived social support ... This link has special significance in terms of the model since it may represent the simplest connection between personality and motivation'.

Whether we believe that our levels of social support are adequate then is not to do with anything as messy as lived experience and recalcitrant relatives. Our perceptions of the social support we receive are merely a matter of our DNA. Notably this claim is buttressed, not by a review of the literature on genetic determinants of beliefs about social support (such a literature is sparse, and overlooks the fact – as does all so-called biological psychology – that genes code for proteins and not for beliefs, attitudes or values), but by an extended discussion of studies of 'extraversion with particular attention to the facet of 'sociability', as the enjoyment of social activities, preference for being with others and 'reward sensitivity'.'

From the other side of the 'personality' coin, it is claimed once more that real-world circumstances have little bearing on how persons describe them. Cummins *et al.* (in press) cite a study by Fyrand *et al.* (1997) that reported a 'strong correlation' (for once we are not given a value) between depression and the lack of social support (described as 'an unmet need') in people with arthritis. However, after statistically removing the effects of neuroticism on the relationship, the correlation 'virtually disappeared'. This, it is stated, means that 'neuroticism may, therefore, have caused the perceived lack of social support'. This is the production of persons as 'cultural dopes' (Garfinkel, 1967): depressed people don't know their own lives or circumstances, they cannot reliably report on whether they have adequate social support or not, their 'neuroticism' makes them incapable of telling it like it is. If we cannot trust people's reports on such a matter, surely people's reports of their 'satisfaction', 'happiness' or SWB on measures such as Cummins's own ComQOL should be regarded as equally unreliable.

'Buffers' of Subjective Well-being

Cummins *et al.* (in press) briefly move away from biology to account for the role of 'buffers' in SWB. Noting 'overwhelming evidence that the way people think about and explain what happens in their lives is intimately tied to their level of SWB', they claim that three 'cognitive protective factors' (self-esteem, perceived control and optimism) are crucial to well-being. In a tautologous argument it is suggested that feeling good about yourself (high self-esteem) produces a feeling of subjective well-being (or feeling good) and, contrariwise, feeling bad about yourself produces feeling of subjective ill-being, viz.: 'low self-esteem would be predicted to correlate with low values of the cognitive buffers…reflecting a weak buffering system that is susceptible to homeostatic defeat by negative life events'. Similarly it is contended that 'perceived control is central to life quality', that perceived control is another buffer that 'reinforces' SWB. The buffer's modus operandum is opaque: 'Under normal conditions, where the person believes their environment is under their control, they will evidence internal control. This, in turn, reinforces SWB.' Essentially what this says is that if people believe they are in control they will behave as if they believe they are in control, and probably tell us they believe they are in control. This tells us little: the link to SWB is, in effect, accomplished by authorial fiat. Cummins *et al.* (in press) then clarify:

> however, the extrinsic environment cannot always be perceived as under one's personal control, such as when negative life events must be endured. This is when the perception of external control can act as a buffer. That is, if negative life events were simply accepted as evidence of a complete loss of control this would be indicative of helplessness and very damaging to SWB. If, on the other hand, such events can be understood as simply bad luck (i.e. that the event is unlikely to recur) or the will of God (i.e. that there is a higher, but not understood purpose underlying the event), then the negative feelings associated with the event can be reduced, and the impact on SWB diminished. This is the proposed role of external control, not to directly enhance SWB but to buffer the potential negative impact of negative life events. The capacity of the buffer is, however, limited in this regard, and this capacity will be exceeded by either a strong or protracted negative event. As a consequence, high levels of external control will most commonly be linked to a measurable reduction in SWB, even though the model predicts such a reduction to be less than would be the case in the absence of the external control buffer.

It is somewhat perplexing then that such an account (which it must be remembered is embedded in an unambiguously biological account of a hard-wired brain system controlling SWB – that is, it is proposed that it is as much a condition of being human that SWB is 'not free to vary' as it is that humans have two legs and two arms, not three or four) immediately falls back on matters of cultural belief (and, it must be said, Western common sense) to account for the operation of what is claimed to be a neurological (brain) system. 'Negative life events', the 'will of God' and 'bad luck' too are, presumably, hard-wired into humans, as is the universality of lowered SWB as the inevitable human response to what is held to be 'helplessness'. That Buddhism, for example, enjoins its adherents actively to seek and to celebrate helplessness cannot be accommodated by this account. That one's own death (and presumably Cummins *et al.* (in press) would imagine this as a 'strong' 'negative life event') might be understood by some as a positive and control over its ending as enhancing the value and quality of what remains of it – as shown by van Hooff's (1990) study of self-killing in antiquity, Irish hunger strikers in the 1980s and many young Palestinians more recently – again cannot be accommodated.

Further difficulties arise with the third 'buffer', optimism, 'defined as a perception that the future will be to the perceiver's advantage or for their pleasure' and that 'studies have shown that people view themselves on an upward path of 'life getting better'.' In support of their claim that 'optimism' too acts to 'buffer' SWB, Glatzer's (1991) survey work is cited as evidence of 'optimism as a positive cognitive bias'.

> People were asked to rate their life satisfaction as they remembered it to be 5 years ago, in the present, and as they anticipated it would be 5 years hence. The mean scores, in %SM units, were as follows: past (73, 71, 74), present (78, 77, 77), future (80, 75, 76). These data do not confirm the future bias, perhaps due to the prevailing uncertainty in the country at that time. However, the present greater than the past bias is clearly evident and is consistent with the idea that the optimism buffer helps to maintain SWB through a downward comparison with the past.

Not only does this conclusion seem odd in face of the evidence, but it also demonstrates both the slipperiness of the concepts deployed and the flexibility of Cummins *et al.*'s arguments. Glatzer (1991) appears to have studied remembered, current and projected 'life satisfaction' not 'optimism'. The results cited directly contradict the central notion that people in the 'normal' range of homeostatically controlled SWB (remember this is supposed to be between 70%SM and 80%SM, into which bracket all estimates cited fall) would not be affected by extrinsic circumstances. The data also directly contradict Cummins's (2001b) claim that there is no evidence that levels of life satisfaction in Western nations changed in the period 1980–1990. How, then, did 'prevailing uncertainty in the country at that time' operate to change the reports offered of German life satisfaction? Prevailing uncertainty is a description of circumstances that clearly rules out what is claimed as the *necessary condition* for homeostatic control being 'wrested' out of the control of the brain – the severity of 'extrinsic threat'. Why then did the scores change?

However, suggesting that optimism shows a high relationship with internal control and 'the personality traits and self-esteem', Cummins *et al.* (in press) argue that 'the buffering aspect of optimism lies within the global expectation that things are going to get better with time and in the tendency to perceive things in a more positive light than may be objectively true'. It seems that these constructs are extremely hard to disentangle. Clarification follows:

> self-esteem, control and optimism buffers appear to display the necessary characteristics to justify their role [in the homeostatic model]. Each one has strong links to SWB consistent with SWB being a product of both the buffers and personality … In addition, the buffers are highly correlated, consistent with the proposal that they constitute a single buffering system for the purpose of SWB output. While it has also been argued that these buffers, through the influence of personality, can be linked to motivation, the most central source of motivation is likely to be the cognitive appraisal of needs.

This account, then, presents putative 'buffers' as simultaneously separable and as a singular system, as 'highly correlated' (and hence conceptually overlapping) but as, in some sense, sufficiently discriminable to be distinct 'things'. They both 'produce' 'SWB output' in collaboration with 'personality' and yet are – at the same time – junior partners to personality when it comes to being 'influenced' about matters of 'motivation'. Such supposed aspects of persons are, as we have seen, understood as fixed, biologically given matters.

Motivation, Needs and Subjective Well-being

When it comes to motivation, earlier the well-spring for human action, a priori traits, buffers and personality types take second place to ratiocination. 'The most central source of motivation' we read 'is likely to be the cognitive appraisal of needs'. That basic needs, such as for food and drink, are not 'cognitive' but rather physical states, and that the logical grammar of statements such as 'I am thirsty' is such that they do not describe a 'cognitive state' but rather a physiological one (cf. Wittgenstein, 1953; Coulter, 1999) is unrecognized. Further to argue that 'unmet needs provide the basis for motivation … the idea that they are directly linked to SWB levels is problematic' is itself problematic. How being unable to satisfy a basic need, for food say, could *not* be related to SWB as ordinary persons would understand the term is difficult to comprehend. And indeed precisely this point is later conceded. Cummins *et al.* write that 'What may, however, affect the levels of SWB is the presence of a strong, chronic, unmet need that acts to compromise the buffers, and thereby to reduce

SWB. For example, a person who is chronically very hungry or insecure is likely to have a level of SWB that lies below the normal range.'

The grounds offered for the counter-intuitive suggestion that SWB is all but impervious to anything but 'chronic unmet needs' is based on an acceptance of Maslow's (1954) theory of a hierarchy of needs. They argue that 'as most basic needs are met, higher level needs arise which, in Maslow's hierarchy, culminate in needs of self-actualization'. Cummins *et al.* (in press) then claim that, given the 'remarkable level of stability' SWB shows, 'to account for such stability it must be assumed either that some needs cannot be met or that met needs are seamlessly replaced by unmet needs, so as to maintain an average SWB level of 75%SM. Both of these ideas seem implausible.'

Not only are Cummins *et al.* (in press) conflating levels of analysis (*population* mean SWB levels and *individuals'* potential 100% SWB minus a supposed need to 'self-actualize'), but also their argument depends upon the prior assumption that Maslow's theory is itself a plausible account of human universals. Again one is reminded that Buddhism and variants of Islam encourage their adherents not to self-actualize but to self-negate, that as Rose (1992: 110) points out, the notion that the 'need' to 'self-actualize' was 'a part of human nature' was only invented in the West in the 1950s, and that, from a Wittgensteinian perspective, the logical grammar of the term 'need' refers not to putative internal states, but rather to conditions of deficit in the external world: for example the statement 'I need a pencil to sign my name' *cannot* index an intra-psychic state.[2]

Problems with the Assumption of Met Needs

Further, the argument depends on uncritically accepting that the idea that 'some needs cannot be met is implausible' is itself plausible. The argument here depends on the further acceptance of the claims that as:

> the majority of people in Western society do not experience chronic unmet needs at the lower levels of Maslow's hierarchy, and have their relationship needs reasonably well met, the assumption of 'unmet' needs, required to fulfil the average 25%SM deficit from complete life satisfaction, must be maintained via unmet 'self-actualization' needs. There is no evidence of which we are aware to support such an idea.

Of course, if one looks at 'hard' evidence relating to divorce rates, levels of domestic violence, homelessness, poverty, inequality of income distribution and lack of access to affordable healthcare across most of the Western world – all of which directly coincide with the 'lower levels of Maslow's hierarchy', and all of which show a steady worsening over the last twenty years (World Bank, 2000) – one might not so readily accept the contention that 'the majority of people in Western society do not experience chronic unmet needs … and have their relationship needs reasonably well met'.

For example, the National Centre for Social and Economic Modelling in Australia has suggested that 'there is strong evidence that income inequality has increased between the late 1980s and mid-1990s and there is some evidence to suggest that it has continued increasing since then; this increase has been driven by a decline in the income share of the bottom 10 per cent of Australians … and an increase in the income share of the top 10 per cent' (Harding and Greenwell, 2001: 22). World Health Organization projections for depression suggest that the global 'burden of disease' caused by depression will increase by at least 50 per cent by 2020 and will be the second most important cause of disability worldwide (WHO, 2001). The UK government has estimated that nearly 20 per cent of British adults have a 'neurotic disorder' (most commonly anxiety and depression) and that these rates have been static since the early 1990s (Ferriman, 2001). These figures suggest a generally widespread low-level misery.

Of course, if it is accepted for a moment that for a considerable number of people in the West there are very real difficulties with meeting basic subsistence and relational needs – as reports such as Harding and Greenwell's (2001) suggest – the argument about putative 25%SM self-actualization deficits runs into difficulties. A considerable body of work demonstrates that high levels of objective threat to the most basic of needs, life itself, are negatively correlated with mean ratings of happiness at the population level. Veenhoven (1997), for example, reports, across 48 countries, that levels of malnutrition, accessibility of safe drinking water, murder rates and lethal accident rates are negatively correlated with happiness. It is, of course, also the case that in Western society, where we are told 'most people do not experience chronic unmet needs…and have their relationship needs reasonably well met', respected psychiatrists such as Wolpert (1999) have described a huge increase in levels of depression since 1980 – an era when, pace Cummins, apparently world levels of SWB have not changed.

There are a number of further problems with this account. The first of these is that – as we all know – our personal estimates of how good life is are, in practice, likely to fluctuate over time. Contra Cummins *et al.* (in press) who object that if unmet needs had a major bearing on SWB, 'SWB would show marked fluctuations as unmet needs arise, and are then met. But this does not occur', data they have already drawn upon to make their argument shows precisely that SWB *does* fluctuate in response to events – such as serious injury or life-threatening illness – which challenge people's abilities to meet their basic needs (Bach and Tilton, 1994; Bloom *et al.*, 1991).

Secondly, it only makes sense to speak of automata or alien beings as exhibiting an 'average 25%SM deficit from complete life satisfaction' as if this were a steady state of being-in-the-world. It is hard to imagine what 100%SM life satisfaction could actually mean, and, if Cummins is right that humans cannot biologically exceed 80%SM, then, ipso facto, 80%SM is as happy as one could be: in effect, this quantum actually represents 100 per cent satisfaction. However, if we talk about real-life human beings (presumably who the model is trying to account for), everyday members' understandings tell us that life is a dynamic process, not a steady state.

Thirdly, SWB may well be 'remarkably stable' when large population averages, derived from cross-sectional ('snapshot') studies, taken from different eras and sourced from completely different people, are what we are trying to explain. But such population averages are *abstractions*: they do not relate to any individual judgments of satisfaction with life and, again, it is surely this that we are trying to explain. Indeed, while Cummins *et al.* (in press) here and elsewhere maintain that SWB is stable, in Cummins (2001) it is suggested that: 'Rodgers (1982) ... reviewed national USA survey data from 1957 to 1978. He reported a slight but significant decrease up to the early 1970s followed by a gradual recovery. This latter increase was also reported by Andrews (1991) in respect of data derived from a life-as-a-whole survey conducted in 1972 and again in 1988' (Cummins, 2001b).

Similarly, in their discussion of the effects that needs being met have on the 'buffers' (which, following an exercise model, it is held 'strengthens' them) Cummins *et al.* (in press) discuss a study reported by Wolinski *et al.* (1985). Wolinski and co-workers found that, over a one-year study, people with high or low levels of SWB at the start of the study scored lower and higher, respectively, five or 12 months later. With socio-economic status (SES) overriding the regression to the mean effect, Cummins *et al.* (in press) acknowledge that a *direct relationship* between socio-economic status and SWB improvement over the course of the study exists. Wolinski *et al.* (1985) conclude that their results 'suggest a vicious cycle wherein lower SES elderly people will increasingly face declining SWB, while their higher SES counterparts will somehow be able to avoid and/or compensate for the circumstances and problems that would otherwise result in reducing their subjective well-being' (p. 102). This is described as: 'consistent with that emerging from the aforementioned review ... the perception of whether or not important needs are being met is strongly influenced by personality' (Cummins, *et al.*, in press). That high SES may be linked to access to resources and the ability to operate materially on the world is not canvassed: rather, again, we see that such matters (despite the contrary evidence Wolinski *et al.* provide) are overridden by 'personality'.

In summarizing their account Cummins *et al.* (in press) thus maintain, as shown in Figure 8.3, that:

> SWB is under the direct control of personality and the indirect control of the buffers, which together act to maintain SWB within its normal range ... chronic met needs will normally have little influence on SWB levels ... in such circumstances, the buffers will typically not be activated ... Consequently, the level of SWB will remain determined by the

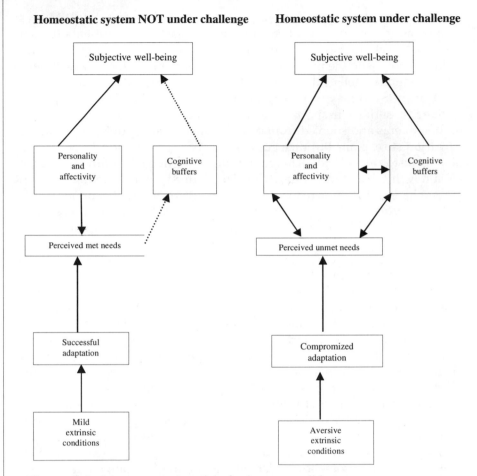

Figure 8.3 A homeostatic model of subjective well-being.
Source: Cummins *et al*. (in press).

dispositional set-point-range ... To summarize, it is proposed that, in the absence of strong unmet needs, the SWB homeostatic system will deliver a level of SWB that is within its set-point-range. The presence of strong unmet needs can defeat this system and, therefore, cause SWB to fall below its normal range ... The differential strength of the buffers combines to absorb the impact of threats causing needs to no longer be met, and as a consequence, act to maintain SWB within homeostatically determined levels.

Adaptation to Life and Subjective Well-being

One other matter needs to be addressed: adaptation. Having stated that 'personality provides a steady affective background that determines the set-point-range for the whole homeostatic system' and that 'a set of cognitive buffers, together with personality, create subjective well-being', Cummins *et al.* (in press) introduce the concept of adaptation as 'the most basic process in the homeostatic model', and describe adaptation as 'a psychological process that allows people, over some period of time, to experience a reduced reaction to some changed life circumstance that comes to represent their extrinsic experience'.

The fundamental postulate of Adaptation Level Theory (Helson, 1964) is that an individual's judgment of their current 'stimulation' level (whether that be positive or negative) is relative to the level to which they are accustomed. So, if current stimulation is higher than accustomed, change is experienced. Cummins *et al.* (in press) suggest that adaptation may be defined as the process by which the future experience of this new level of stimulation comes to seem unremarkable: that is an upward shift in adaptation level occurs 'because the novel stimulation has been added to the "accustomed" level of stimulation'. Secondly, habituation takes place: the idea being that people get used to (or become accustomed to) a given level of 'stimulation', and habituation is the term used to describe 'the idea that events are judged by the extent to which they deviate from adaptation level'.

While adaptation and habituation are usually concepts employed in behavioural psychological research looking at the way rats, for example, show decreased responsivity to painful stimuli over time, or the manner in which humans no longer consciously hear background noise after a certain period of exposure (and hence the use of the rather incongruous sounding term 'stimulation'), a number of studies have transplanted these concepts from the laboratory to examine the ideas of adaptation and habituation in relation to happiness and SWB. As Cummins *et al.* (in press) note, perhaps the most frequently cited study is that of Brickman *et al.* (1978) who compared the reported happiness of lottery winners, people with spinal injuries and a 'no-event' control group. When the happiness of the three groups was compared up to a year and a half later only minor differences in SWB could be found. Cummins *et al.* (in press) explain:

> the lottery winners' initial euphoria and changed life-style caused a massive upward shift in adaptation level ... new pleasures lost their capacity to excite, and the ordinary events of their previous lives, that had been sources of pleasure, were now unable to do so because they fell below the new adaptation level. In contrast, the reduced level of positive stimulation experienced by people who had acquired paraplegia, caused their adaptation level to fall ... these people increasingly experienced pleasure from minor positive events that would have previously gone unnoticed ... due to the changed adaptation levels of these groups, their levels of happiness had returned close to the levels they had experienced prior to their life event.

Such an account, while sounding entirely plausible, does so only as long as it is assumed that 'happiness' is, actually, a static *thing* amenable to precision measurement. The account offered here, by *forcing* happiness into such a mould, neglects that whatever the measure of happiness suggests in terms of a producible quantum, it is not the same 'thing' or set of 'things' that was measured across time. As Cummins *et al.* (in press) note, the spinally injured participants 'increasingly experienced pleasure from minor positive events that would have previously gone unnoticed' whereas, for the lottery winners, the 'new pleasures lost their capacity to excite, and the ordinary events of their previous lives, that had been sources of pleasure, were now unable to do so'. So again, contra their argument, what we see is that what 'happiness' *consists in* changes in keeping with the circumstances of people's individual lives. If entirely different criteria are being used by the participants, at the different moments of measurement, to arrive at a happiness quantum – as Cummins *et al.*'s (in press) exposition so clearly suggests – then we are comparing apples with oranges.

Such confusion continues in the summary of adaptation research. It is suggested that 'data confirming the validity of Adaptation Level Theory in relation to SWB are unimpressive', but despite this Cummins *et al.* conclude that, as the theory is said to 'have a strong level of acceptance' and as 'no telling argument or data have been provided that reasonably question the validity of the main tenets … it seems logical to incorporate the theory… into our Homeostatic model'. It must be noted at this point that Creationism has a 'strong level of acceptance' in many American educational circles, as did Lysenkoism in Soviet genetics and as did the ideas of phlogiston and the earth being a flat disc supported by tortoises in earlier times.

Subjective Well-being, Joy and Depression

The final aspect of the theory of SWB homeostasis concerns 'homeostatic maintenance and failure'. This aspect of the theory is described as 'speculative at this stage', but is necessitated by the fact that 'the maintenance of SWB within its set-point-range requires some kind of feedback loop'. Drawing on Carver (2000), it is suggested that human action is goal-directed and managed by two types of feedback loop: 'goal seekers' and 'anti-goal' avoiders. Checking the match between current conditions and goals, the loops adjust action as necessary. This theoretical speculation affords the insight that, in consequence 'people tend to do what they intend to do … and avoid doing the things they regard as unpleasant'. The same is held to be true for how people feel, but with the added complication that the speed with which goals are being met is also at issue. Carver (2000: 339) suggests that 'if the sensed velocity is less than the reference point, the result is negative affect; if it exceeds the reference point, the result is positive affect' (Cummins *et al.* (in press) apply this logic to subjective well-being. They conjecture that:

> SWB lying either above or below the set-point-range constitutes a deviation from the velocity goal. Such deviations will then lead to internal adjustments that will, eventually, restore SWB to a level within its set-point-range ... Levels of SWB lying above the set-point-range should lead to 'coasting' ... to withdrawal of some effort, basking, or turning to some other behavioural domain. Levels of SWB lying below the set-point-range should lead to the more intense goal-seeking motivation or behaviour.

Lest the idea gain hold that 'coasting, basking' or lazing is under the control of human agency rather than under the direction of automated brain mechanisms whirring away inside their passive human vehicles, Cummins *et al.* (in press) quickly dispel such a thought. In considering 'joy' they note that this experience should be considered neither epihanous, transcendental nor exceptional. It is, rather, a mundane and temporary aberration, a consequence of 'acute homeostatic failure'. It is suggested that 'higher than normal SWB can be induced in the short-term by meeting a need (e.g., having a satisfying meal) or experiencing a highly positive life event (e.g., being promoted at work). Such situations represent homeostatic failure at the level of the cognitive buffers.' Such a notion also represents failure at the level of an account of *human* experience. Similarly with despair: 'depression', it is suggested:

> is conceptualised as the loss of SWB homeostasis ... Provided that some negative influence lacks the power to defeat homeostasis, the symptoms of depression should be virtually absent ... under conditions of homeostatic defeat, the symptoms of depression (i.e. scores on depression indices) are coincident with low values within the buffer systems and related personality trait constellations ... In summary, both joy and depression can be regarded as consequences of homeostatic failure. However, whereas joy is inevitably an acute state, defeated by homeostatic processes, depression can be chronic, representing the failure of homeostasis in the face of powerful and persistent negative experience.

Such an account of the (un)happiness or (dis)satisfaction of persons is flawed on a number of levels. To begin with 'having a satisfying meal' or 'being promoted at work' are not the kinds of events sensibly describable as engendering 'joy' in the usually accepted usage of the term. Secondly, why 'powerful and persistent negative experience' should be capable of producing chronic homeostatic control failure and 'powerful and persistent positive experience' should not, similarly, be capable of producing 'chronic' 'joy' – especially if all it takes is a decent meal – is unspecified.

Furthermore, 'scores on depression indices', which are here held to be 'coincident with low values within the [cognitive] buffer systems', are more often than not derived by asking people primarily about their *actions and bodily experiences*, not about their feelings or 'cognitions'. As such quite how sleeping more or less than usual, or losing or gaining weight, are supposed to be 'coincident with' low levels of optimism, self-esteem and perceived control is opaque. Secondly, just what 'depression' is thought to be happens to be extremely variable across cultures (Wolpert, 1999) and hence both 'symptoms of depression and scores on depression indices' will only have locally specific relationships (if any at all) to putative values of speculative 'cognitive buffers' rather than the universal connection which Cummins *et al.* (in press) wish to claim.

Finally, if SWB is, as Cummins *et al.* (in press) claim, controlled primarily by personality and 'cognitive buffering', it is entirely unclear how, and by what process, 'powerful and persistent negative experience' should overpower the mechanism whereby 'levels of SWB lying below the set-point-range should lead to the more intense goal-seeking motivation or behaviour'. Such an account adds nothing to common-sense understandings of everyday contentment, satisfaction with life or subjective well-being, still less to everyday conceptions of either ecstasy or misery: it merely repackages these in a depersonalized cognitive psychological terminology of 'feedback loops', 'velocity goals' and 'homeostatic failure'. As was noted above, to speak in such a manner of persons is to reduce being human to being a faulty radiator, robot or guided missile.

In Summary

The idea that biology determines lived experience is pervasive in contemporary psychology. Although a powerful and apparently persuasive account of how things stand with persons, it is an extraordinarily problematic position, for all sorts of reasons. This chapter has sought to show how the assumptions underpinning one theory of QOL can be identified and unpacked. As such, this chapter has tried to demonstrate *how* it is possible to take a critical stance towards impressive sounding statistics and the elaborate psychological theories – which make up so much of our current common sense of ourselves. As Foucault (1978) observed, it is precisely *because* psychological ideas determine so much of how we understand ourselves that these notions, which after all are *only hypotheses*, demand detailed critical attention.

Notes

1. In brief Kant's *Critique of Judgement* (1978) attempts to reconcile the paradoxical view of human beings as rational animals, whereby pure reason and everyday earthly practical reason, become via the capacity for judgment a set of checks and balances on each other.
2. My thanks to Alec McHoul for this observation.

Study Questions

- What are the political, practical and ethical implications of understanding subjective well-being as a biological brain state?
- Is my QOL homeostatically controlled?
- How can we *know* how animals (or other persons) feel about themselves or the quality of their lives?
- How much reliance can we place on people's verbal reports of their happiness?

Suggestions for Further Reading

Butler, P. V. (1998) Psychology as history, and the biological renaissance: a brief review of the science and politics of psychological determinism, *Australian Psychologist*, 33, 1: 40–6.

Edwards, D. (1997) *Discourse and Cognition*. London: Sage.

Potter, J. (1996) *Representing Reality: Discourse, Rhetoric and Social Construction*. London: Sage.

Rose, S., Lewontin, R. C. and Kamin, L. J. (1984) *Not in Our Genes: Biology, Ideology and Human Nature*. London: Pelican.

CHAPTER 9

Should We 'Hang up Quality of Life as a Hopeless Term'?

Patients who are dying may find some quality in life, even when their quality of life as assessed by current measures is abysmal. (Farsides and Dunlop, 2001: 1481)

Malcolm: Nothing in his life / Became him like the leaving of it:
he died / As one that had been studied in his death /
To throw away the dearest thing he ow'd as t'were a careless trifle. (*Macbeth*, Act 1, Scene 4, 7–11)

In her foreword to the second American Association on Mental Retardation volume on quality of life (Schalock, 1997) Luckasson (1997: ix) noted that she had moved, over ten years, from being a sceptic about the value of quality of life research, to being at least persuadable that 'quality of life/ happiness, as a guide to good, may be absolutely appropriate'. Potter (2000) observed that, after one hundred years of psychological research, nearly all of the important questions were yet to be asked, let alone answered. In this final Chapter I outline a position congruent with both of these observations. In QOL research I believe, as with Potter's view of psychology, that we have yet to get any where near beginning to comprehend what asking serious questions about the quality of (a) life may mean – as the quotes heading this chapter suggest. Of course, Farsides and Dunlop's (2001) observation may be taken as an indication that what we need are measures or scales that more accurately measure the quality of life of the dying. Such a reading would, I believe, be to miss the point, and, below, I sketch a way forward which respects the view that, as Malcolm noted of the Thane of Cawdor's departure, the quality of a life (or death) is, in the end, a qualitative, or aesthetic, judgment.

So, with Luckasson, I have come to believe that the concept of QOL – or, as Taylor (1990) would have it, a definitively lower case 'quality of life' – may offer not so much a formalized, psychometric, conceptual framework for understanding quality of life as a (biological) human universal. Rather quality of life may offer us a 'sensitizing concept' for thinking through the purpose and methods of delivery of human services, or ways to enhance the 'liveability' of our particular communities in a democratic, inclusive and 'emancipatory' way. This final chapter then draws together the preceding discussion and summarizes the key philosophical, conceptual and methodological issues covered. Some avenues for further research are identified.

Rethinking Quality of Life

In his biography of Ludwig Wittgenstein, Monk (1991) describes the period, during the Second World War, when Wittgenstein collaborated with Grant and Reeve at Guy's Hospital in London. Grant and Reeve were studying the effects of injuries sustained by soldiers in battle and civilians in air raids. The project had begun as an attempt to specify more closely the nature of a condition, first identified in the Great War, described as 'wound shock'. Monk (1991: 445) writes that:

> Grant and Reeve's initial problem was that, in spite of a detailed study of the scientific literature, there seemed to be no satisfactory way of defining clinically the condition of 'wound shock'. Some authors identified the condition on the basis of haemoconcentration (the development of an abnormally high concentration of red blood cells in the blood thought to be due to the leakage of plasma from the blood into the tissue), while others recognized it as a syndrome of low blood pressure, skin pallor and rapid pulse.

The parallels with the social scientific research on quality of life reviewed in this book are striking. Despite claims of consensus, and what many see as inappropriate foreclosure in terms of theoretical models, it seems to be the case, that – as with 'wound shock' in the 1940s – 'in spite of a detailed study of the scientific literature, there seem[s] to be no satisfactory way of defining … the condition'. Instead there exists a bewildering variety of different 'conditions', on the basis of which the construct is inferred. By the time of the final report of the 'wound shock' project, the project team had come to the conclusion, which gives every appearance of having been written by Wittgenstein himself, that:

> in practice we found that the diagnosis of shock seemed to depend on the personal views of the individual making it rather than on generally accepted criteria. Unless we were acquainted with these views we did not know what to expect when called to the bedside. The label alone did not indicate what signs and symptoms the patient displayed, how ill he was or what treatment he required. The *only common ground* for diagnosis that we could detect was that the patient seemed *ill*. We were led, therefore, to discard the word 'shock' in its varying definitions. We have not since found it to be of any value in the study of injury; it has rather been a hindrance to unbiased observation and a cause of misunderstanding. (Monk, 1999: 452, my emphasis)

'Wound shock' and 'quality of life' then share the quality that, while specific instances of the use of the terms seem to depend on the views of the individual using it, nevertheless, these usages show what Wittgenstein

(1953) calls, in the *Philosophical Investigations*, a 'family resemblance': in all cases 'the patient seemed *ill*'. The mistake with 'wound shock' was to look *beyond* the family resemblance, to imagine that an underlying relationship between the multiplicity of manifestations of illness was implied by the existence of a term which appeared to unite them into a singular entity. To pursue the family resemblance argument for a moment, it is clear that the terms 'mother', 'father', 'brother' and 'sister' can all be collected up into the superordinate category 'family' – or, by analogy with 'wound shock', can be seen as different manifestations of the condition 'family', and could be imagined as different forms of 'illness'. But while family members may indeed bear a family resemblance, to say that 'beneath' external appearances, all of these instances of 'family' are 'the same' is to make as little sense as holding that all forms of 'illness' are 'the same'.

If the logical grammar of the term 'quality of life' is examined it too can be seen to operate in this manner. Instances of the usage share a family resemblance with each other: but they do not point to a singular underlying 'thing' or entity. Pace Watson, we cannot make a term mean what we want it to mean. Thus while the field of quality of life research may show immense vigour and huge productivity, at the same time argument continues to rage about what QOL 'really is'. Paradoxically, the need for the field to produce 'consensus documents' points to the *absence* of any serious consensus on the central object of study. It is difficult to imagine any of the mature sciences, such as physics, needing to convene an expert working group to produce a consensus document on a basic concept. One doesn't, therefore, see publications entitled 'The Atom: A consensus document'.

Proponents of QOL research, however, argue that such documents are required because of the youth of the field. Cummins *et al.* (in press), for example, end their account of the homeostatic model of subjective well-being with the claim: 'Other data may cause a re-evaluation of the structure that has been described. We look forward to such developments and offer this homeostatic model only as a first step in out understanding of how it is that SWB is so effectively maintained.' Similarly, in their Preface to the *soi-disant* 'consensus document', *Quality of Life: Its Conceptualization, Measurement and Application* prepared for the International Association for the Study of Intellectual Disability, Schalock and Parmenter (2000: 5) write that 'concepts and models presented in this Consensus Document will potentially vary from country to country … The cross-cultural understanding of the concept of quality of life is still in its infancy'. In their conclusion to the same document Felce *et al.* (2000: 31) *begin* by stating that: 'It is important to point out that the concept of quality of life is still emerging in the field.'

In the *Philosophical Investigations*, Wittgenstein (1953: 232) remarks of psychology that:

the confusion and barrenness of psychology is not to be explained by calling it a 'young science'; its state is not comparable with that of physics, for instance, in its beginnings. (Rather with that of certain branches of mathematics. Set Theory.) For in psychology there are experimental methods and *conceptual confusion*. (As in the other case conceptual confusion and methods of proof.) The existence of the experimental method makes us think we have the means of solving the problems which trouble us; though problem and method pass one another by.

The field of quality of life, it would seem, has the distinction of demonstrating the problems of both set theory and of psychology. As we have seen, it has 'experimental methods' and 'methods of proof' aplenty but, unlike physics in its beginnings, it is assailed by conceptual confusion. Despite the immense outpouring of QOL studies since the 1960s we are no closer to knowing how to answer questions such as 'what is quality of life'. As suggested above, this may be in part because, to paraphrase Wittgenstein, the existence of methods of study makes us think we have the means of solving the problems which trouble us, despite problem and method passing one another by. It is arguable that, in quality of life research across the social sciences, problem and method pass one another by, not so much because 'the science is undeveloped but because the methods it employs are inappropriate to its task' (Monk, 1991: 549).

Given that method is always already theory in disguise, the problem of method may be more to do with the way we theorize *persons*. Theories of the person are almost always implicit (if addressed at all) in currently dominant psychologistic theorizing across the social sciences (in whatever discipline), and the endeavour to measure the 'amount' of quality of life that persons 'have' trades on an entirely unstated theory of the person. The currently dominant theory of the person in the West holds that, after Descartes and Kant, to be human is to have a body and a psyche, a psyche, which may – indeed must – be disaggregated into parts for the purposes of (meaningful) counting. Thus we see that current efforts to measure the quality of life of individuals presuppose that there are such psychical *things* as 'life satisfaction', 'subjective well-being' and the rest, pre-existing inside people's heads, and that they too are subjectable to further disaggregation (into 'domains' or 'facets') that permit direct measurement.

That is – like memories, attitudes and beliefs – such objects exist, and along with the other inventoried 'contents' of the psyche, they *drive human acts*. The provision by a research participant of an answer to a social scientist's question about their quality of life, under such an account, is not then the *act* of a *person* but the act of a being that may, more accurately, be likened to a gas meter. The 'levels' of subjective well-being, satisfaction with relationships and the rest reported by persons are merely *readings* of objectified, 'inner', psychical dials. This surely is a misunderstanding not only of what it means to be a *person*, but also of what it means to *act*.

In *Being and Time* Martin Heidegger (1996: 44–5) writes that:

Acts are nonpsychical. Essentially the person exists only in carrying out intentional acts, and is thus essentially *not* an object. Every psychical objectification, and thus every comprehension of acts as something psychical, is identical with depersonalization. In any case, the person is given as the agent of intentional acts which are connected with the unity of a meaning. Thus psychical being has nothing to do with being a person. Acts are carried out, the person carries them out.

In order then to understand what human acts – such as individuals' descriptions, demonstrations or avowals of the quality of their life – may mean, it is necessary either to rethink our theories of personhood or to accept that currently given psychologistic theories of quality of life cannot, under this account, be theories of the quality of life of *persons*. Paradoxically, then, given their avowed purpose of furnishing an explanation of the quality of life which people experience, while current theories may (or may not) offer compelling accounts of depersonalized (and entirely hypothetical) homeostatically controlled cognitive componentry, they cannot tell us anything about the meaning of the quality of life, as a state of being-in-the-world, of *persons*. Such a state of affairs, it would seem, requires both that we suspend our habitual, a priori, beliefs about the nature of ourselves, and also that we retheorize not only the object of our enquiry (persons, and the quality of their lives), but also the procedures whereby we investigate ourselves.

Quality of Life as a Member's Term

There is, furthermore, another difficult problem to address which follows from the above. That is, debates about definitional matters, objective and subjective indices of QOL, whether subjective well-being is best understood as a function of self or circumstance and the rest, distract attention from a more fundamental issue – namely what is at stake in the everyday-life, normal, practical grounding of the concept of 'quality of life'. If we ask what it means, in ordinary practice, to 'assess someone's quality of life' we must immediately pause. We sense that there is something wrong with the question; that is we do not, in the very ordinary life which is meant both to warrant, and to be explained by, QOL research, 'assess' *anyone's* quality of life at all. To ask the question that way, and indeed to ask the closely related question 'what is quality of life' (on which more later), is to recast what are always already dynamic and interactional phenomena in terms which suggest formality, regularity and standardization (Garfinkel, 1967). QOL *qua* QOL, or 'quality of life' deployed as an *official* or *technical* term, operates in the same manner as all other social-scientific terms. That is it cannot but *homogenize* that which it intends (and claims) to pick apart.

However, 'assessing' the quality of life (whether in people's 'own words' (cf. Edgerton, 1990; Bryant *et al.*, 2001) or, in Edgerton's words, via 'simple scalar instruments' (cf. World Health Organization, 1997; Cummins, 2001c) suggests a range of practices which share a language-game similarity (Wittgenstein, 1953) with folk enquiries, but which have very different motivations, sources of evidence and consequences. That is, there will be circumstances in everyday life under which we care about some particular person's well-being sufficiently to listen out for worries they express and perhaps to check a range of things (whether they are eating and sleeping properly, have enough money to get their groceries and so on), all with the possible upshot (say) of encouraging them to see the doctor, apply for a particular job or take a holiday. Equally, we might read in the newspaper or hear on the radio that this or that group of people seems to be having a bad time of things, that thousands of workers in a particular industry have lost their jobs, that residents of a particular locality have had their homes destroyed by a natural disaster or whatever and talk to friends about it – all with the consequence of (say) warranting a certain argumentative position in casual political talk, organizing a petition or encouraging people to donate towards a relief operation. Note how these mundane examples of everyday occasions when someone's well-being, or some group of people's quality of life, is of concern have to be described in their local and particular details (even at this level of generalization) and how they wholly resist, within the commonsensically understood meaning and usage of the term, being cast as a generalized 'assessment' of 'quality of life'.

On either an ethnomethodological, or an 'ordinary language philosophy', reading it seems clear that each of these 'assessments' (or, to pre-empt a later point, 'appreciations') is occasioned by local demands and has its own motivations, sources of evidence and consequences. In other words, there seems to be in operation a template very like that which Sacks calls those sets of question forms which Members use, one of which is 'Why do you want to do X?' (Sacks, 1992: 33). The general template is familiar, but it has its particular effect from what goes through it locally – and here the template is understandable as 'Are you happy with/about X?' The difference between these ordinary forms of asking about people's 'quality of life' in various domains (are you happy with/about X?) and the form of the question in social scientific QOL research represents a paradox in Sack's (1992) sense. That is, it is precisely contrary to the prevailing social scientific QOL research enterprise that, in everyday life, assessment should be so particular, so local and so unsystematic. The very abstraction and formalism – not only of the term 'assessment of quality of life' – but also of the procedures and practices that most research in the social sciences is committed to – demand standardization, replicability and generality; but *none of these* are routine features of ordinary concerns about some particular person's, or group of persons', particular sort of well-being, for (someone's) particular reasons.

It is possible then that a question like 'what is quality of life' is not the sort of a question that can, sensibly, be asked within a social *scientific* framework as the framework of social *science* is conventionally understood. It is possible that the routine procedures of normal science (Kuhn, 1973) in the social scientific disciplines have misled us about what sort of question it is that we are actually asking when we enquire of people how 'satisfied' they are with their lives. As we have seen, debate rages in the literature about whether such judgments are 'affective' or 'cognitive' (see Cummins *et al.*, in press) or some blend of the two, about the correct methods of calibrating responses and the (conflicting) relationship of these responses to 'variables' of every imaginable stripe. But perhaps to ask someone about the quality of their life is not to request a 'cognitive', rational judgment derived from a calculus of wants and needs, met and unmet. Perhaps it is not, either, to seek a raw, emotional, 'affective' appraisal. Perhaps in seeking a telling about the quality of a life we are not asking such sorts of questions at all: rather perhaps we are asking for a qualitative *appreciation* of how things stand. As such, then, maybe asking about the quality of life amounts to a request for an *aesthetic judgment*.

In his discussion of Wittgenstein's (1978) *Lectures and Conversations on Aesthetics, Psychology and Religious Belief*, Monk (1991) offers an account of Wittgenstein's intellectual project there in 'rescuing' questions of appreciation from the idea that there could be a science of aesthetics, and from the broader project of the West – the 'idol worship', in Wittgenstein's words, of 'Science and the Scientist' (Wittgenstein, 1978: 27). Monk suggests that:

> rather than trying to answer the traditional questions of aesthetics ('What is beauty?' etc.), Wittgenstein gives a succession of examples to show that [artistic] appreciation does not consist (as one might think from reading some philosophical discussions of aesthetics) in standing before a painting and saying: 'That is beautiful'. Appreciation takes a bewildering variety of forms, which differ from culture to culture, and quite often will not consist in *saying* anything. Appreciation will be *shown*, by actions as often as by words, by certain gestures of disgust or satisfaction, by the way we read a work of poetry or play a piece of music, by how often we read or listen to the same piece, and how we do so. These different forms of appreciation do not have any one thing in common that one can isolate in answer to the question 'What is artistic appreciation?' They are, rather linked by a complicated series of 'family resemblances'.

Thus inasmuch as 'appreciation does not consist ... in standing before a painting and saying: "That is beautiful"', perhaps appreciating the quality of one's life does not consist in standing in front of a social scientist and saying '75 ± 2.5 per cent'. Equally, as we saw in Chapter 3, it is perfectly possible to see that people with intellectual disabilities understand Wittgenstein's point that 'appreciation takes a bewildering variety of forms, which differ from culture to culture, and quite often will not consist in *saying* anything. Appreciation will be *shown*, by actions as often as by words, by certain gestures of disgust or satisfaction.' That is, showing appreciation may not be a one-off event, but rather an extended process – as we also saw in the discussion of Koch's (2001) work in Chapter 6. Recall that, in Chapter 3, Bob displayed a comprehensive appreciation of the high quality of his life *not* by *saying* anything about the quality of his life *as such*, and most certainly not in a manner which could contribute to the 'scientific' measurement of his appreciation, satisfaction or whatever. Rather, Bob *displayed* the quality of his life by *showing*, over the course of an extended period – for example in his singing of 'Santa Claus is coming to town' – his warm and positive appreciation of his life circumstances.

Monk goes on to point out that, crucially, in attempting to find answers to the question of aesthetic understanding, we are not looking for a reductive, *causal* explanation. Inasmuch as there is no science of aesthetics, equally the methods, procedures and results of another science, such as physics, or what he terms 'some pseudo-science, such as psychology' (Monk, 1991: 405), cannot sensibly be addressed to these questions. The question of reductionism imported into the analysis of aesthetic questions by the adoption of (pseudo)scientific methods is also eloquently addressed in the *Lectures and Conversations*. There Wittgenstein notes that, although making the statement: 'If we boil Redpath at 200 degrees C. all that is left when the water vapour is gone is some ashes, etc. This is all Redpath really is', has a certain charm, 'it is misleading to say the least' (Wittgenstein, 1978: 24). In talking of appreciation or an aesthetic judgment, then, Wittgenstein observes that: 'it is not only difficult to describe what appreciation consists in, but impossible. To describe what it consists in we would have to describe the whole environment' (Wittgenstein, 1978: 11). And that project is, despite the willingness of the Australian Bureau of Statistics (as we saw in Chapter 2) to contemplate 'mapping the whole of life', in practice a very different, and non-statistical, undertaking.

In an analogous analysis, Leudar and Thomas (2000) discuss the ways in which the 'pseudo-sciences' have approached the puzzling phenomenon of 'auditory hallucinations', or 'hearing voices'. They conclude their magisterial historical survey of the experience – from the reports of Achilles in the *Iliad* to the present day – with a sobering reflection on the problems caused by the practice in the 'pseudo-sciences' of asking questions about lived human experience in the form: '*what is x?*'

> The timeless and universal question 'what is hearing voices? period' is therefore not a happy one – it impoverishes the phenomenon studied. It impoverishes it because it treats as incidental and unimportant its context-

contingent aspects. In psychology, which aims at biological and evolutionary explanations of mind, the timeless question implies there is a basic, raw experience of hearing voices ... This position is clearly not supported by the materials ... As there are no mechanical behaviours (except in abstractions) which become intentional conduct when combined with psychological phenomena, so there are no raw experiences which become meaningful under descriptions but can be lived without them ... So the general conclusion is really that local concepts are constitutive of local experiences and there cannot be a psychology or psychiatry which can do without them. (Leudar and Thomas, 2000: 209)

That is, if we read 'quality of life' for 'hearing voices' in Leudar and Thomas's account, it is difficult to escape coming to identical conclusions. To paraphrase: there is no raw experience of quality of life which becomes meaningful under descriptions but can be lived without them ... local concepts (of quality of life) are constitutive of local experiences (of quality of life) and there cannot be a psychology or psychiatry which can do without them.

Ways Forward

One aspect of a very different project that understanding quality of life might become is outlined by Rose (1992) when he calls for the development of a 'critical ontology of ourselves' (Rose, 1992: 160). Chapter 5 has offered a 'worked example' of what a contribution to such a project might look like. Rose suggests that the investigations of the forms of self that are presupposed within modern social, economic and political relations evokes a 'central question addressed by Max Weber ... a sustained reflection on *Mentschentum*, the history of what humans are in their nature and how human lives are conducted' (Rose, 1992: 160). Such a project is consonant with Foucault's (1986) suggestion that the central task of philosophy after Kant was to describe both the nature of our present and the nature of ourselves in that present. It is, says Rose (1992: 161):

to recognize the importance of historical investigations into the events through which we have come to recognize ourselves and act upon ourselves as certain kinds of subject. It is to interrogate what we have become, as subjects, in our individuality, and the nature of the present in which we are. Such an investigation would not attempt a psychological diagnosis of the modern soul. Rather it would seek to document the categories and explanatory schemes according to which we think ourselves, the criteria and norms we use to judge ourselves and one another in order to make particular kinds of being. We would, that is to say, endeavour to describe the historical *a priori* of our existence as subjects.

And, perhaps, we should take as a starting point the notions of subjectivity, autonomy and freedom themselves.

It is precisely because notions such as subjectivity, autonomy and freedom are so massively pervasive in the ways in which we think ourselves that it is essential that they be subject to scrutiny. The notion of quality of life too is becoming, if it has not already, so much a part of the mundane present, so closely bound up with 'the criteria and norms we use to judge ourselves and one another', that it is essential that this notion, too, be subject to critical scrutiny and analysis. Here too the purpose is emphatically not to 'attempt a psychological diagnosis of the modern soul' (there is more than enough literature essaying precisely that) but rather to understand the manner in which accounts of the 'modern soul' *as* an object amenable to psychological diagnosis and statistical modelling have come to be, how such accounts are constructed in order to persuade, and the relations between such accounting, the norms and criteria developed therein (such as ideas that, because happiness is homeostatically controlled, humans can and must be at best 75–80 per cent satisfied with their lives) and the forms of governmentality and the technologies of the self which flow from, and are naturalized by, such accounts.

In terms of the use of the QOL construct, in a 'scientific' manner, for example to gauge the success or otherwise of policy initiatives, human service structures or individualized care, the upshot of the current dominance of views which see QOL as an individualized aspect of the modern day psyche is paradoxical. If, pace Cummins *et al.* (in press) and Edgerton (1990), we are to believe that individuals' claims to contentment are, in some sense, not theirs to make – but rather are driven by temperamental, or biological, constraints and processes over which they, as persons, have no control – then, as Wolfensberger (1994) and Erikson (1993) have suggested, the practical utility of using measures of QOL as an index of policy success or service quality approximates to nil.

Of course this does not mean that seeking comments on aspects of personal experience which may be directly tied to the quality of health or social care interventions are of no value. In spite of the deprecation heaped on health-related quality of life because of its failure to employ a generic definition and measure of QOL (by Cummins, 1997b, for example), it is precisely the close relationship between, for example, matters such as the closeness of the car park to the outpatient oncology department and the experience of undergoing chemotherapy as more or less bearable which makes many measures in the HRQOL field of direct use in the evaluation of patient satisfaction. That 'patient satisfaction' and 'quality of life' are, in this literature, most often employed interchangeably, and that 'quality of life' here is used in its vernacular, or everyday, usage is only a problem if one wishes to claim a special technical status for what is always already a Member's term. This is not to suggest that other developments in HRQOL are unproblematic: as discussed in Chapter 6, the notions of QALYs and DALYs are not only deeply conceptually and methodologically difficult, they are also – for many – ethically unacceptable. I return to this point again below.

In assessing such matters, however, we have much to gain (as, for example, Thompson and Gifford's (2001) study discussed in Chapter 2 showed us) from the greater use of qualitative methods in the evaluation of quality of life. Edgerton (1990) has drawn the conclusion, from his close ethnographic study of the lives of people with intellectual disabilities, that we should be prepared to 'uncouple' objective standards of quality from subjective appraisals of the quality of life. The difficulties entailed by insisting on firm a priori categorizations of lived experience essential to quantitative work are well illustrated by public health researcher Eberhard Wenzel (2001) in the Internet diary he published up until his death from cancer in late 2001.

Wenzel writes of his first moments as a confirmed cancer patient (http://www.ldb.org/cancer/c1.htm). 'Objectively' he has – at the moment of his formal diagnosis – moved from the category of 'non-patient' into another: he has now become 'A Cancer Patient', and hence, by understood standards of HRQOL research, one might expect that this categorical membership would bestow a quality of life correspondingly reduced to whatever the 'disability weight' of oesophageal cancer is. However, in answer to the question 'how does it feel to be a C patient?', Wenzel notes that: 'Well, I don't know, because I don't feel like a C patient … people call me and ask "how do you feel?", probably expecting me to respond with "uh, not so good …". But that's not true for the time being. It may change though, who knows?' That is, we must be careful with the uncritical use of categories, and specifically the categorical (and dogmatic) use of diagnostic group labels and the values assigned to them. Wenzel shows very clearly that simply being objectively describable as a 'cancer patient' need not necessarily imply that one, 'subjectively', is a cancer patient. Thus, while Edgerton's work is specifically related to people with intellectual disabilities, there are no good reasons for assuming that his conclusions do not apply more widely. He notes (Edgerton, 1996: 88) that:

> improving the quality of a person's life may increase his or her sense of wellbeing, or it may not. That remains an empirical question and a difficult one to answer … We should continue every effort to ensure that persons … have access to better housing, health care, recreational activities, dignified employment, and everything else that an enlightened society can provide for its citizens. But we must never forget that all a society should do is provide options … Nor should it imagine that all who accept its array of life-quality options will experience a greater sense of well-being than they did before, or that all who reject these options in favour of an alternative life-style will be less satisfied.

In a similar vein, in a letter to the editor, published by the *British Medical Journal*, the chair of the UK's Depression Alliance, Dr Chris Manning, wrote to express his disbelief at official government statistics which suggested that levels of everyday misery ('neurosis') had not increased in Britain over the course of the 1990s. In his letter Manning captures one of the major difficulties both with the use of aggregated statistics of population well-being per se, and with the use of what may be described as measures of individual, personal (un)happiness as indicators of the effectiveness of government policy. He suggests that:

> there may be areas of the country where neurosis is increasing and others where it is decreasing. An average would cancel this out. A man sitting with one foot in a bowl of ice and one of boiling water has his feet in water of averagely aggregated warmth – but that will not do justice to *his* description of [his] level of comfort. (Manning, 2001)

As such, there is much to commend – in my view at least – the 'Scandinavian' approach to matters of life quality. If it is (as Perry *et al.* (2000) and Cummins (2001c) would suggest on the basis of 'hard' empirical data) impossible to establish clear-cut and explicit links between human service structures, processes and activities and the expressed happiness or life satisfaction of service recipients, then it seems to make very little sense indeed to employ that happiness, or otherwise, as a measure of how well the service is serving its 'customers'. Of course, if, as I have suggested above, estimations of the quality of one's life are anyway primarily aesthetic, there is no reason to presuppose that 'hard data' would provide any connection in the first place. What such findings do suggest, however, is that whether or not service structures themselves have any bearing on the individual life satisfaction of service users, it is possible to devise sets of publicly verifiable desirable standards for the delivery of services that maximize the quality, or aesthetic, of their use. This is, in my view, a fruitful area for future research.

That is, following Taylor (1990), there is no reason at all that service planners, providers and evaluators, as well as governmental policy-makers, should not use 'quality of life' as a sensitizing notion. However, in the case of using QOL as a formally operationalized and measurable construct, it seems clear that the problems involved probably outweigh the putative benefits. That is to say, there is no reason why we should not set about designing human services by asking ourselves about how this or that service process or this or that service structure might affect the quality of the lived experience of persons served in such a way or such a place. As we saw earlier, in one HRQOL study the key factor determining the 'quality' of patients' cancer treatment experience was found to be the closeness and convenience of the public car park to the outpatients' department. That 'parking proximity' is not identified anywhere else in the literature (at least to my knowledge) as a domain of 'quality of life' is, in the final analysis, irrelevant. That convenience of access made a large contribution to the quality of the treatment experience of a specific group of people is, while a fairly unremarkable and possibly entirely unsurprising finding, a helpful contribution to our knowledge about ways of designing services such that future groups of patients experience a qualitatively different (and better) service. Research possibilities here are extensive, and entirely in keeping with the increasing 'consumerist' focus of health and social care services. In this regard, studies evaluating the outcomes and effectiveness of projects such as the UK Department of Health's 'Expert Patient' initiative are clearly needed. Questions might include: What maximizes doctors' take up of 'expert patients' advice? What factors act as barriers? What effect on medical practice do 'expert patients' have?

Similarly, while methodologically and ethically problematic as a metric for large-scale funding decisions, the Patil *et al.* (2000) study (Chapter 6) showed that the *joint* estimation of hepatitis C disease state and treatment utilities by patients and their doctors may have much to contribute as a method for establishing an explicit base upon which mutually cooperative helping relationships can be forged. An exploration of the comparative utilities of doctors and their patients in a wider range of illnesses, the analysis of the use of cooperative ratings as a possible technique to maximize doctor–patient communication, and the value of the employment of utility evaluation techniques in medical education are clearly exciting areas for further field research.

Furthermore, a range of approaches to the use of social indicators is available, at both the local level (such as the projects described by Salvaris in Chapter 2) and also at a national and supra-national level (such as the EUSI described in Chapter 2), which permit the collection of data which can be *coherently quantified* and *sensibly aggregated* to tell a story about the living conditions of the nation-state (levels of unemployment, income disparities, percentage of women in the labour force, proportion of population with access to fresh drinking water, adherence to international conventions, crime rates and so on). We saw in Chapter 2 some of the key areas for development in the social indicators field: detailed research projects looking at the use of community-derived quality of life indicators are clearly needed.

There is insufficient space here to argue the case in detail, but the adoption of conceptually coherent sets of such indicators at the national and international levels, I would argue, rules out the use of notions like DALYs, particularly in estimates of the 'global burden' of human misery or 'psychiatric disorder'. In the light of the documented disparities between doctors and patients in the 'utility' they assign to various states of health, the methodological and ethical difficulties of their measurement and calculation, and the questionable intellectual coherence of guesses at utilities for hypothetical states as a method of estimating anything (other than, as noted above, immediate and local preferences), the QALY and the DALY should, in my view, be regarded as a misleading and possibly dangerous development. If, as they do, open democratic societies' need mechanisms for the 'rationing' or allocation of healthcare funding, then in my view the preferred site for the making of such decisions is the public forum, and the preferred method is ethical debate. That is, as Luckasson (1997) noted, as a *guide to good*, in the making of what are always already *moral* choices, quality of life might be absolutely appropriate as a ethical or aesthetic concept. Such an approach may have the virtue of reinstating into the debate, explicitly, the fact that when we discuss the quality of people's lives we are engaged in the weighing of moral questions, not simply the dry dissection of putative biological mechanisms or hypothetical statistical abstractions.

That is, efforts to press Member's terms like 'quality of life' into the mould of 'hard science' are probably misguided. The forced quantification of qualitative experience permits the rhetorical invocation of ghostly 'market mechanisms' driven by cost-utility analysis, and the grinding out of impressive-looking, but publicly incomprehensible, utility values to the nth decimal place. Even the WHO has noted that this process serves to distract attention from more important matters (Sayers and Fliedner, 1997). As, in psychology, does the search for equally ghostly 'cognitive mechanisms' which, whirring away all by themselves, 'maintain SWB output'.

As Erikson (1993) put it, the place for citizens to comment on the success or otherwise of governments in raising their personal well-being, or quality of life, is at elections. And, as Ludwig Wittgenstein also clearly put it, on those matters of which we cannot speak, we must remain silent.

Study Questions

- Is the quality of one's life best considered as a psychological (cognitive and/or affective) brain state or as an aesthetic judgment?
- Is enhancing the quality of life, happiness or life satisfaction of individuals the proper role of the state or its institutions?
- How might the scientific study of 'quality of life' proceed?
- Should we 'hang up quality of life as a hopeless term' as Wolfensberger (1994) has suggested?

Suggestions for Further Reading

Heidegger, Martin (1996) *Being and Time*, trans. by J. Stambaugh. Albany, NY: State University of New York Press.

McHoul, A. and Rapley, M. (2001) Culture, psychology and 'being human', *Culture and Psychology*, 7, 4: 433–51.

Wittgenstein, Ludwig (1953) *Philosophical Investigations*, (eds) G. E. M. Anscombe and R. Rhees. Cambridge: Blackwell.

Transcription Conventions

The transcription conventions used here were derived from those developed by Gail Jefferson (see Atkinson and Heritage, 1984).

(.) (..) (...)	Pauses of, approximately, a fifth of a second, half a second and one second.
(2 secs)	A roughly timed period of no speech.
.hh	A dot before an 'h' denotes speaker in-breath. The more h's, the longer the in-breath.
hh	An 'h' denotes an out-breath. The more h's, the longer the out-breath.
hehh hahh	Laughter syllables with some attempt to capture 'colour'.
Go(h)d	(h) This denotes 'laughter' within words.
((slurps))	A description enclosed in double brackets indicates a non-speech sound.
cu-	A dash denotes a sharp cut-off of a prior word or sound.
lo::ng	Colons show that the speaker has stretched the preceding letter or sound.
(guess)	Material within brackets represents the transcriber's guess at an unclear part of the tape.
?	A question mark denotes a rising intonation. It does not necessarily indicate a question.
=	The 'equals' sign denotes utterances that run on.
↑↓	Arrows indicate rising or falling intonational shift. They are placed before the onset of such a shift. Double arrows indicate very marked shifts.

under	Underlining indicates emphasis.
CAPITALS	Capital letters indicate a section of speech that is noticeably louder than that surrounding it.
° soft°	Degree signs indicate speech noticeably quieter than the surrounding talk.
>fast< <slow>	'Greater than' and 'less than' signs indicate that the talk they encompass was produced noticeably more quickly than the surrounding talk; the reverse for 'slow' talk.
he ⌈llo ⌊hello	Square brackets between adjacent lines of concurrent speech show overlapping talk.
[^t]	Dental 'click'.

Introduction

WHOQOL-BREF

INTRODUCTION

**ADMINISTRATION, SCORING AND
GENERIC VERSION OF THE ASSESSMENT**

Field Trial Version December 1996

PROGRAMME ON MENTAL HEALTH

WORLD HEALTH ORGANIZATION

GENEVA

This manual was drafted by Alison Harper on behalf of the WHOQOL group. The WHOQOL group comprises a coordinating group, collaborating investigators in each of the field centres and a panel of consultants. Dr J. Orley directs the project. He has been assisted in this by Professor M. Power, Dr W. Kuyken, Professor N. Sartorius, Dr M. Bullinger and Dr A. Harper. The field centres involved in initial piloting of the WHOQOL were: Professor H. Herrman, Dr H. Schofield and Ms B. Murphy, University of Melbourne, Australia; Professor Z. Metelko, Professor S. Szabo and Mrs M. Pibernik-Okanovic, Institute of Diabetes, Endocrinology and Metabolic Diseases and Department of Psychology, Faculty of Philosophy, University of Zagreb, Croatia; Dr N. Quemada and Dr A. Caria, INSERM, Paris, France; Dr S. Rajkumar and Mrs Shuba Kumar, Madras Medical College, India; Dr S. Saxena and Dr K. Chandiramani, All India Institute of Medical Sciences, New Delhi, India; Dr M. Amir and Dr D. Bar-On, Ben-Gurion University of the Negev, Beer-Sheeva, Israel; Dr Miyako Tazaki, Department of Science, Science University of Tokyo, Japan and Dr Ariko Noji, Department of Community Health Nursing, St Luke's College of Nursing, Japan; Dr G. van Heck and Mrs J. De Vries, Tilburg University, The Netherlands; Professor J. Arroyo Sucre and Professor L. PicardAmi, University of Panama, Panama; Professor M. Kabanov, Dr A. Lomachenkov and Dr G. Burkovsky, Bekhterev Psychoneurological Research Institute, St. Petersburg, Russia; Dr R. Lucas Carrasco, University of Barcelona, Spain; Dr Yooth Bodharamik and Mr Kitikorn Meesapya, Institute of Mental Health, Bangkok, Thailand; Dr S. Skevington, University of Bath, United Kingdom; Professor D. Patrick, Ms M. Martinand, Ms D. Wild, University of Washington, Seattle, USA and; Professor W. Acuda and Dr J. Mutambirwa, University of Zimbabwe, Harare, Zimbabwe.

New centres using the field version of the WHOQOL-100 are: Dr S. Bonicato, FUNDONAR, Fundacion Oncologica Argentina, Argentina; Dr A.E. Molzahn, University of Victoria, Canada; Dr G. Yongping, St Vincent's Hospital, Victoria, Australia; Dr G. Page, University of Quebec at Rimouski, Canada; Professor J. Fang, Sun Yat-Sen University of Medical Sciences, People's Republic of China; Dr M. Fleck, University of the State of Rio Grande do Sul, Brazil; Professor M.C. Angermeyer, Dr R. Kilian, Universitatsklinikum Klinik and Poliklinik für Psychiatrie, Leipzig, Germany; Mr Kwok Fai Leung, Hospital Authority, Hong Kong; Dr B.R. Hanestad, University of Bergen, Norway; Dr M.H. Mubbashar, Rawalpindi General Hospital, Pakistan; Dr J. Harangozo, Semelweis University of Medicine, Budapest & Dr L. Kullman, National Institute of Mental Rehabilitation, Budapest, Hungary; Professor I. Wiklund, Health Economics & Quality of Life, Astra Hassle AB, Sweden; Dr C. Fidaner, Dr Behget Uz Paediatric Hospital, Balqova/Izmir, Turkey; Dr G. de Girolamo, Servizio Salute Mentale USL 27, Italy; Professor P. Bech, Frederiksborg

General Hospital, Denmark; Dr R.S. Pippalla, Howard University, College of Pharmacy and Pharmaceutical Sciences, Washington, DC, USA and Dr H. Che Ismail, School of Medical Sciences, Kelantan, Malaysia.

Further information can be obtained from:
Dr John Orley
Programme on Mental Health
World Health Organization
CH-1211 Geneva 27, Switzerland

WHOQOL-BREF Introduction, Administration, Scoring and Generic Version of the Assessment

Introduction

The WHOQOL-100 quality of life assessment was developed by the WHOQOL Group with fifteen international field centres, simultaneously, in an attempt to develop a quality of life assessment that would be applicable cross-culturally. The development of the WHOQOL-100, has been detailed elsewhere (i.e. Orley & Kuyken, 1994; Szabo, 1996; WHOQOL Group 1994a, 1994b, 1995). This document gives a conceptual background to the WHOQOL definition of quality of life and describes the development of the WHOQOL-BREF, an abbreviated version of the WHOQOL-100. It also includes a generic English language version of the WHOQOL-BREF, instructions for administering and scoring, and proposed uses for this short form of the WHOQOL.

Rationale for the development of the WHOQOL-100

WHO's initiative to develop a quality of life assessment arose for a number of reasons. In recent years there has been a broadening in focus in the measurement of health, beyond traditional health indicators such as mortality and morbidity (e.g. World Bank, 1993; WHO, 1991), to include measures of the impact of disease and impairment on daily activities and behaviour (e.g. Sickness Impact Profile; Bergner, Bobbitt, Carter et al, 1981), perceived health measures (e.g. Nottingham Health Profile; Hunt, McKenna and McEwan, 1989) and disability/functional status measures (e.g. the MOS SF-36, Ware et al, 1993). These measures, whilst beginning to provide a measure of the impact of disease, do not assess quality of life *per se*, which has been aptly described as "the missing measurement in health" (Fallowfield, 1990). Second, most measures of health status have been developed in North America and the UK, and the translation of these measures for use in other settings is time-consuming, and unsatisfactory for a number of reasons (Sartorius and Kuyken, 1994; Kuyken, Orley, Hudelson and Sartorius, 1994). Third, the increasingly mechanistic model of medicine, concerned only with the eradication of disease and symptoms, reinforces the need for the introduction of a humanistic element into health care. By calling for quality of life assessments in health care, attention is focused on this aspect of health, and resulting interventions will pay increased attention to this aspect of patients' well-being. WHO's initiative to develop a quality of life assessment arises from a need for a genuinely international measure of quality of life and a commitment to the continued promotion of an holistic approach to health and health care.

Steps in the development of the WHOQOL-100

The WHOQOL-100 development process consisted of several stages. These are explained in brief within this document. For a detailed description, the reader is referred to the WHOQOL Group (1994a, 1994b, in preparation). In the first stage, concept clarification involved establishing an agreed upon definition of quality of life and an approach to international quality of life assessment.

Quality of life is defined as individuals' perceptions of their position in life in the context of the culture and value systems in which they live and in relation to their goals, expectations, standards and concerns.

This definition reflects the view that quality of life refers to a subjective evaluation which is embedded in a cultural, social and environmental context. Because this definition of quality of life focuses upon respondents' "perceived" quality of life, it is not expected to provide a means of measuring in any detailed fashion symptoms, diseases or conditions, but rather the effects of disease and health interventions on quality of life. As such, quality of life cannot be equated simply with the terms "health status", "life style", "life satisfaction", "mental state" or "well-being". The recognition of the multi-dimensional nature of quality of life is reflected in the WHOQOL-100 structure.

In the second stage of development, exploration of the quality of life construct within 15 culturally diverse field centres was carried out to establish a list of areas/facets that participating centres considered relevant tb the assessment of quality of life. This involved a series in meetings of focus groups which included health professionals, patients and well subjects. A maximum of six specific items for exploring each proposed facet were generated by each centre's focus group. To enable the collaboration to be genuinely international the 15 field centres were selected world-wide to provide differences in level of industrialisation, available health services, and other markers relevant to the measurement of quality of life (e.g. role of the family, perception of time, perception of self, dominant religion). In the third stage of development, questions from each centre were assembled into a global pool. After clustering semantically equivalent questions, 236 items covering 29 facets were included in a final assessment. Pilot work involved administration of this standardised assessment to at least 300 respondents within each centre. Following field testing in these 15 centres, 100 items were selected for inclusion in the WHOQOL-100 Field Trial Version. These included four items for each of 24 facets of quality of life, and four items relating to the 'overall quality of life and general health' facet (see Table 1). The method by which these 100 items were selected is fully documented elsewhere (The WHOQOL Group, in preparation). The WHOQOL-100 Field Trial Version is currently being tested in new centres world-wide (these centres are outlined on page 6 of this document). The initial conceptual framework for the WHOQOL-100 proposed that the 24 facets relating to quality of life should be grouped into 6 domains. Recent analysis of available data, using structural equation modelling, has shown a four domain solution to be more appropriate. For a more detailed explanation of this, the reader is referred to The WHOQOL Group (in preparation). The WHOQOL-BREF is therefore based on a four domain structure (see Table 1).

Table 1: WHOQOL-BREF domains

Domain	Facets incorporated within domains
1. Physical health	Activities of daily living Dependence on medicinal substances and medical aids Energy and fatigue Mobility Pain and discomfort Sleep and rest Work Capacity
2. Psychological	Bodily image and appearance Negative feelings Positive feelings Self-esteem Spirituality / Religion / Personal beliefs Thinking, learning, memory and concentration
3. Social	Personal relationships Social support Sexual activity
4. Environment	Financial resources Freedom, physical safety and security Health and social care: accessibility and quality Home environment Opportunities for acquiring new information and skills Participation in and opportunities for recreation / leisure activities Physical environment (pollution / noise / traffic / climate) Transport

Development of the WHOQOL-BREF

The WHOQOL-100 allows detailed assessment of each individual facet relating to quality of life. In certain instances however, the WHOQOL-100 may be too lengthy for practical use. The WHOQOLBREF Field Trial Version has therefore been developed to provide a short form quality of life assessment that looks at Domain level profiles, using data from the pilot WHOQOL assessment and all available data from the Field Trial Version of the WHOQOL-100. Twenty field centres situated within eighteen countries have included data for these purposes (see Table 2). The WHOQOL-BREF contains a total of 26 questions. To provide a broad and comprehensive assessment, one item from each of the 24 facets contained in the WHOQOL-100 has been included. In addition, two items from the Overall quality of Life and General Health facet have been included.

Table 2: Centres included in development of the WHOQOL-BREF

Centres in the pilot version of the WHOQOL	Centres in the field trial of the WHOQOL-100
Bangkok, Thailand	Bangkok, Thailand
Beer Sheva, Israel	Beer Sheva, Israel
Madras, India	Madras, India
Melbourne, Australia	Melbourne, Australia
New Delhi, India	New Delhi, India
Panama City, Panama	Panama City, Panama
Seattle, USA	Seattle, USA
Tilburg, The Netherlands	Tilburg, The Netherlands
Zagreb, Croatia	Zagreb, Croatia
Tokyo, Japan	Tokyo, Japan
Harare, Zimbabwe	Harare, Zimbabwe
Barcelona, Spain	Barcelona, Spain
Bath, UK	Bath, UK
St Petersburg, Russia	Hong Kong
Paris, France	Leipzig, Germany
	Mannheim, Germany
	La Plata, Argentina
	Port Alegre, Brazil

The WHOQOL-BREF is available in 19 different languages. The appropriate language version, and permission for using it, can be obtained from The WHOQOL Group, Programme on Mental Health, World Health Organisation, CH-1211 Geneva 27, Switzerland. Under no circumstances should the WHOQOL-BREF be used without consultation with The WHOQOL Group. A methodology has been developed for new centres wishing to develop a further language version of the WHOQOL-100 or the

WHOQOL-BREF. This can be obtained from The WHOQOL Group, Programme on Mental Health, World Health Organisation, CH-1211, Geneva 27, Switzerland.

Questions should appear in the order in which they appear in the example WHOQOL-BREF provided within this document, with instructions and headers unchanged. Questions are grouped by response format. The equivalent numbering of questions between the WHOQOL-BREF and the WHOQOL-100 is given in the example version of the WHOQOL-BREF to enable easy comparison between responses to items on the two versions. The WHOQOL-100 field test permitted centres to include national items or facets that were thought to be important in assessing quality of life. Where centres wish to include additional national items or modules to the WHOQOL-BREF, these should be included on a separate sheet of paper and not scattered amongst the existing 26 items. There are three reasons for this:

1. To control for item order effects which could occur and change item meaning.
2. The WHOQOL-BREF represents an agreed upon core set of international items.
3. The WHOQOL-BREF is likely to be used where quality of life is amongst one of several parameters being assessed. Therefore additional national information can be obtained by including additional modules and measures.

Administration of the WHOQOL-BREF

For any new centre not previously involved in either the development or field testing of the WHOQOL-100, the procedure being followed to field test the WHOQOL-BREF should be identical to that used to field test the WHOQOL-100. The instrument should be piloted on at least 300 people. This figure is based on the required numbers of respondents needed for analysis of pilot data. The sample of respondents to whom the assessment should be administered ought to be adults, with 'adult' being culturally defined. While stratified samples are not essential, a sampling quota should apply with regard to:

- Age   (50% = <45 years, 50% = 45+ years)
- Sex   (50% = male, 50% = female)
- Health status (250 persons with disease or impairment; 50 well persons)

With respect to persons with disease or impairment, this group should contain a cross-section of people with varied levels of quality of life. One way of attempting this would be to include some people with quite severe and disabling chronic diseases, some people in contact with health facilities for more transient conditions, possibly some attending a family practitioner, and others who are in contact with the health service for reasons that are not likely to impinge upon their quality of life to any great extent. By sampling patients from a cross-section of primary care settings, hospitals and community care settings this could most likely be achieved.

The WHOQOL-BREF should be self-administered if respondents have sufficient ability: otherwise, interviewer-assisted or interview-administered forms should be used. Standardised instructions, given on the second page of the WHOQOL-BREF example assessment, should be read out to respondents in instances where the assessment is interviewer-administered.

For centres who have already participated in the development and field testing of the WHOQOL100, the above option of testing the WHOQOL-BREF is preferred, but not imperative where specific studies of patient groups are planned.

Frame of reference and time frame

A time frame of two weeks is indicated in the assessment. It is recognised that different time frames may be necessary for particular uses of the instrument in subsequent stages of work. For example, in the assessment of quality of life in chronic conditions, such as arthritis, a longer time frame such as four weeks may be preferable. Furthermore, the perception of time is different within different cultural settings and therefore changing the time scale may be appropriate.

Proposed uses of the WHOQOL-100 and the WHOQOL-BREF

It is anticipated that the WHOQOL assessments will be used in broad-ranging ways. They will be of considerable use in clinical trials, in establishing baseline scores in a range of areas, and looking at changes in quality of life over the course of interventions. It is expected that the WHOQOL assessments will also be of value where disease prognosis is likely to involve only partial recovery or remission, and in which treatment may be more palliative than curative.

For epidemiological research, the WHOQOL assessments will allow detailed quality of life data to be gathered on a particular population, facilitating the understanding of diseases, and the development of treatment methods. The international epidemiological studies that would be enabled by instruments such as the WHOQOL-100 and the WHOQOL-BREF will make it possible to carry out multi-centre quality of life research, and to compare results obtained in different centres. Such research has important benefits, permitting questions to be addressed which would not be possible in single site studies (Sartorius and Helmchen, 1981). For example, a comparative study in two or more countries on the relationship between health care delivery and quality of life requires an assessment yielding cross-culturally comparable scores. Sometimes accumulation of cases in quality of life studies, particularly when studying rare disorders; is helped by gathering data in several settings. Multi-centre collaborative studies can also provide simultaneous multiple replications of a finding, adding considerably to the confidence with which findings can be accepted.

In clinical practice the WHOQOL assessments will assist clinicians in making judgements about the areas in which a patient is most affected by disease, and in making treatment decisions. In some developing countries, where resources for health care may be limited, treatments aimed at improving quality of life through palliation, for example, can be both effective and inexpensive (Olweny, 1992). Together with other measures, the WHOQOL-BREF will enable health professionals to assess changes in quality of life over the course of treatment.

It is anticipated that in the future the WHOQOL-100 and the WHOQOL-BREF will prove useful in health policy research and will make up an important aspect of the routine auditing of health and social services. Because the instrument was developed cross-culturally, health care providers, administrators and legislators in countries where no validated quality of life measures currently exist can be confident that data yielded by work involving the WHOQOL assessments will be genuinely sensitive to their setting.

Scoring the WHOQOL-BREF

The WHOQOL-BREF (Field Trial Version) produces a quality of life profile. It is possible to derive four domain scores. There are also two items that are examined separately: question 1 asks about an individual's overall perception of quality of life and question 2 asks about an individual's overall perception of their health. The four domain scores denote an individual's perception of quality of life in each particular domain. Domain scores are scaled in a positive direction (i.e. higher scores denote higher quality of life). The mean score of items within each domain is used to calculate the domain score. Mean scores are then multiplied by 4 in order to make domain scores comparable with the scores used in the WHOQOL-100. Explicit instructions for checking and cleaning data, and for computing domain scores, are given in Table 3. A method for the manual calculation of individual scores is given on page 1 of the WHOQOL-BREF assessment form. The method for converting raw scores to transformed scores when using this method is given in Table 4, on page

11 of these instructions. The first transformation method converts scores to range between 4–20, comparable with the WHOQOL-100. The second transformation method converts domain scores to a 0–100 scale.

Where more than 20% of data is missing from a assessment, the assessment should be discarded (see Step 4 in Table 3). Where an item is missing, the mean of other items in the domain is substituted. Where more than two items are missing from the domain, the domain score should not be calculated (with the exception of domain 3, where the domain should only be calculated if ≤ 1 item is missing).

Any national items should be scored separately from the core 26 item of the BREF. During the analysis the performance of any national items will be examined for possible use in alter national studies. At this stage of field testing national and core items must not be mixed in administration or scoring of the BREF.

le 3: Steps for checking and cleaning data and computing domain scores

)s	SPSS syntax for carrying out data checking, cleaning and computing total scores
Check all 26 items from assessment ..ave a range of 1–5	RECODE QI Q2 Q3 Q4 Q5 Q6 Q7 Q8 Q9 Q10 Q11 Q12 Q13 Q14 Q15 Q16 Q17 Q18 Q19 Q20 Q21 Q22 Q23 Q24 Q25 Q26 (1=1) (2=2) (3=3) (4=4) (5=5) (ELSE=SYSMIS). (This recodes ull data outwith the range 1–5 to system missing).
everse 3 negatively hrased items	RECODE Q3 Q4 Q26 (1=5) (2=4) (3=3) (4=2) (5=1). (This transforms negatively framed questions to positively framed questions)
Compute domain cores	COMPUTE DOM1=MEAN.6(Q3,Q4,Q10,QI5,Q16,QI7,Q18)*4. COMPUTE DOM2=MEAN.5(Q5,Q6,Q7,QI 1,Q19,Q26)*4. COMPUTE DOM3=MEAN.2(Q20,Q21,Q22)*4. COMPUTE DOM4=MEAN.6(Q8,Q9,Q12,Q13,Q14,Q23,Q24, Q25)*4. (These equations calculate the domain scores. All scores are multiplied by 4 so as to be directly comparable with scores derived from the WHOQOL-100. The '.6' in 'mean.6' specifies that 6 items must be endorsed for the domain score to be calculated).
elete cases with 20% missing data	COUNT TOTAL=Q1 TO Q26 (1 THRU 5). (This command creates a new column 'total'. 'Total' contains a count of the WHOQOL-100 items with the values I–5 that have been endorsed by each subject. The 'Q1 TO Q26' means that consecutive columns from 'Q1', the first item, to 'Q26', the last item, are included in the count. It therefore assumes that data is entered in the order given in the assessment). FILTER OFF. USE ALL. SELECT IF (TOTAL > = 21). EXECUTE. (This second command selects only those cases where 'total', the total number of items completed, is greater or equal to 80%. It deletes the remaining cases from the data set).
heck domain cores	DESCRIPTIVES VARIABLES=DOMI DOM2 DOM3 DOM4 /STATISTICS=MEAN STDDEV MIN MAX. (Running descriptives should display values of all domain scores within the range 4–20).
ive data set	Save data set with a new file name so that the original remains intact.

Table 4: Method for converting row scores to transformed scores

DOMAIN 1			DOMAIN 2			DOMAIN 3			DOMAIN 4		
Raw Score	Transformed scores		Raw Score	Transformed scores		Raw Score	Transformed scores		Raw Score	Transformed scores	
	4–20	0–100		4–20	0–100		4–20	0–100		4–20	0–100
7	4	0	6	4	0	3	4	0	8	4	0
8	5	6	7	5	6	4	5	6	9	5	6
9	5	6	8	5	6	5	7	19	10	5	6
10	6	13	9	6	13	6	8	25	11	6	13
11	6	13	10	7	19	7	9	31	12	6	13
12	7	19	11	7	19	8	11	44	13	7	19
13	7	19	12	8	25	9	12	50	14	7	19
14	8	25	13	9	31	10	13	56	15	8	25
15	9	31	14	9	31	11	15	69	16	8	25
16	9	31	15	10	38	12	16	75	17	9	31
17	10	38	16	11	44	13	17	81	18	9	31
18	10	38	17	11	44	14	19	94	19	10	38
19	11	44	18	12	50	15	20	100	20	10	38
20	11	44	19	13	56				21	11	44
21	12	50	20	13	56				22	11	44
22	13	56	21	14	63				23	12	50
23	13	56	22	15	69				24	12	50
24	14	63	23	15	69				25	13	56
25	14	63	24	16	75				26	13	56
26	15	69	25	17	81				27	14	63
27	15	69	26	17	81				28	14	63
28	16	75	27	18	88				29	15	69
29	17	81	28	19	94				30	15	69
30	17	81	29	19	94				31	16	75
31	18	88	30	20	100				32	16	75
32	18	88							33	17	81
33	19	94							34	17	81
34	19	94							35	18	88
35	20	100							36	18	88
									37	19	94
									38	19	94
									39	20	100
									40	20	100

References

Bergner, M., Bobbitt, R.A., Carter, W.B. *et al.* (1981) The Sickness Impact Profile: Development and final revision of a health status measure. *Medical Care,* **19**, 787–805.

Fallowfield, L. (1990) *The Quality of Life: The Missing Measurement in Health Care.* Souvenir Press.

Hunt, S.M., McKenna, S.P. and McEwan, J. (1989) *The Nottingham Health Profile. Users Manual.* Revised edition.

Kuyken, W., Orley, J., Hudelson, P. and Sartorius, N. (1994) Quality of life assessment across cultures. *International Journal of Mental Health,* **23** (2), 5–27.

Olweny, C. L. M. (1992) Quality of life in developing countries. *Journal of Palliative Care, 8,* 25–30.

Sartorius, N. and Helmchen, H. (1981) Aims and implementation of multi-centre studies. *Modern Problems of Pharmacopsychiatry,* **16,** 1–8.

Sartorius, N. and Kuyken, W. (1994) Translation of health status instruments. In J. Orley and W. Kuyken (Eds) *Quality of Life Assessment: International Perspectives.* Heidelberg: Springer Verlag.

Szabo, S. (1996) The World Health Organisation Quality of Life (WHOQOL) Assessment Instrument. In *Quality of Life and Pharmaeconomics in Clinical Trials* (2nd edition, Edited by Spilker B.) Lippincott-Raven Publishers, Philadelphia, New York.

The WHOQOL Group. The World Health Organization Quality of Life assessment (WHOQOL): position paper from the World Health Organization. *Soc. Sci. Med.,* **41**, 1403, 1995.

Ware, J. E., Snow, K., K., Kosinski, M. and Gandek, B. (1993) SF-36 *Health Survey: Manual and Interpretation Guide.* New England Medical Center, MA, USA.

World Bank. (1993) *World Development Report: Investing in Health.* New York: Oxford University Press.

World Health Organization. (1991) *World Health Statistics Annual.* Geneva: WHO.

The WHOQOL Group. (1994a) Development of the WHOQOL: Rationale and current status. *International Journal of Mental Health,* **23** (3), 24–56.

The WHOQOL Group. (1994b) The development of the World Health Organization quality of life assessment instrument (the WHOQOL) In J. Orley and W. Kuyken (Eds) *Quality of Life Assessment: International Perspectives.* Heidelberg: Springer Verlag.

The WHOQOL Group. (In preparation) The World Health Organisation Quality of Life Assessment (WHOQOL): Development and General Psychometric Properties.

WHOQOL-BREF

PROGRAMME ON MENTAL HEALTH
WORLD HEALTH ORGANIZATION
GENEVA

For office use only

Equations for computing domain scores		Raw score	Transformed scores*
Domain 1	(6-Q3)+(6-Q4)+ Q10 + Q15 + Q16 + Q17 + Q18 □ + □ + □ + □ + □ + □ + □ =		4–20 0–100
Domain 2	Q5 + Q6 + Q7 + Q11 + Q19 +(6-Q26) □ + □ + □ + □ + □ + □ =		
Domain 3	Q20 + Q21 + Q22 □ + □ + □ =		
Domain 4	Q8 + Q9 + Q12 + Q13 + Q14 + Q23 + Q24 + Q25 □ + □ + □ + □ + □ + □ + □ + □ =		

* Please see Table 4 on page 10 of the manual, for converting raw scores to transformed scores.

OUT YOU

I.D. number ☐ ☐ ☐ ☐

e you begin we would like to ask you to answer a few general questions about yourself: by
ng the correct answer or by filling in the space provided.

is your **gender**?   Male   Female

is your **date of birth**?   _____ / _____ / _____
                                Day   Month   Year

is the highest **education** you received?   None at all
                                               Primary school
                                               Secondary school
                                               Tertiary

is your **marital status**?   Single   Separated
                                Married   Divorced
                                Living as married   Widowed

ou currently **ill**?   Yes   No

ething is wrong with your health what do you think it is?_____illness/ problem

uctions

ssessment asks how you feel about your quality of life, health, or other areas of your life.
e **answer all the questions**. If you are unsure about which response to give to a question,
e **choose the one** that appears most appropriate. This can often be your first response.

keep in mind your standards, hopes, pleasures and concerns. We ask that you think about
fe **in the last two weeks**. For example, thinking about the last two weeks, a question might

	Not at all	Not much	Moderately	A great deal	Completely
Do you get the kind of support from others that you need?	1	2	3	4	5

ould circle the number that best fits how much support you got from others over the last
eeks. So you would circle the number 4 if you got a great deal of support from others as
s.

	Not at all	Not much	Moderately	A great deal	Completely
Do you get the kind of support from others that you need?	1	2	3	4	5

ould circle number 1 if you did not get any of the support that you needed from others in the
o weeks.

Please read each question, assess your feelings, and circle the number on the scale for each question that gives the best answer for you.

		Very poor	Poor	Neither poor nor good	Good	Very good
I (G1)	How would you rate your quality of life?	1	2	3	4	5

		Very dissatisfied	Dissatisfied	Neither satisfied nor dissatisfied	Satisfied	Very satisfied
2 (G4)	How satisfied are you with your health?	1	2	3	4	5

The following questions ask about **how much** you have experienced certain things in the last two weeks.

		Not at all	A little	A moderate amount	Very much	An extreme amount
3 (F1.4)	To what extent do you feel that physical pain prevents you from doing what you need to do?	1	2	3	4	5
4 (F11.3)	How much do you need any medical treatment to function in your daily life?	1	2	3	4	5
5 (F4.1)	How much do you enjoy life?	1	2	3	4	5
6 (F24.2)	To what extent do you feel your life to be meaningful?	1	2	3	4	5

		Not at all	A little	A moderate amount	Very much	Extremely
7 (F5.3)	How well are you able to concentrate?	1	2	3	4	5
8 (F16.1)	How safe do you feel in your daily life?	1	2	3	4	5
9 (F22.1)	How healthy is your physical environment?	1	2	3	4	5

The following questions ask about **how completely** you experience or were able to do certain things in the last two weeks.

		Not at all	A little	Moderately	Mostly	Completely
10 (F2.1)	Do you have enough energy for everyday life?	1	2	3	4	5
11 (F7.1)	Are you able to accept your bodily appearance?	1	2	3	4	5
12 (F18.1)	Have you enough money to meet your needs?	1	2	3	4	5
13 (F20.1)	How available to you is the information that you need in your day-to-day life?	1	2	3	4	5
14 (F21.1)	To what extent do you have the opportunity for leisure activities?	1	2	3	4	5

		Very poor	Poor	Neither poor nor good	Good	Very good
15 (F9.1)	How well are you able to get around?	1	2	3	4	5

The following questions ask you to say how **good or satisfied** you have felt about various aspects of your life over the last two weeks.

		Very dissatisfied	Dissatisfied	Neither satisfied nor dissatisfied	Satisfied	Very satisfied
16 (F3.3)	How satisfied are you with your sleep?	1	2	3	4	5
17 (F10.3)	How satisfied are you with your ability to perform your daily living activities?	1	2	3	4	5
18 (F12.4)	How satisfied are you with your capacity for work?	1	2	3	4	5
19 (F6.3)	How satisfied are you with yourself?	1	2	3	4	5
20 (F13.3)	How satisfied are you with your personal relationships?	1	2	3	4	5
21 (F15.3)	How satisfied are you with your sex life?	1	2	3	4	5
22 (F14.4)	How satisfied are you with the support you get from your friends?	1	2	3	4	5

23 (F17.3)	How satisfied are you with the conditions of your living place?	1	2	3	4	5
24 (F19.3)	How satisfied are you with your access to health services?	1	2	3	4	5
25 (F23.3)	How satisfied are you with your transport?	1	2	3	4	5

The following question refers to **how often** you have felt or experienced certain things in the last two weeks.

		Never	Seldom	Quite often	Very often	Always
26 (F8.1)	How often do you have negative feelings such as blue mood, despair, anxiety, depression?	1	2	3	4	5

Did someone help you to fill out this form?..

How long did it take to fill this form out? ....

Do you have any comments about the assessment?

....

....

THANK YOU FOR YOUR HELP

An SPSS syntax file that automatically checks, recodes data and computes domain scores may be obtained from Professor Mick Power, Department of Psychiatry, Royal Edinburgh Hospital, Morningside Park, Edinburgh, EH10 5HF (email: mj@srv2.med.ed.ac.uk; fax: + 131 447 6860)

Resources

The following resources offer some useful places to start in thinking about QOL research.

Websites

Australian Centre for Quality of Life (ACQOL)
   <http://acqol.deakin.edu.au/>
International Society for Quality of Life Studies
   <http://www.cob.vt.edu/market/isqols/>
Internet Resources – Quality of Life Assessment in Medicine
   <http://www.QLMed.org/url.htm>
Quality of Life Assessment in Medicine
   <http://www.QLMed.org/LIST/index.html>
Social Indicators: an annotated bibliography on trends, sources and
   developments, 1960–1998
   <http://www.ag.iastate.edu/centers/rdev/indicators/anbib.html>
Social Indicators Europe
   <http://www.gesis.org/en/social_monitoring/social_indicators/EU_
   Reporting/eusi.htm>
UK National Statistics
   <http://www.statistics.gov.uk/>
World Bank Group – World Development Indicators
   <http://www.worldbank.org/data/wdi/>
World Database of Happiness
   <http://www.eur.nl/fsw/soc/database.happiness>
World Health Organization
   <http://who.int/>

Journals

Social Indicators Research
   <http://www.wkap.nl/journalhome.htm/0303-8300>
Quality of Life Research
   <http://www.wkap.nl/journalhome.htm/0962-9343>

Societies and Research Units

International Society for Quality of Life Studies
    <http://www.cob.vt.edu/market/isqols/>
University of Toronto Quality of Life Research Unit
    <http: //www.utoronto.ca/dol/unit.htm>
Redefining Progress
    <http://www.rprogress.org/index.html>

Quantitative Methods

Cummins, R. A. (2001) *Directory of Instruments to Measure Quality of Life and Cognate Areas*, 6th edn. Melbourne: School of Psychology, Deakin University,<http://acqol.deakin.edu.au/instruments/instrument.php>.

Nussbaum, M. and Sen, A. (eds) (1993) *The Quality of Life*. Oxford: Clarendon Press.

Sarantkos, S. (1993) *Social Research*. Melbourne: Macmillan Academic.

Staquet, M., Hays, R. and Fayers, P. (eds) (1998) *Quality of Life Assessment in Clinical Trials: Methods and Practice*. Oxford: Oxford University Press.

Lyons, J. S., Howard, K. I., O'Mahoney, M. T. and Lish, J. (1997) *The Measurement and Management of Clinical Outcomes in Mental Health*. New York: Wiley.

Qualitative Methods

Bernard, B. (1994). *Research Methods in Anthropology. Qualitative and Quantitative approaches*. London: Altamira Press.

Lepper, G. (2000) *Categories in Text and Talk: A Practical Introduction to Categorization Analysis*. London: Sage.

McHoul, A. and Rapley, M. (eds) (2002) *How to Analyse Talk in Institutional Settings: A Casebook of Methods*. London and New York: Continuum International.

Patton, M. Q. (1990) *Qualitative Evaluation and Research Methods*. Newbury Park, CA: Sage.

Puchta, C. and Potter, J. (1999) Asking elaborate questions: focus groups and the management of spontaneity, *Journal of Sociolinguistics*, 3: 314–35.

Richardson, J. T. E. (ed.) (1996) *Handbook of Qualitative Research Methods for Psychology and the Social Sciences*. Leicester: BPS Books.

Silverman, D. (1997) *Qualitative Methods: Theory, Method and Practice*. London: Sage.

tenHave, P. (1999) *Doing Conversation Analysis: A Practical Guide*. London: Sage.

Yates, S., Taylor, S. and Wetherell, M. (2001) *Discourse as Data: A Guide for Analysis*. London: Sage.

REFERENCES

Aaronsson, N. K., Ahmedzai, S., Bergman, B., Bullinger, M., Cull, A., Duez, N. J. *et al.* (1993) The European Organization for Research and Treatment of Cancer QLQ-C30: a quality of life instrument for use in international clinical trials in oncology, *Journal of the National Cancer Institute*, 85: 365–76.

AbouZahr, C. and Vaughan, J. P. (2000) Assessing the burden of sexual and reproductive ill-health: questions regarding the use of disability-adjusted life years, *Bulletin of the World Health Organization*, 78, 5: 655–66.

Adams, D. (1979) *The Hitch Hikers' Guide to the Galaxy*. London: Pan Books.

Addington-Hall, J. and Kalra, L. (2001) Who should measure quality of life? *British Medical Journal*, 322: 1417–20.

Ager, A. and Hatton, C. (1999) Discerning the appropriate role and status of 'quality of life' assessment for persons with an intellectual disability: a reply to Cummins, *Journal of Applied Research in Intellectual Disabilities*, 12: 335–9.

Ahuvia, A. C. and Friedman, D. C. (1998) Income, consumption, and subjective well-being: toward a composite macromarketing model, *Journal of Macromarketing*, 18: 153–68.

Aksoy, S. (2000) Can the 'quality of life' be used as a criterion in health care services? *Bulletin of Medical Ethics*, October: 19–22.

Albrecht, G. L. and Devlieger, P. J. (1998) The Disability Paradox: high quality of life against all odds, *Social Science and Medicine*, 48: 977–88.

Alderson, P. (2001) Down's syndrome: cost, quality and value of life, *Social Science and Medicine*, 53, 5: 627–38.

Anderson, R. L. and Lewis, D. A. (2000) Quality of life of persons with severe mental illness living in an intermediate care facility, *Journal of Clinical Psychology*, 56, 4: 575–81.

Andrews, F. M. (ed.), (1986) *Research on the Quality of Life*. Ann Arbor: MI: Institute for Social Research.

Andrews, F. M. (1989) The evolution of a movement, *Journal of Public Policy*, 9: 401–5.

Andrews, F. M. (1991) Stability and change in levels and structure of subjective well-being: USA 1972 and 1988, *Social Indicators Research*, 25: 1–30.

Andrews, F. M and Withey, S. B. (1976) *Social Indicators of Well-Being: Americans' Perceptions of Life Quality*. New York: Plenum.

Anson, J. and Anson, O. (2001) Death rests a while: holy day and Sabbath effects on Jewish mortality in Israel, *Social Science and Medicine*, 52: 83–97.

Antaki, C. (1994) *Explaining and Arguing: The Social Organisation of Accounts*. London: Sage.

Antaki, C. (1999) Assessing quality of life of persons with a learning disability: how setting lower standards may inflate well-being scores, *Qualitative Health Research*, 9: 283–300.

Antaki, C. and Houtkoop-Steenstra, H. (1998) Creating happy people by asking yes–no questions, *Research on Language and Social Interaction*, 30: 285–314.

Antaki, C. and Rapley, M. (1996a) 'Quality of Life' talk: the liberal paradox of psychological testing, *Discourse and Society*, 7, 3: 293–316.

Antaki, C. and Rapley, M. (1996b) Questions and answers to psychological assessment schedules: hidden troubles in 'quality of life' interviews, *Journal of Intellectual Disability Research*, 40, 5: 421–37.

Antaki, C., Condor, S. and Levine, M. (1996) Identities in talk: speakers' own orientations, *British Journal of Social Psychology*, 35: 473–92.

Antaki, C., Houtkoop-Steenstra, H. and Rapley, M. (2000) 'Brilliant. Next question ...': high-grade assessment sequences in the completion of interactional units, *Research on Language and Social Interaction*, 33: 235–62.

Arendt, H. (1958) *The Human Condition*. Chicago: University of Chicago Press.

Arnesen, T. and Nord, E. (1999) The value of DALY life: problems with ethics and validity of disability adjusted life years, *British Medical Journal*, 319: 1423–5.

Atkinson, D. (1988) Research interviews with people with mental handicaps, *Mental Handicap Research*, 1, 1: 75–90.

Atkinson, J. M. and Heritage, J. (eds.), (1984) *Structures of Social Action: Studies in Conversation Analysis*. Cambridge: Cambridge University Press.

Australian Bureau of Statistics (2001) *Measuring Wellbeing: Frameworks for Australian Social Statistics*. Canberra: Australian Government Printing Service.

Australia Institute and City of Newcastle (2000) *Indicators of a Sustainable Community: Improving Quality of Life in Newcastle*. Newcastle: Newcastle City Council.

Bach, J. R. and Tilton, M. C. (1994) Life satisfaction and well-being measures in ventilator assisted individuals with traumatic tetraplegia, *Archives of Physical Medicine and Rehabilitation*, 75: 626–32.

Baldwin, S., Godfrey, C. and Propper, C. (eds), (1990a) *Quality of Life: Perspectives and Policies*. London: Routledge.

Baldwin, S., Godfrey, C. and Propper, C. (1990b) Introduction, in S. Baldwin, C. Godfrey, and C. Propper (eds.) *Quality of Life: Perspectives and Policies*. London: Routledge.

Barnes, M., Mercer, G. and Shakespeare, T. (1999) *Exploring Disability: A Sociological Introduction*. Oxford: Polity Press.

Barry, M. M. and Crosby, C. (1996) Quality of life as an evaluative measure in assessing the impact of community care on people with long-term psychiatric disorders, *British Journal of Psychiatry*, 168: 210–16.

Bauer, R. A. (ed.) (1966) *Social Indicators*. Cambridge, MA, and London: MIT Press.

Beasley, F., Hewson, S., Mansell, J., Hughes, D. and Stein, J. (1993) *MTS: Handbook for Observers*. Canterbury: Centre for the Applied Psychology of Social Care, University of Kent at Canterbury.

Berger-Schmitt, R. and Jankowitsch, B. (1999) *Systems of Social Indicators and Social Reporting*, EuReporting Working Paper No. 1. Mannheim: Centre for Survey Research and Methodology.

Berger-Schmitt, R. and Noll, H. -H. (2000) *Conceptual Framework and Structure of a European System of Social Indicators*, EuReporting Working Paper No. 9. Mannheim: Centre for Survey Research and Methodology. Available from: <http://www.gesis.org/en/social_monitoring/social_indicators/EU_ Reporting/concept. htm>.

Bergner, M., and Rothman, M. L. (1987) Health status measures: an overview and guide for selection, *Annual Review of Public Health*, 8: 191–210.

Bergner, M., Bobbitt, R. A., Carter, W. B. and Gilson, B. S. (1981) The Sickness Impact Profile: Development and final revision of a health status measure, *Medical Care*, 19, 8: 787–805.

Bernard, B. (1994) *Research Methods in Anthropology: Qualitative and Quantitative Approaches*. London: Altamira Press.

Billig, M. (1991) *Ideology and Opinions: Studies in Rhetorical Psychology*, London: Sage.

Blass, J. P. (1985) Mental status tests in geriatrics, *Journal of the American Geriatric Society*, 33: 461–2.

Bloom, J. R., Fobair, P., Spiegel, D., Cox, R. S., Varghese, A. and Hoppe, R. (1991) Social supports and the social well-being of cancer survivors, *Advances in Medical Sociology*, 2: 95–114.

Blunden, R. (1988) Quality of life in persons with disabilities: issues in the development of services. In R. I. Brown (ed), *Quality of Life for Handicapped People*. London: Croom Helm. pp. 37–55.

Boden, D. and Zimmerman, D. H. (eds), (1991) *Talk and Social Structure*. Cambridge: Polity Press.

Bonicatto, S. C., Dew, M. A., Zaratiegui, R., Lorenzo, L. and Pecina, P. (2001) Adult outpatients with depression: worse quality of life than in other chronic medical diseases in Argentina, *Social Science and Medicine*, 52: 911–19.

Bowd, A. D. (1989) Client satisfaction and normalization of residential services for persons with developmental handicaps, *Canadian Journal of Community Mental Health*, 8, 1: 63–73.

Bowling, A. (1995) What things are important in people's lives? A survey of the public's judgments to inform scales of health related quality of life, *Social Science and Medicine*, 41: 1447–62.

Bowling, A. (1996) Associations with changes in life satisfaction among three samples of elderly people living at home, *International Journal of Geriatric Psychiatry*, 11: 1077–87.

Boyle, M. (1990) *Schizophrenia: A Scientific Delusion?* London: Routledge.

Boyle, M. (2002) *Schizophrenia: A Scientific Delusion?* 2nd edn. London: Routledge.

Brickman, P., Coates, D. and Janoff-Bulman, R. (1978) Lottery winners and accident victims: is happiness relative? *Journal of Personality and Social Psychology*, 36: 917–27.

Brock, D. (1993) Quality of life measures in health care and medical ethics. In M. Nussbaum and A. Sen (eds), *The Quality of Life*. Oxford: Clarendon Press.

Brown P. (2001) Effective treatments for mental illness not being used, WHO says, *British Medical Journal*, 323: 769.

Brown, R. I. (ed) (1997) *Quality of Life for People with Disabilities: Models, Research and Practice*, 2nd edn. Cheltenham: Stanley Thornes.

Brown, R. I. (2000) Quality of life: Challenges and confrontation, In: K. D. Keith and R. L. Schalock (eds), *Cross-cultural Perspectives on Quality of Life*. Washington: AAMR. pp. 347– 62

Browne, S., Clarke, M., Gervin, M., Waddington, J. L., Larkin, C. and O'Callaghan, E. (2000) Determinants of quality of life at first presentation with schizophrenia, *British Journal of Psychiatry*, 176: 173–6.

Bryant, L. L, Corbett, K. K. and Kutner, J. S. (2001) In their own words: a model of healthy aging, *Social Science and Medicine*, 53: 927–41.

Butterworth, J., Steere, D. E and Whitney-Thomas, J. (1997) Using person-centred planning to address personal quality of life, In: Robert L. Schalock (ed), *Quality of Life: Volume II: Application to Persons with Disabilities*. Washington, DC: AAMR, pp. 5–23.

Button, G., Coulter, J., Sharrock, W. and Lee, J. (1997) *Computers, Minds and Conduct*. Cambridge: Polity Press.

Cagney, K. A., Wu, A. W., Fink, N. E., Jenckes, M. W., Meyer, K. B., Bass, E. B. *et al.* (2000) Formal literature review of quality-of-life instruments used in end-stage renal disease, *American Journal of Kidney Diseases*, 36, 2: 327–36.

Campbell, A. (1976) Subjective measures of well-being, *American Psychologist*, 31: 117–24.

Campbell, A. and Converse, P. E. (1972) *The Human Meaning of Social Change*. New York: Russell Sage Foundation.

Campbell, A., Converse, P. E. and Rodgers, W. L. (1976) *The Quality of American Life: Perceptions, Evaluations, and Satisfactions*. New York: Russell Sage Foundation.

Carley, M. (1981) *Social Measurement and Social Indicators: Issues of Policy and Theory*. London: George Allen and Unwin.

Carr, A. J. and Higginson, I. J. (2001) Are quality of life measures patient centred? *British Medical Journal*, 322: 1357–60.

Carr, A. J., Gibson, B. and Robinson, P. G. (2001) Is quality of life determined by expectations or experience? *British Medical Journal*, 322: 1240–3.

Carroll, L. (1982) *Alice's Adventures in Wonderland and Through the Looking-glass and What Alice Found There*, ed. and intro. Roger Lancelyn Green, illust. John Tenniel, Oxford and New York: Oxford University Press.

Carver, C. S. (2000) On the continuous calibration if happiness, *American Journal on Mental Retardation*, 105: 336–42.

Cattell, V. (2001) Poor people, poor places, and poor health: the mediating role of social networks and social capital, *Social Science and Medicine*, 52: 1501–16.

Cattermole, M., Jahoda, A. and Marková, I. (1988) Leaving home: The experience of people with a mental handicap, *Journal of Mental Deficiency Research*, 32, 1: 47–57.

Centers for Disease Control and Prevention (2000) *Measuring Healthy Days*. Atlanta, GA. CDC.

Chamie, M. (1995) What does morbidity have to do with disability? *Disability and Rehabilitation*, 17: 323–37.

Chassany, O., Bergmann, J. F. and Caulin, C. (1999) Authors are creating a database of quality of life questionnaires (letter), *British Medical Journal*, 318: 1142.

Chorover, S. (1979) *From Genesis to Genocide: The Meaning of Human Nature and the Power of Behaviour Control*. Cambridge, MA: MIT Press.

Clements, J., Rapley, M. and Cummins, R. A. (1999) On, to, for or with? Vulnerable people and the practices of the research community, *Behavioural and Cognitive Psychotherapy*, 27, 2: 103–16.

Coast, J., Peters, T. J., Richards, S. H. and Gunnell, D. J. (1997) Use of the EuroQOL among elderly acute care patients, *Quality of Life Research*, 7, 1: 1–10.

Coates, A. S., Kaye, S. B., Sowerbutts, T., Frewin, C., Fox, R. N. and Tattersall, M.

H. N. (1983) On the receiving end: patient perceptions of side-effects of cancer chemotherapy, *European Journal of Clinical Oncology*, 13: 203–8.

Cobb, C., Goodman, G. S. and Kliejunas, J. C. M. (2000) *Blazing Sun Overhead and Clouds on the Horizon: The Genuine Progress Report for 1999*. Oakland, CA: Redefining Progress.

Coid, J. W. (1993) Quality of life for patients detained in hospital, *British Journal of Psychiatry*, 162: 611–20.

Collins, J. (1992) *When the Eagles Fly: A Report on Resettlement of People with Learning Difficulties from Long-stay Institutions*. London: Values Into Action.

Collins, J. (1993) *The Resettlement Game: Policy and Procrastination in the Closure of Mental Handicap Hospitals*. London: Values Into Action.

Costantini, M., Mencaglia, E., Giulio, P. D., Cortesi, E., Roila, F., Ballatori, E. *et al.* (2000) Cancer patients as 'experts' in defining quality of life domains: A multi-centre survey by the Italian Group for the Evaluation of Outcomes in Oncology (IGEO), *Quality of Life Research*, 9, 2: 151–9.

Coulter, J. (1979) *The Social Construction of Mind: Studies in Ethnomethodology and Linguistic Philosophy*. London: Macmillan.

Coulter, J. (1999) Discourse and mind, *Human Studies*, 22: 163–81.

Crooker, K. J. and Near, J. P. (1998) Happiness and satisfaction: measures of affect and cognition? *Social Indicators Research*, 44, 2: 195–224.

Cubbon, J. (1991) The principle of QALY maximisation as the basis for allocating health care resources, *Journal of Medical Ethics*, 17: 181–4.

Cummins, R. A. (1995) On the trail of the gold standard for life satisfaction, *Social Indicators Research*, 35: 179–200.

Cummins, R. A. (1996) The domains of life satisfaction: an attempt to order chaos, *Social Indicators Research*, 38: 303–28.

Cummins, R. A. (1997a) *The Comprehensive Quality of Life Scale – Intellectual Disability, Fifth Edition (ComQol-ID5): Manual*. Toorak: Deakin University School of Psychology.

Cummins, R. A. (1997b) Assessing quality of life, in: R. I. Brown (ed), *Quality of Life for People with Disabilities: Models, Research and Practice*, 2nd edn. Cheltenham: Stanley Thornes, pp. 116–50.

Cummins, R. A. (1997c) Self-rated quality of life scales for people with an intellectual disability: a review, *Journal of Applied Research in Intellectual Disability*, 10: 199–216.

Cummins, R. A. (1998a) *Use of proxy responding in QOL measures*. Paper presented at the Annual Conference of the Australian Society for the Study of Intellectual Disability, Adelaide, SA, August.

Cummins, R. A. (1998b) The second approximation to an international standard for life satisfaction, *Social Indicators Research*, 43: 307–34.

Cummins, R. A. (2000a) Objective and subjective quality of life: an interactive model, *Social Indicators Research*, 52: 55–72.

Cummins, R. A. (2000b) A homeostatic model for subjective quality of life, *Proceedings, Second Conference on Quality of Life in Cities*. Singapore: National University of Singapore, pp. 51–9.

Cummins, R. A. (2001a) Self-rated quality of life scales for people with an intellectual disability: A reply to Ager and Hatton, *Journal of Applied Research in Intellectual Disabilities*, 14: 1–11.

Cummins, R. A. (2001b) Life satisfaction: measurement issues and a homeostatic model, in B. Zumbo (ed), *Social Indicators and Quality of Life Research Methods: Methodological Developments and Issues, Yearbook, 1999*. Amsterdam: Kluwer Academic.

Cummins, R. A. (2001c) Living with support in the community: predictors of satisfaction with life, *Mental Retardation and Developmental Disabilities Research Reviews*, 7: 99–104.

Cummins, R. A., Gullone, E. and Lau, A. L. D. (in press) A model of subjective well-being homeostasis: the role of personality, in E. Gullone and R. A. Cummins (eds), *The Universality of Subjective Well-Being Indicators*. Dordrecht: Kluwer Academic.

Cummins, R. A., McCabe, M. P., Romeo, Y., Reid, S., and Waters, L. (1997) An initial evaluation of the Comprehensive Quality of Life Scale – Intellectual Disability, *International Journal of Disability, Development and Education*, 44: 7–19.

Cummins, R. A., Andelman, R., Board, R. Carman, L., Ferriss, A., Friedman, P. *et al.* (1998), *Quality of Life Definition and Terminology: A Discussion Document from the International Society for Quality-of-Life Studies*. The International Society for Quality-of-Life Studies (ISQOLS).

Davis, J. A. (1984) New money, an old man/lady and 'two's company': Subjective welfare in the NORC General Social Survey, *Social Indicators Research*, 15: 319–51.

De Neve, K. M. (1999) Happy as an extraverted clam? The role of personality for subjective well-being, *Psychological Science*, 8: 141–4.

De Vries, J., Seebregts, A. and Drent, M. (2000) Assessing health status and quality of life in idiopathic pulmonary fibrosis: which measure should be used? *Respiratory Medicine*, 94, 3: 273–8.

Debats, D. L. (1996) Meaning in life: clinical relevance and predictive power, *British Journal of Clinical Psychology*, 35: 503–16.

Department of Health (1989) *Caring for People: Community Care in the Next Decade and Beyond*, Cmnd. 849. London: HMSO.

Department of Health (1991) *Stephen Dorrell's MENCAP Speech/Statement on Services for People with Learning Disabilities – Tuesday 25 June 1991*. London: HMSO.

Department of Health (1992) *Social Care for Adults with Learning Disabilities (Mental Handicap)* LAC (92) 15. London: HMSO.

Department of Health (1993) *Services for People with Learning Disabilities and Challenging Behaviour or Mental Health Needs* (Chairman: Professor J. Mansell). London: HMSO.

Department of Health (2001) *The Expert Patient – A New Approach to Chronic Disease Management for the 21st Century*. London: HMSO.

Department of Health and Social Security (1969) *Report of the Committee of Inquiry into Allegations of Ill-treatment of Patients and Other Irregularities at the Ely Hospital*. Cardiff: HMSO.

Department of Health and Social Security (1971) *Better Services for the Mentally Handicapped*, Cmnd, 4683 London: HMSO.

Department of Health and Social Security (1979) *Report of the Committee of Enquiry into Mental Handicap Nursing and Care*, Vols. I and II, Cmnd. 7468-I, 7468-II. (Chairman: Mrs. P. Jay). London: HMSO.

Department of Health and Social Security (1980) *Mental Handicap: Progress, Problems and Priorities – A Review of Mental Handicap Services in England Since the*

1971 *White Paper 'Better Services for the Mentally Handicapped'*. London: HMSO.

Department of Health and Social Security (1981a) *Care in the Community: A Consultative Document on Moving Resources for Care in England*, HC(81)9/ LAC(81)5. London: HMSO.

Department of Health and Social Security (1981b) *Care in Action: A Handbook of Policies and Priorities for the Health and Personal Social Services in England*, Cmnd. 8173. London: HMSO.

Department of Health and Social Security (1983) *Care in the Community and Joint Finance*, HC(83)21/LAC(83)15. London: HMSO.

Derogatis, L. R. (n. d.) *Manual for the Symptom Checklist 90-Revised*. Minneapolis: NCI.

Derogatis, L. and Cleary, P. (1977) Confirmation of the dimensional structure of the SCL-90: a study in construct validation, *Journal of Clinical Psychology*, 33: 981–9.

Derogatis L., Lipman, R. S., Rickels, K., *et al.* (1974) The Hopkins Symptom Checklist (HSCL): a self-report symptom inventory, *Behavioral Science*, 19: 1–13.

Deutscher, I. (1973) *What We Say/What We Do: Sentiments and Acts*. Glenview, IL: Scott Foresman.

Devinsky, O., Vickrey, B. G., Cramer, J., Perrine, K., Hermann, B. P., Meador, K. *et al.* (1995) Development of the Quality of Life in Epilepsy Inventory, *Epilepsia*, 39: 399–406.

Dickerson, F. B., Parente, F. and Ringel, N. (2000) The relationship among three measures of social functioning in outpatients with schizophrenia, *Journal of Clinical Psychology*, 56: 1509–19.

Dolan, P., Gudex, C., Kind, P. and Williams, A. (1996) The time trade-off method – results from a general population survey, *Health Economics*, 5: 141–54.

Drenowski, J. (1974) *On Measuring and Planning the Quality of Life*. The Hague: Mouton de Gruyter.

Drew, P. and Heritage, J. (eds) (1992) *Talk At Work: Interaction in Institutional Settings*. Cambridge: Cambridge University Press.

Dubos, R. (1959) *Mirage of Health*. New York: Harper Row.

Duckett, P. S. and Fryer, D. (1998) Developing empowering research practices with people who have learning disabilities, *Journal of Community and Applied Social Psychology*, 8: 57–65.

Easterlin, R. (1973) Does money buy happiness? *The Public Interest*, 30: 3–10.

Eckermann, L. (2000) Gendering indicators of health and well-being: is quality of life gender neutral? *Social Indicators Research*, 52, 1: 29–54.

Eckersley, R. (1998) Redefining progress: shaping the future to human needs, *Family Matters*, 51: 6–12.

Edgerton, R. B. (1990) Quality of Life from a longitudinal research perspective, In: R. L. Schalock (ed), *Quality of Life: Perspectives and Issues*. Washington: AAMR pp. 149–60.

Edgerton, R. B. (1996) A longitudinal-ethnographic research perspective on quality of life, In: R. L. Schalock (ed), *Quality of Life: Volume I: Conceptualization and Measurement*. Washington: AAMR, pp. 83–90.

Edgerton, R. and Gaston, J. (1993) *I've Seen it All!* Cambridge: Brookline Books.

Edwards, D. (1997) *Discourse and Cognition*. London: Sage.

Edwards, D. and Potter, J. (1992) *Discursive Psychology*. London: Sage.

Edwards, D. and Potter, J. (2002) Discursive psychology, In: A. McHoul and M. Rapley (eds), *How to Analyse Talk in Institutional Settings: A Casebook of Methods*. London and New York: Continuum International.

Edwards, D., Ashmore, M. and Potter, J. (1995) Death and furniture: the rhetoric, politics and theology of bottom-line arguments against relativism, *History of the Human Sciences*, 8, 2: 25–49.

Ehrs, P. O., Åberg, H. and Larsson, K. (2001) Quality of life in primary care asthma, *Respiratory Medicine*, 95, 1: 22–30.

Emerson, E. and Hatton, C. (1994) *Moving Out: Relocation from Hospital to Community*. London: HMSO.

Emerson, E. and Hatton, C. (1996) Deinstitutionalisation in the UK and Ireland: outcomes for service users, *Journal of Intellectual and Developmental Disabilities*, 231, 1: 17–37.

Ergene, E., Behr, P. K. and Shih, J. J. (2001) Quality-of-life assessment in patients treated with vagus nerve stimulation, *Epilepsy and Behavior*, 2, 3: 284–7.

Erikson, R. and Uusitalo, H. (1987) *The Scandinavian Approach to Welfare Research*, Reprint Series No. 181. Stockholm: Swedish Institute for Social Research.

Erikson, R. (1993) Descriptions of inequality: the Swedish approach to welfare research, in: M. Nussbaum and A. Sen (eds), *The Quality of Life*. Oxford: Clarendon Press, pp. 67–87.

Estes, R. J. (1984) *The Social Progress of Nations*. New York: Praeger.

Estes, R. J. (1997) Social development trends in Europe, 1970–1994: development prospects for the new Europe, *Social Indicators Research*, 42, 1: 1–19.

EuroQOL Group (1990) EuroQOL – a new facility for the measurement of health-related quality of life, *Health Policy*, 16: 199–208.

Evans, G., Beyer, S. and Todd, S. (1987) *Evaluating the Impact of the All-Wales Strategy on the Lives of People with a Mental Handicap: A Report of a Survey Methodology*, Research Report No. 21. Cardiff: Mental Handicap in Wales – Applied Research Unit.

Evans, G., Todd, S., Beyer, S., Felce, D. and Perry, J. (1994) Assessing the impact of the All-Wales Mental Handicap Strategy: a survey of four districts, *Journal of Intellectual Disability Research*, 38, 109–33.

Fairclough, N. (1993) Critical discourse analysis and the marketisation of public discourse: the universities, *Discourse and Society*, 4: 133–59.

Fairclough, N. (2002) Critical discourse analysis, in A. McHoul and M. Rapley (eds), *How to Analyse Talk in Institutional Settings: A Casebook of Methods*. London and New York: Continuum International, pp. 25–38.

Farlinger, S. (1996) Quality of life for women, *Social Indicators Research*, 39, 1: 109–19.

Farsides, B. and Dunlop, R. J. (2001) Is there such a thing as a life not worth living? *British Medical Journal*, 322: 1481–3.

Fayers, P. and Bjordal, K. (2001) Should quality-of-life needs influence resource allocation? *The Lancet*, 357, 9261: 978.

Felce, D. (1986) Evaluation by direct observation, In: J. Beswick, T. Zadik and D. Felce (eds), *Evaluating Quality of Care*. Kidderminster: BIMH Publications.

Felce, D. and Perry, J. (1993) *Quality of Life: A Contribution to its Definition and Measurement*. Mental Handicap in Wales – Applied Research Unit, University of Wales College of Medicine.

Felce, D. and Perry, J. (1995) Quality of Life: its definition and measurement, *Research in Developmental Disabilities*, 16, 1: 51–74.

Felce, D. and Perry, J. (1996a) Assessment of quality of life, In: R. L. Schalock (ed), *Quality of Life: Volume I: Conceptualization and Measurement*. Washington: AAMR, pp. 63–72.

Felce, D. and Perry, J. (1996b) Adaptive behaviour gains in ordinary housing for people with intellectual disabilities, *Journal of Applied Research in Intellectual Disabilities*, 9, 2: 101–14.

Felce, D., Matikka, L. and Schalock, R. L. (2000) Conclusion: In the Special Interest Research Group on Quality of Life of the International Association for the Scientific Study of Intellectual Disabilities (ed), *Quality of Life: Its Conceptualization, Measurement, and Application. A Consensus Document*. Washington: IASSID.

Ferrans, C. E. (1990) Quality of life: conceptual issues, *Seminars in Oncology*, 6: 248–54.

Ferriman, A. (2001) Levels of neurosis remained static in the 1990s, *British Medical Journal*, 323: 130.

Ferriss, A. L. (1988) The uses of social indicators, *Social Forces*, 66: 601–17.

Feyerabend, P. (1974) *Against Method*. London: Verso.

Finkelstein, V. (1993) Disability: a social challenge or an administrative responsibility? In: J. Swain, V. Finkelstein, S. French and M. Oliver (eds), *Disabling Barriers – Enabling Environments*. London: Sage.

Flanagan, J. C. (1978) A research approach to improving our quality of life, *American Psychologist*, 33: 138–47.

Forbes, A. and Wainwright, S. P. (2001) On the methodological, theoretical and philosophical context of health inequalities research: a critique, *Social Science and Medicine*, 53: 801–16.

Fordham Institute: (1999) *Index of Social Health*. Tarrytown, NY: Fordham Graduate Center.

Foucault, M. (1970) *The Order of Things: An Archaeology of the Human Sciences*. London: Tavistock.

Foucault, M. (1973) *The Birth of the Clinic: An Archaeology of Medical Perception*. New York: Pantheon.

Foucault, M. (1977) *Discipline and Punish: The Birth of the Prison*. London: Allen Lane.

Foucault, M. (1978) *The History of Sexuality Volume 1: An Introduction*. New York: Pantheon.

Foucault, M. (1985) *The Use of Pleasure*. New York: Pantheon.

Foucault, M. (1986) *The Care of the Self: The History of Sexuality Volume 3*. New York: Pantheon.

Franz, M., Lis, S., Pluddemann, K. and Gallhofer, B. (1997) Conventional versus atypical neuroleptics: subjective quality of life in schizophrenic patients, *British Journal of Psychiatry*, 170: 422–5.

Frey, R. S. and Al-Roumi, A. (1999) Political democracy and the physical quality of life: the cross-national evidence, *Social Indicators Research*, 47,1: 73–97.

Fyrand, L., Wichstom, L., Moum, T., Glennas, A. and Kvien, T. K. (1997) The impact of personality and social support on mental health for female patients with rheumatoid arthritis, *Social Indicators Research*, 40: 285–98.

Garfinkel, H. (1967) *Studies in Ethnomethodology*, Englewood Cliffs, NJ: Prentice Hall.

Garro, L. C. (1992) Chronic illness and the construction of narratives, In: M. D. Good, B. J. Brodwin, B. J. Good and A. Kleinman (eds), *Pain as Human Experience: An Anthropological Perspective*. Berkeley, CA: University of California Press, pp. 100–37.

Garro, L. C. (1994a) Individual or societal responsibility? Explanations of diabetes in an Anishinaabe (Ojibway) community, *Social Science and Medicine*, 40, 1: 37–46.

Garro, L. C. (1994b) Narrative representations of chronicling experience: cultural models of illness, mind and body in stories concerning the temporomandibular joint, *Social Science and Medicine*, 38: 775–88.

Gergen, K. (1992) Organization theory in the postmodern era, In: M. Reed and M. Hughes (eds), *Rethinking Organization: Directions in Organization Theory and Analysis*. London: Sage, pp. 207–26.

Gilbert, P. (1986) *The Holocaust: The Jewish Tragedy*. London: William Collins.

Gill, T. M. and Feinstein, A. R. (1994) A critical appraisal of the quality of quality-of-life measurements, *Journal of the American Medical Association*, 272, 6: 619–26.

Glaser, B. G. and Strauss, A. L. (1967) *The Discovery of Grounded Theory: Strategies for Qualitative Research*. New York: Aldine.

Glatzer, W. (1991) Quality of life in advanced industrialized countries: the case of West Germany. In: F. Strack, M. Argyle and N. Schwarz (eds), *Subjective Well-being: An Interdisciplinary Perspective*. New York: Plenum Press, pp. 261–79.

Glover, J. (1977) *Causing Death and Saving Lives*. Harmondsworth: Penguin.

Good, B. J. (1994) *Medicine, Rationality and Experience: An Anthropological Perspective*. Cambridge: Cambridge University Press.

Goode, D. A. (ed) (1994a) *Quality of Life for Persons with Disabilities: International Perspectives and Issues*. Cambridge: Brookline Books.

Goode, D. A. (1994b) The national quality of life for persons with disabilities project: a quality of life agenda for the United States, In: D. A. Goode (ed), *Quality of Life for Persons with Disabilities: International Perspectives and Issues*. Cambridge: Brookline Books.

Goodinson, S. M. and Singleton, J. (1989) Quality of life: a critical review of current concepts, measures and their clinical implications, *International Journal of Nursing Studies*, 26: 327–41.

Goodley, D. (1996) Tales of hidden lives: a critical examination of life history research with people who have learning difficulties, *Disability and Society*, 11, 3: 333–48.

Goodley, D. (2000) *Self-advocacy in the Lives of People with Learning Difficulties: The Politics of Resilience*, Buckingham: Open University Press.

Goodley, D. and Rapley, M. (2001) How do you understand 'learning difficulties'? Towards a social theory of impairment, *Mental Retardation*, 39, 3: 229–32.

Goodwin, C. and Heritage, J. (1990) Conversation analysis, *Annual Review of Anthropology*, 19: 283–307.

Green, S. B., Salkind, N. J. and Akey, T. M. (1997) *Using SPSS for Windows: Analyzing and Understanding Data*. Upper Saddle River, NJ: Prentice Hall.

Greig, R. (1993) *The replacement of hospital services with community services based on individual need: Where are we now?* Paper presented at Hester Adrian Research Centre Conference: Resettlement: New Directions in Services for People with Learning Disabilities, University of Manchester, Manchester, UK. November.

Griffiths, R. (1988) *Community Care: Agenda for Action*. London: HMSO.

Groenewoud, J. H., van der Maas, P. J., van der Wal, G., Hengeveld, M. W., Tholen, A. J., Schudel, W. J. *et al.* (1996) Physician-assisted death in psychiatric practice in the Netherlands, *New England Journal of Medicine*, 336: 1795–801.

Groot, W. and VandenBrink, M. (2000) Life satisfaction and preference drift, *Social Indicators Research*, 50: 315–29.

Groulx, R., Doré, R. and Doré, L. (2000) My quality of life as I see it, In: K. D. Keith and R. L. Schalock (eds), *Cross-cultural Perspectives on Quality of Life*. Washington: AAMR, pp. 23–7.

Gudex, C. (1990) The QALY: how can it be used? In: S. Baldwin, C. Godfrey and C. Propper (eds), *Quality of Life: Perspectives and Policies*. London: Routledge, pp. 218–30.

Gullone, E. and Cummins, R. A. (eds) (2002) *The Universality of Subjective Well-Being Indicators*. Dordrecht: Kluwer.

Haase, J. and Rostad, M. (1994) Experiences of completing cancer treatments: child perspectives, *Oncology Nursing Forum*, 21: 1483–94.

Haase, J. E., Heiney, S. P., Ruccione, K. S. and Stutzer, C. (1999) Research triangulation to derive meaning-based quality-of-life theory: adolescent resilience model and instrument development, *International Journal of Cancer*, 12 (supplement): 125–31.

Habich, R. and Noll, H. -H. (1994) *Soziale Indikatoren und Sozialberichterstattung. Internationale Erfahrungen und gegenwrtiger Forschungsstand*. Bern: Bundesamt für Statistik.

Hagerty, M. R., Naik, P. and Tsai, C.-L. (2000) The effects of quality of life on national elections: a multi-country analysis, *Social Indicators Research*, 49, 3: 347–62.

Hagerty, M. R., Cummins, R. A., Ferriss, A. L., Land, K., Michalos, A. C., Peterson, M. *et al.* (2001) Quality of life indexes for national policy: review and agenda for research, *Social Indicators Research*, 55: 1–96.

Hakim, Z. and Pathak, D. S. (1999) Modelling the EuroQol data: a comparison of discrete choice conjoint and conditional preference modelling, *Health Economics*, 8: 103–16.

Hammerlid, E. and Taft, C. (2001) Health-related quality of life in long-term head and neck cancer survivors: a comparison with general population norms, *British Journal of Cancer*, 84, 2: 149–56.

Hansson, L., Eklund, M. and Bengtsson-Tops, A. (2001) The relationship of personality dimensions as measured by the temperament and character inventory and quality of life in individuals with schizophrenia or schizoaffective disorder living in the community, *Quality of Life Research*, 10, 2: 133–9.

Harding, A. and Greenwell, H. (2001) *Trends in Income and Expenditure: Inequality in the 1980s and 1990s*. Canberra: National Centre for Social and Economic Modelling/University of Canberra.

Harris, J. (1987) QALY-fying the value of life, *Journal of Medical Ethics*, 13: 117–23.

Harris, J. (1991) Unprincipled QALYs: a response to Cubbon, *Journal of Medical Ethics*, 17: 185–8.

Harris, J. (1995) Double jeopardy and the veil of ignorance: a reply, *Journal of Medical Ethics*, 21: 151–7.

Hatton, C. (1995) Linking quality of life to service provision: squaring the quality circle, *Clinical Psychology Forum*, 79: 25–8.

Hatton, C. (1998) Whose quality of life is it anyway? Some problems with the emerging quality of life consensus, *Mental Retardation*, 36: 104–15.

Hays R. D., Sherbourne, C. D. and Mazel, R. M. (1993) The RAND 36-Item Health Survey 1. 0, *Health Economics*, 2: 217–27.

Hays, R. D., Kallich, J. D., Mapes, D. L., Coons, S. J. and Carter, W. B. (1994) Development of the Kidney Disease Quality of Life (KDQOL) Instrument, *Quality of Life Research*, 3: 329–38.

Hays, R. D., Kallich, J. D., Mapes, D. L., Coons, S. J. and Carter, W. B. (1997) *Kidney Disease Quality of Life Short Form (KDQOL-SF), Version 1. 3: A Manual for Use and Scoring.* Santa Monica, CA: RAND.

Headey, B., and Wearing, A. (1989) Personality, life events, and subjective well-being: toward a dynamic equilibrium model, *Journal of Personality and Social Psychology*, 57: 731–9.

Headey, B. and Wearing, A. (1992) *Understanding Happiness: A Theory of Subjective Well-being.* Melbourne: Longman Cheshire.

Headey, B., Veenhoven, R. and Wearing, A. (1991) Top-down versus bottom-up theories of subjective well-being, *Social Indicators Research*, 24: 81–100.

Heal, L. W. and Sigelman, C. K. (1990) Methodological issues in measuring the Quality of Life of individuals with mental retardation. In: R. L. Schalock (ed), *Quality of Life: Perspectives and Issues.* Washington: AAMR, pp. 161–76.

Heidegger, M. (1996) *Being and Time*, trans. J. Stambaugh. Albany, NY: State University of New York Press.

Heinrichs, D. W., Hanlon, T. E. and Carpenter, W. T. Jr (1984) The Quality of Life Scale: an instrument for rating the schizophrenia syndrome, *Schizophrenia Bulletin*, 10: 388–98.

Helson, H. (1964) *Adaptation-level Theory.* New York: Harper and Row.

Hendriks, A. H. C., De Moor, J. M. H., Oud, J. H. L. and Savelberg, M. M. H. W. (2000) Perceived changes in well-being of parents with a child in a therapeutic toddler class, *Research in Developmental Disabilities*, 21: 455–68.

Hermann, B. P., Seidenberg, M., Bell, B., Woodard, A., Rutecki, P. and Sheth, R. (2000) Comorbid psychiatric symptoms in temporal lobe epilepsy: association with chronicity of epilepsy and impact on quality of life, *Epilepsy and Behavior*, 1: 184–90

Hester, S. and Francis, D. (2002) Is institutional talk a phenomenon? In: A. McHoul and M. Rapley (eds), *How to Analyse Talk in Institutional Settings: A Casebook of Methods.* London and New York: Continuum International, pp. 209–20.

Hickey, A. M., Bury, G., O'Boyle, C. A., Bradley, F., O'Kelly, F. D. and Shannon, W. (1996) A new short form individual quality of life measure (SEIQoL-DW): application in a cohort of individuals with HIV / AIDS, *British Medical Journal*, 313: 29–33.

Higginson, I. J. (1993) *Clinical Audit in Palliative Care.* Oxford: Radcliffe Medical Press.

Higginson, I. J. and Carr, A. J. (2001) Using quality of life measures in the clinical setting, *British Medical Journal*, 322: 1297–300.

Hogenraad, R. and Grosbois, T. (1997) A history of threat in Europe and Belgium (1920–1993) *Social Indicators Research*, 42, 2: 221–44.

Houtkoop-Steenstra, H. (2000) *Interaction and the Standardised Interview: The Living Questionnaire*. Cambridge: Cambridge University Press.

Hughes, C., Hwang, B., Kim, J. H., Eisenman, L. T. and Kilian, D. J. (1995) Quality of life in applied research: a review and analysis of empirical measures, *American Journal on Mental Retardation*, 99, 6: 623–41.

Hyder, A. A., Rotllant, G. and Morrow, R. H. (1998) Measuring the burden of disease: healthy life-years, *American Journal of Public Health*, 88, 2: 196–202.

Idler, E. L. and Benyamini, Y. (1997) Self-rated health and mortality: a review of twenty-seven community studies, *Journal of Health and Social Behavior*, 38: 21–37.

James, O. (1997) *Britain on the Couch*. London: Century/Random House.

Johnston, D. F. (1988) Toward a comprehensive 'quality of life' index, *Social Indicators Research*, 20: 473–96.

Jones-Lee, M., Hammerton, M. and Phillips, P. R. (1985) The value of safety: results of a national sample survey, *Economic Journal*, 95: 49–72.

Jordan, T. E. (1998) John O'Neill, Irish bootmaker: a biographical approach to quality of life, *Social Indicators Research*, 48, 3: 297–317.

Jordan, T. E. (2001) Quality of life, hegemony, and social change in rural Ireland: W. Bence Jones, 'A Landlord Who Tried to do His Duty', *Social Indicators Research*, 55, 2: 199–221.

Joseph, G. A. and Rao, P. S. S. S. (1999) Impact of leprosy on the quality of life, *Bulletin of the World Health Organization*, 77, 6: 515–7.

Juster, F. T. and Land, K. C. (eds) (1981) *Social Accounting Systems: Essays on the State of the Art*. New York: Academic Press.

Kaiser, W. (2000) Cognitive effects of antipsychotics in schizophrenia and relationship to quality of life, *British Journal of Psychiatry*, 176: 92–3.

Kaiser, W., Priebe, S., Barr, W., Hoffman, K., Isermann, M., der-Wanner, U-U. *et al.* (1998) Profiles of subjective quality of life in schizophrenic in-and out-patient samples, *Psychiatry Research*, 66: 153–66.

Kant, I. (1978 [1798]) *Anthropology from a Pragmatic Point of View*, trans. V. L. Dowdell, rev. and ed. H. H. Rudnick. Carbondale, IL: Southern Illinois University Press.

Keith, K. D. (1990) Quality of life: issues in community integration, In: R. L. Schalock (ed), *Quality of Life: Perspectives and Issues*. Washington: AAMR.

Keith, K. D. and Schalock, R. L. (eds) (2000) *Cross-cultural Perspectives on Quality of Life*. Washington: AAMR.

Kemmler, G., Holzner, B., Neudorfer, C., Meise, U. and Hinterhuber, H. (1997) General life satisfaction and domain-specific quality of life in chronic schizophrenic patients, *Quality of Life Research*, 6, 3: 265–73.

Kendall, G. and Wickham, G. (1999) *Using Foucault's Methods*. London: Sage.

Kind, P. (1990) Issues in the design and construction of a quality of life measure, In: S. Baldwin, C. Godfrey and C. Propper (eds), *Quality of Life: Perspectives and Policies*. London: Routledge.

Kind, P., Dolan, P., Gudex, C. and Williams, A. (1998) Variations in population health status: results from a United Kingdom national questionnaire survey, *British Medical Journal*, 316: 736–41.

King's Fund Centre (1980/1982) *An Ordinary Life: Comprehensive Locally Based Services for Mentally Handicapped People*. Project Paper No. 24, London: King's Fund.

Klarman, H. E., O'Francis, J. and Rosenthal, G. D. (1968) Cost-effectiveness analysis applied to the treatment of chronic renal disease, *Medical Care*, 6, 1: 48–54.

Klassen, A. F., Newton, J. N. and Mallon, E. (2000) Measuring quality of life in people referred for specialist care of acne: comparing generic and disease-specific measures, *Journal of the American Academy of Dermatology*, 43, 2: 229–33.

Knapp, M. (1988) Construction and expectation: themes from the care in the community initiative, in P. Cambridge and M. Knapp (eds), *Demonstrating Successful Care in the Community*. Canterbury: University of Kent/PSSRU.

Koch, T. (1994) *A Place in Time: Care Givers for Their Elderly*. New York: Praeger.

Koch, T. (2000) Future states: the axioms underlying prospective, future-oriented, health planning instruments, *Social Science and Medicine*, 52: 453–65.

Kuczewski, M. G. (1999) Narrative views of personal identity and substituted judgment in surrogate decision making, *Journal of Law, Medicine and Ethics*, 27, 1: 32–5.

Kuhn, T. S. (1970) *The Structure of Scientific Revolutions*, 2nd edn. Chicago: University of Chicago Press.

Kuhse, H. and Singer, P. (1985) *Should the Baby Live?* Oxford: Oxford University Press.

Land, K. C. (1975) Theories, models and indicators of social change, *International Social Science Journal*, 27: 7–37.

Land, K. C. (1983) Social Indicators, *Annual Review of Sociology*, 9: 1–26.

Land, K. (2000) *Social indicators*. Available from <http://www.cob.vt.edu/market/isqols/kenlandessay. htm> [accessed 08. 11. 01].

Landesman, S. (1986) Quality of life and personal life satisfaction: definition and measurement issues, *Mental Retardation*, 24: 141–3.

Landgraf, J. M., Abetz, L. and Ware, J. E. (1996) *The CHQ User's Manual*. Boston: Health Institute, New England Medical Center.

LaPointe, L. L. (2001) Quality of Life with brain damage, *Brain and Language*, 71: 135–7.

Lauritzen, S. O. and Sachs, L. (2001) Normality, risk and the future: implicit communication of threat in health surveillance, *Sociology of Health and Illness*, 23, 4: 497–516.

Lehman, A. F (1988) A quality of life interview for the chronically mentally ill, *Evaluation and Program Planning*, 11: 51–62.

Lehman, A. F (1996) Measures of quality of life among persons with severe and persistent mental disorders, *Social Psychiatry and Psychiatric Epidemiology*, 31: 78–88.

Lehman, A. F., Ward, N. C., and Linn, L. S. (1982) Chronic mental patients: the quality of life issue, *American Journal of Psychiatry*, 139, 10: 1271–6.

Lehman, A. F., Possidente, S. and Hawker, F. (1986) The quality of life of chronic patients in a state hospital and in community residences, *Hospital and Community Psychiatry*, 37,9: 901–7.

Leidy, N. K. and Haase, J. E. (1999) Functional status from the patient's perspective: the challenge of preserving personal integrity, *Research in Nursing and Health*, 22: 67–77.

Lennon, J. and McCartney, P. (1964) Can't Buy Me Love, From *A Hard Day's Night*, London: Parlophone/EMI. CDP7-46437-2. Recorded by The Beatles 29 January 1964.

Levene, H. (1960) Robust tests for equality of variance. In: I. Olkin (ed), *Contributions to Probability and Statistics*, Palo Alto, CA: Stanford University Press.

Leudar, I. and Thomas, P. (2000) *Voices of Reason, Voices of Insanity: Studies of Verbal Hallucinations*, London: Routledge.

Levinson, S. (1983) *Pragmatics*. Cambridge, Cambridge University Press.

Lewis, G. and Wilkinson, G. (1993) Another British disease? A recent increase in the prevalence of psychiatric morbidity, *Journal of Epidemiology and Community Health*, 47: 358–361.

Loomes, G. and McKenzie, L. (1990) The scope and limitations of QALY measures, In: S. Baldwin, C. Godfrey and C. Propper (eds), *Quality of Life: Perspectives and Policies*. London: Routledge.

Lovett, H. (1993) Foreword, In: P. Kinsella *Supported Living: A New Paradigm*. Manchester: National Development Team.

Lowe, K., dePaiva, S. and Felce, D. (1993) Effects of a community-based service on adaptive and maladaptive behaviours: a longitudinal study, *Journal of Intellectual Disability Research*, 37: 3–22.

Luckasson, R. (1997) Foreword, In: R. L. Schalock (ed.), *Quality of Life: Volume II: Application to Persons with Disabilities*. Washington: AAMR, pp. vii-x.

Lyons, J. S., Howard, K. I., O'Mahoney, M. T. and Lish, J. (1997a) *The Measurement and Management of Clinical Outcomes in Mental Health*. New York: Wiley.

Lyons, J. S., O'Mahoney, M. T., Miller, S. I., Neme, J., Kabat, J. and Miller, F. (1997b) Predicting readmission to the psychiatric hospital in a managed care environment: implications for quality indicators, *American Journal of Psychiatry*, 154: 337–40.

McCormick, R. (1978) The quality of life, the sanctity of life, *Hastings Center Report*, 8: 32.

McGee, H. M., O'Boyle, C. A., Hickey, A., O'Malley, K. and Joyce, C. R. B. (1991) Assessing the quality of life of the individual: the SEIQol with a healthy and a gastroenterology unit population, *Psychological Medicine*, 21: 749– 59.

McHorney, C. A, Ware, J. J. and Raczek, A. E. (1993) The MOS 36-Item Short-Form Health Survey (SF-36): II. Psychometric and clinical tests of validity in measuring physical and mental health constructs, *Medical Care*, 31: 247–63.

McHoul, A. and Rapley, M. (2002b) 'Should we make a start then?' A strange case of (delayed) client-initiated psychological assessment. *Research on Language and Social Interaction*, 35, 1, 73–91.

McHoul, A. and Rapley, M. (2001) Culture, psychology and 'being human', *Culture and Psychology*, 7, 4: 433–51.

McHoul, A. and Rapley, M. (eds) (2002a) *How to Analyse Talk in Institutional Settings: A Casebook of Methods*. London and New York: Continuum International.

Mackenzie, G. (2001) Neurosis may be increasing (e-letter), *British Medical Journal*, <http://www. bmj. com/cgi/eletters/323/7305/130/a#EL3> [accessed 16/10/01].

McLintock, A. (1992) The angel of progress, *Social Text*, 10, 2 and 3: 84–98.

McNamee, D. and Horton, R. (1996) Lies, damn lies, and reports of RCTs, *Lancet*, 348: 562.

MacRae, D., Jr (1985) *Policy Indicators: Links Between Social Science and Public Policy.* Chapel Hill, NC: University of North Carolina Press.

Maguire, P., Booth, K., Elliot, C. and Jones, B. (1996) Helping health care professionals involved in cancer care acquire key interviewing skills: the impact of workshops, *European Journal of Cancer*, 32 (suppl.): 1486–9.

Mahoney, F. I., and Barthel, D. W. (1965) Functional evaluation: the Barthel Index, *Maryland State Medical Journal*, 14, 2: 61–5.

Mallard, A. G. C., Lance, C. E. and Michalos, A. C. (1997) Culture as a moderator of overall life satisfaction-life facet of satisfaction relationships, *Social Indicators Research*, 40: 259–84.

Manning, C. (2001) I don't believe the figures (e-letter), *British Medical Journal*, <http://www. bmj. com/cgi/eletters/323/7305/130/a#EL3> [accessed 16/ 10/01].

Martin, C. R. and Thompson, D. R. (2001) Does dialysis adequacy impact on the quality of life of end-stage renal disease patients? *Clinical Effectiveness in Nursing*, 5, 2: 57–65.

Martin, A. R., Lookingbill, D. P., Botek, A., Light, J., Thiboutot, D. and Girma, C. J. (2001) Health-related quality of life among patients with facial acne – assessment of a new acne-specific questionnaire, *Clinical and Experimental Dermatology*, 26: 380–5.

Maslow, A. H. (1954) *Motivation and Personality.* New York: Harper.

Mattes, R. and Christie, J. (1997) Personal versus collective quality of life and South Africans' evaluations of democratic government, *Social Indicators Research*, 41, 1/3: 205–28.

Megone, C. B. (1990) The quality of life: starting from Aristotle, In: S. Baldwin, C. Godfrey, and C. Propper (eds), *Quality of Life: Perspectives and Policies*. London: Routledge, pp. 28–41.

Michalos A. C. (1985) Multiple discrepancies theory (MDT), *Social Indicators Research*, 16: 347–413.

Miller, P. (1986) Critical sociologies of madness, In: P. Miller and N. Rose (eds), *The Power of Psychiatry*. Cambridge: Polity Press.

Miller, T. and McHoul, A. (1998) *Popular Culture and Everyday Life.* London: Sage.

Missenden, K., Oliver, N., Carson, J., Holloway, F., Towey, A., Dunn, L. *et al.* (1995–6) Understanding quality of life: a comparison between staff and patients, *Social Work and Social Sciences Review*, 6, 2: 117–29.

Monk, R. (1991) *Ludwig Wittgenstein: The Duty of Genius.* London: Random House.

Morreim, H. (1992) The impossibility and the necessity of quality of life research, *Bioethics*, 6, 3: 218–32.

Morris, J. and Durand, A. (1989) *Category Rating Methods: Numerical And Verbal Scales.* York: Centre for Health Economics, University of York (mimeograph).

Mozes, B., Maor, Y. and Shmueli, A. (1999) Do we know what global ratings of health-related quality of life measure? *Quality of Life Research*, 8, 3: 269–73.

Muldoon, M. F., Barger, S. D., Flory, J. D. and Manuck, S. B. (1998) What are quality of life measurements measuring? *British Medical Journal*, 316: 542–5.

Mulkay, M., Ashmore, M. and Pinch, T. (1987) Measuring the quality of life, *Sociology*, 21: 541–64.

Murphy, G. (1987) Direct observation as an assessment tool in functional analysis and treatment, In: J. Hogg and N. V. Raynes (eds), *Assessment in Mental Handicap*. Beckenham: Croom-Helm.

Murray, C. J. L (1994) Quantifying the burden of disease: the technical basis for disability-adjusted life years, *Bulletin of the World Health Organization*, 72, 3: 429–45.

Murray, C. J. L (1996) Rethinking DALYs, In: C. J. L. Murray and A. D. Lopez (eds), *The Global Burden of Disease: A Comprehensive Assessment of Mortality and Disability from Diseases, Injuries, and Risk Factors in 1990 and projected to 2020 – Summary*. Cambridge, MA: Harvard School of Public Health, pp. 1–98.

Murray, C. J. L. and Acharya, A. K. (1997) Understanding DALYs, *Journal of Health Economics*, 16: 703–30.

Murray, C. J. L. and Lopez, A. D. (eds) (1996) *The Global Burden of Disease: A Comprehensive Assessment of Mortality and Disability from Diseases, Injuries, and Risk Factors in 1990 and projected to 2020 – Summary*. Cambridge, MA: Harvard School of Public Health.

Murray, C. J. L, Salomon, J. A. and Mathers. C. (1999) *A Critical Examination of Summary Measures of Population Health*, GPE Discussion Paper No. 2, Geneva: World Health Organization.

Navarro, V. and Shi, L. (2001) The political context of social inequalities and health, *Social Science and Medicine*, 52: 481–91.

Nihira, K., Foster, R., Shellhaas, M. and Leland, H. (1975) *AAMD Adaptive Behaviour Scale*. Washington: American Association on Mental Deficiency.

Noll, H.-H. (2000) Social indicators and social reporting: the international experience, <http://www. ccsd. ca/noll1. html> [accessed 17. 09. 01].

Noll, H.-H. and Zapf, W. (1994) Social indicators research: societal monitoring and social reporting, in I. Borg and P. Mohler (eds), *Trends and Perspectives in Empirical Social Research*, New York: Walter de Gruyter.

Nord, E. (1991) The validity of a visual analogue scale in determining social utility weights for health states, *International Journal of Health Planning and Management*, 6: 234–42.

Nord, E. (1992a) An alternative to QALYs: the saved young life equivalent, *British Medical Journal*, 305: 875–8.

Nord, E. (1992b) Methods for quality adjustment of life years, *Social Science and Medicine*, 34: 559–69.

Nord, E. (1999) *Cost-Value Analysis in Health Care*. Cambridge: Cambridge University Press.

O'Boyle, C. A., McGee, H., Hickey, A., Joyce, C. R. B., Browne, J. and O'Malley, J. (1993) *The Schedule for the Evaluation of Individual Quality of Life Administration Manual*. Dublin: Department of Psychology, Royal College of Surgeons in Ireland.

O'Connor, R. (1993) *Issues in the Measurement of Health-related Quality of Life*, Working Paper 30. Melbourne: National Center for Health Program Evaluation.

Oliver, J. P. J., Huxley, P. J., Priebe, S. and Kaiser, W. (1997) Measuring the quality of life of severely mentally ill people using the Lancashire Quality of Life Profile, *Social Psychiatry Epidemiology*, 32, 76–83.

Oliver, N., Carson, J., Missenden, K., Towey, A., Dunn, L., Collins, E., and Holloway, F. (1996) Assessing the quality of life of the long-term mentally-ill: a comparative study of two measures, *International Journal of Methods in Psychiatric Research*, 6: 161–6.

Oliver, M. (1996) *Understanding Disability: From Theory to Practice.* Chatham: McKays.

Organization for Economic Cooperation and Development (2001) *The Well-being of Nations: The Role of Human and Social Capital.* Paris: OECD.

Organization for Economic Cooperation and Development (1982) *The OECD List of Social Indicators,* OECD Social Indicator Development Programme. Paris: OECD.

Ostroot, N. and Snyder, W. (1996) The quality of life in historical perspective. France: 1695–1990, *Social Indicators Research,* 38, 2: 109–28.

Owens, D. K., Cardinalli, A. B. and Nease, R. F. (1997) Physicians' assessments of the utility of health states associated with Human Immunodeficiency Virus (HIV) and Hepatitis B Virus (HBV) Infection, *Quality of Life Research,* 6. 1: 77–86.

Parker, I. (ed) (1998) *Social Constructionism, Discourse and Realism.* London: Sage.

Patil, R., Cotler, S. J., Banaad-Omiotek, G., McNutt, R. A., Brown, M. D., Cotler, S. *et al.* (2001) Physicians' preference values for hepatitis C health states and antiviral therapy: a survey, *BioMed Central Gastroenterology,* 1: 6. <http://www.biomedcentral. com/1471-230X/1/6> [accessed 02. 08. 01].

Patton, M. Q. (1990) *Qualitative Evaluation and Research Methods.* Newbury Park, CA: Sage.

Peräkylä, A. (1997) Reliability and validity in research based on transcripts, In: David Silverman (ed.), *Qualitative Methods: Theory, Method and Practice.* London: Sage, pp. 201–20.

Perry, J. and Felce, D. (1995) Objective indicators of quality of life: how much do they agree with each other? *Journal of Community and Applied Social Psychology,* 5: 1–19.

Perry, J., Felce., D. and Lowe, K. (2000) *Subjective and Objective Quality of Life Assessment: Their Interrelationship and Determinants.* Cardiff: Welsh Centre for Learning Disabilities – Applied Research Unit/University of Wales College of Medicine.

Personal Social Services Research Unit (1987) Consumerism and care in the community, *Care in the Community Newsletter, No. 7.* Canterbury: University of Kent/PSSRU.

Petersen, A. and Lupton, D. (1996) *The New Public Health: Health and Self in the Age of Risk.* London: Sage.

Phillips, C. and Thompson, G. (1998) *What is a QALY?* London: Hayward.

Pilgrim, D. and Bentall, R. (1999) The medicalisation of misery: a critical realist analysis of the concept of depression, *Journal of Mental Health,* 8, 3: 261–74.

Plato (1903) *The Four Socratic Dialogues of Plato,* trans. B. Jowett, with a preface by E. Caird. Oxford: Clarendon Press.

Pollard, B. and Johnston, M. (2001) Problems with the Sickness Impact Profile: a theoretically based analysis and a proposal for a new method of implementation and scoring, *Social Science and Medicine,* 52: 921–34.

Polsky, D., Willke, R. J., Scott, K., Schulman, K. A. and Glick, H. A. (2001) A comparison of scoring weights for the EuroQol derived from patients and the general public, *Health Economics,* 10: 27–37.

Potter, J. (1996) *Representing Reality: Discourse, Rhetoric and Social Construction,* London: Sage.

Potter, J. (2001) Beyond cognitivism, *Research on Language and Social Interaction*, 32, 1/2: 119–27.

Potter, J. and Wetherell, M. (1987) *Discourse and Social Psychology: Beyond Attitudes and Behaviour*. London: Sage.

Pretty, G. M. H., Andrewes, C. C. and Collet, C. (1994) Exploring adolescents' sense of community and its relationship to loneliness, *Journal of Community Psychology*, 22: 346–58.

Priebe, S., Oliver, J. P. J. and Kaiser, W. (eds), (1999) *Quality of Life and Mental Health Care*. Petersfield: Wrightson Biomedical.

Prieto, L., Santed, R., Cobo, E. and Alonso, J. (1999) A new measure for assessing the health-related quality of life of patients with vertigo, dizziness or imbalance: the VDI questionnaire, *Quality of Life Research*, 8, 1/2: 131–9.

Prince, P. N. and Gerber, G. J. (2001) Measuring subjective quality of life in people with serious mental illness using the SEIQoL-DW, *Quality of Life Research*, 10, 2: 117–22.

Puchta, C. and Potter, J. (1999) Asking elaborate questions: focus groups and the management of spontaneity, *Journal of Sociolinguistics*, 3: 314–35.

Puchta, C. and Potter, J. (forthcoming) *Focus Group Practice: Moderating Interaction in Market Research Focus Groups*. London: Sage.

Putnam, R. (1995) Bowling alone: America's declining social capital, *Journal of Democracy*, 6, 1 (Jan.): 65–78.

Putnam, R. (2002) Bowling together, *The American Prospect*, 11 February: 20–22.

Ramsey, P. (1978) *Ethics at the Edges of Life*. New Haven, CT: Yale University Press.

Rapley, M. (2001) Policing happiness, In: C. Newnes, G. Holmes, and C. Dunn, (eds), *This is Madness Too*. Ross-on-Wye: PCCS Books.

Rapley, M. and Antaki, C. (1996) A conversation analysis of the 'acquiescence' of people with learning disabilities, *Journal of Community and Applied Social Psychology*, 6: 207–27.

Rapley, M. and Beyer, S. (1996) Daily activity, community activity and quality of life in an ordinary housing network, *Journal of Applied Research in Intellectual Disabilities*, 9, 1: 31–9.

Rapley, M. and Beyer, S. (1998) Daily activity, community activity and quality of life in an ordinary housing network: a two-year follow-up, *Journal of Applied Research in Intellectual Disabilities*, 11, 1: 34–43.

Rapley, M. and Hopgood, L. (1997) Quality of life in a community-based service in rural Australia, *Journal of Intellectual and Developmental Disability*, 22, 2: 124–41.

Rapley, M. and Lobley, J. (1995) Factor analysis of the Schalock and Keith (1993) Quality of Life Questionnaire: a replication, *Mental Handicap Research*, 8, 3: 194–202.

Rapley, M. and Ridgway, J. (1998) Quality of Life talk: the corporatisation of intellectual disability, *Disability and Society*, 13, 3: 451–71.

Rapley, M., Kiernan, P. and Antaki, C. (1998) Invisible to themselves or negotiating identity? The interactional management of 'being intellectually disabled', *Disability and Society*, 13, 5: 807–27.

Rapley, M., Ridgway, J. and Beyer, S. (1998) Staff : staff and staff : client reliability of the Schalock and Keith (1996) Quality of Life Questionnaire, *Journal of Intellectual Disability Research*, 42, 1: 37–43.

Ravenscroft, A. J. and Bell, M. D. D (2000) 'End-of-life' decision making within intensive care – objective, consistent, defensible? *Journal of Medical Ethics*, 26: 435–40.

Raynes, N. V., Sumpton, R. C. and Pettipher, C. (1989a) *The Index of Participation in Domestic Life*. Manchester: Manchester University Department of Social Policy and Social Work.

Raynes, N. V., Sumpton, R. C. and Pettipher, C. (1989b) *The Index of Community Involvement*. Manchester: Manchester University Department of Social Policy and Social Work.

Reicher, S. (2001) Studying psychology, studying racism, In: M. Augoustinos and K. Reynolds (eds), *Understanding Prejudice, Racism and Social Conflict*. London: Sage, pp. 273–98.

Reiter, S. and Bendov, D. (1996) The self concept and quality of life of two groups of learning disabled adults living at home and in group homes, *British Journal of Developmental Disabilities*, xlii, 2, 83: 97–111.

Richardson, J. T. E. (1996) *Handbook of Qualitative Research Methods for Psychology and the Social Sciences*. Leicester: BPS Books.

Rodgers, W. (1982) Trends in reported happiness within demographically defined subgroups, 1957–78. *Social Forces*, 60: 826–42.

Rogers-Clark, C. (1998) Women and health, In: C. Rogers-Clark and A. Smith (eds), *Women's Health: A Primary Health Care Approach*. Sydney: MacLennan & Petty.

Rose, N. (1986) Psychiatry: the discipline of mental health, In: P. Miller and N. Rose (eds), *The Power of Psychiatry*. Cambridge: Polity Press.

Rose, N. (1992) Governing the enterprising self, In: P. Heelas and P. Morris (eds), *The Values of Enterprise Culture: The Moral Debate*. London: Routledge.

Rose, N. (1999) *Governing the Soul: The Shaping of the Private Self*, 2nd edn. London: Free Association Books.

Rosen, M. (1986) Quality of life for persons with mental retardation: a question of entitlement, *Mental Retardation*, 24: 365–6.

Rothwell, P. M., McDowell, Z., Wong, C. K. and Dorman, P. J. (1997) Doctors and patients don't agree: cross-sectional study of patients' and doctors' perceptions and assessments of disability in multiple sclerosis, *British Medical Journal*, 314: 1580–3.

Ruggieri, M., Bisoffi, G. and Fontecedro, L. (2001) Subjective and objective dimensions of quality of life in psychiatric patients: a factor analytic approach, *British Journal of Psychiatry*, 178: 268–75.

Ryle, G. (1949) *The Concept of Mind*. Oxford: Clarendon Press.

Sacks, H. (1992) *Lectures on Conversation, vols 1 and 2*, ed. G. Jefferson, intro. E. A. Schegloff. Oxford: Blackwell.

Sadana, R., Mathers, C. D., Lopez, A. D., Murray, C. J. L. and Iburg, K. (n. d.) *Comparative Analyses of More than 50 Household Surveys on Health Status*, GPE Discussion Paper Series No. 15. Geneva: World Health Organization.

Sahlberg-Blom, E., Ternestedt, B.-M. and Johansson, J.-E. (2001) Is good 'quality of life' possible at the end of life? An explorative study of the experiences of a group of cancer patients in two different care cultures, *Journal of Clinical Nursing*, 10: 550–62.

Salkeld, G., Cameron, I. D., Cumming, R. G., Easter, S., Seymour, J., Kurrle, S. E. *et al.* (2000) Quality of life related to fear of falling and hip fracture in older women: a time trade-off study, *British Medical Journal*, 320: 241–6.

Salomon, J. A., Mathers, C. D. and Murray, C. J. L. (2001) Applying DALYs to the burden of infectious disease (letter) *Bulletin of the World Health Organization*, 79, 3: 268.

Salvaris, M. (2000) *Community and Social Indicators: How Citizens Can Measure Progress. An Overview of Social and Community Indicator Projects in Australia and Internationally*. Hawthorn: Institute for Social Research, Swinburne University of Technology.

Samli, A. C. (1987) *Marketing and the Quality-of-Life Interface*. Westport, CT: Quorum Books.

Sanders, C., Eggerm, M., Donovan, J., Tallon, D. and Frankel, S. (1998) Reporting on quality of life in randomised controlled trials: bibliographic study, *British Medical Journal*, 317: 1191–4.

Sands, D. J., Kozleski, E. B. and Goodwin, L. D. (1991) Whose needs are we meeting? Results of a consumer satisfaction survey of persons with developmental disabilities in Colorado, *Research in Developmental Disabilities*, 12: 297–314.

Sarantkos, S. (1993) *Social Research*. Melbourne: Macmillan Academic.

Sawyer, M., Antoniou, G., Toogood, I. and Rice, M. (1999) A comparison of parent and adolescent reports describing the health-related quality of life of adolescents treated for cancer, *International Journal of Cancer*, 12 (supplement): 39–45.

Sayers, B. M. and Fliedner, T. M. (1997) The critique of DALYs: a counter-reply, *Bulletin of the World Health Organization*, 75: 383–4.

Schalock, R. L (1994) The concept of quality of life and its current applications in the field of mental retardation/developmental disabilities, In: D. A. Goode (ed), *Quality of Life for Persons with Disabilities: International Perspectives and Issues*. Cambridge: Brookline Books, pp. 266–84.

Schalock, R. L. (ed) (1996) *Quality of Life: Volume I: Conceptualization and Measurement*. Washington: AAMR.

Schalock, R. L. (ed) (1997) *Quality of Life: Volume II: Application to Persons with Disabilities*. Washington: AAMR.

Schalock, R. L. and Keith, K. D. (1993) *Quality of Life Questionnaire*. Worthington, OH: IDS Publishing Corporation.

Schalock, R. L. and Parmenter, T. (2000) Preface, In: *Quality Of Life: Its Conceptualization, Measurement, and Application A Consensus Document*. Washington: IASSID.

Schalock, R. L., Bonham, G. S. and Marchand, C. B. (2000) Consumer-based quality of life assessment: a path model of perceived satisfaction, *Evaluation and Program Planning*, 23, 1: 77–87.

Schalock, R. L., Keith, K. D. and Hoffman, K. (1990) *Quality of Life Questionnaire: Standardization Manual*. Hastings, NE: Mid-Nebraska Mental Retardation Services.

Schrecker, T., Acosta, L., Somerville, M. A. and Bursztajn, H. J. (2001) The ethics of social risk reduction in the era of the biological brain, *Social Science and Medicine*, 52: 1677–87.

Selai, C. E. and Trimble, M. R. (1997) Patients' assessments of disability in multiple sclerosis, *British Medical Journal*, 315: 1305 (letter).

Sharma, T. (1999) Cognitive effects of conventional and atypical antipsychotics in schizophrenia, *British Journal of Psychiatry*, 174 (suppl. 38): 44–51.

Shaw, C., McColl, E. and Bond, S. (2000) Functional abilities and continence: the use of proxy respondents in research involving older people, *Quality of Life Research*, 9, 10: 1117–26.

Shea, W. R. (1976) Introduction: the quest for a high quality of life, In: W. R. Shea and J. King-Farlow (eds), *Values and the Quality of Life*. New York: Science History Publications, pp. 1–5.

Sheldon, T. (2000) Dutch GP cleared after helping to end man's 'hopeless existence', *British Medical Journal*, 321: 1174.

Shepherd, G., Muijen, M., Dean, R. and Cooney, M. (1996) Residential care in hospital and in the community – quality of care and quality of life, *British Journal of Psychiatry*, 168: 448–56.

Sigelman, C. K., Budd, E. C., Spanhel, C. L. and Schoenrock, C. J. (1981) When in doubt, say 'yes': acquiescence in interviews with mentally retarded persons, *Mental Retardation*, 19: 53–8.

Silverman, D. (1997) Towards an aesthetics of research, In: D. Silverman (ed.), *Qualitative Methods: Theory, Method and Practice*. London: Sage, pp. 239–53

Silverman, D. (1998) *Harvey Sacks: Social Science and Conversation Analysis*. Cambridge: Polity Press.

Simpson, C. J., Hyde, C. E. and Faragher, E. B. (1989) The chronically mentally ill in community facilities: a study of quality of life, *British Journal of Psychiatry*, 154: 77–82.

Singer, P., McKie, J., Kuhse, H. and Richardson, J. (1995) Double jeopardy and the use of QALYs in health care allocation, *Journal of Medical Ethics*, 21: 144–50.

Sirgy, M. J. and Samli, A. C. (eds) (1996) *New Dimensions in Marketing/Quality-of-Life Research*, Westport, CT: Quorum Books.

Skantze, K., Malm, U., Dencker, S. J., May, P. R. and Corrigan, P. (1992) Comparison of quality of life with standard of living in schizophrenic outpatients, *British Journal of Psychiatry*, 161: 797–801.

Skevington, S. M. and Wright, A. (2001) Changes in the quality of life of patients receiving antidepressant medication in primary care: validation of the WHOQOL-100, *British Journal of Psychiatry*, 178: 261–7.

Slaughter, J. G., Lehman, A. F., and Myers, C. P. (1991) Quality of life of severely mentally ill adults in residential care facilities, *Adult Residential Care Journal*, 5, 2: 97–111.

Slevin, M. L., Plant, H., Lynch, D., Drinkwater, J. and Gregory, W. M. (1988) Who should measure quality of life, the doctor or the patient? *British Journal of Cancer*, 57: 109–12.

Smith, J. A, (1995) Semi-structured interviewing and qualitative analysis, In: J. A. Smith, R. Harré and L. Van Langenhove (eds), *Rethinking Methods in Psychology*. London: Sage.

Spencer, B., Leplège, A. and Ecosse, E. (1999) Recurrent genital herpes and quality of life in France, *Quality of Life Research*, 8, 4: 365–71.

Spitzer, W. O. (1987) State of science 1986: quality of life and functional status as target variables for research, *Journal of Chronic Diseases*, 40: 465–71.

Sprangers, M. A. G., de Regt, E. B., Andries, F., van Agt, H. M. E., Bijl, R. V., de Boer, J. B., *et al.* (2000) Which chronic conditions are associated with better or poorer quality of life? *Journal of Clinical Epidemiology*, 53, 9: 895–907.

Staquet, M., Hays, R. and Fayers, P. (eds) (1998) *Quality of Life Assessment in Clinical Trials: Methods and Practice*. Oxford: Oxford University Press.

Stein, R. and Jessop, D. (1990) Functional Status II(R) A measure of child health status, *Medical Care*, 28: 1041–55.

Stein, R. and Jessop, D. (1991) *Manual for the Functional Status II(R) Measure*. New York: Albert Einstein College of Medicine of Yeshiva University.

Stein, J. and Mansell, J. (1992) *MTSTAB: A Program for Analysing the Output of MTS on the PC*. Canterbury, Centre for the Applied Psychology of Social Care, University of Kent at Canterbury.

Stein, R. E. K. and Riessman, C. K. (1980) The development of an impact-on-family scale: preliminary findings, *Medical Care*, 18: 465–72.

Stones, M. J., Hadjistavropoulos, T., Tuuko, J. and Kozma, A. (1995) Happiness has traitlike and statelike properties, *Social Indicators Research*, 36: 129–44.

Swales, J. M. and Rogers, P. S. (1995) Discourse and the projection of corporate culture: the mission statement, *Discourse and Society*, 6: 223–42.

Switzky, H. N. (1999) Intrinsic motivation and motivational self-system processes in persons with mental retardation: a theory of motivational orientation, In: E. Zigler and D. Bennet-Gates (eds), *Personality Development in Individuals with Mental Retardation*. Cambridge: Cambridge University Press, pp. 70–106.

Tabachnick, B. G. and Fiddell, L. S. (1989) *Using Multivariate Statistics*, 2nd edn. New York: Harper and Row.

Taylor, S. J. (1994) In support of research on Quality of Life, but against QOL, In: D. Goode (ed) *Quality of Life for Persons with Disabilities: International Perspectives and Issues*. Cambridge: Brookline Books, pp. 260–65.

Taylor, S. J. and Bogdan, R. (1990) Quality of Life and the individual's perspective, In: R. L. Schalock (ed), *Quality of Life: Perspectives and Issues*. Washington: AAMR. pp. 27– 40.

Taylor, R. E., Leese, M., Clarkson, P., Holloway, F. and Thornicroft G. (1998) Quality of life outcomes for intensive versus standard community mental health services, PRiSM Psychosis Study, *British Journal of Psychiatry*, 173: 416–22.

tenHave, P. (2002) Applied conversation analysis, In: A. McHoul, and M. Rapley (eds), *How to Analyse Talk in Institutional Settings: A Casebook of Methods*. London and New York: Continuum International, pp. 3–11.

Testa, M. A. and Nackley, J. F. (1994) Methods for quality-of-life studies, *Annual Review of Public Health*, 15: 535–59.

Thompson, S. J. and Gifford, S. M. (2000) Trying to keep a balance: the meaning of health and diabetes in an urban Aboriginal community, *Social Science and Medicine*, 51: 1457–72.

Treadwell, J. R., Kearney D. and Davila, M. (2000) Health profile preferences of hepatitis C patients, *Digest of Disease Science*, 45: 345–50.

Tsevat, S. N., Sherman, D. P. A. and McElwee, J. A. (1999) The will to live among HIV-infected patients, *Annals of Internal Medicine*, 131, 3: 194–8.

United Nations (1975) *Towards a System of Social and Demographic Statistics*. New York: United Nations.

United Nations (1995) *Human Development Report 1995*. New York and Oxford: Oxford University Press.

United Nations Human Development Program (UNHDP) (1990) *Human Development Report*. New York and Oxford: Oxford University Press.

United States Department of Health, Education, and Welfare (1969) *Toward a Social Report*. Washington, DC: US Government Printing Office.

van der Maas, P. J., van der Wal, G., Haverkate, I., de Graaff, C. L. M., Kester, J. G. C., Onwuteaka-Philipsen, B. D. *et al.* (1996) Euthanasia, physician-assisted suicide, and other medical practices involving the end of life in the Netherlands, 1990–1995, *New England Journal of Medicine*, 335: 1699–705.

van Hooff, A. J. L. (1990) *From Autothanasia to Suicide: Self-killing in Classical Antiquity*. London: Routledge.

van Thiel, G. J. M. W., van Delden, J. J. M., de Haan, K. and Huibers, A. K. (1997) Retrospective study of doctors' 'end of life' decisions in caring for mentally handicapped people in institutions in the Netherlands, *British Medical Journal*, 315: 88–91.

Veenhoven, R. (1984) *Conditions of Happiness*. Reidel: Dordrecht.

Veenhoven, R. (1991) Is happiness relative? *Social Indicators Research*, 24: 299–313.

Veenhoven, R. (1994) Is happiness a trait? Tests of the theory that a better society does not make people any happier, *Social Indicators Research*, 33: 101–60.

Veenhoven, R. (1996) Happy Life-expectancy: a comprehensive measure of quality-of-life in nations, *Social Indicators Research*, 39: 1–58.

Veenhoven, R. (1997) Advances in the understanding of happiness, *Revue Québécoise de Psychologie*, 18: 267–93.

Veenhoven, R. (1998) Two state-trait discussions on happiness: a reply to Stones *et al.*, *Social Indicators Research*, 43: 211–25.

Verri, A., Cummins, R. A., Petito, F., Vallero, E., Monteath, S., Gerosa, E. *et al.* (1999) An Italian-Australian comparison of quality of life among people with intellectual disability living in the community, *Journal of Intellectual Disability Research*, 43, 6: 513–222.

Verrips, G. H. W., Vogels, A. G. C., den Ouden, A. L., Paneth, N. and Verloove-Vanhorick, S. P. (2000) Measuring health-related quality of life in adolescents: agreement between raters and between methods of administration, *Child: Care, Health and Development*, 26, 6: 457–69.

Virginia Tech Center for Survey Research (1998) *Quality of Life in Virginia: 1998*. Blacksburg, VA: Center for Survey Research, Virginia Polytechnic Institute and State University.

Vogels, A. G. C., Verrips, S. P., Verloove-Vanhorick, M., Fekkes, R. P., Kamphuis, H. M., Koopman, H. *et al.* (1998) Young children's health related quality of life: development of the TACQOL, *Quality of Life Research*, 7: 457–65.

Walker, S. R. (1992) Quality of life measurement: an overview, *Journal of the Royal Society of Health*, 112: 265.

Walker, S. R. and Rosser, R. M. (eds) (1988) *Quality of Life: Assessment and Application*. Lancaster: MTP Press.

Wallcraft, J. and Michaelson, J. (2001) Developing a survivor discourse to replace the 'psychopathology' of breakdown and crisis, In: C. Newnes, G. Holmes and C. Dunn (eds), *This Is Madness Too*. Ross-on-Wye: PCCS Books.

Ware, J. J. and Sherbourne, C. D. (1992) The MOS 36-item short-form health survey (SF–36) I. Conceptual framework and item selection, *Medical Care*, 30: 473–83.

Warr, J. E. Jr, Kosinski, M. and Keller, S. D. (1998) *SF-12: How to Score the SF-12 and Mental Health Summary Scales*. Lincoln, RI: Quality Metric Inc. and The Health Assessment Lab.

Watson, D. R. (2000) The anthropology of communication: foundations, futures and the analysis of 'constructions' of space, in T. Lask (ed), *Social Constructions of Space: The Territories of the Anthropology of Communication*. Liège: Presses Universitaires de Liège.

Wearing, A. (1992) *Understanding happiness: A Theory of Subjective Well-being*. Melbourne: Longman Cheshire.

Webb, N. L. and Drummond, P. D. (2001) The effect of swimming with dolphins on human well-being and anxiety, *Anthrozoös*, 14, 2: 81–6.

Welsh Office (1991) *The Review of the All-Wales Mental Handicap Strategy: Proposals for Development from April 1993*. Cardiff: HMSO.

Wenzel, E. (2001) *The Big 'C' Report*. <http://www. ldb. org/cancer/c1. htm> [accessed 18. 10. 01].

Westerhof, G. J., Dittmann-Kohli, F. and Thissen, T. (2001) Beyond life satisfaction: lay conceptions of well-being among middle-aged and elderly adults, *Social Indicators Research*, 56, 2: 179–203.

WHOQOL Group (1993) *WHOQOL Study Protocol*. Geneva: WHO.

WHOQOL Group (1996) *WHOQOL-BREF: Field Trial Version: Introduction, Administration, Scoring and General Version of the Assessment*. Geneva: WHO.

WHOQOL Group (1998) The World Health Organization Quality of Life Assessment (WHOQOL): development and general psychometric properties, *Social Science and Medicine*, 46, 12: 1569–85.

Wiklund, I., Lindvall, K. and Swedberg, K. (1986) Assessment of quality of life in clinical trials, *Acta Medica Scandinavia*, 220: 1–3.

Willig, C. (2001) *Introducing Qualitative Research in Psychology: Adventures in Theory and Method*. Buckingham: Open University Press.

Wilkinson, G., Hesdon, B., Wild, D., Cookson, R., Farina, C., Sharma, V. *et al.* (2000) Self-report quality of life measure for people with schizophrenia: the SQLS, *British Journal of Psychiatry*, 177: 42–6.

Witt, D. D., Lowe, G. D., Peek, C. W. and Curry, E. W. (1979) The changing relationship between age and happiness: emerging trend or methodological artefact? *Social Forces*, 58: 1302–7.

Wittgenstein, L. (1953) *Philosophical Investigations*, trans. G. E. M. Anscombe and R. Rhees. Oxford: Blackwell.

Wittgenstein, L. (1961) *Tractatus Logico-Philosophicus*, trans. D. F. Pears and B. F. McGuinness. London: Routledge.

Wittgenstein, L. (1978) *Lectures and Conversations on Aesthetics, Psychology and Religious Belief*, ed. C. Barrett. Oxford: Blackwell.

Wolfensberger, W. (1972) *The Principle of Normalization in Human Services*. Toronto: National Institute of Mental Retardation.

Wolfensberger, W. (1994) Lets hang up 'Quality of Life' as a hopeless term, In: D. Goode (ed) *Quality of Life for Persons with Disabilities: International Perspectives and Issues*. Cambridge: Brookline Books.

Wolinsky, F. D., Roe, R. M., Miller, D. K. and Prendergast, J. M. (1985) Correlates of change in subjective well-being among the elderly, *Journal of Community Health*, 10: 93–107.

Wolpert, L. (1999) *Malignant Sadness*. London: Faber and Faber.

Woodill, G., Renwick, R., Brown, I. and Raphael, D. (1994) Being, belonging, becoming: an approach to the quality of life of persons with developmental disabilities. In: D. A. Goode (ed), *Quality of Life for Persons with Disabilities: International Perspectives and Issues.* Cambridge: Brookline Books, pp. 57–67.

Woodrow, P. (2001) Measuring quality of life, *Journal of Medical Ethics,* 27: 205.

World Bank (1997) *World Development Indicators.* Washington, DC: World Bank.

World Bank (2000) *World Development Report 2000/2001: Attacking Poverty.* Oxford: Oxford University Press and the World Bank. <http://publications. worldbank. org/ecommerce/catalog/product?item_id=217116> [accessed 25. 09. 01].

World Health Organization (1997) *WHOQOL: Measuring Quality of Life.* Geneva: WHO.

World Health Organization (2001) *World Health Report 2001: New Understanding, New Hope.* Geneva: WHO.

Wu, A. W., Fink, N. E., Cagney, K. A., Bass, E. B., Rubin, H. R., Meyer, K. B. *et al.* (2001) Developing a health-related quality-of-life measure for end-stage renal disease: the CHOICE health experience questionnaire, *American Journal of Kidney Diseases,* 37, 1: 11–21.

Young, J. M. and McNicoll, P. (1998) Against all odds: positive life experiences of people with advanced amyotrophic lateral sclerosis, *Health and Social Work,* 23, 1: 253–260.

Young, J. M., Marshall, C. L. and Anderson, E. J. (1994) Amyotrophic lateral sclerosis patients' perspectives on use of mechanical ventilation, *Health and Social Work,* 19, 4: 253–60.

Zapf, W. (1977) Soziale Indikatoren – eine Zwischenbilanz, In: H. -J. Krupp and W. Zapf (eds), *Sozialpolitik und Sozialberichterstattung.* Frankfurt am Main and New York: Campus, pp. 231–246.

Zapf, W. (1984) Individuelle Wohlfahrt: Lebensbedingungen und wahrgenommene Lebensqualität in der Bundesrepublik, In: W. Glatzer and W. Zapf (eds), *Lebensqualität in der Bundesrepublic.* Frankfurt am Main and New York: Campus, pp. 13–26.

INDEX

1662 7787

MECHANICAL AND CHEMICAL
ENGINEERING

Multidimensional Signals, Circuits & Systems

Although research on general multidimensional systems theory has been developing rapidly in recent years, this is the first research text to appear on the subject since the early 1980s. The field is closely related to control, systems, circuits and signal/image processing. This text describes the current state of the art of nD systems and sets out a number of open problems, and gives several different perspectives on the subject. It presents a number of solutions to major theoretical problems as well as some very interesting practical results.

The book comprises a selection of plenary and other lectures given at The First International Workshop On Multidimensional (nD) Systems (NDS-98) held in 1998 in Poland, and is written by leading world specialists in the field.

Krzysztof Gałkowski is a Professor in the Institute of Control & Computation Engineering at the Technical University of Zielona Góra, Poland. He works particularly in nD systems and circuit analysis.

Jeffrey Wood is a Royal Society University Research Fellow and Research Lecturer in the Department of Electronics and Computer Science at the University of Southampton, UK. His principal research interests are in algebraic and behavioural approaches to systems theory, particularly multidimensional systems.

The series publishes high quality textbooks and reference works in diverse areas of control theory and control applications. Topics of the past and future volumes include adaptive control, nonlinear systems and robust multivariable control. A particular emphasis is placed on expository texts where theory, experiment and application come together to provide a unifying whole to the subject matter.

Multidimensional Signals, Circuits & Systems

K. Gałkowski & J. Wood

TAYLOR & FRANCIS
Founded 1798

First published 2001
By Taylor & Francis
11 New Fetter Lane, London EC4P 4EE

Simultaneously published in the USA and Canada
by Taylor & Francis Inc,
29 West 35th Street, New York 10001

Taylor & Francis is an imprint of the Taylor & Francis Group

Publisher's Note
This book has been prepared from camera-ready copy provided by the authors

Printed and bound in Great Britain by TJ International Ltd, Padstow, Cornwall

Every effort has been made to ensure that the advice and information in this book is true and accurate at the tim of going to press. However, neither the publishers nor the authors can accept any legal responsibility or liability fo any errors or omissions that may be made. In the case of drug administration, any medical procedure or the use o technical equipment mentioned within this book, you are strongly advised to consult the manufacturer' guidelines.

British Library Cataloguing in Publication Data
A catalogue record for this book is available from the British Library

Library of Congress Cataloging in Publication Data
 A catalogue record for this book has been requested

ISBN 0-415-25363-2 (hbk)

Contents

Preface

The field of multidimensional (nD) systems is an extremely rapidly developing area of systems theory, with applications in a cross-section of Control, Circuits and Signal Processing. The characteristic feature of multidimensional (nD) systems is the presence of more than one, i.e. $n > 1$, independent variables, corresponding to different directions in which information can be propagated. Thus in general multidimensional systems are described by partial differential rather than ordinary differential equations, or the discrete equivalent. These systems are not to be confused with the more classical 1D MIMO systems, which are systems with multiple inputs and outputs (dependent variables). An nD system may be either SISO or MIMO.

The first work in nD systems is generally dated to the early 1960s, when it was shown that networks of constant and linearly variable elements may be described in the framework of two-variable rational transfer functions. A virtually identical result was obtained a few years later for networks of lumped elements and transmission lines of commensurate delays. This evoked great interest from researchers in circuit theory due to a wide variety of possible applications. Many efforts have been devoted to the problem of synthesis of two-variable rational transfer functions and to the problem of stability.

The introduction of the Roesser and Fornasini/ Marchesini state-space models for 2D/ nD systems was probably the next essential step in the development of 2D/nD systems work. This innovation extended the arena of the approach to include multidimensional signal processing and image processing. Also, due to the importance of being able to handle space-time or 3D images it provided the first reason for studying nD systems with n more than 2. In addition, it suggested the idea of developing special nD circuits, for example, multidimensional filters.

At this time there also appeared new application areas such as systems with delays, and it became clear that nD systems can also be used to study partial differential equations. The application of nD tools to these areas proved very effective and is still the subject of on-going work.

Finally, nD systems became the subject of interest of control. One area in which nD tools have proved very effective is in the study of so-called repetitive processes, which enable the handling in a 2D manner of real or algorithmic plants/processes characterized by a series of sweeps, passes or iterations. These applications include the popular field of iterative learning control.

In the interim, there appeared new interesting nD system application possibilities too numerous to list. For example, one of the recent and promising is to systems with uncertainty.

The large number of highly diverse applications led inevitably to the development of a general nD systems theory, in which the general features of these new objects have been studied. A new self-contained discipline with its own notions and methodologies arose. It has been shown many times that multidimensional systems theory is not a simple extension of the standard 1D theory, since so many relationships between systems concepts fail to generalize to n dimensions. The need to develop new tools in the study of nD systems has evoked the interest of the mathematician. One recent extension of perhaps the greatest influence for the long-term future of nD systems research is the extension to the nD case of the new so-called behavioural approach to systems theory.

Multidimensional systems work has appeared in the systems literature for many years, as the subject of many monographs, journal papers and conference presentations. In the last case, nD systems work has in recent years been presented at almost all major circuits, control, systems and signal processing conferences, often either in thematic sessions or as the subject of special workshops. However, for a long time there were no specialized nD systems conferences. The first such meetings were two one day colloquia organized in 1996 and 1998 in London, under the auspices of the IEE. In 1998, the first Workshop devoted to nD systems theory and applications, NDS-98, was held in Łagow near Zielona Gora, Poland, and attracted a great number of nD system researchers. This book is based on the NDS-98 conference and contains a choice of its carefully reviewed presentations. The need of publishing of this book arose from the great importance of the topics of the conference, by the fact that nD systems science has moved on considerably from the time of the last such publication, and, of course, by the high technical quality of the presentations.

The book have been partitioned into three sections related to the main nD system areas:

- Multidimensional Systems – General,

- Control of Multidimensional Systems and Applications, and

- Multidimensional Circuits and Signal Processing.

The section chapters are ordered with the intention of maximizing readability for both general and specialist readers.

PART ONE

Multidimensional Systems – General

This section is devoted to a choice of general aspects of nD systems theory and applications. It opens with a paper by N. K. Bose (State University of Pennsylvania, USA) giving an overview of two decades of research in nD systems. This paper revisits the current open problems and highlights possible future trends in the field.

Next, A. Dzieliński (Warsaw University of Technology) presents some new, numerically related results on application of nD sampling to modeling of 1D nonlinear systems, using MATLAB and SIMULINK. Finally in this section, J. Wood (Southampton, UK), E. Rogers (Southampton, UK) and D. H. Owens (Exeter, UK) present an introduction to the recently emerging behavioural approach to nD systems theory, including an explanation of the use of algebraic tools in this area.

CHAPTER ONE

Two Decades of Multidimensional Systems Research and Future Trends

Nirmal K. Bose

Department of Electrical Engineering,
Pennsylvania State University, USA
nkb@stspbkn.ee.psu.edu

Abstract

The subject of multidimensional systems is concerned with mathematical issues designed to tackle a broad range of paradigms whose analysis or synthesis require the use of functions and polynomials in several complex variables. The areas of signal, image, and video processing, linear multipass processes, iterative learning control systems, lumped-distributed networks, and geophysical exploration, to name a few, have all benefited from the tools available in the developed theory of multidimensional systems. This paper summarizes briefly the past accomplishments, describes the progress made towards the solution of certain open problems documented a decade or so back and identifies avenues of challenging research which need to be more fully traversed in the future.

1.1   INTRODUCTION

Research that had been started and conducted in the areas of multivariate network realizability theory (since about 1960), two-dimensional digital filters (since about 1970) and multidimensional transform analysis of nonlinear systems representable by Volterra series that out-dates the preceding two areas just cited was included within a framework that was christened *multidimensional systems* in June 1977, when a Special Issue, guest edited by the author, was published by The Proceedings of the IEEE. A fertile arena for application of the developed theoretical results in multidimensional systems is multidimensional signal, image, and video processing. Another Special Issue of The Proceedings of the IEEE was guest edited by this author in April 1990 and this one was devoted exclusively to the topic of multidimensional signal processing. The reader may wish to read the opening paper (Bose 1990) in that Special Issue to grasp the fundamental limitations as well as scopes for generalizations of one dimensional signal processing theory in various spatio-temporal signal processing applications.

The concept of positive real functions (Bose 1982) is pervasive in network realizability theory and is also encountered in other areas including the frequency domain approach towards stability of nonlinear dynamic systems (Popov's approach). In an unusually innovative dissertation at M.I.T. in 1930, Otto Brune not only introduced the mathematical characterization of what he called a positive real function in one complex variable but also showed its necessity as well as sufficiency for the realization of driving point functions of any lumped, linear, finite, passive, time-invariant and bilateral network, In a remarkable paper (Koga 1968) that was considered for sometime to be the best paper of the 1960s, Koga claimed to have proved the necessity as well as sufficiency of multivariate positive realness in the synthesis of finite, passive multiports. About the time that multidimensional systems theory was born the falsity of this conclusion was demonstrated through the deployment of technical devices in positive linear maps and sum-of-squares representations (Bose 1982), (Bose 1976), (Bose 1977). In spite of this, Koga's paper continues to inspire researchers in multidimensional systems theory for its early adaptation and use in electrical engineering of results in several complex variables, algebraic geometry, and algebraic function theory. In (Bose & Jury 1974) and (Anderson *et al.* 1975) the applicability of elementary decision algebra and the first-order theory of predicate calculus for ascertaining the existence as well as construction of solutions to a large number of open problems in systems theory was established. This landmark result led to the satisfactory tackling of the following important problems.

- Tests for absence of zeros of a multivariate polynomial in several complex variables (with prescribed numerical coefficients) in a closed polydisk (Bose 1982), on the polydisk distinguished boundary (Bose & Basu 1978) and other compact (as well as noncompact) polydomains required in the tests for various types of stability of discrete and continuous linear and shift-invariant multidimensional filters (Bose 1982), (Bose 1985), stiff differential systems (Genin 1974), multipass processes (Edwards & Owens 1982) etc.

- Tests for global and nonglobal positivity and nonnegativity of a multivariate polynomial in several real variables (with prescribed numerical coefficients) required for ascertaining stability of nonlinear dynamic systems, existence of limit cycles and a host of other applications (Bose 1982).

- The complete solution to the primitive factorization problem (Guiver & Bose 1982) for polynomial matrices whose entries are polynomials in two complex variables with coefficients in an arbitrary but fixed field was shown to be possible. Importantly, it was established that the computations to implement the algorithm for that task could be performed in the ground field i.e. an extension field is not required. It was further shown that primitive factorization for polynomial matrices does not hold, in general, when the number of complex variables exceeds two unlike in the scalar case (Youla & Gnavi 1979). There is considerable scope for applying these results to the feedback stabilization problem of multidimensional control systems using coprime matrix fraction descriptions (see, for instance, (Xu *et al.* 1994) in the 2-D case and (Lin 1998), (Bose & Charoenlarpnopparut 1998a) in the n-D case).

- Investigations into boundary implications in parameter space of sets of polynomials from a small subset of fixed coefficient extreme polynomials were initiated and complete results identifying interesting classes where vertex implications in parameter space hold for various properties like positivity and stability of different types are being identified (Bose 1988), (Basu 1979), (Kharitonov & Torres Munõz 1999), (Kharitonov *et al.* 1999).

- The theory for structure and representation of multidimensional systems, with emphasis in the 2-D case, based on the behavioral approach was advanced (Rocha &

Willems 1989), canonical computational forms for autoregressive 2-D systems delineated (Rocha & Willems 1990) and the problem of the minimal number of trajectories determining a shift-invariant, linear multidimensional system was investigated (Oberst 1993). These results are awaiting applications in various problems in signal processing and control.

- The fundamental limitation caused by the inadmissibility of the Euclidean division algorithm in the multidimensional systems framework was combatted through realization of the scope in multidimensional systems theory of the Buchburger algorithm for construction of Gröbner basis (Bose 1985).

This particular paper documents the presentation in the Opening Plenary Lecture at the First International Workshop on N-D Systems (held at Lagow, Poland in July 1998). The topics chosen during that presentation remain the same. The description is more detailed with updates of related results and references in order to present the state-of-the-art and delay inevitable ultimate obsolescence as much as possible. For the sake of brevity, no attempt is made to trace the chronological development of the subject-matter discussed. The non-specialist will be able to acquire that information from the papers that could not be cited here but which can be extracted without difficulty from the references supplied. The following items will be singled out for special emphasis because of the current interest in tackling difficult but important applications that are likely to benefit significantly from the more recent developments in multidimensional systems theory.

- Implementation of decision algebra by cylindrical algebraic decomposition has been inspired by the development of computer algebra for symbolic and algebraic manipulations. Recent research on multivariate polynomial positivity tests when the coefficients are symbolic (literal) and not numeric will be summarized for applications in robust system design.

- The use of Gröbner basis for realization in particular topologies (like ladder) of multivariate transfer functions involving multiband analysis and synthesis filters will be explained with reference to problems in image and video data compression.

- Progress towards the solution of some open problems that were documented in (Bose 1985).

- The recent progress in the use of concepts in multidimensional systems theory for the processing of multispectral multiframe images acquired through multisensors will be explained and future research involving, for example, the use of multi-dimensional wavelets for simultaneous coding and processing of video images will be summarized.

1.2 MULTIVARIATE POLYNOMIAL POSITIVITY TESTS: LITERAL COEFFICIENTS

Tests for global and local positivity of multivariate polynomials with numerical coefficients, which find applications in several control theory problems, are documented in (Bose 1982). A set of necessary and sufficient conditions for a quartic univariate polynomial with literal coefficients to have only nonnegative values is delineated in (Lazard 1988). The procedure in (Lazard 1988) is problem-specific and is unsuitable for generalization to the higher-degree and multivariate cases. A systematic scheme that leads to a set of inequalities involving the free variables, whose satisfaction will be necessary and sufficient for global positivity or nonnegativity of any specified polynomial with literal coefficients, has been developed, recently (Bose & Charoenlarpnopparut 1998b). In particular, a procedure was advanced to determine a set of necessary and sufficient conditions for an univariate polynomial of arbitrary but fixed degree to be globally nonnegative in terms of the literal coefficients of the polynomial based on the theory of quantifier elimination by the method of resultant and subresultants (Bose & Charoenlarpnopparut 1998b). That effort continued the resurgence of research in the further development of quantifier elimination procedures (Bose 1997) by cylindrical algebraic decomposition of the multidimensional Euclidean space into semi-algebraic cells such that the value of any multivariate polynomial in a set of such polynomials has constant sign (positive, negative, or zero). For lower degree polynomials the result in (Bose & Charoenlarpnopparut 1998b) is explicit in terms of the literal coefficients and provides a direct independent verification of the result in (Lazard 1988) for the fourth degree case. However, in general the conditions arrived at are expressible as inequalities involving polynomial functions of the coefficients.

Central to the procedure delineated in (Bose & Charoenlarpnopparut 1998b) is the resultant matrix (inner matrix) $R(a, a')$ of the polynomial

$$a(x) = a_m x^m + a_{m-1} x^{m-1} + \ldots + a_1 x + a_0, \quad a_m > 0,$$

and its derivative a', whose inner determinants $\Delta_1, \Delta_3, \ldots, \Delta_{2m-1}$ are computed and worked with. The matrix $R(a, a')$ of order $2m - 1$ may be expressed uniquely in terms of submatrices R_1, R_2, R_3 and R_4 whose, respective orders are indicated below.

$$R(a, a') = \begin{array}{cc} & \begin{array}{cc} m-1 & m \end{array} \\ \left[\begin{array}{cc} R_1 & R_2 \\ R_3 & R_4 \end{array} \right] & \begin{array}{c} m-1 \\ m \end{array} \end{array}$$

The Schur-complement is defined by

$$(R/R_1) = R_4 - R_3 R_1^{-1} R_2.$$

Without loss of generality, set $a_m = 1$ for notational brevity. It was pointed out that the Schur complement and Bezoutian matrices, each of which is about half the order of the resultant matrix (Sylvester matrix or inner matrix), could also be used to generate inequalities identical to the inner determinantal polynomial inequalities. The advantage of lower computational complexity is somewhat offset by the need to compute the elements of the matrices by operating on the coefficients. An approach based on the related Sturm-Habicht algorithm was also considered by González-Vega.

Necessary and sufficient conditions for bounded-input bounded-output (BIBO) type of stability for multidimensional systems in terms of literal coefficients are only known for low-order 'all-pole' (autoregressive) models (Bose 1982). Denoting the set of independent complex variables by $\{z_i\}_{i=1}^n$, where z_i represents the unit delay along the ith dimension, necessary and sufficient conditions for BIBO stability of the multidimensional filter $\frac{1}{B(z_1,\ldots,z_n)}$ are known for special cases like (Bose 1982)

$$B(z_1, z_2, z_3) = 1 + az_1 + bz_2 + cz_3 + dz_1 z_2 + ez_2 z_3 + fz_3 z_1 + gz_1 z_2 z_3,$$

where the literal coefficients are self-evident. Some other recent efforts at obtaining stability conditions in the presence of literal coefficients include the efforts documented in (Takahashi 1993) for 2-D systems.

The link between stability and positivity has been appreciated for sometimes. In fact the research of Takahashi was influenced considerably by the possibility for reducing the stability condition for n-D digital filters to the $(n-1)$−variate polynomial positivity problem. More recently, the problem of robust D-stability, where D is any open simply connected region, of an univariate polynomial with coefficients that are continuous in several uncertain system parameters has been studied via positivity. The citations in (Siljak & Stipanovic 1998) give the history of the approach and the use of Bernstein expansion algorithm as a numerical means to determine whether or not a specified multivariate polynomial in several real variables is positive within a specified boxed domain.

1.3 GRÖBNER BASIS FOR REALIZATION

For clarity, we denote an arbitrary but fixed field as $\mathcal{K}$ any of the sets of integers as $(\mathcal{Z})$, positive integers as $(\mathcal{Z}_+)$, rationals as $(\mathcal{Q})$, reals as $(\mathcal{E})$ or complex numbers as $(\mathcal{C})$. The elements of the matrices that characterize the multiband filter banks are polynomials whose coefficients belong to $\mathcal{Q}$ or $\mathcal{E}$ or $\mathcal{C}$ or, for that matter, any arbitrary but fixed field.

In a recent paper (Bose & Charoenlarpnopparut 1998b) the algebraic results by Youla & Gnavi (1979) concerned with the existence of solutions to the Bezout-type of multivariate polynomial matrix equations along with the constructive methods in the theory of Gröbner bases were combined to construct the complete class of solutions to the multivariate polynomial matrix right or left inverse problem considered separately in (Park & Woodburn 1995). The tests for zero and minor primeness were implemented algorithmically while some progress towards the difficult problem of multivariate matrix greatest factor extraction, under the tacit assumption of its existence, was also reported. Unlike zero and minor primeness and coprimeness, the notion of factor primeness cannot be characterized exclusively by the variety of the ideal generated by the maximal minors in the ring $\mathcal{K}[z_1, \ldots, z_n], n \geq 3$ and also the exclusive consideration of the matrix full rank condition is not sufficient. Oberst (1990) showed that for $n \geq 3$, a multivariate rational transfer matrix might have two minimal matrix fraction-descriptions or realizations that are not comparable. Unlike in the $n = 1$ or $n = 2$ cases, it is not possible to speak of greatest common polynomial matrix divisors as these may not be unique up to unimodularity when $n \geq 3$. However, under the hypothesis of existence, constructive algorithmic procedures like Gröbner bases have been used to obtain the factor provided specific constraints are met as in (Bose & Charoenlarpnopparut 1998a) A by-product of the techniques deployed based the use of Gröbner bases for rings and modules is the progress towards the solution of an outstanding problem in minimax control using rate feedback.

The possibility of perfect reconstruction even when the coefficients and the results of multiplications in the various stages of design of ladder structures are quantized was first discussed in (Bruekers & van den Emden 1992). Generic networks for the two-band and three-band cases for perfect inversion and reconstruction were given in an ad hoc manner in (Bruekers & van den Emden 1992). In (Tolhuizen *et al.* 1995), the possibility of applying Euclidean division algorithm for polynomials with coefficients in a ground field to systematically generate and realize each generic ladder structure in the two-band case was demonstrated. The multidimensional case was considered but complete results were not reported. The viewpoint in (Tolhuizen *et al.* 1995) that the ladder structure of two-band filter banks can be determined by decomposing suitable polynomial matrices was also emphasized in (Marshall 1997), where the two-dimensional case was confined to the obtaining of a realization from the underlying one-dimensional structure by a 1-D to 2-D transformation.

1.3.1 Problem formulation

Here the realization problem of multidimensional multiband biorthogonal filter banks is considered by proceeding from the univariate case and then pointing to the implications of certain mathematical results on the solution of the multidimensional problem. The following definitions are standard (Tolhuizen *et al.* 1995) prerequisites for the task undertaken here.

Definition 1.1

1. *An* elementary *matrix, E, is a square matrix with ones on its main diagonal and elements from $\mathcal{K}$ in either its upper or lower triangular-block.*

2. *A matrix is called* realizable *if it can be written as a product of elementary matrices.*

3. *When the maximal minors of a matrix with entries in a polynomial ring generates the unit ideal in that ring, the matrix is called* unimodular.

Elementary matrices are, necessarily, unimodular because their determinants are units in the ring of interest. The transpose and inverse of any specified elementary matrix is also elementary. The following results are useful preludes to the development of a realization procedure for a unimodular matrix with entries in a Euclidean domain by deploying a cascaded ladder topology.

Fact 1.2 *(Newman 1972):　Let $\alpha_1, \alpha_2, \ldots, \alpha_n$ be scalar elements of a principal ideal ring $\mathcal{I}$ and let δ_n be their greatest common divisor. Then, there exists a matrix D_n of order n with first row, $[\alpha_1 \; \alpha_2 \; \ldots \; \alpha_n]$, and determinant δ_n.*

When the principal ideal ring is a Euclidean domain, Euclid's algorithm can be used to construct D_n, as described in the unimodular matrix completion strategy in (Newman 1972). From Fact 1.2, it follows that the elements in the top row of a unimodular matrix are relatively prime. For convenience in later usage, the procedure for constructing a unimodular matrix from a specified top row will be called *matrix completion*. Furthermore, the following result is known to hold.

Fact 1.3 *(Tolhuizen* et al. *1995):　Any unimodular matrix of order 2 whose elements belong to a Euclidean domain is realizable as a cascade of ladder structures.*

As a generalization to the solution offered in (Tolhuizen *et al.* 1995) for the two-band case, the objective here is to identify a square unimodular (realizable) matrix from a specified top row of relatively prime polynomials and to simultaneously provide generic ladder structures for the analysis and synthesis filter banks associated with this matrix and its inverse. The procedure is then extended to realize any unimodular matrix with (or without) an identical top row. The results and mode of exposition below were arrived at in collabora-tion with Chalie Charoenlarpnopparut. Though done independently of recent publications on the subject (Kofidis *et al.* 1996), it has pedagogic value and provides easier entry to the multidimensional multiband case.

1.3.2   Ladder structure of multiband filter bank

In the application of subband coding, a discrete-time signal is analysed (decomposed) at the transmitter and synthesized at the receiver. The process of efficiently splitting the signal makes it suitable for video transmission over ATM networks, where a base layer and an enhancement layer can be utilized without incurring any overhead (van Dyck *et al.* 1996). This idea of using multiband filter banks is crucial not only in the case of 1-D filter banks but also for multidimensional filter banks since the sampling factor of multidimensional systems, which can be determined from the determinant of the sampling matrix associated with the chosen sampling raster (rectangular, hexagonal, etc.), is not always in the form $2^n, n \in \mathcal{Z}_+$. Due to its computational efficiency, the ladder structure has been shown to be useful in subband coding applications (Tolhuizen *et al.* 1995), (van Dyck *et al.* 1996). The ladder structure generated from the extraction of an elementary matrix of order 2, which gives the input and output description,

$$\begin{bmatrix} y_1 \\ y_2 \end{bmatrix} = \begin{bmatrix} 1 & 0 \\ a & 1 \end{bmatrix} \begin{bmatrix} x_1 \\ x_2 \end{bmatrix} \tag{1.1}$$

is called a branch and has been considered systematically for the case of two bands in (Tolhuizen *et al.* 1995). The matrix element $a \in \mathcal{K}$ is called the ladder component. Each of the components in the ladder branches that are cascaded to form the analysis structure as well as each of those components in the corresponding inverse (synthesis) structure is required to be a one-sided finite impulse response (FIR) filter. It will be shown that each of the ladder branches in the multiband cascade (analysis and synthesis) can also be formed from the elementary matrix extracted at a particular stage of matrix factorization. Note that the number of ladder components in an elementary matrix of order m is at most $m(m-1)/2$. The extension of the two-band ladder structure to the multiband case can be shown to be possible by providing the realization associated with an elementary matrix of order m, where m is the number of bands. Note that the coefficients of the inverse structure are negatives of those in the analysis structure. This configuration is not only convenient from the implementational and computational points of view but is also extendable to an elementary matrix of arbitrary order m.

1.3.3   Algorithm for elementary matrix decomposition

The purpose of the algorithm is to identify a square unimodular (realizable) matrix from a specified top row of a set $\{a_i^0\}_{i=1}^m$ of relatively prime univariate polynomials with coeffi-cients in a field. In the $(k+1)^{th}$ iteration, $k = 0, 1, 2, \ldots$, a polynomial in the set $\{a_i^k\}_{i=1}^m$, having the lowest degree and occurring in the left-most column of the row is selected to be the divisor in the ensuing steps. Denote the selected divisor by a_I^k for $i = I$, where k is the index of iteration. If $I < m/2$ $(I > m/2)$, replace the element a_j^k in the jth column by the remainder r_j^k obtained following the application of the division step with a_I^k as divisor and a_j^k as dividend, for $j > I$ $(j < I)$. The elementary matrix E_k at the kth iteration is formed by replacing the Ith row of the identity matrix I_m of order m by the negatives of the quotients in the division steps i.e.

$$[\ 0\ \cdots\ 0\ 1\ -q^k_{I+1}\ -q^k_{I+2}\ \cdots\ -q^k_m\ ],\quad j>I,$$

$$[\ -q^k_1\ -q^k_2\ \cdots\ -q^k_{I-1}\ 1\ 0\ \cdots\ 0\ ],\quad j<I.$$

Basically, as the recursive step continues, any polynomial of the top row, which has its degree higher than the degree of the divisor will be replaced by the remainder polynomial of lower degree, following the application of the division step. The algorithm will stop when all but one of the elements in the top row are zero. For each loop (iteration) of the algorithm, an elementary matrix is generated, which as a factor of the unimodular matrix, is realized as a branch of at most $m(m-1)/2$ components, each of which is a causal FIR filter. The decomposition into a product of elementary matrices allows us to directly realize the filter as a ladder structure. The next example illustrates the algorithm for matrix completion and simultaneous realization as a cascaded ladder configuration.

Example 1.4 *Let us consider a problem of completing the matrix with the given top row*

$$M^0 = [\ a^0_1\ a^0_2\ a^0_3\ ] = [\ 2z^2+3z+2\ \ z+1\ \ z+5\ ], \tag{1.2}$$

where, for notational brevity, z (and not z^{-1}) denotes unit delay.

First, set $k = 0$ and then find the smallest i, denoted as I, such that $\deg(a^k_i)$ is minimum. In this case, $i = 2$ gives desired minimum so that $I = 2$. Since $I \geq m/2$, therefore for $j < I$, the division step on a^0_j leads to

$$a^0_1 = 2z^2 + 3z + 2 = (2z+1)(z+1) + 1. \tag{1.3}$$

After the first iteration ($k = 0$), the elementary matrix E_1, associated with the above division step and the modified top row $M^1 = M^0 E_1$ are

$$E_1 = \begin{bmatrix} 1 & 0 & 0 \\ -2z-1 & 1 & 0 \\ 0 & 0 & 1 \end{bmatrix}, \tag{1.4}$$

$$M^1 = M^0 E_1 = [\ 1\ \ z+1\ \ z+5\ ]. \tag{1.5}$$

The next and, in this case, the final iteration similarly yields

$$E_2 = \begin{bmatrix} 1 & -z-1 & -z-5 \\ 0 & 1 & 0 \\ 0 & 0 & 1 \end{bmatrix}, \tag{1.6}$$

$$M^2 = M^1 E_2 = [\ 1\ \ 0\ \ 0\ ]. \tag{1.7}$$

Thus, the following relationship is obtained,

$$[\ 1\ \ 0\ \ 0\ ] = [\ 2z^2+3z+2\ \ z+1\ \ z+5\ ] \times$$
$$\begin{bmatrix} 1 & 0 & 0 \\ -2z-1 & 1 & 0 \\ 0 & 0 & 1 \end{bmatrix}\begin{bmatrix} 1 & -z-1 & -z-5 \\ 0 & 1 & 0 \\ 0 & 0 & 1 \end{bmatrix} \tag{1.8}$$

The resulting matrix A, defined as $E_2^{-1} E_1^{-1}$, has a top row that is identical to the one in Eq. 1.2.

$$A = \begin{bmatrix} 2z^2 + 3z + 2 & z + 1 & z + 5 \\ 2z + 1 & 1 & 0 \\ 0 & 0 & 1 \end{bmatrix} \tag{1.9}$$

This matrix can be realized as a cascade of two branches (each realizing an elementary matrix in Eq.1.8) of ladder structures.

It has been shown how a row vector of relatively prime univariate polynomials with coefficients in an arbitrary but fixed field can be operated upon via the Euclidean division algorithm to produce a unimodular matrix whose realization in a cascade of ladder topology is simultaneously obtained. Subsequently, a square but otherwise arbitrary unimodular matrix possessing the same top row can be realized systematically using the generic topology of cascaded ladder. The realization of the inverse unimodular matrix is generated in a straightforward manner from the realized unimodular matrix. The procedure advanced generalizes the earlier contributions in references (Bruekers & van den Emden 1992), (Tolhuizen *et al.* 1995), and (Marshall 1997) to the multiband case (see also (Kofidis *et al.* 1996)). The advantage of the generic topology in terms of computational complexity of implementation noticed for the two-band case has been seen to hold in the multiband situation. The algorithmic approach to realization of the generic structure makes it suitable for computer-aided design of multiband filter banks with satisfactory performance evaluation.

1.3.4 Ladder structure of biorthogonal multidimensional multiband filter bank

Let $\mathcal{R}$ denote a ring and let $\mathcal{SL}_m(\mathcal{R})$ be the group of all matrices each of order m and determinant 1, whose entries are elements of $\mathcal{R}$. An elementary matrix E_{ij} over $\mathcal{R}$ is a square matrix whose diagonal elements are unity and all other elements are zero except for the element e_{ij} in the ith row and j^{th} column which is a nonzero element of $\mathcal{R}$. Let $\mathcal{E}_m(\mathcal{R})$ be the subgroup of $\mathcal{SL}_m(\mathcal{R})$ that is generated as a product of a finite number of elementary matrices. Of particular interest to us is the ring $\mathcal{K}[z_1, z_2, \cdots, z_n]$ of n-variate polynomials with coefficients in an arbitrary but fixed field $\mathcal{K}$. The notions of zero primeness, unimodular matrix completion and polynomial matrix inverse, considered in the realization strategy of the previous subsection, are linked, in the multivariate setting by the Quillen-Suslin proof of the fact that projective modules over polynomial rings are free (referred to in the literature as Serre's conjecture) (Lam 1978). The central question in this subsection is the following.

'When is an element of $\mathcal{SL}_m(\mathcal{R})$ expressible as a product of elementary matrices over the ring $\mathcal{R}$ or, in other words, when does it also belong to $\mathcal{E}_m(\mathcal{R})$?'

When the answer to the above question for a specified matrix is in the affirmative, the matrix is said to be *realizable* and it can be synthesized in the ladder topology. Any matrix in $\mathcal{SL}_m(\mathcal{R})$ when $\mathcal{R}$ is a Euclidean domain is realizable, Thus, though any element of $\mathcal{SL}_m(\mathcal{K}[z_1])$ is realizable for any positive integer m, the fact that not all elements of $\mathcal{SL}_2(K[z_1, z_2])$ are realizable follows directly from the work of Cohn (1966) who showed that the matrix,

$$\mathbf{V}(\mathbf{z_1, z_2}) = \begin{bmatrix} 1 + z_1 z_2 & z_1^2 \\ -z_2^2 & 1 - z_1 z_2 \end{bmatrix} \tag{1.10}$$

cannot be written as a product of elementary matrices. It can be proved (Park & Woodburn 1995) that though the above matrix, is not realizable as a product of 2×2 elementary matrices over the base ring $\mathcal{K}[z_1, z_2]$, it can be embedded in the matrix

$$\mathbf{V_a(z_1, z_2)} = \begin{bmatrix} 1 + z_1 z_2 & z_1^2 & 0 \\ -z_2^2 & 1 - z_1 z_2 & 0 \\ 0 & 0 & 1 \end{bmatrix},$$

which is realizable in the group $\mathcal{SL}_3(\mathcal{K}[z_1, z_2])$ of all (3×3) unimodular matrices over the base ring. As a matter of fact, Park & Woodburn (1995) produced an algorithm that expresses any square matrix of order m, where $m \neq 2$, whose entries are in ring $\mathcal{K}[z_1, z_2, \cdots, z_n]$ as a product of elementary matrices with entries in the same ring thus providing an algorithmic proof of the *Suslin stability theorem* which asserts that

$$\mathcal{SL}_m(\mathcal{K}[z_1, z_2, \cdots, z_n]) = \mathcal{E}_m(\mathcal{K}[z_1, z_2, \cdots, z_n]), m \geq 3,$$

where the subgroup of $\mathcal{SL}_m(\mathcal{R})$ generated by $m \times m$ elementary matrices is denoted by $\mathcal{E}_m(\mathcal{R})$.

1.3.5 Minimax controller and Gröbner bases

Given a plant $F(s) = 1/m(s)$, where

$$m(s) = \prod_{i=1}^{n} (s^2 + \beta_i), \quad 0 < \beta_i < \beta_{i+1}$$

is an even polynomial with simple roots on the imaginary axis, in the complex s-plane, the problem is to find from the uncountably infinite set of odd polynomials $\{n_i(s)\}$, whose generic element has the form

$$n_i(s) = k_i s \prod_{l=1}^{n-1} (s^2 + \gamma_{l(i)}), \quad k_i > 0, \beta_l < \gamma_{l(i)} < \beta_{l+1}$$

the one, denoted for brevity, by

$$n(s) = ks \prod_{l=1}^{n-1} (s^2 + \gamma_l), \quad k > 0, \beta_l < \gamma_l < \beta_{l+1}$$

so that the characteristic polynomial, $m(s) + n(s)$, of the resulting optimal rate feedback system has the fastest slowest mode among the set of strict Hurwitz polynomials, $\{m(s) + n_i(s)\}$. In other words, the right most roots of $m(s) + n(s)$ are required to be the farthest to the left of the imaginary axis in comparison to similar roots for any other polynomial in the set $\{m(s) + n_i(s)\}$.

The complete analytic characterization and solution construction (either explicitly or by recursion) for the minimax control problem using optimal rate feedback was given very recently (Bose & Charoenlarpnopparut 1999) for the case when the plant consists of a known fixed set of coupled oscillators of cardinality not exceeding three. The tools used are those originating in realizability theory (especially with respect to the determination of qualitative properties of solutions of polynomial equations) and Gröbner bases in polynomial ideal theory. The computations for reaching the optimal design are recursive in nature and easily implementable with arbitrary precision. When the plant is of higher order, the construction of an optimal solution is analytically and computationally intractable necessitating the need for numerical methods for generating suboptimal solutions.

1.4 PROGRESS TOWARDS SOLUTION OF OPEN PROBLEMS SINCE 1985

A list of open problems in multidimensional systems theory were compiled in (Bose 1985). The progress made towards their solution are summarized next.

1.4.1 Nonessential singularities of the second kind (NSSK)

In Open Problem 1 (Bose 1985), conjectures on the precise effect on BIBO stability of nonessential singularities of the second kind (NSSK), when present on the unit polydisk distinguished boundary (T^n), and the existence of a BIBO stable rational function with a BIBO stable inverse in the presence of such type of singularity was made. Though stability issues with NSSK present have not been fully tackled, some progress has been reported. In (Lin & Bruton 1989), it was shown that a BIBO stable bivariate rational function in reduced form (and, therefore, having a finite number of common zeros) could have a BIBO stable inverse. It was shown that stable systems, in the 3-D case, can admit uncountably infinite NSSKs in T^3 and $T \times T \times U$, where T denotes the unit circle and U denotes the interior of the unit disk (Wang *et al.* 1992). A sufficient condition for the inverse of a stable transfer function with uncountably infinite NSSKs in those domains to be unstable was also given in the same paper. However, Conjecture 1 in Open Problem 1 (Bose 1985) remains unanswered, even under the finiteness assumption made there, in the n-D, $n > 2$, case and Conjecture 2 in Open Problem 1 (Bose 1985) which was made without restricting the NSSK to finite cardinality remains to some extent unsettled.

1.4.2 Feedback stabilization

In Open Problem 6 (Bose 1985), the following question was posed (remember that in this manuscript $\mathcal{E}$ denotes the real-closed field of real numbers):

Given the transfer function of the plant, $p = \frac{f}{g}$, in reduced form, where f and g belong to the multivariate polynomial ring $\mathcal{E}[z_1, z_2, \ldots, z_n]$, when is there a stabilizing compensator $c = \frac{h_1}{h_2}$, with, first, $h_1, h_2 \in \mathcal{E}[z_1, z_2, \ldots, z_n]$? If this is found to be true, the second part seeks the answer to the same question when h_1, h_2 are further restricted to belong to $\mathcal{Q}[z_1, z_2, \ldots, z_n]$.

The first part of the above question was answered as a generalization of the Guiver-Bose result for the 2-D case ((Bose 1985), Chapter 3). Making use of the fact that the number of common zeros in any two relatively prime bivariate polynomials is finite, Guiver and Bose were able to construct a desired compensator after equating the stabilizability issue of the plant to the criterion for absence of zeros in the closed unit bidisk of the numerator and denominator polynomials of the plant transfer function. They also posed the second question with some supporting arguments in the 2-D case. To generalize the first part of the 2-D result to n-D, where the common zeros of two relatively prime n-variate polynomials need not be isolated and, indeed, can belong to a $(2n - 4)$-dimensional real Euclidean space, Shankar & Sule (1992), employing mathematical resources available in commutative algebra and topology, obtained necessary and sufficient conditions for stabilizability in an arbitrary compact polydomain (obviously, including the polydisk) of plants whose transfer functions are fractions over a general integral domain. Their result, expressible in terms of coprimeness of ideals instead of zero-coprimeness of polynomials is a generalization of the 2-D result over unit bidisks. Thus, their approach is coordinate-free in the sense that a particular coprime fraction description is not required because the ideals are invariant with respect to the fractional representation in the ring of, say stable causal transfer functions (instead of just the polynomial ring). They also studied robustness issues after defining a topology on the set of transfer functions and concluded that the stabilizability property is not generic for the transfer function set. The problem of construction, however, was not addressed in (Shankar & Sule 1992).

1.4.3 Robust continuous system stability

A polynomial or a rational function (matrix), characterizing a single-input single-output (multi-input multi-output) system, has the coefficients for parameters. The number of such free parameters defines the dimension of the space and a system with fixed parameters may be represented by a point in such a space. If the coefficients vary about the nominal values, a region in parameter space is generated. This region characterizes a family of systems instead of one fixed system. When the coefficients vary independently of each other within specified compact intervals, an *interval system* is generated. A well explored case when the coefficients do not vary independently occurs when the region in parameter space is a bounded polyhedral set. A *polyhedral set* is formed from the intersection of a finite number of closed half-spaces and could be unbounded. A bounded polyhedral set is a convex polytope and vice versa. For an interval system, the polytope degenerates into a boxed domain or a hyper-rectangle. Extensive documentation of research results concerned with the extraction of information about the complete polytope from a very small subset of the polytope with respect to the property of stability for both continuous-time and discrete-time systems is available in several recent texts ((Kogan 1995), for example), since Kharitonov's trend-setting publications.

Open Problem 8 (Bose 1985) was concerned with the obtaining of multivariate counterparts of Kharitonov's celebrated theorems on vertex implications (in the case of boxed domains in parameter space) for inferring invariance of the strict Hurwitz property of interval polynomials in both the real and complex coefficient cases. A degree-independent vertex-implication result in parameter space (like Kharitonov's, where a small number, independent of polynomial degree, of points in parameter-space allows the test for invariance of a property of interest to be implemented for the complete boxed domain associated with the interval system) on a bivariate interval polynomial for invariance of the scattering Hurwitz property was proved in (Bose 1988), where also the n-variate result was conjectured. This n-variate conjecture was proved in (Basu 1979). In (Basu 1979), a subclass of scattering Hurwitz (stable) polynomials called strict sense Hurwitz (stable) polynomials was also studied for robust interval strict sense Hurwitz stability. In the univariate case the scattering Hurwitz and strict sense Hurwitz definitions coincide. More recently (Kharitonov & Torres Munõz 1999), the maximal class of real and complex coefficient multivariate polynomials were defined such that polynomials from this class do not lose the particular stability property under small coefficient variations. All the coefficients of any polynomial in this maximal class must be of like sign, a property which implies that such a polynomial cannot be lacunary. It is also noted that an univariate strict Hurwitz polynomial (devoid of any zero in the closed right-half plane) cannot have missing coefficients and, therefore, cannot be lacunary. In (Kharitonov *et al.* 1999), it was further shown that the maximal class of polynomials referred to satisfy edge implications in parameter space for polytopic coefficient (parameter) variations and vertex implications for interval and diamond families of polynomials. The zero sets of families of multivariate polynomials as well as quasipolynomials are also considered, albeit briefly, in (Kogan 1995) and a Special Issue of *Multidimensional Systems and Signal Processing* (vol. 5, no. 4, 1994) was entirely devoted to the topic of robustness of multidimensional systems.

1.4.4 Robust discrete system stability

In response to Open Problem 9 (Bose 1985), it was shown via a counterexample (Bose & Zeheb 1986) that vertex implication for discrete-time stability does not hold because, in general, an interval polynomial cannot be inferred to belong to the Schur class (for a set of polynomials to belong to this class, any element of the set must have all its zeros inside the unit circle) by testing only a finite number of extreme polynomials. It was, however, shown that the edge implication in parameter space holds not only for univariate interval polynomials but also for polynomials with polytopic variation of coefficients (Bartlett *et al.* 1988). Some results applicable in the stability analysis of robust multidimensional systems have been reported in (Basu 1979). Constructive methods for the robust stability analysis of nonaffine families of multivariate polynomials need to be developed. Extreme point algorithms for construction of the minimal testing sets need also to be synthesized in that case at least for particular classes.

1.4.5 Robust wavenumber response

Robustness property is crucial in the performance evaluation of spatio-temporal systems used to process analog video signals, multidimensional transform-based coding and in multidimensional filtering for picture quality improvement. Bounds on the wavenumber response of multidimensional digital filters, where the uncertainty structure for the coefficients could be of the interval, polytopic, and nonlinear types are important to obtain. Such filters are important in video data processing. The purpose of the filtering, which can be one, two, and three-dimensional is to improve NTSC by limiting the crosstalk that would otherwise occur between luminance and chrominance components. Finite impulse response (FIR) filters that are widely used because of their linear phase properties are inherently stable. For greater speed of implementation, when infinite impulse response (IIR) filters are employed, the analysis of robust wavenumber response should be coupled with robust stability. The wavenumber response of a two-dimensional (2-D) finite impulse response (FIR) filter, characterized by the unit impulse response bisequence $\{h[k_1, k_2]\}$ of finite support is

$$H(\omega_1, \omega_2) = \sum_{k_1} \sum_{k_2} h[k_1, k_2] exp(-j(\omega_1 k_1 + \omega_2 k_2)).$$

The Fourier transform of the bisequence $\{h[k_1, k_2]\}$ given above contains trigonometric terms of the following four types:

$$cos\ (\omega_1 k_1)cos\ (\omega_2 k_2),\ sin\ (\omega_1 k_1)sin\ (\omega_2 k_2),$$

$$cos\ (\omega_1 k_1)sin\ (\omega_2 k_2),\ sin\ (\omega_1 k_1)cos\ (\omega_2 k_2).$$

In the special case, when for all indices k_1 and k_2 that define the region of support of the filter unit impulse response,

$$h[k_1, k_2]\ =\ h_1[k_1]h_2[k_2],$$

holds, the wavenumber response simplifies to a product of 1-D filter frequency responses and the 2-D filter is then called product *separable*. Otherwise, the filter is *nonseparable*. The 3-D and n-D counterparts of the preceding formulations are straightforward. In general, fewer operations are required to realize a separable 2-D (or n-D) filter than an arbitrary 2-D (or n-D) filter of the same order. However, the price to be paid is a potential loss in performance because of constraints on the type of response that can be achieved. In particular, if filters with rapid cut-offs are desired, the passband of separable filters will have a rectangular shape, which may be inadequate if circular, aster, or diamond-shaped passbands are desired as in multidimensional sampling for image and video applications.

Some degree-dependent vertex implication results are available when the property of interest is the frequency-wavenumber response. Interval trigonometric polynomials and the ratios of such polynomials are useful for assessing the robust frequency responses of, respectively, FIR and IIR digital filters. For such studies it has been concluded that degree-dependent vertex-implication results hold in the univariate case (Bose & Kim 1991). Such degree-dependent vertex implication results hold also for some special classes of two-dimensional interval digital filters, called product separable filters. Latest results are documented in (Bose & Yang 1999), where consequences of imposing various symmetry conditions in the unit impulse response of multidimensional FIR filters on the bounds of wavenumber responses of such filters are investigated. Fourfold and eightfold symmetry constraints on the unit impulse response are satisfactorily tackled for lower order filters. Higher order cases and the twofold symmetry case remains a difficult open problem from the computational complexity standpoint. Amplitude and phase envelopes of an interval rational transfer function of continuous-time systems have also been considered recently (Levkovich & Zeheb 1995).

1.5 MULTISPECTRAL MULTIFRAME MULTISENSOR PROCESSING

The focus of image analysis research is the pursuit of theories and algorithms which will lead to the design of robust automatic systems as well as the development of methods to validate the performance of such systems. This is crucial not only in defense applications such as automatic target recognition (ATR) in which the background of the scene is cluttered, the objects are far away, and the view may be obscured or blurred but also in consumer needs such as the compression and processing of a sequence of undersampled, blurred and noisy multispectral frames in video and television.

A procedure (Boo & Bose 1997) has recently been advanced to restore a single color image, which has been degraded by a linear shift-invariant blur in the presence of additive noise. Four sensors are needed, followed by the application of the RGB-YIQ transformation. Subsequently, one 3-D Wiener filtration is required on a sequence of two luminance components and a 2-D Wiener filter is then applied to each of the two chrominance components. For the procedure to be successful, the imposition of a strongly coprime condition on the wavenumber response of two distinct sensor blur functions is necessary because this artifice converts an ill-posed deconvolution problem to a well-posed one. The resulting well-conditioned problem is subsequently shown to provide high quality color image.

1.5.1 Reconstruction from image sequences

Single image processing methods often provide unacceptable results because of the ill-conditioned nature of associated inverse problems. Therefore, multiple image processing has developed into an active research area because multiple deconvolution operators can be used to make the problem well-posed. Rapid progress in computer and semiconductor technology is making it possible to implement multiple image processing tasks reasonably quickly, but the need for processing in real time requires attention to design of robust algorithms for implementation on current and future generations of computational architectures.

Image sequences are produced from several snapshots of an object or a scene, while multispectral images are captured by using multiple sensors with wavelength-sensitive optical filters. The sources of blur may be diffraction effects, imaging system aberrations, defocused lenses, relative motion between the image and object planes, and atmospheric turbulence. Noise is commonly modeled as either additive white Gaussian in simple cases or additive signal-dependent in more complex noisy environments. To remove blur and noise, multiple image processing algorithms not only use intra-image correlations as in single image processing methods but also inter-image crosscorrelation information.

Following the research described above on a single color image, a novel spatio-temporal filter was described (Boo & Bose 1998) for a sequence of monochrome image sequences with signal-dependent noise by considering both spatial and temporal correlations. With the assumptions of spatio-temporal separability and temporal stationarity it was shown that a motion-compensated group of frames can be decorrelated by the Karhunen-Loeve transform (KLT). Practical filters that work well on a variety of image sequences were developed by first applying either the sub-optimal but computationally-expedient Hadamard transform (HT) or the Discrete Cosine transform (DCT) (depending on the type of noise sources) along the temporal direction. Subsequently, the parametric adaptive Wiener filter was applied to each of the resulting approximately decorrelated transformed images for noise removal. These transformed images were classified into an average image and a remaining set of residual images, which provide interesting and useful interpretations of the type of original image sequence. The noise reduction scheme can reduce signal-dependent noise if observed pixels have either temporal or spatial correlations with their neighborhoods in 3-D. The filter performance was evaluated by considering different types of image sequences in the database. The results reported in (Boo & Bose 1998) are suitable for generalization to the case of a sequence of multispectral images where the RGB-YIQ transform is required in addition either to the other transforms considered in (Boo & Bose 1998) or their variants. Further investigations in this area are required.

1.5.2 Processing of intensity-varying image sequences

Boo & Bose (1998) describes a noise reduction scheme for image sequences with signal-dependent noise, using temporal interframe and spatial intraframe correlation information. It is shown that temporally correlated image sequences can be decorrelated into a set of images by the Karhunen–Loevé transform (KLT). Subsequently, the computationally intensive optimal KLT is approximated by either the Hadamard transform (HT) or the Discrete Cosine Transform (DCT), depending on the type of noise sources. Then, noise in each of the decorrelated images is removed by the parametric Wiener filter whose operation depends on local statistics. The noise reduction scheme can reduce signal-dependent noise if observed pixels have either temporal or spatial correlations with their neighborhoods in 3-D.

In applications such as TV broadcasting, teleconferencing, videophone, and scientific imaging, the light intensity is almost constant over a number of correlated frames and the proposed algorithm in (Boo & Bose 1998) works well for a variety of noise sources. However, in other applications such as magnetic-resonance imaging (MRI) used in medical imaging and with potential for ordnance/mine detection and recognition, a sequence of images generated by the multiple spin-echo technique shows a noticeable change in light intensity, depending on relaxation times (Soltanian-Zadeh *et al.* 1995).

1.5.3   Image processing based on the wavelet transform

The HT and DCT may not be appropriate for decorrelation of intensity-varying images because they can produce large energy in residual images. On the other hand, in case of MRI sequences, the improvement of region of interest only is usually desired for interpretation of MRI scenes. One objective of future research should be, first, to concentrate on the development of a specific noise-reduction algorithm based on the prescribed characteristics of MRI scenes with proper choice of the mother wavelet in wavelet transform and, second, to test the noise reduction scheme on a variety of noise corrupted image sequences for comparison with single image noise reduction techniques.

Though the wavelet transform (WT) (Jawerth & Sweldens 1994, Rioul & Vetterli 1991) has been successfully applied to image coding, it is still premature in areas of image enhancement and restoration. However, as the WT is a general version of the discrete Fourier transform (DFT), it seems that the WT can also be applicable to many interesting image processing problems. With respect to the FT, the WT has some flexibilities for incorporating multidimensional signal processing. For example, the WT can be applicable to space-variant systems. Future work will consider image processing schemes based on the WT, where the characterizing matrix is usually sparse.

1.5.4   Neurocomputing-based multidimensional signal processing

Neurocomputing is becoming increasingly popular as a viable alternative to classical computing in computation-intensive tasks like image processing. Zhou *et al.* (1988) proposed a deterministic Hopfield neural network (Bose & Liang 1996) model for the restoration of gray level images degraded by a known shift-invariant blur and additive Gaussian noise. In conventional image processing, where the blur can be modeled by a linear shift-invariant function, the characterizing matrix in the deconvolution problem has a block-Toeplitz structure.

While approximation of a block Toeplitz with Toeplitz blocks (BTTB) matrix **H** (in the case of linear shift-invariant blur) with a preconditioner **C**, which is block circulant with circulant blocks (BCCB), is indispensable in classical computing to benefit from the applicability of the FFT and better convergence, in neurocomputing such an approximation leads to increase in storage as well as time because **C** is usually much less sparse than **H** and the number of connections in the neural network also increases. This simple discussion underscores the differing needs and requirements of neurocomputing from that of classical computing. This serves to remind the reader that routine application of strategies from classical computing to neurocomputing might prove disastrous especially in multidimensional problems, where the computational chores tend to be high.

1.6 OPEN PROBLEMS

Multidimensional systems continues to be a fertile arena for continued development of theoretical and computational tools for application in multidimensional signal, image and video processing, multidimensional feedback systems design, multidimensional convolutional codes (Fornasini & Valcher 1997), solutions of linear systems of multi-shift difference equations in the discrete case or partial differential equations in the continuous case and related problems. With progresses towards either complete or partial solutions of problems identified earlier, a sequence of new open problems have emerged and some of these are cited next.

- The approach based on resultants/subresultants for studying global positivity (with local and semi-local ramifications) needs to be investigated within the framework of the D-stability and literal coefficient stability problems.

- The stabilizability problem of multi-input/multi-output (MIMO) 2-D systems and classification of all stabilizing compensators based on the theory of matrix-fraction description (Guiver & Bose 1982) was also addressed in (Bose 1985). The approach in (Shankar & Sule 1992) was applied to MIMO n-D systems in (Sule 1994). The question whether stabilizable n-D systems have doubly-coprime fractions raised in (Sule 1994) remains unsettled in general.

- Algorithmic approaches based on the construction and use of Gröbner bases over $\mathcal{K}[z_1, z_2, \cdots, z_n]$ and modules over such n-variate polynomial rings have expanded the domain of application of the developed theories. However, limitations in the implementation of Gröbner basis-based algorithms exist when dealing with the fundamental problem of polynomial matrix greatest common factor existence and extraction, doubly-coprime factorization of a multivariate rational matrix, when it exists, and related issues when $n \geq 3$. Refer to (Charoenlarpnopparut & Bose 1999, Example 1) for an illustration of the fact that in spite of its existence, the trivariate greatest common factor has an order smaller than the number of columns in the reduced Gröbner basis matrix which generates the same module as that generated by the columns of the specified polynomial matrix. if that is at all possible.

- Algebraic aspects of multidimensional convolutional codes, which can be studied in the setting of a ring $\mathcal{F}_q[z_1, z_2, \cdots, z_n]$, where $\mathcal{F}_q$ is a finite field with q elements has attracted some attention recently because of the potentials of n-D convolutional codes in the encoding and decoding of multidimensional data (Fornasini & Valcher 1994), (Fornasini & Valcher 1997). The resources of multidimensional systems theory including the different notions of primeness, were summarized in (Wood *et al.* 1998) for the ring $\mathcal{K}[z_1, z_2, \cdots, z_n]$ (and the Laurent polynomial ring where the indeterminates occur with their respective inverses), when the field of coefficients is arbitrary of characteristic zero (later algebraic closure was assumed). A detailed study of the various notions of matrix primeness as one proceeds from $n = 2$ to $n \geq 3$ is required when the field of coefficients is finite because the characterization of primeness may become field-dependent.

- In applications, computational issues in implementation of numerical and symbolic algebra-based algorithms are crucial. For example, though the algorithmic proof (Park & Woodburn 1995) of the Suslin stability criterion leads to the ladder realization of biorthogonal multidimensional multiband filter banks, the actual implementation is usually very slow and computation-intensive. Heuristic algorithms are often found to be very useful in practice (like the syzygy based algorithm for unimodular matrix completion by H. Park applied to the design of orthogonal perfect reconstruction filter banks) and more attention should be directed towards their development.

- Bose *et al.* (1993) considered low-resolution images with displacement errors and formulated a recursive total least squares (TLS) algorithm for the construction of high-resolution images. An important objective of current research is to develop efficient algorithms based upon ideas for the large and highly structured TLS problems that arise in image processing, thus leading to efficient TLS software for the recovery of high resolution images.

1.7   CONCLUSIONS

The presentation here has been exclusively in terms of transfer operators that provide the input/output description. A state-space description can also be pursued for which earlier results are summarized in ((Bose 1982), Chapter 4) and recent documentations are extensive (Galkowski 1997), (Oberst 1990), (Zerz & Oberst 1993). It was observed (Oberst 1998) that the solution in a special case of the Cauchy problem was given as early as 1910 in a book (Riquier 1910), which interestingly contained the essence of the Gröbner basis algorithm not only for polynomials but even for differential operators with coefficients in the differential field of rational functions. An algebraic analysis of linear multidimensional systems has been conducted recently by J. F. Pommaret and A. Quadrat (personal correspondence with the second author, 1998) by exploiting the duality existing between the theory of differential modules and the formal theory of systems of partial differential equations. This module-theoretic approach, also adopted by Oberst in his seminal paper (Oberst 1990), though requiring considerable algebraic machineries, permit clarification and unification of existing tools in multidimensional systems theory. For example, the consequences of various notions of coprimeness (zero, minor, factor) in multivariate polynomial matrix algebra can be better understood by applying module theory. Of course, the problem of zero coprimeness and unimodular matrix completion is linked to the Quillen-Suslin proof (1976) of Serre's celebrated conjecture that projective modules over polynomial rings are free and the equivalence of minor and factor primeness when matrix elements are drawn from the ring $\mathcal{K}[z_1, z_2]$, follows from the fact that a finitely generated module over such a ring is reflexive, or equivalently, is a second syzygy (Evans & Griffith 1985). The next major result appeared in the form of *Suslin's Stability Theorem* under which any square unimodular matrix with entries in a multivariate polynomial ring can be expressed as a product of elementary matrices. This result provides the machinery for biorthogonal multiband filter bank realization for perfect reconstruction using the ladder topology. The case when both perfect reconstruction and linear phase constraints (or other like paraunitary) are enforced, is still, in general, an open problem. The recent solution given for the two-band 2-D case (Basu 1998), has been shown to be not extendable, in general, to the multiband $m \geq 3$ case. However, using Gröbner bases, not only a simple alternate proof of the resultant matrix based proof for the two-band 2-D case in (Basu 1998) can be given but this result may easily be generalized directly to the two-band n-D case. These and other results on the further use of Gröbner bases to solve an expanding horizon of problems in multidimensional systems and signal processing are reported elsewhere in the book of which this chapter is a part.

ACKNOWLEDGEMENT

The research reported here was conducted under the sponsorship of National Science Foundation Grants ECS-9508620 and ECS-9711590.

REFERENCES

B. D. O. Anderson, N. K. Bose, and E. I. Jury, 1975, Output feedback stabilization and related problems - solution via decision methods. *IEEE Trans. on Automatic Control*, 20:53–66.

A. C. Bartlett, C. V. Hollot, and H. Lin, 1988, Root location of an entire polytope of polynomials. *Mathematics of Controls, Signals and Systems*, 1:61–71.

S. Basu, 1979, On boundary implications of stability and positivity properties of multidimensional systems. *Proceedings of the IEEE*, 78:614–626.

S. Basu, 1998, Multi-dimensional filter banks and wavelets – a system theoretic perspective. *Journal of the Franklin Institute*, 335B:1367–1409.

K. J. Boo and N. K. Bose, 1997, Multispectral image restoration with multisensors. *IEEE Trans. on Geoscience and Remote Sensing*, 35:1160–1170.

K. J. Boo and N. K. Bose, 1998, A motion-compensated spatio-temporal filter for image sequences with signal-dependent noise. *IEEE Trans. on Circuits and Systems for Video Technology*, 8(3):287–298.

N. K. Bose, 1976, New techniques and results in multidimensional problems. *Journal of the Franklin Institute*, 301:83–101.

N. K. Bose, 1977, Problems and progress in multidimensional system theory. *Proceedings of the IEEE*, 65:824–840.

N. K. Bose, 1982, *Applied Multidimensional Systems Theory*. Van Nostrand Reinhold Co., New York, NY.

N. K. Bose, 1985, *Multidimensional Systems Theory: Progress, Directions, and Open Problems*. D. Reidel Publishing Co., Dordrecht, The Netherlands.

N. K. Bose, 1988, Robust scattering multivariate Hurwitz polynomials. *Linear Algebra and Its Applications*, 98:123–136.

N. K. Bose, 1990, Multidimensional digital signal processing: problems, progress, and future scopes. *Proceedings of the IEEE*, 78:590–597.

N. K. Bose, 1997, Past, present, and future of quantifier elimination procedures in system theory. *Proc. Amer. Control Conf.*, 4:1828–1832.

N .K. Bose and S. Basu, 1978, Tests for polynomial zeros on a polydisc distinguished boundary. *IEEE Trans. on Circuits and Systems*, CAS-25(9):684–693.

N. K. Bose and C. Charoenlarpnopparut, 1998a, Multivariate matrix factorization: new results. *Proc. Mathematical Theory of Networks and Systems.*, pages 97–100.

N. K. Bose and C. Charoenlarpnopparut, 1998b, Test for nonnegativity of polynomials with literal coefficients by quantifier elimination. *Proc. Amer. Control Conf.*, 4:1879–1880.

N. K. Bose and C. Charoenlarpnopparut, 1999, Minimax controller design using rate feedback. *Circuits Systems and Signal Processing*, 18:17–25.

N. K. Bose and E. I. Jury, 1974, Positivity and stability tests for multidimensional filters. *IEEE Trans. on Acoust., Speech, and Signal Process.*, 22:174–180.

N. K. Bose, H.C. Kim, and H. M. Valenzuela, 1993, Recursive total least squares algorithm for image reconstruction from noisy, undersampled frames. *Multidimensional Systems and Signal Processing*, 4:253–268.

N. K. Bose and K. D. Kim, 1991, Boundary implications for frequency response of interval FIR and IIR filters. *IEEE Trans. on Signal Processing*, 39:2167–2173.

N. K. Bose and P. Liang, 1996, *Neural Network Fundamentals with Graphs, Algorithms, and Applications.* McGraw-Hill, Inc., New York, NY.

N. K. Bose and C. Yang, 1999, Robust wavenumber response of multidimensional FIR filters. In *Advances in Control*, pages 285–292, Highlights of European Control Conference, Karlsruhe, Germany, Springer-Verlag.

N. K. Bose and E. Zeheb, 1986, Kharitonov's theorem and stability test of multidimensional digital filters. *Proceedings of the IEE Circuits and Systems, Part G*, 133:187–190.

F. A. M. L. Bruekers and A. W. M. van den Emden, 1992, New networks for perfect inversion and perfect reconstruction. *IEEE J. Select. Areas in Commun*, 10:130–137.

C. Charoenlarpnopparut and N. K. Bose, 1999, Multidimensional FIR filter bank design using Gröbner bases. *IEEE Trans. on Circuits and Systems II*, 46:1475–1486.

P. M. Cohn, 1966, On the structure of GL_2 of a ring. *Inst. Hautes Etudes Sci. Publ. Math.*, 30:365–413.

R. E. Van Dyck, Jr., T.G. Marshall, M. Chin, and N. Moayeri, 1996, Wavelet video coding with ladder structures and entropy-constrained quantization. *IEEE Trans. on Circuits and Systems for Video Technology*, 4:1879–1880.

J. B. Edwards and D. H. Owens, 1982, *Analysis and Control of Multipass Processes.* Research Studies Press, Chichester, England.

E. G. Evans and P. Griffith, 1985, *Syzygies.* Cambridge University Press, Cambridge, England.

E. Fornasini and M. E. Valcher, 1994, Algebraic aspects of 2-D convolutional codes. *IEEE Trans. on Inform. Theory*, 40:1068–1082.

E. Fornasini and M. E. Valcher, 1997, n-D polynomial matrices with applications to multidimensional signal analysis. *Multidimensional Systems and Signal Processing*, 8:387–408.

K. Gałkowski, 1997, Elementary operation approach to state-space realizations of 2-D systems. *IEEE Trans. on Circuits and Systems*, 44:120–129.

Y. V. Genin, 1974, An algebraic approach to A-stable linear multistep multiderivative integration formulas. *BIT*, 14:382–406.

J. P. Guiver and N. K. Bose, 1982, Polynomial matrix primitive factorization over arbitrary coefficient field and related results. *IEEE Trans. on Circuits and Systems*, 29:649–657.

B. Jawerth and W. Sweldens, 1994, An overview of wavelet based multiresolution analysis. *SIAM Review*, 36:377–412.

V. L. Kharitonov and J. A. Torres Munõz, 1999, Robust stability of multivariate polynomials, Part I: small coefficient perturbations. *Multidimensional Systems and Signal Processing*, 10:7–20.

V. L. Kharitonov, J. A. Torres Munõz, and M. I. Ramirez-Sosa, 1999, Robust stability of multivariate polynomials, Part II: polytopic coefficient variations. *Multidimensional Systems and Signal Processing*, 10:21–32.

E. Kofidis, S. Theodoridis, and N. Kalouptsidis, 1996, On the perfect reconstruction problem in N-band multirate maximally decimated FIR filter banks. *Signal Processing*, 44:2439–2455.

T. Koga, 1968, Synthesis of finite passive n-ports with prescribed positive real matrices of several variables. *IEEE Trans. on Circuit Theory*, 15:2–23.

J. Kogan, 1995, *Robust Stability and Convexity.* Springer-Verlag, London, Great Britain.

T. Y. Lam, 1978, *Serre's Conjecture.* Springer-Verlag, Berlin, Germany.

D. Lazard, 1988, Quantifier elimination: optimal solution for two classical examples. *Journal of Symbolic Computation*, pages 261–266.

A. Levkovich and E. Zeheb, 1995, Frequency response envelopes of a family of uncertain continuous systems. *IEEE Trans. on Circuits and Systems*, 42:156–165.

Z. Lin, 1998, Feedback stabilizability of MIMO n-D linear systems. *Multidimensional Systems and Signal Processing*, 9:149–172.

Z. Lin and L. T. Bruton, 1989, BIBO stability of inverse 2-D digital filters in the presence of nonessential singularities of the second kind. *IEEE Trans. on Circuits and Systems*, 36:244–254.

T. G. Marshall, 1997, Zero-phase filter bank and wavelet code matrices: properties, triangular decompositions, and a fast algorithm. *Multidimensional Systems and Signal Processing*, 8:71–88.

M. Newman, 1972, *Integral Matrices*. Academic Press, Inc., New York, NY.

U. Oberst, 1990, Multidimensional constant linear systems. *Acta Applicandae Mathematicae*, 20:1–175.

U. Oberst, 1993, On the Minimal Number of Trajectories Determining a Multidimensional System. *Mathematics of Control, Signals and Systems*, 6:264–288.

U. Oberst, 1998, Transfer operators and state spaces for discrete multidimensional linear systems: I. In *Proc. Mathematical Theory of Networks and Systems.*, Padova, Italy.

H. Park and C. Woodburn, 1995, An algorithmic proof of Suslin's stability theorem for polynomial rings. *Journal of Algebra*, 176:277–298.

O. Rioul and M. Vetterli, 1991, Wavelets and signal processing. *IEEE SP Magazine*, 8:14–38.

C. Riquier, 1910, *La methode des fonctions majorantes et les systemes d'equations aux derivees partialles*. Gauthiers-Villars, Paris, France.

P. Rocha and J. C. Willems, 1989, State for 2-D system. *Linear Algebra and Its Applications*, 122:1003–1008.

P. Rocha and J. C. Willems, 1990, Canonical computational forms for AR 2-D systems. *Multidimensional Systems and Signal Processing*, 1:271–278.

S. Shankar and V. R. Sule, 1992, Algebraic geometric aspects of feedback stabilization. *SIAM J. Control and Optimization*, 30:11–30.

D. D. Siljak and D. M. Stipanovic, 1998, Robust D-stability via positivity. *Proc. Amer. Control Conf.*, 4:2502–2509.

H. Soltanian-Zadeh, J. P. Windham, and A. E. Yagle, 1995, A multidimensional nonlinear edge-preserving filter for magnetic resonance image restoration. *IEEE Trans. on Image Processing*, 4(2):147–161.

V. R. Sule, 1994, Feedback stabilization over commutative ring: the matrix case. *SIAM J. Control and Optimization*, 32:1675–1695.

S. Takahashi, 1993, The stable conditions of literal coefficients for linear 2-D digital systems. *The Sixth Karuizawa Workshop on Circuits and Systems, Japan*, 98:31–36.

L. Tolhuizen, H. Hollmann, and T. A. C. M. Kalker, 1995, On the realizability of biorthogonal, m-dimensional two-band filter banks. *Signal Processing*, 43:640–648.

L. Wang, D. Xiyu, and F. Xia, 1992, Nonessential singularities of the second kind and stability of multidimensional digital filters. *Multidimensional Systems and Signal Processing*, 3:363–380.

J. Wood, E. Rogers, and D. H. Owens, 1998, A formal theory of matrix primeness. *Mathematics of Controls, Signals and Systems*, 11:40–78.

L. Xu, O. Saito, and K. Abe, 1994, Output feedback stabilizability and stabilization algorithms for 2-D systems. *Multidimensional Systems and Signal Processing*, 5:41–60.

D. C. Youla and G. Gnavi, 1979, Notes on n-dimensional system theory. *IEEE Trans. on Circuits and Systems*, 26:105–111.

E. Zerz and U. Oberst, 1993, The canonical Cauchy problem for linear systems of partial difference equations with constant coefficients over the complete r-dimensional integral lattice Z^r. *Acta Applicandae Mathematicae*, 31:249–273.

Y. T. Zhou, R. Chellappa, and B. F. Jenkins, 1988, Image restoration using a neural network. *IEEE Trans. on Acoust., Speech, and Signal Process.*, 36:1141–1151.

CHAPTER TWO

MATLAB Package for N-D Sampling-Based Modelling of Nonlinear Systems

Andrzej Dzieliński

Institute of Control and Industrial Electronics (ISEP)
Warsaw University of Technology, Poland
DZIELINSKI@nov.isep.pw.edu.pl

Abstract

The method and software described here are based on the N-D nonuniform sampling approach which led to the Fourier Analysis-based feedforward neural networks. Motivation and conceptual framework of the methodology are described. The mathematical foundations and necessary engineering approximations are then explained. The resulting computer-oriented algorithm follows and the actual software implementation in MATLAB is described.

2.1 INTRODUCTION

The method and software described in this section are based on the N-D nonuniform sampling approach which led to the Fourier Analysis-based feedforward neural network.

The presentation is organized as follows. In Section 2.2 motivation and conceptual framework of the methodology are described. The mathematical foundations and necessary engineering approximations are explained in Section 2.3. The resulting computer-oriented algorithm follows in Section 2.4 and the actual software implementation done for the NACT project is described in Section 2.5. The presentation is concluded with an example application of the software to modelling of a real life nonlinear system in Section 2.6.

2.2 BACKGROUND

Motivation and conceptual framework of the methodology is depicted in Figure 2.1. The main scientific sources were: multi-dimensional Fourier Analysis, feedforward neural networks and nonuniform N-D sampling theory. The basic idea was originally proposed by Sanner & Slotine, but has been substantially revised and advanced by the NACT project, resulting in a more widely applicable and sophisticated algorithm.

The algorithm (see Figure 2.2) assumes a discrete-time NARX (Nonlinear Auto Regressive with eXogenous input) model of known order, but unknown right-hand side (RHS) and its aim is to reconstruct the RHS. Also, the realistic assumption of boundedness of input and output is made, thus defining the RHS on a rectangle. The algorithm makes

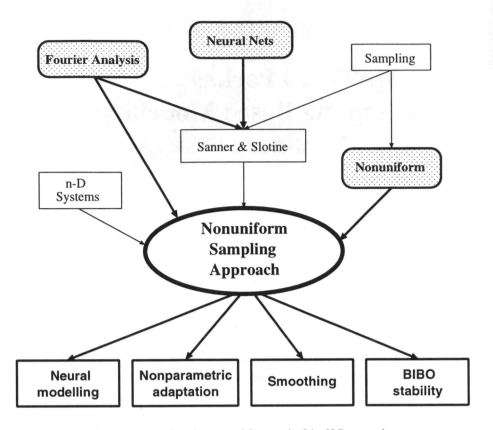

Figure 2.1: Genesis and conceptual framework of the N-D approach.

extensive use of Fourier Analysis and is effectively equivalent to representing the RHS as multi-dimensional Fourier series. The coefficients of the series are computed from an approximation of the Fourier Transform, which in turn is calculated from multi-dimensional samples of the RHS.

2.3 METHOD DESCRIPTION

We begin by briefly describing our approach (Dzieliński & Żbikowski 1996, Żbikowski & Dzieliński 1996b, Żbikowski & Dzieliński 1996a) to identification of a deterministic, non-linear, single-input single-output (SISO) system given by the discrete-time, $t \in \mathbb{Z}_+$, input-output NARX (Leontaritis & Billings 1985, Chen & Billings 1989) model

$$y(t+1) = f(y(t), \dots, y(t-n+1), u(t), \dots, u(t-m+1)) \qquad (2.1)$$

with $y \in [a, b] \subset \mathbb{R}$, $u \in [c, d] \subset \mathbb{R}$ and $f : D \to [a, b]$ with the domain of definition $D = [a, b]^n \times [c, d]^m$. It is physically natural that output y and input u assume only finite values on a connected set and can attain their bounds (this does not preclude stability and boundedness issues). In (2.1) we assume that $f \in L^1(D) \cap L^2(D)$ is unknown, but we can measure current and past inputs $u(t), u(t-1), \dots$ and outputs $y(t), y(t-1), \dots$ at any t.

Put $N = m + n$. Given the samples

$$\lambda_k = (\lambda_{1,k_1}, \ldots, \lambda_{N,k_N}) = (y_t, \ldots, y_{t-n+1}, u_t, \ldots, u_{t-m+1}) \quad \text{and} \quad f(\lambda_k), \qquad (2.2)$$

where we put $y_t = y(t)$ etc. for brevity ($t \in \mathbb{Z}_+$) and $k = (k_1, k_2, \ldots, k_N)$, the issue is to reconstruct the multivariable function f, a problem from multi-dimensional (N-D) Signal Processing. The approach was introduced by Sanner & Slotine, (Sanner & Slotine 1992) but they assumed that the multi-dimensional samples are uniform, i.e., regularly distributed in the domain D of f. This seems to be a simplification, as the dynamics of (2.1) manifest themselves through irregular samples (Dzieliński & Żbikowski 1995). Sanner & Slotine also required f to be analytic.

Let us now present a brief summary of our approach to modelling of (2.1) in the context of N-D irregular sampling.

We are going to use Fourier Transform in several variables, (Stein & Weiss 1971), so $f\colon D \to \mathbb{R}$ must be first extended to $\mathbb{R}^N$. We do it by the space-limited extension

$$\tilde{f}(x) = \begin{cases} f(x), & \text{if } x \in D; \\ 0, & \text{otherwise.} \end{cases} \qquad (2.3)$$

Thus, $\tilde{f}$ is of bounded support and its Fourier Transform is

$$\tilde{F}(w) = \int_{\mathbb{R}^N} \tilde{f}(x) e^{-j\omega \cdot x} dx = \int_D f(x) e^{-j\omega \cdot x} dx, \qquad (2.4)$$

where $\omega \cdot x = \sum_{j=1}^N \omega_j x_j$, so $\tilde{F}$ is a Paley-Wiener function of regular growth (Żbikowski & Dzieliński 1996b).

We are given a *finite* number of non-uniformly spread samples $\tilde{f}(\lambda_k)$, where $\lambda_k = (\lambda_{1,k_1}, \ldots, \lambda_{N,k_N})$, of the nonlinear function $\tilde{f} = \tilde{f}(x)$, with $x = (x_1, \ldots, x_N) = (y_t, y_{t-1}, \ldots, y_{t-n+1}, u_t, u_{t-1}, \ldots, u_{t-m+1})$, i.e., $N = m + n$. We want to find the function $\tilde{f}$, which in general can only be done approximately due to finiteness of data.

The main idea of our method is replacing the nonuniform sampling problem in the space domain by a uniform problem in the Fourier Transform domain. The aim is to reconstruct $\tilde{F}$ and then, by its inversion, $\tilde{f}$. Therefore, our solution consists of two basic steps. First, we find an approximation of $\tilde{F}$ on the basis of given non-uniformly sampled values of $\tilde{f}$, i.e., $\tilde{f}(\lambda_k)$. Then we find the Fourier inverse of the approximation of $\tilde{F}$ to get an approximation of $\tilde{f}$.

For simplicity and clarity we show the reasoning for $D = [a, b] \times [c, d]$, i.e., $m = n = 1$, so that $N = 2$. Cases $m \neq n$ and $N > 2$ are straightforward generalizations of the 2-D derivation, but require more elaborate notations.

The Fourier Transform $\tilde{F}$ of $\tilde{f}$ can be represented by its Shannon series, (Papoulis 1962), since $\tilde{f}$ is space-limited, see (2.3). The actual formula can be computed (emulating the reasoning in (Petersen & Middleton 1962)) for rectangular sampling geometry, i.e., by sampling arguments ω_1 and ω_2 of $\tilde{F}$ independently. It follows that the minimal (Shannon) frequencies are

$$\omega_{S_1} = \frac{2\pi}{b - a}, \qquad (2.5)$$

$$\omega_{S_2} = \frac{2\pi}{d - c} \qquad (2.6)$$

and the corresponding exact representation of $\tilde{F}$ by the Shannon (cardinal) series is

$$
\begin{aligned}
\tilde{F}(\omega_1, \omega_2) \quad = \quad & e^{-j\frac{b+a}{2}\omega_1} e^{-j\frac{d+c}{2}\omega_2} \times \\
& \times \sum_{k_1=-\infty}^{\infty} \sum_{k_2=-\infty}^{\infty} e^{j\frac{b+a}{2}k_1\omega_{S_1}} e^{j\frac{d+c}{2}k_2\omega_{S_2}} \tilde{F}(k_1\omega_{S_1}, k_2\omega_{S_2}) \times \\
& \times \operatorname{sinc}[\frac{b-a}{2}(\omega_1 - k_1\omega_{S_1})]\operatorname{sinc}[\frac{d-c}{2}(\omega_2 - k_2\omega_{S_2})], \quad (2.7)
\end{aligned}
$$

where $\operatorname{sinc}(x) = \frac{\sin x}{x}$. Note that if D is centred at the origin, i.e., $a = -b$ and $c = -d$, then (2.7) becomes the (iterated) standard reconstruction formula:

$$
\tilde{F}(\omega_1, \omega_2) = \sum_{k_1=-\infty}^{\infty} \sum_{k_2=-\infty}^{\infty} \tilde{F}(k_1\omega_{S_1}, k_2\omega_{S_2})\operatorname{sinc}[b(\omega_1 - k_1\omega_{S_1})]\operatorname{sinc}[d(\omega_2 - k_2\omega_{S_2})],
$$

where $\omega_{S_1} = \pi/b$ and $\omega_{S_2} = \pi/d$. Also, in order for (2.7) to uniquely represent $\tilde{F}$ for any $(\omega_1, \omega_2) \in \mathbb{R}^2$ the sampling frequencies ω_{S_1} and ω_{S_2} cannot be smaller than (2.5)–(2.6), but may be larger (oversampling).

In principle, the Sanner & Slotine approach (Sanner & Slotine 1992) of replacing (2.7) with an approximating Gaussian neural network can be used. While this seems to be motivated in their case by an attempt to relax the assumption of band-limitness of f, it is not needed here, due to the space-limited extension (2.3).

An advantage of representing $\tilde{F}$ by (2.7) is that by taking the inverse transform of (2.7) we get a representation of $\tilde{f}$ in terms of samples $\tilde{F}(k_1\omega_{S_1}, k_2\omega_{S_2})$

$$
\tilde{f}(x_1, x_2) = \frac{1}{(b-a)(d-c)} \times
\begin{cases}
\sum_{k_1} \sum_{k_2} \tilde{F}(k_1\omega_{S_1}, k_2\omega_{S_2})e^{jk_1\omega_{S_1}x_1}e^{jk_2\omega_{S_2}x_2}, & (x_1, x_2) \in D; \\
0, & \text{otherwise.}
\end{cases}
$$
$$(2.8)$$

Since the summations in (2.8) are symmetric (from $-\infty$ to $+\infty$), the reconstructed $\tilde{f}$ will be real for all $(x_1, x_2) \in \mathbb{R}^2$. For if $\tilde{R}$ denotes the real and $\tilde{I}$ imaginary part of $\tilde{F}$, $\tilde{F}(\omega_1, \omega_2) = \tilde{R}(\omega_1, \omega_2) + j\tilde{I}(\omega_1, \omega_2)$, then $\tilde{R}$ is even, $\tilde{R}(\omega_1, \omega_2) = \tilde{R}(-\omega_1, -\omega_2)$, and $\tilde{I}$ odd, $\tilde{I}(\omega_1, \omega_2) = -\tilde{I}(-\omega_1, -\omega_2)$.

If $\tilde{f}$ is known, then the above reasoning is a tautology and (2.8) is not needed. However, our problem is that $\tilde{f}$ is unknown, but we have its samples $\tilde{f}(\lambda_{1,k_1}, \lambda_{2,k_2}) = \tilde{f}(y_{t-1}, u_{t-1})$, where $t = 1, 2, \ldots, T$. Since $\tilde{f}$ is space-limited, its Fourier Transform $\tilde{F}$ can be, in principle, reconstructed from (2.7), for which only samples of $\tilde{F}$ are needed. Thus, the core issue is how to obtain these from $\tilde{f}(y_{t-1}, u_{t-1})$. Of course, this can be done only approximately, as we have finite data. From the definition of the Fourier Transform we approximate the integral (2.4) by the finite Riemann-like sum

$$
\begin{aligned}
\tilde{F}_T(\omega_1, \omega_2) \quad &= \quad \sum_{t=1}^{T} \tilde{f}(y_{t-1}, u_{t-1})e^{-j(\omega_1 y_{t-1} + \omega_2 u_{t-1})} A_t \\
&= \quad \sum_{t=1}^{T} y_t e^{-j(\omega_1 y_{t-1} + \omega_2 u_{t-1})} A_t, \quad (2.9)
\end{aligned}
$$

where T is the horizon of observation and A_t is the area associated with (y_{t-1}, u_{t-1}) with $\sum_{t=1}^{T} A_t = (b - a)(d - c)$. While the summation in (2.9) is over one index, t, it is an approximation of the double ($N = 2$) integral (2.4), which manifests itself in (y_{t-1}, u_{t-1}) and A_t.

Note that (2.9) is a non-standard approximation of (2.4), for (y_{t-1}, u_{t-1}) are distributed non-uniformly, i.e., they are not nodes of a rectangular grid (ordinary Riemann sum). Therefore, we have to allocate area A_t to each (y_{t-1}, u_{t-1}) according to the density of the points in D, which may be viewed as weighting of (2.9). One possible approach is to use Voronoi diagrams, for which linear-time computational methods exist; (Okabe *et al.* 1992); thus A_t would be the area of the Voronoi polygon generated by (y_{t-1}, u_{t-1}). This can be extended to $N > 2$ dimensions, as well (Dwyer 1991). Another approach, implemented in our software, is to preprocess the samples to make them quasi-equidistributed and apply the Monte Carlo method, (Stroud 1971), effectively setting $A_t = (b - a)(c - d)/T$ (here T is the number of samples after preprocessing).

It should be emphasized that if nonuniformity is such that the points are evidently not equidistributed, then the approximation of (2.9) is inaccurate. An example of this situation is when the points cluster in a few regions of D, leaving the rest of the rectangle with only very few points. Such an outlier gives little information about the values of $\tilde{f}$ in its neighbourhood, but the area allocated to it is a relatively large fraction of $(b - a)(d - c)$, thus amplifying the uncertainty. There are two possible remedies in such a situation. One is to shrink D, eliminating the regions with little information and another is to try to generate the missing data. As the data are obtained from the dynamical system (2.1), the latter means designing a better identification experiment, while the former that D is a superset of the true domain.

When a reasonable approximation $\tilde{F}_T$ is obtained, then it can be substituted to (2.7) and then to (2.8). In order to obtain a computationally feasible approximation the sums in thus modified (2.8) must be symmetrically truncated to, say, $(2L_1 + 1)(2L_2 + 1)$ terms. Then the approximate reconstruction formula is 0 for (x_1, x_2) outside D and for $(x_1, x_2) \in D$ it yields

$$
\begin{aligned}
\tilde{f}^a(x_1, x_2) &= \frac{1}{(b-a)(d-c)} \Bigg\{ R(0,0) + \\
&\quad 2 \sum_{k_1=1}^{L_1} R(k_1 \omega_{S_1}, 0) \cos(k_1 \omega_{S_1} x_1) - I(k_1 \omega_{S_1}, 0) \sin(k_1 \omega_{S_1} x_1) + \\
&\quad 2 \sum_{k_2=1}^{L_2} R(0, k_2 \omega_{S_2}) \cos(k_2 \omega_{S_2} x_2) - I(0, k_2 \omega_{S_2}) \sin(k_2 \omega_{S_2} x_2) + \\
&\quad 2 \sum_{k_1=1}^{L_1} \sum_{\substack{k_2=-L_2 \\ k_2 \neq 0}}^{L_2} \Big[R(k_1 \omega_{S_1}, k_2 \omega_{S_2}) \cos(k_1 \omega_{S_1} x_1 + k_2 \omega_{S_2} x_2) - \\
&\quad I(k_1 \omega_{S_1}, k_2 \omega_{S_2}) \sin(k_1 \omega_{S_1} x_1 + k_2 \omega_{S_2} x_2) \Big] \Bigg\}.
\end{aligned}
\tag{2.10}
$$

Here R is the real and I imaginary part of $\tilde{F}_T$ of (2.9), i.e., $\tilde{F}_T(\omega_1, \omega_2) = R(\omega_1, \omega_2) + jI(\omega_1, \omega_2)$ and the assumptions that R is even and I odd are made.

Note that L_1, L_2 above are independent of T of (2.9), for L_1, L_2 result from a symmetric truncation of (2.7), while T defines the number of data points available. In principle, increasing L_1, L_2 should improve accuracy of the approximation (2.10), but there are limitations imposed by accuracy of $\tilde{F}_T$ of (2.9) and computational resources available.

Formula (2.10) is in essence a rectangular partial sum of multiple Fourier series with coefficients expressed by (an approximation of) the Fourier transform of $\tilde{f}$. Hence the Gibbs' phenomenon will occur on ∂D; this can be alleviated by artificially enlarging D (see section 2.4 below).

Finally, note that (2.10) is an interpolation formula valid for all points of D, but obtained from the samples (y_{t-1}, u_{t-1}). The latter define R and I in (2.10) via (2.9).

The main features of the algorithm are as follows:

- use of real-world data from an input-output, discrete-time NARX model;

- relative computational simplicity: only (2.9) and (2.10) are needed;

- mild assumptions: m, n in (2.1) known, $f \in L^1(D) \cap L^2(D)$ and availability of measurements (2.2).

2.4 ALGORITHM DESCRIPTION

The data required are N-D samples formed by the current and past outputs and past inputs (block **1** in Figure 2.2). These samples can be easily measured and are necessarily multidimensional and nonuniform.

From them an approximation of the Fourier Transform (FT) is to be computed (block **5**) using the Monte Carlo integration method which gives best results when the samples are equidistributed. Therefore, the data gathered are decimated (block **2**) in order to: (i) eliminate dense clusters and (ii) reduce computational load (less points to be processed). Since the implicit representation of the RHS is by the N-D Fourier series, the Gibbs' phenomenon will occur on the boundaries of the original domain (rectangle). As this would cause distortion of the reconstructed surface, the domain is artificially enlarged. For convenience the augmentation assumes that the RHS is linear in the immediate neighbourhood of the original rectangle and the required additional samples are generated accordingly. This is symbolized by block **3** in Figure 2.2. Finally, to decrease the influence of the reconstruction error on the dynamics of the resulting approximate NARX model, data are regularised by considering the corresponding finite differences model[1] (block **4**). This means that the model output will now be the difference $\Delta y_t = y_t - y_{t-1}$ of the current, y_t, and previous, y_{t-1}, outputs and not the current output. If the system is close to an equilibrium (or dynamics is slow), then y_t differs little from y_{t-1} and thus Δy_t is small. Hence reconstruction error for the RHS g (see footnote 1) will be relatively much smaller for the sought RHS f (see footnote 1). This is a regularisation of an ill-posed problem, as indicated in block **4** in Figure 2.2.

Blocks **2–4** perform data preprocessing, which serves two practical purposes:

1. improving accuracy and speed of the FT approximation; block **2**;

---

[1] For the first order system the NARX model is $y_t = f(y_{t-1}, u_{t-1})$ and the corresponding finite differences model is $y_t - y_{t-1} = f(y_{t-1}, u_{t-1}) - y_{t-1}$, or $\Delta y_t = g(y_{t-1}, u_{t-1})$; here $\Delta y_t = y_t - y_{t-1}$ and $g(y_{t-1}, u_{t-1}) = f(y_{t-1}, u_{t-1}) - y_{t-1}$.

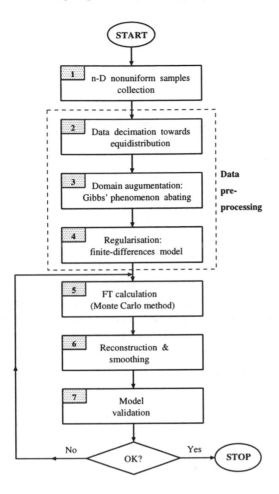

Figure 2.2: Algorithm of the N-D approach.

2. improving accuracy of the RHS reconstruction and dynamics approximation; blocks **3** and **4**.

With data economised and better conditioned, the algorithm proceeds to the essential step (block **5**) of FT calculation. It is an approximation of the corresponding multidimensional integral on the basis of the N-D nonuniform samples. This is a non-standard numerical integration problem, for it is not clear which part of the domain area should be assigned to each sample.[2] However, as the samples are roughly equidistributed (no dense clusters), the Monte Carlo method can be used, which effectively assigns the same area to each sample.

Having computed FT in block **5**, the algorithm does the main step: reconstruction of the

---

[2] The Fourier Transform integral is $\int_D f(x) \exp(-i\omega \cdot x)dx$, where $D \subset \mathbb{R}^N$, and its approximation $\sum_k f(x_k) \exp(-i\omega \cdot x_k)A_k$, where A_k is the area (volume) corresponding to the kth sample $(x_k, f(x_k))$. The key issue is how to generate A_k, so that (i) all A_k add up to the area of D and (ii) each sample gets the right proportion of D; the latter is non-trivial due to nonuniformity of the samples.

NARX model right-hand side (block **6**). Since this is done via multi-dimensional Fourier series, there occur oscillations on the reconstructed surface. These are smoothed, which is done by using Cesáro summability,[3] so that reconstruction and smoothing are inseparable parts of this step. Not only improves this the quality of reconstruction, but also handles noise in data.

The next step, model validation (block **7**), is obviously useful, but also plays an additional role of facilitating the adaptive character of the algorithm. While it is straightforward to compute the reconstruction error (with respect to any useful norm), it is not necessarily the best measure of the quality of the model. This is because we are interested in *dynamics* identification and multi-variable function approximation is only a vehicle for that. A qualitative measure of dynamics is the number and character (attractor/repeller) of equilibria; if the reconstructed function preserves these, while not being too 'wild' elsewhere, the obtained model is useful. The validation procedures implement the reasoning; this entails examination of the low-dimensional cross-sections of the reconstructed surface for the equilibria and data fit. Also, the resulting transients can be generated (via a MATLAB S-function) and investigated both qualitatively and quantitatively. If these procedures indicate that the obtained approximation is not satisfactory, then it is possible to come back to step **5** and increase the number of FT points to be used in the reconstruction (effectively increasing the number of terms in the series). The limit of this adaptation is the number of points passed to **5** from the data pre-processing phase **2–4**.

2.5   SOFTWARE DESCRIPTION

The software implementing the algorithm described in the previous section (Section 2.4) was written in MATLAB and Simulink. The data preprocessing routines, FT calculation, reconstruction and smoothing and qualitative model validation are MATLAB functions, while the resulting model can be used for simulations (and quantitative validation) via a Simulink S-function.

The functional structure of the software, Figure 2.3, decomposes naturally into:

1. the data preparation module, and

2. the reconstruction and validation module.

Module 1 encompasses the MATLAB code for data preprocessing routines and FT calculation on the basis of the preprocessed data (blocks **1–5** in Figure 2.2). The FT information can then be used in two ways in module 2:

1. N-D function reconstruction and validation. The RHS of the identified NARX system is a function of N variables and the algorithm performs its approximation. Different facets of this process can be analysed from the point of view of data fit, using MATLAB code.

---

[3] Representing a function f by a series of functions, $f(x) = \sum_k b_k(x)$, means forming the sequence of partial sums: $s_1(x) = b_1(x), s_2(x) = b_1(x) + b_2(x), s_3(x) = b_1(x) + b_2(x) + b_3(x), \ldots$ with $s_k(x) \to f(x)$. We can also form the sequence of averages of the partial sums, i.e., $r_1(x) = s_1(x), r_2(x) = [s_1(x) + s_2(x)]/2, r_3(x) = [s_1(x) + s_2(x) + s_3(x)]/3, \ldots$; it then follows that $r_k(x) \to f(x)$ and f is said to be Cesàro summable, or (C,1). Ordinary convergence, $s_k(x) \to f(x)$, is simply (C,0)-summability. Since $r_k(x)$ involve averaging, the (C,1) representation is smoother than (C,0) and handles noise better, but requires a larger computational effort.

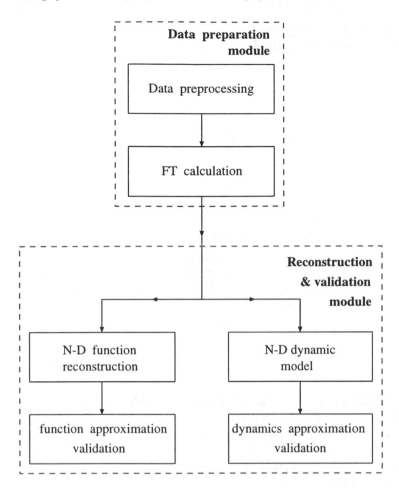

Figure 2.3: Structure of N-D software.

2. N-D dynamic model. The ultimate purpose of the reconstruction of the RHS is to use it for approximation of *dynamics*. Therefore, a different approach is needed to assess the influence of the reconstruction error on the output of the model. The validation must be done with respect to equilibria (qualitative analysis with MATLAB code) and time signals (quantitative analysis with Simulink S-functions).

2.6   APPLICATION

In this section we describe an application of the N-D software to modelling of a nonlinear system. The data points were generated using a model of the real plant – a vehicle; the model was extensively tested and validated. The model under consideration has the form

$$y(t + 1) = f(y(t), u(t)), \tag{2.11}$$

where f is different for different gears; nonlinearity is most pronounced for gear 1. The dynamic vehicle model was subjected to a range of test inputs in order to generate input-output data widely covering the operational space. Our task is to reconstruct f using the simulated input-output data. The data are plotted in Figure 2.4.

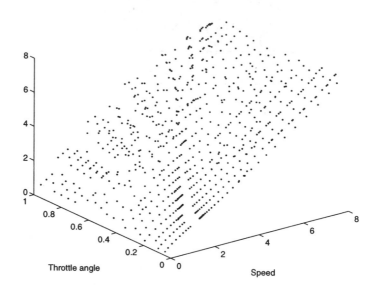

Figure 2.4: All simulated data points

We feed the given data to the pre-processing module which performs two important groups of actions. First, the data points are decimated in order to avoid clustering and to obtain quasi-equidistribution (see Figure 2.5). Then the decimated data are augmented to abate Gibbs' phenomenon and finally they are changed into their differenced version to regularise the underlying ill-posed problem as in Figure 2.6. This figure also illustrates the underlying nonlinearity.

The next step of the algorithm is executed by the Fourier Transform calculation module. An example of the graphical output of this module is given in Figure 2.7. Having calculated the Fourier Transform, we may now proceed to the function reconstruction module which will give the RHS of the NARX model in the form of a 2-D function as in Figure 2.8.

Further validation steps require computation of the cross-sections of the given data and the reconstructed surface. These are obtained in the function validation module and have the form given in Figure 2.9 for this example. Finally, the dynamics validation module is able to evaluate the suitability of the obtained RHS reconstruction for control purposes. The SIMULINK system used for this evaluation is given in Figure 2.11. This system can be used for dynamic simulation.

2.7   SUMMARY OF SIMULATION EXPERIMENTS

The software package described in previous sections has been used for simulation of the N-D nonuniform sampling approach to nonlinear systems modelling. This approach resulted in the Fourier Analysis-based feedforward neural network which is implemented in the software.

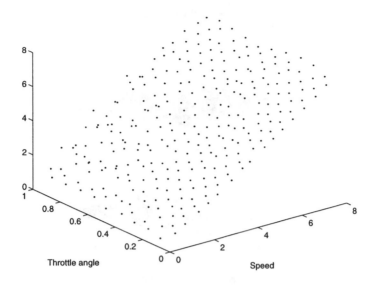

Figure 2.5: Pre-processed data points.

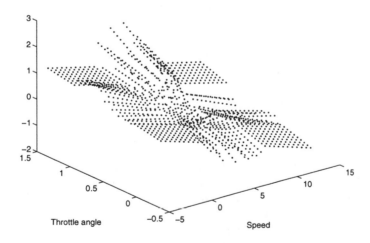

Figure 2.6: Augmented, differenced data points.

2.7.1 Description of experiments

In this summary the main simulation experiments results for the system described are presented. For selected input (α) values 0.1, 0.3, 0.7, 0.85 we obtained the following results of the tests.

In each case the cross-sections of the reconstructed right-hand side of NARX model for the selected input value together with given data points and identity mapping are presented (see 2.9). This test shows how accurate the proposed approximation is, i.e. how well given

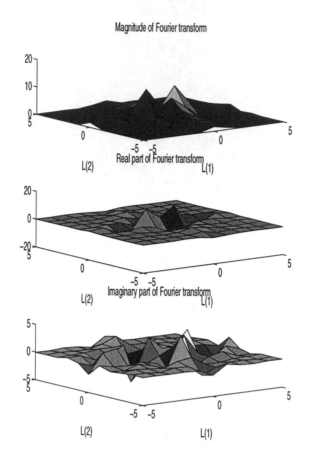

Figure 2.7: 2-D Fourier Transform for vehicle data.

data points fit the surface obtained in N-D approach. Second figure (see Figure 2.10) gives time plots of ND model compared with those of an exact model for the same input signal and the same two initial outputs: y_{min} minimum and y_{max} maximum allowed for given gear. Relative error plots (difference between the output values of the models expressed as a percentage of maximum output value) accompany the time plots. Moreover, mean square error (MSE) values, as a synthetic error measure were calculated in each case. These tests evaluate the dynamic behaviour of the NARX model with the RHS obtained in N-D approach.

Looking at example of the cross-section figures we may notice that for different input values the reconstruction of the RHS is good, i.e. reconstructed curve reasonably well fits into the given data points. Because of smoothing procedure applied (Cesáro summation instead of ordinary summation of Fourier series involved), the curve obtained is not trying 'desperately' to fit all the data points. It is rather trying to interpolate between them smoothly and as accurately as possible. This is a nice feature, because it means that the method is capable, to a certain degree, of dealing with the outliers and noise. All the cross-section figures contain also an identity mapping which allows us to localize the equilibrium

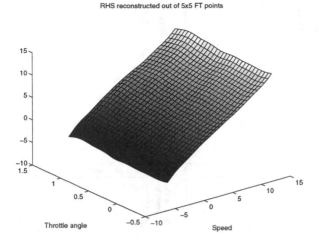

Figure 2.8: Surface plot of reconstructed RHS as a 2-D function.

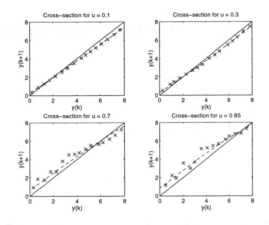

Figure 2.9: Cross-sections of data points and reconstructed 2-D function, where x: given data points; 2–2: cross-section of reconstructed RHS; −: identity mapping.

point. We may see that in some cases even if reconstruction error is reasonably small the placement of equilibrium is different from that for given data points. This results in modelling error which is quantified in time plots figures.

Time plots supplement the cross-sections with the explicit information on dynamic behaviour of the ND model in comparison to exact model. The figures give us not only time plots, but also data points placement on input-output plane.

In general the ND model behaves in a similar way to the exact model. The error between the two depends on input and ranges from about 2% in the best case to about 17% in the worst case. Basic dynamical properties of the underlying nonlinear system were captured to within the degree of accuracy varying for different inputs.

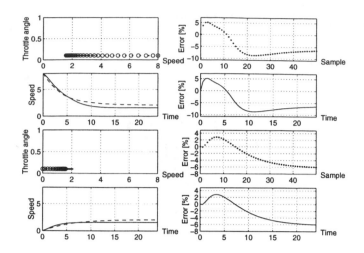

Figure 2.10: Simulation result of dynamic model validation. *Left-hand side plots:* acceleration. *Right-hand side plots:* deceleration.

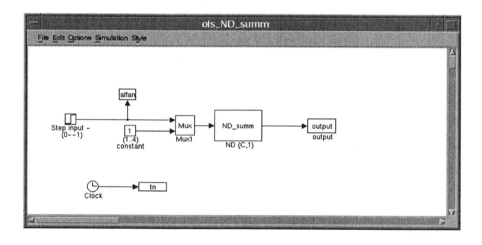

Figure 2.11: SIMULINK diagram for dynamic simulation.

2.7.2   Conclusions

The paper describes a technique for nonlinear system identification from a general model represented by Equation (2.1). Because of the generality the problem is tackled by approximation, prominently manifested in Equation (2.9). The main topic of the paper however is in the MATLAB implementation of the approach, described in detail.

Here are the conclusions which follow the simulation experiments carried out for the N-D sampling based method of nonlinear systems modelling. The presented approach is definitely an interesting choice in case of non-parametric identification of a model without a reasonable linear-in-the-parameters parameterization. Several possible ways of improving the accuracy of the method were investigated. These include: replacing the Monte-Carlo based calculation of the FT with the one based on more sophisticated data space partitioning, i.e., Voronoi diagrams.

Fourier Analysis based neural networks (N-D sampling approach) are capable of modelling the nonlinear system under consideration to within a certain degree of accuracy. The validation was based on evaluation of the approximation accuracy through reconstructed surface cross-sections and what is more important in our case through comparison of N-D model results with those obtained for exact model.

Surface reconstruction turned out to be reasonably accurate in majority of cases under consideration. The cross-sections of reconstructed surface tend to fit data points not only accurately but also taking into account possible outliers and noise.

The major issue is a dynamic modelling error. From the tests presented we may note that this error depends on the input value. The best steady state value of dynamic modelling error achieved is 2% for the input signal 0.35. The worst error values are about 17% for the input signal 0.55.

The synthetic measure of dynamic modelling error was also introduced. This is mean square error (MSE) between the N-D model and exact model. The best MSE values were achieved for the first gear. The lowest MSE value is for input value 0.35 which corresponds to the best case of the dynamic error.

Future work on the method may be pursued, among other possibilities, along the following lines

- Proceed from general to specific by tackling nonlinearities like bilinear, multilinear, polynomic etc. for which documented results in the literature may be exploited

- Error analysis by working with upper and lower bounds on the hypervolumes for the approximation in Equation (2.9)

REFERENCES

S. Chen and S. A. Billings, 1989, Representation of non-linear systems: the NARMAX model. *International Journal of Control*, 49:1013–1032.

R. A. Dwyer, 1991, Higher-dimensional Voronoi diagrams in linear expected time. *Discrete & Computational Geometry*, 6(4):343–367.

A. Dzieliński and R. Żbikowski, 1995, Multidimensional sampling aspects of neurocontrol with feedforward networks. In *Proceedings of the 4th International Conference on Artificial Neural Networks*, pages 240–244, Cambridge, England, 26–28 June 1995.

A. Dzieliński and R. Żbikowski, 1996, A new approach to neurocontrol based on Fourier analysis and nonuniform multi-dimensional sampling. *Applied Mathematics and Computer Science*, 6(3):101–121.

I. J. Leontaritis and S. A. Billings, 1985, Input-output parametric models for non-linear systems. Part I: deterministic non-linear systems. *International Journal of Control*, 41(2):303–328.

A. Okabe, B. Boots, and K. Sugihara, 1992, *Spatial Tessellations. Concepts and Applications of Voronoi Diagrams*. John Wiley & Sons, Chichester.

A. Papoulis, 1962, *The Fourier Integral and Its Applications*. McGraw-Hill, New York.

D. P. Petersen and D. Middleton, 1962, Sampling and reconstruction of wave-number-limited functions in n-dimensional euclidean spaces. *Information and Control*, 5:279–323.

R. M. Sanner and J.-J. E. Slotine, 1992, Gaussian networks for direct adaptive control. *IEEE Transactions on Neural Networks*, 3(6):837–863.

E. M. Stein and G. Weiss, 1971, *Introduction to Fourier Analysis on Euclidean Spaces*. Princeton University Press, Princeton, NJ.

A. H. Stroud, 1971, *Approximate Calculation of Multiple Integrals*. Prentice-Hall, Englewood Cliffs, NJ.

R. Żbikowski and A. Dzieliński, 1996, Fourier transform symmetry and invariance for neurocontrol of NARMA models. *Proceedings of the Second World Congress of Nonlinear Analysis, WCNA-96*, Athens, Greece, 10–17 July 1996.

R. Żbikowski and A. Dzieliński, 1996, Nonuniform sampling approach to control systems modelling with feedforward networks. In R. Żbikowski and K. J. Hunt, editors, *Neural Adaptive Control Technology*, World Scientific series in Robotics and Intelligent Systems, Vol. 15, pages 71–112. World Scientific, Singapore, London.

CHAPTER THREE

Behaviours, Modules, and Duality

Jeffrey Wood[†], Eric Rogers[†] and David H. Owens[‡]

[†] Dept. Electronics and Comp. Science,
University of Southampton, UK
jjw@ecs.soton.ac.uk,
etar@ecs.soton.ac.uk,

[‡] Dept. of Auto. Control and Syst. Eng.
University of Sheffield, UK
d.h.owens@sheffield.ac.uk

The first author has been supported by EPSRC grant no. GR/K 18504
and is currently a Royal Society University Research Fellow.

Abstract

In this chapter we provide an introduction to the behavioural theory of nD systems, with emphasis on the duality between finitely generated modules and differential/ difference behaviours. We provide examples of important problems which have been solved using this approach. Specifically, we look at the Cauchy problem, free variables, exponential trajectories, autonomous systems, and transfer classes.

3.1 INTRODUCTION

Experience has shown that there are a great many problems in generalizing classical 1D systems theory to multidimensional (nD) systems. Some of these problems are fundamentally algebraic in nature, e.g. the distinction in the nD case between factor primeness, minor primeness and zero primeness, or the lack of a Euclidean division algorithm. Other problems concern the apparent absence of relationships between important concepts that are strongly related in the 1D case, e.g. controllability, observability and minimality.

This fragmentation of the theory has resulted in a similar fragmentation of the nD systems theory community, with many researchers considering only a specific aspect of the whole picture. The community would benefit from the introduction of a framework in which all the important concepts of systems theory can be expressed. We believe that the behavioural approach of Willems (1991) is such a framework. Under the behavioural framework, a system is studied in terms of its associated trajectories, with the system equations playing a secondary role. This greatly clarifies the relationship between different sets of system equations (do they represent the same system, or a different system with the same transfer function matrix, or an entirely unrelated system?). It also allows an easy distinction between intrinsic properties of the system and properties of the system representation only.

A further reason for using the behavioural approach is that it allows a strong duality between module theory and nD linear systems theory to be exploited. Under this duality, many important system-theoretic concepts have counterparts in the theory of finitely generated modules over polynomial rings. In this chapter, we describe some of the progress made to date using this approach to nD systems theory, and we look at some specific applications of the duality in more detail.

3.2 DUALITY OF MODULES AND BEHAVIOURS

The behavioural approach to systems theory is due to Willems (Willems 1986, Willems 1991), and centres on the concept of the system behaviour, which is the set of associated trajectories. We propose the following formalism: a *system* is a triple $(\mathcal{A}, q, \mathcal{B})$, where $\mathcal{A}$ is the *signal space*, normally a vector space over some field k, q is the number of system variables (e.g. inputs plus outputs) and $\mathcal{B} \subseteq \mathcal{A}^q$ is the *behaviour*.

We consider (linear, shift-invariant) *differential/ difference behaviours*, which are those which can be described by a finite set of linear differential/ difference equations with constant coefficients. Such behaviours have formerly been termed *autoregressive (AR)*.

Differential/ difference behaviours can be written as the kernel of a polynomial matrix: $\mathcal{B} = \ker_{\mathcal{A}} E, E = k[z_1, \ldots, z_n]^{g,q}$ for some g. Here the ring action of each indeterminate z_i is a backward shift (discrete case) or a partial derivative operator $\partial/\partial t_i$ (continuous case). For example, the 2D differential behaviour with 3 variables described by the single PDE:

$$\frac{\partial w_1}{\partial t_1}(t_1, t_2) + \frac{\partial w_1}{\partial t_2}(t_1, t_2) - \frac{\partial^2 w_2}{\partial t_1 t_2}(t_1, t_2) - 2\frac{\partial^3 w_3}{\partial t_1^3}(t_1, t_2) + w_3(t_1, t_2) = 0$$

can be written as

$$\mathcal{B} = \ker_{\mathcal{A}} E, \qquad E = ((z_1 + z_2) \quad (-z_1 z_2) \quad (1 - 2z_1^3))$$

We say that E is a *kernel representation* of $\mathcal{B}$.

We denote by $\mathcal{R}$ the polynomial ring $k[z_1, \ldots, z_n]$. In the case $\mathcal{A} = k^{\mathbb{Z}^n}$, which allows forward shifts, it is necessary instead to use the Laurent polynomial ring $\mathcal{R} = k[z_1, \ldots, z_n, z_1^{-1}, \ldots, z_n^{-1}]$.

Polynomial row vectors $v \in \mathcal{R}^{1,q}$ now have a natural interpretation as functions on the behaviour. Two such functions v_1, v_2 are equal if their difference, $v_1 - v_2$, is in the *orthogonal module* $\mathcal{B}^{\perp}$, defined as the set of all system equations in $\mathcal{R}^{1,q}$. The set of *system observables*, i.e. distinct functions on the behaviour, is then naturally identified with the factor module $\mathcal{R}^{1,q}/\mathcal{B}^{\perp}$. The concept of a system observable was first formally introduced by Pommaret (1992). The *module of system observables*, termed the *system dynamics* by Fliess (1990), is denoted by $M := \mathcal{R}^{1,q}/\mathcal{B}^{\perp}$. M is a finitely generated module over the ring $\mathcal{R}$.

We can establish the following direct relationship between M and $\mathcal{B}$:

Theorem 3.1 *(Oberst 1990, 2.13)* *A differential/ difference behaviour $\mathcal{B}$ is related to its module of observables by:*

$$\mathcal{B} = D(M) := \text{Hom}_{\mathcal{R}}(M, \mathcal{A}) \tag{3.1}$$

In this situation, we call $\mathcal{B}$ the *dual* of M. There is also a suitable notion of the dual of a map $\phi : M_1 \mapsto M_2$ of finitely generated $\mathcal{R}$-modules; we have $D(\phi) : D(M_2) \mapsto D(M_1)$ defined for any $f \in D(M_2)$ by $D(\phi)f := f \circ \phi$. In the important case where $\phi : \mathcal{R}^{1,g} \mapsto \mathcal{R}^{1,q}$ is the natural left action of a polynomial matrix, we can show that $D(\mathcal{R}^{1,g}) = \mathcal{A}^g$,

$D(\mathcal{R}^{1,q}) = \mathcal{A}^q$, and the dual map $D(\phi) : \mathcal{A}^q \mapsto \mathcal{A}^g$ is the action of the same polynomial matrix given on the signal space $\mathcal{A}^q$ as described previously.

The main fundamental result, due to Oberst, depends upon the choice of signal space $\mathcal{A}$. It holds for example in the discrete cases $\mathcal{A} = k^{\mathbb{N}^n}, k^{\mathbb{Z}^n} (k = \mathbb{R}, \mathbb{C})$, and in the continuous cases $\mathcal{A} = \mathcal{C}^{\infty}(\mathbb{R}^n, k), \mathcal{D}'(\mathbb{R}^n, k), (k = \mathbb{R}, \mathbb{C})$.

Theorem 3.2 *(Oberst 1990, 2.54) Let $\mathcal{A}$ be one of the signal spaces listed above. Then duality is contravariant and faithfully exact. In other words, given a complex of modules*

$$\cdots \xrightarrow{\phi_{i+2}} F_{i+1} \xrightarrow{\phi_{i+1}} F_i \xrightarrow{\phi_i} F_{i-1} \xrightarrow{\phi_{i-1}} \cdots, \tag{3.2}$$

i.e. a set of maps $\phi_i : F_i \mapsto F_{i-1}$ with im $\phi_{i+1} \subseteq \ker \phi_i$ for all i, and its dual complex

$$\cdots \xrightarrow{D(\phi_{i-1})} D(F_{i-1}) \xrightarrow{D(\phi_i)} D(F_i) \xrightarrow{D(\phi_{i+1})} D(F_{i+1}) \xrightarrow{D(\phi_{i+2})} \cdots, \tag{3.3}$$

we have that (3.2) is exact (i.e. im $\phi_{i+1} = \ker \phi_i$ for all i) if and only if (3.3) is exact.

This seemingly abstract result has a multitude of powerful consequences. For example, it follows (Oberst 1990, 2.48) that the orthogonal module $\mathcal{B}^{\perp}$ is the set of all $\mathcal{R}$-linear combinations of any given set of system equations, i.e. in the continuous case the set of all equations obtainable from these by addition, scalar multiplication, and differentiation. Formally, we have

$$\mathcal{B} = \ker_{\mathcal{A}} E \quad \Rightarrow \quad \mathcal{B}^{\perp} = \mathrm{Im}_{\mathcal{R}} E, \quad M = \mathrm{Coker}_{\mathcal{R}} E, \tag{3.4}$$

where

$$\mathrm{Im}_{\mathcal{R}} E := \{v \in \mathcal{R}^{1,q} \mid v = xE \text{ for some } x \in \mathcal{R}^{1,g}\}, \tag{3.5}$$

$$\mathrm{Coker}_{\mathcal{R}} E := \mathcal{R}^{1,q} / \mathrm{Im}_{\mathcal{R}} E \tag{3.6}$$

This does not hold for all classes of systems; e.g. in the delay-differential case (Glüsing-Lüerßen 1997, Ex. 2.3).

The power of Theorem 3.2 comes from the fact that many structural properties can be expressed in terms of exact sequences. For example, any property which can be expressed by identifying the kernel or image of a given map is equivalent to the exactness of a given sequence (complex). Remarkably, properties of system behaviours which appear at first sight to be purely analytic can often be described in this way. Accordingly, we obtain a strong correspondence between system-theoretic properties and module-theoretic properties, and we can use the vast and powerful machinery of commutative algebra to develop nD behavioural theory.

Here are some examples of important questions which have been answered using the behavioural approach in combination with module duality:

1. How can we find an initial condition set for a discrete behaviour, and how can we compute a trajectory from a set of initial conditions?

2. What are controllability and observability, and how can we characterize them?

3. What does it mean for a system to be autonomous, and how can we characterize it?

4. How many free variables does a given behaviour have (i.e. to how many components can we make an arbitrary assignment within the signal space)?

5. What is a pole (decoupling zero, etc) of an nD system?

6. What is the transfer matrix of an nD system, and under what conditions do two systems have the same transfer matrix?

7. How can we measure the complexity of an nD system?

These questions and others have been answered (some for discrete systems and others for both continuous and discrete systems) in (Fornasini *et al.* 1993, Fornasini & Valcher 1995, Oberst 1990, Pillai & Shankar 1999, Rocha 1990, Wood *et al.* 1999a, Wood *et al.* 1999b, Zerz 1996) and other works.

Let us now review the answers to some of these problems.

3.3 THE CAUCHY PROBLEM

The Cauchy problem for a system is to find a complete set of independent initial conditions, the values of which determine any system trajectory. In the discrete case $B \subseteq (k^q)^{\mathbb{N}^n}$, this amounts to finding a subset T_1 of $\{1, \ldots, q\} \times \mathbb{N}^n$ such that the values of a trajectory on the points of T_1 are unconstrained, and these values determine the rest of the trajectory completely. For (linear, shift-invariant) difference behaviours, Oberst has provided a family of solutions to this problem (Oberst 1990, para. 5). His solution has been extended to behaviours with the signal space $k^{\mathbb{Z}^n}$ by several authors (Pauer & Unterkircher 1997, Pauer & Zampieri 1996, Zampieri 1994, Zerz & Oberst 1993).

Oberst's solution to the Cauchy problem is as follows. Take a behaviour $B = \ker_A E \subseteq \mathcal{A}^q$, and consider a monomial ordering on $\mathcal{R}^{1,q}$, i.e. a total ordering $\geq$ of the monomials of $\mathcal{R}^{1,q}$ such that if m_1 and m_2 are monomials of $\mathcal{R}^{1,q}$ and $x \notin k$ is a monomial of $\mathcal{R}$ then $m_1 \geq m_2$ implies $xm_1 \geq xm_2 > m_2$. We identify the monomials of $\mathcal{R}^{1,q}$ with the points of $\{1, \ldots, q\} \times \mathbb{N}^n$ in the natural way. Now for any system equation $v \in B^{\perp}$, the initial term, denoted $\text{in}_\geq v$, is defined to be that term of v corresponding to the highest monomial of v under $\geq$. The module generated by the initial terms of all $v \in B^{\perp}$ is called the *initial term module* and denoted by $\text{in}_\geq B^{\perp}$.

A classical result of Macaulay is that the monomials of $\mathcal{R}^{1,q}$ which are outside $\text{in}_\geq B^{\perp}$ form a k-basis for $M = \mathcal{R}^{1,q}/B^{\perp}$ (Eisenbud 1995). From this result we obtain the following:

Theorem 3.3 *(Oberst 1990, para. 5) Let $\geq$ be a monomial ordering on $\mathcal{R}^{1,q}$, and $B \subseteq \mathcal{A}^q$ a differential/ difference behaviour. Let $\text{in}_\geq B^{\perp}$ be the initial term module with respect to $\geq$ of the orthogonal module. Then the set of points of $\{1, \ldots, q\} \times \mathbb{N}^n$ corresponding to monomials of $\mathcal{R}^{1,q}$ outside $\text{in}_\geq B^{\perp}$ are a complete initial condition set for B.*

Furthermore, we can construct the given initial condition set by finding a *Gröbner basis* for $B^{\perp}$, i.e. a generating set for $B^{\perp}$ whose initial terms generate $\text{in}_\geq B^{\perp}$. This can be done via Buchberger's algorithm (Buchberger 1985, Cox *et al.* 1996, Eisenbud 1995). The equations of a Gröbner basis can be used to generate any trajectory from its initial condition values.

As an example, consider the 2D discrete behaviour (defined on $\mathbb{N}^2$) given by

$$\mathcal{B} = \ker_{\mathcal{A}} \begin{pmatrix} z_1^3 \\ z_1^2 z_2 + z_1 z_2^2 \end{pmatrix}$$

In this case, $\mathcal{B}^\perp \subseteq \mathcal{R}$ is the ideal $(z_1^3, z_1^2 z_2 + z_1 z_2^2)$. Choosing $\geq$ to be the lexicographic ("dictionary") ordering with $z_1 > z_2$, we find that $\{z_1^3, z_1^2 z_2 + z_1 z_2^2\}$ is not a Gröbner basis of $\mathcal{B}^\perp$ with respect to this ordering, because the initial term of the element $z_1 z_2^3 \in \mathcal{B}^\perp$ is not generated by the initial terms of the two given generators. Applying Buchberger's algorithm, a Gröbner basis is constructed as $\{z_1^3, z_1^2 z_2 + z_1 z_2^2, z_1 z_2^3\}$. The initial terms are $\{z_1^3, z_1^2 z_2, z_1 z_2^3\}$, and the monomials outside $\text{in}_{\geq} \mathcal{B}^\perp$ are those monomials which are not divisible by any of the given initial terms. By Theorem 3.3, an initial condition set for $\mathcal{B}$ is given by

$$\{(0, a_2) \mid a_2 \in \mathbb{N}\} \ \cup \ \{(1,0), (1,1), (1,2), (2,0)\}$$

It is not hard to see how the Gröbner basis can be used to compute a trajectory from its values on this set.

In the continuous case, similar techniques have been derived for finding the formal power series solutions of a set of PDEs; see e.g. the introduction to (Pommaret 1994) for a discussion.

3.4 FREE VARIABLES

A set of system variables $w_{i_1}, \ldots, w_{i_l} \in \{w_1, \ldots, w_q\}$ is said to be *free* if these variables can take any value in $\mathcal{A}^l$. In the following result, $e_1, \ldots, e_q$ denote the natural basis vectors of $\mathcal{R}^{1,q}$.

Lemma 3.4 *(Wood et al. 1999b, proof of Lemma 5)* Let $\mathcal{B} = D(M) \subseteq \mathcal{A}^q$ *be a differential/ difference behaviour, and let* $\Phi \subseteq \{1, \ldots, q\}$. *Then the set of variables* $\{w_i \mid i \in \Phi\}$ *is free if and only if the observables* $\{e_i + \mathcal{B}^\perp \mid i \in \Phi\}$ *are linearly independent over* $\mathcal{R}$.

It follows that the (maximum) *number of free variables* of $\mathcal{B}$ is equal to the maximum number of linearly independent elements of M. We write this quantity as $m(\mathcal{B})$. It is also known that $m(\mathcal{B}) = q - \text{rank } E$ (Oberst 1990, Thm. 2.69), which means in particular that the rank of a kernel representation is independent of the representation.

For any of the given signal spaces, consider the 2D behaviour

$$\mathcal{B} = \ker_{\mathcal{A}} \begin{pmatrix} z_1^2 - 1 & z_1 z_2 - z_2 & 0 \\ z_1 z_2 + z_2 & z_2^2 & z_1 \end{pmatrix}$$

From the equation

$$(0 \ \ 0 \ \ z_1 - z_1^2) = z_2(z_1^2 - 1 \ \ z_1 z_2 - z_2 \ \ 0) - (z_1 - 1)(z_1 z_2 + z_2 \ \ z_2^2 \ \ z_1)$$

we see that the observable $e_3 + \mathcal{B}^\perp$ is not linearly independent in M (a multiple of e_3 is in $\mathcal{B}^\perp$). Accordingly, $\{w_3\}$ is not a set of free variables in $\mathcal{B}$. However, $\{w_1\}$ and $\{w_2\}$ are sets of free variables. The number of free variables is 1, and the rank of the given kernel representation is $3 - 1 = 2$.

Furthermore, we discover that the number of free variables is additive (Wood *et al.* 1999b), i.e. given an exact sequence

$$0 \longrightarrow \mathcal{B}_1 \longrightarrow \mathcal{B}_2 \longrightarrow \mathcal{B}_3 \longrightarrow 0$$

of behaviours, we have

$$m(\mathcal{B}_2) = m(\mathcal{B}_1) + m(\mathcal{B}_3)$$

This has interesting consequences; for example, for any sub-behaviours $\mathcal{B}_1, \mathcal{B}_2$ of $\mathcal{A}^q$, we have

$$m(\mathcal{B}_1) + m(\mathcal{B}_2) = m(\mathcal{B}_1 + \mathcal{B}_2) + m(\mathcal{B}_1 \cap \mathcal{B}_2) \tag{3.7}$$

3.5 EXPONENTIAL TRAJECTORIES AND AUTONOMOUS SYSTEMS

Exponential trajectories are of course of great importance in the study of poles, zeros, stability, etc. For simplicity we assume here that $k = \mathbb{C}$; the real case is more complex(!) but can be dealt with similarly. By an *exponential trajectory of frequency* $\underline{a} \in \mathbb{C}^n$, we shall therefore mean a trajectory of the form

$$w(\underline{t}) = v_0 e^{a_1 t_1 + \cdots + a_n t_n}, \qquad v_0 \in \mathbb{C}^q \tag{3.8}$$

in the continuous case, or

$$w(\underline{t}) = v_0 a_1^{t_1} \cdots a_n^{t_n}, \qquad v_0 \in \mathbb{C}^q \tag{3.9}$$

in the discrete case (Oberst 1995, Wood *et al.* 1999a). For the discrete case $\mathcal{A} = k^{\mathbb{Z}^n}$ it is appropriate throughout this discussion to restrict attention to points $\underline{a} \in (\mathbb{C}\backslash 0)^n$.

Algebraically, the significance of an exponential trajectory $w(\underline{t})$ of frequency $\underline{a}$ is that it is killed by the operators $z_1 - a_1, \ldots, z_n - a_n$. In other words, the *annihilator* of w contains the (maximal) ideal generated by $z_1 - a_1, \ldots, z_n - a_n$, and is equal to this ideal provided that $w \neq 0$.

Annihilators are of great importance in algebraic systems theory. The *annihilator* of an arbitrary module M, denoted ann M, is the ideal of all elements $r \in \mathcal{R}$ such that $rx = 0$ for all $x \in M$. Thus the annihilator of a behaviour $\mathcal{B}$ is the set of all equations satisfied by each system variable (independently of the values of the others). We have the following useful result:

Lemma 3.5 *(Wood* et al. *1999a) For any finitely generated module M,*

$$\text{ann } M = \text{ann } D(M) \tag{3.10}$$

The concept of an annihilator is already known from classical 1D linear systems theory. If we have a linear state-space model $\dot{x}(t) = Ax(t) - Bu(t)$, then the behaviour with input $u(t)$ equal to zero is given in the current formalism by $\mathcal{B}_{x,0} = \ker_{\mathcal{A}}(zI - A)$. The annihilator of this behaviour is equal to the ideal generated by the well-known annihilating polynomial or minimal polynomial of the matrix A (Kalman *et al.* 1969). In (Wood *et al.* 1998), it is shown that the annihilator can be used to characterize the "degree of primeness" of an nD polynomial matrix, and in particular that the well-known concept of a Bézout identity is intimately connected with annihilators.

The *characteristic variety* of B, written $V(\text{ann } B)$, is the set of all points $\underline{a} \in \mathbb{C}^n$ at which every point in the annihilator of B vanishes (Wood *et al.* 1999a); this concept comes from the theory of PDEs. Now if B contains a non-zero exponential trajectory w with frequency $\underline{a}$, then ann $B \subseteq$ ann $w = (z_1 - a_1, \ldots, z_n - a_n)$, and so $\underline{a}$ is a point in the characteristic variety. The converse also holds.

Furthermore, if $B = \ker_A E$, then the ideal of qth order minors of E and the annihilator of B have the same "radical" (Eisenbud 1995, Prop. 20.7) and therefore vanish at the same points. Putting all this together, we have:

Theorem 3.6 *(Wood* et al. *1999a) Let $B = D(M)$ be a behaviour with kernel representation E, and let $\underline{a} \in \mathbb{C}^n$. The following are equivalent:*

1. $\underline{a} \in V(\text{ann } B) = V(\text{ann } M)$.

2. $E(\underline{a})$ *has less than full column rank.*

3. B *contains a non-zero exponential trajectory with frequency $\underline{a}$.*

Consider for example the following behaviour over the signal space $\mathcal{A} = \mathcal{C}^\infty(\mathbb{R}^2, \mathbb{R})$:

$$B = \ker_A E, \qquad E = \begin{pmatrix} z_2 + 1 & z_1 + 2 \\ z_1 - 1 & -z_2 \\ 0 & z_1 z_2 \end{pmatrix}$$

The order 2 minors of E are $(-z_2^2 - z_2 - z_1^2 - z_1 + 2)$, $z_1 z_2(z_2 + 1)$ and $z_1 z_2(z_1 - 1)$. The characteristic variety consists in this case of a finite number of points, where these minors vanish:

$$V(\text{ann } B) = \{(1, -1), (0, 1), (0, -2), (1, 0), (-2, 0)\}$$

and we can soon check that B contains the following exponential trajectories:

$$\begin{pmatrix} 1 \\ 0 \end{pmatrix} e^{t_1 - t_2}, \quad \begin{pmatrix} 1 \\ -1 \end{pmatrix} e^{t_2}, \quad \begin{pmatrix} 2 \\ 1 \end{pmatrix} e^{-2t_2}, \quad \begin{pmatrix} 3 \\ -1 \end{pmatrix} e^{t_1}, \quad \begin{pmatrix} 0 \\ 1 \end{pmatrix} e^{-2t_1}$$

Theorem 3.6 is the basis for a theory of poles of nD behaviours, which covers concepts analogous to input and output decoupling zeros, etc (Wood *et al.* 1999a).

Another consequence of the relationship between the ideal of qth order minors of E and the annihilator of $B = \ker_A E = D(M)$ is the following:

Lemma 3.7 *Let $B = D(M)$ be a behaviour with kernel representation E. Then the following are equivalent:*

1. B *has no free variables.*

2. E *has full column rank.*

3. ann $B \neq 0$.

4. ann $M \neq 0$; *equivalently, M is a torsion module, i.e. has no linearly independent elements.*

The above conditions are both necessary and sufficient for a discrete behaviour to be *autonomous* in the sense of a trajectory definition given in (Fornasini *et al.* 1993, Wood *et al.* 1999b). Another equivalent condition is that the characteristic variety of B is not equal to $\mathbb{C}^n$, a property proposed as a definition of autonomy for continuous behaviours in (Pillai & Shankar 1999).

The complementary concept to autonomy is controllability, which again admits a behavioural definition (Pillai & Shankar 1999, Wood *et al.* 1999b, Wood & Zerz 1999); it is interesting that controllability is equivalent to the algebraic property of torsionfree-ness (see (Wood *et al.* 1999a) and the references given in the discussion of controllability).

3.6 TRANSFER CLASSES

Consider a behaviour with a partitioning of system variables $B = B_{u,y}$ described by $P(\underline{z})y = Q(\underline{z})u$, i.e. a kernel representation is $B_{u,y} = \ker_A (-Q \ P)$. Suppose further that rank $(-Q \ P) = $ rank P and that P has full column rank p. In this situation, we call the partitioning of system variables a *free input/output structure on B*. Equivalently, we have that the behaviour $B_{0,y} \cong \ker_A P$ of all trajectories with $u = 0$ has no free variables, but that the number of free variables of B is equal to $q - $ rank $(-Q \ P) = q - p$. Thus a free input/ output structure describes the situation where the variables u are a maximal set of free variables, the 'inputs', which determine the 'outputs' y to within an autonomous behaviour.

In this situation, the columns of Q are $\mathcal{R}$-linearly dependent on the columns of P, and so there exists a (unique) rational function matrix G with $PG = Q$. This matrix is called the *transfer matrix* of the behaviour (with respect to the given free input/output structure) (Oberst 1990, Thm. 2.69). Note that, in the case where $(-Q \ P)$ has full row rank, this reduces to the well-known case of a left matrix fraction description $G = P^{-1}Q$.

This leads to the question: under what circumstances do two behaviours with the same free input/output structure have the same transfer matrix?

Theorem 3.8 *(Oberst 1990, Thms. 2.94,7.17,7.21) If $B_1 = D(M_1)$ and $B_2 = D(M_2)$, then B_1 and B_2 have a common free input/output structure, and the same transfer matrix with respect to that structure, if and only if $Q(\mathcal{R}) \otimes_\mathcal{R} M_1 = Q(\mathcal{R}) \otimes_\mathcal{R} M_2$, where $Q(\mathcal{R}) = k(z_1, \ldots, z_n)$. In this situation, we say that B_1 and B_2 have the same transfer class. In particular, the transfer class of a behaviour is independent of the free input/output structure considered.*

Each transfer class has a unique element which is minimal with respect to set inclusion, called the minimal realization of the transfer matrix. Given a behaviour $B = D(M)$ with transfer matrix G, the minimal realization of G is given by $D(M/tM)$, where $tM \subseteq M$ is the torsion submodule of M, i.e. the set of all elements of M which have a non-zero annihilator.

Note that M/tM is always torsionfree, and so minimal realizations are always controllable, and conversely, i.e. minimality (in the transfer class) is equivalent to controllability. This may seem odd, given the classical theory in which minimality is equivalent to controllability plus observability. However in the current framework, we have not introduced states, and so observability does not play a role. Another point to note is that since duality reverses the arrows of mappings, $D(M/tM)$ is a sub-behaviour of $D(M)$, as expected.

Going back to the behaviour considered in section 3.4, and taking w_1 to be the (single) input, we find

$$P = \begin{pmatrix} z_1 z_2 - z_2 & 0 \\ z_2^2 & z_1 \end{pmatrix}, \quad Q = \begin{pmatrix} -(z_1^2 - 1) \\ -(z_1 z_2 + z_2) \end{pmatrix}$$

$$\Rightarrow \quad G = P^{-1}Q = \begin{pmatrix} \frac{z_1 + 1}{-z_2} \\ 0 \end{pmatrix},$$

the minimal realization of which is given by the following sub-behaviour of $\mathcal{B}$:

$$\mathcal{B}^c = \begin{pmatrix} z_1 + 1 & z_2 & 0 \\ 0 & 0 & 1 \end{pmatrix}$$

It is not hard to check that the rows of this matrix are torsion elements in $\mathcal{R}^{1,q}/\mathcal{B}^\perp$.

3.7 CONCLUSIONS

We have given a brief introduction to nD behavioural theory and in particular the duality theory due to Oberst, and we have illustrated the scope of the theory by considering a variety of different nD systems problems. We conclude by giving a number of reasons for including algebraic methods in any cohesive approach to nD systems theory.

1. The algebraic characterizations of system-theoretic concepts are generally concise and easy to manipulate. For example, the algebraic characterization of autonomy of a behaviour is simply ann $\mathcal{B} \neq 0$.

2. Development of the duality allows difficult results from algebra to be applied to systems theory, generally providing easier proofs than arguments from first principles.

3. The duality also suggests non-obvious relationships between behavioural concepts, through the known relationships between the corresponding algebraic concepts.

4. Algebraic properties are representation-independent in the strong sense that they are unaffected by changes of basis or re-embeddings of a behaviour $\mathcal{B} \subseteq \mathcal{A}^q \hookrightarrow \mathcal{A}^{q+1}$. Furthermore, it becomes possible to consider constructions such as factors of behaviours, which are useful in certain proofs, without having a system-theoretic interpretation of such objects.

5. In some cases, commutative algebra is the only practical language in which to express results in nD systems theory (e.g. Oberst's solution of the Cauchy problem).

6. The algebraic community has produced algorithms, largely using Gröbner bases, for computing many objects of interest in module theory. These algorithms can be applied to many system-theoretic problems. Specialist commutative algebra packages exist, many of which are in the public domain. Indeed, it is possible to construct initial condition sets, annihilators and minimal realizations, and test for controllability and autonomy, etc, by applying algorithms in these packages.

REFERENCES

B. Buchberger, 1985, Gröbner bases: An algorithmic method in polynomial ideal theory. In N.K. Bose, editor, *Multidimensional Systems Theory*, pages 184–232. D. Reidel.

D. Cox, J. Little, and D. O'Shea, 1996, *Ideals, Varieties and Algorithms*. Springer-Verlag, 2nd edition.

D. Eisenbud, 1995, *Commutative Algebra with a View Toward Algebraic Geometry*, volume 150 of *Graduate Texts in Mathematics*. Springer-Verlag .

M. Fliess, 1990, Some basic structural properties of generalized linear systems. *Systems and Control Letters*, 15:391–396 .

E. Fornasini, P. Rocha, and S. Zampieri, 1993, State space realization of 2-D finite-dimensional behaviours. *SIAM J. on Contr. and Opt.*, 31(6):1502–1517 .

E. Fornasini and M.E. Valcher, 1995, A polynomial matrix approach to the behavioural analysis of nD systems. In *Proc. ECC'95*, pages 1757–1762 .

H. Glüsing-Lüerßen, 1997, A behavioral approach to delay-differential systems. *SIAM J. Control Optim.*, 35(2):480–499 .

R.E. Kalman, P.L. Falb, and M.A. Arbib, 1969, *Topics in Mathematical Systems Theory*. International Series in Pure and Applied Mathematics. McGraw-Hill.

U. Oberst, 1990, Multidimensional constant linear systems. *Acta Applicandae Mathematicae*, 20:1–175.

U. Oberst, 1995, Variations on the fundamental principle for linear systems of partial differential and difference equations with constant coefficients. *Applicable Algebra in Engineering, Communication and Computing*, 6(4/5):211–243.

F. Pauer and A. Unterkircher, 1997, Gröbner bases for ideals in Laurent polynomial rings and their application to systems of difference equations. Preprint.

F. Pauer and S. Zampieri, 1996, Gröbner bases with respect to generalized term orders and their application to the modelling problem. *J. Symbolic Computation*, 21:155–168.

H. Pillai and S. Shankar, 1999, A behavioral approach to control of distributed systems. *SIAM J. on Contr. and Opt.*, 37(2):388–408.

J.-F. Pommaret, 1992, New perspectives in control theory for partial differential equations. *IMA Journal on Mathematical Control and Information*, 9:305–330.

J.-F. Pommaret, 1994, *Partial Differential Equations and Group Theory: New Perspectives for Applications*, volume 293 of *Mathematics and Its Applications*. Kluwer, Dordrecht.

P. Rocha, 1990, *Structure and Representation of 2-D Systems*. PhD thesis, University of Groningen, The Netherlands.

J.C. Willems, 1986, From time series to linear system — part I: Finite-dimensional linear time invariant systems. *Automatica*, 22(5):561–580.

J.C. Willems, 1991, Paradigms and puzzles in the theory of dynamical systems. *IEEE Trans. on Auto. Contr.*, 36(3):259–294.

J. Wood, U. Oberst, E. Rogers, and D.H. Owens, 2000, A behavioural approach to the pole structure of 1D and nD linear systems. *SIAM Journal of Control and Optimization*, 32(8):627–661.

J. Wood, E. Rogers, and D.H. Owens, 1998, A formal theory of matrix primeness. *Mathematics of Control, Signals and Systems*, 11(1):40–78.

J. Wood, E. Rogers, and D.H. Owens, 1999, Controllable and autonomous nD linear systems. *Mult. Systems and Signal Processing*, 10(1):33–69.

J. Wood and E. Zerz, 1999, Notes on the definition of behavioural controllability. *Systems and Control Letters*, 37:31–37.

S. Zampieri, 1994, A solution of the Cauchy problem for multidimensional discrete linear shift-invariant systems. *Linear Algebra and Its Applications*, 202:143–162.

E. Zerz, 1996, Primeness of multivariate polynomial matrices. *Systems and Control Letters*, 29(3):139–146.

E. Zerz and U. Oberst, 1993, The canonical Cauchy problem for linear systems of partial difference equations with constant coefficients over the complete r-dimensional integral lattice $\mathbb{Z}^r$. *Acta Applicandae Mathematicae*, 31(3):249–273.

PART TWO

Control of Multidimensional Systems and Applications

The section presents a selection of both theoretically and practically oriented aspects of nD systems control.

First, Zhiping Lin (Nanjang, Singapore) revisits output feedback stabilizability and stabilization of linear nD systems.

Next, Li Xu (Asahi, Japan) and Osami Saito (Chiba, Japan) review recent results in nD systems control theory in the so-called practical sense, which means here that the input and output signals are permitted to be unbounded in at most one dimension. This situation occurs frequently in practical applications.

The next paper by E. Rogers (Southampton, UK) and D. H. Owens (Sheffield, UK) discusses two decades of research in linear repetitive processes, sketches current open problems and provides a perspective for future research in this area. The following paper by K. Galkowski (Zielona Gora, Poland), E. Rogers (Southampton, UK), A. Gramacki (Zielona Gora, Poland), J. Gramacki (Zielona Gora, Poland) and D. H. Owens (Sheffield, UK), relates also to repetitive processes, and provides some new insight to discrete versions of these processes with so-called dynamic boundary conditions, a situation which is unknown in the classical 1D theory.

The last two chapters in this section are devoted to the extremely important problem of the optimal control of 2D systems. Firstly, M. Dymkov (National Academy of Sciences, Belarus) studies this problem for continuous-discrete 2D systems. Secondly, D. Idczak and S. Walczak (Łódź, Poland) approach the question in the context of continuous Roesser models.

CHAPTER FOUR

Output Feedback Stabilizability and Stabilization of Linear n-D Systems

Zhiping Lin

School of Electrical and Electronic Engineering
Nanyang Technological University, Singapore
EZPLin@ntu.edu.sg

Abstract

This chapter gives an overview of output feedback stabilizability and stabilization of linear multidimensional (n-D) discrete systems. The emphasis is on multi-input–multi-output systems and the matrix fraction description approach. The discussion will focus on three topics: 1. *Stabilizability*. Determine whether a given linear n-D system is output feedback stabilizable. 2. *Stabilization*. Construct a stabilizing compensator for a stabilizable system. 3. *Parametrization*. Parametrize all stabilizing compensators for a stabilizable system. After reviewing the progress and the state of the art in these topics, a number of related issues are briefly mentioned. Some open problems are then posed at the end of the chapter.

4.1 INTRODUCTION

The problem of output feedback stabilizability and stabilization of linear 1-D as well as n-D systems has drawn much attention in the past years because of its importance in control and systems (see , e.g., (Bisiacco 1985, Bisiacco *et al.* 1985, Bisiacco *et al.* 1986a, Bisiacco *et al.* 1986b, Bisiacco *et al.* 1988, Bisiacco *et al.* 1989, Fornasini 1988, Guiver & Bose 1985, Lin 1988a, Lin 1998, Lin 1999a, Raman & Liu 1984, Raman & Liu 1986, Shankar & Sule 1992, Sule 1994, Vidyasagar 1985, Xu *et al.* 1994b, Xu *et al.* 1998, Youla *et al.* 1976) and the references therein). The matrix fraction description (MFD) approach is probably one of the best known methods for attacking this problem since it embraces, within a single framework, various linear systems such as continuous as well as discrete systems, lumped as well as distributed systems, 1-D as well as n-D systems, etc. (see, e.g., (Vidyasagar 1985)). Consider the feedback system shown in Figure 4.1, where P represents a plant (system) and C represents a compensator. The relationship between $\mathbf{u}_1$, $\mathbf{u}_2$ and $\mathbf{e}_1$, $\mathbf{e}_2$ can be expressed as:

$$
\begin{bmatrix} \mathbf{e}_1 \\ \mathbf{e}_2 \end{bmatrix} = \underbrace{\begin{bmatrix} (I+PC)^{-1} & -P(I+CP)^{-1} \\ C(I+PC)^{-1} & (I+CP)^{-1} \end{bmatrix}}_{H_{eu}} \begin{bmatrix} \mathbf{u}_1 \\ \mathbf{u}_2 \end{bmatrix} \tag{4.1}
$$

A given plant P is said to be (output) feedback stabilizable if and only if there exists a compensator C such that the feedback system H_{eu} is stable, i.e., each entry of H_{eu} has

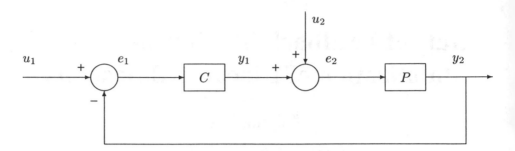

Figure 4.1: Feedback system.

no poles in the unstable region (Vidyasagar 1985). For a linear n-D discrete system, the feedback system is structurally stable[1] if and only if each entry of H_{eu} has no poles in the closed unit polydisc $\overline{U}^n = \{(z_1, \ldots, z_n) : |z_1| \leq 1, \ldots, |z_n| \leq 1\}$ (Bose 1982, Jury 1986).

In this chapter, we give an overview of output feedback stabilizability and stabilization of linear n-D ($n \geq 2$) discrete systems. The emphasis is on multi-input-multi-output (MIMO) systems and the matrix fraction description (MFD) approach. The discussion will focus on three topics:

1) *Stabilizability.* Determine whether a given linear n-D system is feedback stabilizable.

2) *Stabilization.* Construct a stabilizing compensator for a stabilizable system.

3) *Parametrization.* Parametrize all stabilizing compensators for a stabilizable system.

The progress and the state of the art in these topics will be reviewed in Sections 4.2 to 4.4. Section 4.2 is about 2-D systems, while Sections 4.3 and 4.4 are on n-D ($n \geq 3$) SISO (single-input–single-output) and MIMO systems, respectively. A number of related issues will then be briefly mentioned in Section 4.5. Finally, some open problems will be posed in Section 4.6.

Some notation is required before moving to the next section. We shall denote $\mathbf{R(z)} = \mathbf{R}(z_1, \ldots, z_n)$ the set of rational functions in complex variables $z_1, \cdots, z_n$ with coefficients in the field of real numbers $\mathbf{R}$; $\mathbf{R[z]}$ the set of polynomials in complex variables $z_1, \cdots, z_n$ with coefficients in $\mathbf{R}$; $\mathbf{R}^{m \times l}[\mathbf{z}]$ the set of $m \times l$ matrices with entries in $\mathbf{R[z]}$, *etc.* Throughout this chapter, the arguments $(\mathbf{z})$ is omitted whenever its omission does not cause confusion.

4.2   2-D SYSTEMS

The problem of feedback stabilization of 2-D systems using the MFD approach has attracted much attention for over a decade (Bisiacco 1985, Bisiacco *et al.* 1985, Bisiacco *et al.* 1986a, Bisiacco *et al.* 1986b, Bisiacco *et al.* 1988, Bisiacco *et al.* 1989, Fornasini 1988, Guiver & Bose 1985, Lin 1988a, Raman & Liu 1984, Raman & Liu 1986, Xu *et al.* 1994b), mainly around the period between 1985 and 1990. Xu *et al.* gave a good introduction on

---

[1]In this chapter, stability means structural stability rather than BIBO stability (Jury 1986).

this topic in (Xu *et al.* 1994b). Since 2-D SISO systems are a special case of 2-D MIMO systems and most of the results to be reviewed are valid for both 2-D SISO and MIMO systems, we shall be mainly concerned with 2-D MIMO systems in this section.

4.2.1 Stabilizability

Throughout Section 4.2, we assume that $P(z_1, z_2) \in \mathbf{R}^{m \times l}(z_1, z_2)$ and has MFDs

$$P(z_1, z_2) = N(z_1, z_2) D^{-1}(z_1, z_2) = \tilde{D}^{-1}(z_1, z_2) \tilde{N}(z_1, z_2),$$

where $D(z_1, z_2)$ and $N(z_1, z_2)$ are 2-D polynomial matrices which are already right minor coprime, and $\tilde{D}(z_1, z_2)$ and $\tilde{N}(z_1, z_2)$ are left minor coprime (Morf *et al.* 1977).

Let $\mathcal{I}$ denote the ideal generated by the $l \times l$ minors, $a_1, \ldots, a_\beta$, of $F = [D^T \ N^T]^T$, $\tilde{\mathcal{I}}$ the ideal generated by the $m \times m$ minors, $\tilde{a}_1, \ldots, \tilde{a}_\beta$, of $\tilde{F} = [\tilde{D} \ \tilde{N}]$, and let $\mathcal{V}(\mathcal{I})$ denote the variety of $\mathcal{I}$, $\mathcal{V}(\tilde{\mathcal{I}})$ the variety of $\tilde{\mathcal{I}}$.

Fact 4.1 *(Bisiacco* et al. *1986a): $\mathcal{V}(\mathcal{I}) = \mathcal{V}(\tilde{\mathcal{I}})$.*   ∎

Theorem 4.2 *(Stabilizability) (Guiver & Bose 1985, Bisiacco* et al. *1986a): $P(z_1, z_2)$ is feedback stabilizable if and only if $\mathcal{V}(\mathcal{I}) \cap \overline{U}^2 = \emptyset$, or equivalently, $F(z_1, z_2)$ is of full rank for all $(z_1, z_2) \in \overline{U}^2$.*   ∎

As $\mathcal{V}(\mathcal{I})$ is of zero dimension when $D(z_1, z_2)$ and $N(z_1, z_2)$ are minor right coprime, it is not difficult in principle to explicitly compute $\mathcal{V}(\mathcal{I})$ and then test whether or not all of these finite number of points are outside $\overline{U}^2$. However, the direct computation of $\mathcal{V}(\mathcal{I})$ may be quite troublesome. Hence, more efficient methods for stabilizability tests have been proposed (Bisiacco *et al.* 1988), (Fornasini 1988, Xu *et al.* 1994b). We now review two methods for testing stabilizability.

Let $\mathcal{G} = (g_1, g_2, \ldots, g_h)$ denote a Gröbner basis (Buchberger 1985) of the ideal $\mathcal{I}$. Then the set $\{p_1 = 1, p_2, \ldots, p_v\}$ of monic monomials in z_1 and z_2 that are not multiple of the leading power product of any of the polynomials in $\mathcal{G}$ is finite. The corresponding residue classes modulo $\mathcal{I}$, $\bar{p}_1$, constitute a basis for the vector space $\mathbf{R}[z_1, z_2]/\mathcal{I}$. Consider now the following maps:

$$\mathcal{Z}_1 : \mathbf{R}[z_1, z_2]/\mathcal{I} \to \mathbf{R}[z_1, z_2]/\mathcal{I}, q + \mathcal{I} \to z_1 q + \mathcal{I},$$

$$\mathcal{Z}_2 : \mathbf{R}[z_1, z_2]/\mathcal{I} \to \mathbf{R}[z_1, z_2]/\mathcal{I}, q + \mathcal{I} \to z_2 q + \mathcal{I}.$$

These are well defined, commuting linear transformations on the $\mathbf{R}$-space $\mathbf{R}[z_1, z_2]/\mathcal{I}$. This implies that when $\mathbf{R}[z_1, z_2]/\mathcal{I}$ is represented onto $\mathbf{R}^v$, $\mathcal{Z}_1$ and $\mathcal{Z}_2$ are represented by a pair of commuting matrices M_1 and M_2 in $\mathbf{R}^{v \times v}$. The actual construction of M_1 and M_2 is a little involved and the reader is referred to (Bisiacco *et al.* 1988), (Fornasini 1988) for the details.

Method 3.1. (Bisiacco *et al.* 1988, Fornasini 1988): Suppose that M_1 and M_2 are a pair of commutative (constant) matrices as described above and constructed in (Bisiacco *et al.* 1988, Fornasini 1988). The following statements are equivalent:

1) $P(z_1, z_2)$ is feedback stabilizable.

2) Any common eigenvector of M_1 and M_2 refers to a pair of eigenvalues (α_1, α_2) such that $|\alpha_1| > 1$ and/or $|\alpha_2| > 1$.

3) For any pair (t_{ii}^1, t_{ii}^2) in the triangular form of M_1 and M_2, we have $|t_{ii}^1| > 1$ and/or $|t_{ii}^2| > 1$.   ∎

Based on the same commutative matrices M_1 and M_2 as in Method 3.1, Bisiacco *et al.* (1988) have further reduced the stabilizability test to the solution of a finite number of Lyapunov equations and thus can be accomplished in a finite number of steps. The derivation is however, rather involved, and the reader is directed to their paper (Bisiacco *et al.* 1988) for more details. Furthermore, it is not clear how to generalize Method 3.1 to the n-D ($n \geq 3$) case.

Xu *et al.* (1994b) have proposed an alternative method for testing the stabilizability of a given 2-D system. Their method is now reviewed after some notation and definitions.

Let

$$\tilde{F} = [\tilde{D}\ \tilde{N}] = [\tilde{\mathbf{f}}_1 \cdots \tilde{\mathbf{f}}_k],$$

where $k = m + l$, and $\tilde{\mathbf{f}}_i$ ($i = 1, \ldots, k$) is an $m \times 1$ 2-D polynomial vector.

An n-D polynomial is said to be stable if all its zeros are outside $\overline{U}^n$, and completely unstable if all its zeros are in $\overline{U}^n$. A diagonal polynomial matrix is said to be stable if all its diagonal elements are stable, and is completely unstable if all its diagonal elements are completely unstable (Xu *et al.* 1994b).

Method 3.2. (Xu *et al.* 1994b): Construct 2-D polynomial matrices X_1, Y_1, X_2, Y_2 such that

$$\tilde{D}(z_1, z_2)X_1(z_1, z_2) + \tilde{N}(z_1, z_2)Y_1(z_1, z_2) = V_1(z_1),$$

$$\tilde{D}(z_1, z_2)X_2(z_1, z_2) + \tilde{N}(z_1, z_2)Y_2(z_1, z_2) = V_2(z_2),$$

where $V_1(z_1)$ and $V_2(z_2)$ are some diagonal 1-D polynomial matrices. Since $\tilde{D}$ and $\tilde{N}$ are minor left coprime, the above construction of X_1, Y_1, X_2, Y_2 is possible (Morf *et al.* 1977). Factorize V_i ($i = 1, 2$) as a product of stable and completely unstable diagonal polynomial matrices V_{is} and V_{iu} ($i = 1, 2$)

$$V_1(z_1) = V_{1s}(z_1)V_{1u}(z_1),$$

$$V_2(z_2) = V_{2s}(z_2)V_{2u}(z_2).$$

Define

$$\Gamma\{\det V_{1u}(z_1), \det V_{2u}(z_2)\} = \\ \{(z_1, z_2) \in \mathbf{C}^2 | \det V_{1u}(z_1) = 0, \det V_{2u}(z_2) = 0\}.$$

The following statements are equivalent:

1) $P(z_1, z_2)$ is feedback stabilizable.

2) For any $(z_{10}, z_{20}) \in \Gamma\{\det V_{1u}(z_1), \det V_{2u}(z_2)\}$, $\tilde{F}(z_{10}, z_{20})$ is of full rank.

3) A nonzero constant is an element in the Gröbner basis (Buchberger 1985) of the ideal generated by $\det V_{1u}(z_1)$, $\det V_{2u}(z_2)$, and $a_1, \ldots, a_\beta$.

4) For $i = 1, \ldots, m$, $\mathbf{e}_i$ is an element of the Gröbner basis of the module generated by

$$
\left\{ \tilde{\mathbf{f}}_1, \ldots, \tilde{\mathbf{f}}_k, \begin{bmatrix} 0 \\ \vdots \\ 0 \\ \det V_{1u}(z_1) \\ 0 \\ \vdots \\ 0 \end{bmatrix} *, \begin{bmatrix} 0 \\ \vdots \\ 0 \\ \det V_{2u}(z_2) \\ 0 \\ \vdots \\ 0 \end{bmatrix} * \right\}
$$

where $\mathbf{e}_i$ is an $m \times 1$ vector having 1 at the ith position and 0 at the other positions, and $*$ denote the ith position of the associated vector. ∎

The advantage of the above method is that it can be easily generalized to the n-D ($n \geq 3$) case provided that the ideal $\mathcal{I}$ is of zero dimension (Xu *et al.* 1994b, Xu *et al.* 1998).

4.2.2 Stabilization

Once a given 2-D system $P(z_1, z_2)$ is tested to be stabilizable, the next step is to construct a 2-D stabilizing compensator $C(z_1, z_2)$. It has been shown (Guiver & Bose 1985, Bisiacco *et al.* 1986a) that the construction of $C(z_1, z_2)$ can be carried out by solving one of the following two 2-D polynomial matrix equations:

$$X(z_1, z_2)D(z_1, z_2) + Y(z_1, z_2)N(z_1, z_2) = V(z_1, z_2) \tag{4.2}$$

and

$$\tilde{D}(z_1, z_2)\tilde{X}(z_1, z_2) + \tilde{N}(z_1, z_2)\tilde{Y}(z_1, z_2) = \tilde{V}(z_1, z_2) \tag{4.3}$$

for some $V(z_1, z_2)$ and $\tilde{V}(z_1, z_2)$ with $\det V(z_1, z_2)$ and $\det \tilde{V}(z_1, z_2)$ being stable polynomials. A stabilizing compensator is then given by $C(z_1, z_2) = X^{-1}(z_1, z_2)Y(z_1, z_2)$, or $C(z_1, z_2) = \tilde{Y}(z_1, z_2)\tilde{X}^{-1}(z_1, z_2)$.

In the literature there are several methods available for solving either (2) or (3) (Bisiacco 1985, Bisiacco *et al.* 1985, Bisiacco *et al.* 1986a, Bisiacco *et al.* 1986b, Bisiacco *et al.* 1988, Bisiacco *et al.* 1989, Fornasini 1988, Guiver & Bose 1985, Lin 1988a, Raman & Liu 1984, Raman & Liu 1986, Xu *et al.* 1994b). Three typical methods are reviewed in the following.

Method 3.3. (Bisiacco 1985, Bisiacco *et al.* 1985, Bisiacco *et al.* 1986a, Bisiacco *et al.* 1986b, Bisiacco *et al.* 1988, Bisiacco *et al.* 1989, Fornasini 1988, Guiver & Bose 1985):

(1) Calculate first the variety $\mathcal{V}(\mathcal{I})$, denoted by $(z_{11}, z_{21}), \ldots, (z_{1r}, z_{2r})$. Construct a 2-D polynomial $s(z_1, z_2) = \Pi_{i=1}^{r}(z - z_{1i})^{i_1}(z - z_{2i})^{i_2}$, where $i_1 = 1$ if $|z_{1i}| > 1$, otherwise, $i_1 = 0$, and similarly for i_2. It is easy to see that $s(z_1, z_2)$ is stable and vanishes at $\mathcal{V}(\mathcal{I})$.

(2) By Hilbert's Nullstellensatz, there exist some $\lambda_1, \ldots, \lambda_\beta$, and some integer r such that

$$\sum_{i=1}^{\beta} \lambda_i a_i = s^r.$$

The construction of $\lambda_1, \ldots, \lambda_\beta$ can be done using Gröbner bases (Buchberger 1985).

3) For $i = 1, \ldots, \beta$, construct polynomial matrix B_i from F such that $B_i F = a_i I_l$, and then construct $H = \sum_{i=1}^{\beta} \lambda_i B_i$ such that $HF = s^r I_l$.

4) Partition $H = [X \; Y]$.   ∎

Remarks. Methods for construction of stable polynomial $s(z_1, z_2)$ have also been proposed without explicit computation of the variety $\mathcal{V}(\mathcal{I})$ (Bisiacco *et al.* 1986b, Bisiacco *et al.* 1988, Fornasini 1988).

The advantage of the above method is that it can be generalized to the n-D ($n \geq 3$) as long as a suitable stable n-D polynomial can be constructed, e.g., if the ideal $\mathcal{I}$ is of zero dimension. However, the disadvantages of the method is the explicit calculation of all the $l \times l$ minors, $a_1, \ldots, a_\beta$, and the restricted form $V(z_1, z_2) = s^r(z_1, z_2) I_l$. An alternative method was proposed in (Raman & Liu 1986) for 2-D SISO systems and generalized to 2-D MIMO systems in (Lin 1988a), which has certain advantages over Method 3.3. The method of (Lin 1988a) is now reviewed.

Method 3.4. (Lin 1988a):

1) Construct 2-D polynomial matrices X_0, Y_0 such that:

$$X_0 D + Y_0 N = V_0$$

for some $V_0 = \text{diag}\,\{v_1(z_1), \ldots, v_l(z_1)\}$ (Morf *et al.* 1977).

2) Decompose $v_1(z_1) = v_{1s}(z_1) v_{1u}(z_1)$, where $v_{1s}(z_1)$ is stable and $v_{1u}(z_1)$ is completely unstable. Factorize $v_{1u}(z_1) = (z_1 - z_{11}) \ldots (z_1 - z_{1n})$. 'Replace', one after another, the unstable factor $(z_1 - z_{1i})$ by a stable polynomial $r_{1i}(z_2)$ for $i = 1, \ldots, n$. In particular, when $i = n$, we can construct X_n, Y_n such that:

$$X_n D + Y_n N = V_n$$

where V_n is the same as V_0 except that $v_1(z_1)$ now becomes $v_{1s}(z_1) s_1(z_2)$ where $s_1(z_2) = r_{11}(z_2) \ldots r_{1n}(z_2)$ is a stable polynomial. Notice that $r_{1i}(z_2)$ depends on $(z_1 - z_{1i})$ ($i = 1, \ldots, n$) and $D(z_1, z_2), N(z_1, z_2)$, but can always be chosen to be stable when $P(z_1, z_2)$ is stabilizable.

3) Repeating step 2) for $v_2, \ldots, v_l$ successively, we arrive at

$$XD + YN = V$$

where V is a stable diagonal matrix.   ∎

Method 3.4 does not require the explicit calculation of $a_1, \ldots, a_\beta$, and allows $V(z_1, z_2)$ to have a more general form. As a result, in general $X(z_1, z_2)$ and $Y(z_1, z_2)$ are of lower degree in z_1 and z_2 (Lin 1988a). However, the disadvantages of this method is that explicit calculation of all the zeros of $\det V_0(z_1)$ is required and the method is rather difficult to be extended to the n-D ($n \geq 3$) case.

To overcome the disadvantages of Methods 3.3 and 3.4, and at the same time retain the advantages of these two methods, a new method for constructing a 2-D stabilizing compensator has recently been proposed by Xu *et al.* (1994b). This method is now reviewed.

Method 3.5. (Xu *et al.* 1994b):

1) Construct a stable 2-D polynomial $s(z_1, z_2)$ that vanishes at $\mathcal{V}(\mathcal{I})$. The construction of $s(z_1, z_2)$ can be carried out employing the long division method for a 1-D polynomial without explicitly computing its zeros.

2) Solve the following equation using the Gröbner basis approach:

$$\tilde{x}_{1,1}(z_1, z_2, t)\tilde{\mathbf{f}}_1(z_1, z_2) + \cdots + \tilde{x}_{1,k}(z_1, z_2, t)\tilde{\mathbf{f}}_k(z_1, z_2)$$

$$+\tilde{x}_1(z_1, z_2, t) \begin{bmatrix} 1 - t\,s(z_1, z_2) \\ 0 \\ \vdots \\ 0 \end{bmatrix} = \begin{bmatrix} 1 \\ 0 \\ \vdots \\ 0 \end{bmatrix},$$

where t is a new indeterminate. Substituting $t = 1/s$ into the above equation and clearing out the denominators gives

$$\tilde{F}\mathbf{f}_1 = [s^{r_1}, 0, \ldots, 0]^T$$

where $\mathbf{f}_1$ is a $k \times 1$ 2-D polynomial vector and r_1 is a non-negative integer. Notice the unwanted term associated with $\tilde{x}_1(z_1, z_2, t)$ has vanished after the substitution of $t = 1/s$.

3) Repeating step 2) for $2, \ldots, m$ gives

$$\tilde{F}[\mathbf{f}_1 \ldots \mathbf{f}_m] = \begin{bmatrix} s^{r_1} & & \\ & \ddots & \\ & & s^{r_m} \end{bmatrix} = S.$$

4) Partitioning $[\mathbf{f}_1 \ldots \mathbf{f}_m]$ as $\tilde{X}$ and $\tilde{Y}$, we have

$$\tilde{D}\tilde{X} + \tilde{N}\tilde{Y} = S,$$

where $\det S = s^{r_1} \cdots s^{r_m}$ is clearly a stable polynomial. ∎

The above method can also be extended to a more general case where $S = \text{diag}\{s_1^{r_{11}} \cdots s_q^{r_{1q}}, \ldots, s_1^{r_{m1}} \cdots s_q^{r_{mq}}\}$, with $s = s_1 \cdots s_q$ (see (Xu *et al.* 1994b) for more details). The advantages of the above method are that explicit calculation of all the $l \times l$ minors $a_1, \ldots, a_\beta$ and all the zeros of $\det V_0$ is not required, and that the method can be easily generalized to the n-D ($n \geq 3$) case when the ideal $\mathcal{I}$ is of zero dimension (Xu *et al.* 1994b, Xu *et al.* 1998). However, a disadvantage of the generalized version of Method 3.5 is that when q is large, the newly introduced indeterminates $t_1, \ldots, t_q$ may result in more complicated computations.

In the synthesis of 1-D as well as n-D feedback system, it is often necessary to construct stabilizing compensators which are causal or even strictly causal (Guiver & Bose 1985, Cadzow 1973).

Recall that a rational function $n(\mathbf{z})/d(\mathbf{z})$ with $n, d \in \mathbf{R}[\mathbf{z}]$ is called causal if $d(\mathbf{0}) = (0, \ldots, 0) \neq 0$. It is called strictly causal if in addition $n(\mathbf{0}) = 0$. A rational function matrix $P \in \mathbf{R}^{m \times l}(\mathbf{z})$ is called causal if all its entries are causal. It is called strictly causal if all its entries are strictly causal (Guiver & Bose 1985, Cadzow 1973, Lin 1998).

To construct a causal stabilizing compensator, the plant $P(z_1, z_2)$ is usually assumed to be strictly causal (Bisiacco 1985, Bisiacco *et al.* 1985, Bisiacco *et al.* 1986a, Bisiacco *et al.* 1986b, Guiver & Bose 1985). However, Šebek (1985) has shown that it is always possible to obtain a causal stabilizing compensator even when a given SISO 2-D plant is causal but not necessarily strictly causal. Lin (1988a) has generalized Šebek's result and shown that a strictly causal stabilizer always exists for a causal but not necessarily strictly causal 2-D MIMO plant.

Fact 4.3 *(Lin 1988a): Suppose that $P(z_1, z_2)$ is causal and stabilizable. If $X(z_1, z_2)$ and $Y(z_1, z_2)$ are a solution to the 2-D equation (2), then a strictly causal stabilizer is $C(z_1, z_2) = \hat{X}^{-1}(z_1, z_2)\hat{Y}(z_1, z_2)$, where*

$$\hat{X}(z_1, z_2) = X(z_1, z_2) + Y(0, 0)\tilde{D}^{-1}(0, 0)\tilde{N}(z_1, z_2)$$

and

$$\hat{Y}(z_1, z_2) = Y(z_1, z_2) - Y(0, 0)\tilde{D}^{-1}(0, 0)\tilde{D}(z_1, z_2).$$

∎

4.2.3   Parametrization

An advantage of using the MFD approach is that it is relatively easy to obtain a parametrization of all stabilizing compensators for a given stabilizable plant P. A critical step is to show that there exists a double (stable) coprime MFD for P. It is proven in (Guiver & Bose 1985) that a stabilizable 2-D plant $P(z_1, z_2)$ can always be expressed as a fraction of two coprime matrices over the ring of stable 2-D rational functions $\mathbf{R_s}(z_1, z_2)$. A parametrization of all stabilizing compensators for $P(z_1, z_2)$ is then given by (Guiver & Bose 1985):

$$\begin{aligned}
C(z_1, z_2) &= (t_1(z_1, z_2)X(z_1, z_2) - T_2(z_1, z_2)\tilde{N}(z_1, z_2))^{-1}(t_1(z_1, z_2)Y(z_1, z_2) \\
&\quad + T_2(z_1, z_2)\tilde{D}(z_1, z_2))
\end{aligned} \tag{4.4}$$

where $t_1(z_1, z_2)$ is an arbitrary stable polynomial, and $T_2(z_1, z_2)$ is an arbitrary polynomial matrix.

In the 1-D case, the parametrization of all stabilizing compensators for a given stabilizable plant has found wide applications in control system synthesis (Vidyasagar 1985). With the increasing interests in the control of 2-D systems (see, e.g., (Bisiacco 1995)), it is hoped that the parametrization of all stabilizing compensators for a given 2-D plant will soon have similar applications.

4.3 n-D ($n \geq 3$) SISO SYSTEMS

Unlike 2-D systems, little attention has been directed to the feedback stabilization problem for n-D ($n \geq 3$) SISO systems (Raman & Liu 1984, Shankar & Sule 1992). One of the reasons is probably due to the similarity between a 2-D SISO system and its n-D ($n \geq 3$) counterpart. Therefore, our review on this area will be brief as most of the results presented in the previous section can be easily carried over to n-D ($n \geq 3$) SISO systems, and some results to be presented in the next section for n-D ($n \geq 3$) MIMO systems can also be specialized to the SISO case.

Let $p(z_1, \ldots, z_n) = p(\mathbf{z}) = n(\mathbf{z})/d(\mathbf{z})$, where $d(\mathbf{z})$ and $n(\mathbf{z})$ are factor coprime.

Stabilizability (Raman & Liu 1984, Shankar & Sule 1992): $d(\mathbf{z})$ and $n(\mathbf{z})$ do not have common zeros in $\overline{U}^n$.

Stabilization (Raman & Liu 1984, Berenstein & Struppa 1986, Shankar & Sule 1992): If $p(\mathbf{z})$ is stabilizable, there exist $x(\mathbf{z})$ and $y(\mathbf{z})$ such that

$$x(\mathbf{z})d(\mathbf{z}) + y(\mathbf{z})n(\mathbf{z}) = v(\mathbf{z})$$

where $x(\mathbf{z}) \neq 0$ and $v(\mathbf{z}) \neq 0$ for any $(\mathbf{z}) \in \overline{U}^n$. A stabilizing compensator is $c(\mathbf{z}) = y(\mathbf{z})/x(\mathbf{z})$.

Parametrization: All stabilizing compensators for $p(\mathbf{z})$ are given by:

$$c(\mathbf{z}) = (t_1(\mathbf{z})y(\mathbf{z}) + t_2(\mathbf{z})d(\mathbf{z}))/(t_1(\mathbf{z})x(\mathbf{z}) - t_2(\mathbf{z})n(\mathbf{z}))$$

where $t_1(\mathbf{z})$ is an arbitrary stable polynomial, and $t_2(\mathbf{z})$ is an arbitrary polynomial.

4.4 n-D ($n \geq 3$) MIMO SYSTEMS

It has been well known that there exist some fundamental differences between 2-D and n-D ($n \geq 3$) MIMO systems (Fornasini & Valcher 1997, Lin 1988b, Youla & Gnavi 1979). For the problem of feedback stabilization, results on 2-D MIMO systems or n-D ($n \geq 3$) SISO systems cannot be directly extended to n-D ($n \geq 3$) MIMO systems.[2] The main obstacle is that a given n-D transfer matrix $P(\mathbf{z})$ does not always have a right or a left minor coprime MFD (Youla & Gnavi 1979, Lin 1988b), and hence the MFD approach cannot be readily applied to n-D MIMO systems. Nevertheless, with the introduction of some new tools and techniques, the problem of feedback stabilization of n-D MIMO systems has attracted increasing attention recently (Sule 1994, Lin 1998, Xu *et al.* 1998, Lin 1999a), and a review on new concept and results will be given in this section.

Definition 4.4   *(Youla & Gnavi 1979):   Let $D \in \mathbf{R}^{l \times l}[\mathbf{z}]$, $N \in \mathbf{R}^{m \times l}[\mathbf{z}]$, and $F = [D^T \ N^T]^T$. Then D and N are said to be:*

(i) minor right coprime (MRC) if the $l \times l$ minors of F are factor coprime.

(ii) factor right coprime (FRC) if in any polynomial decomposition $F = F_1 F_2$, the $l \times l$ matrix F_2 is a unimodular matrix, i.e., $\det F_2 = k \in \mathbf{R}^*$.   ∎

---

[2]Throughout this section, the term 'n-D' implies $n \geq 3$ unless otherwise indicated.

Minor left coprimeness (MLC) etc. can be similarly defined.

Fact 4.5   *(Youla & Gnavi 1979):*

(i) For MIMO systems, MRC $\equiv$ FRC for $n = 2$ but not for $n \geq 3$.

(ii) For SISO systems, MRC $\equiv$ FRC for all n.

In all cases, MRC $\Rightarrow$ FRC.   ∎

The generalization of results on stabilizability and stabilization of 2-D MIMO systems to their n-D counterparts is not trivial. In particular, if $P(\mathbf{z})$ does not have a right or a left minor coprime MFD, new difficulty arises. Hence, we need to introduce some new concepts for solving the problem of feedback stabilization of n-D systems. In the remainder of Section 4.4, we assume that the plant transfer matrix $P(\mathbf{z}) = N(\mathbf{z})D^{-1}(\mathbf{z})$, where $D(\mathbf{z})$ and $N(\mathbf{z})$ are not necessarily minor right coprime.

4.4.1   Stabilizability

Definition 4.6   *(Lin 1988b):   Let $a_1(\mathbf{z}), \ldots, a_\beta(\mathbf{z})$ denote the $l \times l$ minors of the matrix $F(\mathbf{z}) = [D^T(\mathbf{z})\ N^T(\mathbf{z})]^T$. Extracting a greatest common divisor (g.c.d.) $d(\mathbf{z})$ of $a_1(\mathbf{z}), \ldots, a_\beta(\mathbf{z})$ gives:*

$$a_i(\mathbf{z}) = d(\mathbf{z})b_i(\mathbf{z}), \qquad i = 1, \ldots, \beta.$$

Then, $b_1(\mathbf{z}), \ldots, b_\beta(\mathbf{z})$ are called the 'generating polynomials' (or the 'family of reduced minors' (Sule 1994)) of $F(\mathbf{z})$.   ∎

Remarks. The term 'reduced minors' is probably more accurate than the term 'generating polynomials'. It is therefore recommended that 'reduced minors' instead of 'generating polynomials' should be adopted in future.

Fact 4.7   *(Sule 1994, Lin 1988b):   Any left MFD and right MFD of $P(\mathbf{z})$ have the same reduced minors.*   ∎

Remarks. Fact 4.1 turns out to be a special case of Fact 4.7.

Sule (1994) also introduced another useful concept, called the 'family of elementary factors', which is closely related to the family of reduced minors. Denote

$$F = \begin{bmatrix} N \\ D \end{bmatrix}, \qquad \tilde{F} = [\tilde{N}\ \tilde{D}] \tag{4.5}$$

Definition 4.8   *(Sule 1994):   Let $F_1, \ldots, F_r$ denote the family of all nonsingular $l \times l$ submatrices of the matrix F defined in (5), and for each index j, let $B_j = F(F_j)^{-1}$, where the entries of B_j are already in the reduced form. Let t_j be the radical of the least common multiple of all the denominators of B_j. $T = \{t_1, \ldots, t_r\}$ is called the family of elementary factors of the matrix F. Similarly, let $G = \{g_1, \ldots, g_q\}$ denote the family of elementary factors of the matrix $\tilde{F}$. $H = \{t_i\, g_j, i = 1, \ldots, r,\ j = 1, \ldots, q\}$ is called the family of elementary factors of the plant transfer matrix P.*   ∎

Remarks. The elementary factors of P defined above are redundant in the sense that any left and right MFD of P have the same elementary factors (Mori & Abe 1997, Lin 1999b). Therefore, the elementary factors of F (or $\tilde{F}$) alone can be considered as the elementary factors of P. Moreover, a method for computing the elementary factors based on the reduced minors has recently been proposed in (Lin 1999b).

Stabilizability of a given n-D system can now be given in terms of the family of reduced minors or the family of elementary factors.

Method 3.6. (Sule 1994, Lin 1998): Let $b_1(\mathbf{z}), \ldots, b_\beta(\mathbf{z})$ denote the family of reduced minors of $P(\mathbf{z})$. Then $P(\mathbf{z})$ is feedback stabilizable if and only if $b_1(\mathbf{z}), \ldots, b_\beta(\mathbf{z})$ have no common zeros in $\overline{U}^n$. ∎

Method 3.7. (Sule 1994): Let $h_1(\mathbf{z}), \ldots, h_k(\mathbf{z})$ $(k = rt)$ denote the family of elementary factors of $P(\mathbf{z})$. Then $P(\mathbf{z})$ is feedback stabilizable if and only if $h_1(\mathbf{z}), \ldots, h_k(\mathbf{z})$ have no common zeros in $\overline{U}^n$. ∎

4.4.2 Stabilization

Once a given causal n-D system $P(\mathbf{z})$ is known to be stabilizable, the next step is to construct a stabilizing compensator $C(\mathbf{z})$. Sule (1994) has first proposed a method for obtaining a stabilizing compensator based on the family of elementary factors of $P(\mathbf{z})$.

Method 3.8. (Sule 1994):

1) Obtain the family of elementary factors of P, denoted by $H = \{h_1, \ldots, h_k\}$.

2) Let $P = Nq^{-1}$, where q is an n-D polynomial and N is an n-D polynomial matrix. For each h_i in H $(i = 1, \ldots, k)$, obtain rational matrices X_i, Y_i, U_i, V_i such that $X_i N = U_i q$, $Y_i N = V_i q$ and $NY_i = (I - X_i) q$. The denominators of entries of X_i, Y_i, U_i, V_i are integer power of h_i.

3) Find a sufficiently large integer n_i such that $h_i^{n_i} X_i$, $h_i^{n_i} Y_i$, $h_i^{n_i} U_i$ and $h_i^{n_i} V_i$ are polynomial matrices.

4) Find rational function α_i $(i = 1, \ldots, k)$ whose denominator is not equal to zero in $\overline{U}^n$ such that $\sum_{i=1}^k \alpha_i h_i^{n_i} = 1$, or equivalently, find polynomials $\lambda_1, \ldots, \lambda_k$ such that $\sum_{i=1}^k \lambda_i h_i^{n_i} = s$ with $s \neq 0$ in $\overline{U}^n$.

5) Let $\tilde{X} = \sum_{i=1}^k \alpha_i h_i^{n_i} X_i$, $\tilde{Y} = \sum_{i=1}^k \alpha_i h_i^{n_i} Y_i$. Then $C = \tilde{Y} \tilde{X}^{-1}$ is a stabilizing compensator for P. ∎

However, Sule himself pointed out that the computation of the family of elementary factors is much more difficult than the family of reduced minors (Sule 1994). An alternative method for obtaining a stabilizing compensator using only the family of reduced minors of P has recently proposed by Lin (1998).

Method 3.9. (Lin 1998):

1) Obtain the $l \times l$ minors of $F = [D^T \ N^T]^T$, denoted by $a_1, \ldots, a_\beta$, and the family of reduced minors $b_1, \ldots, b_\beta$, where $a_i = db_i$.

2) Find polynomials $\lambda_1, \ldots, \lambda_\beta$ such that $\sum_{i=1}^{\beta} \lambda_i b_i = s$ with $s \neq 0$ in $\overline{U}^n$.

3) Construct H such that $HF = dsI_l$, and $\sum_{i=1}^{\beta} e_i b_i = s_1$ for some stable polynomial s_1, where $e_1, \ldots, e_\beta$ are the family of reduced minors of H. Details for constructing such an H can be found in (Lin 1998).

4) Partition $H = [X \ Y]$. Then $C = X^{-1}Y$ is a stabilizing compensator for P.   ∎

It can be seen that Method 3.9 is computationally much simpler than Method 3.8. A detailed comparison of these two methods can be found in (Lin 1998). As mentioned in (Lin 1998), a very important and difficult part for the design problem of stabilizing n-D compensator for both Method 3.8 and Method 3.9 is the construction of $\lambda_1, \ldots, \lambda_\beta$ such that $\sum_{i=1}^{\beta} \lambda_i b_i = s$, with $s \neq 0$ in $\overline{U}^n$. Although a method for obtaining $\lambda_1, \ldots, \lambda_\beta$ and s has been suggested in (Berenstein & Struppa 1986), this author believes the method is not constructive. The construction of a stable polynomial s for the stabilization of n-D systems is posed as an open problem in Section 4.6.

It is proper at this point to compare methods for stabilizing 2-D and n-D MIMO systems.

For a 2-D system $P(z_1, z_2)$, we decompose $P(z_1, z_2)$ into a minor right coprime MFD $P(z_1, z_2) = N(z_1, z_2)D^{-1}(z_1, z_2)$, and then solve the following 2-D polynomial matrix equation:

$$X(z_1, z_2)D(z_1, z_2) + Y(z_1, z_2)N(z_1, z_2) = V(z_1, z_2) \tag{4.6}$$

such that $\det V(z_1, z_2) \neq 0$ for any $(z_1, z_2) \in \overline{U}^2$.

On the other hand, for an n-D system $P(\mathbf{z})$ and applying Method 3.9, we decompose $P(\mathbf{z})$ into a right MFD $P(\mathbf{z}) = N(\mathbf{z})D^{-1}(\mathbf{z})$ (not necessarily minor right coprime). Now obtain the family of maximal order minors of $F(\mathbf{z}) = [D^T(\mathbf{z}) \ N^T(\mathbf{z})]^T$, denoted by $a_1(\mathbf{z}), \ldots, a_\beta(\mathbf{z})$, and the family of reduced minors $b_1(\mathbf{z}), \ldots, b_\beta(\mathbf{z})$, where $a_i(\mathbf{z}) = d(\mathbf{z})b_i(\mathbf{z})$. Find an n-D polynomial matrix $H(\mathbf{z})$ such that

$$H(\mathbf{z})F(\mathbf{z}) = d(\mathbf{z})s(\mathbf{z})I_l \tag{4.7}$$

and

$$\sum_{i=1}^{\beta} e_i(\mathbf{z})b_i(\mathbf{z}) = s_1(\mathbf{z}) \tag{4.8}$$

where $s_1(\mathbf{z}) \neq 0$ for any $(\mathbf{z}) \in \overline{U}^n$, and $e_1(\mathbf{z}), \ldots, e_\beta(\mathbf{z})$ are the family of reduced minors of $H(\mathbf{z})$.

The main difference is that for the n-D case, $\det(H(\mathbf{z})F(\mathbf{z}))$ may have zeros in $\overline{U}^n$ (due to $d(\mathbf{z})$), and the feedback system is still stable (Lin 1998)!

To end this subsection, we briefly discuss the causality of $P(\mathbf{z})$ and $C(\mathbf{z})$. Sule assumed in (Sule 1994) that $P(\mathbf{z})$ is strictly causal, and obtained a causal stabilizer $C(\mathbf{z})$. On the other hand, Lin (1998) has shown that, as in the 2-D case, it is always possible to construct a strictly causal stabilizer for a given causal but not necessarily strictly causal n-D plant.

Fact 4.9 *(Lin 1998): Let $P(\mathbf{z})$ be causal and stabilizable. If $C = X^{-1}(\mathbf{z})Y(\mathbf{z})$ is a stabilizer for $P(\mathbf{z})$, then a strictly causal stabilizer for $P(\mathbf{z})$ is: $\hat{C}(\mathbf{z}) = \hat{X}^{-1}(\mathbf{z})\hat{Y}(\mathbf{z})$,* where

$$\hat{X}(\mathbf{z}) = X(\mathbf{z}) + \frac{d^{l-1}(\mathbf{z})}{d^{l-1}(0)}Y(0)\tilde{D}^{-1}(0)\tilde{N}(\mathbf{z})$$

and

$$\hat{Y}(\mathbf{z}) = Y(\mathbf{z}) - \frac{d^{l-1}(\mathbf{z})}{d^{l-1}(0)}Y(0)\tilde{D}^{-1}(0)\tilde{D}(\mathbf{z}).$$

∎

The extra factor $\frac{d^{l-1}(\mathbf{z})}{d^{l-1}(0)}$ introduced here (as compared with the 2-D case) is to guarantee that both (7) and (8) are satisfied. Without this factor, (7) can still be satisfied, but not (8). As a result, the feedback system may become unstable (Lin 1998)!

4.4.3 Parametrization

The problem of parametrization of all stabilizing compensators for an arbitrary stabilizable n-D system $P(\mathbf{z})$ is still open (Lin 1998). Recently, this problem has been solved for a class of linear 3-D MIMO systems (Lin 1999a). As in the 2-D case, the key step is to obtain a double (stable) coprime MFD of $P(z_1, z_2, z_3)$.

Method 3.10. (Lin 1999a): Consider a stabilizable 3-D MIMO linear system $P(z_1, z_2, z_3)$.

1) Decompose P into MFDs:
$$P = \tilde{D}^{-1}\tilde{N} = ND^{-1},$$

where $\tilde{D}$, D, $\tilde{N}$, and N are 3-D polynomial matrices of appropriate dimensions, such that the g.c.d. of the $l \times l$ minors of $F = [D^T \ N^T]^T$ is $g(z_1)$ and the g.c.d. of the $m \times m$ minors of $\tilde{F} = [-\tilde{N} \ \tilde{D}]$ is $\tilde{g}(z_1)$.

2) Let $g(z_1) = g_s(z_1)g_u(z_1)$, $\tilde{g}(z_1) = \tilde{g}_s(z_1) \ \tilde{g}_u(z_1)$, where $g_s(z_1)$ and $\tilde{g}_s(z_1)$ are stable and $g_u(z_1)$ and $\tilde{g}_u(z_1)$ are completely unstable. If all the zeros of $g_u(z_1)$ and $\tilde{g}_u(z_1)$ are simple, $g_u(z_1)$ and $\tilde{g}_u(z_1)$ can be 'replaced' by stable polynomials $e(z_2, z_3)$ and $\tilde{e}(z_2, z_3)$ respectively.

3) Obtain MFDs of P:
$$P = \tilde{D}_0^{-1}\tilde{N}_0 = N_0 D_0^{-1}$$

such that the g.c.d. of the $l \times l$ minors of $[D_0^T \ N_0^T]^T$ is $g_s(z_1)e(z_2, z_3)$, and the g.c.d. of the $m \times m$ minors of $[-\tilde{N}_0 \ \tilde{D}_0]$ is $\tilde{g}_s(z_1)\tilde{e}(z_2, z_3)$. ∎

As both $[D_0^T \ N_0^T]^T$ and $[-\tilde{N}_0 \ \tilde{D}_0]$ are now of full rank in $\overline{U}^3$, it is routine to show that $P(z_1, z_2, z_3)$ admits a double (stable) coprime MFD. With minor modification, a parametrization of all stabilizing compensators for $P(z_1, z_2, z_3)$ in this class can be given similarly as for the 2-D case in (4).

4.5   RELATED ISSUES

So far we have given a rather detailed review on the problem of output feedback stabilization of n-D ($n \geq 2$) systems using the MFD approach. As feedback stabilization is one of the fundamental problems in controls and systems, in this section, we mentioned some issues related to feedback stabilization. The discussion is brief and references are not complete as there is a large number of related papers and books in the literature. We shall try to give some representative references for each issue so that the interesting reader can find out more references there.

(i) *Output feedback stabilization using methods other than the MFD approach.* These methods are closely associated with the problem of characteristic polynomial assignment. The basic idea is to specify a desirable characteristic polynomial that is of course stable, and then try to find out an appropriate compensator by solving a set of constant linear equations or some n-D polynomial equation (see (Kaczorek 1985) for more details). In fact, this issue should be included in the main body of the chapter if we do not emphasize the MFD approach. As we pointed out earlier, an advantage of the MFD approach is that it is relatively easy to obtain a parametrization of all stabilizing compensators for a given linear system by the MFD approach, but very difficult or impossible by other methods.

(ii) *Stabilization using state feedback.* This issue has been discussed by many researchers due to the popularity of state feedback for 1-D systems (see e.g. (Kaczorek 1985) or (Tzafestas 1986) for more details). However, unlike the 1-D case where it is sufficient to use static state feedback to stabilize an arbitrary 1-D system without unstable hidden modes, it is well known by now that static state feedback is in general insufficient to stabilize a given stabilizable n-D system. As a result, dynamic state feedback plus a dynamic state observer are usually required. This may lead to a more complicated compensator.

(iii) *Strong stabilizability.* An n-D system is said to be output feedback strong stabilizable if and only if there exists a stable n-D compensator such that the closed loop feedback system is stable. Although methods have been proposed for testing the strong stabilizability of a given n-D system, the problem of constructing a stable stabilizing compensator remains unresolved and more research is required (see (Ying 1998) for more details).

(iv) *Practical stabilizability.* The concept of practical stability was first proposed by Agathoklis & Bruton (1983) and adopted in the context of practical stabilizability by Xu *et al.* (1994a). By restricting at most one of the n dimensions to be unbounded, the practical stabilizability problem has essentially been reduced to a set of 1-D stabilizability problem and thus can be solved using 1-D approach (see (Xu & Saito 1998) for more details).

(v) *Linear systems over rings.* As linear n-D systems may be considered as a special case of linear systems over rings, it is relevant to mention this issue here. Research works on linear systems over rings began as early as in the 1970s and many papers and books can be found in the literature. However, since most of the papers are assuming conditions similar to zero or minor coprimeness, they may not be directly applied to our problem when an n-D plant admits only a factor coprime MFD. Furthermore, unlike research in n-D systems, most of the methods proposed for linear systems over rings are not constructive in nature (see (Shankar & Sule 1992, Sule 1994, Khargonekar & Sontag 1982) for more details).

4.6 OPEN PROBLEMS

Although some progress has been made in the direction of output feedback stabilization of linear n-D ($n \geq 3$) MIMO systems, a few open problems still exist due to the complexity of n-D MIMO systems. They are now posed in the following.

Problem 1. Determine whether or not an unstable but stabilizable n-D MIMO system admits a double (stable) coprime MFD, i.e., $P(\mathbf{z}) = N(\mathbf{z})D^{-1}(\mathbf{z}) = \tilde{D}^{-1}(\mathbf{z})\tilde{N}(\mathbf{z})$ with $[D^T(\mathbf{z})\ N^T(\mathbf{z})]$ and $[\tilde{N}(\mathbf{z})\ \tilde{D}(\mathbf{z})]$ being of full rank in $\overline{U}^n$.

Although this problem has not yet been solved, this author feels that the answer might be positive. Hence, the following conjecture was raised in (Lin 1998).

Conjecture (Lin 1998): If $P(\mathbf{z})$ is stablizable, then $P(\mathbf{z})$ has a double (stable) coprime MFD.

A partial solution was given in (Lin 1999a).

Problem 2. Parametrize all stabilizing compensators for a stabilizable n-D system.

Remarks. Sule (1994) has given a characterization of all stabilizing compensators for a stabilizable system as follows. Consider an MFD $P = N_s d_s^{-1}$ for a stabilizable P, where $N_s \in \mathbf{R_s}^{m \times l}(\mathbf{z})$ and $d_s \in \mathbf{R_s}(\mathbf{z})$. Then solve the following equation:

$$\begin{aligned} X_s N_s &= U_s d_s, \\ Y_s N_s &= W_s d_s, \\ N_s Y_s &= (I_m - X_s)d_s. \end{aligned} \tag{4.9}$$

where $X_s \in \mathbf{R_s}^{m \times m}(\mathbf{z})$, $Y_s \in \mathbf{R_s}^{l \times m}(\mathbf{z})$, $U_s \in \mathbf{R_s}^{m \times l}(\mathbf{z})$, $W_s \in \mathbf{R_s}^{l \times l}(\mathbf{z})$. It was shown in (Sule 1994) that all stabilizing compensators for P are characterized by $C = Y_s X_s^{-1}$ where X_s and Y_s satisfy (9). His characterization is not equivalent to the well known parametrization of (4).

Problem 3. Let $\mathcal{I}$ denote the ideal generated by a finite set of n-D polynomials $b_1(\mathbf{z}), \ldots, b_r(\mathbf{z})$. Find an efficient method to obtain $\mathcal{V}(\mathcal{I})$ or to determine whether or not $\mathcal{V}(\mathcal{I}) \cap \overline{U}^n = \emptyset$.

Problem 4. If $\mathcal{V}(\mathcal{I}) \cap \overline{U}^n = \emptyset$, find a stable polynomial $s(\mathbf{z})$ such that $s(\mathbf{z})$ vanishes on $\mathcal{V}(\mathcal{I})$.

Remarks. If $\mathcal{I}$ is of zero dimension, i.e., $\mathcal{V}(\mathcal{I})$ consists of only a finite number of points, it is not difficult to construct such a $s(\mathbf{z})$ (Xu *et al.* 1998).

Problem 5. Prove the existence of real double (stable) coprime MFDs for the class of 3-D MIMO systems in (Lin 1999a).

ACKNOWLEDGEMENT

This work was done while the author was with DSO National Laboratories, Singapore. The author would like to thank the anonymous reviewer whose insightful and helpful comments have greatly improved the presentation of this chapter.

REFERENCES

P. Agathoklis and L.T. Bruton, 1983, 'Practical-BIBO stability of n-dimensional discrete systems,' *Proc. IEE,* vol. 130, pt. G, pp. 236–242.

C.A. Berenstein and D.C. Struppa, 1986, '1-Inverses for polynomial matrices of non-constant rank,' *Systems & Control Letters*, vol. 6, pp. 309–314.

M. Bisiacco, 1985, 'State and output feedback stabilizability of 2-D systems,' *IEEE Trans. Circuits Syst.,* vol. 32, pp. 1246–1254.

M. Bisiacco, 1995, 'New results in 2D optimal control theory,' *Multidimensional Systems and Signal Processing*, vol. 6, pp. 189–222.

M. Bisiacco, E. Fornasini and G. Marchesini, 1985, 'On some connections between BIBO and internal stability of two-dimensional filters,' *IEEE Trans. Circuits Syst.,* vol. 32, pp. 948–953.

M. Bisiacco, E. Fornasini and G. Marchesini, 1986, 'Controller design for 2D systems,' in *Frequency Domain and State Space Methods for Linear Systems* ' (C.I. Byrnes and A. Lindquist, eds.), North-Holland: Elsevier, pp. 99–113.

M. Bisiacco, E. Fornasini and G. Marchesini, 1986, 'Causal 2D compensators: stabilization algorithms for multivariable 2D systems,' in *Proc. 25th Conf. Decision and Control,* pp. 2171–2174.

M. Bisiacco, E. Fornasini and G. Marchesini, 1988, 'Linear algorithms for computing closed loop polynomials of 2D systems,' in *Proc. IEEE Symp. Circuits and Systems,* Helsinki, Finland, pp. 345–348.

M. Bisiacco, E. Fornasini and G. Marchesini, 1989, '2D systems feedback compensation: an approach based on commutative linear transformations,' *Linear Algebra Appl.,* vol. 121, pp. 135–150.

N. K. Bose, 1982, *Applied Multidimensional Systems Theory*, New York: Van Nostrand Reinhold.

B. Buchberger, 1985, 'Gröbner bases: an algorithmic method in polynomial ideal theory,' in *Multidimensional Systems Theory: Progress, Directions and Open Problems* (N.K. Bose, ed.), Dordrecht: Reidel, p. 184.

J. Cadzow, 1973, *Discrete-Time Systems: An Introduction with Interdisciplinary Applications*, Englewood Cliffs, NJ: Prentice Hall.

E. Fornasini, 1988, 'A note on output feedback stabilizability of multivariable 2D systems,' *Systems & Control Letters*, vol. 10, pp. 45–50.

E. Fornasini and M.E. Valcher, 1997, 'nD polynomial matrices with applications to multi-dimensional signal analysis,' *Multidimensional Systems and Signal Processing*, vol. 8, pp. 387–408.

J. P. Guiver and N. K. Bose, 1985, 'Causal and weakly causal 2-D filters with applications in stabilizations,' in *Multidimensional Systems Theory: Progress, Directions and Open Problems* (N.K. Bose, ed.), Dordrecht: Reidel, p. 52.

E.I. Jury, 1986, 'Stability of multidimensional systems and related problems,' in *Multidimensional Systems: Techniques and Applications* (S.G. Tzafestas, ed.), New York: Marcel Dekker, p. 89.

T. Kaczorek, 1985, *Two-Dimensional Linear Systems*, Berlin: Springer-Verlag.

P.P. Khargonekar and E.D. Sontag, 1982, 'On the relation between stable matrix fraction factorization and regulable realization of linear systems over rings,' *IEEE Trans. Automat. Contr.*, vol. 27, pp. 627–638.

Z. Lin, 1988, 'Feedback stabilization of multivariable two-dimensional linear systems,' *Int. J. Contr.*, vol. 48, pp. 1301–1317.

Z. Lin, 1988, 'On matrix fraction descriptions of multivariable linear n-D systems,' *IEEE Trans. Circuits Syst.*, vol. 35, pp. 1317–1322.

Z. Lin, 1998, 'Feedback stabilizability of MIMO n-D linear systems,' *Multidimensional Systems and Signal Processing*, vol. 9, pp. 149–172.

Z. Lin, 1999, 'Feedback stabilization of MIMO 3-D linear systems,' *IEEE Trans. Automat. Contr.*, vol. 44, pp. 1950–1955.

Z. Lin, 1999, 'On the elementary factors of linear systems over unique factorization domains,' *Systems & Control Letters*, vol. 37, pp. 237–241.

M. Morf, B. C. Lévy and S. Y. Kung, 1977, 'New results in 2-D systems theory, Part I: 2-D polynomial matrices, factorization and coprimeness,' *Proc. IEEE*, vol. 65, pp. 861–872.

K. Mori and K. Abe, 1997, 'Improvement of generalized elementary factors and new criteria of the feedback stabilizability over integral domain,' in *European Control Conference ECC'97*.

V.R. Raman and R. Liu, 1984, 'A necessary and sufficient condition for feedback stabilization in a factorial ring,' *IEEE Trans. Automat. Contr.*, vol. 29, pp. 941–943.

V.R. Raman and R. Liu, 1986, 'A constructive algorithm for the complete set of compensators for two-dim ensional feedback systems design,' *IEEE Trans. Automat. Contr.*, vol. 31, pp. 166-170.

M. Šebek, 1985, 'On 2-D pole placement,' *IEEE Trans. Automat. Contr.*, vol. 30, pp. 819–823.

S. Shankar and V.R. Sule, 1992, 'Algebraic geometric aspects of feedback stabilization,' *SIAM J. Contr. Optim.*, vol. 30, pp. 11–30.

V.R. Sule, 1994, 'Feedback stabilization over commutative rings: the matrix case,' *SIAM J. Contr. Optim.*, vol. 32, pp. 1675–1695.

S.G. Tzafestas, 1986, 'State-feedback control of three-dimensional systems,' in *Multidimensional Systems: Techniques and Applications* (S.G. Tzafestas, ed.), New York: Marcel Dekker, p. 161.

M. Vidyasagar, 1985, *Control System Synthesis: A Factorization Approach*, Cambridge, MA: MIT Press.

L. Xu and O. Saito, 1998, 'Control of nD systems in a practical sense,', presented at the First International Workshop on Multidimensional Systems, Poland, July.

L. Xu, O. Saito and K. Abe, 1994, 'The design of practically stable nD feedback systems,' *Automatica,* vol. 30, pp. 1389–1397.

L. Xu, O. Saito and K. Abe, 1994, 'Output feedback stabilizability and stabilization algorithms for 2-D systems,' *Multidimensional Systems and Signal Processing*, vol. 5, pp. 41–60.

L. Xu, J.Q. Ying and O. Saito, 1998, 'Feedback stabilization for a class of MIMO n-D systems by Gröbner basis approach,' presented at the First International Workshop on Multidimensional Systems, Poland.

J.Q. Ying, 1998, 'Conditions for strong stabilizabilities of n-dimensional systems,' *Multidimensional Systems and Signal Processing*, vol. 9, pp. 125–148.

D. C. Youla and G. Gnavi, 1979, 'Notes on n-dimensional system theory,' *IEEE Trans. Circuits Syst.,* vol. 26, pp. 105–111.

D.C. Youla, H.A. Jabr and J.J. Bongiorno, Jr., 1976, 'Modern Wiener-Hopf design of optimal controllers, Part II: The multivariable case,' *IEEE Trans. Automat. Contr.,* vol. 21, pp. 319–338.

CHAPTER FIVE

A Review of nD System Control Theory in a Certain Practical Sense

Li Xu   and   Osami Saito

Dept. of Inf. Management Science,   Faculty of Engineering,
School of Business Administration,   Chiba University, Japan
Asahi University, Japan
xuli@alice.asahi-u.ac.jp

Abstract

This chapter is aimed to show the state of the art of the practical nD control theory, i.e., the control theory for nD systems in the practical sense that the input and output signals of the systems are unbounded in, at most, one dimension. A brief but overall review will be given on the recent theoretical and methodological results and possible applications related to most fundamental topics such as practical BIBO and internal stabilities, feedback practical stabilization, practical tracking and optimal control.

It is clarified that the nD control problems considered in the noted practical sense can be essentially reduced to the corresponding 1D problems, thus can be solved, compared with the conventional nD system theory, under less restrictive stability conditions and by much simpler 1D methods. In particular, it is shown that the proposed methods for 2D practical tracking control and optimal control in fact provide general design approaches for a class of iterative learning control systems and linear multipass processes. Therefore, the presented control theory for nD systems in the practical sense is of significance not only from the point of view of practical applications of nD system theory but also from that of control of such iterative systems.

5.1 INTRODUCTION

In the last two decades, significant progress has been made in the control theory of nD (multidimensional) systems. In particular, considerable theoretical results and insights have been shown for most fundamental 2D control problems such as algebraic tests of stability and stabilizability, constructive synthesis of feedback stabilizing compensators and tracking control systems (Agathoklis *et al.* 1993, Bisiacco *et al.* 1985, Bose 1993, Fornasini 1988, Guiver & Bose 1985, Hu 1994, Lin 1988, Raman & Liu 1986, Šebek 1989, Xu *et al.* 1990, Xu *et al.* 1994b, Xu *et al.* 1999). As a natural next step, how to apply these theoretical developments to practical applications has become a major research interest in this area, and some efforts have recently been reported (e.g., (Amann 1996, Amann *et al.* 1994, Amann *et al.* 1996, Amann *et al.* 1998, Foda & Agathoklis 1992, Geng *et al.* 1990, Heath 1994, Kurek & Zaremba 1993, Rogers & Owens 1992, Xu *et al.* 1994b, Xu *et al.* 1997a)).

Due to the complexity of the underlying theory, however, some substantial difficulties might be encountered in practical situations. For example, in most cases the 2D optimal control system cannot be constructed by using finite-dimensional local state feedback (Bisiacco 1995, Bisiacco & Fornasini 1990). Also, it seems in general unlikely that the complicated solution algorithms for 2D stabilization (equivalently, 2D unilateral or Diophantine equation) may be utilized in a self-tuning strategy on-line (Heath 1994).

On the other hand, however, it has been found that the prerequisite condition tacitly assumed in 2D (nD) system theory that all the independent variables are totally unbounded does not agree with the actual situations for a lot of practical applications. As a matter of fact, it has been observed that in many practical situations of nD signal processing, such as seismic and image processing, the independent variables $i_1, \ldots, i_n$ of an nD signal $x(i_1, \ldots, i_n)$ are usually spatial variables bounded in finite domains, except that perhaps one variable is the unbounded temporal variable. Based on this feature, Agathoklis & Bruton (1983) introduced the concept of practical BIBO (bounded-input bounded-output) stability for nD discrete systems, and revealed that practical BIBO stability is less restrictive and more relevant for practical applications than the conventional one. Further, it has also been well known that a large class of iterative learning control systems and linear multipass processes can be described by 2D system models (Boland & Owens 1980, Geng *et al.* 1990). As a common feature of these systems, it is noted again that, though the iteration index is not subject to any boundary condition, the dynamical processes on each trial or pass are always restricted in finite time intervals. It is natural, therefore, to expect that it would be possible to establish a simple and unified approach for the control of these systems under less restrictive stability conditions derived in some practical sense.

Since practical BIBO stability conditions are much weaker than the conventional ones, there exist systems that are practical BIBO stable but which are not conventional BIBO stable (Agathoklis & Bruton 1983). This fact means that the current design methods for nD systems (Lin 1998, Xu *et al.* 1994b), developed under the conventional BIBO stability concept, cannot be applied to design practical BIBO stable feedback systems (Xu *et al.* 1994a). In fact, many new problems need to be investigated if we want to deal with the control problems of nD systems in such a practical sense.

Motivated by these facts, the authors have recently investigated some fundamental control problems of nD systems, such as internal stability (Xu *et al.* 1996a), feedback stabilization (Xu *et al.* 1994a, Xu *et al.* 1996b) and asymptotic tracking control (Xu *et al.* 1994b, Xu *et al.* 1997a), in the practical sense of (Agathoklis & Bruton 1983), i.e, under the assumption that the system input and output signals are unbounded in, at most, one dimension. The obtained results show that nD control problems in the practical sense can be essentially reduced to corresponding 1D problems, and solved by the well-known 1D approaches. This property is of special significance for practical applications for it implies that in some cases nD control problems may be unsolvable under the conditions of conventional stability, but can be solved under the less restrictive practical stability and meanwhile by much simpler 1D methods. It should also be emphasized here, however, that the practical nD theory is entirely build on the assumption given above and should only be considered as a branch of the whole field of nD system theory where techniques totally different from the standard 1D theory are usually required.

This chapter aims to show the state of the art of the practical nD control theory, i.e., the control theory for nD systems in the noted practical sense, by giving a concise but overall review on the recent theoretical and methodological results and their possible applications.

The chapter is organized as follows. Section 5.2 reviews the results on practical BIBO stability and practical internal stability. Section 5.3 is devoted to treatments of the problem of practical stabilization by both matrix fractional description (MFD) algebraic approach and state-space approach. In Section 5.4, results on 2D practical tracking problem and its applications to iterative learning control systems and linear multipass processes will be summarized. Optimal control for 2D systems under the condition that one (fixed) variable is bounded and the other is unbounded and the related possible applications are investigated in Section 5.5.

Throughout the chapter, the following notation will be used. $\mathbf{R}$: the field of real numbers; $\mathbf{C}$ the field of complex numbers; $\mathbf{R}[z_1, \ldots, z_n]$: commutative ring of nD polynomials in $z_1, \ldots, z_n$ with coefficients in $\mathbf{R}$; Z_+: the set of non-negative integers; $Z_+^n = \{(i_1, \ldots, i_n) \mid i_1, \ldots, i_n \in Z_+\}$; $Z_+^{-n} = \{(i_1, \ldots, i_n) \mid i_1, \ldots, i_n \in Z_+, \text{ but if } i_j = +\infty, \text{ then } i_k < +\infty, k = 1, 2, \ldots, n, k \neq j \}$; $U, \bar{U}, T$: the open, closed unit disc and the unit circle in $\mathbf{C}$, respectively; $U^n, \bar{U}^n, T^n$: the open, closed unit polydisc and the unit torus in $\mathbf{C}^n$, respectively; A^T or x^T: transpose of matrix A or the vector x; I_m: $m \times m$ identity matrix; $(i_1, \ldots, 0_j, \ldots, i_n) \triangleq (i_1, \ldots, i_{j-1}, 0, i_{j+1}, \ldots, i_n)$; $(0, \ldots, i_j, \ldots, 0) \triangleq (0, \ldots, 0, i_j, 0, \ldots, 0)$.

5.2 PRACTICAL STABILITIES

Consider the class of SISO (single-input single-output) linear shift invariant nD discrete systems characterized by the nD convolution sum

$$y(i_1, \ldots, i_n) = \sum_{k_1=0}^{\infty} \cdots \sum_{k_n=0}^{\infty} h(i_1 - k_1, \ldots, i_n - k_n)u(k_1, \ldots, k_n) \qquad (5.1)$$

where $u(i_1, \ldots, i_n)$, $y(i_1, \ldots, i_n)$ are the input and output respectively, and $h(i_1, \ldots, i_n)$ is the impulse response. Further, denote the transfer function of (5.1) by

$$H(z_1, \ldots, z_n) = \frac{n(z_1, \ldots, z_n)}{d(z_1, \ldots, z_n)}. \qquad (5.2)$$

where $n, d \in \mathbf{R}[z_1, \ldots, z_n]$.

Definition 5.1 (Agathoklis & Bruton 1983) *nD system (5.1) is practical BIBO stable iff, for all bounded input signals $u(i_1, \ldots, i_n) \, \forall (i_1, \ldots, i_n) \in Z_+^{-n}$, the output $y(i_1, \ldots, i_n)$ is also bounded $\forall (i_1, \ldots, i_n) \in Z_+^{-n}$.*

The difference to the conventional BIBO stability defined on Z_+^n is that the behavior of the system at the points where more than one of the indeterminates take infinite value are not considered (see (Agathoklis & Bruton 1983).

The following necessary and sufficient conditions for the practical BIBO stability of nD systems are given in (Agathoklis & Bruton 1983)).

Theorem 5.2 *nD discrete system (5.1) is practical BIBO stable iff the n inequalities*

$$\sum_{i_1=0}^{N_1} \sum_{i_2=0}^{N_2} \cdots \sum_{i_k=0}^{N_k=\infty} \cdots \sum_{i_n=0}^{N_n} |h(i_1, i_2, \ldots, i_k, \ldots, i_n)| < \infty, \quad k = 1, 2, \ldots, n \qquad (5.3)$$

are satisfied where $N_1, \ldots, N_{k-1}, N_{k+1}, \ldots, N_n$ are any finite integers.

Theorem 5.3 *nD system described by* (5.2) *is practical BIBO stable iff*

$$d(0, \ldots, z_k, \ldots, 0) \neq 0 \quad \forall z_k \in \bar{U}, \quad k = 1, 2, \ldots, n. \tag{5.4}$$

The condition of (5.4) reveals that practical BIBO stability is in fact equivalent to the stabilities of n 1D systems which is much weaker than the condition for conventional BIBO stability (Goodman 1977, Swamy *et al.* 1985).

On the other hand, consider the nD Roesser state-space model (Kaczorek 1985, Kurek 1985) given by

$$\boldsymbol{x}'(i_1, \ldots, i_n) \;=\; A\boldsymbol{x}(i_1, \ldots, i_n) + B\boldsymbol{u}(i_1, \ldots, i_n) \tag{5.5}$$

$$\boldsymbol{y}(i_1, \ldots, i_n) \;=\; C\boldsymbol{x}(i_1, \ldots, i_n) + D\boldsymbol{u}(i_1, \ldots, i_n) \tag{5.6}$$

where $\boldsymbol{u}(i_1, \ldots, i_n) \in \mathbf{R}^m$ and $\boldsymbol{y}(i_1, \ldots, i_n) \in \mathbf{R}^p$ are the input and output vectors, respectively; $\boldsymbol{x}(i_1, \ldots, i_n) \in \mathbf{R}^{\tilde{n}}$ is the local state vector and $\boldsymbol{x}'$ denotes

$$\boldsymbol{x}'(i_1, i_2, \ldots, i_n) = \begin{bmatrix} \boldsymbol{x}_1(i_1 + 1, i_2, \cdots, i_n) \\ \boldsymbol{x}_2(i_1, i_2 + 1, \cdots, i_n) \\ \vdots \\ \boldsymbol{x}_n(i_1, i_2, \cdots, i_n + 1) \end{bmatrix}$$

with $\boldsymbol{x}_i(i_1, \ldots, i_n) \in \mathbf{R}^{n_i}$ $(i = 1, \ldots, n, \; \tilde{n} = \sum_{i=1}^n n_i)$ being the ith (sub-)vector of $\boldsymbol{x}(i_1, \ldots, i_n)$; and

$$A = \begin{bmatrix} A_{11} & \cdots & A_{1n} \\ \vdots & \ddots & \vdots \\ A_{n1} & \cdots & A_{nn} \end{bmatrix}, \qquad B = \begin{bmatrix} B_1 \\ \vdots \\ B_n \end{bmatrix},$$

$$C = [C_1 \; \cdots \; C_n]$$

with A_{ij}, B_i, C_i and D being constant real matrices of suitable dimensions, in particular, $A_{ii} \in \mathbf{R}^{n_i \times n_i}$ $(i = 1, \ldots, n)$.

Define the following nD z-transform for $f(i_1, \ldots, i_n) = 0$ for all $(i_1, \ldots, i_n) \notin Z_+^n$ (Bisiacco *et al.* 1989)

$$F(z_1, \ldots, z_n) = \sum_{i_1 + \ldots + i_n \geq 0} f(i_1, \ldots, i_n) z_1^{i_1} \cdots z_n^{i_n}. \tag{5.7}$$

Applying it to nD system (5.6) yields

$$\boldsymbol{x}(z_1, \ldots, z_n) = (I - ZA)^{-1}(ZB\boldsymbol{u}(z_1, \ldots, z_n) + \mathcal{X}_0)$$

$$\boldsymbol{y}(z_1, \ldots, z_n) = C\boldsymbol{x}(z_1, \ldots, z_n) + D\boldsymbol{u}(z_1, \ldots, z_n)$$

where $Z = \text{block diag}(z_1 I_{n_1}, z_2 I_{n_2}, \cdots, z_n I_{n_n})$, and $\mathcal{X}_0 = \sum_{i_1 + \ldots + i_n = 0} \boldsymbol{x}(i_1, \ldots, i_n)$ $z_1^{i_1} \cdots z_n^{i_n}$. Let $\mathcal{X}_0 = 0$, then we obtain the input/output relation

$$\boldsymbol{y}(z_1, \ldots, z_n) = G(z_1, \ldots, z_n)\boldsymbol{u}(z_1, \ldots, z_n), \tag{5.8}$$

where $G(z_1, \ldots, z_n) = C(I - ZA)^{-1}ZB + D$ is the transfer matrix.

The characteristic polynomial of nD system (5.6) is defined as

$$\rho(z_1, \ldots, z_n) = \det(I - ZA), \tag{5.9}$$

and the following relation holds (Xu *et al.* 1996a).

$$\rho(0, \ldots, z_k, \ldots, 0) = \det(I_{n_k} - z_k A_{kk}), \quad k = 1, \ldots, n. \tag{5.10}$$

To investigate the internal stability of (5.6), it is enough to consider only the SISO case with $m = l = 1$. Introduce the notation:

$$\tilde{X}_r = \left\{ x(i_1, \ldots, i_n) \in \mathbf{R}^{\tilde{n}} \; \middle| \; \sum_{j=1}^{n} i_j = r \right\}, \tag{5.11}$$

where it is assumed that $x(i_1, \ldots, i_n) = 0$ when $(i_1, \ldots, i_n) \notin Z_+^n$, and $x_j(i_1, \ldots, 0_j, \ldots, i_n) = 0$ $(j = 1, \ldots, n)$ except $x(0, \ldots, 0)$. Further, denote by $\|x(i_1, \ldots, i_n)\|$ the Euclidean norm of $x(i_1, \ldots, i_n)$ in the state space $\mathbf{R}^{\tilde{n}}$ and define, in the practical sense of (Agathoklis & Bruton 1983), the following norm for $\tilde{X}_r$:

$$\|\tilde{X}_r\|_{h_0} = \max_{h \le h_0} \left\{ \|x(i_1, \ldots, i_{j-1}, r-h, i_{j+1}, \ldots, i_n)\| \; \middle| \; h = \sum_{\substack{k=1 \\ k \ne j}}^{n} i_k, \; j = 1, \ldots, n \right\}, \tag{5.12}$$

where h_0 is an arbitrary finite positive integer. For brevity, let $\|\tilde{X}_r\| = \|\tilde{X}_r\|_{h_0}$ in the sequel.

Definition 5.4 (Xu *et al.* 1996a) *For nD system (5.6), suppose that $u = 0$ and $\|\tilde{X}_0\|$ is finite. Then the system is said to be practically internally (or asymptotically) stable if $\|\tilde{X}_r\| \to 0$ as $r \to \infty$ for any finite h_0.*

This definition of practical internal stability in fact implies that, for any finite $\|\tilde{X}_0\|$, $\|x(i_1, \ldots, i_n)\|$ approaches zero as (any) one of the variables $i_1, \ldots, i_n$ goes to infinity but all the others are finite, or equivalently, as $r = i_1 + \ldots + i_n \to \infty$ but $(i_1, \ldots, i_n) \in Z_+^{-n}$ (Xu *et al.* 1996a).

Theorem 5.5 (Xu *et al.* 1996a) *The nD system (5.6) is practically internally stable (or asymptotically stable) iff all the matrices A_{kk} $(k = 1, \ldots, n)$ are stable in the 1D sense, i.e.,*

$$\rho(0, \ldots, z_k, \ldots, 0) = \det(I_{n_k} - z_k A_{kk}) \ne 0, \quad \forall z_k \in \bar{U}, \quad k = 1, \ldots, n. \tag{5.13}$$

Theorem 5.5 shows that the practical internal stability of an nD system is also equivalent to the stabilities of n 1D systems, just like the case of practical BIBO stability. When $n = 2$, in particular, a system given by (5.6) is practically internally stable iff $\rho(z_1, 0) \ne 0$, $\rho(0, z_2) \ne 0$, $\forall z_1, z_2 \in \bar{U}$. In contrast with this, a 2D system is internally stable in the conventional sense (Ahmed 1980, Fornasini & Marchesini 1979) iff $\rho(z_1, z_2) \ne 0, \forall (z_1, z_2) \in \bar{U}^2$, which is obviously much more restrictive.

It has been clarified in (Xu *et al.* 1996a) that a state-space realization of a practical BIBO stable system is practically internally stable iff it is practically stabilizable and practically detectable (see Section 5.3.2). Moreover, it has also been shown that, for a practical BIBO stable 2D system given by $b(z_1, z_2)/a(z_1, z_2)$, a practically internally stable (Roesser or Fornasini-Marchesini model) realization can always be obtained (Xu *et al.* 1996a).

5.3   PRACTICAL STABILIZATION

This section briefly summarizes some results on practical stabilization of nD systems by algebraic and state-space approaches. By practical stabilization, we mean to find a output or local state feedback compensator such that the resultant closed-loop system is practically stable. A connection between the state-space representation and the doubly coprime MFD on **H** has been shown in (Xu *et al.* 1996b), however it is omitted here for brevity.

5.3.1   Algebraic approach

Let **G** be the ring of nD causal rational function, **H** be the ring of nD practically-stable rational function, i.e., $\mathbf{G} = \{n/d \mid n, d \in \mathbf{R}[z_1, \ldots, z_n],\ d(0, \ldots, 0) \neq 0\}$, $\mathbf{H} = \{n/d \in \mathbf{G} \mid d(0, \ldots, z_k, \ldots, 0) \neq 0\ \forall z_k \in \bar{U},\ k = 1, 2, \ldots, n\}$, and let $\mathbf{I} = \{h \in \mathbf{H} \mid h^{-1} \in \mathbf{G}\}$, $\mathbf{J} = \{h \in \mathbf{H} \mid h^{-1} \in \mathbf{H}\}$. Denote by $\mathbf{M}(*)$ the set of matrices with entries in set $*$ (e.g., **G**, **H**). An element of $\mathbf{M}(\mathbf{H})$ is then said to be **G**-unimodular (respectively **H**-unimodular) iff it is square and its determinant belongs to **I** (**J**). If $P \in \mathbf{M}(\mathbf{G})$ can be written as $P = N_p D_p^{-1}$, where $D_p, N_p \in \mathbf{M}(\mathbf{H})$ and D_p is **G**-unimodular, we refer to such $N_p D_p^{-1}$ as a right MFD of P (on $\{\mathbf{G}, \mathbf{H}, \mathbf{I}, \mathbf{J}\}$).

Definition 5.6 *For right MFD $N_p D_p^{-1}$, we say that N_p and D_p are right coprime on **H** and that $N_p D_p^{-1}$ is a right coprime MFD on **H** iff there exist $W, V \in \mathbf{M}(\mathbf{H})$ that satisfy the Bezout equation*

$$W D_p + V N_p = I. \tag{5.14}$$

The dual definitions on the left are given analogously. It is easy to see that for any $P \in \mathbf{M}(\mathbf{G})$, we can always find $N_p, D_p \in \mathbf{M}(\mathbf{R}[z_1, \ldots, z_n]) \subset \mathbf{M}(\mathbf{H})$ with $\det D_p \in \mathbf{I}$ such that $P = N_p D_p^{-1}$, but N_p and D_p are not necessarily right coprime on **H**. The following theorem gives a necessary and sufficient condition for the existence of right coprime MFD of P on **H**. Suppose, without loss of generality, $N_p, D_p \in \mathbf{M}(\mathbf{R}[z_1, \ldots, z_n])$ and $\det D_p \in \mathbf{I}$. Let $\mathcal{I}_k$ denote the ideal generated by the all maximal order minors of the matrix

$$\left[\begin{array}{c} D_p(0, \ldots, z_k, \ldots, 0) \\ N_p(0, \ldots, z_k, \ldots, 0) \end{array} \right] \tag{5.15}$$

and $\mathcal{V}(\mathcal{I}_k)$ be the algebraic variety of $\mathcal{I}_k$, i.e., the set of common zeros of the minors, where $k = 1, 2, \ldots, n$.

Theorem 5.7 (Xu *et al.* 1994a) *For $N_p D_p^{-1}$ where $N_p, D_p \in \mathbf{M}(\mathbf{R}[z_1, \ldots, z_n])$ and $\det D_p \in \mathbf{I}$, D_p and N_p is right coprime on **H** iff*

$$\mathcal{V}(\mathcal{I}_k) \cap \bar{U} = \emptyset, \qquad k = 1, 2, \ldots, n. \tag{5.16}$$

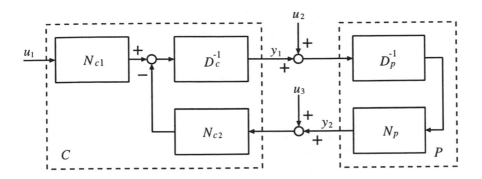

Figure 5.1: nD Feedback Control System

The proof of this theorem in (Xu *et al.* 1994a) gives a constructive solution algorithm for the Bezout equation (5.14), which can also be found in (Xu *et al.* 1997a).

Using the right and left coprime MFDs on **H**, a doubly coprime MFD relation on **H** in the form

$$\begin{bmatrix} W & V \\ -\tilde{N}_p & \tilde{D}_p \end{bmatrix} \begin{bmatrix} D_p & -\tilde{V} \\ N_p & \tilde{W} \end{bmatrix} = \begin{bmatrix} I & 0 \\ 0 & I \end{bmatrix} \tag{5.17}$$

can be obtained as well (Xu *et al.* 1994a).

Consider now the MIMO (multi-input multi-output) nD feedback system shown in Fig. 5.1 where $N_p D_p^{-1}$, with N_p, $D_p \in \mathbf{M}(\mathbf{R}[z_1, \ldots, z_n])$, is a right MFD on **H** for the plant $P \in \mathbf{M}(\mathbf{G})$, and $D_c^{-1}[N_{c1} \ N_{c2}]$, with $D_c, N_{c1}, N_{c2} \in \mathbf{M}(\mathbf{H})$, is a left MFD on **H** for the controller $C \in \mathbf{M}(\mathbf{G})$. Let $y = [y_1 \ y_2]^T$, $u = [u_1 \ u_2 \ u_3]^T$. It is then easy to see (Vidyasagar 1985)

$$y = H_{yu} u \tag{5.18}$$

where

$$H_{yu} = \begin{bmatrix} D_p \Delta^{-1} N_{c1} & -I + D_p \Delta^{-1} D_c & -D_p \Delta^{-1} N_{c2} \\ N_p \Delta^{-1} N_{c1} & N_p \Delta^{-1} D_c & -N_p \Delta^{-1} N_{c2} \end{bmatrix} \tag{5.19}$$

and

$$\Delta = N_{c2} N_p + D_c D_p. \tag{5.20}$$

If $\det \Delta \neq 0$ and $H_{yu} \in \mathbf{M}(\mathbf{H})$, we say that the nD feedback system of Fig. 5.1 is practically stable, and P is practically stabilizable and further C is a practically stabilizing compensator for P.

Theorem 5.8 *nD plant $P = N_p D_p^{-1} \in \mathbf{M}(\mathbf{G})$, where D_p and N_p are right factor coprime on $\mathbf{R}[z_1, \ldots, z_n]$, is practically stabilizable if D_p and N_p are right coprime on $\mathbf{H}$. For $n \leq 2$, the condition is also necessary.*

The sufficiency can be shown by using the results of Theorem 5.7 as the proof for the sufficiency of Theorem 5 in (Xu *et al.* 1994a) and the necessity for the 2D case can be shown in similar way as (Guiver & Bose 1985). However, it should be indicated that the claim for the necessity of Theorem 5 in (Xu *et al.* 1994a) is not correct for the cases of $n \geq$ 3. In fact, cancellation between (unstable) zeros and poles may lead to a practically stable

H_{yu} even if D_p and N_p are not right coprime on H. Special attention should be paid to the fact that such cancellation may occur in a transfer matrix even when the corresponding MFD to it is factor coprime on $\mathbf{R}[z_1, \ldots, z_n]$, as is impossible in the cases of $n = 1, 2$ (Lin 1988, Lin 1998).

The parameterization of all nD (output feedback) practically stabilizing compensators can be given under the assumption that both right and left coprime MFD on H exist for the considered plant.

Theorem 5.9 (Xu *et al.* 1994a) *Suppose that $N_p D_p^{-1}$ and $\tilde{D}_p^{-1} \tilde{N}_p$ are respectively any right and left coprime MFD on $\mathbf{H}$ for a given plant $P \in \mathbf{M}(\mathbf{G})$, and that $W, V \in \mathbf{M}(\mathbf{H})$ satisfy $W D_p + V N_p = I$. Then the set of all practically stabilizing compensators of P is given by*

$$C \in \{(W + S\tilde{N}_p)^{-1}[Q \;\; V - S\tilde{D}_p] \mid$$
$$Q, S \in \mathbf{M}(\mathbf{H}), \; \det(W + S\tilde{N}_p) \in \mathbf{I}\} \tag{5.21}$$

and the set of all possible practically-stable transfer matrices is in the form

$$\begin{bmatrix} D_p Q & D_p(W + S\tilde{N}_p) - I & -D_p(V - S\tilde{D}_p) \\ N_p Q & N_p(W + S\tilde{N}_p) & -N_p(V - S\tilde{D}_p) \end{bmatrix}. \tag{5.22}$$

5.3.2   State-space approach

First, we see some basic properties in the practical sense of (Agathoklis & Bruton 1983) for an nD system described by Roesser state-space model.

Consider linear nD system (5.6) with the boundary conditions

$$\bar{\mathcal{X}}_0 = \{x_j(i_1, \ldots, 0_j, \ldots, i_n) \mid i_k \in Z_+, k, j = 1, \ldots, n\}. \tag{5.23}$$

The practical controllability (reachability) and the practical observability are respectively defined as follows.

Definition 5.10 (Xu *et al.* 1996b) *nD system (5.6) is said to be practically controllable (equivalently, practically reachable) iff, for all $p = 1, \ldots, n$, there exist $t_p \geq 0$ such that for any finite $i_k \geq 0$, $k = 1, \ldots, n$, $k \neq p$, local state $x_p(i_1, \ldots, t_p, \ldots, i_n)$ can be reached from $\bar{\mathcal{X}}_0 = 0$ by using the input signal sequence $\{u(i_1, \ldots, i_p, \ldots, i_n) \mid 0 \leq i_p < t_p\}$.*

Definition 5.11 (Xu *et al.* 1996b) *nD system (5.6) is said to be practically observable iff, for all $p = 1, \ldots, n$, there exist $s_p > 0$ such that whenever $u = 0$ and $\bar{\mathcal{X}}_0 = 0$ except $x_p(i_1, \ldots, 0_p, \ldots, i_n) \neq 0$ for any finite $i_k \geq 0$, $k = 1, \ldots, n$, $k \neq p$, $y(i_1, \ldots, s_p, \ldots, i_n)$ is not the same as when $x_p(i_1, \ldots, 0_p, \ldots, i_n) = 0$.*

The following necessary and sufficient conditions for practical controllability and practical observability have been shown in (Xu *et al.* 1996b).

Theorem 5.12 *nD system (5.6) is practically controllable iff the pairs (A_{ii}, B_i) are controllable in the 1D sense for all $i = 1, \ldots, n$.*

Theorem 5.13 *nD system (5.6) is practically observable iff the pairs (A_{ii}, C_i) is observable in the 1D sense for all $i = 1, \ldots, n$.*

It is easy to see the duality between the practical controllability and the practical observability.

nD system (5.6) is said to be practically internally (or asymptotically) stabilizable, or simply practically stabilizable, if there exists a local state feedback such that the resultant feedback system is practically internally stable, and practically detectable if there exists an asymptotic observer for the local state $x(i_1, \ldots, i_n)$ whose estimate error vanishes as $i_1 + \cdots + i_n \to \infty$ but $(i_1, \ldots, i_n) \in Z_+^{-n}$.

Define the local state feedback:

$$u(i_1, \ldots, i_n) = v(i_1, \ldots, i_n) - Kx(i_1, \ldots, i_n), \qquad (5.24)$$

where $v \in \mathbf{R}^m$ is a new input vector and $K = [K_1 \cdots K_n]$, $K_i, i = 1, \ldots, n$, are real feedback gain matrices of appropriate dimensions. Substituting (5.24) into (5.6) yields the closed-loop system:

$$x'(i_1, \cdots, i_n) = A_c x(i_1, \cdots, i_n) + Bv(i_1, \ldots, i_n) \qquad (5.25)$$

where $A_c \triangleq A - BK$. Then the closed-loop characteristic polynomial is given by

$$\rho_c(z_1, \ldots, z_n) = \det(I - ZA_c). \qquad (5.26)$$

The following theorem gives necessary and sufficient conditions for nD system (5.6) to be practically stabilizable, or equivalently, for the closed-loop nD system (5.25) to be practically stable.

Theorem 5.14 (Xu *et al.* 1996b) *The following conditions are equivalent:*

(i) *nD system (5.6) is practically stabilizable;*

(ii) *All the pairs* (A_{kk}, B_k), $k = 1, \ldots, n$, *are stabilizable in the 1D sense, i.e.,*

$$\mathrm{rank}[I_{n_k} - z_k A_{kk} \quad z_k B_k] = n_k \quad \forall z_k \in \bar{U},$$
$$k = 1, \ldots, n \qquad (5.27)$$

(iii) *The matrices* $(I - ZA)$ *and* ZB *are left coprime on* $\mathbf{H}$, *i.e. there exist* $X(z_1, \ldots, z_n)$, $Y(z_1, \ldots, z_n) \in \mathbf{M(H)}$ *such that*

$$(I - ZA)X(z_1, \ldots, z_n) + (ZB)Y(z_1, \ldots, z_n) = I. \qquad (5.28)$$

Theorem 5.14 reveals that the practical stabilization problem of nD system (5.6) by state feedback (5.24) is equivalent to the stabilization problems of n 1D systems described by (A_{ii}, B_i), $i = 1, \ldots, n$. Therefore, the feedback gain matrices K_i, $i = 1, \ldots, n$, can be determined by the well-known 1D methods.

The zeros of $\rho(0, \ldots, z_k, \ldots, 0)$, for $k = 1, \ldots, n$, are called the practical zeros of $\rho(z_1, \ldots, z_n)$, or the practical poles of system (5.6), and the problem to locate the closed-loop practical poles $\{z_k \mid \rho_c(0, \ldots, z_k, \ldots, 0) = 0, k = 1, \ldots, n\}$ of system (5.6) is called practical pole assignment problem. It should be clear that these practical poles are arbitrarily assignable iff the system (A, B) is practically controllable (Xu *et al.* 1996b).

To realize the state feedback we may need to construct an observer to estimate the states if they cannot be completely measured. Consider an nD observer described by

$$\hat{x}'(i_1,\ldots,i_n) = A\hat{x}(i_1,\ldots,i_n) + Bu(i_1,\ldots,i_n)$$
$$+ F\{y(i_1,\ldots,i_n) - \hat{y}(i_1,\ldots,i_n)\}$$
$$\hat{y}(i_1,\ldots,i_n) = C\hat{x}(i_1,\ldots,i_n) \tag{5.29}$$

where $\hat{x}(i_1,\ldots,i_n) \in \mathbf{R}^{\tilde{n}}$ is the local state vector, $\hat{y}(i_1,\ldots,i_n) \in \mathbf{R}^l$ is the output vector of the observer, and $F = [F_1^T \cdots F_n^T]^T$, $F_i, i = 1,\ldots,n$, are real matrices with suitable dimensions. To estimate the local state $x(i_1,\ldots,i_n)$, we should choose F such that the error

$$e(i_1,\ldots,i_n) = x(i_1,\ldots,i_n) - \hat{x}(i_1,\ldots,i_n) \tag{5.30}$$

can be properly controlled. From (5.6) and (5.29), the error $e(i_1,\ldots,i_n)$ obeys the equation

$$e'(i_1,\ldots,i_n) = (A - FC)e(i_1,\ldots,i_n). \tag{5.31}$$

According to the results of Theorem 5.5, if there exists some F such that (5.31) is practically asymptotically stable, the estimate error $e(i_1,\ldots,i_n) \to 0$ as $i_1 + \cdots + i_n \to \infty$ but $(i_1,\ldots,i_n) \in Z_+^{-n}$, i.e., nD system (5.6) will be practically detectable.

Theorem 5.15 (Xu *et al.* 1996b) *The following conditions are equivalent:*

(i) *nD system (5.6) is practically detectable;*

(ii) *All the pairs (A_{kk}, C_k), $k = 1,\ldots,n$, are detectable in the 1D sense, i.e.,*

$$\operatorname{rank}\begin{bmatrix} C_k \\ I_{n_k} - z_k A_{kk} \end{bmatrix} = n_k \quad \forall z_k \in \bar{U},$$
$$k = 1,\ldots,n \tag{5.32}$$

(iii) *The matrices $(I - ZA)$ and C are right coprime on $\mathbf{H}$, i.e. there exist $W(z_1,\ldots,z_n)$, $V(z_1,\ldots,z_n) \in \mathbf{M}(\mathbf{H})$ such that*

$$W(z_1,\ldots,z_n)(I - ZA) + V(z_1,\ldots,z_n)C = I \tag{5.33}$$

Theorem 5.15 shows that observer for nD system (5.6) in the practical sense can be constructed by using 1D approaches. It is also obvious that the practical zeros of $\det(I - Z(A - FC))$ can be arbitrarily assigned iff nD system (A, C) is practically observable. Moreover, it is easy to see that, just as the 1D case, the controller and the observer can be designed independently (Xu *et al.* 1997a).

5.4 PRACTICAL TRACKING CONTROL AND ITS APPLICATIONS

Solutions to the nD practical tracking control problem, i.e., the tracking control problem for nD systems in the practical sense of (Agathoklis & Bruton 1983) are shown based on the concept of skew primeness on $\mathbf{H}$ and a solution algorithm for the skew prime equation, which can be regarded as a kind of generalization of the results of 1D case (Wolovich 1978). It is also shown that the obtained results can be applied, as a unified and general design approach, to iterative learning control systems and linear multipass processes under much less restrictive convergence or stability conditions and without requiring any *a priori* restriction on the structure of controllers.

5.4.1 Skew primeness over H

Definition 5.16 *Consider matrices $D, N \in \mathbf{M}(\mathbf{H})$. D and N are said to be (externally) skew prime on $\mathbf{H}$ iff there exist $X, Y \in \mathbf{M}(\mathbf{H})$ such that*

$$DX + YN = I \tag{5.34}$$

It is easy to see that, when studying the skew primeness of D, N on $\mathbf{H}$, one can limit D and N to be polynomial matrices without loss of generality (Xu *et al.* 1997a). In what follows, therefore, we assume that $D, N \in \mathbf{M}(\mathbf{R}[z_1, \ldots, z_n])$.

Theorem 5.17 (Xu *et al.* 1997a) *Consider D, $N \in \mathbf{M}(\mathbf{R}[z_1, \ldots, z_n])$ and let D be non-singular. Then, D and N are skew prime on $\mathbf{H}$ if there exist $\bar{D}, \bar{N} \in \mathbf{M}(\mathbf{H})$ such that*

$$ND = \bar{D}\bar{N} \tag{5.35}$$

where D, $\bar{N}$ are right coprime and N, $\bar{D}$ are left coprime on $\mathbf{H}$. When $n \leq 2$, the condition is also necessary.

In view of Theorem 5.17, a solution to the skew prime equation (5.34) will be directly obtained if $\bar{D}$ and $\bar{N}$ satisfying (5.35) can be found (Xu *et al.* 1997a). For the 2D case, a constructive procedure has been given in (Xu *et al.* 1997a) for the determination of $\bar{D}$ and $\bar{N}$ under the assumptions that $D, N \in \mathbf{M}(\mathbf{R}[z_1, z_2])$ and D is square and nonsingular.

Suppose, without loss of generality, that D and N are square matrices of equal order, say $D, N \in \mathbf{R}^{p \times p}[z_1, z_2]$. Then, we can always find $\hat{D}$ and $\hat{N}$ such that

$$ND = \hat{D}\hat{N} \tag{5.36}$$

with $\det \hat{D} = \det D$ (Xu *et al.* 1990, Xu *et al.* 1997a) and the following theorem can be obtained.

Theorem 5.18 (Xu *et al.* 1997a) *Consider a pair of square matrices $D, N \in \mathbf{M}(\mathbf{R}[z_1, z_2])$ of equal order with D nonsingular. Let $ND = \hat{D}\hat{N}$ with $\det \hat{D} = \det D$, then D and N are skew prime on $\mathbf{H}$ iff D and $\hat{N}$ are right coprime on $\mathbf{H}$, or N and $\hat{D}$ are left coprime on $\mathbf{H}$.*

5.4.2 Practical tracking control

Consider a plant characterized by the input/output relation

$$y(z_1, z_2) = A_p^{-1}B_p u(z_1, z_2) + A_p^{-1}C_p y_0(z_1, z_2) \tag{5.37}$$

where $A_p, B_p, C_p \in \mathbf{M}(\mathbf{R}[z_1, z_2])$; A_p is $\mathbf{G}$-unimodular; u, y are vectors over $\mathbf{R}[z_1, z_2]$ corresponding to the input and output sequences, respectively; and y_0 is a vector over $\mathbf{R}[z_1, z_2]$ denoting arbitrary initial or boundary conditions of the considered plant. Let

$$A_p^{-1}B_p = \tilde{B}_p \tilde{A}_p^{-1} \tag{5.38}$$

with $\tilde{B}_p$ and $\tilde{A}_p$ right factor coprime.

Similarly, let the class of 2D reference signals $r(z_1, z_2)$ be given by the equation

$$r(z_1, z_2) = A_s^{-1}B_s r_0(z_1, z_2) \tag{5.39}$$

where A_s, $B_s \in \mathbf{M}(\mathbf{R}[z_1, z_2])$, and r_0 corresponds to the initial or boundary conditions of the reference generator.

A general linear 2D controller can be described by

$$
\begin{aligned}
u(z_1, z_2) &= A_c^{-1} B_{c1} r(z_1, z_2) - A_c^{-1} B_{c2} y(z_1, z_2) \\
&\quad + A_c^{-1} C_c u_0(z_1, z_2)
\end{aligned}
\tag{5.40}
$$

where A_c, B_{c2}, $B_{c1} \in \mathbf{M}(\mathbf{H})$, and u_0 depends on the initial or boundary conditions of the controller.

The practical tracking problem is defined as: given A_p, B_p, A_s, find A_c, B_{c1} and B_{c2} for arbitrary $C_p y_0$, $B_s r_0$ and $C_c u_0$ such that

- the resultant closed-loop feedback system

$$
\begin{aligned}
y(z_1, z_2) &= \tilde{B}_p (A_c \tilde{A}_p + B_{c2} \tilde{B}_p)^{-1} B_{c1} r(z_1, z_2) \\
&\quad + [I - \tilde{B}_p (A_c \tilde{A}_p + B_{c2} \tilde{B}_p)^{-1} B_{c2}] A_p^{-1} C_p y_0(z_1, z_2) \\
&\quad + \tilde{B}_p (A_c \tilde{A}_p + B_{c2} \tilde{B}_p)^{-1} C_c u_0(z_1, z_2)
\end{aligned}
\tag{5.41}
$$

  is stable, and

- the output y asymptotically tracks the reference signal r

in the practical sense of (Agathoklis & Bruton 1983).

In view of the results of practical internal stability and the remarks on its relation to practical BIBO stability in Section 5.2, it is easy to see that the practical tracking problem is equivalent to the one: under the given conditions, find A_c, B_{c1}, B_{c2} such that the output $y(z_1, z_2)$ of the closed-loop system and the tracking error $e(z_1, z_2) = r(z_1, z_2) - y(z_1, z_2)$ are vectors with entries in $\mathbf{H}$, for any $C_p y_0$, $B_s r_0$ and $C_c u_0$.

It follows from (5.39) and (5.41) the relation

$$
\begin{aligned}
e(z_1, z_2) &= [I - \tilde{B}_p (A_c \tilde{A}_p + B_{c2} \tilde{B}_p)^{-1} B_{c1}] A_s^{-1} B_s r_0(z_1, z_2) \\
&\quad - [I - \tilde{B}_p (A_c \tilde{A}_p + B_{c2} \tilde{B}_p)^{-1} B_{c2}] A_p^{-1} C_p y_0(z_1, z_2) \\
&\quad - \tilde{B}_p (A_c \tilde{A}_p + B_{c2} \tilde{B}_p)^{-1} C_c u_0(z_1, z_2).
\end{aligned}
\tag{5.42}
$$

The following theorem gives a sufficient condition for the solution of the practical tracking problem.

Theorem 5.19 (Xu *et al.* 1997a) *Suppose that A_p and B_p are left factor coprime on $\mathbf{R}[z_1, z_2]$, and A_s and B_s are left coprime on $\mathbf{H}$. Then, the practical tracking problem is solvable if and only if the plant (5.37) is practically stabilizable, i.e., A_p and B_p are left coprime on $\mathbf{H}$, and $\tilde{B}_p$ and A_s are skew prime on $\mathbf{H}$.*

The following procedure can be utilized to design a practical tracking control system (Xu *et al.* 1997a).

Procedure 1:

Step 1. For given A_p, B_p, verify whether they are left coprime on $\mathbf{H}$ according to Theorem 5.7. If it is the case, then find $\tilde{A}_p$ and $\tilde{B}_p \in \mathbf{M}(\mathbf{R}[z_1, z_2])$ which satisfy $A_p^{-1} D_p = \tilde{B}_p \tilde{A}_p^{-1}$ and are right factor coprime by the methods of, e.g., (Guiver & Bose 1982, Morf *et al.* 1977).

Step 2. Solve the Bezout equation

$$A_c \tilde{A}_p + B_{c2} \tilde{B}_p = I \qquad (5.43)$$

by the algorithm given in (Xu *et al.* 1994a). Here, first find a particular solution $X, Y \in M(H)$ such that $X \tilde{A}_p + Y \tilde{B}_p = I$, then construct the following general solution to (5.43)

$$
\begin{aligned}
A_c &= X + SB_p & (5.44) \\
B_{c2} &= Y - SA_p & (5.45)
\end{aligned}
$$

where $S \in M(H)$ is an arbitrary matrix satisfying $\det A_c(0,0) \neq 0$.

Step 3. Verify the solvability of the skew prime equation

$$\tilde{B}_p B_{c1} + Q A_s = I \qquad (5.46)$$

and, if it is solvable, find the solution $B_{c1}, Q \in M(H)$, by the methods given in Section 5.4.1.

5.4.3 Application to linear multipass processes

Multipass processes are a class of dynamic systems characterized by a series of passes, through a set of dynamics defined over a finite time interval, with the output of previous passes contributing to the output of the later passes (see (Rogers & Owens 1992) and references therein).

Connections between linear multipass processes and 2D systems have been considered by several researchers (Boland & Owens 1980, Galkowski *et al.* 1997, Rocha *et al.* 1996, Rogers & Owens 1992, Xu *et al.* 1994c, Xu *et al.* 1997a). In what follows, we just show how we can apply the results for practical tracking control to design a control system for multipass processes.

Consider the non-unit memory discrete linear multipass processes described by the state-space model (Rogers & Owens 1992)

$$
x_{k+1}(i+1) = A x_{k+1}(i) + B u_{k+1}(i) + \sum_{j=1}^{M} B_{j-1} y_{k+1-j}(i) \qquad (5.47)
$$

$$
y_{k+1}(i) = C x_{k+1}(i) + D_0 u_{k+1}(i) + \sum_{j=1}^{M} D_j y_{k-j}(i) \qquad (5.48)
$$

$$
0 \leq i \leq N, \, x_k(0) = d_k, \quad k \geq 0
$$

where $u_k(i) \in \mathbf{R}^l$, $y_k(i) \in \mathbf{R}^m$, and $x_k(i) \in \mathbf{R}^p$ are the input, output and state vectors on the k-th pass respectively; A, B, C, B_j, D_j are constant matrices with suitable dimensions, and the pass length N is a fixed finite constant.

Define

$$
\xi(i,k) = [x_k^T(i), \, y_{k-1}^T(i), \, \ldots, \, y_{k-M}^T(i)]^T \in \mathbf{R}^{p+mM} \qquad (5.49)
$$

Then, (5.47) can be expressed as the 2D Fornasini-Marchesini model:

$$
\begin{aligned}
\xi(i+1, k+1) &= \tilde{A}_1 \xi(i, k+1) + \tilde{A}_2 \xi(i+1, k) \\
&\quad + \tilde{B}_1 u(i, k+1) + \tilde{B}_2 u(i+1, k) \qquad (5.50) \\
y(i, k) &= \tilde{C} \xi(i, k) + D_0 u(i, k) \qquad\qquad (5.51)
\end{aligned}
$$

where

$$
\tilde{A}_1 =
\begin{bmatrix}
A & B_0 & B_1 & \cdots & B_{M-1} \\
0 & 0 & 0 & \cdots & 0 \\
0 & 0 & \ddots & & 0 \\
\vdots & & & \ddots & \vdots \\
0 & 0 & 0 & \cdots & 0
\end{bmatrix},
$$

$$
\tilde{A}_2 =
\begin{bmatrix}
0 & 0 & \cdots & 0 & 0 \\
C & D_1 & \cdots & D_{M-1} & D_M \\
0 & I & \cdots & 0 & 0 \\
\vdots & & \ddots & 0 & 0 \\
0 & 0 & \cdots & I & 0
\end{bmatrix}
$$

$$
\tilde{B}_1 = [B^T, \, 0, \, \ldots, \, 0]^T, \qquad \tilde{B}_2 = [0, \, D_0, \, 0, \, \ldots, 0]^T,
$$

$$
\tilde{C} = [C, \, D_1, \, \ldots, D_M]
$$

It can be shown that the transfer matrix $G(z_1, z_2)$ of (5.51) satisfy the relation

$$
\begin{aligned}
G(z_1, z_2) &= \tilde{C}(I_{p+mM} - z_1 \tilde{A}_1 - z_2 \tilde{A}_2)^{-1}(z_1 \tilde{B}_1 + z_2 \tilde{B}_2) + D_0 \\
&= (I_m - \sum_{j=1}^{M} G_j(z_1) z_2^j)^{-1} G_0(z_1) \qquad\qquad (5.52)
\end{aligned}
$$

where

$$
\begin{aligned}
G_0(z_1) &= C(I_p - z_1 A)^{-1} z_1 B + D_0 \qquad\qquad (5.53) \\
G_j(z_1) &= C(I_p - z_1 A)^{-1} z_1 B_{j-1} + D_j, \qquad\qquad (5.54)
\end{aligned}
$$

and z_1, z_2 can be regarded as backward shift operators. Note that the 2D Fornasini-Marchesini model of (5.51) directly corresponds to a Roesser model which is simply equivalent to the ones shown in (Rocha *et al.* 1996) and (Galkowski *et al.* 1997). It is thus clear that the class of multipass processes is a special case of the standard 2D systems, and the results developed for 2D systems can be applied directly.

For $G(z_1, z_2)$ given by (5.52), it is trivial to see

$$
G(z_1, 0) = G_0(z_1) \qquad\qquad (5.55)
$$

$$
G(0, z_2) = \mathrm{adj}\left(I_m - \sum_{j=1}^{M} D_j z_2^j\right) D_0 / \rho(z_2) \qquad\qquad (5.56)
$$

We then have that $G(z_1, z_2)$ is practically stable iff $G(z_1, 0)$ and $G(0, z_2)$ are both 1D stable. In particular, the latter is equivalent to condition for the asymptotic stability for linear multipass processes given in (Rogers & Owens 1992). Further, by practical stability theory, if we need also to consider the stability as the pass length $N \to \infty$ but the iteration index k is finite, then the 1D stability condition of $G(z_1, 0)$ has to be satisfied. That is reasonable to consider such situation since it has been observed (also see (Kurek & Zaremba 1993) for a similar situation) that, if the pass length N is large, there may exist the cases where the system outputs value are excessively large for large time i and small iteration number k. Practical stability theory, therefore, not only shows some significant insights but also supplies a rather reasonable design requirement for linear multipass processes.

In the following, a solution will be shown to the control problem of linear multipass processes under the condition of practical stability, i.e., the problem how to find an (output) feedback controller for a given multipass process such that the resultant closed-loop system is (asymptotically) stable and the output converges to a sequence of specified reference signals with finite pass length.

In fact, the above problem can be easily formulated to the practical tracking problem stated in Section 5.4.2. A reference signal $r_k(i)$ for multipass processes with finite pass length N can be regarded as 2D signal $r(i, k)$ in the form

$$r(i, k) = \begin{cases} r_k(i) & (0 \le i \le N) \\ 0 & (i > N) \end{cases} \tag{5.57}$$

Applying 2D z-transform to $r(i, k)$ yields

$$r(z_1, z_2) = \sum_{i=0}^{N} \sum_{k=0}^{\infty} r(i, k) z_2^k z_1^i \in \mathbf{M}(\mathbf{R}(z_2)[z_1]) \tag{5.58}$$

i.e., the entries of $r(z_1, z_2)$ are polynomials in z_1 having polynomial fractions in z_2 as coefficients. Therefore, we can always have

$$r(z_1, z_2) = A_s^{-1}(z_2) B_s(z_1, z_2) \tag{5.59}$$

where $A_s(z_2) \in \mathbf{M}(\mathbf{R}[z_2])$ and $B_s(z_1, z_2) \in \mathbf{M}(\mathbf{R}[z_1, z_2])$. Suppose that $A_s(z_2)$ and $B_s(z_1, z_2)$ are left coprime on $\mathbf{H}$, which means that the matrices $[A_s(z_2) \quad B_s(0, z_2)]$ and $[A_s(0) \quad B_s(z_1, 0)]$ are full rank for any $z_1, z_2 \in \bar{U}$.

Letting $G(z_1, z_2) = A_p^{-1}(z_1, z_2) B_p(z_1, z_2)$, we see that the considered problem is a special case of the 2D practical tracking problem with a reference signal specified by (5.59), so Procedure 1 can be applied directly.

5.4.4 Application to iterative learning control systems (ILCS)

A discrete iterative learning control system (ILCS) for a given (1D) plant is demanded to repetitively track a specified output trajectory $y_d(i)$ on a finite discrete-time interval $i \in [1, N]$ with the system performance improved based on the evaluation of the performance on previous iterations. Some design approaches for ILCS have been proposed based on either conventional 1D system design principles or artificial intelligence (see e.g. (Geng *et al.* 1990, Moore 1993) and the references therein). Since it is in general difficult to unitedly characterize by a 1D system model the two kinds of dynamics in ILCS, i.e., the dynamics of the control system itself on the time interval and the behavior of the learning process along the direction of iterations, most approaches for convergence analysis and learning system design based on 1D techniques are of an *ad hoc* type and usually adopt a fixed learning law for a particular task (Geng *et al.* 1990). In fact, most fundamental properties of ILCS such as the interaction between the two different dynamics of ILCS and their effects to stability, learning convergence and performance of ILCS have not yet been fully understood (Amann *et al.* 1996, Amann *et al.* 1998, Geng *et al.* 1990).

On the other hand, recent research results based on 2D approaches have shown that 2D system theory may offer a highly promising approach to ILCS (Amann *et al.* 1996, Amann *et al.* 1998, Geng *et al.* 1990, Kurek & Zaremba 1993, Xu *et al.* 1994b, Xu *et al.* 1997a, Yamada *et al.* 1999b). In particular, the entire dynamics involved in ILCS can be easily represented by a 2D model, and 2D stability theory provides a natural and useful method for analysis of learning convergence and stability of ILCS. However, although (Geng *et al.* 1990) proposed a general type of learning controller structure based on 2D model and showed a convergence condition for the learning controller in terms of 2D stability, no constructive procedures were provided for the test of the condition and the design of such general learning controller, except for a very restricted particular case. In fact, it would be extremely difficult, if not impossible, to find such general procedures under the convergence condition given by (Geng *et al.* 1990) since the condition itself contains the as yet undetermined parameters of the controller under design. Further, the feature that the length of the time interval is finite was not taken into account in (Geng *et al.* 1990) and the conventional 2D stability was directly applied to the analysis of learning convergence, which is in fact overly restrictive as indicated in (Kurek & Zaremba 1993).

It has been shown that it is possible to design a ILCS, by the method proposed for 2D practical tracking systems, under the less restrictive conditions of practical stability and without requiring a *priori* restriction on the controller structure (Xu *et al.* 1997a).

Consider the 1D system given by

$$x(i+1) = Ax(i) + Bu(i) \tag{5.60}$$

$$y(i) = Cx(i) + Du(i) \tag{5.61}$$

where u, y, x are the input, output and state vectors, respectively; A, B, C, D are real matrices with suitable dimensions.

The problem may now be formulated as follows. Given system (5.61) with boundary condition $x(0) = x_0$, and a reference output trajectory $y_d(i)$ $(i = 1, \ldots, N)$, find a learning control scheme such that the tracking error $y(i) - y_d(i)$ for all $i \in [1, N]$ asymptotically converges to zero along the direction of learning iterations.

Denote by j the iteration number, and by $\tilde{u}(i, j)$, $\tilde{y}(i, j)$, $\tilde{x}(i, j)$ the values of the input, output and state vectors at the time point i of the jth iteration, respectively. Then, the plant (5.61) can be viewed as a 2D discrete system in the form

$$\tilde{x}(i+1, j) = A\tilde{x}(i, j) + B\tilde{u}(i, j) \tag{5.62}$$

$$\tilde{y}(i, j) = C\tilde{x}(i, j) + D\tilde{u}(i, j) \tag{5.63}$$

where the boundary conditions are $\tilde{x}(i, 0), 0 \le i \le N$ and $\tilde{x}(0, j), j \ge 0$. Similarly, denote by $\tilde{y}_d(i, j)$ the reference trajectory. Since the identical $y_d(i)$ is used for all iterations, $\tilde{y}_d(i, j)$ can be represented as follows.

$$\tilde{y}_d(i, j) = \begin{cases} y_d(i) & (0 \le i \le N) \\ 0 & (i > N) \end{cases} \tag{5.64}$$

Further, define the tracking error $\tilde{e}(i,j)$ as

$$\tilde{e}(i,j) = \tilde{y}_d(i,j) - \tilde{y}(i,j). \tag{5.65}$$

Applying 2D z-transform to (5.63) gives

$$\tilde{Y}(z_1, z_2) = [C(I - z_1 A)^{-1} z_1 B + D] \tilde{U}(z_1, z_2)$$
$$+ C(I - z_1 A)^{-1} \sum_{j=0}^{\infty} \tilde{x}(0,j) z_2^j \tag{5.66}$$

Find $D_p(z_1), C_p(z_1) \in \mathbf{M}(\mathbf{R}[z_1])$ that satisfy $C(I - z_1 A)^{-1} = D_p^{-1}(z_1) C_p(z_1)$ and $\det D_p(0) \neq 0$ and are left coprime. Then, (5.66) can be rewritten as

$$\tilde{Y}(z_1, z_2) = D_p^{-1}(z_1) N_p(z_1) \tilde{U}(z_1, z_2) + D_p^{-1}(z_1) C_p(z_1) \tilde{X}_0(z_2) \tag{5.67}$$

where $N_p(z_1) = C_p(z_1) z_1 B + D_p(z_1) D$ and $\tilde{X}_0(z_2) = \sum_{j=0}^{\infty} \tilde{x}(0,j) z_2^j$.
The 2D z-transform of (5.64) is

$$\tilde{Y}_d(z_1, z_2) = (1 - z_2)^{-1} \sum_{i=0}^{N} \tilde{y}_d(i,0) z_1^i = (1 - z_2)^{-1} \sum_{i=0}^{N} y_d(i) z_1^i$$
$$\triangleq (1 - z_2)^{-1} Y_d(z_1) \tag{5.68}$$

Obviously, the entries of $Y_d(z_1)$ are 1D polynomials of N degree in z_1.

Considering that a general learning controller may depend on the information of the input and the tracking error in both the present iteration and a finite number of previous iterations, we use a general linear controller structure as follows.

$$\tilde{U}(z_1, z_2) = D_c^{-1}(z_1, z_2) N_{c1}(z_1, z_2) \tilde{Y}_d(z_1, z_2) - D_c^{-1}(z_1, z_2) N_{c2}(z_1, z_2) \tilde{Y}(z_1, z_2) \tag{5.69}$$

where $D_c, N_{c1}, N_{c2} \in \mathbf{M}(\mathbf{H})$.

Similarly as previous discussions for multipass processes, besides the convergence of ILCS in the direction of learning iterations, it is also reasonable to consider the stability of the system in the time direction $(i \to \infty)$ at a fixed iteration. It should be clear that, in this case, the considered problem is just a special case of the 2D practical tracking problem.

In view of Procedure 1, D_c and N_{c2} can be determined by solving the equation

$$D_c(z_1, z_2) \tilde{D}_p(z_1) + N_{c2}(z_1, z_2) \tilde{N}_p(z_1) = I \tag{5.70}$$

where $\tilde{N}_p(z_1) \tilde{D}_p^{-1}(z_1) = D_p^{-1}(z_1) N_p(z_1)$, $\tilde{D}_p(z_1), \tilde{N}_p(z_1) \in \mathbf{M}(\mathbf{R}[z_1])$, $\det \tilde{D}_p(0) \neq 0$.
If the 1D plant (5.61) is stabilizable, there exist $X_1, Y_1, \Phi_1 \in \mathbf{M}(\mathbf{R}[z_1])$ such that

$$X_1(z_1) \tilde{D}_p(z_1) + Y_1(z_1) \tilde{N}_p(z_1) = \Phi_1(z_1) \tag{5.71}$$

with $X_1(0) = I, Y_1(0) = 0, \det \Phi_1(z_1) \neq 0, \forall z_1 \in \bar{U}$.

It is clear $\Phi_1(0) = \tilde{D}_p(0)$. On the other hand, since $\tilde{D}_p(0)$ and $\tilde{N}_p(0)$ are real matrices, the equation

$$X_2(z_2) \tilde{D}_p(0) + Y_2(z_2) \tilde{N}_p(0) = \Phi_2(z_2) \tag{5.72}$$

will always be solvable for the solution $X_2(z_2) = I, Y_2(z_2) = 0, \Phi_2(z_2) = \tilde{D}_p(0)$ and $\det \Phi_2(z_2) = \det D_p(0) \neq 0$. Therefore, the following general solution to (5.70) can be obtained.

$$D_c(z_1, z_2) = \Phi_1^{-1}(z_1)X_1(z_1) + S(z_1, z_2)N_p(z_1) \qquad (5.73)$$

$$N_{c2}(z_1, z_2) = \Phi_1^{-1}(z_1)Y_1(z_1) - S(z_1, z_2)D_p(z_1) \qquad (5.74)$$

where $S(z_1, z_2) \in \mathbf{M}(\mathbf{H})$ is an arbitrary matrix satisfying $\det D_c(0, 0) \neq 0$.

Further, due to Theorem 5.19 and (5.68), N_{c1} can be obtained by solution of

$$\tilde{N}_p(z_1)N_{c1}(z_1, z_2) + T(z_1, z_2)(1 - z_2) = I \qquad (5.75)$$

Several features of the proposed approach can be observed (Xu *et al.* 1997a). In most existing design methods for ILCS, the up-dating control input

$$\tilde{u}(i, j) = \tilde{u}(i, j - 1) + \Delta\tilde{u}(i, j - 1) \qquad (5.76)$$

is used and the input modification $\Delta\tilde{u}$ is usually restricted to rather simple structure in order to make the design possible (see, e.g. (Moore 1993) by 1D approach and (Geng *et al.* 1990) by 2D approach). However, in this way, it would be difficult to answer the question whether or not more general controllers exist when one failed in the design. In fact, most (1D) design approaches for (5.76) require the invertibility of the plant in order to obtain a zero tracking error (Moore 1993), but the presented approach does not require this condition and thus can also be applied to non-minimum phase plant. A more general learning controller has also been given in (Moore 1993) which can be represented in the following form for the case considered here.

$$U_{k+1}(z_1) = T_u(z_1)U_k(z_1) + T_e(z_1)(Y_d(z_1) - Y_k(z_1)) \qquad (5.77)$$

where $T_u \neq I$ (if $T_u = I$, then it will just be the same as (5.76)). Though it has been shown that by a learning controller in this form it is possible to avoid the problem of plant invertibility, while still making the learning iteration convergent, the tracking error $e_k = y_d - y_k$ will not converge to zero now (Moore 1993). In contrast to this, the presented approach gives a constructive design procedure for the most general linear learning controller (5.69), which obviously contains (5.76) and (5.77) as special cases, without *a priori* restriction on its structure. Another obvious advantage of (5.69) is that it has both feedback and feedforward structures and may provide the possibility to improve robustness of the designed system to disturbances and plant modeling error, while (5.76) has only a feedforward structure in the direction of learning iterations (see (Xu *et al.* 1997b) and similar discussions in (Amann *et al.* 1996, Amann *et al.* 1998)).

It should also be noted that the proposed procedure does not require any information on the value of the reference trajectory. As a matter of fact, besides the model of the plant, what we need is just to know that the reference signal is restricted in a finite time interval and it does not vary with the iterations. This means that, for a given plant, it is possible to design a learning scheme such that the resultant ILCS repetitively tracks an arbitrary trajectory as long as it is restricted in a finite time interval (Xu *et al.* 1997a).

5.5 2D OPTIMAL CONTROL IN A PRACTICAL SENSE

Since the results on 2D practical tracking control shown in the previous section are mainly based on the consideration of steady-state performance of the resultant control systems, no guarantee is provided in general for the transient performance. Optimal control and model following control would be naturally considered as an effective strategy to improve the system transient performance (Furuta & Komiya 1982). As a special case of 2D LQR (linear quadratic regulator) problem, 2D minimum-energy problem in the finite-horizon case (both the two variables bounded) and its application to multipass processes have been considered in, e.g., (Kaczorek & Klamka 1986, Li & Fadali 1991). The optimal control obtained for this case, however, is an open-loop one. 2D LQR problem in the infinite-horizon case (both variables unbounded) have also been considered in (Bisiacco & Fornasini 1990, Bisiacco 1995) where, however, a substantial difficulty is encountered that infinite-dimensional global state feedback is in general required. Therefore, we see that, for practical applications, it would be more reasonable and practicable to consider 2D optimal control in the practical sense of allowing only one variable unbounded.

The authors have recently solved 2D optimal control and model-following servo problems for the case that one of the two variables of the considered 2D systems is unbounded, and the other one is bounded (Yamada *et al.* 1999b, Yamada *et al.* 1999a). This case is slightly different with the practical sense we have had in the previous sections where either of the two variables may take an infinite value but they cannot be infinite simultaneously. For brevity, we only summarize here some basic results on the 2D optimal control in the above mentioned practical sense, and refer the interested readers to (Yamada *et al.* 1999b) for the 2D model-following servo control.

5.5.1   Problem formulation and solution

Consider a 2D plant given by the 2D Roesser state-space model:

$$\begin{aligned} x'(i,j) &= Ax(i,j) + Bu(i,j) \\ y(i,j) &= Cx(i,j) \end{aligned} \tag{5.78}$$

where $x(i,j) = [x^{hT}(i,j) \ x^{vT}(i,j)]^T \in \mathbf{R}^{\bar{n}}$ is the local state vector with $x^h(i,j) \in \mathbf{R}^{n_h}, x^v(i,j) \in \mathbf{R}^{n_v}$, $n = n_h + n_v$. $u(i,j) \in \mathbf{R}^m$ and $y(i,j) \in \mathbf{R}^p$ are the input and output vectors, respectively.

$$A = \begin{bmatrix} A_{11} & A_{12} \\ A_{21} & A_{22} \end{bmatrix} \in \mathbf{R}^{\bar{n}\times\bar{n}}, \ B = \begin{bmatrix} B_1 \\ B_2 \end{bmatrix} \in \mathbf{R}^{\bar{n}\times m},$$

$$C = \begin{bmatrix} C_1 & C_2 \end{bmatrix} \in \mathbf{R}^{p\times\bar{n}}$$

The boundary condition is given as

$$\begin{aligned} x^h(0,j) &= x_0^j, \ j = 0,1,\dots,N \\ x^v(i,0) &= 0, \ i = 0,1,\dots \end{aligned}$$

The assumption $x^v(i,0) = 0$ is made for the purpose to make $x(i,j) \to 0$ as $i \to \infty$ in the following problem.

Problem 4.1: For the given system (5.78), find a control input that minimize the performance index

$$J = \sum_{i=0}^{\infty} \sum_{j=0}^{N} \|y(i,j)\|_Q + \sum_{i=1}^{\infty} \sum_{j=0}^{N} \|u(i,j)\|_R \tag{5.79}$$

where $\|a(i,j)\|_M$ denotes $a^T(i,j)Ma(i,j)$, and $Q \in \mathbf{R}^{p \times p}$, $R \in \mathbf{R}^{m \times m}$ are symmetric positive definite matrices.

It is first shown that Problem 4.1 can be reduced to a 1D LQR problem and thus can be solved by using the well-known 1D approaches. Calculating $x(i+1,1)$, $x(i+1,2)$, ..., $x(i+1,N)$ from (5.78) and carrying out sequential substitutions, we can have the following equivalent description of the system (5.78).

$$x^h(i+1,0) = A_{11}x^h(i,0) + B_1u(i,0) \tag{5.80}$$

$$x(i+1,j) = (A^{0,1})^j \bar{A}^{1,0} x^h(i,0) + \sum_{l=1}^{j}(A^{0,1})^{j-l}A^{1,0}x(i,l)$$

$$+ \sum_{l=0}^{j}(A^{0,1})^{j-l}B^{1,0}u(i,l)$$

$$+ \sum_{l=0}^{j-1}(A^{0,1})^{j-l-1}B^{0,1}u(i+1,l), \quad j = 1,2,\ldots,N \tag{5.81}$$

where

$$A^{1,0} = \begin{bmatrix} A_{11} & A_{12} \\ 0 & 0 \end{bmatrix}, \quad A^{0,1} = \begin{bmatrix} 0 & 0 \\ A_{21} & A_{22} \end{bmatrix}$$

$$\bar{A}^{1,0} = \begin{bmatrix} A_{11} \\ 0 \end{bmatrix}, \quad B^{1,0} = \begin{bmatrix} B_1 \\ 0 \end{bmatrix}, \quad B^{0,1} = \begin{bmatrix} 0 \\ B_2 \end{bmatrix}.$$

By defining the vectors

$$\tilde{x}(i) = \left[x^{hT}(i,0)\, x^T(i,1) \cdots x^T(i,N) \right]^T \in \mathbf{R}^{n_h+N\tilde{n}},$$

$$\tilde{u}(i) = \left[u^T(i,0)\, u^T(i,1) \cdots u^T(i,N) \right]^T \in \mathbf{R}^{(N+1)m},$$

$$\tilde{y}(i) = \left[y^T(i,0)\, y^T(i,1) \cdots y^T(i,N) \right]^T \in \mathbf{R}^{(N+1)p},$$

we can express (5.78) as a 1D system in the form

$$\tilde{x}(i+1) = \tilde{A}\tilde{x}(i) + \tilde{B}_1\tilde{u}(i) + \tilde{B}_2\tilde{u}(i+1)$$
$$\tilde{y}(i) = \tilde{C}\tilde{x}(i) \tag{5.82}$$

with

$$\tilde{A} = \begin{bmatrix} A_{11} & 0 & \cdots & 0 \\ A^{0,1}\bar{A}^{1,0} & A^{1,0} & \cdots & 0 \\ (A^{0,1})^2\bar{A}^{1,0} & A^{0,1}A^{1,0} & \cdots & 0 \\ \vdots & \vdots & \ddots & \vdots \\ (A^{0,1})^N\bar{A}^{1,0} & (A^{0,1})^{N-1}A^{1,0} & \cdots & A^{1,0} \end{bmatrix},$$

$$\tilde{B}_1 = \begin{bmatrix} B_1 & 0 & \cdots & 0 \\ A^{0,1}B^{1,0} & B^{1,0} & \cdots & 0 \\ (A^{0,1})^2B^{1,0} & A^{0,1}B^{1,0} & \cdots & 0 \\ \vdots & \vdots & \ddots & \vdots \\ (A^{0,1})^NB^{1,0} & (A^{0,1})^{N-1}B^{1,0} & \cdots & B^{1,0} \end{bmatrix},$$

$$\tilde{B}_2 \; = \; \begin{bmatrix} 0 & 0 & \cdots & 0 & 0 \\ B^{0,1} & 0 & \cdots & 0 & 0 \\ A^{0,1}B^{0,1} & B^{0,1} & \cdots & 0 & 0 \\ \vdots & \vdots & \ddots & \vdots & \vdots \\ (A^{0,1})^{N-1}B^{0,1} & (A^{0,1})^{N-2}B^{0,1} & \cdots & B^{0,1} & 0 \end{bmatrix},$$

$$\tilde{C} \; = \; \text{block diag}\,(C_1,\, C,\ldots, C).$$

The boundary condition for (5.82) is given by

$$\tilde{x}(0) = \begin{bmatrix} x_0^T & x^T(0,1) \cdots x^T(0,N) \end{bmatrix}^T \tag{5.83}$$

where

$$x(0,j) \; = \; \begin{bmatrix} x_0^j \\ \displaystyle\sum_{l=0}^{j-1}(A_{22})^{j-l-1}A_{21}x_0^l \\ + \displaystyle\sum_{l=0}^{j-1}(A_{22})^{j-l-1}B_2u(0,l) \end{bmatrix}, \tag{5.84}$$

$$j = 1, 2, \ldots, N.$$

Note that $\tilde{u}(0)$ is also involved in the boundary condition and thus should be given previously.

For there exists an extra term $(\tilde{B}_2\tilde{u}(i+1))$ in the right-hand side of (5.82) compared with a standard 1D system model, the approach for 1D LQR problem cannot yet be directly applied.

Applying the following feedback control law to (5.82)

$$\tilde{u}(i) = -K_1\tilde{x}(i-1) - K_2\tilde{u}(i-1) \tag{5.85}$$

gives

$$\begin{aligned} \tilde{x}(i+1) & = \; \tilde{A}\tilde{x} + \tilde{B}_1\tilde{u}(i) + \tilde{B}_2\{-K_1\tilde{x}(i) - K_2\tilde{u}(i)\} \\ & = \; (\tilde{A} - \tilde{B}_2K_1)\tilde{x}(i) + (\tilde{B}_1 - \tilde{B}_2K_2)\tilde{u}(i). \end{aligned} \tag{5.86}$$

Thus, from (5.85) and (5.86) we get the closed-loop system:

$$\begin{aligned} \begin{bmatrix} \tilde{x}(i) \\ \tilde{u}(i) \end{bmatrix} & = \begin{bmatrix} \tilde{A} - \tilde{B}_2K_1 & \tilde{B}_1 - \tilde{B}_2K_2 \\ -K_1 & -K_2 \end{bmatrix} \begin{bmatrix} \tilde{x}(i-1) \\ \tilde{u}(i-1) \end{bmatrix} \\ & = \left\{ \begin{bmatrix} \tilde{A} & \tilde{B}_1 \\ 0 & 0 \end{bmatrix} - \begin{bmatrix} \tilde{B}_2 \\ I_{(N+1)m} \end{bmatrix} \begin{bmatrix} K_1 & K_2 \end{bmatrix} \right\} \begin{bmatrix} \tilde{x}(i-1) \\ \tilde{u}(i-1) \end{bmatrix} \end{aligned} \tag{5.87}$$

In view of the form of (5.87), we see that the problem to find the feedback law (5.85) for the system (5.82) can be regarded as a problem to find the feedback

$$\tilde{u}(i) = -K_a x_a(i) \tag{5.88}$$

for the (open-loop) system

$$\begin{aligned} x_a(i+1) & = \; A_a x_a(i) + B_a \tilde{u}(i) \\ \tilde{y}(i) & = \; C_a x_a(i) + D_a \tilde{u}(i) \end{aligned} \tag{5.89}$$

where

$$x_a(i) = \begin{bmatrix} \tilde{x}(i-1) \\ \tilde{u}(i-1) \end{bmatrix} \in \mathbf{R}^{N(\tilde{n}+m)+n_h+m},$$

$$A_a = \begin{bmatrix} \tilde{A} & \tilde{B}_1 \\ 0 & 0 \end{bmatrix}, \quad B_a = \begin{bmatrix} \tilde{B}_2 \\ I_{(N+1)m} \end{bmatrix},$$

$$C_a = \begin{bmatrix} \tilde{C}\tilde{A} & \tilde{C}\tilde{B}_1 \end{bmatrix}, \quad D_a = \tilde{C}\tilde{B}_2$$

$$K_a = \begin{bmatrix} K_1 & K_2 \end{bmatrix}. \tag{5.90}$$

The boundary condition for (5.89) is

$$x_a(1) = \begin{bmatrix} \tilde{x}^T(0) & \tilde{u}^T(0) \end{bmatrix}^T. \tag{5.91}$$

Further, it is also ready to show that the performance index (5.79) can be rewritten in the 1D form

$$J = \sum_{i=0}^{\infty} \tilde{y}^T(i)Q_a\tilde{y}(i) + \sum_{i=1}^{\infty} \tilde{u}^T(i)R_a\tilde{u}(i) \tag{5.92}$$

where,

$$Q_a = \text{block diag}(\overbrace{Q,\ldots,Q}^{N+1}),$$

$$R_a = \text{block diag}(\overbrace{R,\ldots,R}^{N+1}) \tag{5.93}$$

Let

$$\bar{C}_a = \begin{bmatrix} \tilde{C} & 0 \end{bmatrix} \tag{5.94}$$

then (5.92) becomes

$$J = \sum_{i=1}^{\infty} \left\{ x_a^T(i)\bar{C}_a^T Q_a \bar{C}_a x_a(i) + \tilde{u}^T(i)R_a\tilde{u}(i) \right\} \tag{5.95}$$

Due to the definition of Q,R, we see that Q_a, R_u are symmetric positive definite matrices. It is now clear that Problem 4.1 has been reduced to the following problem:

Problem 4.2:   Find a control input for the system (5.89) such that the performance index (5.95) is minimized.

It follows immediately from 1D optimal control theory that:

Lemma 5.20 (Yamada *et al.* 1999a) *If $(A_a, B_a, \bar{C}_a)$ is stabilizable and detectable, Problem 4.2 is solvable and the optimal control input which minimizes the performance index (5.95) is given by*

$$\tilde{u}(i) = -(R_a + B_a^T PB_a)^{-1}B_a^T PA_a x_a(i) \tag{5.96}$$

where P is a symmetric positive semidefinite solution to the Riccati equation

$$P = A_a^T PA_a + \bar{C}_a^T Q_a \bar{C}_a - A_a^T PB_a(R_a + B_a^T PB_a)^{-1}B_a^T PA_a \tag{5.97}$$

A natural question arises now: what does the (1D) condition given in Lemma 5.20 mean for the original 2D system?

Due to the results of Theorems 9, 10, we see that, for the case where a certain variable, say i_j ($j \in \{1, 2, \ldots, n\}$), is fixed to be unbounded while all the other ones are always bounded to finite region, the practical stabilizability and detectability of the nD system (5.6) are equivalent to the 1D stabilizability and detectability of (A_{jj}, B_j, C_j). Therefore, we will call the nD system (5.6) practically stabilizable, or respectively, practically detectable, in the direction of i_j iff (A_{jj}, B_j, C_j) is 1D stabilizable, or detectable.

Now we have the following results.

Lemma 5.21 (Yamada *et al.* 1999a) *(A_a, B_a) is stabilizable iff 2D system (5.78) is practically stabilizable in the direction of i, i.e., (A_{11}, B_1) is 1D stabilizable.*

Lemma 5.22 (Yamada *et al.* 1999a) *$(\bar{C}_a, A_a)$ is detectable iff the 2D system (5.78) is practically detectable in the direction of i, i.e., (C_1, A_{11}) is 1D detectable.*

Based on the above results, then, we have the following theorem.

Theorem 5.23 (Yamada *et al.* 1999a) *When the 2D system (5.78) is practically stabilizable and detectable in the direction of i, i.e., (A_{11}, B_1, C_1) is 1D stabilizable and detectable, an optimal control in the form of (5.85) that minimizes the performance index (5.79) is given by*

$$
\begin{aligned}
K_1 &= (R_a + B_a^T P B_a)^{-1} B_a^T P_1 \tilde{A} \\
K_2 &= (R_a + B_a^T P B_a)^{-1} B_a^T P_1 \tilde{B}_1
\end{aligned} \tag{5.98}
$$

where $P_1 \in \mathbf{R}^{\{N(n+m)+n_h+m\} \times (n_h+Nn)}$ is obtained from the symmetric positive semidefinite solution $P = [P_1 \; P_2]$ of the Riccati equation (5.97).

Proof: In view of Lemmas 5.21, 5.22, if (A_{11}, B_1, C_1) is stabilizable and detectable, $(A_a, B_a, \bar{C}_a)$ will be, too. Then, it follows from Lemma 5.20 that the optimal control input minimizing the performance index (5.95), or equivalently (5.79), is given by (5.96) which can be written in the form

$$
\begin{aligned}
\tilde{u}(i) &= -(R_a + B_a^T P B_a)^{-1} B_a^T P A_a x_a(i) \\
&= -(R_a + B_a^T P B_a)^{-1} B_a^T \begin{bmatrix} P_1 & P_2 \end{bmatrix} \begin{bmatrix} \tilde{A} & \tilde{B}_1 \\ 0 & 0 \end{bmatrix} \begin{bmatrix} \tilde{x}(i-1) \\ \tilde{y}(i-1) \end{bmatrix} \\
&= -(R_a + B_a^T P B_a)^{-1} B_a^T \left\{ P_1 \tilde{A} \tilde{x}(i-1) + P_1 \tilde{B}_1 \tilde{u}(i-1) \right\}.
\end{aligned} \tag{5.99}
$$

Then, the result of (5.98) is obtained from (5.99) and (5.85). ∎

5.5.2 Application to ILCS

For convenience, we rewrite here the plant of ILCS in the 2D form of (5.63):

$$
\begin{aligned}
x(k, t+1) &= A_l x(k, t) + B_l u(k, t) \tag{5.100} \\
y(k, t) &= C_l x(k, t) + D_l u(k, t) \tag{5.101}
\end{aligned}
$$

Consider the updating control input

$$u(k+1,t) = u(k,t) + \Delta u(k,t) \tag{5.102}$$

where $\Delta u(k,t)$ is the input modification.

(5.101) and (5.102) give a kind of 2D system description for ILCS where the control input is $\Delta u(k,t)$. Assume that the boundary condition for (5.101) and (5.102) are given as

$$
\begin{aligned}
x(k,0) &= x_0, \ k = 0,1,\ldots \\
u(0,t) &= 0, \ t = 0,1,\ldots,N
\end{aligned}
$$

Let

$$e(k,t) = y_r(t) - y(k,t) \tag{5.103}$$

Then, it follows from (5.101), (5.103) that

$$
\begin{aligned}
e(k+1,t) - e(k,t) &= \{y_r(t) - y(k+1,t)\} - \{y_r(t) - y(k,t)\} \\
&= -\{C_l x(k+1,t) + D_l u(k+1,t)\} + \{C_l x(k,t) + D_l u(k,t)\} \\
&= -C_l \{x(k+1,t) - x(k,t)\} - D_l \{u(k+1,t) - u(k,t)\} \tag{5.104}
\end{aligned}
$$

Defining

$$\eta(k,t) = x(k+1,t) - x(k,t), \tag{5.105}$$

we have

$$e(k+1,t) = e(k,t) - C_l \eta(k,t) - D_l \Delta u(k,t). \tag{5.106}$$

Further, from (5.101), (5.105) we see

$$\eta(k,t+1) = A_l \eta(k,t) + B_l \Delta u(k,t) \tag{5.107}$$

Therefore, we obtain a Roesser model for ILCS as

$$
\begin{aligned}
\bar{x}'(k,t) &= \bar{A}\bar{x}(k,t) + \bar{B}\Delta u(k,t) \tag{5.108} \\
e(k,t) &= \bar{C}\bar{x}(k,t) \tag{5.109}
\end{aligned}
$$

where

$$\bar{x}(k,t) = \begin{bmatrix} e(k,t) \\ \eta(k,t) \end{bmatrix} \in \mathbf{R}^{n_l+p_l}, \ \bar{x}' = \begin{bmatrix} e(k+1,t) \\ \eta(k,t+1) \end{bmatrix},$$

$$\bar{A} = \begin{bmatrix} I_p & -C_l \\ 0 & A_l \end{bmatrix}, \ \bar{B} = \begin{bmatrix} -D_l \\ B_l \end{bmatrix}, \ \bar{C} = \begin{bmatrix} I_p & 0 \end{bmatrix}$$

and the boundary condition is given by

$$
\begin{aligned}
e(0,t) &= y_r(t) - y(0,t) = y_r(t) - C_l A_l^t x_0, \quad t = 0,1,\ldots,N \\
\eta(k,0) &= x(k+1,0) - x(k,0) = x_0 - x_0 = 0, \quad k = 0,1,\ldots
\end{aligned}
$$

If there exists some control input such that $y(k,t) \to y_r(t)$, $t = 0,1,\ldots,N$ as $k \to \infty$, then we would have $\lim_{k\to\infty} e(k,t) = 0$. This also means that the control input approaches certain constant value, i.e., $\lim_{k\to\infty} \Delta u(k,t) = 0$. Therefore, for design of ILCS, it is reasonable to set the following performance index

$$J = \sum_{k=0}^{\infty}\sum_{t=0}^{N}\|e(k,t)\|_{Q_l} + \sum_{k=1}^{\infty}\sum_{t=0}^{N}\|\Delta u(k,t)\|_{R_l} \tag{5.110}$$

where Q_l, R_l are symmetric positive definite matrices.

Now, we see that the design problem of ILCS under the performance index (5.110) can be viewed as the 2D optimal control problem:

Problem 4.3: For system (5.109), find a control input $\Delta u(k,t)$ that minimizes the performance index (5.110).

Theorem 5.24 *If D_l is full row rank, the optimal control input $\Delta u(k,t)$ to (5.109) that minimizes the performance index (5.110) can be constructed, and correspondingly the updating control input (5.102) to (5.101) is determined by the equation*

$$\bar{u}(k) = -K_1 \mathcal{X}(k-1) - K_2 \bar{u}(k-1), \quad k = 1,2,\dots \tag{5.111}$$

where

$$\bar{u}(k) = [u^T(k,0) \ \dots \ u^T(k,N)]^T, \tag{5.112}$$

$$\mathcal{X}(0) = \begin{bmatrix} 0 & 0 & (A_l x_0)^T & \cdots & 0 & (A_l^N x_0)^T \end{bmatrix}^T,$$

$$\mathcal{X}(k) = \left[\sum_{j=0}^{k-1} e^T(j,0) \ \sum_{j=0}^{k-1} e^T(j,1) \ x^T(k,1) \ \cdots \ \sum_{j=0}^{k-1} e^T(j,N) \ x^T(k,N) \right]^T,$$

$$k = 1,2,\dots$$

$$K_1 = (\bar{R}_a + \bar{B}_a^T \bar{P} \bar{B}_a)^{-1} \bar{B}_a^T \bar{P}_1 \bar{A}_a$$

$$K_2 = (\bar{R}_a + \bar{B}_a^T \bar{P} \bar{B}_a)^{-1} \bar{B}_a^T \bar{P}_1 \bar{B}_1$$

and $\bar{A}_a, \bar{B}_1, \bar{R}_a, \bar{B}_a, \bar{P}_1$ correspond to the matrices $\tilde{A}, \tilde{B}_1, R_a, B_a, P_1$ given in Theorem 5.23, respectively.

Proof: Due to Theorem 5.23, Problem 4.3 is solvable if the system (5.109) is practical stabilizable and detectable in the k direction, i.e., $(I_p, -D_l, I_p)$ is 1D stabilizable and detectable. It is trivial to see that $(I_p, -D_l, I_p)$ is always detectable and stabilizable if D_l is full row rank.

Therefore, it follows from Theorem 5.23 that the optimal control input minimizing (5.110) is given by

$$\tilde{u}(k) = -K_1 \tilde{x}(k-1) - K_2 \tilde{u}(k-1) \tag{5.113}$$

where

$$\tilde{u}(k) = [\Delta u^T(k,0) \ \dots \ \Delta u^T(k,N)]^T,$$
$$\tilde{x}(k) = [e^T(k,0) \ e^T(k,1) \ \eta^T(k,1) \dots e^T(k,N) \ \eta^T(k,N)]^T.$$

Making a summation of the two-sides of (5.113) from $k = 1$ up to $k = k'$ yields

$$
\begin{bmatrix}
u(k'+1,0) \\
u(k'+1,1) \\
\vdots \\
u(k'+1,N)
\end{bmatrix}
=
\begin{bmatrix}
u(1,0) \\
u(1,1) \\
\vdots \\
u(1,N)
\end{bmatrix}
- K_1
\begin{bmatrix}
0 \\
0 \\
x(0,1) \\
\vdots \\
0 \\
x(0,N)
\end{bmatrix}
$$

$$
- K_1
\begin{bmatrix}
\sum\limits_{j=0}^{k'-1} e^T(j,0) \\
\sum\limits_{j=0}^{k'-1} e^T(j,1) \\
x^T(k',1) \\
\cdots \\
\sum\limits_{j=0}^{k'-1} e^T(j,N) \\
x^T(k',N)
\end{bmatrix}
- K_2
\begin{bmatrix}
u(k',0) \\
u(k',1) \\
\vdots \\
u(k',N)
\end{bmatrix}
\tag{5.114}
$$

$$\tag{5.115}$$

Define $\bar{u}(k)$ as in (5.112) and let, without loss of generality,

$$
\bar{u}(1) \triangleq -K_1
\begin{bmatrix}
0 \\
0 \\
x(0,1) \\
\vdots \\
0 \\
x(0,N)
\end{bmatrix}
= -K_1
\begin{bmatrix}
0 \\
0 \\
A_l x_0 \\
\vdots \\
0 \\
A_l^N x_0
\end{bmatrix}.
\tag{5.116}
$$

Then the result of (5.111) follows immediately.   ∎

Though the above approach is proposed for the system without time delay (i.e., $D_l \neq 0$ in (5.101)), it can also be applied to systems with time delay ($D_l = 0$) by introducing some minor modifications (Yamada *et al.* 1999a).

It has been verified through numerical and simulation examples that by using the proposed optimal approach it is possible to achieve better transient performance and faster convergence than the approach shown in previous section (Yamada *et al.* 1999a). There is, however, an obvious problem for the implementation of this approach because the number of N may be in general large for practical cases so that the involved calculations would be costly. To avoid such problem, therefore, more efficient procedures, if possible in certain 2D style, are desired. Recent research results (Amann *et al.* 1994, Amann 1996, Amann *et al.* 1996, Amann *et al.* 1998) should be particularly noted which provide some useful insights and solution approaches to the learning controller design problem based on the techniques of norm optimization in a Hilbert space setting and predictive control.

5.6 CONCLUDING REMARKS

Recent theoretical and methodological results and possible applications have been reviewed for the control of nD systems in the practical sense that the system inputs and outputs are unbounded in, at most, one dimension. Numerical examples on practical stabilities, practical stabilization, practical tracking control, optimal control and model-following servo systems and their applications can be found in e.g. (Agathoklis & Bruton 1983, Xu *et al.* 1994a, Xu *et al.* 1996b, Xu *et al.* 1997a, Yamada *et al.* 1999a) and thus were omitted for brevity.

It has been clarified that the nD control problems considered in the practical sense can be essentially reduced to the corresponding 1D problems, thus can be solved, compared with the conventional nD system theory, under less restrictive stability conditions and by much simpler methods. In particular, it is shown that the proposed method for 2D practical tracking control in fact provides a general design approach for a class of iterative learning control systems and linear multipass processes. Therefore, the presented control theory for nD systems in the practical sense is of significance not only from the point of view of practical applications of nD system theory but also from that of control of such iterative systems.

It should be remarked that the problems considered in this chapter are the most basic ones for the control of nD systems in the practical sense, and there remain many problems to be solved for actual applications. In particular, the following problems would be some important and interesting directions for further research. For actual situations, the ability to obtain, in an appropriate way, the model of the underlying system is of great importance. Therefore, various techniques for 2D model identification, parameter estimation and adaptive scheme would be desirable. To this end, some efforts and interesting results have recently been reported and the interested readers can be referred to e.g. (Heath 1994, Geng *et al.* 1990, Mikhael & Yu 1995, Zhang 1991). Closed-loop system robustness and performance in the presence of uncertainty are also extremely important for practical applications. Though these problems are substantially difficult and there would still be a long way to go, some rather interesting results have been given very recently (Xie 1999). Moreover, as the final goal, applying 2D theoretical results to actual control of various real systems will undoubtedly become the most active division of the field, and related to this the preparation of an integral CAD environment will surely be indispensable (Gramacki *et al.* 1999, Xu *et al.* 1999).

REFERENCES

P. Agathoklis and L. Bruton, 1983, Practical-BIBO stability of n-dimensional discrete systems. *IEE Proc. G. Electron. Circuits & Systems*, 130(6):236–242.

P. Agathoklis, E. I. Jury, and M. Mansour, 1993, Algebraic necessary and sufficient conditions for the stability of 2-D discrete systems. *IEEE Circuits and Systems II: Analog and Digital Signal Processing*, 40(4):251–258.

A. R. E. Ahmed, 1980, On the stability of two-dimensional discrete systems. *IEEE Trans. Automat. Control*, 25(3):551–552.

N. Amann, 1996, Optimal algorithms for iterative learning control. In *PhD thesis*, School of Engineering, University of Exeter, UK.

N. Amann, D. H. Owens, and E. Rogers, 1994, Non-minimum phase plants in iterative learning control. In *Proc. 2nd Int. Conf. on Intelligent System Engineering*, pages 107–112, Hamburg-Harburg, Germany.

N. Amann, D. H. Owens, and E. Rogers, 1996, Iterative learning control using optimal feedback and feedforward actions. *Int. J. Control*, 65:277–293.

N. Amann, D. H. Owens, and E. Rogers, 1998, Predictive optimal iterative learning control. *Int. J. Control*, 69:203–226.

M. Bisiacco. New Results in 2D Optimal Control Theory. *Multidimensional Systems and Signal Processing*, 6(3):189–222, 1995.

M. Bisiacco and E. Fornasini, 1990, Optimal control of two-dimensional systems. *SIAM J. Control and Optimization*, 28(3):582–601.

M. Bisiacco, E. Fornasini, and G. Marchesini, 1985, On some connections between BIBO and internal stability of two-dimensional filters. *IEEE Trans. Circuits and Systems*, 32:948–953.

M. Bisiacco, E. Fornasini, and G. Marchesini, 1989, Dynamic regulation of 2D systems: a state-space approach. *Linear Algebra Appl.*, 122/123/124:195–218.

F. M. Boland and D. H. Owens, 1980, Linear multipass processes: a two-dimensional interpretation. *IEE Proc.*, 127, Pt. D-5:189–193.

N. K. Bose, 1993, Simplification of a multidimensional digital filter stability test. *Journal of the Franklin Institut*, 330(5):905–911.

S. Foda and P. Agathoklis, 1992, Control of the metal rolling process: a multidimensional system approach. *J. Franklin Inst.*, 329(2):317–332.

E. Fornasini, 1988, A note on output feedback stabilizability of multivariable 2D systems. *Syst. & Control Letters*, 10:45–50.

E. Fornasini and G. Marchesini, 1979, On the internal stability of two-dimensional filters. *IEEE Trans. Automat. Control*, 24(1):129–130.

K. Furuta and K. Komiya, 1982, Design of model-following servo controller. *IEEE Trans. Automat. Control*, 27(3):725–727.

K. Galkowski, E. Rogers, and D. Owens, 1997, Basic systems theory for discrete linear repetitive processes using 2D Roesser model interpretations. *Appl. Math. and Comp. Sci.*, 7(1):101–116.

Z. Geng, R. Carroll, and J. Xie, 1990, Two-dimensional model and algorithm analysis for a class of iterative learning control systems. *Int. J. Control*, 52(4):833–862.

D. Goodman, 1977, Some stability properties of two-dimensional linear shift-invariant digital filters. *IEEE Trans. Circuits and Systems*, 24:201–208.

J. Gramacki, A. Gramacki, K. Galkowski, E. Rogers, and D. H. Owens, 1999, MAT-LAB based tools for 2D linear systems with application to iterative learning control schemes. In *Proc. of CACSD'99*, pages 410–415, Hawaii.

J. P. Guiver and N. K. Bose, 1982, Polynomial matrix primitive factorization over arbitrary coefficient field and related results. *IEEE Trans. Circuits and Systems*, 29(10):649–657.

J. P. Guiver and N. K. Bose, 1985, Causal and weakly causal 2-D filters with applications in stabilization. In N. K. Bose, editor, *Multidimensional Systems Theory*, page 52. Dordrecht: Reidel.

W. P. Heath, 1994, *Self-tuning control for two-dimensional processes*. Research Studies Press Ltd., Taunton, Somerset, England.

X.H. Hu, 1994, On two-dimensional filter stability test. *IEEE Trans. Circuits and Systems—II: Analog and Digital Signal Processing*, 41:457–462.

T. Kaczorek, 1985, *Two-Dimensional Linear Systems*. Springer-Verlag, Berlin.

T. Kaczorek and J. Klamka, 1986, Minimum energy control of 2-D linear systems with variable coefficients. *Int. J. Control*, 44(3):645–650.

J. E. Kurek, 1985, Basic properties of q-dimensional linear digital systems. *Int. J. Control*, 42(1):119–128.

J. E. Kurek and M. B. Zaremba, 1993, Iterative learning control synthesis based on 2-D system theory. *IEEE Trans. Automat. Control*, 38(1):121–125.

C. Li and M. S. Fadali, 1991, Optimal control of 2-D systems. *IEEE Trans. Automat. Control*, 36(2):223–228.

Z. Lin, 1988, Feedback stabilization of multivariable two-dimensional linear systems. *Int. J. Control*, 48(3):1301–1317.

Z. Lin, 1998, Feedback stabilizability of MIMO n-D linear systems. *Multidimensional Systems and Signal Processing*, 9(2):149–172.

W. B. Mikhael and H. Yu, 1995, Two-dimensional, frequency domain, adaptive system modeling using three-dimensional spatiotemporal inputs. *IEEE Trans. on Circuits and Systems II: Analog and Digital Signal Processing*, 42(5):317–325.

K. L. Moore, 1993, *Iterative Learning Control for Deterministic Systems*. Springer Verlag.

M. Morf, B. Levy, and S. Y. Kung, 1977, New result in 2-D systems theory, Part I: 2-D polynomial matrices, factorization and coprimeness. *Proc. IEEE*, 65(6):861–872.

V. R. Raman and R. Liu, 1986, A constructive algorithm for the complete set of compensators for two-dimensional feedback systems design. *IEEE Trans. Automat. Control*, 31:166–170.

P. Rocha, E. Rogers, and D. H. Owens, 1996, Stability of discrete non-unit memory linear repetitive processes – a two-dimensional systems interpretation. *Int. J. Control*, 63(3):457–482.

E. Rogers and D. H. Owens, 1992, *Stability Analysis for Linear Repetitive Processes*. Springer Verlag, Berlin.

M. Šebek, 1989, Two-sided equations and skew primeness for n-D polynomial matrices. *Syst. & Control Letters*, 12:331–337.

M. N. Swamy, L. M. Roytman, and E. I. Plotkin, 1985, On stability properties of three- and higher dimensional linear shift-invariant digital filters. *IEEE Trans. Circuits and Systems*, 32(9):888–891.

M. Vidyasagar, 1985, *Control System Synthesis: A Factorization Approach.* MIT Press.

W. A. Wolovich, 1978, Skew prime polynomial matrices. *IEEE Trans. Automat. Control*, 23(5):880–887.

L. Xie, 1999, LMI approach to output feedback stabilization of 2-D discrete systems. *Int. J. Control*, 73:97–106.

L. Xu, O. Saito, and K. Abe, 1990, Bilateral polynomial matrix equations in two indeterminates. *Multidimensional Systems and Signal Processing*, 1(4):363–379.

L. Xu, O. Saito, and K. Abe, 1994, The design of practically stable nD feedback systems. *Automatica*, 30(9):1389–1397.

L. Xu, O. Saito, and K. Abe, 1994, Output feedback stabilizability and stabilization algorithms for 2D systems. *Multidimensional Systems and Signal Processing*, 5(1):41–60.

L. Xu, O. Saito, and K. Abe, 1996, Practical internal stability of nD discrete systems. *IEEE Trans. Automat. Control*, 41(5):756–761.

L. Xu, O. Saito, and K. Abe, 1996, Design of practically stable nD feedback systems: a state-space approach. *Int. J. Control*, 64(1):29–39.

L. Xu, O. Saito, and K. Abe, 1997, nD control systems in a practical sense. *Applied Mathematics and Computer Science*, 7(4):907–941.

L. Xu, O. Saito, and J. Ying, 1999, 2D feedback system design: the tracking and disturbance rejection problems. In *Proc. of ISCAS'99*, volume V, pages 13–16, Orlando, Florida.

L. Xu and M. Yamada and O. Saito, 1997, Practical tracking problem of nD systems. *Trans. SICE*, 33(9):897–904 (in Japanese).

L. Xu, M. Yamada, O. Saito, and K. Abe, 1994, Practical tracking problem of nD systems and its applications to iterative control systems. In *Proc. 1st Asian Contr. Conf.*, pages III 447–450, Tokyo, Japan.

M. Yamada, L. Xu, and O. Saito, 1999, 2D optimal control in a certain practical sense. *Systems, Information and Control*, 12(12) (in Japanese).

M. Yamada, L. Xu, and O. Saito, 1999, 2D model-following servo system. *Multidimensional Systems and Signal Processing*, 10(1):71–91.

X. D. Zhang, 1991, On the estimation of two-dimensional moving average parameters. *IEEE Trans. Automat. Control*, 36(10):1196–1199.

CHAPTER SIX

Two Decades of Research on Linear Repetitive Processes

Eric Rogers[†] and David H. Owens[‡]

† Department of Electronics and Computer Science,
University of Southampton, UK
etar@ecs.soton.ac.uk

‡ Department of Automatic Control and Systems Engineering,
University of Sheffield, UK
D.H.Owens@sheffield.ac.uk

Abstract

Repetitive processes are a distinct class of 2D systems of both practical and algorithmic interest. Their unique characteristic is repeated sweeps, or passes, through a set of dynamics defined over a finite duration with explicit interaction between the outputs, or pass profiles, produced as the process evolves. Experience has shown that these processes cannot be studied/controlled by direct application of existing theory (in all but a few very restrictive special cases). This fact, and the growing list of application areas, has prompted an on-going research programme into the development of a 'mature' systems theory for these processes for onward translation into reliable generally applicable controller design algorithms. This chapter provides a critical survey of the major developments to-date together with discussion of some current work and directions for future research.

6.1 INTRODUCTION

The essential unique characteristic of a repetitive, or multipass, process can be illustrated by considering machining operations where the material or workpiece involved is processed by a sequence of passes of the processing tool. Assuming that the pass length α (i.e. the duration of a pass of the processing tool) is finite and constant, the output vector, or pass profile, $y_k(t)$, $0 \leq t \leq \alpha$, (t being the independent spatial or temporal variable) produced on the kth pass acts as a forcing function on the next pass and hence contributes to the dynamics of the new pass profile $y_{k+1}(t)$, $0 \leq t \leq \alpha$, $k \geq 0$. A more general case arises when it is the previous $M > 1$ pass profiles which contribute to the current one. The integer M is termed the memory length and such processes are simply termed non-unit memory and unit memory in the case when $M = 1$.

Repetitive processes as a subject area has its origins in the coal mining industry and, in particular, long-wall coal cutting which is the main method of extracting coal from deep cast mines in Great Britain. In this method (see (Edwards 1974) for a detailed treatment) roadways are machined and kept open at either end of the coal seam and the coal is removed by a series of sweeps of a cutting machine along the coal face (which is perpendicular to the roadways in a plan view). The cutter is borne on the so-called armored face conveyor, a collection of loosely joined steel pans, which rests on the newly cut floor profile. Hydraulic rams in the supporting roof structure are used to steer the cutting heads within the undulating confines of the coal seam as the machine passes along the coal face, where the basic objective is to maximize coal extraction without penetrating the stone coal interface (to be avoided on both safety and economic grounds).

In the simplest form of operation, the machine cuts in one direction only — more advanced bi-directional cutting is only really feasible in very rich seam mines. At the end of each pass, the cutting machine is hauled back in reverse (a high speed operation) to the start of the pass and hydraulic rams are used to push over the complete installation (i.e. machine, armored face conveyor and supporting roof structure) so that it now rests on the newly cut floor profile ready for the start of the next pass. A study of its basic geometry and dynamics immediately confirms that long-wall coal cutting is indeed a repetitive process.

The basic unique control problem for repetitive processes is that the output sequence of pass profiles can contain oscillations that increase in amplitude in the pass to pass direction (i.e. in the k-direction in the notation for variables used here). Such behavior is easily generated in simulation studies and in experiments on scaled models of industrial examples such as long-wall coal cutting (see (Edwards 1974) and (Smyth 1992) for a detailed treatment). In long-wall coal cutting this problem appears (in its worst form) as severe undulations in the newly cut floor profile which means that cutting operations (i.e. productive work) must be suspended to enable their manual removal. This problem is one of the key factors behind the 'stop/start' cutting pattern of a typical working cycle in a coal mine.

Early approaches to stability analysis and controller design for (linear) repetitive processes, and, in particular, long-wall coal cutting, were based on first converting the system into an infinite-length single-pass process (Edwards 1974). This resulted in a scalar differential/algebraic delay system to which standard scalar inverse-Nyquist stability criteria were then applied. In general, however, it was soon established that this approach to stability analysis and hence controller design would, except in a few very restrictive special cases, lead to incorrect conclusions (Owens 1977). The basic reason for this is that such an approach effectively neglects their finite pass length repeatable nature and the effects of resetting the initial conditions before the start of each pass.

To remove these deficiencies, a rigorous stability theory has been developed (Owens 1977, Rogers & Owens 1992c). This theory is based on an abstract model of the dynamics in a Banach space setting which includes all processes with linear dynamics and a constant pass length as special cases. In effect, this theory consists of the distinct concepts of asymptotic stability and stability along the pass, and necessary and sufficient conditions for these properties are available. These are expressed in terms of conditions on the bounded linear operator in the abstract model which describes the contribution of the previous pass dynamics to those of the current one.

Coal mining in Great Britain is now a 'greatly reduced' industry relative to the 1970s and in recent years the focus applications-wise has been on problem areas where adopting a repetitive process perspective has major advantages over alternatives — so-called algorithmic examples. This is especially true for classes of iterative learning control schemes (Amann *et al.* 1996, Amann *et al.* 1998) and of iterative solution algorithms for classes of nonlinear dynamic optimal control problems based on the maximum principle (Roberts 1996).

The objectives of this chapter are to (i) undertake a critical review of the progress to-date

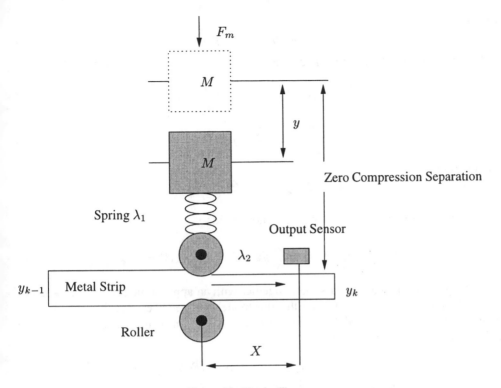

Figure 6.1: Metal rolling process.

on the development of a rigorous control and systems theory for linear constant pass length repetitive processes, (ii) illustrate the application of elements of this theory to iterative learning control and nonlinear optimal control, and (iii) highlight some areas for short to medium term further research. We begin in the next section by introducing the important sub-classes of so-called differential and discrete linear repetitive processes and the general abstract model on which the stability theory is based.

6.2 DIFFERENTIAL AND DISCRETE LINEAR REPETITIVE PROCESSES

Figure 6.1 is a schematic diagram of a metal rolling process where the basic objective is to reduce the width of the strip to a predefined value by a series of passes through the roll mill. The parameters in this model are defined as follows: $y_k(t)$ is the roll gap thickness on pass k, F_m is the force developed by the motor, M is the lumped mass of the roll-gap adjusting mechanism, λ_1 is the stiffness of the adjusting mechanism spring, λ_2 is the hardness of the metal strip, and $\lambda = \frac{\lambda_1 \lambda_2}{\lambda_1 + \lambda_2}$ is the composite stiffness of the metal strip and the roll mechanism. Clearly the width after each pass will have a major effect on what happens next time through and it is easy to see that this operation is indeed a repetitive process.

With this notation, the force developed by the motor can, under well defined assumptions, be modeled by

$$F_m = F_s + M\ddot{y}(t) \tag{6.1}$$

where

$$F_s = \lambda_2 \left[y_{k-1}(t) - y_k(t) \right] \tag{6.2}$$

and, since F_s is also the force applied to the metal strip by the rollers, it follows that

$$\lambda_2 \left[y_{k-1}(t) - y_k(t) \right] = \lambda_1 \left[y(t) + y_k(t) \right] \tag{6.3}$$

Also

$$y(t) = \frac{F_s}{\lambda_1} - y_k(t) \tag{6.4}$$

and therefore

$$y(t) = \frac{\lambda_2}{\lambda_1} y_{k-1}(t) - \frac{\lambda_1 + \lambda_2}{\lambda_1} y_k(t) \tag{6.5}$$

Combining these equations and rearranging now yields

$$M\ddot{y}_k(t) + \lambda y_k(t) = M\frac{\lambda}{\lambda_1}\ddot{y}_{k-1}(t) + \lambda y_{k-1}(t) - \frac{\lambda}{\lambda_2}F_m \tag{6.6}$$

Taking F_m as the current pass input together with an appropriate set of state variables (for both $y_k(t)$ and $y_{k-1}(t)$) it is clear that this model is a special case of the following one which is the state space model of a so-called differential linear repetitive process whose dynamics evolve over $0 \leq t \leq \alpha$, $k \geq 0$.

$$\begin{aligned}
\dot{x}_{k+1}(t) &= A x_{k+1}(t) + B u_{k+1}(t) + B_0 y_k(t) \\
y_{k+1}(t) &= C x_{k+1}(t) + D u_{k+1}(t) + D_0 y_k(t)
\end{aligned} \tag{6.7}$$

Here on pass k, $x_k(t)$ is the $n \times 1$ state vector, $y_k(t)$ is the $m \times 1$ pass profile vector, and $u_k(t)$ is the $l \times 1$ vector of control inputs.

To complete the process description, it is necessary to specify the 'initial conditions' — termed the boundary conditions here, i.e. the state initial vector on each pass and the initial pass profile. The simplest possible form for these is

$$\begin{aligned}
x_{k+1}(0) &= d_{k+1}, \ k \geq 0 \\
y_0(t) &= y(t), \ 0 \leq t \leq \alpha
\end{aligned} \tag{6.8}$$

where d_{k+1} is an $n \times 1$ vector with constant entries and $y(t)$ is an $m \times 1$ vector whose entries are known functions of t.

In some cases, the boundary conditions of (6.8) are simply not strong enough to 'adequately' model the underlying dynamics — even for preliminary simulation/control analysis. In actual fact, see the next section, the form of the boundary conditions has a crucial effect on the stability properties of these processes. Consequently we start with the most general form of these and then specialize as required for a given example. Other work (Smyth 1992) has concluded that this set results from replacing $x_{k+1}(0)$, $k \geq 0$, in (6.8) by

$$x_{k+1}(0) = d_{k+1} + \sum_{j=1}^{M} K_j y_k(t_j) \tag{6.9}$$

where $0 \leq t_1 < t_2 < \cdots < t_M \leq \alpha$ are M sample points along the previous pass profile, and K_j, $1 \leq j \leq M$, are $n \times m$ matrices with constant entries.

To introduce the structure of a so-called discrete linear repetitive process, it is instructive to consider briefly the work of Roberts (Roberts 1996, Roberts 1998) who has shown that such a structure arises in the analysis of the local convergence and stability properties of iterative algorithms for solving (classes of) nonlinear dynamic optimal control problems. In these algorithms a trial solution is updated from iteration to iteration which gives rise to an inherent 2D/repetitive process structure where one direction of information propagation is the time horizon of the dynamic response and the other is the iteration number. Applying these ideas to particular algorithms based on dynamic integrated system optimization and parameter estimation, for the background see (Becerra & Roberts 1996, Roberts 1993, Roberts 1994), for the solution of continuous and discrete optimal control problems subject to model reality differences has resulted in direct application of discrete linear repetitive process theory to study the stability and convergence properties of the resulting iterative solution algorithms.

Consider now the unconstrained nonlinear optimal discrete control problem (following the notation of Roberts (1993))

$$\min_{u(i)} J = \sum_{i=0}^{N-1} L(x(i), u(i), i) \ \text{ s.t. } \ x(i+1) = f(x(i), u(i), i), \ x(0) = x_0 \qquad (6.10)$$

where $x(i) \in \mathbb{R}^n$, $u(i) \in \mathbb{R}^l$ are the system state and control vectors respectively, and x_0 is a defined initial condition vector. Then it is a standard fact that application of the maximum principle requires the solution of the following two point boundary value problem

$$
\begin{aligned}
\hat{x}(i+1) &= f(\hat{x}(i), \hat{p}(i), i), \ \hat{x}(0) = x_0; \ i \in [0, N-1] \\
\hat{p}(i+1) &= g(\hat{x}(i), \hat{p}(i), i), \ \hat{p}(N) = 0; \ i \in [0, N-1]
\end{aligned}
\qquad (6.11)
$$

where $p(i) \in \mathbb{R}^n$ is the costate vector and the 'hat' symbol denotes an optimal value. The optimal control is obtained in the form

$$\hat{u}(i) = h(\hat{x}(i), \hat{p}(i), i) \qquad (6.12)$$

Given that the boundary conditions are mixed, the solution of a problem of the above form is usually determined iteratively by applying methods such as quasilinearization or a gradient method in a function space. In general, such algorithms can be written in the form:

Step 1: Select or compute a nominal solution $Y_0^T(i) = [u_0^T(i), x_0^T(i), p_0^T(i)]^T$ and set the iteration counter $k = 0$.

Step 2: Compute an estimate of the optimal control by solving:

$$
\begin{aligned}
X_k(i+1) &= \begin{bmatrix} \hat{x}_k(i+1) \\ \hat{p}_k(i+1) \end{bmatrix} = F(X_k(i), Y_k(i)), \ X_k(0) = d_{0_k} \\
\hat{u}_k(i) &= h(X_k(i)), \ i \in [0, N-1]
\end{aligned}
\qquad (6.13)
$$

Step 3: Update the estimated solution:

$$Y_{k+1}(i) = G(X_k(i), Y_k(i)) \qquad (6.14)$$

Step 4: Increment $k = k + 1$ and repeat steps 1-3 above until convergence is achieved.

Note that the vector $Y_k(i)$ is not necessarily full (e.g. $Y_k^T(i) = [x_k^T(i), p_k^T(i)]^T$ in the quasilinearization algorithm or $Y_k(i) = u_k(i)$ in a gradient function space algorithm), and the initial condition d_{0_k} changes from iteration to iteration. This algorithm is clearly in the form of a nonlinear discrete repetitive process where $Y_k(i)$, $i \in [0, N]$, acts as a driving input from iteration to iteration.

Discrete dynamic integrated system optimization and parameter estimation is a technique for solving discrete optimal control problems where there are differences in structure and parameters between reality and the model employed in the computations. This approach was originally developed in continuous time (Roberts 1993) and then extended to discrete time (Becerra 1994). The main property of the procedure is that by iterating on appropriately modified model based problems the correct optimal solution is achieved despite the presence of model-reality differences. Algorithms are available in both domains (continuous and discrete time respectively) for a general nonlinear optimal control problem with terminal weighting, mixed free and specified terminal conditions, and bounded controls. Here in order to highlight the (linear) repetitive process aspects we only briefly consider a free end point problem with no terminal weighting or control constraints.

Consider the optimal control problem defined by (6.10) which is denoted as the real optimal control problem (ROP):

$$\min_{u(i)} J = \sum_{i=0}^{N-1} L^*(x(i), u(i), i) \text{ s.t. } x(i+1) = f^*(x(i), u(i), i), \ x(0) = x_o \quad (6.15)$$

where $L^* : \mathbb{R}^n \times \mathbb{R}^l \times \mathbb{R} \mapsto \mathbb{R}$ is the real performance measure function and $f^* : \mathbb{R}^n \times \mathbb{R}^l \times \mathbb{R} \mapsto \mathbb{R}^n$ represents reality. Owing to modeling uncertainties and system complexity, this problem is not solved directly but instead the following, possibly simplified, model based optimal control problem (MOP) is considered:

$$\min_{u(i)} J = \sum_{i=0}^{N-1} L(x(i), u(i), \gamma(i)) \text{ s.t } x(i+1) = f(x(i), u(i), \alpha(i)), \ i \in [0, N-1] \quad (6.16)$$

with $x(0) = x_0$ where $\alpha(i) \in \mathbb{R}^r$ and $\gamma(i) \in \mathbb{R}$ are discrete parameters, $L : \mathbb{R}^n \times \mathbb{R}^m \times \mathbb{R} \mapsto \mathbb{R}$ is the model performance measure function, and $f : \mathbb{R}^n \times \mathbb{R}^m \times \mathbb{R}^r \mapsto \mathbb{R}^n$ represents the model.

By expanding MOP to include additional equality constraints to match the model with reality and then examining the overall optimality conditions, it can be shown that the solution of ROP can be found by iterating on the modified model based problem (MMOP) (Becerra 1994):

$$\min_{u(i)} J = \sum_{i=0}^{N-1} [L(x(i), u(i), \gamma(i)) - \lambda^T(i)u(i) - \beta^T(i)x(i)$$

$$+ \frac{1}{2}r_1 \|u(i) - v(i)\|^2 + \frac{1}{2}r_2 \|x(i) - z(i)\|^2]$$

$$\text{s.t.} \quad x(i+1) = f(x(i), u(i), \alpha(i)); \ i \in [0, N-1], \ x(0) = x_0 \quad (6.17)$$

under specified $\alpha(i)$ and $\gamma(i)$, specified multipliers $\lambda(i)$ and $\beta(i)$, and specified $v(i)$ and $z(i)$, which are updated between iterations using the relationships:

$$f(z(i), v(i), \alpha(i)) = f^*(z(i), v(i), i)$$

$$L(z(i), v(i), \gamma(i)) = L^*(z(i), v(i), i); \ i \in [0, N-1]$$

$$\lambda(i) = -\left[\frac{\partial f^*(.)}{\partial v(i)} - \frac{\partial f(.)}{\partial v(i)}\right]^T p(i+1) - \left[\frac{\partial L^*(.)}{\partial v(i)} - \frac{\partial L(.)}{\partial v(i)}\right]^T$$

$$\beta(i) = -\left[\frac{f^*(.)}{\partial z(i)} - \frac{\partial f(.)}{\partial z(i)}\right]^T \hat{p}(i+1) - \left[\frac{\partial L^*(.)}{\partial z(i)} - \frac{\partial L(.)}{\partial z(i)}\right]^T$$

$$v(i) = u(i)$$

$$z(i) = x(i) \qquad\qquad (6.18)$$

where $p(i)$ is the costate variable obtained from the solution of MMOP. The terms proportional to the scalars r_1 and r_2 are introduced in MMOP to provide convexification argumentation and hence improve convergence. Convergence and stability is also regulated by using a relaxation scheme to satisfy (6.18).

From this basis it is possible to develop an iterative based algorithm which, assuming convergence, will solve ROP by repeated solutions of MMOP. The resulting algorithm, termed DDISOPE by Becerra (1994), can also be formulated as a nonlinear unit memory repetitive process but subsequent analysis is not really feasible. Instead, insight into the local convergence properties of the technique can be obtained by considering the special case when the real and model based problems are both linear with quadratic performance indices.

Consider, therefore, the problems ROP and MOP defined by (6.15) and (6.16) and let:

$$f^*(x(i), u(i), i) = A^* x(i) + B^* u(i)$$

$$L^*(x(i), u(i), i) = \frac{1}{2}(x^T(i)Q^* x(i) + u^T(i)R^* u(i)) \qquad (6.19)$$

and

$$f(x(i), u(i), \alpha(i)) = A x(i) + B u(i) + \alpha(i)$$

$$L(x(i), u(i), \gamma(i)) = \frac{1}{2}(x^T(i)Q x(i) + u^T(i)R u(i)) + \gamma(i) \qquad (6.20)$$

Then, within the iterative scheme, the modified model based optimal control problem becomes:

$$\min_{u(i)} J = \sum_{i=0}^{N-1} \frac{1}{2}(x^T(i)Q x(i) + u^T(i)R u(i)) + \gamma_i(i)$$

$$- \lambda_k^T(i)u(i) - \beta_k^T(i)x(i) + \frac{1}{2}(r_1 \|u(i) - u_k(i)\|^2 + r_2 \|x(i) - x_k(i)\|^2)$$

$$\text{s.t} \quad x(i+1) = A x(i) + B u(i) + \alpha_k(i), \ i \in [0, N-1], \ x(0) = x_0 \qquad (6.21)$$

It can now be shown that the local behavior of this algorithm can be described by a special case of the following which is the state space model of a so-called discrete linear repetitive process over $0 \leq i \leq \alpha, k \geq 0$

$$x_{k+1}(i+1) = A x_{k+1}(i) + B u_{k+1}(i) + B_0 y_k(i)$$

$$y_{k+1}(i) = C x_{k+1}(i) + D u_{k+1}(i) + D_0 y_k(i) \qquad (6.22)$$

The most general form of pass initial conditions in this case is the discrete counterpart of (6.9), i.e.

$$x_{k+1}(0) = d_{k+1} + \sum_{j=1}^{M} K_j y_k(p_j), \ 0 \le p_1 < p_2 \cdots < p_M \le \alpha, \ k \ge 0$$

$$y_0(p) = y(p), \ 0 \le p \le \alpha \tag{6.23}$$

Standard optimality conditions now give the estimates of the optimal control, state and costate sequences on the kth iteration as:

$$\hat{u}_k(i) = \overline{R}^{-1}[-B^T \hat{p}_k(i+1) + \lambda_k(i) + r_1 u_k(i)]$$
$$\hat{x}_k(i+1) = A\hat{x}_k(i) + B\hat{u}_k(i) + \alpha_k(i), \ \hat{x}_k(0) = x_0$$
$$\hat{p}_k(i+1) = -A^{-T}[\overline{Q}\hat{x}_k(i) - \hat{p}_k(i) - \beta_k(i) - r_2 x_k(i)], \ \hat{p}_k(N) = 0 \tag{6.24}$$

where $\overline{R} = R + r_1 I_m$, $\overline{Q} = Q + r_2 I_n$. Also the model parameter and multiplier vectors become:

$$\lambda_k(i) = -[B^* - B]^T \hat{p}_k(i+1) - [R^* - R]u_k(i)$$
$$\beta_k(i) = -[A - A^*]^T \hat{p}_k(i+1) - [Q^* - Q]x_k(i)$$
$$\alpha_k(i) = [A^* - A]x_k(i) + [B^* - B]u_k(i) \tag{6.25}$$

Note also that it is not necessary to calculate $\gamma(k)$.

Now define

$$x_k(i) = \begin{bmatrix} \hat{x}_k(i) \\ \hat{p}_k(i) \end{bmatrix}, \ y_k(i) = \begin{bmatrix} u_k(i) \\ x_k(i) \\ p_k(i+1) \end{bmatrix} \tag{6.26}$$

Then, after some routine manipulations to eliminate $\alpha_k(i)$, $\lambda_k(i)$ and $\beta_k(i)$, it can be shown that this linearized solution algorithm is capable of determining the correct solution of the real optimal control problem despite model-reality differences.

In a later section, we will see how both differential and discrete linear repetitive processes underpin the analysis of important classes of iterative learning control schemes. This requires the stability theory for linear constant pass length linear repetitive processes which we describe in the next section.

6.3 STABILITY THEORY AND TESTS

The stability theory for linear constant pass length repetitive processes developed by Rogers & Owens (1992c) is based on an abstract model of these processes in a Banach space setting which includes all such processes as special cases. The formal definition of this model is as follows.

Definition 6.1 *A linear repetitive process $S(E_\alpha, W_\alpha, E_\alpha)$ of constant pass length $\alpha > 0$ consists of a Banach space E_α, a linear subspace W_α of E_α, and a bounded linear operator L_α mapping E_α into itself. The system dynamics are described by linear recursion relations of the form*

$$y_{k+1} = L_\alpha y_k + b_{k+1}, \ k \ge 0 \tag{6.27}$$

where $y_k \in E_\alpha$ is the pass profile on pass k and $b_{k+1} \in W_\alpha$. Here the term $L_\alpha y_k$ represents the contribution from pass k to pass $k+1$ and b_{k+1} represents initial conditions, disturbances and control input effects on pass $k+1$.

Note 6.2 *In what follows $||.||$ is used to denote both the norm on E_α and the induced operator norm.*

In the case of a differential process described by (6.7) and (6.9) choose $E_\alpha = L_2^m[0, \alpha] \cap L_\infty[0, \alpha]$. Then it is easy to see that

$$(L_\alpha y)(t) = Ce^{At}\hat{y} + C \int_0^t e^{A(t-\tau)} B_0 y(\tau) \, d\tau + D_0 y(t), \ 0 \leq t \leq \alpha \qquad (6.28)$$

where

$$\hat{y} = \sum_{j=1}^{M} K_j y(t_j) \qquad (6.29)$$

and

$$b_{k+1} = Ce^{At}d_{k+1} + C \int_0^t e^{A(t-\tau)} Bu_{k+1}(\tau) \, d\tau + Du_{k+1}(t), \ 0 \leq t \leq \alpha, \ k \geq 0 \quad (6.30)$$

For the discrete case of (6.22) and (6.23), choose $E_\alpha = \ell_2^m[0, \alpha]$ — the space of sequences of real $m \times 1$ vectors of length α (corresponding to $i = 1, 2, \cdots, \alpha$). Then the corresponding formulas are:

$$(L_\alpha y)(i) = CA^i(\sum_{j=1}^{M} K_j y(p_j)) + \sum_{r=0}^{i-1} CA^{i-1-r} B_0 y(r) + D_0 y(i), \ 1 \leq i \leq \alpha \quad (6.31)$$

$$b_{k+1}(i) = CA^i d_{k+1} + \sum_{r=0}^{i-1} CA^{i-1-r} Bu_{k+1}(r) + Du_{k+1}(i), \ 1 \leq i \leq \alpha \qquad (6.32)$$

The stability theory for linear repetitive processes consists of two distinct concepts termed asymptotic stability and stability along the pass respectively, where asymptotic stability is defined as follows.

Definition 6.3 $S(E_\alpha, W_\alpha, L_\alpha)$ *is said to be asymptotically stable if $\exists$ a real scalar $\delta > 0$ such that, given any initial profile y_0 and any disturbance sequence $\{b_k\}_{k \geq 1} \in W_\alpha$ bounded in norm (i.e. $||b_k|| \leq c_1$ for some constant $c_1 \geq 0$ and $\forall \, k \geq 0$), the output sequence generated by the perturbed process*

$$y_{k+1} = (L_\alpha + \gamma)y_k + b_{k+1}, \ k \geq 0 \qquad (6.33)$$

is bounded in norm whenever $||\gamma|| \leq \delta$.

This definition is easily shown to be equivalent to the requirement that $\exists$ finite real scalars $M_\alpha > 0$ and $\lambda_\alpha \in (0, 1)$ such that

$$||L_\alpha^k|| \leq M_\alpha \lambda_\alpha^k, \ k \geq 0 \qquad (6.34)$$

A necessary and sufficient condition for (6.34) to hold is that the spectral radius, $r(L_\alpha)$, of L_α satisfies

$$r(L_\alpha) < 1 \tag{6.35}$$

Introduce for the differential case, with $D = 0$, $D_0 = 0$, for simplicity

$$M(z) := \sum_{j=1}^{M} K_j C e^{\hat{A}(z)t_j} \tag{6.36}$$

where

$$\hat{A}(z) = A + z^{-1} B_0 C, \ z \neq 0 \tag{6.37}$$

Then the following results, for the proofs see (Owens & Rogers 1999a), characterize asymptotic stability in this case.

Theorem 6.4 *Suppose* $\{A, B_0\}$ *is controllable, then* $S(E_\alpha, W_\alpha, L_\alpha)$ *generated by (6.7) and (6.9) has operator* L_α *with spectral radius*

$$r(L_\alpha) = max\{0, sup \, |z| \ : \ z \neq 0 \ \& \ |zI_n - M(z)| = 0\} \tag{6.38}$$

Corollary 6.5 $S(E_\alpha, W_\alpha, L_\alpha)$ *generated by (6.7) and (6.9) with* $D = 0$, $D_0 = 0$, *is asymptotically stable if, and only if, all solutions of*

$$|zI_n - M(z)| = 0 \tag{6.39}$$

have modulus strictly less than unity.

Note: In the case when the state initial vector sequence has the form of (6.8) (or its discrete counterpart), asymptotic stability holds if, and only if, $r(D_0) < 1$.

Further simplification (reduction in dimension) is possible in some special cases, e.g. the following.

Corollary 6.6 *Consider the linear repetitive process* $S(E_\alpha, W_\alpha, L_\alpha)$ *generated by (6.7) and (6.9) (with* $D = 0$, $D_0 = 0$) *in the special case when* $K_j = KT_j$, $1 \leq j \leq M$, *where* K *is an* $n \times m$ *matrix with constant entries and* T_j, $1 \leq j \leq M$, *are* $m \times m$ *matrices with constant entries. Then this process is asymptotically stable if, and only if, all solutions of*

$$|zI_m - \sum_{j=1}^{M} T_j C e^{\hat{A}(z)t_j} K| = 0 \tag{6.40}$$

have modulus strictly less than unity.

Consider now the case when the boundary conditions and, in particular, the state initial vector sequence are of the simple form (6.8). Then we have the 'counter-intuitive' result that asymptotic stability is independent of the process dynamics and, in particular, the eigenvalues of the matrix A. This is due entirely to the fact that the pass length α is finite and of constant value for all passes. This situation will change drastically if (as below) we let $\alpha \rightarrow +\infty$.

In general, these results show that the property of asymptotic stability for differential (and discrete — see below) linear repetitive processes is critically dependent on the structure of $x_{k+1}(0)$, $k \geq 0$. Suppose also that this sequence is incorrectly modeled as in (6.8)

instead of a special case of the form given in (6.9). Then the process could well be interpreted as asymptotically stable when in actual fact it is asymptotically unstable. This fact
is a key distinguishing feature of these repetitive processes and is the key reason why, in
particular, discrete linear repetitive processes cannot simply be analyzed by direct application of Roesser (Roesser 1975) or Fornasini Marchesini (Fornasini & Marchesini 1978)
state space model based 2D linear systems theory.

The above analysis provides necessary and sufficient conditions for asymptotic stability
but no really 'useful' information concerning transient behavior and, in particular, about the
behavior of the output sequence of pass profiles as the process evolves from pass to pass
(i.e. in the k direction). The limit profile introduced next provides a characterization of
process behavior after a 'large number' of passes have elapsed.

Suppose that $S(E_\alpha, W_\alpha, L_\alpha)$ is asymptotically stable and let $\{b_k\}_{k \geq 1}$ be a disturbance
sequence that converges strongly to a disturbance b_∞. Then the strong limit

$$y_\infty := \lim_{k \to +\infty} y_k \tag{6.41}$$

is termed the limit profile corresponding to this disturbance. Also it can be shown (Rogers
& Owens 1992c) that y_∞ is uniquely given by

$$y_\infty = (I - L_\alpha)^{-1} b_\infty \tag{6.42}$$

Note also that (6.42) can be formally obtained from (6.27) (which describes the dynamics
of $S(E_\alpha, W_\alpha, L_\alpha)$) by replacing all variables by their strong limits.

Corollary 6.7 *In the case when $S(E_\alpha, W_\alpha, L_\alpha)$ generated by (6.7) and (6.9) with $D =
0$, $D_0 = 0$, is asymptotically stable, the resulting limit profile is*

$$
\begin{aligned}
\dot{x}_\infty(t) &= (A + B_0 C)x_\infty(t) + B u_\infty(t) \\
y_\infty(t) &= C x_\infty(t) \\
x_\infty(0) &= (I_n - M(1))^{-1} d_\infty
\end{aligned}
\tag{6.43}
$$

where d_∞ is the strong limit of $\{d_k\}_{k \geq 1}$.

Proof: Replace all variables by their strong limits and note that, by considering the
unforced case, we can write

$$x_\infty(0) = (I_n - M(1))^{-1} d_\infty \tag{6.44}$$

where the inverse exists by asymptotic stability. ∎

Asymptotic stability of processes described by (6.7) and (6.9) guarantees the existence
of a limit profile which is described by a standard, or 1D, linear systems state space model.
Hence, in effect, if the process under consideration is asymptotically stable, then its repetitive dynamics can, after a 'sufficiently large' number of passes, be replaced by those of a
1D linear time invariant system. This result has obvious implications in terms of the design
of control schemes for these processes (see later).

Owing to the finite pass length (over which duration even an unstable 1D linear system
can only produce a bounded output), asymptotic stability cannot guarantee that the resulting limit profile has 'acceptable' along the pass dynamics, where in this case the basic

requirement is stability as a 1D linear system. As a simple example to demonstrate this fact, consider the differential process defined by $A = -1$, $B = 1$, $B_0 = 1 + \beta$, $C = 1$, $x_{k+1}(0) = 0$, $k \geq 0$ where $\beta > 0$ is a real scalar. Then the resulting limit profile dynamics are described by the unstable 1D linear system

$$\dot{y}_\infty(t) = \beta y_\infty(t) + u_\infty(t), \ 0 \leq t \leq \alpha \tag{6.45}$$

The natural definition of stability along the pass for the above example is to ask that the limit profile is stable in the sense that $\beta < 0$ if we let the pass length α become infinite. This intuitively appealing idea is, however, not applicable to cases where the limit profile resulting from asymptotic stability is not described by a 1D linear systems state space model. Consequently stability along the pass for the general model $S(E_\alpha, W_\alpha, L_\alpha)$ has been defined in terms of the rate of approach to the limit profile as the pass length α becomes infinitely large. One of several versions of the formal definition is as follows.

Definition 6.8 $S(E_\alpha, W_\alpha, L_\alpha)$ *is said to be stable along the pass if, and only if, $\exists$ real numbers $M_\infty > 0$ and $\lambda_\infty \in (0, 1)$ which are independent of α and satisfy*

$$\|L_\alpha^k\| \leq M_\infty \lambda_\infty^k, \ \forall \, \alpha > 0, \ \forall \, k \geq 0 \tag{6.46}$$

Necessary and sufficient conditions for (6.46) are that

$$r_\infty := \sup_{\alpha > 0} r(L_\alpha) < 1 \tag{6.47}$$

and that

$$M_0 := \sup_{\alpha > 0} \sup_{|z| \geq \lambda} \|(zI - L_\alpha)^{-1}\| < \infty \tag{6.48}$$

for some real number $\lambda \in (r_\infty, 1)$.

In terms of $S(E_\alpha, W_\alpha, L_\alpha)$ generated by (6.7) and (6.9), there are two cases to deal with. The first of these is that as $\alpha \to +\infty$ we allow $M \to +\infty$ and $t_j \to +\infty$ and the second of these is that as $\alpha \to +\infty$ we keep M and t_j fixed. Of these cases, the second is the most practically relevant and hence only this case is considered further here — see (Owens & Rogers 1999b) for the first case. In what follows, we assume that M and t_j are fixed at the outset.

To obtain necessary and sufficient conditions for stability along the pass, the route is to examine the equation $(zI - L_\alpha)y = f$ in E_α where $\alpha \geq t_M$ and $f \in E_\alpha$. We require that (i) $r(L_\alpha) < 1$, $\forall \, \alpha \geq t_M$ which, due to the assumption above, holds if, and only if, Corollary 6.1 holds, and
(ii) $\exists \lambda \in (r_\infty, 1)$ such that the map $f \mapsto y$ is defined and uniformly bounded with respect to $\alpha \geq t_M$ and $|z| \geq \lambda$.

Clearly, a necessary condition for these properties is that the matrix A is stable in the 1D sense. In effect, this demands that the first pass profile is uniformly bounded (with respect to α) and is therefore taken as an assumption in the following result which gives necessary and sufficient conditions for stability along the pass.

Theorem 6.9 *Suppose that $\{A, B_0\}$ is controllable, $\{C, A\}$ is observable, and the matrix A is stable. Then $S(E_\alpha, W_\alpha, L_\alpha)$ generated by (6.7) and (6.9) with $D = 0$, $D_0 = 0$, is stable along the pass if, and only if,*

(a) Corollary 6.5 holds, and
(b)

$$\sup_{\omega \geq 0} r(G(\imath\omega)) < 1 \tag{6.49}$$

where

$$G(s) := C(sI_n - A)^{-1}B_0 \tag{6.50}$$

Consider now the problem of testing the conditions of Theorem 6.9 for a given example. Then in the case of boundary conditions of the form (6.8), it follows immediately that this task can be completed using standard 1D linear systems stability tests. Note, however, that even if 'Nyquist like' tests are used then, unlike the 1D case, they provide no really useful information as to expected system performance — either open loop or closed loop under appropriate control action. This area is the subject of the next section.

In the differential case when the boundary conditions are of the form (6.9), the problem of developing computationally efficient stability tests is still an open question. Consider, however, the discrete case with state initial vectors of the (most general) form

$$x_{k+1}(0) = d_{k+1} + \sum_{j=0}^{\alpha-1} K_j y_k(j) \, k \geq 0 \tag{6.51}$$

Then it will be shown in a later section that the resulting conditions for stability along the pass can also be tested using only 1D linear systems tests. The route is via a 1D equivalent linear systems state space model of the process dynamics.

6.4 PERFORMANCE PREDICTION

This general problem area has been addressed by two routes — so-called 1D and 2D Lyapunov equations (Benton *et al.* 1999, Owens & Rogers 1995, Rogers & Owens 1996) and simulation based methods (Rogers & Owens 1992b, Rogers & Owens 1992a, Rogers & Owens 1993) respectively. In the 1D Lyapunov equation case, we now give the main results which also produce stability tests which can be implemented by computations on matrices with constant entries. Note also that all of the results currently available for the 1D Lyapunov equation approach assume the simplest possible form of boundary conditions, where no loss of generality arises from setting $d_{k+1} = 0$, $k \geq 0$.

A discrete process of the form (6.22) under these boundary conditions is stable along the pass if, and only if, $r(D_0) < 1$, $r(A) < 1$, and all eigenvalues of the transfer function matrix

$$G(z) = C(zI_n - A)^{-1}B_0 + D_0 \tag{6.52}$$

have modulus strictly less than unity $\forall \, |z| = 1$. The only potential difficulty in testing these conditions for a given example arises with the last one which requires the computation of the eigenvalues of a possibly large dimension matrix with complex valued entries for all points on the unit circle in the complex plane. The following result is the first step in developing stability tests which only involve computations on matrices with constant entries. This result is from (Rogers & Owens 1996) and uses the so-called (see below) 1D Lyapunov equation.

Theorem 6.10 *Suppose that the pair $\{A, B_0\}$ is controllable and the pair $\{C, A\}$ is observable. Then $S(E_\alpha, W_\alpha, L_\alpha)$ generated by (6.22) with $x_{k+1}(0) = 0$, $k \geq 0$, is stable along the pass if, and only if, $r(D_0) < 1$, $r(A) < 1$, and $\exists$ a rational polynomial matrix solution $P(z)$ of the Lyapunov equation*

$$G^T(z^{-1})P(z)G(z) - P(z) = -I \tag{6.53}$$

bounded in an open neighborhood of the unit circle $\hat{T} = \{z : |z| = 1\}$ in the complex plane with the properties that $P(z) \equiv P^T(z^{-1})$ and

$$\beta_2^2 I \geq P(z) = P^T(z^{-1}) \geq \beta_1^2 I, \ \forall \, z \in \hat{T} \tag{6.54}$$

for some choices of real scalars $\beta_i \geq 1$, $i = 1, 2$.

The scalars β_i play no role in stability analysis but, as described next, are the key to obtaining bounds on expected system performance.

Suppose that (6.22) is stable along the pass. Then factorization techniques enable $P(z)$ to be written as $P(z) = F^T(z^{-1})F(z)$ where $F(z)$ is both stable and minimum phase and hence has a stable minimum phase inverse. Given these facts, return to (6.22) and consider the case when the current pass input terms are deleted. Then it follows that the process dynamics can be written in terms of the standard (1D) z transform as

$$Y_{k+1}(z) = G(z)Y_k(z), \ k \geq 0 \tag{6.55}$$

Also let

$$\hat{Y}_k(z) = F(z)Y_k(z), \ \ k \geq 0 \tag{6.56}$$

denote 'filtered' (by properties of $F(z)$) outputs. Then the following result gives bounds on expected system performance.

Theorem 6.11 *Suppose that $S(E_\alpha, W_\alpha, L_\alpha)$ generated by (6.22) with $x_{k+1}(0) = 0$, $k \geq 0$, is stable along the pass. Then, $\forall \, k \geq 0$,*

$$\|\hat{Y}_{k+1}\|^2_{\ell_2^m(0,+\infty)} = \|\hat{Y}_k\|^2_{\ell_2^m(0,+\infty)} - \|Y_k\|^2_{\ell_2^m(0,+\infty)} \tag{6.57}$$

and hence the filtered output sequence $\{\|\hat{Y}_k\|^2_{\ell_2^m(0,+\infty)}\}_{k\geq 0}$ is strictly monotonically decreasing to zero and satisfies, for $k \geq 0$, the inequality

$$\|\hat{Y}_k\|_{\ell_2^m(0,+\infty)} \leq \lambda^k \|\hat{Y}_0\|_{\ell_2^m(0,+\infty)} \tag{6.58}$$

where

$$\lambda := (1 - \beta_2^{-2})^{\frac{1}{2}} < 1 \tag{6.59}$$

Also the actual output sequence $\{\|Y_k\|_{\ell_2^m(0,+\infty)}\}_{k\geq 0}$ is bounded by

$$\|Y_k\|_{\ell_2^m(0,+\infty)} \leq M\lambda^k \|Y_0\|_{\ell_2^m(0,+\infty)} \tag{6.60}$$

where

$$M := \beta_2 \beta_1^{-1} \geq 1 \tag{6.61}$$

This result provides computable (see below) information concerning the convergence of the output sequence of a discrete linear repetitive process under stability along the pass to the resulting limit profile. The main features are as follows.

- The sequence of filtered outputs $\{\hat{Y}_k\}_{k\geq 0}$ consists of monotone signals converging to zero at a computable rate in $\ell_2^m(0, +\infty)$.

- The actual output sequence $\{Y_k\}_{k\geq 0}$ converges at the same geometric rate but is no longer necessarily monotonic. Also the deviation from monotonicity is described by the parameter M computed from the solution of the 1D Lyapunov equation.

To solve the 1D Lyapunov equation (and hence stability tests only involving computations on matrices with constant entries) in the general case requires the use of the Kronecker product, denoted $\otimes$, for matrices. In particular, assuming the first two conditions of Theorem 6.10 hold, the example under consideration is stable along the pass if, and only if, $\exists$ a positive definite Hermitian matrix (denoted P. D. H.) $P(e^{i\theta})$ which solves the following equivalent version of (6.53) $\forall\, \theta \in [0, 2\pi]$

$$(I_{m^2} - G^T(e^{-i\theta}) \otimes G^T(e^{i\theta}))S[P(e^{i\theta})] = S[I] \tag{6.62}$$

where $S[.]$ denotes the stacking operator. The following is a new set of conditions for stability along the pass.

Theorem 6.12 *Suppose that the controllability and observability assumptions of Theorem 6.10 hold. Then $S(E_\alpha, W_\alpha, L_\alpha)$ generated by (6.22) with $x_{k+1}(0) = 0$, $k \geq 0$, is stable along the pass if, and only if, $r(D_0) < 1$, $r(A) < 1$, $P \equiv P(e^{i\theta_0})$ – the solution of*

$$P - G^T(e^{-i\theta_0})PG(e^{i\theta_0}) = I \tag{6.63}$$

is positive definite for any $\theta_0 \in [0, 2\pi]$; and

$$det(I_{m^2} - G^T(e^{-i\theta}) \otimes G^T(e^{i\theta})) \neq 0, \ \forall\, \theta \in [0, 2\pi] \tag{6.64}$$

Finally, we have the following result which gives conditions for stability along the pass which can be tested by computations with matrices which have constant entries.

Theorem 6.13 *Suppose that the controllability and observability assumptions of theorem 6.4 hold. Then $S(E_\alpha, W_\alpha, E_\alpha)$ generated by (6.22) with $x_{k+1}(0) = 0$, $k \geq 0$, is stable along the pass if, and only if, $r(D_0) < 1$, $r(A) < 1$, $r(G(e^{i\theta_0})) < 1$ for an arbitrary $\theta_0 \in [0, 2\pi]$; and*

$$det(\lambda^2 X_1 + \lambda X_2 + X_3) \neq 0, \ \forall\, |\lambda| = 1 \tag{6.65}$$

In this last result, the matrices X_i, $1 \leq i \leq 3$, are composed of compatibly dimensioned zero matrices, identity matrices, and matrices whose block entries are defined by compatibly dimensioned Kronecker products of the matrices A, B_0, C and D_0 respectively. A minor complication is that the matrix X_1 is singular and hence further development is required for the separate cases when A is singular and non-singular. The development required in both cases is extensive, but routine, algebraic manipulations to obtain an equivalent to (6.65) which can easily be tested using existing software for solving a particular class of generalized eigenvalue problems.

The term '1D' for the Lyapunov equation of Theorems 6.10–6.12 refers to the fact that it has an identical structure to that for discrete 1D linear time invariant systems but with defining matrices which are functions of a complex variable. In the case of 2D linear systems and both differential and discrete linear repetitive processes, it is also possible to use a so-called 2D Lyapunov equation to study stability properties. Considering again the discrete case, define the so-called augmented plant matrix for (6.22) as

$$\Phi = \begin{bmatrix} A & B_0 \\ C & D_0 \end{bmatrix} \tag{6.66}$$

Then the 2D Lyapunov equation for (6.22) has the form

$$\Phi^T W \Phi - W = -Q \tag{6.67}$$

where W is the direct sum, denoted $\oplus$, of the $n \times n$ symmetric matrix W_1 and the $m \times m$ symmetric matrix W_2, i.e. $W = W_1 \oplus W_2 := \text{diag}\{W_1, W_2\}$, and Q is an $(n+m) \times (n+m)$ symmetric matrix. The stability result is as follows.

Theorem 6.14 $S(E_\alpha, W_\alpha, L_\alpha)$ *generated by (6.22) with* $x_{k+1}(0) = 0$, $k \geq 0$, *is stable along the pass if* $\exists$ *symmetric positive definite matrices* W *and* Q *which solve the 2D Lyapunov equation (6.67).*

The 2D Lyapunov equation gives, in general, sufficient but not necessary conditions for stability along the pass. (This fact can be established by a counter-example (Benton 2000).) A number of special case do exist, however, where it is both necessary and sufficient – (arguably) the most relevant of which is single-input single-output processes. Despite its conservativeness, the 2D Lyapunov equation has a (potentially) major role to play in the analysis of discrete linear repetitive processes in terms of stability margins and robust stability theory as discussed briefly next.

Consider first relative stability in the case when $r(D_0) < 1$ and $r(A) < 1$. Then if the 2D Lyapunov equation holds this is a sufficient condition for the so-called characteristic polynomial of (6.22)

$$\rho(z_1, z) := \det \begin{pmatrix} I_n - z_1 A & -z_1 B_0 \\ -zC & I_m - zD_0 \end{pmatrix} \tag{6.68}$$

to satisfy

$$\rho(z_1, z) \neq 0, \ \forall \ |z_1| \leq 1, \ |z| \leq 1 \tag{6.69}$$

Using this last result, stability margins can now be defined using the smallest bidisc where $\rho(z_1, z)$ has no roots, i.e.

$$\begin{aligned} \rho(z_1, z) &\neq \quad \text{in } D^2_{\sigma_1} \\ \rho(z_1, z) &\neq \quad \text{in } D^2_{\sigma_2} \\ \rho(z_1, z) &\neq \quad \text{in } D^2_{\sigma} \end{aligned} \tag{6.70}$$

where

$$\begin{aligned} D^2_{\sigma_1} &= \{(z_1, z) : |z_1| < 1 + \sigma_1, |z| < 1\} \\ D^2_{\sigma_2} &= \{(z_1, z) : |z_1| < 1, |z| < 1 + \sigma_2,\} \\ D^2_{\sigma} &= \{(z_1, z) : |z_1| < 1 + \sigma, |z| < 1 + \sigma\} \end{aligned} \tag{6.71}$$

Considerable effort has been directed towards the development of algorithms for computing σ_1, σ_2, and σ in the 2D discrete linear systems case. This work has yielded numerous algorithms based on different starting points. For example, one set is based on minimizing the distance between the roots of $\rho(z_1, z)$ and the boundary of the unit bidisc $\hat{T}^2 = \{(z_1, z) : |z_1| = 1, |z| = 1\}$. Alternatively, algorithms based on the so-called resultant matrix could be used. Also it has been shown that the stability margin is related (in a well defined sense) to the minimal norm of ρ.

A completely different approach is based on the premise that it is not always necessary to know the exact value of the stability margin(s). Instead it suffices to know that it is greater than certain lower limits where one such limit (in each of the three cases) can be obtained as a function of the positive definite solution of the 2D Lyapunov equation. The details are in (Benton *et al.* 1999) and it should also be noted that this complete area, although highly promising, still requires much further development work — see also the conclusions section of this chapter.

To-date, virtually no work has been reported on the key problem of robust stability for differential and discrete linear repetitive processes. In the case of 2D discrete linear systems described by, for example, the Roesser model, this general area has been studied under two types of perturbation in the matrices which define the state space model. As per the 1D case, these are as follows.

- Structured perturbations where the perturbation model structure and bounds on the individual elements of the perturbation matrix are known.

- Unstructured perturbations where, at most, a spectral norm bound on the perturbation is known.

One approach in the second case here is to use the 2D Lyapunov equation under the following additive perturbation structure for the augmented plant matrix

$$\Phi_{\text{per}} = \Phi + \Delta\Phi \tag{6.72}$$

where

$$\Delta\Phi = \begin{bmatrix} \Delta A & \Delta B_0 \\ \Delta C & \Delta D_0 \end{bmatrix} \tag{6.73}$$

If the nominal system is assumed to be stable along the pass and the associated 2D Lyapunov equation holds for some W and Q, it is then possible to derive conditions under which the perturbed system is stable along the pass. Some early results in this area can again be found in (Benton *et al.* 1999) but note also that this area is also in need of much further research effort.

As an alternative to the 1D Lyapunov equation approach discussed earlier in this section, it is possible to obtain time domain (also termed 'simulation based' in the literature) performance bounds. Here we survey the main ideas and results for the differential case based on (Rogers & Owens 1992b, Rogers & Owens 1992a). The discrete case is treated in (Rogers & Owens 1993).

Consider first the 1D linear time invariant system parameterized by the state space quadruple $\{A, B_0, C, D_0\}$ or, in input output terms,

$$(LY)(t) = \int_0^t H(\tau)U(t - \tau)\, d\tau + D_0 U(t) \tag{6.74}$$

where $H(t)$ is the $m \times m$ impulse response matrix

$$H(t) = Ce^{At}B_0 \tag{6.75}$$

Then it is assumed that the step response matrix

$$W(t) = \int_0^t H(\tau)\,d\tau + D_0, \ t \geq 0 \tag{6.76}$$

is available and it is convenient to write this matrix in the form

$$W(t) = \begin{bmatrix} W_{11}(t) & \cdots & W_{1m}(t) \\ \vdots & \ddots & \vdots \\ W_{m1}(t) & \cdots & W_{mm}(t) \end{bmatrix} \tag{6.77}$$

where $W_{pq}(t)$ denotes the response of the pth output channel to a unit step applied at $t = 0$ in the qth input channel. Also it is required that $W(t)$ is a stable response. Formally we require that

$$\|W(t)\|_m \leq \int_0^\infty \|H(\tau)\|_m\,d\tau + \|D_0\|_m < +\infty \tag{6.78}$$

where $\|.\|_m = \max_i \sum_j |(.)_{ij}|$ is the matrix norm induced by the vector norm $\|.\|_m = \max_i |(.)|_m$ in $\mathbb{R}^m$. Under the standard controllability and observability assumptions, this condition holds if, and only if, all eigenvalues of the matrix A have strictly negative real parts.

To proceed, the following lemma is required.

Lemma 6.15 *Consider the case when $g \in L_1(0, T)$, d is a real scalar and*

$$f(t) = d + \int_0^t g(t')\,dt' \tag{6.79}$$

is bounded and continuous on the infinite open interval $0 < t < \infty$ with local maxima or minima at times $t_1 < t_2 \cdots$ satisfying $\sup_{t_j} = +\infty$ in the extended half-line $t > 0$. Then, with $t_0 = 0$

$$|d| + \int_0^T |g(t)|\,dt = N_T(f) \tag{6.80}$$

where

$$N_T(f) := |f(0^+)| + \sum_{j=1}^{j^*} |f(t_j) - f(t_{j-1})| \tag{6.81}$$

and

$$N_\infty(f) := \sup_{T \geq 0} N_T(f) \tag{6.82}$$

where j^* is the largest integer satisfying $t_j < T$.

The application of Lemma 6.15 to a given signal is a simple and numerically well conditioned operation which is illustrated in Figure 6.2. Suppose also that $\|X\|_p$ denotes the nonnegative matrix obtained from the $p \times q$ matrix X by replacing each element by its absolute value. Also let $\geq$ be the partial ordering on $p \times q$ matrices defined by $X \leq Y$ if, and only if, $X_{ij} \leq Y_{ij}$ for all elements (i, j). Then $\|X\|_p$ has a number of 'norm like' properties under this partial ordering, the most important of which here are

(i) $||X||_p \geq 0$

(ii) $||\gamma X||_p \leq |\gamma| ||X||_p$ ∀ complex scalars γ

(iii) (for matrices of the same dimension) $||X + Y||_p \leq ||X||_p + ||Y||_p$

(iv) if Y is a matrix compatible for premultiplication by X then $||XY||_p \leq ||X||_p ||Y||_p$,

(v) if X and Y are square matrices (of the same dimensions) then $0 \leq ||X||_p \leq Y \Rightarrow r(X) \leq r(||X||_p) \leq r(Y)$

(vi) if X is an $n_1 \times n_1$ matrix then $(I_{n_1} - ||X||_p)^{-1}$ exists and is nonnegative if, and only if, $r(||X||_p) < 1$.

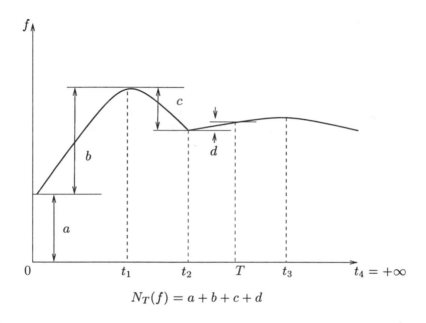

$$N_T(f) = a + b + c + d$$

Figure 6.2: $N_T(f)$ — The Total Variation of f

Suppose now that the result of Lemma 6.15 is applied to each element in turn of the step response matrix $W(t)$ on $(0, +\infty)$ and denote the resulting nonnegative matrix by $||\hat{L}||_p$. Then it follows immediately from the partial ordering $\geq$ that

$$||L_\alpha||_p \leq ||\hat{L}||_p, \ 0 < \alpha < +\infty \tag{6.83}$$

and the following result can now be established.

Theorem 6.16 $S(E_\alpha, L_\alpha, W_\alpha)$ *generated by* (6.22) *with* $x_{k+1}(0) = 0$, $k \geq 0$, *is stable along the pass if*

$$r(||\hat{L}||_p) < 1 \tag{6.84}$$

The numerical procedures required to implement this test consist, in effect, of (i) obtaining the step response matrix $W(t)$, and (ii) the computation of $||\hat{L}||_p$ and its spectral radius. In terms of Lemma 6.15, it is easily shown that, for each f, $N_T(f)$ is monotonically increasing and continuous as a function of f. Hence $N_\infty(f)$ can be obtained as $\lim_{T \to +\infty} N_T(f)$. Note also that

$$\lim_{T \to +\infty} |N_T(f) - N_\infty(f)| = 0 \tag{6.85}$$

and it follows immediately that $N_\infty(f)$ can be estimated to arbitrary accuracy using data on a 'long enough' interval $0 < t \leq T$. On such an interval, the continuity of f as a function of the stationary points $t_1, t_2, \cdots$ indicates that it is insensitive to errors in their estimation — see (Smyth 1992) and (Smyth *et al.* 1994) for a detailed treatment of these aspects and numerical examples.

This simulation based test is sufficient but not necessary and hence there will exist examples which are stable along the pass but where Theorem 6.16 produces an inconclusive result. This, however, is largely offset by the fact that it produces, at no extra computational cost, definitive computable information on the following key aspects of expected process performance to given input signals.

- The rate of approach of the output sequence of pass profiles $\{y_k\}_{k \geq 1}$ to the limit profile.

- The error $y_k - y_\infty$ on any pass k.

Given the clear structural links with 1D linear systems, it is natural to judge the systems response for control purposes in terms of 'benchmark' choices of $u_{k+1}(t)$ (reference signals under feedback control). An obvious choice is

$$u_{k+1}(t) \equiv u_\infty(t) = e_i, \ 0 \leq t \leq \alpha, \ k \geq 0 \tag{6.86}$$

where e_i is the $l \times 1$ column vector consisting of zeros everywhere except the ith position, which consists of a unit element. Equivalently, a unit step is applied at $t = 0$ on each pass in this channel with all others identically zero. Such an input is a special case of a constant disturbance sequence (i.e. $b_{k+1} \equiv b_\infty$, $k \geq 0$) and the following result can now be established.

Theorem 6.17 *Suppose that $S(E_\alpha, L_\alpha, W_\alpha)$ generated by (6.22) with $x_{k+1}(0) = 0$, $k \geq 0$, is stable along the pass with $r(||\hat{L}||_p) < 1$. Suppose also that the control input sequence applied is constant from pass to pass, i.e. $u_{k+1} \equiv u_\infty$, $k \geq 0$, and hence $b_{k+1} \equiv b_\infty$ in (6.27). Then, for $\alpha \in (0, +\infty)$ there exists an $m \times m$ nonnegative matrix W and a real scalar $\gamma \in (r(||\hat{L}||_p), 1)$ such that the error $y_k - y_\infty$, $k \geq 0$ satisfies*

$$||y_k - y_\infty||_p \leq W\gamma^k \{||y_0||_p + (I_m - ||\hat{L}||_p)^{-1}||b_\infty||_p\} \tag{6.87}$$

Suppose therefore that the real scalar γ is chosen as any number in the range $r(||\hat{L}||_p) < \gamma < 1$. Then it follows immediately that the output sequence of pass profiles $\{y_k\}_{k \geq 1}$ approach the limit profile y_∞ at a geometric rate governed by this computable scalar.

In the case of the error $y_k - y_\infty$, it is first necessary to compute $||b_\infty||_p$. In which case, first note that b_∞ is the response of the stable of the 1D linear system

$$\begin{aligned} \dot{x}(t) &= Ax(t) + Bu_\infty(t), \ x(0) = 0 \\ b_\infty(t) &= Cx(t) + Du_\infty(t) \end{aligned} \tag{6.88}$$

Then it follows immediately that

$$||b_\infty||_p = \begin{bmatrix} b_1 & b_2 & \cdots & b_m \end{bmatrix}^T \tag{6.89}$$

with

$$b_i := \sup_{t \geq 0} |b_\infty^i(t)|, \ 1 \leq i \leq m \tag{6.90}$$

where $b_\infty^i(t)$ denotes the ith element of $b_\infty(t)$.

At this stage, introduce

$$P_k = (I_m - ||\hat{L}||_p)^{-1}||\hat{L}||_p^k||b_\infty||_p := ||M_k||_p||b_\infty||_p \qquad (6.91)$$

and denote the ith entry in this vector by P_k^i. Also denote the ith entry in $y_k(t)$ and $y_\infty(t)$ by $y_k^i(t)$ and $y_\infty^i(t)$ respectively, $1 \leq i \leq m$. Then, with $y_0(t)$ set equal to zero for simplicity, it follows immediately from theorem 6.9 that $y_k^i(t)$ lies in the computable 'band' defined by

$$y_\infty^i(t) - P_k^i \leq y_k^i(t) \leq y_\infty^i(t) + P_k^i \qquad (6.92)$$

This band has an obvious graphical interpretation and is obviously compatible with computer aided analysis/design. Also its width from pass to pass is effectively governed by the relationship

$$||M_{k+1}||_p = ||M_k||_p||\hat{L}||_p \qquad (6.93)$$

Numerous alternatives to this result exist — see the cited references for a detailed treatment. One other advantage of this approach is that, unlike the other stability tests, it can be extended to examples where it is necessary to include so-called inter-pass smoothing effects in the basic model. In particular, this approach can be extended to the case where the inter-pass smoothing is modeled by an integral kernel representation of the form

$$\dot{x}_{k+1}(t) = Ax_{k+1} + Bu_{k+1}(t) + B_0 \int_0^\alpha K(t,\tau)y_k(\tau)\,d\tau$$

$$y_{k+1}(t) = Cx_{k+1}(t), \ x_{k+1}(0) = 0, \ k \geq 0, \ 0 \leq t \leq \alpha \qquad (6.94)$$

where the inter-pass interaction term $B_0 \int_0^\alpha K(t,\tau)\,y_k(\tau)d\tau$ represents a 'smoothing out' of the previous pass profile in a manner governed by the properties of the kernel $K(t,\tau)$. Note also that the particular choice of $K(t,\tau) = \delta(t - \tau)I_m$ where δ denotes the Dirac delta function reduces (6.94) to the case of (6.7) (with $D = 0$, $D_0 = 0$).

Some productive work has already been undertaken on the use of these simulation based tests in the specification and design of control schemes for these processes. This topic is considered again in a later section.

6.5 SYSTEMS THEORETIC CONCEPTS

Discrete linear repetitive processes has strong structural links with 2D discrete linear systems described by the well known Fornasini Marchesini (Fornasini & Marchesini 1978) and Roesser (Roesser 1975) state space models. Note, however, that repetitive processes are uniquely characterized by a finite pass length and hence well developed 2D linear systems theory cannot be directly applied to characterize, for example, what (if anything) is meant by controllability for these processes. It is, however, still feasible to exploit such theory given an equivalent 2D Roesser or Fornasini Marchesini state space model description of the process dynamics.

The latter approach has been the subject of considerable research in recent years — see (Gałkowski *et al.* 1998, Rogers *et al.* 1998). This has shown that the appropriate starting point is the so-called augmented state vector

$$Z(k,p) := \left[x_k^T(p), y_k^T(p) \right]^T \qquad (6.95)$$

and then the dynamics of (6.22) can be written in the form

$$EZ(k+1, p+1) = A_1 Z(k+1, p) + A_2 Z(k, p) + B_1 u(k+1, p) \tag{6.96}$$

which is one of several singular versions of the Fornasini Marchesini model. In 2D linear systems theory, it is possible to write standard or singular Fornasini Marchesini models in Roesser form. In the case of discrete linear repetitive processes, this is also possible by introducing the following transformations into (6.96)

$$\eta(k, p) \;=\; EZ(k, p+1) - A_1 Z(k, p) \tag{6.97}$$
$$\gamma(k, p) \;=\; \eta(k, p) - B_1 u(k, p) \tag{6.98}$$

where the role of (6.98) to avoid the undesirable feature of a shift in the input vector indexes. The result of this operation is the following singular 2D linear systems Roesser model interpretation for the dynamics of discrete linear repetitive processes

$$\begin{bmatrix} I_{n+m} & 0 \\ 0 & E \end{bmatrix} \begin{bmatrix} \gamma(k+1, p) \\ Z(k, p+1) \end{bmatrix} = \begin{bmatrix} 0 & A_2 \\ I & A_1 \end{bmatrix} \begin{bmatrix} \gamma(k, p) \\ Z(k, p) \end{bmatrix} + \begin{bmatrix} 0 \\ B_1 \end{bmatrix} u(k, p) \tag{6.99}$$

In this model, both state $\{x\}$ and the pass profile $\{y\}$, which form the augmented state vector Z, constitute the information transmitted in one direction. Suppose also that the following transformations are introduced into (6.22) (where to conform with the 2D systems literature, $x(k, p) \equiv x_k(p)$, $y(k, p) \equiv y_k(p)$, and $u(k, p) \equiv u_k(p)$)

$$\eta(k, p) \;:=\; x(k, p+1) - Ax(k, p) - Bu(k, p) \tag{6.100}$$
$$\mu(k, p) \;:=\; y(k, p) - Cx(k, p) - Du(k, p) \tag{6.101}$$

Then the result can be written as

$$\begin{bmatrix} x(k, p+1) \\ \mu(k+1, p) \\ \eta(k+1, p) \end{bmatrix} = \begin{bmatrix} A & 0 & I \\ D_0 C & D_0 & 0 \\ B_0 C & B_0 & 0 \end{bmatrix} \begin{bmatrix} x(k, p) \\ \mu(k, p) \\ \eta(k, p) \end{bmatrix} + \begin{bmatrix} B \\ D_0 D \\ B_0 D \end{bmatrix} u(k, p) \tag{6.102}$$

which is a standard (also termed nonsingular) Roesser model whose state dimension is $2n + m$ as opposed to $2(n + m)$ for the singular Roesser model interpretation.

The 2D systems interpretations have led to the following advances in terms of systems theory for discrete linear repetitive processes.

- The standard model has led to a formal equivalence between stability along the pass and bounded-input bounded-output stability of the Roesser (and hence Fornasini Marchesini) state space model interpretation of the process dynamics.

- The singular model has been used to develop a transition matrix, or fundamental matrix sequence, and hence a general response formula for calculating the process response to a given input sequence and boundary conditions (of the form $x_{k+1}(0) = d_{k+1}$, $k \geq 0$, but a generalization to the general form of (6.23) should be possible). This has then led to the characterization, in terms of matrix rank conditions for certain reachability/controllability properties as discussed below.

In order to define so-called local reachability and controllability for discrete linear repetitive processes, the following partial ordering of two-tuple integers will be used.

$$
\begin{aligned}
(i,j) &\leq (k,p) \text{ iff } i \leq k \text{ and } j \leq p \\
(i,j) &= (k,p) \text{ iff } i = k \text{ and } j = p \\
(i,j) &< (k,p) \text{ iff } (i,j) \leq (k,p) \text{ and } (i,j) \neq (k,p)
\end{aligned}
\tag{6.103}
$$

Also the dynamics of discrete linear repetitive processes evolve over

$$
D_e := \{(k,p) : k \geq 0, \, 0 \leq p \leq \alpha\}
\tag{6.104}
$$

but in practice only a finite number of passes, say K^*, will actually be completed. Hence a natural way to define reachability/controllability properties for these processes is to ask if it is possible to 'reach' all possible vectors in the rectangle whose boundary in the pass-to-pass direction is given by $0 \leq k \leq K^*$ and in the along the pass direction by $0 \leq p \leq \alpha$. Next we formalize this intuitive idea in terms of so-called local reachability and controllability properties of (6.22) (with $x_{k+1}(0) = d_{k+1}$, $k \geq 0$) where for $(a,b) < (c,d)$ the rectangle $[(a,b),(c,d)]$ is defined as follows.

$$
[(a,b),(c,d)] := \{(a,b) \leq (i,j) \leq (c,d)\}
\tag{6.105}
$$

In general, as in the 2D linear systems case, local reachability and controllability of discrete linear repetitive processes are quite distinct concepts. The formal definitions are as follows.

Definition 6.18 *The dynamics of discrete linear repetitive processes modeled by (6.96) are said to be locally reachable in the rectangle $[(0,0),(f,h)]$, $0 \leq f \leq K^*$, $0 \leq h \leq \alpha$ if for every $z_r \in \mathbb{R}^{n+m} \, \exists$ a sequence of control input vectors defined on $(0,0) \leq (i,j) \leq (f,h)$ such that $Z(f,h) = z_r$.*

Definition 6.19 *The dynamics of discrete linear repetitive processes modeled by (6.96) are said to be locally controllable in the rectangle $[(0,0),(f,h)]$, $0 \leq f \leq K^*$, $0 \leq h \leq \alpha$, if there exists a sequence of control vectors $u(i,j)$ defined on $(0,0) \leq (i,j) \leq (f,h)$ such that $Z(f,h) = 0$.*

The characterization of both these properties in terms of conditions on the rank of constant matrices can be found in (Rogers *et al.* 1998). Note that local reachability implies local controllability but the converse is not necessarily true. Hence it is of interest to establish exactly when local controllability implies local reachability — it is expected that results by Kaczorek (1994) for the corresponding 2D systems case will be of direct use in this respect.

In common with 2D discrete linear systems, at least one other distinct definition of reachability/controllability for discrete linear repetitive processes can be formulated. For example, preliminary work (Smyth 1992) has highlighted the need for so-called simultaneous, or pass, reachability/controllability of discrete linear repetitive processes. The controllability definition is as follows (see (Kaczorek 1992) for a related concept for 2D linear systems described by the Roesser model).

Definition 6.20 *Let K^* be an arbitrarily chosen pass index for the discrete linear repetitive process (6.22). Then examples described by this model are said to be simultaneously, or pass, controllable if $\exists$ control input vectors $u_{k+1}(p)$, $0 \leq p \leq \alpha$, $0 \leq k \leq K^*$, which will drive the process to a pre-specified pass profile on pass K^*.*

Consider now the problem of characterizing this property using the equivalent 2D linear systems state space descriptions of the dynamics of (6.22) described above. Then, in fact, it is not possible to completely characterize this property using this approach. The basic reason for this is that pass controllability plays the same role for discrete linear repetitive processes as the so-called global controllability of 2D Roesser/Fornasini Marchesini systems. In particular, global controllability for such 2D linear systems is expressed in terms of the global state vector with entries along the entire separation set, but, in the case of (6.22) this collection of local state vectors is finite by definition.

Pass controllability for (6.22) can be completely characterized by using a recently developed (Gałkowski *et al.* 1998) 1D linear systems state space interpretation of the underlying dynamics. The resulting conditions are expressed in terms of rank properties of matrices with constant entries. Such 1D models have also been developed for 2D Roesser/Fornasini Marchesini systems (Aravena *et al.* 1990) but the resulting descriptions are 'time varying' in the sense that the dimensions of the matrices and vectors which define them increase as the system evolves. This fact alone has severely restricted their onward use in systems analysis.

In the case of discrete linear repetitive processes, however, it is possible to develop an equivalent 1D model description defined by matrices and vectors with constant dimensions. The details are in (Gałkowski *et al.* 1998) and it suffices to note here that this model is expressed in terms of the so-called pass profile, state and input super-vectors respectively which are defined as follows.

$$Y(k) := \left[y_k^T(0), \dots, y_k^T(\alpha - 1) \right]^T$$

$$X(k) := \left[x_k^T(1), \dots, x_k^T(\alpha) \right]^T$$

$$U(k) = \left[u_k^T(0), \dots, u_k^T(\alpha - 1) \right]^T \qquad (6.106)$$

Also it leads immediately (as noted above) to a characterization of pass controllability in terms of conditions on the rank properties of constant matrices — again see (Gałkowski *et al.* 1998).

Another major use for the 1D model is the development of stability tests for the discrete case when the state initial vector on each pass has the form (6.51). In particular, use of this 1D equivalent model leads to stability tests when can be implemented by direct application of 1D linear systems tests. The details are in (Rogers *et al.* 1998). Finally, note that the full potential of this 1D model has not yet been realized (see also the conclusions section of this chapter).

6.6 CONTROL OF DIFFERENTIAL AND DISCRETE LINEAR REPETITIVE PROCESSES

In general, only certain aspects of this very general problem area have yet been addressed. Also the area where the most substantial progress to-date has been achieved is iterative learning control (ILC). In this section, we survey the work which has been completed and then discuss some areas for short to medium term further research. We begin with the simplest possible control structures which are based on direct extension of 1D linear systems feedback control schemes.

Some effort has been directed at the development of suitable control objectives for differential and discrete linear repetitive processes (Smyth 1992). One result of this has been the so-called limit profile design problem (LPDP). This, as the names suggests, has its origins in the fact that the limit profile for a differential (respectively discrete) linear repetitive process is a 1D differential (respectively discrete) linear system. Its basic requirements can be stated as follows, where these are to be independent of the pass length α and hence stability along the pass is a prerequisite.

- The resulting limit profile dynamics should satisfy such additional 1D linear systems performance criteria as deemed appropriate.

- The output sequence of pass profiles $\{y_k\}_{k \geq 1}$ must be within a specified 'band' of y_∞ after a specified number of passes, say k^*, have elapsed and remain within it $\forall k > k^*$.

- The error $y_k - y_\infty, 0 \leq k \leq k^*$ must be 'acceptable'.

Clearly the terms in quotation marks here must be refined into design criteria appropriate for the particular application under consideration. In terms of the structure of possible control schemes, the strong structural links with 1D linear systems, strongly suggests the use of appropriately defined feedback control schemes. Such schemes can be classified in general terms as follows.

1. Those which only explicitly use current pass information — termed memoryless.

2. Those which explicitly use information from the current and/or previous pass profiles, state vectors, or input vectors.

The first class here have the simplest possible structure in terms of the information which must be logged/stored in order to actuate the controller(s). Hence it is clear that the potential of such schemes should be fully evaluated before recourse to those in the second class or alternatives.

Results of the underlying theory of these memoryless feedback control schemes for differential and discrete linear repetitive processes can be found in (Rogers & Owens 1995) and (Rogers & Owens 1994) respectively. One particular scheme in this class is the so-called memoryless dynamic unity negative feedback controller. In effect, this is just the 1D linear systems dynamic unity negative feedback controller applied on the current pass and is discussed further next for the differential case.

Suppose that $r_{k+1}(t) \in \mathbb{R}^m$ is a new external reference vector taken to represent desired behavior on pass $k + 1$, $k \geq 0$. Also define the so-called current pass error vector as

$$e_{k+1}(t) = r_{k+1}(t) - y_{k+1}(t), \ 0 \leq t \leq \alpha, \ k \geq 0 \qquad (6.107)$$

Then a memoryless dynamic unity negative feedback controller for the differential linear repetitive process (6.7) constructs the input $u_{k+1}(t)$, $0 \leq t \leq \alpha$, $k \geq 0$ as the output from

$$\begin{aligned} \dot{x}^c_{k+1}(t) &= A^c x^c_{k+1}(t) + B^c e_{k+1}(t) \\ u_{k+1}(t) &= C^c x^c_{k+1}(t) + D^c e_{k+1}(t) \end{aligned} \qquad (6.108)$$

where $x^c_{k+1}(t) \in \mathbb{R}^{n_1}$ denotes the internal state vector of the controller.

To illustrate the potential of this general approach, consider the case when the 1D subsystem of (6.7) formed by the quadruple $\{A, B, C, D\}$ has the structure of a so-called multivariable first order lag (Owens 1978). Then it is easy to show that the dynamics in this case can be described by

$$\dot{y}_{k+1}(t) = -A_0^{-1}A_1 y_k(t) + A_0^{-1}u_{k+1}(t) + \hat{B}_0 y_k(t), \ 0 \leq t \leq \alpha, \ k \geq 0 \qquad (6.109)$$

where A_0 and A_1 are $m \times m$ matrices with A_0 nonsingular.

By analogy with the 1D case, consider the use of a proportional forward path controller with the structure

$$u_{k+1}(t) = (\rho A_0 - A_1)e_{k+1}(t), \ 0 \leq t \leq \alpha, \ k \geq 0 \qquad (6.110)$$

where $\rho > 0$ is a scalar gain to be selected. In which case, it is easy to see that the condition on the eigenvalues of the matrix A closed loop holds $\forall \rho > 0$. Suppose also that the simulation based route is used. Then

$$||L^c||_p = \frac{||\hat{B}_0||_p}{\rho} \qquad (6.111)$$

and hence closed loop stability along the pass if

$$\rho > r(||\hat{B}_0||_p) \qquad (6.112)$$

which can always be satisfied by choosing a 'high enough' value of ρ (i.e. high gain).

Given this last result, theorem 6.9 can be used to conclude that $\{y_k\}_{k \geq 1}$ approaches y_∞ at a geometric rate governed by the computable scalar

$$\gamma \in (r(\frac{||\hat{B}_0||_p}{\rho}), 1) \qquad (6.113)$$

Also it is easily shown that the closed loop limit profile is described in Laplace transform terms by

$$(sI_m + \rho(I_m - \frac{\hat{B}_0}{\rho}))Y_\infty(s) = \rho(I_m - \frac{A_0^{-1}A_1}{\rho})R_\infty(s) \qquad (6.114)$$

which is a stable 1D linear system. Finally, interpreting (6.87) gives the error band for each element of $y_k - y_\infty$, $k \geq 0$.

As a final point, consider the case $\rho \to +\infty$ (high gain). Then in this case, $y_\infty(t)$ is arbitrarily close to the inverse Laplace transform of

$$Y_\infty(s) = \frac{\rho}{s + \rho}I_m R_\infty(s) \qquad (6.115)$$

which is a totally non-interacting 1D linear system with zero steady-state error to a unit step applied at $t = 0$ in any channel. Further, it follows immediately that the limit profile dynamics are reached to within arbitrary accuracy on the first pass under this condition. Also other special cases within this setting exist — see, for example, (Benton *et al.* 1998).

Iterative learning control (ILC) is an application area which has seen the most progress to-date in terms of the development of control schemes for differential and discrete linear repetitive processes. In particular, the use of (2D) predictive control has been the subject of considerable productive research effort. Next we give an overview of progress to-date in the differential case starting with some background on ILC.

In essence, ILC is a technique to control systems operating in a repetitive mode with the additional requirement that a specified output trajectory $r(t)$ on a finite interval $[0, T]$ is followed to a high precision. Examples of such systems are robot manipulators required to repeat a given task, chemical batch processes, or, more generally, the class of tracking systems. Motivated by human learning, the basic idea of ILC is to use information from previous executions of the task in order to improve performance from trial to trial in the sense that the tracking error is sequentially reduced — see (Arimoto *et al.* 1984, Moore 1993) for further background and early work in this general area.

Typical ILC schemes construct the input to the plant on a given trial from the input used on the last trial plus an additive increment that is typically a function of the past values of the observed output error, i.e. the difference between the achieved and desired plant output. The objective of constructing a sequence of input functions $\{u_k(t)\}_k$, $t \in [0, T]$ such that the performance is gradually improving as the task is repeated can be refined into a convergence condition on the input and error:

$$\lim_{k \to \infty} \|e_k\| = 0, \quad \lim_{k \to \infty} \|u_k - u_\infty\| = 0 \qquad (6.116)$$

Here on trial k, $e_k(t) = r(t) - y_k(t)$ (i.e. the error between the reference signal and the kth trial output), and $u_k(t)$ is the system input.

This definition of convergent learning is a stability problem on an infinite-dimensional 2D product space, typically of the form $\mathbb{N} \times L_2[0, T]$. As such, it places the analysis of ILC schemes firmly outside the scope of traditional control theory — instead it must be studied as a fixed-point problem or, more precisely as a linear repetitive process.

Normally, ILC algorithms require only a minimal knowledge of the plant but pay for this high degree of robustness with a (possibly) slow rate of convergence. For example, the original learning law proposed in (Arimoto *et al.* 1984) requires only the (approximate) knowledge of the first Markov parameter of the plant. Convergence can be achieved with this law but a fast reduction in the error cannot be guaranteed. It is, however, natural to aim for a fast rate of convergence since, for example, the ultimate aim may be a reduction in the error by a given factor on each trial, a goal which has not been achieved to-date.

In order to achieve good performance, more knowledge of the plant must be assumed and several approaches based on a complete but uncertain model of the plant have been investigated — see (Amann *et al.* 1996) for an overview of such approaches. Amann *et al.* (1996) also proposed a solution based on using a 'classical' linear quadratic regulator (LQR) performance criterion to compute an optimal feedforward control increment combined with a stabilizing feedback input. This algorithm has a natural feedback-feedforward structure and has the very desirable property of a monotonic reduction of the error (in an L_2-sense) but to a degree that depends on algorithm parameters and, very significantly, plant dynamic structure.

This last point, i.e. the 'negative' effects of the plant structure, motivated the development of so-called predictive optimal ILC where the principal idea is to use a prediction horizon in the computation of the control input, in a similar manner to model predictive control (MPC) or generalized predictive control (GPC). (For background on MPC or GPC see, for example, (Garcia *et al.* 1989) or (Clarke & Mohtadi 1989)). MPC and GPC methods require the solution of a single finite-time LQR problem at each sample and time step, using a receding horizon so that an optimal solution needs to be re-computed at each step. In the predictive optimal ILC algorithm, a set of 1D finite-time LQR problems is solved between each trial (or experiment), also using a receding horizon. The algorithm presented below is hence a form of 2D predictive control.

The cost function used in (Amann *et al.* 1996) had the form (in the notation given above)

$$J_{k+1}(u_{k+1}) = ||e_{k+1}||^2 + ||u_{k+1} - u_k||^2 \qquad (6.117)$$

and the plant was assumed to be modeled by the input-output relation $y_{k+1} = Gu_{k+1}$ where G is a linear operator defined by the plant dynamics. The norms $||.||^2$ are induced norms from the inner products $\langle \cdot \rangle$ of the chosen input and output Hilbert spaces $\mathcal{U}$ and $\mathcal{Y}$ respectively. For example, in the continuous case the norm is typically the $L_2[0, T]$ norm.

Under this choice of norm, the problem posed above is a standard LQR control problem with a well known solution (see, for example, Anderson & Moore (1989)). The resulting ILC control algorithm was termed 'norm-optimal ILC' by Amann *et al.* (1996) who also undertook a detailed analysis of its properties. These include guaranteed convergence with a monotonically decreasing error for all linear, possibly time-varying, processes with good convergence for examples which are minimum phase. The case when there are non-minimum phase zeros has been considered by (Amann & Owens 1994) where it was shown that such zeros of a plant are associated with specific directions in the input space where convergence is very slow.

This last observation was one of the main reasons why so-called predictive optimal ILC was considered. In effect, this approach extends the cost function used in norm-optimal ILC to take future predicted error signals into account. The extended criterion for computing the input u_{k+1} on trial $k + 1$ is taken as

$$J_{k+1,N}(u_{k+1}) = \sum_{i=1}^{N} \lambda^{i-1}(||e_{k+i}||^2 + ||u_{k+i} - u_{k+i-1}||^2) \qquad (6.118)$$

This cost function includes the error on the next N trials together with corresponding changes in the input, and the weight parameter $\lambda > 0$ determines the importance of more distant (future) errors and incremental inputs compared with the present ones. By including more future signals into the performance criterion, the algorithm becomes less 'short sighted' and it is expected that the predictive optimal ILC algorithm which solves this problem will have significantly better convergence properties than the one step look ahead algorithm of (Amann *et al.* 1996, Amann *et al.* 1998).

To solve this optimization problem, dynamic programming is used. The starting point is to postulate that the optimal value of $J_{k+1,N}$ is a quadratic form in e_k, i.e.

$$J_{k+1,N}(u_{k+1}) = \langle e_k, Q_N e_k \rangle \qquad (6.119)$$

where the self-adjoint positive operator Q_N is a function of λ, N, and G to be determined. This assumption is known to be valid (Amann *et al.* 1996) for the case of $N = 1$ and routine analysis leads to the following formula for the optimal input on trial $k + 1$

$$u_{k+1} = u_k + G^*(I + \lambda Q_{N-1})e_{k+1} \qquad (6.120)$$

where the superscript $*$ denotes the adjoint operation. The optimal error resulting from this input can be written (pre-multiply by G and use the fact that $Gu_{k+1} - Gu_k = e_k - e_{k+1}$)

$$e_{k+1} = [I + GG^*(I + \lambda Q_{N-1})]^{-1}e_k := L_N e_k \qquad (6.121)$$

This is already the first form of a recursive error evolution law where the operator

$$L_N := [I + GG^*(I + \lambda Q_{N-1})]^{-1} \qquad (6.122)$$

maps the error from one trial to the next and plays a central role in the study of this general class of ILC schemes and is known as the 'error transmission operator'. It is now necessary to determine the operator Q_N for which we have, on exploiting the self adjoint properties of Q_N and L_N,

$$J_{k+1,N} = < e_k, L_N(I + \lambda Q_{N-1})e_k > \qquad (6.123)$$

Comparing this last result with the original postulate (6.119) now yields the following recursive relation for Q_N

$$Q_N = [I + GG^*(I + \lambda Q_{N-1})]^{-1}(I + \lambda Q_{N-1}) \qquad (6.124)$$

with the starting optimal input ($N = 1$) given by

$$u_{k+1} = u_k + G^*e_{k+1} \qquad (6.125)$$

and comparison with (6.120) gives $Q_0 = 0$. It is now possible to derive properties of this algorithm — a key aspect of which is the conversion of the highly symbolic form of (6.120) to an implementable algorithm (see later in this section).

Formally, the analysis just summarized can be stated as follows.

Definition 6.21   *The optimal predictive ILC algorithm with a prediction horizon of N trials is given by the input which minimizes at each trial the cost criterion (6.118). The optimal control input u_{k+1} is given by the update law (6.120) where the self-adjoint, positive operator $Q_N(GG^*, \lambda)$ satisfies the recurrence relation (6.124) with $Q_0 = 0$. This algorithm leads to the recursive error update law (6.121) when applied to the plant $e_{k+1} = r - Gu_{k+1}$.*

In order to state key properties (for the proofs see (Amann *et al.* 1998)) of this ILC algorithm it is first useful to express the learning operator L_N as a recursion relation by eliminating Q_N. The result is, with $H := GG^*$ for notational simplicity,

$$L_N(H, \lambda) = [(1 + \lambda)I + H - \lambda L_{N-1}]^{-1}, \ N = 1, 2, \ldots, \ L_0 = I \qquad (6.126)$$

This equation defines L_N recursively in terms of λ and H, where this last operator is a (more or less) arbitrary linear, self-adjoint, operator from a real Hilbert space – the space of output functions – into itself. By studying properties of L_N in terms of H and λ, it is possible to determine the structural properties of predictive optimal ILC. These are summarized in turn next.

Property 6.22 *All learning operators $L_N(H, \lambda)$, $N = 1, 2, \ldots$ are self-adjoint and commute with each other.*

The next property shows that $L_N : \mathcal{Y} \to \mathcal{Y}$ is positive in the sense that $\langle e, L_N e \rangle > 0$ for all nonzero $e \in \mathcal{Y}$.

Property 6.23 *If H is positive and bounded in norm then the learning operators $L_N(H, \lambda)$ are positive according to the following bound*

$$L_N(H, \lambda) \geq (I + \lambda + H)^{-1} > 0, \ \forall \, 0, \lambda < \infty, \ N = 1, 2, \ldots \qquad (6.127)$$

A lower bound on L_N is of some interest but an upper bound (on the norm of L_N) is more important to ILC convergence analysis since the norm of the error at the kth trial can be bounded by $||e_k|| \leq ||L_N||^k ||e_0||$, i.e. a sufficient condition for convergence is $||L_N|| < 1$. A 'fast' rate of convergence requires that $||L_N||$ is as small as possible. If the plant is bounded below, as in the next property, clear statements can be given.

Property 6.24 *If $\langle e, He \rangle \geq \sigma^2 ||e||^2$ for all $e \in \mathcal{Y}$, then*

$$L_N \leq l_N(\sigma^2, \lambda)I \tag{6.128}$$

where

$$l_N(\sigma^2, \lambda) = \frac{1}{1 + \lambda + \sigma^2 - \lambda l_{N-1}(\sigma^2, \lambda)}, \quad l_0 = 1 \tag{6.129}$$

and the error sequence is bounded by $||e_{k+1}|| \leq l_N(\sigma^2, \lambda)||e_k||$.

Given the definition of the norm of a self-adjoint operator L this last property means that $||L_N|| \leq l_N(\sigma^2, \lambda)$. The smallest value of the 'smallest singular value' σ defined above which holds for the plant is $\sigma = 0$ since $\langle e, He \rangle = ||G^* e||^2 \geq 0$, but the bound l_N for $||L_N||$ gives useful information only if $\sigma > 0$. In this case, the next property specifies the norm of L_N and proves convergence for this case.

Property 6.25 *If $\sigma > 0$, then*

$$||L_N|| < 1, \quad \forall N \geq 0 \tag{6.130}$$

This last result implies that the predictive algorithm converges geometrically if $\sigma > 0$, i.e. the norm of the error on each trial is reduced by a factor of at least $||L_N|| \leq l_N$ and hence $\frac{||e_{k+1}||}{||e_k||} \leq l_N$. The next two properties show the dependence of the learning operator L_N on N and λ.

Property 6.26 *If $H > 0$, then the following monotonicity property holds*

$$L_{N+1}(H, \lambda) < L_N(H, \lambda), \quad \forall N \geq 0, \lambda > 0 \tag{6.131}$$

Property 6.27 *If $H > 0$ and $0 < \lambda' < \lambda$, then*

$$L_N(H, \lambda) < L_N(H, \lambda'), \quad \forall N > 1 \tag{6.132}$$

Note 6.28 *Properties 6.26 and 6.27 can also be stated in terms of $l_N(\sigma^2, \lambda)$ — simply replace H by σ^2 and L_N by l_n.*

Using Property 6.26 it follows immediately that one way of increasing the rate of convergence is to increase the prediction horizon but at the cost of increased computational complexity since the state dimension of the controller is increased by the order of the plant. An alternative way to improve convergence is by increasing the weight λ (follows from Property 6.27). (See the example later in this section for the benefits of increasing N or λ.) In these cases, the benefits predicted by the norm estimate $l_N(\sigma^2, \lambda)$ decrease as σ^2 decreases. The next property establishes the monotonicity of $l_N(\sigma^2, \lambda)$.

Property 6.29 *The bound $l_N(\sigma^2, \lambda)$ is strictly decreasing for increasing σ^2 and fixed $\lambda > 0$, $N \geq 1$.*

The norm bound reaches its maximum at $\sigma = 0$ and has value $l_N(0, \lambda) = 1$. A similar statement can also be made for the learning operator L_N. Properties 6.26 and 6.27 assumed that $H > 0$ which, in turn, implies that the null space of H is only the zero vector. If the null vector contains other vectors then the following property applies where $\mathcal{N}(H)$ and $\mathcal{R}(H)$ denote the null and range spaces of H respectively.

Property 6.30 *For all finite N*

$$L_N(H, \lambda)\bar{e} = \bar{e}, \ \forall \bar{e} \in \mathcal{N}(H) \tag{6.133}$$

This property shows that the learning algorithm does not have any effect for those signals in the null space of $H = GG^*$, i.e. $\forall \bar{e}$ such that $\bar{e} \in \mathcal{N}(G^*)$ or, equivalently, $\bar{e} \in (\mathcal{R}(G))^{\perp}$. This is to be expected since these signals are precisely those for which there exists no input $\bar{u}$ such that $\bar{e} = G\bar{u}$, i.e. they cannot be generated by the plant. It is therefore futile to try to converge to these non-existing inputs by means of any ILC algorithm. Hence it is necessary to ensure that a desired reference signal is in the range of G before starting any ILC sequence — the literature on plant inverses (see, for example, (Silverman 1969)) is of relevance in this respect.

Convergence here is only proved for $\sigma > 0$ (see Property 6.25) and if $\sigma = 0$ a norm-based proof of convergence is not possible if $\mathcal{N}(G) \neq \{0\}$ since $\|L_N\| = 1$. There are, however, cases where $\sigma = 0$ and $\mathcal{N}(H) = \{0\}$, e.g. a continuous plant. In such cases, Property 6.24 is of no use since it states that $\|L_N\| = 1$ and convergence is no longer proved by the norm estimate. The more difficult case of $\sigma = 0$ is considered next.

Suppose that G is compact which is the case for a discrete time plant or a continuous time plant acting on functions defined on a finite time interval. Then the spectral theorem (see, for example, (Kato 1976)) states that for self-adjoint positive-definite operators (satisfied by H and L_N) there exists a finite or infinite orthonormal sequence $\{\psi_j\}$ of eigenvectors of H with corresponding real eigenvalues $\{\sigma^2\}$ such that $\forall e \in \mathcal{Y}$

$$He = \sum_j \sigma_j^2 \langle e, \psi_j \rangle \psi_j \tag{6.134}$$

The sequence $\{\sigma_j^2\}$, if infinite, tends to 0 and this sequence is infinite if the output space $\mathcal{Y}$ is infinite dimensional, e.g. a continuous-time plant with $\mathcal{Y} = L_2[0, T]$. If the sequence is infinite and hence tends to zero then $\sigma = 0$ even if $\mathcal{N}(H) = 0$. Also if $\mathcal{Y}$ is separable, e.g. $L_2[0, T]$, then the sequence $\{\psi_j\}$ is complete, i.e. each error signal $e \in \mathcal{Y}$ can be decomposed by projecting it onto the eigenfunctions ψ_j:

$$e = \sum_j \langle e, \psi_j \rangle \psi_j \tag{6.135}$$

Applying the above analysis now shows that the action of the learning operator L_N on an error signal e_k is as follows:

$$e_{k+1} = L_N e_k = \sum_j l_N(\sigma_j^2, \lambda) \langle e_k, \psi_j \rangle \psi_j \tag{6.136}$$

where $l_N(\sigma_j^2, \lambda)$ is precisely the sequence generated by the recursion (6.129) for each σ_j^2.

Equation (6.136) can now be interpreted in the sense that the learning operator results in a reduction by the factor of (6.129) for that part of the signal e_k in the eigenspace associated with the eigenvalue σ_j^2. Note that the reduction by L_N is less marked for small eigenvalues σ_j^2 corresponding to high frequencies. This means that the algorithm converges most rapidly when tracking smooth signals (consisting of signals with low-frequency content) and is slower when tracking signals with high-frequency content. The following property is a formal statement of this fact.

Property 6.31 *For any $\epsilon > 0$, let the integer $\hat{m}$ be such that the approximation error satisfies $\left\| e_0 - \sum_{j=1}^{\hat{m}} \langle e_0, \psi_j \rangle \psi_j \right\| < \epsilon$. Then under these conditions the following error bound holds*

$$\|e_k\|^2 \le l_N^{2k}(\sigma_m^2, \lambda)\|e_0\|^2 + \epsilon^2 \tag{6.137}$$

This property shows that the predictive algorithm converges even in the case of $\sigma = 0$ (with σ defined in property 6.24) but the convergence is no longer geometric in nature. In particular, the geometric nature only holds in the case when $\epsilon = 0$. The above property does, however, show that the error is reduced geometrically except for an arbitrarily small remainder ϵ. Also combining this with the bounds on l_N — Properties 6.26 and 6.27 — it is clear that arbitrary fast convergence to any given (norm-based) precision $\epsilon > 0$ can be achieved with the predictive algorithm.

The above analysis formulated and solved the ILC problem in terms of the plant represented as any linear operator acting between real Hilbert spaces. For practical application, the abstract results obtained must translated for the particular case under consideration. In what follows we detail this for the case of a linear continuous time plant.

The state space model of the plant is

$$\begin{aligned} \dot{x}_k(t) &= A(t)x_k(t) + B(t)u_k(t), \ x_k(0) = x_0, \ 0 \le t \le T, \ k \ge 0 \\ y_k(t) &= Cx_k(t), \ x_k(t) \in \mathbb{R}^n, \ y_k(t) \in \mathbb{R}^m, \ u_k(t) \in \mathbb{R}^l \end{aligned} \tag{6.138}$$

where, for notational simplicity, the argument time t is omitted from A, B and C in what follows. The input and output spaces $\mathcal{U}$ and $\mathcal{Y}$ respectively are chosen to be $L_2[0, T]$ spaces equipped with the following inner products

$$\begin{aligned} \langle y_1(t), y_2(t) \rangle_{\mathcal{Y}} &= \int_{t=0}^{T} y_1^T(t) Q y_2(t)\, dt + y_1^T(T) F y_2(T) \\ \langle u_1(t), u_2(t) \rangle_{\mathcal{U}} &= \int_{t=0}^{T} u_1^T(t) R u_2(t)\, dt \end{aligned} \tag{6.139}$$

where the matrices Q, R and F are required to be symmetric and positive definite. These matrices are to be selected by the designer to reflect the importance to be placed on either of the signals in an application.

With the norms $\|.\|^2 = \langle \cdot \rangle$, the performance criterion (6.138) becomes a typical LQR cost. The weighted sum of norms can be expressed as a matrix product in a single integral as follows:

$$
J_{k+1,N} = \int_0^T \left\{ \begin{bmatrix} e_{k+1} \\ e_{k+2} \\ \vdots \\ e_{k+N} \end{bmatrix}^T \begin{bmatrix} Q & 0 & \cdots & 0 \\ 0 & \lambda Q & \cdots & 0 \\ \vdots & \vdots & \ddots & \vdots \\ 0 & 0 & \cdots & \lambda^{N-1} Q \end{bmatrix} \begin{bmatrix} e_{k+1} \\ e_{k+2} \\ \vdots \\ e_{k+N} \end{bmatrix} \right.
$$

$$
+ \begin{bmatrix} u_{k+1} - u_k \\ u_{k+2} - u_{k+1} \\ \vdots \\ u_{k+N} - u_{k+N-1} \end{bmatrix}^T \begin{bmatrix} R & 0 & \cdots & 0 \\ 0 & \lambda R & \cdots & 0 \\ \vdots & \vdots & \ddots & \vdots \\ 0 & 0 & \cdots & \lambda^{N-1} R \end{bmatrix} \begin{bmatrix} u_{k+1} - u_k \\ u_{k+2} - u_{k+1} \\ \vdots \\ u_{k+N} - u_{k+N-1} \end{bmatrix} \left. \right\} dt
$$

$$
+ \begin{bmatrix} e_{k+1}(T) \\ e_{k+2}(T) \\ \vdots \\ e_{k+N}(T) \end{bmatrix}^T \begin{bmatrix} F & 0 & \cdots & 0 \\ 0 & \lambda F & \cdots & 0 \\ \vdots & \vdots & \ddots & \vdots \\ 0 & 0 & \cdots & \lambda^{N-1} F \end{bmatrix} \begin{bmatrix} e_{k+1}(T) \\ e_{k+2}(T) \\ \vdots \\ e_{k+N}(T) \end{bmatrix} \qquad (6.140)
$$

In order to exploit a simple numerical implementation it is first necessary to transform this integral into an equivalent but more convenient form by changing the weight matrix of the input as follows. In particular, noting that $(u_{k+j} - u_k) - (u_{k+j-1} - u_k) = u_{k+j} - u_{k+j-1}$, the difference-in-input vector can be equivalently written as

$$
\begin{bmatrix} u_{k+1} - u_k \\ u_{k+2} - u_{k+1} \\ u_{k+3} - u_{k+2} \\ \vdots \\ u_{k+N} - u_{k+N-1} \end{bmatrix} = \begin{bmatrix} 1 & 0 & 0 & \cdots & 0 \\ -1 & 1 & 0 & \cdots & 0 \\ 0 & -1 & 1 & \cdots & 0 \\ \vdots & \vdots & \vdots & \ddots & \vdots \\ 0 & 0 & 0 & \cdots & 1 \end{bmatrix} \begin{bmatrix} u_{k+1} - u_k \\ u_{k+2} - u_k \\ u_{k+3} - u_k \\ \vdots \\ u_{k+N} - u_k \end{bmatrix} \qquad (6.141)
$$

The second term of the integral criterion can now be refined to the form:

$$
J_{k+1,N} = \sum_{j=1}^{N} \lambda^{j-1} \|e_{k+j}\|^2 + \int_0^T \left\{ \begin{bmatrix} u_{k+1} - u_k \\ u_{k+2} - u_k \\ \cdots \\ u_{k+N} - u_k \end{bmatrix}^T \right.
$$

$$
\times \begin{bmatrix} (1+\lambda)R & -\lambda R & \cdots & 0 \\ -\lambda R & (\lambda + \lambda^2)R & \cdots & 0 \\ \vdots & \vdots & \ddots & \vdots \\ 0 & 0 & \cdots & \lambda^{N-1} R \end{bmatrix} \begin{bmatrix} u_{k+1} - u_k \\ u_{k+2} - u_k \\ \vdots \\ u_{k+N} - u_k \end{bmatrix} \left. \right\} dt \quad (6.142)
$$

The actual implementation uses a number of parallel plants — only the first of which is the actual plant with the current input $u_{k+1}(t)$ producing the real output $y_{k+1}(t)$. The other plants are 'virtual' in the sense that they are simulations whose only purpose is to contribute to the computation of the input $u_{k+1}(t)$. The errors $e_{k+j}(t)$, $1 \le j \le N$, are given by $e_{k+j}(t) = r(t) - y_{k+j}(t)$ with $y_{k+j} = Gu_{k+j}$ from (6.138).

In vector form we have

$$
\begin{bmatrix} e_{k+1} \\ e_{k+2} \\ \vdots \\ e_{k+N} \end{bmatrix} = \begin{bmatrix} r \\ r \\ \vdots \\ r \end{bmatrix} - \begin{bmatrix} G & 0 & \cdots & 0 \\ 0 & G & \cdots & 0 \\ \vdots & \vdots & \ddots & \vdots \\ 0 & 0 & \cdots & G \end{bmatrix} \begin{bmatrix} u_{k+1} \\ u_{k+2} \\ \vdots \\ u_{k+N} \end{bmatrix} \tag{6.143}
$$

The structure of the parallel plants is now apparent from this description and using the block diagonal matrix form of the plant description in the last equation, the following extended plant matrices are defined:

$$
A_N = \text{diag}\{A, A, \cdots, A\}, \; B_N = \text{diag}\{B, B, \cdots, B\}, \; C_N = \text{diag}\{C, C, \cdots, C\} \tag{6.144}
$$

with N entries each. Also the following extended weighting matrices are defined.

$$
Q_N = \{Q, \lambda Q, \cdots, \lambda^{N-1}Q\}, \; F_N = \{F, \lambda F, \cdots, \lambda^{N-1}F\} \tag{6.145}
$$

$$
R_N = \begin{bmatrix} (1+\lambda)R & -\lambda R & 0 & \cdots & 0 \\ -\lambda R & (\lambda+\lambda^2)R & -\lambda^2 R & \cdots & 0 \\ 0 & -\lambda^2 R & (\lambda^2+\lambda^3)R & \cdots & 0 \\ \vdots & \vdots & \vdots & \ddots & \vdots \\ 0 & 0 & 0 & \cdots & \lambda^{N-1}R \end{bmatrix} \tag{6.146}
$$

Note that the special structure of R_N results from the re-definition of the input vector in the integral criterion.

At this stage, the optimization problem has been refined into a usual LQR problem. In particular, it is a combination of a tracking problem and a disturbance accommodation problem (see, for example, (Anderson & Moore 1989, Skelton 1988)) whose solution is:

$$
\begin{bmatrix} u_{k+1} \\ u_{k+2} \\ \vdots \\ u_{k+N} \end{bmatrix} = \begin{bmatrix} u_k \\ u_k \\ \vdots \\ u_k \end{bmatrix} - R_N^{-1}B_N^T \left\{ K(t)\left(\begin{bmatrix} x_{k+1} \\ x_{k+2} \\ \vdots \\ x_{k+N} \end{bmatrix} - \begin{bmatrix} x_k \\ x_k \\ \vdots \\ x_k \end{bmatrix} \right) - \zeta_{k+1,N}(t) \right\} \tag{6.147}
$$

where the state feedback gain matrix $K(t)$ is the solution of the well known Riccati differential equation on $[0, T]$:

$$
\dot{K} = -A_N^T K - KA_N + KB_N R_N^{-1}B_N^T K - C_N^T Q_N C_N, \; K(T) = C_N^T F_N C_N \tag{6.148}
$$

The predictive term $\zeta_{k+1,N}$ is generated by solving

$$
\dot{\zeta}_{k+1,N}(t) = -\left[A_N - B_N R_N^{-1}B_N^T K(t)\right]^T \zeta_{k+1,N}(t) - C_N^T Q_N \begin{bmatrix} e_k(t) \\ e_k(t) \\ \vdots \\ e_k(t) \end{bmatrix} \tag{6.149}
$$

with the final condition $\zeta_{k+1,N}(T) = C_N^T F_N [e_k^T(T), e_k^T(T), \cdots, e_k^T(T)]^T$.

This causal solution has its origins in (Amann *et al.* 1996, Amann *et al.* 1998). Note also that the Riccati matrix $K(t)$ is independent of inputs, outputs and states and needs to

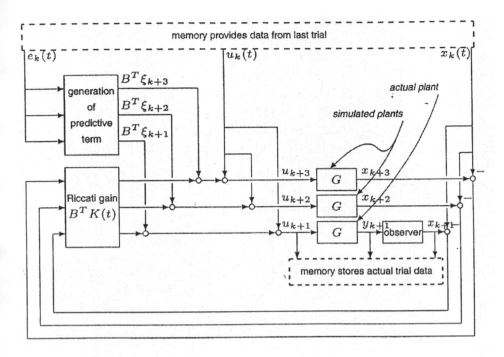

Figure 6.3: Implementation schematic.

be solved only once before the sequence of trials begins. The feedforward term $\zeta_{k+1,N}(t)$, however, must be computed off-line between trials by reverse-time simulation using the data $e_k(t)$ from the last trial. The reformulation of the input vector means that all old data required for the simulation are just the actual data from the last trial, N times repeated. Figure 6.3 shows a schematic of the predicted learning system implemented using the plant and $N-1$ plant models. The staggered structure of plants and repeated data is clearly visible but note that the solution (6.147) requires knowledge of the states. This is only a problem for the state $x_{k+1}(t)$ of the actual plant as the others are directly available from the simulated plants. If the elements of the state vector $x_{k+1}(t)$ are not directly available then it must be estimated by an observer.

To demonstrate the capabilities of the above theory, consider the following plant

$$G(s) = \frac{s-1}{(s+2)(s+3)} \tag{6.150}$$

with reference signal $r(t) = 1-(1+2t)e^{-2t}$. This is a non-minimum phase example where it is known (Amann & Owens 1994) that commonly used gradient based ILC algorithms exhibit a very slow rate of convergence for this type of plant. Indeed, other ILC algorithms may not converge at all for non-minimum phase plants (Curtelin *et al.* 1994).

Consider the following choice of parameters for the predictive ILC algorithm: $Q = 1$, $R = 0.1$, $F = 0.0512$, $\lambda = 10$, and $N = 6$. Figure 6.4 shows the simulation results on

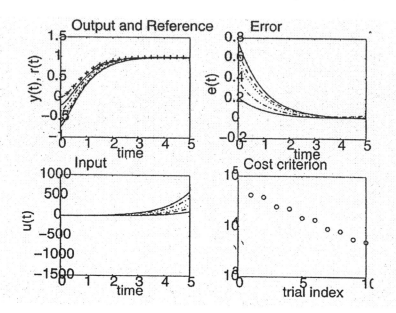

Figure 6.4: Simulation results.

applying the resulting controller. Due to the zero at $s = 1$, the limit input $u_\infty(t)$ contains a term e^t which appears in the plot of the inputs which converge to an exponentially growing input. Aside from the obvious question of whether or not it is physically reasonable to use such an input, this example shows that the algorithm converges in theory even to such an 'unstable' input. Also the algorithm exhibits rapid convergence where the L_2 norm of the error is reduced at each iteration by a factor of 1.2 during the first ten trials.

More detailed work (omitted here for brevity — see (Amann *et al.* 1998) for the details) leads to the conclusion that an exponential rate of convergence can be achieved. (Essentially, this follows from the (roughly) linear decrease in the cost function visible on a semi-logarithmic plot.) This good rate of convergence is in stark contrast to alternatives (such as (Curtelin *et al.* 1994)) which encounter severe difficulties in this respect. It is also possible (again see (Amann *et al.* 1998) for the details) to demonstrate the beneficial influence of λ and N.

It is also possible to consider the case of $N \to \infty$ where, obviously, the formal limit of the controller structure described above corresponds to an infinite-dimensional controller which is difficult to realize in practice. Note, however, that we already know how to approximate it. Also it can be shown, the details are omitted here and can be found in (Amann *et al.* 1998), that in the limit a geometric convergence of a well defined and easily controlled form can be achieved. Knowledge of this limit provides further evidence of the potential benefits of increasing N and clearly identifies the critical role of λ. The main theorem arising from this analysis is stated formally as follows.

Theorem 6.32 *Suppose that $\lambda > 1$. Then, if $N = \infty$, the ILC algorithm leads to an error sequence $\{e_k\}_{k\geq 0}$ in $\mathcal{Y}$ satisfying the norm inequalities*

$$\|e_{k+1}\| \leq \frac{1}{\lambda}\|e_k\|, \quad \|e_{k+1}\| \leq \frac{1}{\lambda^k}\|e_0\| \tag{6.151}$$

If N is finite and G is compact with $\mathcal{N}(G) = \{0\}$, then, for any choice of integer $k^* \geq 1$ and real $\epsilon \in (0, \lambda - 1)$, there is a prediction horizon $N^* \geq 1$ such that

$$\|e_{k+1}\| \leq \frac{1}{\lambda - \epsilon}\|e_k\|, \; 0 \leq k \leq k^* \tag{6.152}$$

for all prediction horizons $N \geq N^*$.

This last result is proved by, in effect, application of the strong limit of a sequence $\{L_N\}$ of operators and of Property 6.31. It states that the use of a finite prediction horizon can, if the horizon is 'sufficiently large', provide an arbitrarily close approximation to the 'ideal' limit performance when $N = \infty$ and this performance can be guaranteed for an arbitrary number of trials. Examples suggest that the prediction horizon need not be excessively large for the predicted performance to be usefully achieved.

6.7 CONCLUSIONS AND FURTHER WORK

This chapter has undertaken a review of two decades on research on the analysis and control of (linear) repetitive processes. The major developments can be summarized as follows.

- A rigorous stability theory has been developed based on an abstract model of the process dynamics in a Banach space setting which includes all linear dynamics constant pass length examples as special cases. This theory is therefore general in nature and removes deficiencies in earlier approaches. Necessary and sufficient conditions for the two distinct stability properties — asymptotic stability and stability along the pass respectively — are expressed in terms of properties of the bounded linear operator in the abstract model which describes the contribution of the dynamics of the previous pass to those of the current one.

- The results of applying the stability theory to a range of sub-classes are known. In particular, when applied to the sub-classes of so-called differential and discrete linear repetitive processes the resulting conditions which can be tested by direct application of 1D linear systems tests. Also each of these conditions has a well defined physical interpretation. The critical importance of the structure of the state initial conditions on each pass to stability has been rigorously established. In particular, these conditions alone can cause instability.

- Possible computational difficulties in implementing one of these stability tests has led to the development of alternatives which only involve computations on matrices with constant entries. The route here is via a so-called 1D Lyapunov equation characterization of stability which also yields computable information on a key aspect of expected system performance — the rate of approach of the sequence of pass profiles of a stable example to the resulting limit profile.

- A so-called 2D Lyapunov equation characterization of stability in the discrete case has also been obtained but, in general, this is sufficient but not necessary. This drawback is (potentially) offset by the fact that the 2D Lyapunov equation is one possible basis for the development of a robust stability/control theory. Some highly promising initial results using this starting point have been obtained but much further work remains to be done before the true potential of this 2D Lyapunov equation can be realistically assessed.

- A so-called simulation based approach to stability analysis for both the differential and discrete cases has been developed. Again the resulting conditions are sufficient but not necessary but if they hold then computable information is available for no extra computational cost concerning (i) the rate of approach of the output sequence to the limit profile, and (ii) the error on any pass between the pass profile and the limit profile. How to fully exploit such information in controller design for these processes is still very much an open area (see below).

- The links between discrete linear repetitive processes and 2D linear systems described by the well known Roesser and Fornasini Marchesini state space models has been the subject of much profitable research in recent years. This has led, in particular, to the development of a transition matrix, or fundamental matrix sequence, and hence to a general response formula for computing the process response to given control inputs and initial conditions. From this has followed the definition and characterization in the form of matrix rank based conditions of so-called local (or point) reachability and controllability which are, in general, distinct concepts. So-called pass controllability has also been defined and characterized in the form of matrix rank tests defined in terms of an equivalent 1D state space model interpretation of the underlying process dynamics. Unlike previously proposed 1D models for 2D systems, the 1D model for discrete linear repetitive processes is defined by matrices and vectors of constant dimensions. This makes this model potentially very powerful in terms of controller design for these processes and is an obvious area for productive research — some highly promising initial results in this area can be found in (Benton 2000) and the relevant cited references.

- Although not covered in this chapter, some work has been done of the generalization of Rosenbrock systems matrix theory for these processes (Johnson *et al.* 1996). Similarly, there is much scope for the use of behavioural theory here — for recent progress on behavioural based systems theory for nD linear systems in general see, for example, (Wood *et al.* 2000) and the relevant cited references. One objective here would be to 'translate' the recently characterized concept of a pole for nD linear systems to the repetitive process case where a 'physically based' interpretation should be possible.

- The general area of the formulation and solution of physically meaningful control problems for these processes is one where much profitable research remains to be done to build on the somewhat 'piecemeal' results currently available. One starting point clearly is the predictive optimal control algorithm developed for the ILC application.

6.8   ACKNOWLEDGMENTS

Our research in this area has benefited greatly from input by research students and colleagues and from collaboration with, in particular, Krzysztof Gałkowski, Artur Gramacki and Jarsolaw Gramacki, Technical University of Zielona Gora, Poland.

REFERENCES

N. Amann and D. H. Owens, 1994, Non-minimum phase plants and iterative learning control. *Proceedings of The 2nd International Conference on Intelligent Systems Engineering*, pages 107–112.

N. Amann, D. H. Owens, and E. Rogers, 1996, Iterative learning control using optimal feedback and feedforward actions. *International Journal of Control*, 65(2):277–293.

N. Amann, D. H. Owens, and E. Rogers, 1998, Predictive optimal iterative learning control. *International Journal of Control*, 69(2):203–226.

B. D. O. Anderson and J. B. Moore, 1989, *Optimal Control – Linear Optimal Control*. Prentice-Hall, Englewood Cliffs, New Jersey, USA

J. L. Aravena, M. Shafiee, and W. A. Porter, 1990, State models and stability for 2-D filters. *IEEE Transactions on Circuits and Systems*, CAS-37:1509–1519.

S. Arimoto, S. Kawamura, and F. Miyazaki, 1984, Bettering operations of robots by learning. *Journal of Robotic Systems*, 1:123–140.

V. Becerra, 1994, *Development and Applications of Novel Optimal Control Algorithms*. City University, London UK.

V. Becerra and P. D. Roberts, 1996, Dynamic integrated system optimization and parameter estimation for discrete time optimal control of nonlinear systems. *International Journal of Control*, 63(2):257–281.

S. E. Benton, 2000, *Analysis and Controller Design for Linear Repetitive Processes, PhD Thesis*. University of Southampton, Southampton UK.

S. E. Benton, E. Rogers, and D. H. Owens, 1998, 1D controllers for a class of 2D systems. *IFAC Conference on System Structure and Control*, 2:321–326.

S. E. Benton, E. Rogers, and D. H. Owens, 1999, Lyapunov stability theory for linear repetitive processes – the 2D equation approach. 1999 *European Control Conference*, CD Rom Proceedings.

D. W. Clarke and C. Mohtadi, 1989, Properties of generalized predictive control. *Automatica*, 25:859–875.

G. Curtelin, B. Caron, and H. Saari, 1994, A specific repetitive control algorithm for continuous and digital systems: study and applications. *Proceedings of IEE International Conference Control 94*, pages 634–639.

J. B. Edwards, 1974, Stability problems in the control of multipass processes. *Proceedings of The Institution of Electrical Engineers*, 121 (11):1425–1431.

E. Fornasini and G. Marchesini, 1978, Doubly-indexed dynamical systems: State space models and structural properties. *Mathematical Systems Theory*, 12:59–72.

K. Gałkowski, E. Rogers, and D. H. Owens, 1998, Matrix rank based conditions for reachability/controllability of discrete linear repetitive processes. *Linear Algebra and its Applications*, 275–276:201–224.

C. E. Garcia, D. M. Prett, and M. Morari, 1989, Model predictive control — a survey. *Automatica*, 25:335–348.

D. S. Johnson, A. C. Pugh, E. Rogers, G. E. Hayton, and D. H. Owens, 1996, A polynomial matrix theory for a certain class of two-dimensional linear systems. *Linear Algebra and its Applications*, 241–243:669–703.

T. Kaczorek, 1992, *Linear Control Systems II*. Research Studies Press, Taunton UK.

T. Kaczorek, 1994, When does the local controllability of the general model of 2D linear systems imply its local reachability? *Systems and Control Letters*, 23:445–452.

T. Kato, 1976, *Perturbation Theory for Linear Operators, second edition*. Springer Verlag, Berlin.

K. L. Moore, 1993, *Iterative Learning Control for Deterministic Systems*. Springer Verlag Advances in Industrial Control Series, London.

D. H. Owens, 1977, Stability of linear multipass processes. *Proceedings of The Institution of Electrical Engineers*, 124 (11):1079–1082.

D. H. Owens, 1978, *Feedback and Multivariable Systems*. Peter Peregrinus.

D. H. Owens and E. Rogers, 1995, Frequency domain Lyapunov equations and performance bounds for differential linear repetitive processes. *Systems and Control Letters*, 26:65–68.

D. H. Owens and E. Rogers, 1999, Stability analysis of a class of 2D continuous-discrete linear systems with dynamic boundary conditions. *Systems and Control Letters*, 37:55–60.

D. H. Owens and E. Rogers, 1999, Stability of differential linear repetitive processes with drifting boundary conditions. *University of Southampton, Department of Electronics and Computer Science, Research Report*, pages 1–19.

P. D. Roberts, 1993, An algorithm for optimal control of nonlinear systems with model reality differences. *Proceedings of 12th IFAC World Congress*, 8:407–412.

P. D. Roberts, 1994, Unit memory repetitive processes and iterative optimal control problems. *IEE International Conference CONTROL 94*, pages 454–459.

P. D. Roberts, 1996, Computing the stability of iterative optimal control algorithms through the use of two-dimensional systems theory. *Proceedings of UKACC International Conference Control 96*, 2:981–986.

P. D. Roberts, 1998, A MATLAB graphical interface for investigating the local stability of iterative optimal control algorithms. *Proceedings of UKACC International Conference CONTROL 98*, pages 1629–1634.

R. P. Roesser, 1975, A discrete state space model for linear image processing. *IEEE Transactions Auto Control*, AC-20:1–10.

E. Rogers, J. Gramacki, K. Galkowski, and D. H. Owens, 1998, Stability theory for a class of 2D linear systems with dynamic boundary conditions. *Proceedings 37th IEEE International Conference on Decision and Control*, pages 2800–2805.

E. Rogers and D. H. Owens, 1992, New stability tests and performance bounds for differential linear repetitive processes. *International Journal of Control*, 56(4):831–856.

E. Rogers and D. H. Owens, 1992, Simulation based stability tests and performance bounds for differential non-unit memory linear repetitive processes. *International Journal of Control*, 56(2):581–606.

E. Rogers and D. H. Owens, 1992, *Stability Analysis for Linear Repetitive Processes*. Springer Verlag, Lecture Notes in Control and Information Sciences Series Vol 175, Berlin.

E. Rogers and D. H. Owens, 1993, Stability tests and performance bounds for a class of 2D linear systems. *Multidimensional Systems and Signal Processing*, 4(4):355–391.

E. Rogers and D. H. Owens, 1994, Output feedback control theory for discrete linear repetitive processes. *IMA Journal of Mathematical Control and Information*, 10:177–193.

E. Rogers and D. H. Owens, 1995, Error actuated feedback control theory for differential linear repetitive processes. *International Journal of Control*, 61(5):981–998.

E. Rogers and D. H. Owens, 1996, Lyapunov stability theory and performance bounds for a class of 2D linear systems. *Multidimensional Systems and Signal Processing*, 7(2):179–194.

L. M. Silverman, 1969, Inversion of multivariable linear systems. *IEEE Transactions on Automatic Control*, pages 270–276.

R. E. Skelton, 1988, *Dynamic Systems Control*. Wiley, New York.

K. J. Smyth, 1992, *Computer Aided Analysis for Linear Repetitive Processes, PhD Thesis*. University of Strathclyde, Glasgow UK.

K. J. Smyth, C. Cao, E. Rogers, and D. H. Owens, 1994, Signal processing based performance measures for differential linear repetitive processes. *International Journal of Adaptive Control and Signal Processing*, 8(4):553–572.

J. Wood, O. Oberst, E. Rogers, and D. H. Owens, 2000, A behavioural approach to the pole structure of 1D and nD linear systems. *SIAM Journal of Control and Optimization*, 32(8):627–661.

CHAPTER SEVEN

Analysis and Control of Discrete Linear Repetitive Processes with Dynamic Boundary Conditions

Krzysztof Gałkowski[†], Eric Rogers[‡], Artur Gramacki[*],
Jaroslaw Gramacki[*] and David H. Owens[#]

† Department of Robotics and Software Engineering,
Technical University of Zielona Gora, Poland
galko@akson.irio.pz.zgora.pl

‡ Department of Electronics and Computer Science,
University of Southampton, UK
etar@ecs.soton.ac.uk

* Department of Electronics and Computer Science,
Technical University of Zielona Gora, Poland
{A.Gramacki,J.Gramacki}@iie.pz.zgora.pl

Department of Automatic Control and Systems Engineering,
University of Sheffield, UK
D.H.Owens@sheffield.ac.uk

Abstract

Repetitive processes are a distinct class of 2D systems of both practical and algorithmic interest. Their essential characteristic is repeated sweeps, or passes, through a set of dynamics defined over a finite duration with explicit interaction between the outputs, or pass profiles, produced as the process evolves. Experience has shown that these processes cannot be studied/controlled by direct application of existing theory (in all but a few very restrictive special cases). This fact, and the growing list of application areas, has prompted an on-going research programme into the development of a 'mature' systems theory for these processes for onward translation into reliable generally applicable controller design algorithms. This contribution gives some important new results on the analysis and control of the sub-class known as discrete linear repetitive processes in the presence of a general set of pass initial conditions, which are termed boundary conditions here.

7.1 INTRODUCTION

The essential unique characteristic of a repetitive process (termed multipass process in the early literature) can be illustrated by considering machining operations where the material or workpiece involved is processed by a sequence of passes of the processing tool. Assuming that the pass length α (i.e. the duration of a pass of the processing tool) is finite and constant, the output vector, or pass profile, $y_k(p)$, $0 \leq p \leq \alpha$, (p being the independent spatial or temporal variable) produced on the kth pass acts as a forcing function on the next pass and hence contributes to the dynamics of the new pass profile $y_{k+1}(p)$, $0 \leq p \leq \alpha$, $k \geq 0$. A more general case arises when it is the previous $M > 1$ pass profiles which contribute to the current one. The integer M is termed the memory length and such processes are simply termed non-unit memory and unit memory in the case when $M = 1$. Here we only consider the unit memory case since all results obtained generalize in a natural manner to the case when $M > 1$.

Industrial examples of these processes include long-wall coal cutting and metal rolling operations — see (Edwards 1974) and (Smyth 1992) for a detailed treatment. Also cases exist where adopting a repetitive process setting has major advantages over alternatives — so-called algorithmic examples. This is especially true for classes of iterative learning control schemes (Amann *et al.* 1996, Amann *et al.* 1998) and of nonlinear dynamic optimal control problems based on the maximum principle (Roberts 1996).

Repetitive processes clearly have a two-dimensional (or 2D) structure, i.e. information propagation from pass to pass (k direction) and along a pass (p direction). Such systems and the natural generalization to information propagation in more than two separate directions, collectively known as multidimensional or, simply, nD systems, have been the subject of a large volume of research over the last three decades. In the 2D case, much effort has been focused on linear systems which can be described by the well known Roesser (Roesser 1975) and Fornasini Marchesini (Fornasini & Marchesini 1978) state space models. The sub-class of so-called discrete linear repetitive processes considered in this contribution are distinct from such 2D linear systems in the sense that information propagation in one of the two separate directions (along the pass) only occurs over a finite duration.

The basic unique control problem for repetitive processes is that the output sequence of pass profiles can contain oscillations that increase in amplitude in the pass to pass direction (i.e. in the k - direction in the notation for variables used here). Such behavior is easily generated in simulation studies and in experiments on scaled models of industrial examples such as long-wall coal cutting (see (Edwards 1974) and (Smyth 1992) for a detailed treatment).

Early approaches to stability analysis and controller design for (linear) repetitive processes, and, in particular, long-wall coal cutting, was based on first converting the system into an infinite-length single-pass process (Edwards 1974). This resulted, for example, in a scalar differential/algebraic delay system to which standard scalar inverse-Nyquist stability criteria were then applied. In general, however, it was soon established that this approach to stability analysis and hence controller design would, except in a few very restrictive special cases, lead to incorrect conclusions (Owens 1977). The basic reason for this is that such an approach effectively neglects their finite pass length repeatable nature and the effects of resetting the initial conditions before the start of each pass.

To remove these deficiencies, a rigorous stability theory has been developed (Owens 1977, Rogers & Owens 1992). This theory is based on an abstract model of the dynamics in a Banach space setting which includes all processes with linear dynamics and a constant pass length as special cases. In effect, this theory consists of the distinct concepts of asymptotic stability and stability along the pass, and necessary and sufficient conditions for these properties are available. These are expressed in terms of conditions on the bounded linear operator in the abstract model which describes the contribution of the previous pass dynamics to the current one.

The results of applying this abstract model based stability theory to a range of sub-classes are known (see, for example, (Rogers & Owens 1992, Rogers & Owens 1995)). These include discrete linear repetitive processes which are the subject of this contribution and, for example, occur in the iterative learning control application. Previous work (Rogers *et al.* 1998, Owens & Rogers 1999) has shown that the structure of the pass initial conditions alone can destroy even the weakest form of stability for these processes. This contribution builds on this work by developing stability tests which can be implemented by direct application of well known 1D linear systems tests. Some basic results on the use of appropriate control action to remove, or reject, the effects of a general form of pass state initial conditions on the dynamics of discrete linear repetitive processes are also given.

7.2 BACKGROUND

The state space model of a sub-class of discrete linear repetitive processes has the form over $0 \leq p \leq \alpha$, $k \geq 0$

$$
\begin{aligned}
x_{k+1}(p+1) &= Ax_{k+1}(p) + Bu_{k+1}(p) + B_0 y_k(p) \\
y_{k+1}(p) &= Cx_{k+1}(p) + Du_{k+1}(p) + D_0 y_k(p)
\end{aligned}
\tag{7.1}
$$

Here on pass k, $x_k(p)$ is the $n \times 1$ state vector, $y_k(p)$ is the $m \times 1$ vector pass profile, and $u_k(p)$ is the $r \times 1$ vector of control inputs.

To complete the process description, it is necessary to specify the 'initial conditions' — termed the boundary conditions here, i.e. the state initial vector on each pass and the initial pass profile. The simplest possible form for these is

$$
\begin{aligned}
x_{k+1}(0) &= d_{k+1}, \ k = 0, 1, \dots \\
y_0(p) &= y(p), \ 0 \leq p \leq \alpha
\end{aligned}
\tag{7.2}
$$

where d_{k+1} is an $n \times 1$ vector with constant entries and $y(p)$ is an $m \times 1$ vector whose entries are known functions of p.

In some cases, the boundary conditions of (7.2) are simply not strong enough to 'adequately' model the underlying dynamics — even for preliminary simulation/control analysis. For example, the optimal control application (Roberts 1996) requires the use of pass state initial vectors which are functions of the previous pass profile. Next we introduce a general set of boundary conditions for discrete linear repetitive processes and then (in the next section) obtain a complete characterization of stability under these conditions.

Clearly it is of prime importance to start with a general form of boundary conditions with subsequent specialization to particular cases as required. Other work (Owens & Rogers 1999) has concluded that the most general set results from replacing $x_{k+1}(0)$, $k \geq 0$, in (7.2) by

$$
x_{k+1}(0) = d_{k+1} + \sum_{j=1}^{N} K_j \, y_k(p_j), \quad k = 0, 1, \dots
\tag{7.3}
$$

where $0 \leq p_1 < p_2 < \cdots < p_N \leq \alpha$ are N sample points along the previous pass profile, and $K_j, 1 \leq j \leq N$, are $n \times m$ matrices with constant entries.

The stability theory for linear constant pass length repetitive processes is based on the following abstract model of the underlying dynamics, where E_α is a suitably chosen Banach space with norm $||.||$ and W_α is a linear subspace of E_α,

$$y_{k+1} = L_\alpha y_k + b_{k+1}, \; k \geq 0 \tag{7.4}$$

In this model $y_k \in E_\alpha$ is the pass profile on pass k, $b_{k+1} \in W_\alpha$, and L_α is a bounded linear operator mapping E_α into itself. The term $L_\alpha y_k$ represents the contribution from pass k to pass $k + 1$ and b_{k+1} represents known initial conditions, disturbances and control input effects. We denote this model by S.

In the case of (7.1) and (7.3), we choose $E_\alpha = \ell_2^m[0, \alpha]$, i.e. the space of sequences of real $m \times 1$ vectors of length α (corresponding to $p = 1, 2, \cdots, \alpha$ in (7.1)). Then it is routine to show that (7.1) and (7.3) can be regarded as a special case of (7.4) with

$$(L_\alpha y)(p) = CA^p \hat{Y} + D_0 y_k(p) + \sum_{r=0}^{p-1} CA^{p-1-r} B_0 y(r), \; 1 \leq p \leq \alpha \tag{7.5}$$

with

$$\hat{Y} = \sum_{j=1}^{N} K_j y(p_j) \tag{7.6}$$

and

$$b_{k+1} = CA^p d_{k+1} + D u_{k+1}(p) + \sum_{r=0}^{p-1} CA^{p-1-r} B u_{k+1}(r), \; 1 \leq p \leq \alpha, \; k \geq 0 \tag{7.7}$$

7.3 STABILITY OF DISCRETE LINEAR REPETITIVE PROCESSES

The process of (7.4) is said to be asymptotically stable (Rogers & Owens 1992) provided $\exists$ a real scalar $\delta > 0$ such that, given any initial profile y_0 and any disturbance sequence $\{b_k\}_{k \geq 1} \subset W_\alpha$ bounded in norm (i.e. $||b_k|| \leq c_1$ for some constant $c_1 \geq 0$ and $\forall \, k \geq 1$), the output sequence generated by the perturbed process

$$y_{k+1} = (L_\alpha + \gamma) y_k + b_{k+1}, \; k \geq 0 \tag{7.8}$$

is bounded in norm whenever $||\gamma|| \leq \delta$. This definition is easily shown to be equivalent to the requirement that $\exists$ finite real numbers $M_\alpha > 0$ and $\lambda_\alpha \in (0, 1)$ such that

$$||L_\alpha^k|| \leq M_\alpha \lambda_\alpha^k, \; k \geq 0 \tag{7.9}$$

where $||.||$ is also used to denote the induced operator norm. A necessary and sufficient condition for (7.9) (for a proof see (Rogers & Owens 1992)) is that the spectral radius, $r(L_\alpha)$, of L_α satisfies

$$r(L_\alpha) < 1 \tag{7.10}$$

It is easy to see that asymptotic stability of (7.1) and (7.2), i.e. $r(D_0) < 1$, is a necessary condition for asymptotic stability of (7.1) and (7.3). Hence, for simplicity, we set $D_0 = 0$ for the remainder of this section and also $D = 0$.

Introduce

$$M(z) = \sum_{j=1}^{N} K_j C \hat{A}^{p_j} \tag{7.11}$$

where

$$\hat{A}(z) = A + z^{-1} B_0 C, \ z \neq 0 \tag{7.12}$$

Then the following result proved in (Gałkowski *et al.* 1999) characterizes asymptotic stability of processes described by (7.1) and (7.3).

Theorem 7.1 *Suppose that $\{A, B_0\}$ is controllable. Then S generated by (7.1) and (7.3) (with $D = 0$, $D_0 = 0$) is asymptotically stable if, and only if, all solutions of*

$$\left| z I_n - \sum_{j=1}^{N} K_j C (A + z^{-1} B_0 C)^{p_j} \right| = 0 \tag{7.13}$$

have modulus strictly less than unity.

Further simplification (reduction in dimension) is possible in some special cases, e.g. the following:

Corollary 7.2 *Consider discrete linear repetitive processes described by (7.1) and (7.3) in the special case when $K_j = K T_j$, $1 \leq j \leq N$, where K is an $n \times m$ matrix with constant entries and T_j, $1 \leq j \leq M$, are $m \times m$ matrices with constant entries. Then S generated in this case (with $D = 0$, $D_0 = 0$) is asymptotically stable if, and only if, all solutions of*

$$\left| z I_m - \sum_{j=1}^{N} T_j C (A + z^{-1} B_0 C)^{p_j} K \right| = 0 \tag{7.14}$$

have modulus strictly less than unity.

Return now to the case when the state initial conditions are of the simple form (7.2). Then we have the 'counter-intuitive' result that asymptotic stability is essentially independent of the process dynamics and, in particular, of the eigenvalues of the matrix A. This situation is due entirely to the fact that the pass length α is finite and fixed by definition and will change drastically if (as below) we let $\alpha \to +\infty$.

In the general case, this result shows that the property of asymptotic stability for discrete linear repetitive processes is completely dependent on the structure of the sequence of pass initial state vectors. In particular, suppose that the initial state vector for an example is incorrectly modeled as (7.2) instead of a special case of (7.3). Then the process could well be interpreted as asymptotically stable when in fact it is asymptotically unstable!

The result of theorem 7.1 provides a necessary and sufficient condition for asymptotic stability but not any really 'useful' information about transient behavior and, in particular, about the behavior of the output sequence of pass profiles as the process evolves from pass to pass (i.e. in the k direction). The limit profile provides a characterization of process behavior after 'a large number of passes' have elapsed.

Suppose that the abstract model (7.4) is asymptotically stable and let $\{b_k\}_{k \geq 1}$ be a disturbance sequence that converges strongly to a disturbance b_∞. Then the strong limit

$$y_\infty := \lim_{k \to +\infty} y_k \tag{7.15}$$

is termed the limit profile corresponding to this disturbance sequence. Also it can be shown (Rogers & Owens 1992) that y_∞ is the unique solution of the linear equation

$$y_\infty = L_\alpha y_\infty + b_\infty \qquad (7.16)$$

Note also that (7.16) can be formally obtained from (7.4) by replacing all variables by their strong limits. In the case of processes described by (7.1) and (7.3), the following corollary of theorem 7.1 defines the limit profile.

Corollary 7.3 *The limit profile for discrete linear repetitive processes defined by (7.1) and (7.3) (with $D = 0$, $D_0 = 0$) is described by the state space model*

$$\begin{aligned}
x_\infty(p+1) &= (A + B_0 C)x_\infty(p) + Bu_\infty(p) \\
y_\infty(p) &= Cx_\infty(p)
\end{aligned} \qquad (7.17)$$

with state initial vector $x_\infty(0)$ given by

$$x_\infty(0) = (I_n - M(1))^{-1} d_\infty \qquad (7.18)$$

where d_∞ is the strong limit of $\{d_k\}_{k \geq 1}$ and the matrix $(I_n - M(1))$ is invertible by asymptotic stability.

Asymptotic stability guarantees the existence of a limit profile which is described by a 1D linear systems state space model. Hence, in effect, if the process under consideration is asymptotically stable, then its repetitive dynamics can, after a 'sufficiently large' number of passes, be replaced by those of a 1D linear time invariant system described by a strictly proper state space model. This result has obvious implications in terms of the design of control schemes for these processes.

Owing to the finite pass length (over which duration even an unstable 1D system can only produce a bounded output), asymptotic stability cannot guarantee that the resulting limit profile has 'acceptable' characteristics and, in particular, that it is stable in the 1D sense. A simple example to illustrate this fact is the following process over $0 \leq p \leq \alpha$, $k \geq 0$

$$\begin{aligned}
x_{k+1}(p+1) &= -0.5x_{k+1}(p) + u_{k+1}(p) \\
&\quad + (0.5 + \beta)y_k(p), \ x_{k+1}(0) = 0 \\
y_{k+1}(p) &= x_{k+1}(p)
\end{aligned} \qquad (7.19)$$

where β is a real scalar. This process is asymptotically stable but the resulting limit profile

$$y_\infty(p+1) = \beta y_\infty(p) + u_\infty(p), \ 0 \leq p \leq \alpha \qquad (7.20)$$

is unstable in the 1D sense if $|\beta| \geq 1$.

Despite this weakness, applications do exist where asymptotic stability is all that is required or can be achieved. For example, in the application of Roberts (1996) (which uses a version of the state initial conditions of (7.3)) the matrix corresponding to A in (7.1) never has all its eigenvalues inside the unit circle in the complex plane. This, as shown below, is a necessary condition for stability along the pass which, in general, is what will be required.

The natural definition of stability along the pass for the above example is to demand that (7.20) defining the limit profile is stable in the sense that $|\beta| < 1$ if we let $\alpha \rightarrow$

$+\infty$. This intuitively appealing idea is, however, not applicable to cases where the limit profile resulting from asymptotic stability is not described by a 1D linear systems state space model. Consequently stability along the pass for the general model of (7.4) has been defined in terms of the rate of approach to the limit profile as the pass length α becomes infinitely large. One of several equivalent formulations of this property is that (7.4) is said to be stable along the pass provided $\exists$ finite real numbers $M_\infty > 0$ and $\lambda_\infty \in (0, 1)$ which are independent of the pass length and satisfy

$$\|L_{\alpha_0}^k\| \leq M_\infty \lambda_\infty^k, \ \forall \, k \geq 0, \ \forall \, \alpha_0 > 0 \tag{7.21}$$

Necessary and sufficient conditions for this to hold are (Rogers & Owens 1992)

$$r_\infty := \sup_{\alpha_0 > 0} r(L_{\alpha_0}) < 1 \tag{7.22}$$

and

$$M_0 := \sup_{\alpha_0 > 0} \sup_{|z| \geq \lambda} \|(zI - L_{\alpha_0})^{-1}\| < \infty \tag{7.23}$$

for some real number $\lambda \in (r_\infty, 1)$.

Note 7.4 *Here we assume that the sample points p_j, $1 \leq j \leq N$, in (7.3) are fixed at the outset along the pass length α and, in particular, do not vary when we are developing stability along the pass criteria by letting $\alpha \to +\infty$. To avoid a source of confusion, α in (7.21)-(7.23) above and where necessary in what follows, has been replaced by α_0.*

Asymptotic stability of (7.4) can be interpreted (see (Rogers & Owens 1992) for a rigorous treatment of this aspect) as bounded-input/bounded-output stability over the finite and fixed pass length α_0 in the sense that disturbance sequences bounded in norm produce bounded in norm sequences of pass profiles. Stability along the pass is stronger in the sense that it demands that boundedness is uniform in α_0. The condition of (7.22) for stability along the pass demands asymptotic stability $\forall \, \alpha_0 > 0$ and is clearly implied by the condition of (7.23). Aside from its physical interpretation, the other main reason for retaining the separate identity of asymptotic stability is that, in a number of the cases considered, it has proved much easier (in relative terms) to interpret than stability along the pass.

If, as assumed here, the sample points in (7.3) are fixed at the outset, (7.22) is equivalent to the condition of theorem 7.1. The condition of (7.23) then reduces to the requirement that the output solution y of $(zI - L_\alpha)y = f$ is bounded (in an ℓ_2^m sense) if $f \in \ell_2^m$.

Suppose now that the pair $\{A, B_0\}$ is controllable and the pair $\{C, A\}$ is observable. Then it follows that this last condition reduces to the requirement that

$$r(\hat{A}(z)) \leq 1 - \epsilon, \ \forall \, |z| \geq \lambda \tag{7.24}$$

and for some $\epsilon > 0$ and $\lambda \in (r_\infty, 1)$. Now introduce

$$\rho(\gamma, z) := |\gamma I_n - A - z^{-1} B_0 C| \tag{7.25}$$

and it is easily seen (consider the case when $|z| = \infty$) that a necessary condition for stability along the pass is that $r(A) < 1$. (Physically this can be interpreted as the requirement that the first pass profile is bounded independent of the pass length.) Also

$$\rho(\gamma, z) = \frac{|\gamma I_n - A||zI_m - G(\gamma)|}{z^m} \tag{7.26}$$

where

$$G(\gamma) = C(\gamma I_n - A)^{-1} B_0 \tag{7.27}$$

and a further necessary condition for stability along the pass is

$$|zI_m - G(\gamma)| \neq 0, \ |z| = \lambda, \ |\gamma| \geq 1 \tag{7.28}$$

which, noting that $\lim_{|\gamma| \to +\infty} G(\gamma) = 0$ and considering the case of $|\gamma| = 1$, implies that all eigenvalues of $G(\gamma)$ with $|\gamma| = 1$ lie in the interior of the unit circle in the complex plane.

Suppose now that theorem 7.1 holds, $r(A) < 1$ and all eigenvalues of $G(\gamma)$ with $|\gamma| = 1$ lie in the open unit circle in the complex plane. Then it is possible to choose $\lambda \in (r_\infty, 1)$ such that both sides of (7.26) are non-zero for $|z| = \lambda$ and $|\gamma| = 1$ and such that all eigenvalues of A have modulus less than λ. Suppose also that the unit circle contour $\{\gamma : |\gamma| = 1\}$ is traversed in a clockwise manner. In which case standard encirclement theorems applied to (7.26) shows that all roots of the characteristic polynomial (7.25) lie in the interior of the circle $|\gamma| < 1, \forall |z| = \lambda$. Hence we have proved the following theorem.

Theorem 7.5 *Suppose that the pair $\{A, B_0\}$ is controllable and that the pair $\{C, A\}$ is observable. Then S generated by (7.1) and (7.3) (with $D_0 = 0$) is stable along the pass if, and only if,*

   1. *theorem 7.1 holds,*

   2. $r(A) < 1$, *and*

   3. *all eigenvalues of the transfer function matrix $G(\gamma)$ have modulus strictly less than unity $\forall |\gamma| = 1$.*

Note 7.6 *The stability conditions for the Roesser 2D linear systems interpretation of the dynamics of discrete linear repetitive processes only gives the correct answer if the initial state vector on each pass has the simple structure of (7.2).*

It is easy to see that stability along the pass does ensure that the limit profile is stable as a standard 1D linear time invariant system. Also in terms of stability tests it is clear that the only real problem arises with the condition for asymptotic stability. This is investigated next through the use of an equivalent 1D linear systems model interpretation of the dynamics of (7.1) and (7.3). In this analysis, we use the following (most general) form of (7.3)

$$x_{k+1}(0) = d_{k+1}(0) + \sum_{j=0}^{\alpha-1} K_j \, y_k(j), \ k = 0, 1, \dots \tag{7.29}$$

which is precisely the pass state initial vector sequence required in, for example, the optimal control application (Roberts 1996).

7.4   1D MODEL AND ANALYSIS

Consider a discrete linear repetitive process described by (7.1) with initial conditions of the form (7.2) or (7.29). Then the basic steps in derivation of 1D equivalent model of the dynamics of this process are given below — for a detailed treatment see (Gałkowski *et al.* 1998).

Step 1

The basic state space model (7.1) is first transformed to the standard 2D linear systems Roesser state space model by applying a simple 'forward transformation' of the pass profile vector followed by a change of variable in the pass number. In particular, set

$$y_{k-1}(p) := v_k(p), \ k \geq 0, 0 \leq p \leq \alpha. \tag{7.30}$$

and

$$l := k + 1 \tag{7.31}$$

respectively. Then on introducing these substitutions into (7.1) the dynamics of a discrete linear repetitive process can be equivalently described by the standard (also termed regular or nonsingular) Roesser state space model

$$
\begin{aligned}
x_l(p+1) &= A\,x_l(p) + B\,u_l(p) + B_0\,v_l(p) \\
v_{l+1}(p) &= C\,x_l(p) + D\,u_l(p) + D_0\,v_l(p).
\end{aligned}
\tag{7.32}
$$

where $l = 1, 2, \ldots, \ p = 0, 1, \ldots, \alpha - 1$ (and it is now more convenient to consider the interval $[0, \alpha - 1]$ rather (see (7.5)-(7.7)) than $[1, \alpha]$ in defining the pass to pass coupling dynamics).

Step 2

To calculate the process response using this equivalent description it is necessary to 'transform' and apply the correct set of boundary conditions. In the case of (7.2) these become

$$
\begin{aligned}
x_l(0) &= d_l(0), \ l = 1, 2, \ldots \\
v_1(p) &= f(p), \ p = 0, 1, \ldots, \alpha - 1.
\end{aligned}
\tag{7.33}
$$

Step 3

Now define the so-called global pass profile, state and input super-vectors for (7.1) as

$$
\mathbf{Y}(l) := \begin{bmatrix} v_l(0) \\ v_l(1) \\ \vdots \\ v_l(\alpha - 1) \end{bmatrix}, \ \mathbf{X}(l) := \begin{bmatrix} x_l(1) \\ \vdots \\ x_l(\alpha) \end{bmatrix}, \ \mathbf{U}(l) := \begin{bmatrix} u_l(0) \\ u_l(1) \\ \vdots \\ u_l(\alpha - 1) \end{bmatrix}
\tag{7.34}
$$

Then dynamics of discrete linear repetitive processes described by (7.1) and (7.2) are equivalently described by the 1D linear systems state space model

$$
\begin{aligned}
\mathbf{Y}(l+1) &= \tilde{\Phi}\mathbf{Y}(l) + \Delta\mathbf{U}(l) + \Theta x_l(0) \\
\mathbf{X}(l) &= \Gamma\mathbf{Y}(l) + \Sigma\mathbf{U}(l) + \Psi x_l(0).
\end{aligned}
\begin{aligned}
&\tag{7.35} \\
&\tag{7.36}
\end{aligned}
$$

where the matrices $\tilde{\Phi}, \Delta, \Theta$ and Γ, Σ, Ψ are defined as follows

$$\tilde{\Phi} = \begin{bmatrix} D_0 & 0 & 0 & \cdots & 0 \\ CB_0 & D_0 & 0 & \cdots & 0 \\ CAB_0 & CB_0 & D_0 & \cdots & 0 \\ \vdots & \vdots & \vdots & \ddots & \vdots \\ CA^{\alpha-2}B_0 & CA^{\alpha-3}B_0 & CA^{\alpha-4}B_0 & \cdots & D_0 \end{bmatrix}_{m\alpha \times m\alpha} \tag{7.37}$$

$$\Delta = \begin{bmatrix} D & 0 & 0 & \cdots & 0 \\ CB & D & 0 & \cdots & 0 \\ CAB & CB & D & \cdots & 0 \\ \vdots & \vdots & \vdots & \ddots & \vdots \\ CA^{\alpha-2}B & CA^{\alpha-3}B & CA^{\alpha-4}B & \cdots & D \end{bmatrix}_{m\alpha \times r\alpha}, \Theta = \begin{bmatrix} C \\ CA \\ \vdots \\ CA^{\alpha-1} \end{bmatrix}_{m\alpha \times n} \tag{7.38}$$

$$\Gamma = \begin{bmatrix} B_0 & 0 & \cdots & 0 \\ AB_0 & B_0 & \cdots & 0 \\ \vdots & \vdots & \ddots & \vdots \\ A^{\alpha-1}B_0 & A^{\alpha-2}B_0 & \cdots & B_0 \end{bmatrix}_{n\alpha \times m\alpha} \tag{7.39}$$

$$\Sigma = \begin{bmatrix} B & 0 & \cdots & 0 \\ AB & B & \cdots & 0 \\ \vdots & \vdots & \ddots & \vdots \\ A^{\alpha-1}B & A^{\alpha-2}B & \cdots & B \end{bmatrix}_{n\alpha \times r\alpha}, \Psi = \begin{bmatrix} A \\ A^2 \\ \vdots \\ A^{\alpha} \end{bmatrix}_{n\alpha \times n}. \tag{7.40}$$

The 1D model of (7.35)-(7.36) is easily extended to the dynamic boundary conditions case by simply inserting (7.29) rewritten in the form

$$x_l(0) = d_l(0) + \sum_{j=0}^{\alpha-1} K_j v_l(j), \quad l = 1, 2, \ldots \tag{7.41}$$

into (7.35)-(7.36) to yield

$$\mathbf{Y}(l+1) = \Phi \mathbf{Y}(l) + \Delta \mathbf{U}(l) + \Theta d_l(0) \tag{7.42}$$

$$\mathbf{X}(l) = \Gamma \mathbf{Y}(l) + \Sigma \mathbf{U}(l) + \Psi d_l(0) \tag{7.43}$$

where

$$\Phi = \left[\tilde{\Phi} + \Theta K\right]_{m\alpha \times m\alpha} \tag{7.44}$$

$$\Gamma = \left[\tilde{\Gamma} + \Psi K\right]_{n\alpha \times m\alpha} \tag{7.45}$$

$$K = [K_0 \ K_1 \ \cdots \ K_{\alpha-1}]_{n \times m\alpha}. \tag{7.46}$$

$$\Phi =$$

$$
\begin{bmatrix}
D_0 + CK_0 & CK_1 & \cdots & CK_{\alpha-1} \\
C(B_0 + AK_0) & (D_0 + CAK_1) & \cdots & CAK_{\alpha-1} \\
CA(B_0 + AK_0) & C(B_0 + A^2K_1) & \cdots & CA^2K_{\alpha-1} \\
\vdots & \vdots & \ddots & \vdots \\
CA^{\alpha-2}(B_0 + AK_0) & CA^{\alpha-3}(B_0 + A^2K_1) & \cdots & (D_0 + CA^{\alpha-1}K_{\alpha-1})
\end{bmatrix} \tag{7.47}
$$

$$\Gamma =$$

$$
\begin{bmatrix}
B_0 + AK_0 & AK_1 & \cdots & AK_{\alpha-1} \\
A(B_0 + AK_0) & (B_0 + A^2K_1) & \cdots & A^2K_{\alpha-1} \\
A^2(B_0 + AK_0) & A(B_0 + A^2K_1) & \cdots & A^3K_{\alpha-1} \\
\vdots & \vdots & \ddots & \vdots \\
A^{\alpha-1}(B_0 + AK_0) & A^{\alpha-2}(B_0 + A^2K_1) & \cdots & (B_0 + A^\alpha K_{\alpha-1})
\end{bmatrix} \tag{7.48}
$$

Previous research in the 2D/nD systems area has also developed a 1D equivalent model for the underlying dynamics — see, for example, (Aravena *et al.* 1990). A key point about the resulting model is that it is 'time varying' in the sense that the dimensions of the matrices and vectors which define it increase as the process evolves over the positive quadrant, and this fact alone has prevented its effective use in the development of a mature systems theory for the 2D/nD processes it describes. This feature is not present in the equivalent 1D model for discrete linear repetitive processes and hence it should be of major use in the development of a 'mature' systems theory for these processes.

An immediate use for this 1D model is to develop tests for stability along the pass and, in particular, the condition of theorem 7.1 (in the case when the state initial vectors have the form (7.29)). The basis for these tests is the following result — for a proof see (Rogers *et al.* 1998).

Theorem 7.7 *Under the assumptions of theorem 7.1, discrete linear repetitive processes described by (7.1) and (7.29) (with $D = 0$, $D_0 = 0$) are stable along the pass if, and only if,*

1. *all eigenvalues of the transfer function matrix $G_1(z)$ have modulus strictly less than unity $\forall \, |z| = 1$ where*

$$G_1(z) = K(zI_{m\alpha} - \tilde{\Phi})^{-1}\Theta \tag{7.49}$$

2. *$r(A) < 1$, and*

3. *all eigenvalues of the transfer function matrix $G(\gamma)$ of (7.27) have modulus strictly less than than unity $|\gamma| = 1$.*

These conditions can be tested by direct application of well known 1D linear systems stability tests.

The use of this 1D model to define and characterize so-called pass controllability for discrete linear repetitive processes is reported in (Gałkowski *et al.* 1998). In the remainder of this contribution, we use this model to develop some basic results on the control of discrete linear repetitive processes by feedback action which aims to decouple the effects of pass initial state vectors of the form (7.29), which alone can cause instability, from the resulting closed loop dynamics. This is based on use of a control law of the form

$$\mathbf{U}(l) = \mathbf{L}x_l(0) + \mathbf{U}^*(l) \tag{7.50}$$

where

$$\mathbf{U}^*(l) := \left[r_l^T(0), r_l^T(1), \cdots, r_l^T(\alpha - 1) \right]^T \tag{7.51}$$

is the vector of external reference signals applied on pass l and

$$\mathbf{L} := \left[L_0^T, L_1^T, \cdots, L_{\alpha-1}^T \right]^T \tag{7.52}$$

is a feedback gain matrix to be selected.

Applying this control law to the 1D model for updating the pass to pass output results in the closed loop state space model

$$\mathbf{Y}(l+1) = \tilde{\Phi}\mathbf{Y}(l) + \Delta\mathbf{U}^*(l) + (\Delta\mathbf{L} + \Theta)x_l(0) \tag{7.53}$$

$$\mathbf{X}(l) = \tilde{\Gamma}\mathbf{Y}(l) + \Sigma\mathbf{U}^*(l) + (\Sigma\mathbf{L} + \Psi)x_l(0) \tag{7.54}$$

or

$$\mathbf{Y}(l+1) = \left[\tilde{\Phi} + (\Delta\mathbf{L} + \Theta)K \right] \mathbf{Y}(l) + \Delta\mathbf{U}^*(l) + (\Delta\mathbf{L} + \Theta)d_l(0) \tag{7.55}$$

$$\mathbf{X}(l) = \left[\tilde{\Gamma} + (\Sigma\mathbf{L} + \Psi)K \right] \mathbf{Y}(l) + \Sigma\mathbf{U}^*(l) + (\Sigma\mathbf{L} + \Psi)d_l(0). \tag{7.56}$$

and hence to decouple the effects of the pass initial state vectors from the pass to pass updating Equation (7.55) requires the existence of an $\mathbf{L}$ such that

$$\Delta_{m\alpha \times r\alpha}\mathbf{L}_{r\alpha \times n} + \Theta_{m\alpha \times n} = \mathbf{0}. \tag{7.57}$$

Also to simultaneously decouple the effects of $x_l(0)$ from the state updating there must exist an $\mathbf{L}$ which solves both (7.57) and

$$\Sigma_{n\alpha \times r\alpha}\mathbf{L}_{r\alpha \times n} + \Psi_{n\alpha \times n} = \mathbf{0} \tag{7.58}$$

Of course, simultaneous decoupling, i.e. both pass to pass and state, will only be possible under stronger conditions than that of pass to pass alone. Here the first objective considered is to decouple the effects of the pass state initial vectors from stability and hence we consider the problem of solving (7.57) alone. In which case, it is easy to see that decoupling in this case requires that $\mathbf{L}$ solves the following set of equations

$$DL_0 + C = 0$$
$$CBL_0 + DL_1 + CA = 0$$
$$CABL_0 + CBL_1 + DL_2 + CA^2 = 0$$
$$\vdots$$
$$CA^{\alpha-2}BL_0 + CA^{\alpha-3}BL_1 + DL_{\alpha-1} \cdots + CA^{\alpha-1} = 0 \tag{7.59}$$

Taking the dimensions of the matrices of (7.57) into consideration, it follows that an exact solution always exists if either the example under consideration is single-input single-output (SISO) or the dimension of the pass profile vector is equal to that of the input vector and the matrix Δ is nonsingular. If, however there are more outputs (pass profiles) m than inputs r, i.e. the defining set of linear equations is over-determined, a unique solution usually does not exist. However, with further constraints, a 'practical' solution can usually be found, such as the solution that minimizes the squared error in $\Delta L + \Theta$ i.e. the least squares solution.

Alternatively, when there are fewer outputs than inputs, i.e. the set of linear equations to be solved is under-determined, an infinite number of solutions exists. Of these solutions, the most relevant are those with either the maximum number of zeros in the elements of **L** or, on computing the pseudo-inverse of Δ, the solution giving the minimum norm of **L**.

Suppose now the the pass profile and input vectors have the same dimension and also that the matrix D is nonsingular. Then in this case, the following recurrence gives the solution

$$
\begin{aligned}
L_0 &= -D^{-1}C \\
L_1 &= L_0 A + L_0 B L_0 \\
L_2 &= L_0 A^2 + L_0 A B L_0 + L_0 B L_0 B L_1 \\
&\vdots \\
L_h &= L_0 A^h + \sum_{i=0}^{h-1} L_0 A^{h-1-i} B L_i, \quad h = 0, 1, \cdots, \alpha - 1 \quad (7.60)
\end{aligned}
$$

Consider now the case when D (and in what follows Δ) is rectangular or square and singular. Then in this case we make use of the pseudo-inverse and some of its basic properties. To summarize these, first recall that the matrix $X^{\#}$ is termed the pseudo-inverse of the matrix X if

$$
X X^{\#} X = X. \quad (7.61)
$$

Also the first equation in (7.59) is solvable if, and only if,

$$
D D^{\#} T_0 = T_0 \quad (7.62)
$$

where

$$
T_0 = -C \quad (7.63)
$$

Lemma 7.8 *If (7.62) holds then the general solution of the first equation of the set (7.59) can be expressed in the form*

$$
\widehat{L}_0 = -D^{\#}C + (I_m - D^{\#}D)P_0. \quad (7.64)
$$

where P_0 is any matrix of compatible dimensions.

Now substitute (7.64) into the second equation in (7.59) to yield

$$
D\widehat{L}_1 = T_1 \quad (7.65)
$$

where

$$
T_1 = -CA + CBD^{\#}C - CB(I_m - D^{\#}D)P_0. \quad (7.66)
$$

Also it is easy to check that if (7.65) holds then

$$
D D^{\#} T_1 = T_1. \quad (7.67)
$$

and from the second equation in the set (7.59) it follows that

$$\widehat{L}_1 = D^\# T_1 + (I_m - D^\# D) P_1. \tag{7.68}$$

where P_1 is any matrix of compatible dimensions. Continuing this process constructively establishes the following result.

Theorem 7.9 *The set of equations (7.59) are solvable if, and only if, the first one is solvable i.e. the condition of (7.62) holds.*

Finally, if (7.62) holds then the solution of (7.59) may be written in recursive form as

$$\widehat{L}_h = D^\# T_h + (I_m - D^\# D) P_h, \quad h = 0, 1, \ldots, \alpha - 1 \tag{7.69}$$

where

$$T_h = -CA^h - \sum_{j=0}^{h-1} CA^j B \widehat{L}_{h-1-j} \tag{7.70}$$

and P_h is any matrix of compatible dimensions.

As noted earlier in this section, to ensure decoupling of the state initial vector from both the pass profile and state equations it is necessary to seek a common solution to (7.57) and (7.58), where (7.58) can be written in partitioned form as

$$
\begin{aligned}
BL_0 + A &= 0 \\
ABL_0 + BL_1 + A^2 &= 0 \\
A^2 BL_0 + ABL_1 + BL_2 + CA^3 &= 0 \\
&\ \vdots \\
A^{\alpha-1} BL_0 + A^{\alpha-2} BL_1 + \cdots + ABL_{\alpha-2} + BL_{\alpha-1} + CA^\alpha &= 0
\end{aligned}
\tag{7.71}
$$

Proceeding as before, the following theorem can now be constructively established.

Theorem 7.10 *The set of equations (7.71) are solvable if, and only if, the first one is solvable i.e. the following condition holds*

$$BB^\# S_0 = S_0 \tag{7.72}$$

where

$$S_0 = -A. \tag{7.73}$$

Hence the necessary and sufficient condition for simultaneous solvability of (7.57) and (7.58) can be stated as follows.

Theorem 7.11 *The set of equations (7.57) and (7.58) (or (7.59) and (7.71)) are solvable if, and only if, the following condition holds.*

$$\begin{bmatrix} D \\ B \end{bmatrix} \begin{bmatrix} D \\ B \end{bmatrix}^\# V_0 = V_0 \tag{7.74}$$

where

$$V_0 = - \begin{bmatrix} C \\ A \end{bmatrix} \tag{7.75}$$

Finally, if (7.74) holds then the recurrent solution of (7.59) and (7.71) may be written as

$$\widehat{L}_h = \left[\begin{array}{c} D \\ B \end{array} \right]^{\#} V_h + \left(I_m - \left[\begin{array}{c} D \\ B \end{array} \right]^{\#} \left[\begin{array}{c} D \\ B \end{array} \right] \right) P_h, \quad h = 0, 1, \ldots, \alpha - 1 \qquad (7.76)$$

where

$$V_k = - \left[\begin{array}{c} C \\ A \end{array} \right] A^h - \sum_{j=0}^{h-1} \left[\begin{array}{c} C \\ A \end{array} \right] A^j B \widehat{L}_{h-1-j} \qquad (7.77)$$

and P_h is any matrix with compatible dimensions.

Note that theorem 7.6 is very restrictive due the fact that the component of the 1D model given by (7.43) is not dynamic, i.e. it does not involve recursive updating of $X(l)$. As such it does not influence asymptotic stability and this simply stresses again the requirement to decouple the effects of the pass state initial conditions from (7.42) using the necessary and sufficient conditions of theorem 7.4. Theorem 7.6 should only be used if simultaneous decoupling from both (7.42) and (7.43) is required. Note also that (7.43) is, in effect, a full order state observer for the underlying discrete linear repetitive process. If the respective sets of equations do not have unique solutions then approximate ones have to be used, where in what follows $\|.\|_2$ denotes the standard Euclidean norm on matrices.

Theorem 7.12 *The norm*

$$\| DL_0 + C \|_2 \qquad (7.78)$$

has minimum value if, and only if,

$$L_0 = -D^{\#}C + (I_m - D^{\#}D)P_0 \qquad (7.79)$$

where $D^{\#}$ is an L-symmetrical pseudo-inverse of the matrix D i.e.

$$L = DD^{\#} \qquad (7.80)$$

is symmetric

Hence, even if the necessary and sufficient condition for solvability of (7.59) does not hold, it is possible to find matrices $\widehat{L}_h$ such that

$$\widehat{L}_h = -D^{\#}T_k + (I_m - D^{\#}D)P_h, \quad h = 0, 1, \ldots, \alpha - 1 \qquad (7.81)$$

where

$$T_h = -CA^h - \sum_{j=0}^{h-1} CA^j B \widehat{L}_{h-1-j} \qquad (7.82)$$

which minimize the norms

$$\| CA^{h-1}BL_0 + CA^{h-2}BL_1 + \cdots + CBL_{h-1} + DL_h + CA^h \|_2, \, k = 0, 1, 2, \cdots, \alpha - 1 \qquad (7.83)$$

and hence decrease the effects of the dynamic pass initial conditions. This point is illustrated in the simulation studies of the next section.

7.5   SIMULATION RESULTS

In this section, two examples which illustrate the effectiveness of decoupling of the influence of the pass state initial conditions are presented.

Example 7.13 *The SISO process defined by the state space matrices* $A = 0.7$, $B = 0.1$, $B_0 = 0.15$, $C = 0.9$, $D = 0.2$, $D_0 = 0.6$

Firstly the initial conditions are assumed to be

$$
\begin{aligned}
x_{k+1}(0) &= 0, \ k \geq 0 \\
y_0(p) &= 1, \ 0 \leq p \leq \alpha
\end{aligned}
$$

and the process is unforced, i.e.

$$
u_k(p) = 0, \ k \geq 0, \ 0 \leq p \leq \alpha.
$$

This SISO model is asymptotically stable $(D_0 = 0.6 < 1)$ *which is confirmed by the pass profile and state dynamics simulations of Figures 1a and b.*

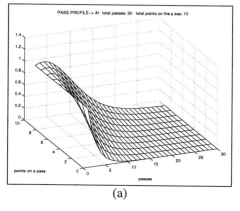 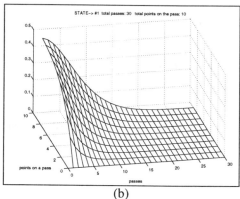

(a)   (b)

Figure 7.1: Simulations for the process with zero state initial conditions

Now suppose that the dynamic pass initial conditions are defined by

$$
K = [2.4, \ -5, \ 12.5, \ -37, \ 68, \ -80, \ 57, \ -25, \ 4, \ 0]
$$

which is easily shown to result in an unstable process (the matrix Φ *of (7.47) in this case has eigenvalues outside the unit circle). This fact is confirmed by the simulations of Figure 7.2 a and b.*

  In this case the equations of (7.59) and (7.71) may not be solvable simultaneously since the conditions of (7.74) of theorem 7.11 do not hold. However, Equations (7.59) or (7.71) considered separately are solvable, i.e. we can only decouple from the pass to pass or state updating equation. Here we choose to decouple the effects from the pass profile dynamics,

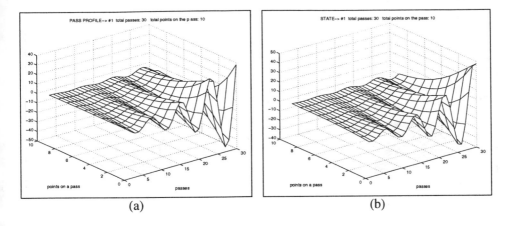

Figure 7.2: Simulations for the process with general pass initial conditions

where solving (7.59) gives the following feedback matrices (see (7.69))

$$L = -[4.5000e + 000, \ 1.1250e + 000, \ 2.8125e - 001, \ 7.0312e - 002,$$
$$1.7578e - 002, \ 4.3945e - 003, \ 1.0986e - 003, \ 2.7466e - 004,$$
$$6.8665e - 005, \ 1.7166e - 005]^{T}$$

The resulting closed loop process simulations are given in Figure 7.3 a and b where it is clear that complete decoupling has only been completely achieved for the pass profile dynamics.

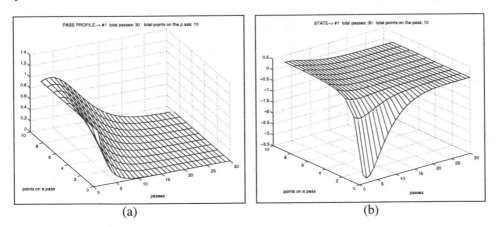

Figure 7.3: Simulations for the process with the effects of the pass initial conditions decoupled in the pass profile dynamics

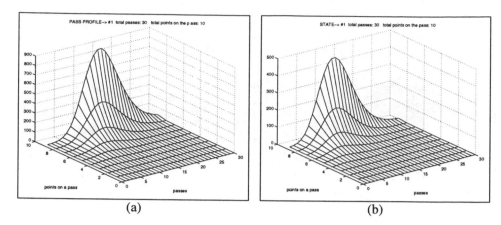

Figure 7.4: Simulations for the initial MIMO process

Example 7.14 *The MIMO process defined by the state space matrices*

$$A = \begin{bmatrix} 0.5 & 0 \\ 0 & 0.4 \end{bmatrix}, \ B = \begin{bmatrix} 1 & 0 & 1 \\ 0 & 0.5 & 0 \end{bmatrix}, \ B_0 = \begin{bmatrix} 1 & 0 & 0 & 0 \\ 0 & 1 & 0 & 1 \end{bmatrix},$$

$$C = \begin{bmatrix} 1 & 0 \\ 0 & 1 \\ 0 & 0 \\ 0 & 1 \end{bmatrix}, \ D = \begin{bmatrix} 1 & 0 & 0 \\ 0 & 0 & 1 \\ 1 & 1 & 0 \\ 1 & 0.5 & 1 \end{bmatrix}, \ D_0 = \begin{bmatrix} 0.5 & 0 & 0 & 0 \\ 0 & 0.4 & 0 & 0 \\ 0.3 & 0 & 0.6 & 0 \\ 1 & 0.5 & 1 & 0.2 \end{bmatrix},$$

with initial conditions

$$x_{k+1}(0) = 0, \ k \geq 0$$
$$y_0(t) = 1, \ 0 \leq t \leq \alpha$$

and the input sequence

$$u_k(p) = 0, \ k \geq 0, \ 0 \leq p \leq \alpha.$$

*This process with the simple structure state initial conditions is asymptotically stable —
see Figure 7.4 a and b.*

*Suppose now that this process is subject to dynamic pass initial conditions defined by
the matrix $K = [\cdots]_{2 \times 40}$*

$$K = \begin{bmatrix} 0.2 & 0 & 0 & 0 & -0.2 & 0 & 0 & 0 & 0 & -0.1 & 0 & 0 & 0 & 0 & 0.1 & 0 & \cdots \\ -0.1 & 0 & 0 & 0 & -0.2 & 0 & 0 & 0 & 0 & -0.1 & 0 & 0 & 0 & 0 & 0.1 & 0 & \cdots \end{bmatrix}$$
$$\begin{bmatrix} 0 & 0 & 0 & 0 \\ 0 & 0 & 0 & 0 \end{bmatrix}$$
$$= \begin{bmatrix} K_0 & | & K_1 & | & K_2 & | & K_3 & | & \cdots & | & K_9 \end{bmatrix}$$

Then it can be shown that process is now unstable (the matrix Φ has eigenvalues outside the unit circle) — see Figure 7.5 a and b. Also it is easily established that Equations (7.59) and (7.71) do not have a common solution, nor do they separately have a solution. Hence it is impossible to decouple the effects of the pass initial conditions in this case from either pass profile or state dynamics. We can, however, apply the approximate decoupling procedure for the pass profile dynamics as described in theorem 7.12. This results in a stable process with some level of decoupling — see Figure 7.6 a and b.

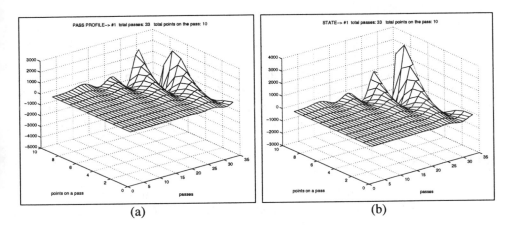

(a) (b)

Figure 7.5: Simulations for the process disturbed by pass initial conditions

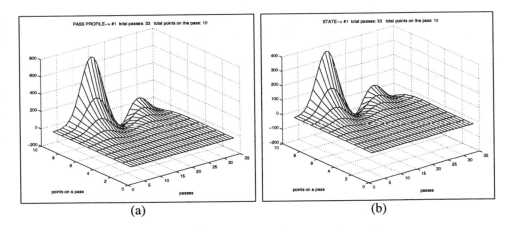

(a) (b)

Figure 7.6: Simulations for the approximately decoupled process

7.6 CONCLUSIONS

This chapter has considered discrete linear repetitive processes in the presence of so-called dynamic boundary conditions arising from a pass initial state vector sequence which is an explicit function of the previous pass profile. Aside from their theoretical interest, such boundary conditions arise naturally in some applications, e.g. nonlinear optimal control. Previous work had shown that such boundary conditions alone can destabilize a discrete linear repetitive process. In particular, if these conditions are not 'adequately' modeled then totally erroneous stability conclusions could be reached.

In this chapter, we have built on previous work and developed stability tests which can be implemented by direct application of well known 1D linear systems stability tests. Also some highly promising initial results on the use of appropriate control action to remove, or reject, the effects of a general form of these boundary conditions have been developed. Much further work remains to be done, however, before the true potential of this approach can be realistically assessed. Areas for immediate attention include further investigation of the numerical aspects of the algorithms used and the role of geometric control theory.

REFERENCES

N. Amann, D. H. Owens, and E. Rogers, 1996, Iterative learning control using optimal feedback and feedforward actions. *International Journal of Control*, 65(2):277–293.

N. Amann, D. H. Owens, and E. Rogers, 1998, Predictive optimal iterative learning control. *International Journal of Control*, 69(2):203–226.

J. L. Aravena, M. Shafiee, and W. A. Porter, 1990, State models and stability for 2-D filters. *IEEE Transactions on Circuits and Systems*, 37(12):1509–1519.

J. B. Edwards, 1974, Stability problems in the control of multipass processes. *Proceedings of The Institution of Electrical Engineers*, 121 (11):1425–1431.

E. Fornasini and G. Marchesini, 1978, Doubly-indexed dynamical systems: State space models and structural properties. *Mathematical Systems Theory*, 12:59–72.

D. Franke, 1998, 2D approach to stability of hybrid systems. *Proceedings of The 3rd International Conference on Automation of Hybrid Systems (ADPM98)* Zaytoon, J. (Ed), 2:159–163.

K. Gałkowski, E. Rogers, and D. H. Owens, 1998, Matrix rank based conditions for reachability/controllability of discrete linear repetitive processes. *Linear Algebra and its Applications*, 275–276:201–224.

K. Gałkowski, E. Rogers, and D. H. Owens, 1999, 1D model based stability analysis for a class of 2D linear systems. *Mathematical Theory of Networks and Systems (Proceedings on MTNS98)*, A. Beghi, L. Finesso and G. Picci (Eds), IL POLIGRAFO Press, Padova, Italy, pages 169–172.

D. H. Owens, 1977, Stability of linear multipass processes. *Proceedings of The Institution of Electrical Engineers*, 124 (11):1079–1082.

D. H. Owens and E. Rogers, 1999, Stability analysis of a class of 2D continuous-discrete linear systems with dynamic boundary conditions. *Systems and Control Letters*, 37:55–60.

P. D. Roberts, 1996, Computing the stability of iterative optimal control algorithms through the use of two-dimensional systems theory. *Proceedings of UKACC International Conference Control 96*, 2:981–986.

R. P. Roesser, 1975, A discrete state space model for linear image processing. *IEEE Transactions Auto Control*, AC-20:1–10.

E. Rogers, J. Gramacki, K. Gałkowski, and D. H. Owens, 1998, Stability theory for a class of 2D linear systems with dynamic boundary conditions. *Proceedings 37th IEEE International Conference on Decision and Control*, pages 2800–2805.

E. Rogers and D. H. Owens, 1992, *Stability Analysis for Linear Repetitive Processes*. Springer Verlag, Lecture Notes in Control and Information Sciences Series Vol 175, Berlin.

E. Rogers and D. H. Owens, 1995, Error actuated output feedback control theory for differential linear repetitive processes. *International Journal of Control*, 61(2):981–998.

K. J. Smyth, 1992, *Computer Aided Analysis for Linear Repetitive Processes, PhD Thesis*. University of Strathclyde, Glasgow UK.

CHAPTER EIGHT

Entire Function Methods for Optimization Problems in Continuous-Discrete 2D Control Systems

M. Dymkov

Institute of Mathematics,
National Academy of Sciences of Belarus,
Minsk, Belarus
dymkov@im.bas-net.by

Abstract

This paper applies the theory of entire functions to $2D$ control systems problems, starting with a discussion of some properties of the space of entire functions relevant to optimization based control schemes. In particular, the so-called maximal deviation problem for 2D continuous-discrete control systems is reduced to the extremal problem for some integral operator in Winner-Paley space. This is followed by an investigation of the optimal control problem for linear 2D continuous-discrete systems with mixed constraints where it is shown that the problem under consideration can be reduced to the linear programming problem in an appropriate Hilbert space of entire functions. Optimality conditions are expressed in terms of solutions to the adjoint system. Also some applications of entire functions to 1D optimization problems are discussed.

8.1 INTRODUCTION

The theory of complex-valued functions is commonly employed in the solution of various engineering and scientific problems. This paper considers the application of aspects of entire function theory to $2D$ (or, more generally, nD, $n > 3$) control systems problems. Attention is restricted to the case of linear dynamics since this is the area where most (initial) progress can be made.

Elements of complex analysis have a long history of application to nD systems problems – for early work see, for example, (Bose 1977, Huang 1972, Roesser 1975). In fact, the transfer function based input-output description of the dynamics of nD linear systems leads directly to the need to analyze multi-parametric complex-valued functions. Also criteria for stability, controllability etc. can be expressed in terms of functions defined in complex plane – see, for example, (Dymkov 1997a, Gaishun 1996, Gałkowski 1997, Rocha & Willems 1991, Rogers & Owens 1992). In particular, a proof of existence of closed-loop optimal control for LQ-optimization problem in $2D$ linear systems can be established by method of analytical extension of the solution of a Riccati equation defined initially on the unit circle in the complex plane (Dymkov 1997a, Fornasini & Marchesini 1976). Note also that for continuous-discrete $2 - D$ control systems defined on unbounded set Z_+ – the set of nonnegative integers – with respect to a discrete parameter infinitely differentiable functions are needed to determine the solution of such systems. These facts serve as motivation for considering the application of the classical theory of analytical (regular) complex-valued functions to 2D systems.

In this work we will employ a partition of regular functions using the classification (Ibragimov 1984) which is based on the presence of singular points. Under this partition, regular bounded functions without singularity in the complex plane $\bar{C}$ are constants and so-called entire functions are those functions that are regular in the complex plane except at the point $z = \infty$. The class of all entire functions has a complicated topological structure, but here we only need a subclass of these functions – the space of entire functions of exponential type and finite degree. Next we give some required mathematical preliminaries.

Let E, V be finite dimensional unitary spaces over a complex field C. We say that the complex function $f : C \to E$ is an entire function of exponential type and finite degree σ if f is regular on C and for any $\varepsilon > 0$ there is a constant $M = M(\varepsilon)$ such that the inequality $M \exp{(\sigma - \varepsilon)|z_s|} < |f(z)|_E < M \exp{(\sigma + \varepsilon)|z_s|}$ holds for all $z \in C$ and some $z_s \in C, z_s \to \infty, s \to \infty$. Let W_E denote the set of entire functions of exponential type and finite degree σ, which is never greater than π, such that its restriction on R – the space of real numbers – are some functions from the space $L_2(R, E)$. Then it is known that W_E is Hilbert space – termed the generalized Winner-Paley space (Ibragimov 1984). An inner product on W_E can be defined as $(f, g)_W = \int_R (f(x), \overline{g(x)})_E dx$, where $(\cdot, \cdot)_E$ denotes an inner product in E, and the overbar denotes the complex conjugate operation. We will also need the Hilbert space $l_2(W_E)$ of square summable sequences of elements from W_E with the usual inner product.

The next section gives some essential background analysis for the main results in this paper.

8.2   BACKGROUND

This chapter makes particular use of properties of Winner-Paley spaces. In particular, according to Winner's theorem, functions in such spaces admit the following description: the set W_E is precisely the set of analytical (regular) extensions $F(z)$ of the Fourier transformations of functions $f(t)$ from $L_2([-\sigma, \sigma], E)$ such that $F(z) = \frac{1}{\sqrt{2\pi}} \int_{-\sigma}^{\sigma} f(t)e^{-izt} dt$.

Also the space W_E is a compact subspace of $L_2(R, E)$.

Consider now the following problem: maximize the functional

$$J(u) = \sup_{s \in R} |(c, x(t^*, s))_E| \longrightarrow \max_{u \in V} \tag{8.1}$$

over the solutions of the system

$$x(t+1, s) = Ax(t, s) + D\partial x(t, s)/\partial s + Bu(t, s), \ t \in T = \{0, 1, ..., t^*\}, \quad s \in R, \tag{8.2}$$

with initial condition $x(0, s) = \varphi(s)$, $s \in R$ and subject to $u \in V$, where

$$V = \left\{ u : T \times C \to C \quad \middle| \quad u(t, \cdot) \in W_\sigma, \ t \in T, \quad \sum_{t \in T} \int_R |u(t, s)|^2 ds \leq 1 \right\}, \quad (8.3)$$

and t^* is a given nonnegative integer.

Definition 8.1 *For given functions $u \in V$, $\varphi \in W_E$ we say that a function $x : T \times C \to E$ is the solution to system (8.2) if $x(t, \cdot) \in W_E$, $t \in T$ and x satisfies (8.2) for all $t \in T$, $s \in R$.*

It is easy to check that for given $u \in V, \varphi \in W_E$ the solution of (8.2) can be written in the form

$$x(t + 1, s) = r(t, \varphi) + \sum_{\tau=0}^{t} \sum_{j=0}^{\tau} P^j(A, D) b \frac{\partial^j u(t - \tau, s)}{\partial^j s}, \quad (8.4)$$

where $r(t, \varphi)$ is some function of φ and its derivatives such that $r(t, 0) = 0$, $P^j(A, D)$ are polynomials of degree j with respect to the matrices A, D with known coefficients.

The optimization problem (8.1)–(8.3) can now be expressed as finding

$$J(u^0) = \sup_{u \in V} \sup_{s \in R} \left| \sum_{\tau=0}^{t^*-1} \sum_{j=0}^{\tau} N(\tau, j) \frac{\partial^j u(t^* - \tau - 1, s)}{\partial^j s} \right|. \quad (8.5)$$

which, in turn, can be reduced to the extremal problem for some integral operator in the space of entire functions. In particular, using the results of (Ibragimov 1984) the solution of this problem is equivalent to that of maximal deviation problem (in the uniform convergence topology) for the integral operator

$$U(f, v) = \frac{1}{2\pi i} \int_{|\xi|=\lambda} \sum_{j=1}^{k} f_j(\xi + v) K_j(\xi) d\xi, \quad (8.6)$$

over the unit ball in W_E^k, denoted here by $W_E^k[1]$. Here $f = (f_1, ..., f_k)$, $f_j \in W_E$, $j = 1, 2, ..., k$, k is a given integer, v is a real parameter, $0 < \lambda < \infty$ is some number, and $K_j \in M$ are given functions. Also M denotes the class of regular functions $K(z)$, for $|z| \geq \lambda$ such that the function $\Phi(t) = \frac{1}{2\pi i} \int_{|\xi|=\lambda} e^{it\xi} K(\xi) d\xi$ belongs to the space $L_2(-\sigma, \sigma)$ for any λ, $0 < \lambda < \infty$. The set $W_E^k[1]$ is the unit ball in the space W_E^k, where $W_E^k = W_\sigma \times ... \times W_\sigma$ is the linear normed space with norm defined by $\|f\|_{2,k} = \left(\sum_{i=1}^{k} \|f_i\|^2 \right)^{1/2}$.

The extremal value for the integral operator $U(f, v)$ can be estimated using the following linear functional defined on W_E^k

$$L(f) = U(f, 0) = \frac{1}{2\pi i} \int_{|\xi|=\lambda} \sum_{j=1}^{k} f_j(\xi) K_j(\xi) d\xi. \quad (8.7)$$

Note also that an element $f \in W_E^k, f \neq 0$ is termed an extremal element for $L(f)$ if $|L(f)| = \|L\| \|f\|$ holds and W_E^k is a strong normed space. Hence, any linear bounded functional defined on W_E^k has no more than one extremal element. Consequently we say that the function $f^0 \in W_E^k$ is extremal for $L(f)$ if the condition $\sup\limits_{f \in W_E^k[1]} L(f) = |L(f^0)| = \|L\|$ holds.

The estimation of extremal value for the integral operator $U(f, v)$ is now given by the following theorem.

Theorem 8.2 *If for $L(f)$ there is the extremal function $f^0(z)$ from the unit ball $W_E^k[1]$ then it is unique and the following inequality*

$$\sup_{f \in W_E^k[1]} \sup_{v \in R} |U(f, v)| = |L(f^0)| \le (2\pi)^{1/2} \left(\sum_{j=1}^k \|\Phi_j\|^2 \right)^{1/2}, \tag{8.8}$$

where $\|\Phi\| = \left(\int\limits_R |\Phi(t)|^2 dt \right)^{1/2}$, holds.

Proof: By the Winner-Paley theorem the function $f \in W_E$ can be written in the form

$$f(z) = \frac{1}{\sqrt{2\pi}} \int\limits_{-\sigma}^{\sigma} e^{izt} \varphi(t) dt, \tag{8.9}$$

where $\varphi \in L_2(-\sigma, \sigma)$ is the Fourier transformation of $f(x)$, $x \in R$ and $\varphi(t) = (2\pi)^{-1/2} \int\limits_{-\sigma}^{\sigma} f(x) e^{-ixt} dx$. Also the inequality $\|\varphi\|_L = \|f\|_W$ holds and hence

$$\begin{aligned} U(f, v) &= \frac{1}{2\pi i} \int\limits_{|\xi| = \lambda} \sum_{j=1}^k K_j(\xi) \frac{1}{\sqrt{2\pi}} \int\limits_{-\sigma}^{\sigma} e^{ivt} e^{i\xi t} \varphi_j(t) dt d\xi \\ &= \frac{1}{\sqrt{2\pi}} \int\limits_{-\sigma}^{\sigma} \sum_{j=1}^k e^{ivt} \varphi_j(t) \Phi_j(t) dt, L(f) \\ &= \frac{1}{\sqrt{2\pi}} \int\limits_{-\sigma}^{\sigma} \sum_{j=1}^k \varphi_j(t) \Phi_j(t) dt. \end{aligned} \tag{8.10}$$

It follows easily that $\sup\limits_{v \in R} |U(f, v)| \ge |U(f, 0)| = |L(f)|$. Use of the Holder inequality now yields

$$\begin{aligned} |L(f)| &\le \sup_{v \in R} |U(f, v)| = \sup_{v \in R} \frac{1}{\sqrt{2\pi}} \left| \int\limits_{-\sigma}^{\sigma} \sum_{j=1}^k e^{ivt} \varphi_j(t) \Phi_j(t) dt \right| \\ &\le \frac{1}{\sqrt{2\pi}} \sum_{j=1}^k \int\limits_{-\sigma}^{\sigma} |\varphi_j(t) \Phi_j(t)| dt \le \frac{1}{\sqrt{2\pi}} \sum_{j=1}^k \|\varphi_j\|^2 \|\Phi_j\|^2 \\ &= \frac{1}{\sqrt{2\pi}} \sum_{j=1}^k \|f_j\|^2 \|\Phi_j\|^2 \le 1/\sqrt{2\pi} \left(\sum_{j=1}^k \|f_j\|^2 \right)^{1/2} \left(\sum_{j=1}^k \|\Phi_j\|^2 \right)^{1/2} \end{aligned}$$

$$= 1/\sqrt{2\pi}\|f\|_{2,k}\left(\sum_{j=1}^{k}\|\Phi_j\|^2\right)^{1/2}. \tag{8.11}$$

It follows that $L(f)$ is a linear bounded functional defined on W_E^k. Also let $f^0 \in W_E^k[1]$ be an extremal function for $L(f)$. Then using the above inequality yields

$$\|U\|^* = \sup_{f\in W_p^k[1]}\sup_{v\in R}|U(f,v)| = |L(f_0)| \le (2\pi)^{-1/2}\left(\sum_{j=1}^{k}\|\Phi\|^2\right)^{1/2}. \tag{8.12}$$

As noted above W_E^k is a strong normed space. Hence the linear bounded functional $L(f)$ has no more than one extremal element on the unit ball $W_E^k[1]$ and the proof is complete.

∎

Remark 8.3 *The above theorem also holds in the more general case when the space W_σ is replaced by $W_{E,p}, (p > 1)$, i.e. the set of entire functions of exponential type and finite degree σ not exceeding π such that its restriction on R are functions from the space $L_p(R, E)$. In this case, the right-hand side of the inequality (8.8) must be multiplied by some constant C.*

The following theorem can also be established but it is only valid for the case of $p = 2$.

Theorem 8.4 *The function $f^0(z) = (f_1^0(z), ..., f_k^0(z))$ from the set $W_\sigma^k[1]$ is extremal for the operator $U(f, v)$ if, and only if, f it can be represented in the form*

$$f_j^0(z) = (2\pi)^{-1/2}e^{i\alpha}\|\Phi\|_{2,k}^{-1}\int_{-\sigma}^{\sigma}e^{izt}\overline{\Phi_j(t)}dt, \quad j = 1, 2, ..., k, \tag{8.13}$$

where $\|\Phi\|_{2,k} = \left(\sum_{j=1-\sigma}^{k}\int^{\sigma}|\Phi_j(t)\|^2\right)^{1/2}$, α is an arbitrary real number, and

$\|U\|^* = \sup_{f\in W_\sigma^k}\sup_{v\in R}|U(f,v)| = \|\Phi\|_{2,k}/\sqrt{2\pi}.$

Proof: We shall prove that the inequality (8.8) is valid as an exact equality, i.e. we shall show that for some function $f \in W_E^k$ the following hold:

$$\begin{aligned}|L(f)| &= \frac{1}{\sqrt{2\pi}}\left|\int_{-\sigma}^{\sigma}\sum_{j=1}^{k}\varphi_j^0(t)\Phi_j(t)dt\right| = \frac{1}{\sqrt{2\pi}}\int_{-\sigma}^{\sigma}\left|\sum_{j=1}^{k}\varphi_j^0(t)\Phi_j(t)\right|dt\\ &= \frac{1}{\sqrt{2\pi}}\sum_{j=1}^{k}\|\varphi_j^0\|\|\Phi_j\| = \frac{1}{\sqrt{2\pi}}\left(\sum_{j=1}^{k}\|f_j^0\|^2\right)^{1/2}\left(\sum_{j=1}^{k}\|\Phi_j\|^2\right)^{1/2}\\ &= \frac{1}{\sqrt{2\pi}}\|\Phi\|_{2,k}.\end{aligned} \tag{8.14}$$

Such a situation is possible in the following cases.

1) $\arg \sum_{j=1}^{k} \varphi_j^0(t)\Phi_j(t) = \alpha$ for almost all $t \in [-\sigma, \sigma]$, where α is a constant.

2) $\arg(\varphi_j^0(t)\Phi_j(t)) = \arg(\varphi_i^0(t)\Phi_i(t))$, $i \neq j$ for almost all $t \in [-\sigma, \sigma]$.

3) $|\varphi_j^0(t)| = A_j|\Phi_j(t)|$, $A_j > 0$, $j = 1, 2, ..., k$.

4) $\|\varphi_j^0\|_2 = \gamma\|\Phi_j\|_2$, where γ is constant for all $j = 1, ..., k$.

5) $\|f^0\|_{2,k} = 1$. Here $\varphi_j^0(t)$ is the Fourier transformation of $f_j(t)$, $j = 1, ..., k$. From conditions 1 and 2 we have that $\arg(\varphi_j^0(t)\Phi_j(t)) = \alpha$ for all $j = 1, ..., k$ and for almost all $t \in [-\sigma, \sigma]$, where α is a constant. From conditions 3 and 4 it follows that $|\varphi_j^0(t)| = A|\Phi_j(t)|$ for all $j = 1, ..., k$ and for almost all $t \in [-\sigma, \sigma]$, where A is a constant. Also it is a simple task to check that the functions $\varphi_j^0(t) = Ae^{i\alpha}|\Phi_j(t)|^2/\Phi_j(t)$, $j = 1, 2, ..., k$, where α is an arbitrary real number, satisfy the required conditions. Condition 5 yields

$$1 = \|f^0\|_{2,k} = \|\varphi\|_{2,k} = A \left(\sum_{j=1}^{k} \int_{-\sigma}^{\sigma} |\Phi_j(t)\|^2 \right)^{1/2} = A\|\Phi\|_{2,k}, \qquad (8.15)$$

i.e. $A = 1/\|\Phi\|_{2,k}$ and the required functions $f_j^0(z)$, $j = 1, ..., k$ are given by the formula (8.9). Note that in accordance with Winner-Paley theorem, these functions belong to the space W_E. Note also the definition of the functions $\Phi_j(t)$ and the fact that the functions $k_j(t) = |\Phi_j(t)|^2/\Phi_j(t) = = \overline{\Phi_j(t)}$ belong to $L_2(-\sigma, \sigma)$.

Using (8.13) we now have that

$$\|U\|^* = \sup_{f \in W_E^k[1]} \sup_{v \in R} |U(f, v)| = |L(f_0)| \leq (2\pi)^{1/2}\|\Phi\|_{2,k}, \qquad (8.16)$$

which proves that $f^0(z)$ is extremal.

Conversely, let $f^0 \in W_E^k[1]$ be an extremal function for $L(f)$. Since W_E^k is a strong normed space, $L(f)$ has a unique extremal element in the unit ball $W_E^k[1]$. Hence (8.14) and (8.16) hold and it follows immediately that $f^0(z)$ is given by (8.13) and the proof is complete. ∎

The optimal control $u^0 = (u_1^0, ..., u_{t^*-1}^0)$ which solves the optimization problem (8.1)–(8.3) can be obtained from theorem 1, once the functions $K_j(z)$ have been determined. For example, in the case when $\dim E = 1$, $\varphi = 0$, these functions can be taken as $K_\tau(z) = \sum_{j=0}^{\tau} j!N(\tau, j)z^{-(j+1)}$, where $N(\tau, j)$ are known numbers. In which case applying residue theory to the integral operator $U(f, v)$ yields

$$U^*(u, v) = \frac{1}{2\pi i} \int_{|\xi|=\lambda} \sum_{\tau=0}^{t^*-1} u(t^* - \tau - 1, \xi + v)K_\tau(\xi)d\xi$$

$$= \sum_{\tau=0}^{t^*-1} \sum_{j=0}^{\tau} j!N(\tau, j) \, Res_{\xi=0} \frac{u(t^* - \tau - 1, \xi + v))}{\xi^{j+1}}$$

$$= \sum_{\tau=0}^{t^*-1} \sum_{j=0}^{\tau} N(\tau, j) \lim_{\xi \to 0} \frac{d^j u(t^* - \tau - 1, \xi + v))}{d\xi^j}$$

$$= \sum_{\tau=0}^{t^*-1} \sum_{j=0}^{\tau} N(\tau, j) \frac{d^j u(t^* - \tau - 1, s)}{ds^j}. \tag{8.17}$$

Also the functions $\Phi_j(t)$ in this case can be written as

$$\Phi_\tau^*(t) = \frac{1}{2\pi i} \int_{|\xi|=\lambda} \sum_{j=0}^{\tau} j! N(\tau, j) e^{i\xi t} / \xi^{j+1} = \sum_{j=0}^{\tau} j! N(\tau, j) \text{Res}_{\xi=0}(e^{i\xi t}/\xi^{j+1})$$

$$= \sum_{j=0}^{\tau} N(\tau, j) \lim_{\xi \to 0} \frac{d^j e^{it\xi}}{d\xi^j} = \sum_{j=0}^{\tau} N(\tau, j)(it)^j. \tag{8.18}$$

Hence in the case when $\dim E = 1, \varphi = 0$ the following result can be established.

Theorem 8.5 *The optimal control for (8.1)–(8.3) ($\dim E = 1, \phi = 0$) is*

$$u^0(t^* - \tau - 1, z) = (2\pi)^{-1/2} e^{i\alpha} / \|\Phi^*\|_{2,t^*} \sum_{j=0}^{\tau} N(\tau, j) R_j(z), \quad \tau \in T, \tag{8.19}$$

where

$$R_j(z) = \begin{cases} (-1)^{j/2} \int_0^{\sigma} t^j \cos(tz) dt, & if \quad j - even, \\ (-1)^{(j+1)/2} \int_0^{\sigma} t^j \sin(tz) dt, & if \quad j - odd, \end{cases} \tag{8.20}$$

and α is a real number. The optimal value is $J(u^0) = (2\pi)^{-1/2} \|\Phi^*\|_{2,t^*}$.

8.3 LINEAR OPTIMAL CONTROL FOR CONTINUOUS-DISCRETE 2D SYSTEMS WITH CONSTRAINTS

First note that the results given below are based on the simple fact that a Winner-Paley space can be considered as a Hilbert space. It is also well-known that this fact is also valid for other classes of regular functions, such as the set $A^2(D)$ of all square summable regular in domain D. The evaluation of the derivatives of such functions is not simple as in the case of a Winner-Paley space and hence such functions are not considered here.

Consider now the following problem: maximize the linear functional

$$J(u, \varphi) = \sum_{t \in Z_+} \int_R \text{Re}(p(t, s), \overline{x(t, s)})_E ds + \int_R \text{Re}(q(s), \overline{\varphi}(s))_E ds \tag{8.21}$$

over the solutions of the system

$$x(t+1, s) = Ax(t, s) + D\partial x(t, s)/\partial s + Bu(t, s), \quad t \in Z_+, \quad s \in R, \tag{8.22}$$

with initial condition $x(0, s) = \varphi(s), s \in R$ subject to

$$Px(t, s) + Qu(t, s) - b(t, s) \in K_1, \quad u(t, s) \in K_2, \quad \varphi(s) \in K_3, \quad t \in Z_+, \quad s \in R. \tag{8.23}$$

Here (as before) Z_+ is the set of nonnegative integers; $p: Z_+ \times C \to E$, $B: Z_+ \times C \to E$ and $q: C \to E$ are given functions from $l_2(W_E)$ and W_E respectively; $u: Z_+ \times C \to V$ is an unknown control function; A, D, P are linear operators mapping E into itself; B, Q are linear operators from V in E; K_1, K_2 and K_3 are convex closed cones in E and V, respectively. Also it is assumed that the interior of K_1 is nonempty.

Definition 8.6 *For given functions $u(t, s)$, $\varphi(s)$ we say that a function x from $l_2(W_E)$ is the solution of system (8.22) if x satisfies (8.22) for all $t \in Z$, $s \in R$.*
The control function $u: Z_+ \times C \to V$ and the initial function $\varphi: C \to E$ will be called admissible if $u \in l_2(W_V)$, $\varphi \in W_E$ and inclusions (8.23) hold.

To establish optimality conditions it is convenient to represent the original problem (8.21)–(8.23) as a linear programming problem in Hilbert space $l_2(W_E)$ (see (Dymkov 1997b) for the details). To do this, we define the linear operator $a: W_E \to W_E$ by the formula $(a\varphi)(z) = A\varphi(z) + Dd\varphi(z)/dz, z \in C$. It is known (Ibragimov 1984) that W_E is invariant with respect to the operation of differentiation, and to estimate the derivatives the inequality $\|\varphi'\|_W \leq \sigma\|\varphi\|_W$ also holds. This establishes the boundedness of the operator A.

The system (8.22) can be rewritten as the discrete equation

$$\alpha(t+1) = a\alpha(t) + \gamma(t), \alpha(0) = \varphi, \alpha(t) \in W_E, t \in Z_+, \tag{8.24}$$

where φ and $\gamma(t), t \in Z_+$ are given elements from W_E. Define the operator $\mathcal{A}: l_2(W_E) \to W_E \times l_2(W_E)$ as follows

$$\mathcal{A}: (\alpha(0), \alpha(1), \alpha(2), \ldots) \to \{(\alpha(0), (\alpha(1) - a\alpha(0), \alpha(2) - a\alpha(1), \ldots)\}.$$

Then it is easy to see that $\mathcal{A}$ is a bounded linear operator. Also (8.24) can be written using $\mathcal{A}$ as

$$\mathcal{A}\alpha = f, \alpha \in l_2(W_E), \tag{8.25}$$

where $f = (\varphi, \gamma)$ is an element from $W_E \times l_2(W_E)$. It can also be shown that in the case when $\|A\| + \sigma\|D\| < 1$, $\mathcal{A}$ has an inverse defined by

$$\mathcal{A}^{-1}: \{\varphi, (\eta(0), \eta(1), \ldots)\} \to (\varphi, \eta(0) + a\varphi, \eta(1) + a\eta(0) + a^2\varphi, \ldots). \tag{8.26}$$

Using this fact, it follows immediately that (8.25), and hence (8.24) and (8.22) have a unique solution $\alpha = \mathcal{A}^{-1}f$ for any φ and u.

In addition to (8.25), consider the following adjoint equation

$$\mathcal{A}^*\beta = g, \beta = (\psi, \xi) \in W_E \times l_2(W_E), g \in l_2(W_E). \tag{8.27}$$

Then it can be shown that $\mathcal{A}^*: W_E \times l_2(W_E) \to l_2(W_E)$ is defined by $\mathcal{A}^*: \{\psi, (\xi(0), \xi(1), \ldots)\} \to (\psi - a^*\xi(0), \xi(0) - a^*\xi(1), \ldots)$. Here the conjugate operator $a^*: W_E \to W_E$ is given by $a^*\psi = A^*\psi - D^*\psi$ since any entire function from a Winner-Paley space vanishes for the points at infinity, and A^*, D^* denote conjugate operators for A and D respectively. Hence, using the representation of $\mathcal{A}^*$ we see that (8.27) can be written as the following system of equations in terms of unknown ψ and ξ:

$$\xi(t) = a^*\xi(t+1) + g(t+1), \psi = a^*\xi(0) + g(0), t \in Z_+, \|\xi(t)\| \to 0, t \to \infty. \tag{8.28}$$

We term (8.28) the adjoint for (8.24) and, using the explicit form of a^*, it can be written as

$$y(t,s) = A^*y(t+1,s) - D^*\partial y(t+1,s)/\partial s + g(t+1,s), \quad \|y(t,\cdot)\|_W \to 0, \quad t \to \infty,$$

$$\psi(s) = A^*y(0,s) - D^*\partial y(0,s)/\partial s + g(0,s), \quad t \in Z_+, \quad s \in R. \tag{8.29}$$

and we term (8.29) the adjoint system for (8.22). The solution of (8.29) is defined in the same manner as the solution of (8.22).

It is now a simple matter to show that in the case of $\|A\| + \sigma\|D\| < 1$, (8.29) has a unique solution for any $g \in l_2(W_E)$. This follows immediately from the well known result that (8.25) has a unique solution for any $f \in W_E \times l_2(W_E)$ if, and only if, the conjugate equation (8.27) has a unique solution for any $g \in l_2(W_E)$.

At this stage it is convenient to represent the original problem (8.1)–(8.3) as a linear programming problem in Hilbert space $l_2(W_E)$. In particular, it is easy to show that (8.22) can be written in the form (8.25), where $g = (\varphi, Bu), \varphi \in W_E, u \in l_2(W_E)$, and the bounded linear operator $B : l_2(W_V) \to l_2(W_E)$ is defined as

$$(Bu)(t,z) = Bu(t,z), \ t \in Z_+, z \in C. \tag{8.30}$$

Define the linear bounded operator $T : W_E \times l_2(W_V) \to l_2(W_E)$ as:

$$(T)(\varphi, u) = (PA^{-1})(\varphi, Bu) + Ju, \quad (\varphi, u) \in W_E \times l_2(W_V), \tag{8.31}$$

Here $P : l_2(W_E) \to l_2(W_E), J : l_2(W_V) \to l_2(W_E)$ are linear operators given by the formula $(Px)(t,z) = Pu(t,z), (Ju)(t,z) = Gu(t,z), t \in Z_+, z \in C$. Use of T yields a representation of constraints of (8.22) in the form

$$T\xi - b \in K_1, \quad \xi \in K_0, \quad \xi = (\varphi, u) \in W_E \times l_2(W_V), \tag{8.32}$$

where K_1, K_0 are cones in $l_2(W_E)$ which, in turn, are defined using cones $K_i, \ i = 1,2,3$ as follows: $K_0 = K_2 \times K_3, K_3 = \{\xi(\cdot) \in W_E, \xi(x) \in K_3 \text{ for any } x \in R\}, K_i = \{\lambda(\cdot) \in l_2(W_E), \lambda(t,x) \in K_i \text{ for any } t \in Z_+, x \in R\}, \ i = 1,2$. Next we prove that $K_i, \ i = 1,2,3$ are closed and convex sets.

It is easy to see that the convexity of these cones follows from convexity of $K_i, \ i = 1,2,3$. To prove that K_3 is closed, let $\{\xi_n(\cdot)\}$ be a sequence from K_3 which converges to $\xi(\cdot)$ such that $\|\xi_n - \xi\|_W^2 = \int_R |\xi_n(x) - \xi(x)|^2 dx \to 0$ as $n \to \infty$. Since $|\xi(x) - P_k(\xi(x))|^2 \le |\xi(x) - \xi_n(x)|^2$ for all n (here $P_k(\xi(x))$ denotes the projection of $\xi(x)$ on the closed convex set K) and P_k is as a known continuous function from E in K, we have that $\int_R |\xi(x) - P_k(\xi(x))|^2 dx \le \|\xi_n - \xi\| \to 0$ as $n \to \infty$. Hence $\xi(x) = P_k(\xi(x))$ or $\xi(x) \in K_3$. Finally, $\xi(\cdot) \in W_E$ since W_E is a total space and the proof is complete. The proof that $K_i, \ i = 0,1,2$ is closed follows immediately on noting that $l_2(W_E)$ is a total space.

At this stage, the problem defined by (8.21)–(8.23) generates the following linear programming problem in the Hilbert space $W_E \times l_2(W_V$: maximize the linear functional

$$f(\xi) = \text{Re}(\tilde{p}, \xi)_{W_E \times l_2(W_V)} \tag{8.33}$$

subject to

$$T\xi - b \in K_1, \quad \xi \in K_0, \quad \xi \in W_E \times l_2(W_V). \tag{8.34}$$

Here $\tilde{p} \in W_E \times l_2(W_V)$ is given by

$$\tilde{p} = \left\{ \sum_{s \in Z_+} a^{*^s} p(s), \left(\sum_{s \in Z_+} B^* a^{*^s} p(s+1), \sum_{s \in Z_+} B^* a^{*^s} p(s+2), \ldots \right) \right\}. \tag{8.35}$$

Consider now the problem: minimize the linear functional

$$r(\eta) = -\mathrm{Re}(b, \eta)_{l_2(W_E)} \tag{8.36}$$

subject to

$$-T^* \eta + \tilde{p} \in \mathcal{K}_0^*, \quad \eta \in \mathcal{K}_1^*, \quad \eta \in l_2(W_E), \tag{8.37}$$

where $\mathcal{K}_i^*$, $i = 0, 1$ are conjugate cones defined as $\mathcal{K}_0^* = \mathcal{K}_2^* \times \mathcal{K}_3^*$ and

$$
\begin{aligned}
\mathcal{K}_i^* &= \{\eta \in l_2(W_E), \mathrm{Re}(\eta, \lambda)_{l_2(W)} \geq 0 \,\forall\, \lambda \in \mathcal{K}_i\}, i = 1, 2 \\
\mathcal{K}_3^* &= \{\eta \in W_E, \mathrm{Re}(\eta, \xi)_W \geq 0 \,\forall\, \xi \in \mathcal{K}_3\}.
\end{aligned} \tag{8.38}
$$

Then this last problem is said to be the dual problem for (8.33)–(8.34).

It is easy to check that the conjugate operator T^* in this case is defined by the formula

$$T^* : (\eta(0), \eta(1), \eta(2), \ldots) \to \left\{ \sum_{s \in Z_+} a^{*^s} \mathcal{P}^* \eta(s), \right.$$

$$\left. \left(\sum_{s \in Z_+} B^* a^{*^s} \mathcal{P}^* \eta(s+1) + \mathcal{J}^* \eta(1), \sum_{s \in Z_+} B^* a^{*^s} \eta(s+2) + \mathcal{J}^* \eta(2), \ldots \right) \right\} \tag{8.39}$$

where the conjugate operators B^*, $\mathcal{P}^*$, $\mathcal{J}^*$ follow from an easy computation. Also it is a simple matter to verify that the conjugate cones are given by $\mathcal{K}_3^* = \{\eta \in W_E, \eta(x) \in K_3^* \,\forall\, x \in R\}, \mathcal{K}_i^* = \{\eta \in l_2(W_E), \eta(t, x) \in K_i^* \,\forall\, t \in Z_+, x \in R\}, i = 1, 2$. Duality theory is now a standard way to obtain optimality conditions for linear extremal problems. Below this method is applied to the problem defined by (8.21)–(8.23).

Introduce the new variable $\lambda = (\psi, y) \in W_E \times l_2(W_E)$ as $\lambda = (\mathcal{A})^{-1*}(\mathcal{P}^* \eta + p)$. Then we have that

$$\psi = \mathcal{P}^* \eta(0) + p(0) + a^* y(0), \quad y(t) = \mathcal{P}^* \eta(t+1) + p(t+1) + a^* y(t+1), \tag{8.40}$$

where $t \in Z_+$, $\|y(t)\| \to 0, t \to \infty$. Here $\psi : C \to E \in W_E$, $y : Z_+ \times C \to E \in l_2(W_E)$. Also write $\eta = (v(0), v(1), \ldots)$, where $v : Z_+ \times C \to E \in l_2(W_E)$.

Using the formulas for a^* and $\mathcal{P}^*$ the above relations can be written in the form:

$$
\begin{aligned}
y(t, s) &= A^* y(t+1, s) - D^* \partial y(t+1, s)/\partial s + P^* v(t+1, s) \\
&\quad + p(t+1, s), \|y(t, \cdot)\|_W \to 0, \quad t \to \infty, \\
\psi(s) &= A^* y(0, s) - D^* \partial y(0, s)/\partial s + P^* v(0, s) + p(0, s), \quad t \in Z, s \in R.
\end{aligned} \tag{8.41}
$$

In this case the constraints (8.37) and the cost functional (8.36) take the form

$$-B^* y(t, s) - Q^* v(t, s) \in K_2^*, \quad v(t, s) \in K_1^*, \quad -q(s) - \psi(s) \in K_3^*, \quad t \in Z_+, s \in R, \tag{8.42}$$

$$r(v) = -\sum_{t \in Z_+} \int_R \mathrm{Re}(b(t, s), \overline{v(t, s)})_E ds. \tag{8.43}$$

Thus, the dual problem for (8.21)–(8.21) is to minimize functional (8.43) over the solutions of (8.41) under the conditions of (8.42). This results in the following theorem.

Theorem 8.7 *Let* $|A| + \sigma|D| < 1$ *and* $u^0(t, s)$, $\varphi^0(s)$, $t \in Z$, $s \in R$ *be an optimal solution for the problem (8.21)–(8.23). Then there exists an optimal solution* $v^0(t, s)$, $t \in Z$, $s \in R$ *for the dual problem (8.41)–(8.43) such that* $J(u^0, \varphi^0) = r(v^0)$ *and* $\text{Re}((Px^0(t, s) + Qu^0(t, s) - b(t, s)), v^0(t, s))_E = 0, \text{Re}(\psi^0(s) + q(s), \varphi^0(s))_E = 0, \text{Re}((B^*y^0(t, s) + Q^*v^0(t, s)), u^0(t, s))_E = 0, t \in Z_+, s \in R$, *where* $x^0(t, s)$ *and* $y^0(t, s)$ *are solutions of (8.22) and (8.41) corresponding to* $u^0(t, s), \varphi(s)$ *and* $v^0(t, s), t \in Z_+, s \in R$, *respectively.*

8.4 CONCLUDING REMARKS

First note that there is another property of Winner-Paley space which can also be applied to optimization problems. In particular, according to the Kotelnikov theorem (Ibragimov 1984) there is an isomorphism between W_E and the space of square summable sequences of complex numbers l_2:

$$f \in W_\sigma \leftrightarrow \{c_k\} \in l_2, \quad f(z) = \sum_{k=-\infty}^{\infty} (-1)^k c_k \frac{\sin \pi z}{\pi(z - k)}. \tag{8.44}$$

Otherwise, the function f is determined by numbers c_k.

To demonstrate the use of such a representation, consider the following 1-D extremal problem:

$$\int_{-\pi}^{\pi} |u(t)|^2 dt \to \min, \quad \dot{x} = Ax + bu, \ t \in [-\pi, \pi], \ x(-\pi) = x_0, \ Hx(\pi) = 0. \tag{8.45}$$

where $x \in \mathcal{R}^n$, A is an $(n \times n)$ matrix, b, x_0 are given $n \times 1$ vectors, $u(t), t \in [-\pi, \pi]$ is the control input vector from the space $L_2[-\pi, \pi]$ of measurable and square summable functions on $[-\pi, \pi]$, H is an $(m \times n)$ matrix. It is also assumed that the system is controllable and the eigenvalues of A are real and distinct. Now introduce $G = [Hb, HAb, ..., HA^{n-1}b]$, $R = -[Hx_0, HAx_0, ..., HA^{n-1}x_0]$; V— $(n \times n)$ and let V denote the Vandermonde matrix generated by eigenvalues $\lambda_1, ..., \lambda_n$ of A. Also introduce $F = GV^{-1}\Lambda$, $f = (2\pi)^{-1/2}RV^{-1}g$, $g = (e^{2\lambda_1\pi}, ..., e^{2\lambda_n\pi})^T$. Then we have the following theorem.

Theorem 8.8 *The Fourier transformation of the optimal control for (8.45) is given by*

$$u^0(z) = \sum_{s=1}^{m} \beta_s \sum_{j=1}^{n} F_{sj} \overline{D(\pi z_j - \pi z)}, \tag{8.46}$$

where the complex numbers $\beta_s = \nu_s + i\gamma_s$, $s = 1, 2, ...$, *are determined by the following algebraic equations*

$$\sum_{s=1}^{m} \beta_s \sum_{j=1}^{n} \sum_{i=1}^{n} F_{lj}F_{sj}\overline{D(\pi z_i - \pi z_j)} = f_l, \quad l = 1, 2, ..., m. \tag{8.47}$$

Here $D(z) = \sin z/z$, $D(0) = 1$, F_{lj}, f_l, $l = 1, 2, ..., m$, $j = 1, 2, ..., n$ *are elements of* $(m \times n)$-*matrix* F *and* m-*vector* f, *respectively.*

It is also possible to show that the Fourier transformation of the optimal control for (8.45) can be represented by a series expansion of $l_k = Q^{-1}(z)(z - k)^{-1} \sin \pi z$, $k = 0, 1, ...$, where $Q(z)$ is some polynomial of finite degree. Hence an approximate solution for (8.45) can be obtained from this expansion. More details on this particular aspect can be found in (Ibragimov 1984).

ACKNOWLEDGMENTS

The author is indebted to Professor K. Gałkowski, Technical University of Zielona Gora, Poland, and Professor E. Rogers, University of Southampton, UK, for their kind encouragement of this work which was partially supported by The Education Ministry of Belarus.

REFERENCES

Bose, N. K. (Ed), 1977, *Multidimensional Systems Theory*, Reidel Publishing Company, Dordrecht/Boston/Lancaster.

Dymkov, M. P., 1997, Quadratic optimization in 2D linear control systems, *Automation and Remote Control*, 56(6) Part 1, pp 944-951.

Dymkov, M. P., 1997, Optimality conditions for linear 2D control systems with constraints, *Applied Mathematics and Computer Science*, 7(3), pp. 495-512.

Fornasini, E. and Marchesini, G., 1976, State space realization of two-dimensional filters, *IEEE Transactions on Automatic Control*, AC-21, pp 484-491.

Gaishun, I. V., 1996, Multi-dimensional control systems – Minsk: *Nauka i Technica*, (In Russian).

Gałkowski, K., 1997, State space realization of multi-input multi-output systems – elementary operations approach, *International Journal of Control*, 66(1), pp 119-140.

Huang, T. S., 1972, Stability of two-dimensional and recursive filters, *IEEE Transactions on Audio and Electroacoustics*, 20, pp. 158-163.

Ibragimov, I. I., 1984, *Selected Problems for Regular Functions Theory*, ELm Publisher-house, (In Russian).

Rocha, P. and Willems, J. C., 1991, Controllability of 2-D systems, *IEEE Transactions on Automatic Control*, AC-36(4), pp. 413-423.

Roesser, R. P., 1975, A discrete state space model for linear image processing, *IEEE Transactions on Automatic Control*, AC-20(1), pp. 1-10.

Rogers, E. and Owens, D. H., 1992, *Stability Analysis for Linear Repetitive Processes*, *Lecture Notes in Control and Information Sciences Series*, Vol 175, Springer-Verlag, Berlin.

CHAPTER NINE

Existence of an Optimal Solution for a Continuous Roesser Problem with a Terminal Condition

Dariusz Idczak and Stanisław Walczak

Faculty of Mathematics,
University of Łódź, Poland
idczak@math.uni.lodz.pl, stawal@math.uni.lodz.pl

Abstract

In the paper, a theorem on the continuous dependence of solutions on controls for a linear nonautonomous continuous Roesser system, in some special spaces of trajectories and controls, is derived. Next, a theorem on the existence of an optimal solution for the above system, with a terminal condition and an integral performance index is proved.

9.1 INTRODUCTION

Let us consider the following control system (the so-called continuous Roesser system)

$$\frac{\partial z^1}{\partial x} = A_{11}(x,y)z^1 + A_{12}(x,y)z^2 + B_1(x,y)u^1 \tag{9.1}$$

$$\frac{\partial z^2}{\partial y} = A_{21}(x,y)z^1 + A_{22}(x,y)z^2 + B_2(x,y)u^2$$

almost everywhere (a.e.) on $\Omega = [0,1] \times [0,1] \subset R^2$, with the boundary conditions

$$z^i(\cdot,0) = z^i(0,\cdot) = 0, \ i = 1,2, \tag{9.2}$$

everywhere on $[0,1] \subset R$ and with the terminal condition

$$(z^1(1,1), z^2(1,1)) = (P^1, P^2). \tag{9.3}$$

We assume that $z^1 \in R^{n_1}$, $z^2 \in R^{n_2}$, $u^1 \in R^{r_1}$, $u^2 \in R^{r_2}$, $A_{11} \in R^{n_1 \times n_1}$, $A_{12} \in R^{n_1 \times n_2}$, $A_{21} \in R^{n_2 \times n_1}$, $A_{22} \in R^{n_2 \times n_2}$, $B_1 \in R^{n_1 \times r_1}$, $B_2 \in R^{n_2 \times r_2}$, $P^1 \in R^{n_1}$, $P^2 \in R^{n_2}$, $n_1, n_2, r_1, r_2 \in N$.

Systems of type (9.1) are the continuous analogue of the well-known discrete 2-D systems of Roesser type (cf. (Roesser 1975), (Kaczorek 1983), (Klamka 1991), (Kaczorek & Klamka 1987), (Kurek 1984)). They are used to describe some chemical processes which hold in the reactor with the changeable activity of a catalyst.

Usually, system (9.1) is investigated in the space (defined below) $U_x^{n_1} \times U_y^{n_2}$ of absolutely continuous, in the appropriate variables, trajectories and in the space of integrable

controls (cf. (Wailiew 1981), (Walczak 1988), (Idczak 1995), (Idczak 1996b)). In mono-
graph (Wailiew 1981) author gives the conditions guaranteeing the existence and uniqueness of a solution to problem (9.1)–(9.2). Some differentiability properties of an integral
cost functional with the constraints given by (9.1)–(9.2) are established too. The maximum principle for system (9.1)–(9.2) with a linear integral cost functional is derived in
(Walczak 1988). In paper (Idczak 1995), a theorem on the existence of an optimal solution
to problem (9.1)–(9.2) with an integral cost functional, in the spaces mentioned above, is
proved. Necessary optimality conditions for a nonlinear continuous Roesser system are
derived in (Idczak 1996b).

In paper (Pieczka 1974), problem (9.1)–(9.2) with the constant coefficients and analytical controls is investigated.

Terminal condition (9.3) causes that the problem must be considered in other spaces of
trajectories and controls (cf. (Idczak 1996a), (Idczak & Walczak 1995)).

We shall consider system (9.1) in the spaces $AC = AC^{n_1} \times AC^{n_2}$ of trajectories and
$U = U_y^{r_1} \times U_x^{r_2}$ of controls, where $AC^{n_i} = \{z^i : \Omega \to R^{n_i};$ there exists $l^i \in L^2(\Omega, R^{n_i})$
such that $z^i(x, y) = \int_0^x \int_0^y l^i(s, t)ds dt$ for $(x, y) \in \Omega\}$, $i = 1, 2$, and $U_y^{r_1} = \{u^1 : \Omega \to$
$R^{r_1};$ there exists $\mu^1 \in L^2(\Omega, R^{r_1})$ such that $u^1(x, y) = \int_0^y \mu^1(x, t)dt$ for $x \in [0, 1]$ a.e.,
$y \in [0, 1]\}$, $U_x^{r_2} = \{u^2 : \Omega \to R^{r_2};$ there exists $\mu^2 \in L^2(\Omega, R^{r_2})$ such that $u^2(x, y) =$
$\int_0^x \mu^2(s, y)ds$ for $y \in [0, 1]$ a.e., $x \in [0, 1]\}$. In the same way $U_y^{n_1 \times r_1} = \{u^1 : \Omega \to$
$R^{n_1 \times r_1};$ there exists $\mu^1 \in L^2(\Omega, R^{n_1 \times r_1})$ such that $u^1(x, y) = \int_0^y \mu^1(x, t)dt$ for $x \in [0, 1]$
a.e., $y \in [0, 1]\}$, $U_x^{n_2 \times r_2} = \{u^2 : \Omega \to R^{n_2 \times r_2};$ there exists $\mu^2 \in L^2(\Omega, R^{n_2 \times r_2})$ such
that $u^2(x, y) = \int_0^x \mu^2(s, y)ds$ for $y \in [0, 1]$ a.e., $x \in [0, 1]\}$.

We shall identify functions belonging to $U_y^{r_1}$ ($U_x^{r_2}, U_y^{n_1 \times r_1}, U_x^{n_2 \times r_2}$) and equal a.e.

Of course, each function belonging to AC satisfies boundary conditions (9.2). Continuity property of elements of AC is important from the point of view of the terminal
condition (9.3).

Let us introduce in AC^{n_i}, $i = 1, 2$, and in $U_y^{r_1}$, $U_x^{r_2}$ the following scalar products

$$(z^i, w^i) = \int_\Omega < \frac{\partial^2 z^i}{\partial x \partial y}(x, y), \frac{\partial^2 w^i}{\partial x \partial y}(x, y) > dx dy$$

for $z^i, w^i \in AC^{n_i}, i = 1, 2$,

$$(u^1, v^1) = \int_\Omega < \frac{\partial u^1}{\partial y}(x, y), \frac{\partial v^1}{\partial y}(x, y) > dx dy$$

for $u^1, v^1 \in U_y^{r_1}$,

$$(u^2, v^2) = \int_\Omega < \frac{\partial u^2}{\partial x}(x, y), \frac{\partial v^2}{\partial x}(x, y) > dx dy$$

for $u^2, v^2 \in U_x^{r_2}$.

It is easy to check that the spaces $AC^{n_i}, i = 1, 2$, and $U_y^{r_1}, U_x^{r_2}$, with the appropriate
scalar products, are complete.

We have the following

Theorem 9.1 *If the functions $A_{11} \in U_y^{n_1 \times n_1}$, $A_{12} \in U_y^{n_1 \times n_2}$, $A_{21} \in U_x^{n_2 \times n_1}$, $A_{22} \in$
$U_x^{n_2 \times n_2}$, $B_1 \in U_y^{n_1 \times r_1}$, $B_2 \in U_y^{n_2 \times r_2}$ are such that $\frac{\partial A_{11}}{\partial y}, \frac{\partial A_{12}}{\partial y}, \frac{\partial A_{21}}{\partial x}, \frac{\partial A_{22}}{\partial x}, \frac{\partial B_1}{\partial y}, \frac{\partial B_2}{\partial x}$
are essentially bounded on Ω, then, for any control $u = (u^1, u^2) \in U$, there exists in the
space AC a unique solution $z_u = (z_u^1, z_u^2)$ of system (9.1).*

Proof: In paper (Idczak 1997), an existence of a unique solution in the space AC to system

$$\frac{\partial z^1}{\partial x} = A_{11}(x,y)z^1 + A_{12}(x,y)z^2 + v^1(x,y)$$

$$\frac{\partial z^2}{\partial y} = A_{21}(x,y)z^1 + A_{22}(x,y)z^2 + v^2(x,y)$$

with $v^1 \in U_y^{n_1}$, $v^2 \in U_x^{n_2}$, is proved. The assertion follows from the fact that if $B_1 \in U_y^{n_1 \times r_1}$, $B_2 \in U_x^{n_2 \times r_2}$ and $\frac{\partial B_1}{\partial y}$, $\frac{\partial B_2}{\partial x}$ are essentially bounded, then, for any $u^1 \in U_y^{r_1}$, $u^2 \in U_x^{r_2}$, the functions $B_1 u^1$, $B_2 u^2$ belong to $U_y^{n_1}$, $U_x^{n_2}$, respectively.

∎

9.2 CONTINUOUS DEPENDENCE OF SOLUTIONS ON CONTROLS

In the sequel we shall assume that the assumptions of theorem 9.1 are satisfied. We have

Theorem 9.2 *If the sequence $(u_n^1, u_n^2)_{n \in N}$ of controls tends in U to a control (u_0^1, u_0^2), then the sequence $(z_n^1, z_n^2)_{n \in N}$ of appropriate solutions to system (9.1) tends in AC to the solution (z_0^1, z_0^2), corresponding to the control (u_0^1, u_0^2).*

Proof: Let us fix a positive integer k and define an equivalent norm in $U_y^{n_1} \times U_x^{n_2}$

$$\|w\|_k = \left(\int_\Omega e^{-2k(x+y)} (|\nu^1(x,y)|^2 + |\nu^2(x,y)|^2) dx dy \right)^{\frac{1}{2}}$$

where $w(x,y) = (w^1(x,y), w^2(x,y))$ with components $w^1(x,y) = \int_0^y \nu^1(x,t)dt$ and $w^2(x,y) = \int_0^x \nu^2(s,y)ds$.

In (Idczak 1997) it is proved that the unique solution $(z_n^1, z_n^2) \in AC^{n_1} \times AC^{n_2}$ to system (9.1), corresponding to a control $(u_n^1, u_n^2) \in U_y^{r_1} \times U_x^{r_2}$, is given by

$$z_n^1(x,y) = \int_0^x w_n^1(s,y)ds,$$

$$z_n^2(x,y) = \int_0^y w_n^2(x,t)dt,$$

where (w_n^1, w_n^2) is a fixed point of the operator

$$S_{(u_n^1, u_n^2)} : U_y^{n_1} \times U_x^{n_2} \to U_y^{n_1} \times U_x^{n_2},$$

$$
\begin{aligned}
S_{(u_n^1, u_n^2)}(w^1, w^2) = {} & \left(A_{11}(x,y) \int_0^x w^1(s,y)ds + A_{12}(x,y) \int_0^y w^2(x,t)dt \right. \\
& + B_1(x,y)u_n^1(x,y), \\
& A_{21}(x,y) \int_0^x w^1(s,y)ds + A_{22}(x,y) \int_0^y w^2(x,t)dt \\
& \left. + B_2(x,y)u_n^2(x,y) \right).
\end{aligned}
$$

It is easy to check that there exist a positive integer k and a constant $0 < \alpha < 1$, such that

$$\left\| S_{(u_n^1, u_n^2)}(\overline{w}^1, \overline{w}^2) - S_{(u_n^1, u_n^2)}(\widetilde{w}^1, \widetilde{w}^2) \right\|_k \leq \alpha \left\| (\overline{w}^1, \overline{w}^2) - (\widetilde{w}^1, \widetilde{w}^2) \right\|_k$$

for $n = 0, 1, \dots$. So

$$
\begin{aligned}
\left\| (w_n^1, w_n^2) - (w_0^1, w_0^2) \right\|_k &= \left\| S_{(u_n^1, u_n^2)}(w_n^1, w_n^2) - S_{(u_0^1, u_0^2)}(w_0^1, w_0^2) \right\|_k \\
&\leq \left\| S_{(u_n^1, u_n^2)}(w_n^1, w_n^2) - S_{(u_n^1, u_n^2)}(w_0^1, w_0^2) \right\|_k \\
&\quad + \left\| S_{(u_n^1, u_n^2)}(w_0^1, w_0^2) - S_{(u_0^1, u_0^2)}(w_0^1, w_0^2) \right\|_k \\
&\leq \alpha \left\| (w_n^1, w_n^2) - (w_0^1, w_0^2) \right\|_k \\
&\quad + \left\| S_{(u_n^1, u_n^2)}(w_0^1, w_0^2) - S_{(u_0^1, u_0^2)}(w_0^1, w_0^2) \right\|_k .
\end{aligned}
$$

Consequently, we have

$$
\begin{aligned}
\left\| (z_n^1, z_n^2) - (z_0^1, z_0^2) \right\|_{AC} &= \left\| (w_n^1, w_n^2) - (w_0^1, w_0^2) \right\|_U \\
&\leq e^{2k} \left\| (w_n^1, w_n^2) - (w_0^1, w_0^2) \right\|_k \\
&\leq \frac{e^{2k}}{1 - \alpha} \left\| S_{(u_n^1, u_n^2)}(w_0^1, w_0^2) - S_{(u_0^1, u_0^2)}(w_0^1, w_0^2) \right\|_k \\
&\leq \frac{e^{2k}}{1 - \alpha} \left(\int_\Omega \left(\left| \frac{\partial}{\partial y}(B_1(x,y)(u_n^1(x,y) - u_0^1(x,y))) \right|^2 \right. \right. \\
&\qquad \left. \left. + \left| \frac{\partial}{\partial x}(B_2(x,y)(u_n^2(x,y) - u_0^2(x,y))) \right|^2 \right) dx dy \right)^{\frac{1}{2}} \\
&\leq \frac{e^{2k}}{1 - \alpha} \left(\int_\Omega \left(\left(\left| \frac{\partial B_1}{\partial y}(x,y)(u_n^1(x,y) - u_0^1(x,y)) \right| \right. \right. \right. \\
&\qquad \left. + \left| B_1(x,y) \left(\frac{\partial u_n^1}{\partial y}(x,y) - \frac{\partial u_0^1}{\partial y}(x,y) \right) \right| \right)^2 \\
&\qquad + \left(\left| \frac{\partial B_2}{\partial x}(x,y)(u_n^2(x,y) - u_0^2(x,y)) \right| \right. \\
&\qquad \left. \left. + \left| B_2(x,y) \left(\frac{\partial u_n^2}{\partial x}(x,y) - \frac{\partial u_0^2}{\partial x}(x,y) \right) \right| \right)^2 \right) dx dy \right)^{\frac{1}{2}}
\end{aligned}
$$

$$
\begin{aligned}
&\leq \frac{e^{2k}}{1 - \alpha} \left(\int_\Omega \left(M^2 \left(|u_n^1(x,y) - u_0^1(x,y)| + \left| \frac{\partial u_n^1}{\partial y}(x,y) - \frac{\partial u_0^1}{\partial y}(x,y) \right| \right)^2 \right. \right. \\
&\qquad \left. \left. + M^2 \left(|u_n^2(x,y) - u_0^2(x,y)| + \left| \frac{\partial u_n^2}{\partial x}(x,y) - \frac{\partial u_0^2}{\partial x}(x,y) \right| \right)^2 \right) dx dy \right)^{\frac{1}{2}} \\
&\leq \frac{2 M e^{2k}}{1 - \alpha} \left(\int_\Omega |u_n^1(x,y) - u_0^1(x,y)|^2 \, dx dy + \int_\Omega \left| \frac{\partial u_n^1}{\partial y}(x,y) - \frac{\partial u_0^1}{\partial y}(x,y) \right|^2 \, dx dy \right. \\
&\qquad \left. + \int_\Omega |u_n^2(x,y) - u_0^2(x,y)|^2 \, dx dy + \int_\Omega \left| \frac{\partial u_n^2}{\partial x}(x,y) - \frac{\partial u_0^2}{\partial x}(x,y) \right|^2 \, dx dy \right)^{\frac{1}{2}},
\end{aligned}
$$

where $M = \max\{$ ess sup B_1, ess sup B_2, ess sup $\frac{\partial B_1}{\partial y}$, ess sup $\frac{\partial B_2}{\partial x}\}$. Since
$\quad\quad\quad\quad\quad\Omega\quad\quad\quad\quad\Omega\quad\quad\quad\quad\Omega\quad\quad\quad\quad\quad\Omega$

$$\|u^1\|_{L^2(\Omega, R^{r_1})} \leq \|u^1\|_{U_y^{r_1}}, \ u^1 \in U_y^{r_1},$$
$$\|u^2\|_{L^2(\Omega, R^{r_2})} \leq \|u^2\|_{U_x^{r_2}}, \ u^2 \in U_x^{r_2},$$

therefore

$$\|(z_n^1, z_n^2) - (z_0^1, z_0^2)\|_{AC} \underset{n\to\infty}{\to} 0$$

and the proof is completed. ∎

9.3 EXISTENCE OF AN OPTIMAL SOLUTION

Now, let us fix a convex compact set $M \subset R^{r_1+r_2}$ and assume that the set

$$U_M^T = \{(u^1, u^2) \in U; \ (\frac{\partial u^1}{\partial y}(x, y), \frac{\partial u^2}{\partial x}(x, y)) \in M \text{ for } (x, y) \in \Omega \text{ a.e.},$$
$$(z_u^1(1, 1), z_u^2(1, 1)) = (P^1, P^2)\}$$

is not empty (some results concerning the controllability of autonomous system (9.1–9.2) were proved in (Idczak & Walczak 1995)).

Let us consider in U_M^T the following optimal control problem (S)

$$\frac{\partial z^1}{\partial x} = A_{11}(x, y)z^1 + A_{12}(x, y)z^2 + B_1(x, y)u^1$$
$$\frac{\partial z^2}{\partial y} = A_{21}(x, y)z^1 + A_{22}(x, y)z^2 + B_2(x, y)u^2,$$

$$z^i(\cdot, 0) = z^i(0, \cdot) = 0, \ i = 1, 2,$$
$$(z^1(1, 1), z^2(1, 1)) = (P^1, P^2),$$

$$J(u) = \int_\Omega f^0(x, y, z_u^1(x, y), z_u^1(x, y), \frac{\partial u^1}{\partial y}(x, y), \frac{\partial u^2}{\partial x}(x, y))dxdy \to \min.,$$

where $f^0 : \Omega \times R^{n_1+n_2} \times R^{r_1+r_2} \to R$ is such that

(A) there exists a constant $L > 0$ such that

$$\left|f^0(x, y, z, \mu) - f^0(x, y, w, \mu)\right| \leq L|z - w|$$

for $(x, y) \in \Omega, \ z, w \in R^{n_1+n_2}, \ \mu \in R^{r_1+r_2},$

(B) for any $z \in R^{n_1+n_2}, \mu \in R^{r_1+r_2}$, the function $f^0(\cdot, \cdot, z, \mu)$ is measurable on Ω; for any $z \in R^{n_1+n_2}, (x, y) \in \Omega$ a.e., the function $f^0(x, y, z, \cdot)$ is continuous on $R^{r_1+r_2}$; for $(x, y) \in \Omega$ a.e., the function $f^0(x, y, \cdot, \cdot)$ is convex on $R^{n_1+n_2} \times R^{r_1+r_2}$,

(C) there exist a function $a \in L^1(\Omega, R_0^+)$ and a constant $b > 0$, such that

$$\left| f^0(x, y, 0, \mu) \right| \leq a(x, y) + b \left| \mu \right|^2$$

for $(x, y) \in \Omega$ a.e., $\mu \in R^{r_1 + r_2}$.

From the assumptions made above it follows that the cost functional J is well defined. Moreover, we have

Theorem 9.3 *If $U_M^T \neq \emptyset$, the assumptions of theorem 9.1 are satisfied and conditions (A), (B), (C) hold, then the optimal control problem (S) possesses an optimal solution in U_M^T.*

In the proof of the above theorem we shall use the following classical result

Lemma 9.4 *Let V be a convex closed bounded subset of a reflexive Banach space. If the functional $J : V \to R$ is convex and lower semicontinuous on V, then there exists an element $u^* \in V$ such that*

$$J(u^*) \leq J(u)$$

for any $u \in V$.

Proof: It is easy to see that U_M^T is convex and bounded subset of the Hilbert space U.
Moreover, if $u_n \in U_M^T, n = 1, 2, ..., u_0 \in U$, are such that $u_n \underset{n \to \infty}{\to} u_0$ in U, then

$u_0 \in U_M^T$. Indeed, from the fact that $\left(\frac{\partial u_n^1}{\partial y}, \frac{\partial u_n^2}{\partial x} \right) \underset{n \to \infty}{\to} \left(\frac{\partial u_0^1}{\partial y}, \frac{\partial u_0^2}{\partial x} \right)$ in $L^2(\Omega, R^{r_1 + r_2})$, from

the closedness of the set $\{l \in L^2(\Omega, R^{r_1 + r_2}); l(x, y) \in M$ for $(x, y) \in \Omega$ a.e.$\}$ in $L^2(\Omega, R^{r_1 + r_2})$, from theorem 9.2 and the fact that convergence in AC imply the uniform convergence on Ω, it follows that $\left(\frac{\partial u_0^1}{\partial y}(x, y), \frac{\partial u_0^2}{\partial x}(x, y) \right) \in M$ for $(x, y) \in \Omega$ a.e. and $z_0^1(1, 1) = P^1, z_0^2(1, 1) = P^2$. So, $u_0 \in U_M^T$.
Convexity of the functional J follows from the linearity of system (9.1) and from the convexity of the function $f^0(x, y, \cdot, \cdot)$.
In view of lemma 9.4, to end the proof it suffices to show that J is lower semicontinuous on U_M^T.
From the assumptions (A),(B),(C) it follows that for any $(z, \mu) \in L^2(\Omega, R^{n_1 + n_2}) \times L^2(\Omega, R^{r_1 + r_2})$ the function $f^0(x, y, z(x, y), \mu(x, y))$ is integrable on Ω. As $f^0(x, y, z, \mu)$ is of Caratheodory type on $\Omega \times R^{n_1 + n_2 + r_1 + r_2}$ (this follows from (A) and (B)), therefore, from the theorem on the continuity of the Nemytskii operator, from theorem 9.2 and the fact that convergence in AC imply the convergence in $L^2(\Omega, R^{n_1 + n_2})$, we obtain the continuity of J on U_M^T.   ∎

REFERENCES

Idczak, D., 1995, Optimal control of a continuous n-D Roesser model, *Bull. Pol. Acad. Sci Tech. Sci.*, vol. 43, no.2, 227-234.

Idczak, D., 1996, The maximum principle for a continuous 2-D Roesser model with a terminal condition, *Proceedings of MMAR'96*, Międzyzdroje, 197-200.

Idczak, D., 1996, Necessary optimality conditions for a nonlinear continuous n-dimensional Roesser model, *Mathematics and Computers in Simulation*, 41, 87-94.

Idczak, D., 1997, Necessary optimality conditions for a nonlinear Roesser problem with a terminal condition, *A Proceedings Volume of the IFAC Workshop – Manufacturing Systems: Modelling, Management and Control*, Vienna, Austria, 197-202

Idczak, D., Walczak, S., 1995, On the controllability of continuous Roesser systems, *Proceedings of MMAR'95*, Międzyzdroje, 115-119.

Kaczorek, 1983, T., *Linear Control Systems, II*, Res. Stud. Press LTD. J. Wiley, New York.

Kaczorek, T., Klamka, J., 1987, Local controllability and minimum energy control of n-D linear systems, *Bull. Pol. Acad. Sci.: Sci. Tech.*, 35, 679-685.

Klamka, J., 1991, *Controllability of Dynamical Systems*, PWN-Kluwer Acad. Publ., Warszawa.

Kurek, J.E., 1984, Stabilities of 2-D linear discrete-time systems, *Preprints IFAC 9th World Congress*, Budapest, July 2-6, 150-154.

Pieczka, W., 1974, On the general solution of some partial differential equations in two-variables domain, *Demonstr. Math.*, 4, 451-461.

Roesser, R.P., 1975, A discrete state-space model for linear image processing, *IEEE Trans. Autom. Contr.*, AC-20, 1-10.

Walczak, S., 1988, On the existence of a solution for some systems of partial differential equations – necessary conditions for optimality, *Bull. Pol. Acad. Sci.: Math.*, 36, 375-384.

Wasiliew, F.P., 1981, *The Methods of Solving of Extremal Problems*, Moscow (in Russian).

PART THREE

Multidimensional Circuits and Signal Processing

This section contains theoretically and practically oriented papers on the applications of nD systems tools to circuits and signal processing.

Multidimensional (nD) circuits are clearly a subclass of multidimensional (nD) systems, differing from classic (1D) circuits in that the dynamics (input, output and state variables) depend on more than one indeterminate and hence information is propagated in many independent directions. The study of multidimensional circuits relates to the wide variety of nD systems applications, of both practical and theoretical interest.

The first significant work on nD systems appeared in the early 1960s in the general area of circuit analysis and synthesis, when it was shown that positive real functions of two or more variables could be used to describe circuits with variable parameters. Then the same approach was developed for application in the analysis and synthesis of networks of transmission lines and lumped reactances, which was of particular interest to electrical and telecommunication engineers studying high frequency networks (microwaves). The use of this theory in studying transmission lines also suggested that it may be applicable to systems with delays.

Another field for nD systems theory, where nD circuits have found significant application is processes modelled by partial differential and/or difference equations. For example, the prominent idea by Fettweis of so-called wave filters turned out to be easily extendible into the nD case and has been fruitfully implemented for the modelling and numerical integration of a class of partial differential equations.

As in the case of classic (1D) circuits, multidimensional (nD) circuits are represented by currents and voltages, which however now are functions of several independent variables. The classical Kirchoff laws are still valid, i.e.

1. The sum of currents in every circuit vertex is zero, and

2. The sum of voltages in every circuit loop is also zero.

The standard steady state notion and symbolic approach enables us to introduce several symbolic frequency variables and, hence, several types of reactance elements related to various complex frequencies. The generalisation of the Laplace or 'z'-transform provides in effect, the transfer function apparatus, which however now uses multivariate rational functions (matrices). Finally, a state-space description of circuits was also derived and is being successfully applied.

Another huge area of possible applications of nD systems and circuits theory, of interest in its own right, is multidimensional (nD) signal/ image processing. In 1D signal processing, the term '1D' refers to the independent variable of which the measured signals are a function. By far the most common case encountered in such signal processing has time as the independent variable. There are, however, a range of nD signal processing problems with more than one independent variable and also these problems need not necessarily involve time as an independent variable. A standard example of 2D signal processing is the restoration of photographic images, and other examples include scanning radar systems, seismology, tomography, and the study of crop treatments in agriculture/ horticulture.

The standard type of signal processing operations required on 2D data from applications such as those listed above (and, more generally, on nD data) can be classified as either filtering or prediction, e.g. image restoration, which requires 2D algorithms which are the equivalent of 1D smoothers and filters. A fundamental question to ask is 'what makes 2D/nD signal processing different from 1D'? The answer is (as in other areas) that it is computationally much more demanding and algorithmically complex.

The contributions to this section on circuits and signal processing are as follows. The first paper is by S. Basu (IBM), who studies the structure of the linear phase perfect reconstruction subclass of multidimensional filter banks. Next, P. Bauer, (Notre Dame, USA) considers the numerical features of discrete multidimensional systems derived by applying the delta type discretization.

The following paper, by A. Aksen and B. S. Yarman (Isik University, Turkey), is devoted to the modelling and processing of systems described by partial differential equations, using nD circuit theory. The authors propose an original method for the synthesis of 2D networks of lumped elements and transmission lines.

The last group of three papers, supplied by F. Boschen, A. Kummert, H. Herzog and W. Zeise (Wuppertal/ Research Centre Jülich KFA, Germany) consist of various aspects of practically motivated nD signal/ image processing. The application areas studied are respectively positron emission tomography, inspection of railroad lines, and virtual environment creation.

CHAPTER TEN

On the Structure of Linear Phase Perfect Reconstruction Quincunx Filter Banks

Sankar Basu

IBM Thomas J. Watson Research Center
Yorktown Heights, USA
sankar@watson.ibm.com

Supported by NSF grant MIP 9696176

Abstract

The paper is motivated by the desire to extend the notion of Quillen-Suslin (Lam 1978) type result on the unimodular completion of polynomial matrices to the context of multi-dimensional finite impulse response (FIR) linear phase (LP) perfect reconstruction (PR) filter bank design. The specific problem is to construct a multidimensional linear phase PR filter bank, given a subset, say, one of the filters of the filter bank. In filter bank terminology, given one of the filters satisfying the linear phase property (and the property that its analysis polyphase components do not have any finite common zero set) the problem is to complete the linear phase filter bank. If linear phase property is not desired, the construction of the PR filter bank follows almost trivially via an application of the Quillen-Suslin theorem. However, since the linear phase property of the filter bank dictates certain symmetries, the matrix completion problem becomes somewhat more constrained. We only deal with the case of the so called quincunx sub-sampling in the two-dimensional (2D) case, and show that in this simple case, Quillen-Suslin type result indeed holds true with the additional linear phase constraint. While the result was previously announced in (Basu 1998) proofs have not appeared in the open literature.

10.1 INTRODUCTION

We begin by considering a multidimensional (k-D) subband coding scheme. We shall follow the notation from standard literature as in (Basu 1998, Vaidyanathan 1992). Associated with each such scheme there is a decimation matrix $\mathbf{M}$ of size $k \times k$. We shall also need to consider a number of parameters associated with $\mathbf{M}$. First, note that $\det \mathbf{M}$ is the ratio of sampling densities of the original signal and the sub-sampled signal, and thus, for critically sampled signals, must be equal to the number of channels m in the subband coding scheme i.e., we have $m = |\det D|$. We also need to consider the lattice $\{\sum_{i=0}^{k} \mu_i \mathbf{u}_i; \ \mu_i \text{ are integers}\}$ generated by $\mathbf{M}$, where $\mathbf{u}_i$'s are the columns of the matrix $\mathbf{M}$ and the unit cell associated with $\mathbf{M}$ defined as $\mathcal{UC}(\mathbf{M}) = \{\sum_{i=0}^{k} \lambda_i \mathbf{u}_i; \ \lambda_i \in [0, 1)\}$.

We use the notation $\mathbf{z}$ for the k-tuple $(z_1, z_2, \cdots z_k)$. By following standard practice in the multidimensional subband coding literature we shall also use $\mathbf{z}^\kappa$, where $\kappa = [\kappa_1, \kappa_2, \cdots \kappa_k]^T$ is an integer column vector to denote the monomial $z_1^{\kappa_1} z_2^{\kappa_2} \cdots z_k^{\kappa_k}$, and the notation $\mathbf{z}^M$ to denote the k-tuple of monomials $(\mathbf{z}^{u_1}, \mathbf{z}^{u_2}, \cdots \mathbf{z}^{u_k})$.

Note that the analysis filters $H_i(\mathbf{z})$, $i = 0, 1, \cdots (m-1)$ and the synthesis filters $G_i(\mathbf{z})$, $i = 0, 1, \cdots (m-1)$ in the filter bank can be decomposed into their polyphase components as :

$$H_i(\mathbf{z}) = \sum_{j=0}^{m-1} \mathbf{z}^{\kappa_j} \mathbf{H_{ij}}(\mathbf{z}^M); \quad \mathbf{G_i}(\mathbf{z}) = \sum_{j=0}^{m-1} \mathbf{z}^{\kappa_j} \mathbf{G_{ij}}(\mathbf{z}^M) \quad (10.1)$$

where the κ_i's belong to $\mathcal{UC}(M)$. The filter bank is said to satisfy the perfect reconstruction (PR) condition (i.e., the reconstructed signal is identical to the original signal except possibly for a delay) if:

$$\mathbf{H}(\mathbf{z})\mathbf{G}(\mathbf{z}) = \mathbf{I} \cdot \mathbf{z}^N \quad (10.2)$$

where the matrices $\mathbf{H}$, $\mathbf{G}$ given as follows

$$\mathbf{H} = \begin{bmatrix} H_{00} & H_{01} & \cdots & H_{0(m-1)} \\ H_{10} & H_{11} & \cdots & H_{1(m-1)} \\ \vdots & \vdots & \ddots & \vdots \\ H_{(m-1)0} & H_{(m-1)1} & \cdots & H_{(m-1),(m-1)} \end{bmatrix} \quad (10.3)$$

$$\mathbf{G} = \begin{bmatrix} G_{0(m-1)} & G_{1(m-1)} & \cdots & G_{(m-1),(m-1)} \\ G_{0(m-2)} & G_{1(m-2)} & \cdots & G_{(m-1),(m-2)} \\ \vdots & \vdots & \ddots & \vdots \\ G_{00} & G_{10} & \cdots & G_{(m-1)0} \end{bmatrix} \quad (10.4)$$

are the so called polyphase matrices (Vaidyanathan 1992) associated with the analysis and synthesis bank respectively, and where $\mathbf{N}$ is a fixed k-tuple of non-negative integers. We shall only be concerned with finite impulse response (FIR) filters i.e., when the filter $H_k(\mathbf{z})$ and $G_k(\mathbf{z})$ are polynomials in the variables $\mathbf{z}$. Clearly, the condition for PR in (10.2) is equivalent to

$$\det \mathbf{H}(\mathbf{z}) = \mathbf{z}^{\mathbf{p}^T}, \quad (10.5)$$

where $\mathbf{p}$ is a non-negative integer vector. With slight abuse of notation we also write $\mathbf{H}(\mathbf{w}) = \mathbf{H}(e^{j\mathbf{w}})$, where $\mathbf{w} = (\omega_1, \omega_2, \cdots, \omega_k)$ has the interpretation of multidimensional frequency (or wavenumber) variable. If filter H_k has the *linear phase property* then by definition it satisfies $H_k(\mathbf{w}) = \pm e^{j\mathbf{w}\mathbf{n}_k^T} H_k(-\mathbf{w})$, or equivalently,

$$H_k(\mathbf{z}) = \pm \mathbf{z}^{\mathbf{n}_k^T} H_k(\mathbf{z}^{-1}) \quad (10.6)$$

for some integer vector $\mathbf{n_k}$. We say that the filter H_k is of index $\mathbf{n_k}$. Note that index generalizes the notion of degree of the polynomial (i.e., FIR filter) H_k, and is the same as the degree of the filter if H_k does not have any monomial factor. We say that the filter bank is LP if all filters H_k, $i = 0, 2, \cdots (m-1)$ in the filter bank has the LP property. If for some integer row vector $\mathbf{m_k}$, we have $\mathbf{n_k^T} = M\mathbf{m_k^T} + \mathbf{k}_\ell^T$; $\mathbf{k}_\ell^T \in \mathcal{U}(M)$ for all filters $k = 0, 1 \ldots m-1$ belonging to the filter bank then, we say that the filter bank is of *type* $\mathbf{k}_\ell$.

The condition for LP in terms of polyphase matrices is given by (Basu 1998):

$$\mathbf{H}(\mathbf{wM}) = D \cdot \Omega_{\mathbf{n}_k} \cdot \mathbf{H}(-\mathbf{wM}) \cdot \mathcal{W}(-\mathbf{w}) \cdot \Delta_l \cdot \mathcal{W}(-\mathbf{w}) \tag{10.7}$$

where $\Delta_l = \frac{1}{m} \mathcal{W}_d^* \cdot \mathcal{L} \cdot \mathcal{W}_d^*$, $\mathcal{W}_d$ is the multidimensional DFT matrix with respect to sampling $\mathbf{M}$ and

$$\mathcal{W}(\mathbf{w}) = Diag[1, \quad e^{j\mathbf{w}\mathbf{k}_1^T}, \quad \cdots \quad , e^{j\mathbf{w}\mathbf{k}_{m-1}^T}]$$

$$\Omega_{\mathbf{n}_k} = Diag[e^{j\mathbf{w}\mathbf{n}_0^T}, \quad e^{j\mathbf{w}\mathbf{n}_1^T}, \quad \cdots, \quad e^{j\mathbf{w}\mathbf{n}_{m-1}^T}]$$

Here, the determinant of Δ_l is 1 or -1 depending on $\mathbf{k}_l$, and the matrix D is a diagonal matrix with ± 1 entries on the diagonal. Further restrictions on the indices of filters arising from (10.7) will be elaborated upon in the following section. Essentially, (10.7) reflects certain *column symmetries* in the matrix $\mathbf{H}$. Given this setup, the following problem was posed in (Basu 1998) in the spirit of Quillen-Suslin theorem (Lam 1978, Vidyasagar 1985, Youla & Pickel 1984):

Given one of the filters with its polyphase components having no common zeros (i.e., the first row of the matrix $\mathbf{H}$ such that the row does not vanish for any $\mathbf{z}$) except possibly at $\mathbf{z} = 0$, find the matrix $\mathbf{H}$ such that the condition (10.5) for PR is satisfied and, in addition, $\mathbf{H}$ satisfies the linear phase condition (10.7).

Without the symmetry requirement, a solution is ensured by Quillen-Suslin theorem (we refer to (Vidyasagar 1985, Youla & Pickel 1984) for a system theoretic exposition). While it can be conjectured that the answer to the question is positive, we provide a proof here only for the case when the subsampling matrix $\mathbf{M}$ is of the quincunx type (more on it later). For a complete solution, however, further detailed study is warranted.

The main goal of this paper is to provide the aforementioned proof of the claim made in (Basu 1998) and other facts stated without proof in (Basu 1998). We start with some preliminaries and then go on to the case of quincunx filter banks. For general discussion of filter banks the reader may be referred to the standard literature (Vaidyanathan 1992, Vetterli & Kovacevic 1995). For further discussion on multidimensional filter banks in general, we refer to (Basu 1998, Kalker & Shah 1998, Kovacevic & Vetterli 1992, Vaidyanathan 1992).

10.2 SOME PRELIMINARIES

The linear phase property together with the PR property imposes certain restrictions on the degrees of the multidimensional filter bank as well as on the admissible number of symmetric and antisymmetric filters. We enumerate these restrictions in the following for the sake of completeness, first for an arbitrary subsampling matrix $\mathbf{M}$ and then for the specific case of quincunx subsampling of interest in this paper.

Fact 10.1 *Let the condition (10.2) for the filter bank to have the PR property be expressed as* $\det \mathbf{H}(\mathbf{w}) = e^{j\mathbf{w}\mathbf{p}^T}$, *in which* $\mathbf{p}$ *is a nonnegative integer vector.*

If filters satisfy the condition for LP then the following necessarily holds true

$$\sum_{i=0}^{m-1} \mathbf{n}_i^T = 2(\mathbf{M}\mathbf{p}^T + \sum_{i=0}^{m-1} \mathbf{k}_i^T) \tag{10.8}$$

The number of symmetric and antisymmetric filters can be determined from the matrix D. However, a more explicit characterization is as follows.

Fact 10.2

1. *If m is odd, the number of symmetric filters exceed the number of antisymmetric filters by one for all k_l.*

2. *If m is even, then in the 2D case, the number of symmetric filters exceeds the number of antisymmetric filters by 0 or 2 or 4. To this end, similar, but more involved, statements can be made for k-D case in general.*

10.2.1 The case of quincunx filter banks:

We now consider the case of quincunx sampling, i.e. when the decimation matrix is given by

$$\mathbf{M} = \begin{bmatrix} 1 & 1 \\ 1 & -1 \end{bmatrix}$$

Then, since the size of $\mathbf{M}$ is (2×2), and $|\det \mathbf{M}| = 2$ the filter bank corresponds to 2D and 2-band. Let the two integer vectors $\mathbf{k}_0$, $\mathbf{k}_1$ in $\mathcal{UC}(\mathbf{M})$ describing the filter type be as $\mathbf{k}_0 = (0,0)$, $\mathbf{k}_1 = (1,0)$. Furthermore, let the integer vectors denoting the indices of analysis filters be $\text{Ind}(H_0) = \mathbf{n}_0 = (n_{00}, n_{01})$ and $\text{Ind}(H_1) = \mathbf{n}_1 = (n_{10}, n_{11})$.

Each of the analysis filters $H_k(z)$; $i = 0, 1$ can be uniquely decomposed into its polyphase components as in (10.1). More specifically,

$$H_k(\mathbf{z}) = \mathbf{z}^{\mathbf{k}_0^T} H_{k,0}(\mathbf{z}^{\mathbf{M}}) + \mathbf{z}^{\mathbf{k}_1^T} H_{k,1}(\mathbf{z}^{\mathbf{M}}) \tag{10.9}$$

where $\mathbf{z}^{\mathbf{M}} = (z_1 z_2, z_1 z_2^{-1})$. Thus, the respective polyphase components are given by

$$H_{k,0}(\mathbf{z}^{\mathbf{M}}) = \frac{1}{2}(H_k(\mathbf{z}) + H_k(-\mathbf{z})); \quad H_{k,1}(\mathbf{z}^{\mathbf{M}}) = \frac{1}{2z_1}(H_k(\mathbf{z}) - H_k(-\mathbf{z})) \tag{10.10}$$

where the obvious notation $\pm \mathbf{z} = (\pm z_1, \pm z_2)$ has been used.

10.2.2 Condition for perfect reconstruction:

Clearly, the condition for PR in (10.5), in this particular case, is equivalent to

$$H_{00}(\mathbf{z})H_{11}(\mathbf{z}) - H_{01}(\mathbf{z})H_{10}(\mathbf{z}) = \mathbf{z}^{\mathbf{p}^T} \tag{10.11}$$

where $\mathbf{p}$ is an integer vector. Given one of the analysis filters, say $H_0(\mathbf{z})$, if its polyphase component pair, say $\{H_0(\mathbf{z}), H_1(\mathbf{z})\}$, have common zeros at (α, β) for $\alpha \neq 0$ and/or $\beta \neq 0$, then (10.11) cannot be satisfied. More generally, we have the following:

Fact 10.3 *The polyphase components of $H_0(\mathbf{z})$ do not have any common zero except possibly for $(z_1, z_2) = (0, \gamma)$ or $(\gamma, 0)$, if and only if there does not exist $\alpha \neq 0$ and/or $\beta \neq 0$ such that $H_0(\alpha, \beta) = H_0(-\alpha, -\beta) = 0$.*

Proof: Sufficiency: Suppose that $H_0(\alpha, \beta) = H_0(-\alpha, -\beta) = 0$ for $\alpha \neq 0$ and/or $\beta \neq 0$. Then, from (10.9) we easily show that $H_{00}(\alpha', \beta') = H_{01}(\alpha', \beta') = 0$ where $\alpha' = \alpha\beta \neq 0$ and/or $\beta' = \alpha/\beta \neq 0$.

Necessity: Suppose that $H_{00}(\alpha, \beta) = H_{01}(\alpha, \beta) = 0$ for $\alpha \neq 0$ and/or $\beta \neq 0$. Then, from (10.10) we can show that $H_0(\alpha', \beta') = H_0(-\alpha', -\beta') = 0$ where $\alpha' = \sqrt{\alpha\beta} \neq 0$ and/or $\beta' = \sqrt{\alpha/\beta} \neq 0$.   ∎

10.2.3 Condition for linear phase

The polyphase components of a (anti)symmetric filter are self- or cross-symmetric depending on the filter type. More specifically, we have the following. Let the filter symmetry be described by (10.6) its polyphase components are related as follows:

Property 10.4 *Let the filter bank be of type $k_0 = (0,0)$, and index of the k-th filter in the filter bank can be expressed as $n_k = m_k \cdot M^T + k_0$ where m_k is an integer vector. Then polyphase components of each filter in the filter bank is self-(anti)symmetric as described by:*

$$H_{k,0}(z) = \pm z^{m_k^T} H_{k,0}(z^{-1}); \quad H_{k,1}(z) = \pm z^{(m_k-(1,1))^T} H_{k,1}(z^{-1}) \qquad (10.12)$$

Proof: Combining (10.6) and (10.9) we obtain

$$H_k(z) = \pm(z^{n_k^T} H_{k,0}(z^{-M}) + z^{(n_k-k_1)^T} H_{k,1}(z^{-M}))$$

We substitute the identity $-k_1 = -(1,1) \cdot M^T + k_1$ into the above equation, and subtract (10.9) from the above equation, and obtain

$$\{H_{k,0}(z^M) \mp z^{M \cdot m_k^T} H_{k,0}(z^{-M})\} + z^{k_1} \{H_{k,1}(z^M) \mp z^{M \cdot (m_k-(1,1))^T} H_{k,1}(z^{-M})\} = 0$$

The last equation implies that each of the braced term must be equal to zero. Thus, we have the desired result. ∎

Property 10.5 *Let the filter bank be of type $k_1 = (1,0)$, and index of the k-th filter in the filter bank can be expressed as $n_k = m_k \cdot M^T + k_0$ where m_k is an integer vector. Then polyphase components of each filter in the filter bank are cross-(anti)symmetric as described by:*

$$H_{k,0}(z) = \pm z^{m_k^T} H_{k,1}(z^{-1}) \qquad (10.13)$$

Proof: Proof is similar to Property 10.4. ∎

In fact, it is easily seen that Property 10.4 and 10.5 are equivalent to the condition for LP given in (10.7).

10.2.4 LP and PR quincunx filter banks:

The following two results must hold in LP and PR filter banks. Proofs can be found from Fact 10.1 and Fact 10.2.

Corollary 10.6 *In LP and PR quincunx filter banks, the number of symmetric and anti-symmetric filters are determined as:*

1. *If the filter bank is of type $k_0 = (0,0)$, then both filters are symmetric.*

2. *If the filter bank is of type $k_1 = (1,0)$, then one filter is symmetric and the other filter is antisymmetric.*

Admissible index constraints

As stated earlier, there exists constraints on admissible values of indices arising both from the PR and LP property. In this vein, the following is immediate from (10.1).

Corollary 10.7 *In LP and PR quincunx filter banks, the sum of indices $\mathbf{n}_0$ and $\mathbf{n}_1$ of the two analysis filters satisfy the following relation:*

$$\mathbf{n}_0 + \mathbf{n}_1 = 2(\mathbf{p} \cdot \mathbf{M}^T + \mathbf{k}_0 + \mathbf{k}_1) \tag{10.14}$$

where $\mathbf{p}$ is an integer vector.

Next, let $\mathbf{n}_k = (n_{k,0}, n_{k,1})$ for $k = 0, 1$. Recalling that $\mathbf{n}_k = \mathbf{m}_k \mathbf{M}^T + \mathbf{k}_\ell$, we have

$$n_{k,0} + n_{k,1} = \begin{cases} \mathbf{m}_k \begin{bmatrix} 2 & 0 \end{bmatrix}^T & \text{if } \mathbf{k}_\ell = \mathbf{k}_0 \\ \mathbf{m}_k \begin{bmatrix} 2 & 0 \end{bmatrix}^T + 1 & \text{if } \mathbf{k}_\ell = \mathbf{k}_1 \end{cases} \tag{10.15}$$

Thus, in view of (10.15), if the filter bank is of type $\mathbf{k}_0$ then sum indices of each filter is necessarily even resulting in the conclusion that either both $n_{k,0}$ and $n_{k,1}$ are even or odd. However, as shown below the latter case must be excluded by the PR property.

Fact 10.8 *If the filter bank is of type $\mathbf{k}_0 = (0,0)$, then indices each filter i.e, $n_{k,0}$ and $n_{k,1}$ for $k = 0, 1$ are necessarily even for perfect reconstruction to be satisfied.*

Proof: In view of the discussion preceding the statement of the fact, we only need to exclude the case that both $n_{k,0}$ and $n_{k,1}$ are odd. For contradiction we assume this to be the case and expand $H_k(z_1, z_2)$ as a polynomial in z_2:

$$H_k(z_1, z_2) = \sum_{i=0}^{n_{k,1}} h_i(z_1) z_2^i \tag{10.16}$$

Due to the symmetry of $H_k(z_1, z_2)$, the coefficients $h_i(z_1)$ are symmetric as well. Thus, $h_i(1) = h_{n_{k,1}-i}(1)$. Substituting $(z_1, z_2) = (1, -1)$ in (10.16) we have $H_k(1, -1) = \sum_{i=0}^{n_{k,1}} h_i(1)(-1)^i$ or alternatively,

$$H_k(1, -1) = \sum_{i=0}^{n_{k,1}} h_{n_{k,1}-i}(1)(-1)^{n_{k,1}-i}.$$

Adding the last two expressions and, subsequently, using the fact that $h_i(1) = h_{n_{k,1}-i}(1)$ we arrive at

$$H_k(1, -1) = \frac{1}{2} \sum_{i=0}^{n_{k,2}} h_i(1)(-1)^i [1 + (-1)^{n_{k,1}-2i}] = 0$$

due to odd character of $n_{k,1}$. It can also be shown in a similar manner that $H_k(-1, 1) = 0$. However, in view of Fact 10.3 this latter situation violates the necessary condition for PR that the polyphase components may not have a common zero for nonzero z_1 and z_2. ∎

If the filter bank is of type $\mathbf{k}_1$ then, in view of (10.15), it is necessary that $n_{k,0} + n_{k,1}$ is odd. Thus, there are four cases such that when n_{00} and n_{01} are even(odd) and odd(even). However, as show below, two of these four cases are eliminated by the PR condition.

Fact 10.9 *If the filter bank is of type $\mathbf{k}_1$, then that the sum of (partial) indices of corresponding variables of the two filters i.e., $n_{0,k} + n_{1,k}$ for $k = 0, 1$ must be necessarily even for PR to hold.*

Proof: Suppose $n_{0,k} + n_{1,k} = $ odd. Since in view of (10.6) two analysis filters have different symmetry, we assume without loss of generality that $H_0(\mathbf{z})$ is symmetric and $H_1(\mathbf{z})$ is antisymmetric. From Property 10.5, their polyphase components are related as

$$H_{00}(\mathbf{z}^M) = z_1^{n_{00}-1} z_2^{n_{01}} H_{01}(\mathbf{z}^M); \quad H_{10}(\mathbf{z}^M) = -z_1^{n_{10}-1} z_2^{n_{11}} H_{11}(\mathbf{z}^M)$$

Then, by substituting $(z_1, z_2) = (1, -1)$ into the above equations, the determinant of the polyphase matrix becomes

$$\det \mathbf{H}(-1, -1) = (-1)^{n_{01}} H_{00}(-1, -1) H_{11}(-1, -1)[1 - (-1)^{n_{01}+n_{11}+1}]$$

Our hypothesis that $n_{0,k} + n_{1,k} = $ odd, then yields that the polyphase matrix $\mathbf{H}(\mathbf{z}^M)$ is singular at $(z_1, z_2) = (1, -1)$, thus violating the PR property (10.5). ∎

A summary of admissible indices of the filters appeared in tabular form in (Basu 1998).

10.2.5 Some interesting special cases

Starting from a given analysis LP filter, say, $H_0(\mathbf{z})$, we want to find the complementary filter $H_1(\mathbf{z})$ such that the associated polyphase matrix satisfies the condition for PR as well as the condition for LP. In other words, the polyphase matrix must have a monomial determinant, and its elements (i.e., polyphase components) satisfy either (10.12) or (10.13) as the case may be.

As mentioned in Fact 10.3, given $H_0(\mathbf{z})$ it is necessary for PR that the polyphase components of $H_0(\mathbf{z})$ do not have any common zero except possibly of the type $(z_1, z_2) = (0, \gamma)$, or $(z_1, z_2) = (\gamma, 0)$ where γ is a constant. However, it is difficult to satisfy this requirement due to the fact that in k-D, arbitrarily chosen k polynomials in k variables almost always have common zeros. Thus, in the quincunx case, for arbitrarily given $H_0(\mathbf{z})$ the two polyphase components of $H_0(\mathbf{z})$ almost always have common zeros. However, as illustrated in the following, one can identify at least two distinct scenarios when the desirable zero-coprime pairs of polyphase components can be deliberately generated. See (Basu 1998, Basu 1999) for more details.

McClellan transformation

Consider the following 1D zero phase filter

$$H_0^{(1)}(z) = \sum_{k=0}^{n} h_k \left(\frac{z + z^{-1}}{2}\right)^k \tag{10.17}$$

A 2D zero phase filter is obtained by replacing $(z + z^{-1})/2$ by $(z_1 + z_1^{-1} + z_2 + z_2^{-1})/4$ in (10.17), replacing h_k by $4^k a_k$ and multiplying by $(z_1 z_2)^n$ as:

$$H_0(z_1, z_2) = \sum_{k=0}^{n} a_k (z_1 z_2)^{n-k} \{(z_1 + z_2)(1 + z_1 z_2)\}^k \qquad (10.18)$$

Thus, if the pair $\{H_0^{(1)}(z), H_0^{(1)}(-z)\}$ is zero co-prime, then the pair $\{H_0(\mathbf{z}), H_0(-\mathbf{z})\}$ may have common zeros only at $(z_1, z_2) = (0, 0)$, satisfying the otherwise stringent requirement that polyphase components of $H_0(\mathbf{z})$ may not have common zeros except possibly at $\mathbf{z} = 0$. Note that a 2D FIR filter obtained by McClellan transformation necessarily belongs to the type $\mathbf{k}_0 = (0, 0)$.

One of the polyphase components is monomial

Suppose that one of the polyphase components is a monomial. Then, two polyphase components obviously do not have any common zero except for $(z_1, z_2) = (0, \gamma)$, or $(\gamma, 0)$ for some γ. Such filters of the type $\mathbf{k}_1$ have the property that both polyphase components are monomials, because they must form a cross-symmetric pair (see Property 10.4). Thus, again the more interesting case is when the filters are of the type $\mathbf{k}_0$.

10.3   LINEAR PHASE FILTER BANK COMPLETION

Next, we consider the main result of the paper, and propose a method for obtaining the entire LP PR filter banks from the given symmetric (and, therefore, linear phase) $H_0(\mathbf{z})$. This is the Quillen-Suslin type filter bank completion problem in the context of quincunx subsampling. Numerical examples demonstrating the procedure have appeared in (Basu 1998). Consider first two 2D polynomials $A(z_1, z_2)$ and $B(z_1, z_2)$:

$$\begin{aligned} A(z_1, z_2) &= \sum_{k=0}^{n} a_k(z_1) z_2^k = \sum_{k=0}^{n'} a_k'(z_2) z_1^k \\ B(z_1, z_2) &= \sum_{k=0}^{m} b_k(z_1) z_2^k = \sum_{k=0}^{m'} b_k'(z_2) z_1^k \end{aligned} \qquad (10.19)$$

Then, the z_1-*resultant matrix* of $\mathbf{R}_{n+m}[A, B](z_1)$ of $A(z_1, z_2)$ and $B(z_1, z_2)$, or simply $\mathbf{R}_{n+m}(z_1)$, is defined as (Bose 1982, Kailath 1980).

$$\mathbf{R}_{n+m}(z_1) = \begin{bmatrix} a_0 & 0 & \cdots & 0 & b_0 & 0 & \cdots & 0 \\ a_1 & a_0 & \cdots & 0 & b_1 & b_0 & \cdots & 0 \\ a_2 & a_1 & \cdots & 0 & b_2 & b_1 & \cdots & 0 \\ \vdots & \vdots & & \vdots & \vdots & \vdots & & \vdots \\ a_{n-1} & a_{n-2} & \cdots & a_0 & b_{m-1} & b_{m-2} & \cdots & b_0 \\ a_n & a_{n-1} & \cdots & a_1 & b_m & b_{m-1} & \cdots & b_1 \\ \vdots & \vdots & & \vdots & \vdots & \vdots & & \vdots \\ 0 & 0 & \cdots & a_n & 0 & 0 & \cdots & b_m \end{bmatrix} \qquad (10.20)$$

where the top braces label the first block of columns as m and the second block as n.

The z_2-resultant matrix $\mathbf{R}_{n'+m'}(z_2)$ is defined in an analogous manner. Furthermore, in our terminology, *resultant* of A and B is the determinant of resultant matrix of A and B. The following is well known (Bose 1982).

Theorem 10.10 *Two 2D polynomials $A(z_1, z_2)$ and $B(z_1, z_2)$ have common zeros at a point $(z_1, z_2) = (\alpha_i, \beta_i)$ for $i = 0, \cdots, k$, if and only if all zeros of z_1-resultant (or z_2-resultant) are $z_1 = \alpha_i$ (or $z_2 = \beta_i$) for $i = 0, \cdots, k$.*

An immediate corollary to this Theorem 10.10 is that if $A(z_1, z_2)$ and $B(z_1, z_2)$ do not have any common zeros except for $(z_1, z_2) = (0, 0)$, then the resultants associated with them must be monomials.

Let us define even and odd parts of $H_0(z_1, z_2)$ as:

$$H_0^e(\mathbf{z}) = H_{00}(\mathbf{z^M}); \quad H_0^o(\mathbf{z}) = z_1 H_{01}(\mathbf{z^M}) \tag{10.21}$$

Thus, in view of (10.10) we have that $H_0(\mathbf{z}) = H_0^e(\mathbf{z}) + H_0^o(\mathbf{z})$, $H_0^e(\mathbf{z})$ and $H_0^o(\mathbf{z})$ are polynomials in $\mathbf{z}$, and furthermore, if $H_0(\mathbf{z})$ and $H_0(-\mathbf{z})$ do not have any common zero except for $(z_1, z_2) = (0, 0)$, then $H_0^e(\mathbf{z})$ and $H_0^o(\mathbf{z})$ do not have any common zero except for $(z_1, z_2) = (0, 0)$, which, in turn, implies that the resultant of $H_0^e(\mathbf{z})$ and $H_0^o(\mathbf{z})$ is a monomial. The condition for PR given in (10.11) can be rewritten in terms of the even and odd parts as follows:

$$H_0^e(\mathbf{z})H_1^o(\mathbf{z}) - H_0^o(\mathbf{z})H_1^e(\mathbf{z}) = z_1^{l_1} z_2^{l_2} \tag{10.22}$$

where $l_k = (n_{0,k} + n_{1,k})/2$ and $\text{Ind}(H_k) = (n_{k,0}, n_{k,1})$ for $k = 0, 1$.

We first find two different filters $H_1^{(0)}(\mathbf{z})$ and $H_1^{(1)}(\mathbf{z})$ each of which are complementary to $H_0(\mathbf{z})$. It is not necessary for the complementary filters $H_1^{(i)}(\mathbf{z})$ to be linear phase, but the even and odd parts of each pair $\{H_0, H_1^{(0)}\}$ and $\{H_0, H_1^{(1)}\}$ must satisfy (10.22). Then, as shown later, a linear phase $H_1(\mathbf{z})$ satisfying (10.22) can be obtained by adding the two solutions just mentioned.

Let us further express the even and odd parts of $H_0(\mathbf{z})$ in (10.21) as:

$$H_0^e(z_1, z_2) = \sum_{k=0}^{n_{01}} a_k(z_1) z_2^k, \quad H_0^o(z_1, z_2) = \sum_{k=0}^{n_{01}} b_k(z_1) z_2^k \tag{10.23}$$

10.3.1 Filter banks of type $\mathbf{k}_0 = (0, 0)$

Due to Corollary 10.6, $H_0(\mathbf{z})$ is symmetric, and due to Property 10.5 the even and odd parts of $H_0(\mathbf{z})$, namely, $H_0^e(\mathbf{z})$ and $H_0^o(\mathbf{z})$ are symmetric as well. This yields,

$$a_k(z_1) = z_1^{n_{00}} a_{n_{01}-k}(z_1^{-1}), \quad b_k(z_1) = z_1^{n_{00}} b_{n_{01}-k}(z_1^{-1}) \tag{10.24}$$

Using the symmetry exhibited in (10.24), we can show that the resultant matrix $\mathbf{R}_{2n_{01}}(z_1)$ (see (10.20) associated with $H_0^e(z_1, z_2)$ and $H_0^o(z_1, z_2)$ in (10.23) also satisfy a certain symmetry as expressed in the following.

$$\mathbf{R}_{2n_{01}}(z_1) = z_1^{n_{00}} \mathbf{J}_{2n_{01}} \cdot \mathbf{R}_{2n_{01}}(z_1^{-1}) \cdot \begin{bmatrix} \mathbf{J}_{n_{01}} & 0 \\ 0 & \mathbf{J}_{n_{01}} \end{bmatrix} \tag{10.25}$$

where $\mathbf{J}_n$ is the skew identity matrix of size $(n \times n)$.

First solution $H_1^{(0)}(z_1, z_2)$

We assume that the degree of $H_1^{(0)}(z_1, z_2)$ in z_2 is n_{01}. We write the even and odd components of $H_1^{(0)}(z_1, z_2)$ as

$$H_1^{e(0)}(z_1, z_2) = \sum_{k=0}^{n_{01}} c_k(z_1) z_2^k, \quad H_1^{o(0)}(z_1, z_2) = \sum_{k=0}^{n_{01}} d_k(z_1) z_2^k \tag{10.26}$$

Then by substituting (10.23) and (10.26) in (10.22) and equating coefficients of like powers of z_2, one obtains a set of $2n_{01} + 1$ polynomial equations written in matrix form as:

$$\left[\begin{array}{c|c} \mathbf{R}_{2n_{01}} & \mathbf{A} \\ \hline \mathbf{0} & a_{n_{01}} \; b_{n_{01}} \end{array} \right] \cdot \left[\begin{array}{c} \mathbf{d} \\ -\mathbf{c} \\ d_{n_{01}} \\ -c_{n_{01}} \end{array} \right] = \left[\begin{array}{c} \mathbf{0}_{n_{01}} \\ z_1^{l_1} \\ \mathbf{0}_{n_{01}} \end{array} \right] \tag{10.27}$$

where, as state before, $\mathbf{R}_{2n_{01}}(z_1)$ is the resultant matrix of $H_0^e(\mathbf{z})$ and $H_0^o(\mathbf{z})$, associated with $H_0^e(z_1, z_2)$ and $H_0^o(z_1, z_2)$,

$$\mathbf{A} = \left[\begin{array}{cccccc} \mathbf{0}_{n_{01}} & a_0 & a_1 & \cdots & a_{n_{01}-1} \\ \mathbf{0}_{n_{01}} & b_0 & b_1 & \cdots & b_{n_{01}-1} \end{array} \right]^T$$
$$\mathbf{d} = [d_0 \; d_1 \; \cdots \; d_{n_{01}-1}]^T \tag{10.28}$$
$$\mathbf{c} = [c_0 \; c_1 \; \cdots \; c_{n_{01}-1}]^T$$

The last of the equations in (10.27) is satisfied if we choose the polynomials $d_{n_{01}}(z_1)$ and $c_{n_{01}}(z_1)$ as:

$$d_{n_{01}}(z_1) = b_{n_{01}}(z_1)\beta(z_1), \quad c_{n_{01}}(z_1) = a_{n_{01}}(z_1)\beta(z_1) \tag{10.29}$$

where $\beta(z_1)$ is arbitrary. Substituting (10.29) into (10.27) we obtain:

$$\left[\begin{array}{c} \mathbf{d} \\ -\mathbf{c} \end{array} \right] = \mathbf{R}_{2n_{01}}^{-1} \left(\left[\begin{array}{c} \mathbf{0}_{n_{01}} \\ z_1^{l_1} \\ \mathbf{0}_{n_{01}-1} \end{array} \right] - \mathbf{A} \cdot \beta \left[\begin{array}{c} b_{n_{01}} \\ -a_{n_{01}} \end{array} \right] \right) \tag{10.30}$$

It can be easily shown that if l_1 is odd and $\beta(z_1)$ is an even polynomial, then $H_1^{e(0)}$ and $H_1^{o(0)}$ obtained from (10.29) and (10.30) are respectively even and odd functions of $\mathbf{z} = (z_1, z_2)$. Thus, we choose $n_{10} = n_{00} + 4i + 2$ for each integer $i \geq 0$ so that $l_1 = (n_{00} + n_{10})/2 = n_{00} + 2i + 1$ is odd, and $\beta(z_1)$ such that the first equation in (10.31) is satisfied.

$$\beta(z_1) = \beta(-z_1); \quad \beta(z_1) = z_1^{4i+2}\beta(z_1^{-1}) \quad \text{for integer } i \geq 0 \tag{10.31}$$

Furthermore, we shall require the polynomial $\beta(z_1)$ to satisfy the second equation (10.31). It will be seen later that this symmetry of $\beta(z)$ will be necessary to obtain a symmetric solution for $H_1(\mathbf{z})$, whereas the choice of index of $\beta(z_1)$ will guarantee that $\text{Deg}(c_k, d_k) \leq n_{10}$.

Second solution $H_1^{(1)}(z_1, z_2)$

As before, we assume that the degree of $H_1^{(1)}(z_1, z_2)$ in z_2 is n_{01}, and expand its even and odd parts as polynomials in z_2 as:

$$H_1^{e(1)}(z_1, z_2) = \sum_{k=0}^{n_{01}} e_k(z_1) z_2^k, \quad H_1^{o(1)}(z_1, z_2) = \sum_{k=0}^{n_{01}} f_k(z_1) z_2^k \qquad (10.32)$$

Then by substituting (10.23) and (10.32) in (10.22) and equating coefficients of like powers of z_2, one obtains a set of $2n_{01} + 1$ polynomial equations written in matrix form as:

$$\left[\begin{array}{c|c} \mathbf{0} & a_0 \ b_0 \\ \hline \mathbf{R}_{2n_{01}} & \mathbf{B} \end{array}\right] \cdot \left[\begin{array}{c} \mathbf{f} \\ -\mathbf{e} \\ f_0 \\ -e_0 \end{array}\right] = \left[\begin{array}{c} \mathbf{0}_{n_{01}} \\ z_1^{l_1} \\ \mathbf{0}_{n_{01}} \end{array}\right] \qquad (10.33)$$

where $\mathbf{R}_{2n_{01}}(z_1)$ is the resultant matrix defined earlier, and

$$\mathbf{B} = \left[\begin{array}{ccccc} a_1 & a_2 & \cdots & a_{n_{01}} & \mathbf{0}_{n_{01}} \\ b_1 & b_2 & \cdots & b_{n_{01}} & \mathbf{0}_{n_{01}} \end{array}\right]^T$$
$$\mathbf{f} = [f_1 \ f_2 \ \cdots \ f_{n_{01}-1} \ f_{n_{01}}]^T \qquad (10.34)$$
$$\mathbf{e} = [e_1 \ e_2 \ \cdots \ e_{n_{01}-1} \ e_{n_{01}}]^T$$

In fact, viewed as a system of scalar polynomial equations, (10.33) is identical to (10.27) if e_k and f_k are replaced by c_k and d_k respectively. However, it is possible to obtain an alternate solution by partitioning the coefficient matrix in a different manner. The first of the set of $2n_{01} + 1$ equations in (10.33), can be automatically satisfied by choosing the polynomials f_0 and e_0 as:

$$f_0(z_1) = b_0(z_1)\beta(z_1), \quad e_0(z_1) = a_0(z_1)\beta(z_1) \qquad (10.35)$$

where we choose $\beta(z_1)$ as in (10.31). Substituting (10.35) into (10.33), we obtain

$$\left[\begin{array}{c} \mathbf{f} \\ -\mathbf{e} \end{array}\right] = \mathbf{R}_{2n_{01}}^{-1} \left(\left[\begin{array}{c} \mathbf{0}_{n_{01}-1} \\ z_1^{l_1} \\ \mathbf{0}_{n_{01}} \end{array}\right] - \mathbf{B} \cdot \beta \left[\begin{array}{c} b_0 \\ -a_0 \end{array}\right]\right) \qquad (10.36)$$

Now, if $H_0(\mathbf{z})$ and $H_0(-\mathbf{z})$ do not have any common zero (z_1, z_2) other than the type $(\gamma, 0)$ or $(0, \gamma)$, then by Theorem 10.10, the resultant $\det \mathbf{R}_{2n_{01}}$ is a monomial in z_1. Thus, by properly choosing i, and $\beta(z_1)$ satisfying (10.31), we can find polynomial solutions for $\mathbf{c}$, $\mathbf{d}$ in (10.30) and $\mathbf{e}$, $\mathbf{f}$ in (10.36).

We next show how by combining the two specific solutions to (10.22) just obtained, neither of which produce linear phase filters, per se, we can produce a linear phase solution to (10.22).

Claim 10.11 *Consider the two even-odd pairs* $\{H_1^{e(0)}(z_1, z_2), H_1^{o(0)}(z_1, z_2)\}$ *in (10.26) and* $\{H_1^{e(1)}(z_1, z_2), H_1^{o(1)}(z_1, z_2)\}$ *in (10.32) obtained via the above procedure and the use of* $\beta(z_1)$ *as in (10.31). Let*

$$H_1^e(z_1, z_2) = \sum_{k=0}^{n_{01}} s_k(z_1) z_2^k, \quad H_1^o(z_1, z_2) = \sum_{k=0}^{n_{01}} t_k(z_1) z_2^k \qquad (10.37)$$

where

$$s_k = (c_k + e_k)/2, \quad t_k = (d_k + f_k)/2; \quad k = 0, 1, \cdots, n_{01}. \tag{10.38}$$

Then, the filter given by

$$H_1(z_1, z_2) = H_1^e(z_1, z_2) + H_1^o(z_1, z_2) \tag{10.39}$$

provides a solution to the linear phase quincunx filter bank completion problem. In particular, the filter H_1 with index $(n_{00} + 4i + 2, n_{01})$ forms a linear phase PR filter bank together with the prescribed H_0, having the pair $\{H_0^e(z_1, z_2), H_0^o(z_1, z_2)\}$ as its even and odd parts.

Proof: Clearly, since we have

$$H_1^e(z_1, z_2) = (H_1^{e(0)}(z_1, z_2) + H_1^{e(1)}(z_1, z_2))/2$$

and

$$H_1^o(z_1, z_2) = (H_1^{o(0)}(z_1, z_2) + H_1^{o(1)}(z_1, z_2))/2$$

if the pairs
$\{H_1^{e(0)}(z_1, z_2), H_1^{o(0)}(z_1, z_2)\}, \{H_1^{e(1)}(z_1, z_2), H_1^{o(1)}(z_1, z_2)\}$ satisfy condition (10.22) for PR then the pair $\{H_0^e(z_1, z_2), H_0^o(z_1, z_2)\}$ satisfies the same condition as well. It remains to show the linear phase property. Using (10.24), (10.25) and (10.31), we can rewrite (10.36) as

$$\mathbf{R}_{2n_{01}} \cdot \begin{bmatrix} z_1^{n_{10}} \mathbf{J}_{n_{01}} \cdot \mathbf{f}(z_1^{-1}) \\ -z_1^{n_{10}} \mathbf{J}_{n_{01}} \cdot \mathbf{e}(z_1^{-1}) \end{bmatrix} + \mathbf{A} \cdot \beta \begin{bmatrix} b_{n_{01}}(z_1) \\ -a_{n_{01}}(z_1) \end{bmatrix} = \begin{bmatrix} \mathbf{0}_{n_{01}} \\ z_1^{l_1} \\ \mathbf{0}_{n_{01}-1} \end{bmatrix}$$

Subtracting the last equation from (10.30), we obtain

$$\mathbf{R}_{2n_{01}}(z_1) \cdot \begin{bmatrix} \mathbf{d}(z_1) - z_1^{n_{10}} \mathbf{J}_{n_{01}} \cdot \mathbf{f}(z_1^{-1}) \\ -\mathbf{c}(z_1) + z_1^{n_{10}} \mathbf{J}_{n_{01}} \cdot \mathbf{e}(z_1^{-1}) \end{bmatrix} = \mathbf{0}$$

Since the normal rank (Kailath 1980) of $\mathbf{R}_{2n_{01}}(z_1)$ is full, we have

$$\mathbf{d}(z_1) = z_1^{n_{10}} \mathbf{J}_{n_{01}} \cdot \mathbf{f}(z_1^{-1}), \quad \mathbf{c}(z_1) = z_1^{n_{10}} \mathbf{J}_{n_{01}} \cdot \mathbf{f}(z_1^{-1})$$

or, equivalently,

$$d_k(z_1) = \begin{cases} z_1^{n_{10}} f_{n_{01}-k}(z_1^{-1}) & \text{for } k = 0, 1, \cdots, n_{01} - 1 \\ b_{n_{01}}(z_1)\beta(z_1) & \text{for } k = n_{01} \end{cases} \tag{10.40}$$

and

$$c_k(z_1) = \begin{cases} z_1^{n_{10}} e_{n_{01}-k}(z_1^{-1}) & \text{for } k = 0, 1, \cdots, n_{01} - 1 \\ a_{n_{01}}(z_1)\beta(z_1) & \text{for } k = n_{01} \end{cases} \tag{10.41}$$

The above relations show that $\text{Deg}(c_k, d_k, e_k, f_k) \le n_{01} = n_{00} + 4i + 2$.

Since for all $k = 0, 1, \cdots, n_{01}$, we have $s_k(z_1) = (c_k(z_1) + e_k(z_1))/2$ and $t_k(z_1) = (d_k(z_1) + f_k(z_1))/2$, it follows by using (10.40), (10.41), (10.29) and (10.35) that:

$$s_k(z_1) = z_1^{n_{10}} s_{n_{01}-k}(z_1^{-1}), \quad t_k(z_1) = z_1^{n_{10}} t_{n_{01}-k}(z_1^{-1})$$

where $n_{10} = n_{00} + 4i + 2$ i.e., $s_k(z_1)$ and $t_k(z_1)$ are self-symmetric polynomials with index $n_{10} = n_{00} + 4i + 2$. Thus, both $H_1^e(z_1, z_2) = \sum_{k=0}^{n_{01}} s_k(z_1) z_2^k$ and $H_1^o(z_1, z_2) = \sum_{k=0}^{n_{01}} t_k(z_1) z_2^k$ are symmetric polynomials with index $(n_{00} + 4i + 2, n_{01})$. Consequently, the filter $H_1(\mathbf{z}) = H_1^e(\mathbf{z}) + H_1^o(\mathbf{z})$ is symmetric linear phase (cf. Property 10.4 and part 1 of Corollary 10.6). ∎

10.3.2 Filter banks of type $k_1 = (1, 0)$

Our treatment here will be brief. The even and odd parts of $H_0(\mathbf{z})$, in view of (10.5), are cross-symmetric, and when expanded as in (10.21), are related by:

$$a_k(z_1) = z_1^{n_{00}} b_{n_{01}-k}(z_1^{-1}), \quad k = 0, 1, \cdots, n_{01} \tag{10.42}$$

Using (10.20) and (10.42), we can show that

$$\mathbf{R}_{2n_{01}}(z_1) = z_1^{n_{00}} \mathbf{J}_{2n_{01}} \cdot \mathbf{R}_{2n_{01}}(z_1^{-1}) \cdot \mathbf{J}_{2n_{01}} \tag{10.43}$$

We follow exactly same procedure described as in the previous subsection, except that now the requirements on $\beta(z_1)$ are:

$$\beta(z_1) = \beta(-z_1) \quad \text{and} \quad \beta(z_1) = -z_1^{4i}\beta(z_1^{-1}) \quad \text{for integer } i \geq 0 \tag{10.44}$$

Claim 10.12 *Consider the filter H_1 as in (10.39) obtained as in Claim 10.11 via the use of (10.30), (10.36), (10.37) and (10.38), but now with $\beta(z_1)$ as in (10.44). Then, the desired anti-symmetric linear phase complementary filter is given by $H_1(z_1, z_2)$ and has index $(n_{00} + 4i, n_{01})$.*

Proof: Using (10.42), (10.43) and (10.44), we can rewrite (10.36) as

$$\mathbf{R}_{2n_{01}}(z_1) \cdot \begin{bmatrix} -z_1^{n_{10}} \mathbf{J}_{n_{01}} \cdot \mathbf{e}(z_1^{-1}) \\ z_1^{n_{10}} \mathbf{J}_{n_{01}} \cdot \mathbf{f}(z_1^{-1}) \end{bmatrix} + \mathbf{A} \cdot \beta(z_1) \begin{bmatrix} b_{n_{01}}(z_1) \\ -a_{n_{01}}(z_1) \end{bmatrix} = \begin{bmatrix} \mathbf{0}_{n_{01}} \\ z_1^{l_1} \\ \mathbf{0}_{n_{01}-1} \end{bmatrix}$$

Subtracting the last equation from (10.30), we obtain

$$\mathbf{R}_{2n_{01}}(z_1) \cdot \begin{bmatrix} \mathbf{d}(z_1) + z_1^{n_{10}} \mathbf{J}_{n_{01}} \cdot \mathbf{e}(z_1^{-1}) \\ -\mathbf{c}(z_1) - z_1^{n_{10}} \mathbf{J}_{n_{01}} \cdot \mathbf{f}(z_1^{-1}) \end{bmatrix} = \mathbf{0}$$

Since the normal rank (Kailath 1980) of $\mathbf{R}_{2n_{01}}(z_1)$ is full, we have for $k = 0, 1, \cdots, n_{01}$:

$$c_k(z_1) = -z_1^{n_{10}} f_{n_{01}-k}(z_1^{-1}), \quad d_k(z_1) = -z_1^{n_{10}} e_{n_{01}-k}(z_1^{-1}) \tag{10.45}$$

The above relation also shows that $\text{Deg}(c_k, d_k, e_k, f_k) \leq n_{10} = n_{00} + 4i$. Since $s_k = (c_k + e_k)/2$ and $t_k = (d_k + f_k)/2$, equations (10.45) yields:

$$s_k(z_1) = -z_1^{n_{10}} t_{n_{01}-k}(z_1^{-1})$$

Therefore $H_1^e(z_1, z_2) = \sum_{k=0}^{n_{01}} s_k(z_1) z_2^k$ and $H_1^o(z_1, z_2) = \sum_{k=0}^{n_{01}} t_k(z_1) z_2^k$ form a cross-antisymmetric pair with index $(n_{00}+4i, n_{01})$. Thus, $H_1(z_1, z_2) = H_1^e(z_1, z_2) + H_1^o(z_1, z_2)$ is antisymmetric linear phase with index $(n_{00} + 4i, n_{01})$ (cf. Property 10.5 and part 2 of Corollary 10.6). ∎

10.4 CONCLUSIONS

The main purpose of the present paper has been to provide a detail proof of a Quillen-Suslin type result originally announced in (Basu 1998) on filter bank completion in the quincunx linear phase context. Since then, several authors have reportedly studied the problem in the broader context of multichannel filter banks. Notable among these are (Lawton & Lin 1999) and (Bose 1999). Based on these studies the conjectured validity of linear phase filter bank completion may be questioned without hitherto unknown additional restrictions (that are automatically satisfied in the quincunx case) on the filters. This is especially true for filters with low degree. In view of this, the following questions remain open and deserves further study.

1. What are the necessary and sufficient conditions for the existence of solution to the problem of finding a *column symmetric* extension **H** from one of its rows i.e., to find the entire LP, PR, k-D filter bank from one of the filters. The cases $k = 1$ with arbitrary m (Basu & Choi 1999) and $k = 2$ with **M**=quincunx are fully understood.

2. How to obtain efficient algorithms for finding the solution to the problem mentioned above? Groebner basis techniques could provide a viable approach (Bose 1999, Park *et al.* 1997).

3. What is the smallest degree solution, and what are the restrictions on allowed degrees of the other filters in the filter bank? See (Lawton & Lin 1999) in particular.

4. Issue of uniqueness of solution, and tractable parameterization of all solutions of higher degree.

5. How to use this last mentioned parameterization to satisfy other practical objectives e.g., frequency shaping of the filters, or to impose regularity of the wavelets associated with the filter bank (we refer to (Cohen & Daubechies 1996) for this later topic).

REFERENCES

S. Basu, 1998, Multidimensional filter banks and wavelets — a system theoretic perspective, *Journal of the Franklin Institute*, invited paper, Special issue on Signal Processing, pp.1367-1409, vol. 335B.

S. Basu, 1999, New Results in Multidimensional Linear Phase Filter Bank Design, *Proc. Int. Symp. on Cir.& Sys.*, Orlando, Florida.

S. Basu, Han-Mook Choi, 1999, Hermite reduction methods for generation of a complete class of linear phase perfect reconstruction filter banks — Part I: theory, *IEEE Trans. on Circuits and Systems II*, 46(4):434–447.

N. K. Bose, 1982, *Applied Multidimensional Systems Theory*, Van Nostrand Reinhold.

N. K. Bose, 1999, Private communication.

A. Cohen and I. Daubechies, 1996, A new technique to estimate the regularity of refinable functions, *Revista Mathematica Iberoamericana*, 12, pp. 527-92.

T. Kailath, 1980, *Linear System Theory*, Prentice Hall.

I. A. Kalker, A. A. C. Shah, Algebraic theory of multidimensional filter banks and their design, Phillips Research Lab., Eindhoven, The Netherlands, preprint.

J. Kovacevic and M.Vetterli, 1992, Non-separable multidimensional perfect reconstruction banks and wavelets for R^n, *IEEE Trans. on Information Theory*, vol. 38, no. 2, pp. 533-555.

T. Y. Lam, 1978, *Serre Conjecture, Lecture Notes in Mathematics*, Springer Verlag, vol. 635.

W. M. Lawton and Zhiping Lin, 1999, Matrix completion problems in multidimensional systems, *Int. Symp. on Cir. and Sys.*, Orlando, FL.

H Park, T. Kalker, M. Vetterli, 1997, Gröbner bases and multidimensional multirate filter banks, *Multidimensional Systems and Signal Processing*, vol.8, pp. 11-30.

P. P. Vaidyanathan, *Multirate Systems and Filter Banks*, 1992, Prentice Hall.

M. Vetterli, J. Kovacevic, 1995, *Wavelets and subband Coding*, Prentice Hall.

M. Vidyasagar, 1985, *Control Systems Synthesis: A Factorization Approach*, MIT Press.

D. C. Youla and P. F. Pickel, 1984, The Quillen-Suslin theorem and the structure of n-dimensional polynomial matrices, *IEEE Trans. on Circuits and Systems*, vol. 31, no.6, pp. 513-517.

CHAPTER ELEVEN

Deadbands in m-D Delta-Operator Based Digital Filters with Floating Point Arithmetic

Peter H. Bauer   and   Kamal Premaratne

Department of Electrical Engineering, University of Notre Dame, USA

Department of Electrical and Computer Engineering, University of Miami, USA

Abstract

The effect of floating- and block-floating point arithmetic on the asymptotic response of m-D digital filters in delta-operator form is analyzed. In particular, the existence of incorrect equilibrium points, i.e., DC limit cycles, is investigated and conditions for their existence are formulated. Deadband bounds are constructed and the dependency of these bounds on the sampling rate is analyzed. The results are compared with the fixed point case.

11.1 INTRODUCTION

Delta-operator formulated digital filters are known to have several significant advantages over their shift-operator formulated counterparts. Especially the reduced coefficient sensitivity and quantization noise are noteworthy (Middleton & Goodwin 1990). It has recently been shown (Premaratne & Bauer 1994), that in the case of fixed point arithmetic, a delta-operator formulated digital filter can also have drawbacks such as large amplitude DC limit cycles. This effect is especially pronounced if the sampling time Δ is very small. In fact, it was determined in (Premaratne & Bauer 1994) that this effect often prevents a delta-operator based filter from being implemented on a fixed point machine. In (Bauer & Premaratne 2000) it was shown that m-D delta-operator formulated systems suffer from the same drawbacks.

This paper, therefore explores the effect of other number representation schemes on the asymptotic behavior of m-D digital filters. In particular, the use of floating and block floating point arithmetic will be investigated. Conditions for the existence of incorrect zero input equilibrium points will be derived and the connection between sampling time and deadband size will be investigated.

11.2 PRELIMINARIES

Consider the following m-D delta-operator formulated system model in the form of a Roesser model (Roesser 1975):

$$
\begin{bmatrix} \delta^{(1)}[\mathbf{x}^{(1)}](\mathbf{n}) \\ \vdots \\ \delta^{(m)}[\mathbf{x}^{(m)}](\mathbf{n}) \end{bmatrix} = \begin{bmatrix} A_{11}^{\delta} & \cdots & A_{1m}^{\delta} \\ \vdots & & \vdots \\ A_{m1}^{\delta} & \cdots & A_{mm}^{\delta} \end{bmatrix} \begin{bmatrix} \mathbf{x}^{(1)}(\mathbf{n}) \\ \vdots \\ \mathbf{x}^{(m)}(\mathbf{n}) \end{bmatrix} + \begin{bmatrix} B_1^{\delta} \\ \vdots \\ B_m^{\delta} \end{bmatrix} \mathbf{u}(\mathbf{n})
$$

$$(11.1)$$

$$
\begin{bmatrix} q^{(1)}[\mathbf{x}^{(1)}](\mathbf{n}) \\ \vdots \\ q^{(m)}[\mathbf{x}^{(m)}](\mathbf{n}) \end{bmatrix} = \begin{bmatrix} \mathbf{x}^{(1)}(\mathbf{n}) \\ \vdots \\ \mathbf{x}^{(m)}(\mathbf{n}) \end{bmatrix} + \begin{pmatrix} \Delta_1 & & 0 \\ & \ddots & \\ 0 & & \Delta_m \end{pmatrix} \begin{bmatrix} \delta^{(1)}[\mathbf{x}^{(1)}](\mathbf{n}) \\ \vdots \\ \delta^{(m)}[\mathbf{x}^{(m)}](\mathbf{n}) \end{bmatrix}
$$

$$(11.2)$$

where

$$
q^{(i)}[\mathbf{x}^{(i)}](\mathbf{n}) = \mathbf{x}^{(i)}(n_1, \cdots, n_{i-1}, n_i + 1, n_{i+1}, \cdots, n_m) \tag{11.3}
$$

$$
\delta^{(i)}[\mathbf{x}^{(i)}](\mathbf{n}) = \frac{1}{\Delta_i}(\mathbf{x}^{(i)}(n_1, \cdots, n_{i-1}, n_i + 1, n_{i+1}, \cdots, n_m) - \mathbf{x}^{(i)}(\mathbf{n})) \tag{11.4}
$$

In (11.1)–(11.4) the following notation is used:

$q^{(i)}[\ ]$: shift-operator in direction of the n_i-axis

$\delta^{(i)}[\ ]$: delta-operator in direction of the n_i-axis

$\mathbf{n}$: point in the first hyper-quadrant $\mathbf{n} = (n_1, \cdots, n_m)$

$\mathbf{x}^{(i)}(\mathbf{n})$: portion of state vector $\mathbf{x}(\mathbf{n})$, propagating in direction of the n_i-axis

Δ_i: sampling time in direction n_i

$\mathbf{u}(\mathbf{n})$: m-D input vector

A_{ij}^{δ}: system submatrix coupling i^{th} and j^{th} direction of propagation

B_i^{δ}: input submatrix

From (11.1), (11.2) we obtain the following floating point zero input model

$$
\begin{bmatrix} \delta^{(1)}[\mathbf{x}^{(1)}](\mathbf{n}) \\ \vdots \\ \delta^{(m)}[\mathbf{x}^{(m)}](\mathbf{n}) \end{bmatrix} = Flp \left\{ \begin{bmatrix} A_{11}^{\delta} & \cdots & A_{1m}^{\delta} \\ \vdots & & \vdots \\ A_{m1}^{\delta} & \cdots & A_{mm}^{\delta} \end{bmatrix} \begin{bmatrix} \mathbf{x}^{(1)}(\mathbf{n}) \\ \vdots \\ \mathbf{x}^{(m)}(\mathbf{n}) \end{bmatrix} \right\} \tag{11.5}
$$

$$
\begin{bmatrix} q^{(1)}[\mathbf{x}^{(1)}](\mathbf{n}) \\ \vdots \\ q^{(m)}[\mathbf{x}^{(m)}](\mathbf{n}) \end{bmatrix} = Flp \left\{ \begin{bmatrix} \mathbf{x}^{(1)}(\mathbf{n}) \\ \vdots \\ \mathbf{x}^{(m)}(\mathbf{n}) \end{bmatrix} + \right.
$$

$$\begin{pmatrix} \Delta_1 & & & 0 \\ & \Delta_2 & & \\ & & \ddots & \\ 0 & & & \Delta_m \end{pmatrix} \begin{bmatrix} \delta^{(1)}[\mathbf{x}^{(1)}](\mathbf{n}) \\ \vdots \\ \delta^{(m)}[\mathbf{x}^{(m)}](\mathbf{n}) \end{bmatrix} \Bigg\} \quad (11.6)$$

where $Flp\{\ \}$ stands for floating point computation of the argument. In the case of block floating point we will use the symbol $BFlp\{\}$. The system (11.5,11.6) will be investigated in terms of zero convergence properties for both the regular floating point and the block floating point case.

Two problems will be tackled:

1. Conditions which guarantee the existence of limit cycles will be derived. (These conditions can also be viewed as necessary conditions for stability.)

2. The size of the corresponding deadband bounds will be estimated.

The following definition will be used to describe zero convergence of the first quarter plane causal filter:

Definition 11.1 *(Asymptotic Stability) (Bauer 1992)* *An m-D first hyper-quadrant causal digital filter is asymptotically stable under all finitely extended bounded input signals* $\mathbf{u}(\mathbf{n})$,

$$\begin{aligned} \| \, \mathbf{u}(\mathbf{n}) \, \| \leq S & \qquad \text{for } n_1 + \cdots + n_m \leq D \\ \mathbf{u}(\mathbf{n}) = 0 & \qquad \text{for } n_1 + \cdots + n_m > D \end{aligned}$$

if all the states of the m-D digital filter asymptotically reach zero for $n_1 + \cdots + n_m \to \infty$. *Here,* $n_\nu \geq 0, \nu = 1, \cdots, m$, *S is a non-negative real number and D is a positive integer.* $\| \cdot \|$ *denotes any vector norm.*

Next, we will briefly review the fundamentals of floating and block-floating point arithmetic:

11.2.1 Floating point arithmetic

The implementation of state space equations (11.1,11.2) in floating point format requires the evaluation of inner products, i.e., only multiplications and additions are needed. A floating point number u is represented as

$$u = u_m \cdot 2^{u_E}$$

where $\frac{1}{2} \leq u_m < 1$ and $E_{\min} \leq u_E \leq E_{\max}$.

In the above equation u_m denotes the mantissa and u_E the exponent. The exponent is always an integer and $E_{\min}, E_{\max}$ denote the minimum and maximum exponent respectively. If the condition $u_m \in [\frac{1}{2}, 1)$ is not satisfied, u is said to be in denormalized form. We will further assume that all mantissas will be of length l_m (excluding the sign bit). This applies to all coefficients and signals.

The following floating point reformatting operations are needed for the computation of an inner product:

1. Floating Point Multiplication:
   The coefficient-signal product is computed by multiplying the coefficient mantissa with the signal mantissa and adding the exponents. If the product is not in normalized form, a left shift in the mantissa is needed and the exponent needs to be decremented. The mantissa product can either be stored in its full length or quantized from double length to single length.

2. Floating Point Addition:
   In a sequential addition, the ith product is added to the sum of the previous $(i-1)$ products. This may require denormalization of the mantissa of the smaller operand and a corresponding exponent adjustment. Addition is then carried out by adding mantissas. If the result is not normalized a mantissa register right or left shift in conjunction with the corresponding exponent update is required. If in step 1, double length product registers are available, quantization to a single length mantissa is also needed at this point.

11.2.2 Block floating point arithmetic

In block floating point arithmetic, a set $\mathbf{U} = \{u_1, \cdots, u_m\}$ of number is represented by a set of rational numbers $\hat{\mathbf{U}} = \{\hat{u}_1, \cdots, \hat{u}_m\}$ of the form:

$$\hat{u}_i = \hat{u}_{i,m} \cdot 2^{E_u}, \quad \forall i, \ i = 1, \cdots, m.$$

The set $\hat{\mathbf{U}}$ is produced from $\mathbf{U}$ via some suitable quantization scheme. Note that all elements in $\hat{\mathbf{U}}$ share the same exponent value E_u, i.e., they differ only in the 'block' mantissa $\hat{u}_{i,m}$. This is in contrast to regular floating point arithmetic, where each number has its own exponent register. This 'block' exponent E_u in block floating point arithmetic is chosen such that

$$0 \leq |\hat{u}_{i,m}| < 1, \quad \forall i = 1, \cdots, m$$

and $0.5 \leq \max_i |\hat{u}_{i,m}| < 1$. Consequently, in block floating point arithmetic, only one element is guaranteed to have a normalized mantissa in the sense of regular floating point arithmetic.

For block floating point digital filters it is assumed that all stored signal values (states and possibly inputs and outputs) share the same exponent.

11.3 NECESSARY CONDITIONS FOR GLOBAL ASYMPTOTIC STABILITY — FLOATING POINT ARITHMETIC

In order to obtain necessary conditions for stability of the m-D delta-operator formulated system, we will use a result in (Bauer 1995). This result states that a m-D nonlinear system can only be stable if the m 1-D nonlinear systems, which describe the m-D system on the axes, are stable.

Theorem 11.2 *The global asymptotic stability of the following 1-D systems is necessary for global asymptotic stability of the digital filter in (11.5,11.6):*

$$\delta^{(i)}[\mathbf{x}^{(i)}](n_i) \ = \ Flp\{A_{ii}^{\delta}\mathbf{x}^{(i)}(n_i)\} \tag{11.7}$$

$$q^{(i)}[\mathbf{x}^{(i)}](n_i) \ = \ Flp\{\mathbf{x}^{(i)}(n_i) + \Delta_i\delta^{(i)}[\mathbf{x}^{(i)}](n_i)\}$$

$$i = 1, \cdots, m \tag{11.8}$$

Proof: The proof follows directly from Theorem 1 in (Bauer 1995).   ∎

In the fixed point case, the key for the problem of incorrect equilibria could be found in the update equation, i.e., equation (11.6). If Δ is a small number then the product of Δ and the incremental difference vector can be quantized to the zero vector, thus failing to update the state vector. This results in a so called DC limit cycle.

In floating point arithmetic a similar phenomenon occurs due to the process of denormalization. Since the stability of the 1-D systems in Theorem 11.2 provides a necessary condition for stability, we will from here on, only consider the m 1-D systems of Theorem 11.2, in particular the update equations:

$$q^{(i)}[\mathbf{x}^{(i)}](n_i) \;=\; Flp\{\mathbf{x}^{(i)}(n_i) + \Delta_i \delta^{(i)}[\mathbf{x}^{(i)}](n_i)\}$$
$$i = 1, \cdots, m.$$

A DC limit cycle occurs if the following condition is satisfied.

$$\mathbf{x}^{(i)}(n_i) \;=\; q^{(i)}[\mathbf{x}^{(i)}](n_i) = Flp\{\mathbf{x}^{(i)}(n_i) + \Delta_i \delta^{(i)}[\mathbf{x}^{(i)}](n_i)\}$$
$$\text{for some } i, i = 1, \cdots, m. \tag{11.9}$$

There are a number of possible floating point formats, which for the sake of brevity, cannot all be discussed. Instead of considering various quantization schemes, the worst case is considered. This case occurs if the product $\Delta_i \cdot \delta^{(i)}[\mathbf{x}^{(i)}](n_i)$ is quantized using truncation before addition, i.e., at the point of summation, $\mathbf{x}^{(i)}(n_i)$ and $\Delta_i \cdot \delta^{(i)}[\mathbf{x}^{(i)}](n_i)$ are represented by the same number of mantissa bits, say l_m bits. If the two operands in the summation process have two different exponents, the mantissa of the smaller operand needs to be denormalized in order to match the exponent of the larger operand.

This denormalization requires a right shift of the mantissa and an increase of the exponent. Condition (11.9) is satisfied for certain quantization schemes (e.g., magnitude truncation in single precision) if:

$$|\Delta_i \delta_j^{(i)}[\mathbf{x}^{(i)}]| < 2^{-l_m + E(\mathbf{x}_j^{(i)})} \tag{11.10}$$

for some $i = 1, \cdots, m$ $\forall j = 1, \cdots, N_i$ where N_i denotes the dimensionality of the partial state vector $\mathbf{x}^{(i)}$ and $E(\mathbf{x}_j^{(i)})$ denotes the exponent of $\mathbf{x}_j^{(i)}$ in floating point format. Since (11.10) must be satisfied for every component $\mathbf{x}_j^{(i)}$ of the state equation, this condition is rarely satisfied for large l_m. Some sufficient conditions for (11.10) can be obtained as follows:
From the 1-D system of Theorem 11.2 we obtain for the linear case:

$$\| \delta^{(i)}[\mathbf{x}^{(i)}](n_i) \|_\infty \leq \| A_{ii}^\delta \|_\infty \| \mathbf{x}^{(i)}(n_i) \|_\infty \tag{11.11}$$

Imposing the condition

$$\Delta_i \cdot \| A_{ii}^\delta \|_\infty \| \mathbf{x}^{(i)}(n_i) \|_\infty < 2^{-l_m + \min_j E\{\mathbf{x}_j^{(i)}\}} \tag{11.12}$$
$$\text{for some } i = 1, \cdots, m$$

ensures by virtue of Equation (11.11), that (11.10) is satisfied. Therefore, if (11.12) is satisfied, there will be DC limit cycles, but not vice versa. From inequality (11.12), we obtain a condition on the sampling periods, which will always support DC limit cycles in direction of the n_i axis:

$$\Delta_i < \frac{2^{-l_m + \min\limits_j E\{\mathbf{x}_j^{(i)}\}}}{\| A_{ii}^\delta \|_\infty \cdot \| \mathbf{x}^{(i)}(n_i) \|_\infty} \tag{11.13}$$

The right hand side of inequality (11.13) is maximized for the case

$$\frac{1}{2} \cdot 2^{\min\limits_j E\{\mathbf{x}_j^{(i)}\}} = \| \mathbf{x}^{(i)}(n_i) \|_\infty, \tag{11.14}$$

i.e., for the case when all states in $\mathbf{x}^{(i)}$ have the same exponent. With (11.13) and (11.14) we have

$$\Delta_i < \frac{2^{-l_m + 1}}{\| A_{ii}^\delta \|_\infty} \tag{11.15}$$

Hence we obtain the following theorem:

Theorem 11.3 *The floating point implementation of the delta operator formulated digital filter in (11.5) and (11.6) will exhibit incorrect equilibrium points, if*

$$\Delta_i < \frac{2^{-l_m + 1}}{\| A_{ii}^\delta \|_\infty} \tag{11.16}$$

for some i, $i = 1, \cdots, m$.

Theorem 11.3 shows that the mantissa register length l_m and the $\| \cdot \|_\infty$-norm of the system matrix play a key role. In general, the higher the sampling rate the larger the required mantissa length. This indicates that for delta-operator based systems, precision and sampling rate are connected if floating point arithmetic is used. By simply rewriting Equation (11.13), one can deduce information about the size of the deadband for the considered direction of propagation

$$\| \mathbf{x}^{(i)}(n_i) \|_\infty < \frac{2^{-l_m + \min\limits_j E\{\mathbf{x}_j^{(i)}\}}}{\| A_{ii}^\delta \|_\infty \Delta_i} \tag{11.17}$$

Condition (11.17) is an implicit condition on the state vector $\mathbf{x}(\mathbf{n})$, since $\mathbf{x}$ appears on both sides of the inequality. In case (11.17) leads to a contradiction, i.e.,

$$\| \mathbf{x}^{(i)}(n_i) \|_\infty < \frac{1}{2} 2^{\min\limits_j E\{\mathbf{x}_j^{(i)}\}}$$

then no bound on the deadband is obtained.

Let us now consider a special case, i.e., a particular choice of the exponent.

$$E\{x_j^{(i)}\} = E_{\max}, \text{ for some } i, \text{ and } \forall j = 1, \cdots, N_i. \tag{11.18}$$

With (11.18) and (11.17) we have

$$\| \mathbf{x}^{(i)}(n_i) \|_\infty < \frac{2^{-l_m + E_{\max}}}{\| A_{ii}^\delta \|_\infty \cdot \Delta_i} \tag{11.19}$$

Condition (11.19) does not lead to a contradiction if

$$\frac{2^{-l_m}}{\| A_{ii}^{\delta} \|_{\infty} \Delta_i} > \frac{1}{2} \tag{11.20}$$

which is equivalent to inequality (11.16).

From (11.19) and (11.20) we have

$$\| \mathbf{x}^{(i)}(n_i) \|_{\infty} < (\frac{1}{2}, 1) \cdot 2^{E_{max}} \tag{11.21}$$

as the description for the deadband which demonstrates that the deadband occupies the whole dynamic range. $(\frac{1}{2}, 1)$ describes the open interval with boundaries $\frac{1}{2}$ and 1. Equivalently, the DC limit cycles can occur at any exponent. In (Bauer & Wang 1993) this was referred to as an R2 response type.

Remark 11.4 *The result of Theorem 11.3 shows that sampling time and accuracy in number representation are connected. It is therefore possible to use different wordlength registers for different state vector portions if the sampling rate differs greatly between the directions of propagation. In many applications this is not practical and the largest register length will be used for all directions of propagation.*

11.4 NECESSARY CONDITIONS FOR GLOBAL ASYMPTOTIC STABILITY — BLOCK FLOATING POINT ARITHMETIC

Theorem 11.2 in the previous Section and condition (11.9) for the existence of a DC limit cycle are completely analogous for the block floating point case.

Let us again define l_m as the block mantissa length and E_{min}, E_{max} as the minimum and maximum exponent respectively. The condition for an incorrect equilibrium in direction of the n_i axis is given by

$$\mathbf{x}^{(i)}(n_i + 1) = \mathbf{x}^{(i)}(n_i) = BFlp\{\mathbf{x}^{(i)}(n_i) + \Delta_i \delta^{(i)}[\mathbf{x}^{(i)}](n_i)\} \tag{11.22}$$

Similar to the regular floating point case we will consider only the worst case format, i.e., the format which produces DC limit cycles for the largest values of Δ_i. This again turns out to be quantization after multiplication, using a magnitude truncation scheme (Bauer *et al.* 1995). Other reformatting schemes might tolerate a somewhat smaller sampling period before incorrect nonzero equilibria occur. Equation (11.22) is satisfied for this reformatting scheme if

$$\| \Delta_i \cdot \delta^{(i)}[\mathbf{x}^{(i)}](n_i) \|_{\infty} < 2^{-l_m + E} \tag{11.23}$$

for some i, $i = 1, \cdots, m$ and E being the common block exponent.

Proceeding in an analogous fashion as in the previous section, the condition on the sampling rate which supports DC limit cycles, is given by

$$\Delta_i < \frac{2^{-l_m + E}}{\| A_{ii}^{\delta} \|_{\infty} \| \mathbf{x}^{(i)}(n_i) \|_{\infty}} \tag{11.24}$$

for some $i = 1, \cdots, m$.

The r.h.s. of inequality (11.24) is maximized if

$$\frac{2^E}{\| \mathbf{x}^{(i)}(n_i) \|_\infty} = 2^{l_m},$$

i.e., for the case

$$\| \mathbf{x}^{(i)}(n_i) \|_\infty = 2^{E-l_m}. \tag{11.25}$$

Such a small $\| \cdot \|_\infty$ norm for the ith propagating portion of the state vector $\mathbf{x}(\mathbf{n})$ is possible in block floating point arithmetic since only one component of $\mathbf{x}(\mathbf{n})$ needs to be normalized. This is in sharp contrast to regular floating point arithmetic or even a block floating point scheme, which reserves one block for each portion of the state vector. (It was assumed that all signals in the filter are represented within one block, i.e., by one common exponent.) With (11.24) and (11.25) we have

$$\Delta_i < \frac{1}{\| A_{ii}^\delta \|_\infty};$$

This result is summarized in Theorem 11.5, which is the block floating point counterpart of Theorem 11.3.

Theorem 11.5 *The block floating point implementation of the delta-operator formulated digital filter in (11.5) and (11.6) will exhibit incorrect equilibrium points if*

$$\Delta_i < \frac{1}{\| A_{ii}^\delta \|_\infty} \tag{11.26}$$

for some i, $i = 1, \cdots, m$.

From (11.24) we obtain the following hypercube, which is embedded in the deadband

$$\| \mathbf{x}^{(i)}(n_i) \|_\infty < \frac{2^{-l_m+E}}{\| A_{ii}^\delta \|_\infty \Delta_i} \tag{11.27}$$

Obviously, if

$$\frac{2^{-l_m}}{\| A_{ii}^\delta \|_\infty \Delta_i} > 1 - 2^{-l_m} \tag{11.28}$$

the deadband can occupy the whole dynamic range. (This requires the choice $E = E_{\max}$ in (11.27).) This result is completely analogous to the floating point case, i.e., condition (11.26) by itself will not allow for the deadband to occupy the whole dynamic range. Condition (11.28) which requires a smaller sampling time then (11.26) needs to be satisfied to create a deadband similar to the floating point case.

11.5 CONCLUSION

The phenomenon of incorrect non-zero equilibrium points in zero input m-D digital filters with floating and block-floating point arithmetic has been investigated. It was shown that blockfloating point arithmetic is more susceptible to this phenomenon than regular floating point arithmetic. The derived condition for the existence of DC limit cycles for regular floating point arithmetic requires a by a factor of 2^{-l_m} smaller sampling time than the corresponding block floating point scheme. Although this indicates a substantial difference, the real difference might not be as drastic since both conditions might have different levels of conservatism.

REFERENCES

P. H. Bauer, 1992, Finite Wordlength Effects in M-D Digital Filters with Singularities on the Stability Boundary, *IEEE Trans. on Signal Proc.*, Vol. 40, No. 4, pp. 894–901.

P. H. Bauer, 1995, A Set of Necessary Stability Conditions for M-D Nonlinear Digital Filters, *Journal of Circuits, Systems and Signal Processing*, Vol. 14, No. 4, pp. 555–561.

P. H. Bauer, R. Costañeda and K. Premaratne, 1995, Zero Input Behavior of Fixed Point Digital Filters in Delta-Operator Representation, *Proceedings of the 1995 Asilomar Conference*, Pacific Grove, California.

P. H. Bauer and K. Premaratne, 1997, Limit Cycles in Delta-Operator Formulated 1-D and m-D Discrete-Time Systems with Fixed Point Arithmetic, *IEEE Transactions on Circuits and Systems, Part I*, Vol 44 (6), pp 529–537.

P. H. Bauer and J. Wang, 1993, Limit Cycle Bounds for Floating Point Implementations of Second Order Recursive Digital Filters, *IEEE Trans. on Circuits and Systems – Part II: Analog and Digital Signal Processing*, Vol. 40, No. 8, pp. 493–501.

R. H. Middleton and G. C. Goodwin, 1990, *Digital Control and Estimation: A Unified Approach*, Englewood Cliffs, NJ: Prentice Hall.

K. Premaratne and P. H. Bauer, 1994, Limit Cycles and Asymptotic Stability of Delta-Operator Systems in Fixed Point Arithmetic, *1994 IEEE International Symposium on Circuits and Systems*, London, England, pp. 2461–2464.

R. P. Roesser, 1975, A Discrete State Model for Linear Image Processing, *IEEE Trans. on Aut. Control*, Vol. AC-20, pp. 1–10.

CHAPTER TWELVE

Cascade Synthesis of Two-Variable Lossless Two-Port Networks with Lumped Elements and Transmission Lines: A Semi-Analytic Procedure

Ahmet Aksen and B. Siddik Yarman

Electronic Engineering Dept.,
Isik University, Turkey
aksen@isikun.edu.tr

Abstract

Two-variable characterization of cascades composed of lossless two-port networks with lumped elements and transmission lines is considered. The problems associated with the construction of scattering functions in two variables are discussed and for cascade synthesis of two-variable mixed element networks, a semi-analytic procedure utilizing the topologic restrictions is proposed. Some particular mixed lumped-distributed structures for which the proposed procedure ends up with explicit formulas are addressed and the application of the results in real frequency broadband matching is indicated.

12.1 THE DESIGN PROBLEM OF MIXED LUMPED-DISTRIBUTED NETWORKS

Because of its increasing importance in the present day microwave monolithic integrated circuit (MMIC) technology, design problem of mixed lumped-distributed networks, in conjunction with radio frequency analog circuits such as microwave filters, matching networks and interconnects, has received a great deal of attention for a long time in the literature. Unfortunately, a design theory for those structures incorporating both lumped and distributed elements, comparable in precision to the one available in the lumped element case, still does not exist.

In most of the existing studies, the particular interest is devoted to a practical network configuration consisting of cascaded lossless lumped elements and ideal commensurate transmission lines or unit elements (UE) (Fig. 12.1). The multivariable approach to describe such networks is based on the Richards transformation $\lambda = \tanh p\tau$), which converts the transcendental functions of distributed transmission lines with delay length into rational functions of λ (Richards 1948). In this way, the network functions of the structure under consideration can be written as rational functions of two complex variables p and λ, where λ is used for distributed parameter elements and the standard complex frequency variable p is taken for lumped parameter elements. As a matter of fact, the problem is actually a

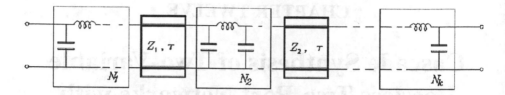

Figure 12.1: Generic form of cascaded lumped and distributed two-ports

single variable one, because of the hyperbolic dependence of the complex variables p and λ. However, if p and λ are assumed to be independent variables, then the problem can be treated using multivariable techniques based on the fundamental correspondence between the realizability of rational multivariable functions and the realizability of single variable transcendental functions established in (Bose 1982).

In the last decade, there have been several contributions on the synthesis and realizability of multivariable network functions (Bose 1982, Scanlan & Baher 1979, Swamy & Reddy 1986, Youla *et al.* 1972). Although multivariable generalization of some network theoretical concepts had been introduced in the literature, a general realizability theory, similar to the classical single variable case is still not available (Darlington 1939). Some attractive results on the general cascade synthesis problem have been obtained after the multivariable generalization of the scattering description of multidimensional lossless two-ports and multivariable Hurwitz polynomials (Basu & Fettweis 1988, Fettweis 1982, Kummert 1989). The existing studies elaborating this issue indicated that, although the positive real or bounded real conditions are necessary and sufficient in the single variable case, this is not true for the multivariable functions if passivity together with the cascade topology is to be captured (Bose 1982). For cascade synthesis of mixed-lumped distributed structures, additional conditions imposing the topological restrictions are required. This fact constitutes one of the major problems in establishing the realizability conditions for multivariable cascade synthesis.

In the present study, based on the two-variable scattering description of mixed lumped-distributed lossless two-port networks, the topological restrictions are utilized to end up with the necessary and sufficient conditions to characterize regular cascade structures. For the construction of lossless ladders composed of lumped elements and commensurate transmission lines a semi-analytical procedure is proposed.

12.2 CONSTRUCTION OF TWO-VARIABLE SCATTERING FUNCTIONS FOR LOSSLESS TWO-PORTS FORMED WITH CASCADED LUMPED AND DISTRIBUTED ELEMENTS

Consider the generic form of a lossless two-port formed with cascade connections of lumped and distributed two-ports shown in Fig. 12.1.

The scattering matrix describing the mixed lumped-distributed element two-port can be expressed in the Belevitch canonical form as (Basu & Fettweis 1988, Fettweis 1982),

$$S(p,\lambda) = \frac{1}{g(p,\lambda)} \begin{pmatrix} h(p,\lambda) & \sigma f(-p,-\lambda) \\ f(p,\lambda) & -\sigma h(-p,-\lambda) \end{pmatrix} . \tag{12.1}$$

where

- $f(p, \lambda), g(p, \lambda)$ and $h(p, \lambda)$ are real polynomials in the complex variables p and λ, ($\lambda = \tanh p\tau$), τ being the delay length of unit elements.)

- $g(p, \lambda)$ is a Scattering Hurwitz polynomial (Fettweis 1982),

- $f(p, \lambda)$ is monic, σ is a unimodular constant $|\sigma| = 1$

- The polynomials are related by

$$g(p, \lambda)g(-p, -\lambda) = h(p, \lambda)h(-p, -\lambda) + f(p, \lambda)f(-p, -\lambda) \qquad (12.2)$$

Let the real polynomials $g(p, \lambda)$ and $h(p, \lambda)$ with partial degrees n_p and n_λ be expressed as follows:

$$g(p, \lambda) = \sum_{i=1}^{n_p} g_i(\lambda)p^i, \qquad h(p, \lambda) = \sum_{i=1}^{n_p} h_i(\lambda)p^i, \qquad (12.3)$$

or equivalently

$$g(p, \lambda) = \mathbf{p}^T \Lambda_g \lambda, \qquad h(p, \lambda) = \mathbf{p}^T \Lambda_h \lambda, \qquad (12.4)$$

where $\mathbf{p}^T = (1 \ p \ p^2 \ \cdots \ p^{n_p})$, $\lambda^T = (1 \ \lambda \ \lambda^2 \ \cdots \ \lambda^{n_\lambda})$, and

$$\Lambda_g = \begin{pmatrix} g_{00} & g_{01} & \cdots & g_{0n_\lambda} \\ g_{10} & g_{11} & \cdots & \\ \vdots & \vdots & \ddots & \vdots \\ g_{n_p 0} & & \cdots & g_{n_p n_\lambda} \end{pmatrix}, \quad \Lambda_h = \begin{pmatrix} h_{00} & h_{01} & \cdots & h_{0n_\lambda} \\ h_{10} & h_{11} & \cdots & \\ \vdots & \vdots & \ddots & \vdots \\ h_{n_p 0} & & \cdots & h_{n_p n_\lambda} \end{pmatrix}. \quad (12.5)$$

As far as the realizability conditions are concerned, in order the scattering matrix $S(p, \lambda)$ to correspond to a lossless network, it should satisfy the properties given above. Furthermore, for the cascade topology under consideration, the scattering matrix and hence the canonical polynomials $f(p, \lambda), g(p, \lambda)$ and $h(p, \lambda)$ have to satisfy some additional independent conditions to ensure the realizability as a passive lossless cascade structure. In this context, regarding the generic form of the cascade topology under consideration, the followings may immediately be remarked:

1. For the mixed element lossless two-port, the polynomial $f(p, \lambda)$ defines the transmission zeros of the cascade and it is given by

$$f(p, \lambda) = f'(p)f''(\lambda), \qquad (12.6)$$

where, $f'(p)$ and $f''(\lambda)$ contain the transmission zeros due to the lumped sections and unit elements in the cascade, respectively. If n_λ unit elements are considered in cascade mode, then $f''(\lambda) = (1 - \lambda^2)^{n_\lambda/2}$ and when these transmission lines are removed from the cascade structure, one would end up with a lumped network whose transmission zeros are defined by $f'(p)$. In most of the practical cases, it is appropriate to choose $f'(p)$ as an even/odd real polynomial, which corresponds to reciprocal lumped structures. A particularly useful case is obtained for $f'(p) = 1$, which corresponds to a typical low-pass structure having transmission zeros only at infinity. In this case the polynomial $f(p, \lambda)$ takes the simple form

$$f(p, \lambda) = (1 - \lambda^2)^{n_\lambda/2} . \qquad (12.7)$$

Another practical case is to choose $f'(p) = p^{n_p}$, which corresponds to a typical high-pass structure having transmission zeros at origin.

2. When the transmission lines are removed from the cascade structure, one would end up with a lumped network whose transmission zeros are defined by $f'(p)$. In this case, the scattering matrix of the resulting lumped prototype can fully be described independently in terms of the real polynomials $f'(p)$, $g_0(p)$ and $h_0(p)$ as in the Belevitch representation (12.1). This would correspond to the boundary case where we set $\lambda = 0$ in the expressions of (12.3) and in the scattering description given by (12.1). In other words, the boundary polynomials $f(p, 0), g(p, 0)$ and $h(p, 0)$ define the cascade of lumped sections which take place in the composite structure, where $g(p, 0)$ is strictly Hurwitz and

$$g(p,0)g(-p,0) = h(p,0)h(-p,0) + f(p,0)f(-p,0) \qquad (12.8)$$

3. When the lumped elements are removed from the cascade structure, one would obtain a lossless two-port formed with typical cascade connection of transmission lines. In this case the resulting distributed prototype whose transmission zeros are defined as $f''(\lambda) = (1 - \lambda^2)^{n_\lambda/2}$ can fully be described independently in terms of the real polynomials $f''(\lambda), g''(\lambda)$ and $h''(\lambda)$ as in the Belevitch representation (12.1). For the particular mixed element structures with low-pass type lumped sections described by (12.7), setting $p = 0$ in the scattering description given by (12.1) corresponds to the boundary polynomials $g''(\lambda) = g_0(\lambda) = g(0, \lambda)$ and $h''(\lambda) = h_0(\lambda) = h(0, \lambda)$. In this case, the boundary polynomials $g(0, \lambda)$ and $h(0, \lambda)$ define the cascade of UEs which take place in the composite structure, where $g(0, \lambda)$ is strictly Hurwitz and

$$g(0, \lambda)g(0, -\lambda) = h(0, \lambda)h(0, -\lambda) + (1 - \lambda^2)^{n_\lambda} \qquad (12.9)$$

The more general cases with finite transmission zeros in lumped sections can also be treated following a similar reasoning. For example, if the lumped sections in the cascade are assumed to consist of high-pass type of elements with transmission zeros at origin, setting $p = \infty$ in (12.1), we end up with the corresponding boundary polynomials $g''(\lambda) = g_{n_p}(\lambda)$ and $h''(\lambda) = h_{n_p}(\lambda)$. In this case the paraunitary relation (12.9) is modified as,

$$g_{n_p}(\lambda)g_{n_p}(-\lambda) = h_{n_p}(\lambda)h_{n_p}(-\lambda) + (1 - \lambda^2)^{n_\lambda} \qquad (12.10)$$

where $g_{n_p}(\lambda)$ is strictly Hurwitz.

4. Note that the single variable boundary polynomials $h(p, 0)$ and $g(p, 0)$ related by the equation (12.8) define the first row entries of the coefficient matrices Λ_h and Λ_g given by (12.5). The boundary polynomials $h(0, \lambda)$, $g(0, \lambda)$ and the relation (12.9)

on the other hand define the entries of the first columns of Λ_h and Λ_g. In this case, the problem is to generate the remaining submatrices with unknown entries, so that the two-variable paraunitary relation (12.2) is satisfied together with the boundary conditions introduced in remarks (a), (b) and (c) above. The submatrices to be determined carry the cascade connection information and hence, they will be called the connectivity submatrices.

5. The essence of the cascade connection information can easily be exhibited by considering the construction of scattering functions via analysis. In the numerical analysis of mixed element cascaded structures, if the topologic connectivity information is fully provided at the outset, construction of the corresponding two-variable scattering functions, and hence generation of the connectivity submatrices of Λ_h and Λ_g can be achieved using the following procedure.

- The boundary polynomial sets $[f(p,0), g(p,0), h(p,0)]$ and $[f(0,\lambda), g(0,\lambda), h(0,\lambda)]$ describe two independent lumped and distributed network prototypes respectively. Those prototypes can be decomposed into their subsections algebraically by the use of transfer matrix factorization (Fettweis 1982), (Aksen 1994). Then the subsections can be sequentially connected as desired to form a cascade, as a result of which the remaining unknown coefficients of Λ_h and Λ_g are generated.

6. For the generation of the connectivity submatrices of Λ_h and Λ_g, which satisfy the boundary conditions given by the remarks (b) and (c), the solution of the two-variable paraunitary relation (12.2) is essential. By equating the coefficients of the same powers of the complex frequency variables in the equality (12.2), we end up with the following set of equations relating the coefficients of the matrices Λ_h and Λ_g:[1]

$$g_{0,k}^2 + 2\sum_{l=0}^{k-1}(-1)^{k-l}g_{0,l}g_{0,2k-l} \;=\;$$

$$h_{0,k}^2 + f_{0,k}^2 + 2\sum_{l=0}^{k-1}(-1)^{k-l}[h_{0,l}h_{0,2k-l} + f_{0,l}f_{0,2k-l}]$$

$$\vdots \quad \text{for} \quad k = 0 \text{ to } n_\lambda \tag{12.11}$$

$$\sum_{j=0}^{i}\sum_{l=0}^{k}(-1)^{i-j-l}g_{j,l}g_{i-j,2k-1-l} \;=\;$$

$$\sum_{j=0}^{i}\sum_{l=0}^{k}(-1)^{i-j-l}[h_{j,l}h_{i-j,2k-1-l} + f_{j,l}f_{i-j,2k-1-l}]$$

$$\vdots \quad \text{for} \quad i = 1,3,\cdots,2n_p - 1, \quad k = 0 \text{ to } n_\lambda \tag{12.12}$$

---

[1] In the equations hereafter one must set $f_{ij} = g_{ij} = h_{ij} = 0$ for $i > n_p$, $j > n_\lambda$.

$$\sum_{j=0}^{i}(-1)^{i-j}\left(g_{j,k}g_{i-j,k}+2\sum_{l=0}^{k-1}(-1)^{k-l}g_{j,l}g_{i-j,2k-l}\right)=\sum_{j=0}^{i}(-1)^{i-j}\left(h_{j,k}h_{i-j,k}\right.$$

$$+f_{j,k}f_{i-j,k}+2\sum_{l=0}^{k-1}(-1)^{k-l}[h_{j,l}h_{i-j,2k-l}+f_{j,l}f_{i-j,2k-l}]\left.\right)$$

$$\vdots \qquad \text{for} \quad i=2,4,\cdots 2n_p-2, \quad k=0 \text{ to } n_\lambda \qquad (12.13)$$

$$g_{n_p,k}^2+2\sum_{l=0}^{k-1}(-1)^{k-l}g_{n_p,l}g_{n_p,2k-l}=$$

$$h_{n_p,k}^2+f_{n_p,k}^2+2\sum_{l=0}^{k-1}(-1)^{k-l}[h_{n_p,l}h_{n_p,2k-l}+f_{n_p,l}f_{n_p,2k-l}]$$

$$\vdots \qquad \text{for} \quad k=0 \text{ to } n_\lambda \qquad (12.14)$$

It is worthwhile to mention that, the solution of the above equation set for the coefficients g_{ij} of the polynomial $g(p, \lambda)$ is equivalent to the factorization of a two-variable polynomial, and therefore, the equation set in (12.11)–(12.14) will be referred to as the fundamental equation set (FES) (Aksen 1994). Since the fundamental equation set is nonlinear, a generalized explicit solution, which results in a scattering Hurwitz polynomial $g(p, \lambda)$ is not clear. Therefore in order to end up with a realizable system, some further properties of FES must be investigated and the necessary constraints leading to an acceptable solution must be established. In this case, the problem is the determination of a particular solution of the fundamental equation set under proper constraints. In two-variable cascade synthesis, the problem is essentially that of determining those solutions of the FES which lead to a realizable cascade structure with positive element values. In this case, in addition to the boundary conditions given by (12.6), (12.8), (12.9) we need to consider additional independent coefficient constraints carrying the cascade connectivity information, in order to be able to come up with a solution.

Based on the above discussion, we end up with the following semi analytic procedure to construct two-variable canonical polynomials, which in turn define the scattering matrices for cascaded lumped-distributed structures.

Procedure:

- Assuming a regular cascaded structure as in Fig. 12.1, determine the complexity and transmission zeros of the structure. That is, set the number of lumped and distributed elements $[n_p, n_\lambda]$ and the polynomial $f(p, \lambda)$.

- Choose the coefficients of the polynomials $h(p, 0)$ and $h(0, \lambda)$ as the independent parameters and generate the strictly Hurwitz polynomials $g(p, 0)$ and $g(0, \lambda)$ using (12.8) and (12.9) respectively.

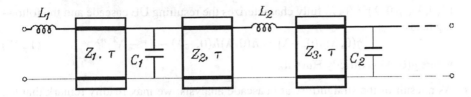

Figure 12.2: Low-pass ladder with unit elements

- In addition to the boundary conditions stated above, if further topologic constraints on the coefficients are invented, then FES given in (12.11)–(12.14) can be solved for the remaining unknown coefficients. This requires the establishment of coefficient constraints reflecting the connectivity information for each class of cascade topology. In case that the invented connectivity constraints are sufficient, we end up with a unique solution of FES. In this context, by straightforward analysis, the coefficient constraints leading to an explicit solution of FES can easily be generated for symmetric structures or those regular structures in which the lumped sections are confined to be simple low-pass, high-pass or band-pass elements (Yarman & Aksen 1992, Aksen & Yarman 1994, Youla *et al.* 1972, Belevitch 1968, Fettweis 1970, Fettweis 1972, Richards 1948, Brune 1931, Darlington 1939, Matthaei *et al.* 1964, Kummert 1989, Basu & Fettweis 1988, Abrie 1999, Sertbas *et al.* 1998).

12.3   CONSTRUCTION OF LOW-PASS LADDERS WITH UNIT ELEMENTS

From the physical implementation point of view, one of the practical circuit configurations is that of low-pass ladder structures with unit elements inserted between the lumped elements (Fig. 12.2).

The semi-analytic procedure discussed in the previous section can easily be applied for the construction of canonical polynomials describing the generic low-pass ladder structures with unit elements (LPLUE) as follows (Aksen & Yarman 1994, Aksen 1994):

1. LPLUE structure includes n_p simple lumped sections with transmission zeros at ∞ and n_λ UEs which introduce transmission zeros at $\lambda = \mp 1$. Thus, the polynomial $f(p, \lambda)$ corresponding to LPLUE structure is in the form

$$f(p, \lambda) = (1 - \lambda^2)^{n_\lambda/2}. \tag{12.15}$$

2. Removing the UEs in the cascade corresponds to setting $\lambda = 0$. In this case, the polynomial set $[f(p, 0), g(p, 0), h(p, 0)]$ fully characterizes the resulting lumped ladder and the following holds;

$$g(p, 0)g(-p, 0) = h(p, 0)h(-p, 0) + 1 \tag{12.16}$$

where $g(p, 0)$ is Strictly Hurwitz.

3. Removing the lumped elements in LPLUE structure, we obtain a cascade connection of UEs, which corresponds to setting $p = 0$. In this case, the polynomial set

$[f(0, \lambda), g(0, \lambda), h(0, \lambda)]$ fully characterizes the resulting UE cascade and the following holds;

$$g(0, \lambda)g(0, -\lambda) = h(0, \lambda)h(0, -\lambda) + (1 - \lambda^2)^{n_\lambda} \qquad (12.17)$$

where $g(0, \lambda)$ is Strictly Hurwitz.

4. As a result of the straightforward cascade analysis, we may readily remark that the coefficient matrices Λ_h and Λ_g have the generic forms;

$$\Lambda_h = \begin{pmatrix} 0 & h_{01} & h_{02} & \cdots & h_{0n_\lambda} \\ h_{10} & h_{11} & h_{12} & \cdots & h_{1n_\lambda} \\ h_{20} & h_{21} & h_{22} & \cdots & 0 \\ \vdots & \vdots & 0 & \ddots & \vdots \\ h_{n_p0} & 0 & 0 & \cdots & 0 \end{pmatrix} \qquad (12.18)$$

$$\Lambda_g = \begin{pmatrix} 1 & g_{01} & g_{02} & \cdots & g_{0n_\lambda} \\ g_{10} & g_{11} & g_{12} & \cdots & g_{1n_\lambda} \\ g_{20} & g_{21} & g_{22} & 0 & 0 \\ \vdots & \vdots & 0 & \ddots & \vdots \\ g_{n_p0} & 0 & 0 & \cdots & 0 \end{pmatrix}, \qquad (12.19)$$

where,

- The nonzero entries of Λ_g are nonnegative real numbers,
- $g_{11} = g_{01}g_{10} - h_{01}h_{10}$,
- $g_{kl} = h_{kl} = 0$ for $k + l > n_\lambda + 1$, $k, l = 0, 1, \cdots n_\lambda$,
- $h_{kl} = \mu g_{kl}$ for $k + l = n_\lambda + 1$, $k, l = 0, 1, \cdots n_\lambda$ where $\mu = \pm 1$,
- If $n_p = n_\lambda + 1$, then $\mu = h_{n_p0}/g_{n_p0} = \pm 1$.

The triangular form of the coefficient matrices and the coefficient relations for the nonzero entries given above can easily be verified by direct cascade analysis of generic LPLUE structure.

It should be noted here that for any other regular cascade topology involving UEs and high-pass or band pass type lumped sections, different sets of coefficient relations and matrix forms will be obtained. That is to say, the coefficient constraints in (12.18–12.19) uniquely describe the alternating connection of first order UEs with series inductors and shunt capacitors, and hence gives the connectivity information of the LPLUE structure under consideration.

5. Using the boundary conditions and the coefficients properties given in the items above, FES has been attempted to be solved algebraically for the unknown coefficients. We were able to come up with the derivation of explicit relations for the coefficients of Λ_h and Λ_g matrices of up to total degree $n_p + n_\lambda = 5$, where the coefficient properties given above constitute also sufficiency and lead to a unique explicit solution. The resulting explicit coefficient relations and the corresponding elementary LPLUE topologies to be accessed are shown in Table 12.1 and Fig. 12.3 respectively. For higher order ladders since direct derivation of coefficient relations becomes highly complicated, one has to solve FES by numerical means.

Table 12.1: Explicit formulas for low-order LPLUE

Degree 2 $n_p = 1$ $n_\lambda = 1$	h_{01}, h_{10} independent coefficients $g_{01} = (1 + h_{01}^2)^{1/2}$ $g_{11} = g_{10}g_{01} - h_{10}h_{01}$ $g_{10} = \|h_{10}\|$ $h_{11} = g_{11}h_{10}/g_{10}$
Degree 3 $n_p = 2$ $n_\lambda = 1$	h_{01}, h_{10}, h_{20} independent coefficients $g_{01} = (1 + h_{01}^2)^{1/2}$ $g_{11} = g_{10}g_{01} - h_{10}h_{01}$ $g_{20} = \|h_{20}\|$ $g_{10} = (h_{10}^2 + 2g_{20})^{1/2}$ $h_{11} = g_{11}g_{20}/h_{20}$
Degree 4 $n_p = 2$ $n_\lambda = 2$	$h_{01}, h_{02}, h_{10}, h_{20}$ independent coefficients $g_{01} = (2 + 2g_{02} + h_{01}^2)^{1/2}$ $g_{11} = g_{10}g_{01} - h_{10}h_{01}$ $h_{12} = \mu g_{12}$ $g_{02} = (1 + h_{02}^2)^{1/2}$ $h_{11} = h_{02}\beta/\alpha + h_{20}\alpha/\beta$ $h_{21} = \mu g_{21}$ $g_{10} = (h_{10}^2 + 2g_{20})^{1/2}$ $g_{12} = (g_{11}g_{02} - h_{11}h_{02})/\alpha$ $g_{20} = \|h_{20}\|$ $g_{21} = (g_{11}g_{20} - h_{11}h_{20})/\beta$ $\alpha = g_{01} - \mu h_{01}$ $\beta = g_{10} - \mu h_{10}$ $\mu = h_{20}/g_{20}$
Degree 5 $n_p = 3$ $n_\lambda = 2$	$h_{01}, h_{02}, h_{10}, h_{20}, h_{30}$ independent coefficients $g_{01} = (2 + 2g_{02} + h_{01}^2)^{1/2}$ $g_{11} = g_{10}g_{01} - h_{10}h_{01}$ $h_{12} = \mu g_{12}$ $g_{02} = (1 + h_{02}^2)^{1/2}$ $h_{11} = h_{02}\beta/\alpha + h_{20}\alpha/\beta$ $h_{21} = \mu g_{21}$ $g_{10} = (h_{10}^2 + 2g_{20})^{1/2}$ $g_{12} = (g_{11}g_{02} - h_{11}h_{02})/\alpha$ $g_{20} = (h_{20}^2 + 2g_{10}g_{30} - 2h_{10}h_{30})^{1/2}$ $g_{30} = \|h_{30}\|$ $g_{21} = (g_{11}g_{20} - h_{11}h_{20} - g_{01}g_{30} + h_{01}h_{30})/\beta$ $\alpha = g_{01} - \mu h_{01}$ $\beta = g_{10} - \mu h_{10}$ $\mu = h_{30}/g_{30}$

12.4 APPLICATION

A major potential area of application of the results obtained is that of computer aided real frequency broadband matching. The real frequency matching involves with the description of the matching network in terms of a set of independent real parameters and then with the numerical determination of these parameters by optimizing the gain performance of the system under load and gain-bandwidth limitations (Chen 1988, Yarman 1985, Yarman & Carlin 1982). In the design of broadband matching networks with mixed lumped and distributed elements, the scattering representation of mixed element matching network is generated from the partially defined polynomial $h(p, \lambda)$ using the procedure discussed above. That is, provided that the complexity and the location of transmission zeros of the matching network is defined by setting $f(p, 0)$ and $f(0, \lambda)$, the coefficients of the polynomials $h(p, 0)$ and $h(0, \lambda)$ are chosen as the independent unknown parameters of the problem and determined to optimize the transducer power gain of the doubly terminated system. The transducer power gain of the doubly terminated mixed element network can be written in two variable formalism at real frequencies as follows: (Aksen 1994, Abrie 1999)

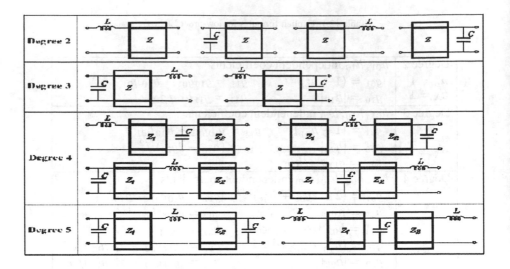

Figure 12.3: Low order LPLUE structures

$$T(\omega) = \frac{(1 - |S_G|^2)(1 - |S_L|^2)|f(\jmath\omega, \jmath\Omega)|^2}{|g(\jmath\omega, \jmath\Omega) - h(\jmath\omega, \jmath\Omega)S_G + \sigma S_L h(-\jmath\omega, -\jmath\Omega) - \sigma S_L S_G g(\jmath\omega, \jmath\Omega)|^2}, \tag{12.20}$$

where, $\Omega = \tan\omega\tau$, τ being the delay length of UEs, S_G and S_L denote the reflection functions of the generator and the load networks to be matched respectively. h, g and f are the two-variable polynomials describing the mixed element matching network.

By close examination of the expression (12.20), we can easily see that the gain $T(\omega)$ is almost inverse quadratic in the chosen unknown coefficients h_{ij} of the polynomials $h(p, 0)$ and $h(0, \lambda)$. Hence a least square optimization technique provides satisfactory results, especially if a flat gain characteristic T_0 is to be approximated. The objective function to be minimized may be defined as

$$\delta = \sum_{k=1}^{N_\omega}[T(\omega_k, \{h_{i0}, h_{0j}\}) - T_0]^2, \qquad i = 1, \dots n_p, \ j = 1, \dots n_\lambda \tag{12.21}$$

where, N_ω denotes the number of sampling frequencies over the matching band.

Once the final forms of $g(p, \lambda)$ and $h(p, \lambda)$ are generated, the mixed element realization can be obtained by employing the algebraic decomposition technique (Basu & Fettweis 1988, Aksen 1994) on the polynomial sets describing the lumped and distributed prototypes independently.

12.4.1 An example

In the following, we present a typical double matching problem to exhibit the application of the design procedure with mixed lumped-distributed elements. In the example, an LPLUE

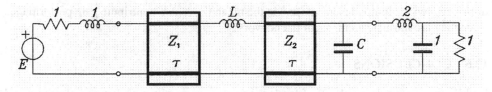

Figure 12.4: Double matching example with lumped-distributed elements, $L = 2.126, C = 0.751, Z_1 = 0.161,$ $Z_2 = 0.341, \tau = 0.21$

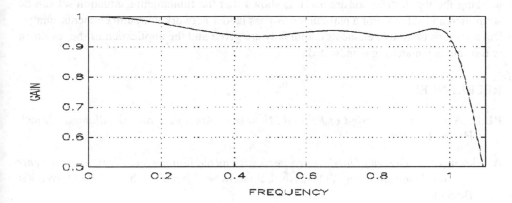

Figure 12.5: Gain performance of double matching example

network of degree four, $(n_p = 2, n_\lambda = 2)$ is employed to match the load and generator impedances shown in Fig. 12.4 over a normalized frequency band of $0 \leq \omega \leq 1$.

In course of optimization process, the coefficients $\{h_{01}, h_{02}, h_{10}, h_{20}\}$, the sign constant μ and the delay length τ of the UEs are chosen as the free parameters, and the explicit expressions given in (12.1) are directly utilized.

Starting with ad hoc choice of initial values for the free parameters, as a result of optimization we obtain the following coefficient matrices which fully describe the scattering functions of the matching network:

$$\Lambda_h = \begin{pmatrix} 0 & -4.325 & -0.824 \\ 0.687 & -3.303 & -20.188 \\ 0.798 & -4.965 & 0 \end{pmatrix}, \quad \Lambda_g = \begin{pmatrix} 1 & 4.827 & 1.296 \\ 1.439 & 9.917 & 20.188 \\ 0.798 & 4.965 & 0 \end{pmatrix}.$$

The final network with the component values and the gain performance of the system are shown in Fig. 12.4 and Fig. 12.5 respectively.

The gain performance of the resulting system is in good agreement with the available lumped element design solutions of the same problem in the literature (Yarman & Fettweis 1990). From the microwave integrated circuit implementation point of view, the available solutions employing solely lumped sections create serious implementation problems due to the physical length of interconnections (Abrie 1999). In our example however, the commensurate transmission line sections (UEs) provide the necessary physical connections between the lumped elements and in the mean time, also contribute gain performance since they are intrinsic elements of the network.

12.5 CONCLUSIONS

In this study, cascade synthesis of lossless two-port networks with lumped elements and transmission lines is investigated. Based on two-variable scattering matrix description of mixed element cascade structures, the fundamental equation set for the determination of the coefficients of canonical polynomials describing the scattering matrix is set up. By utilizing the topological constraints, it is shown that the fundamental equation set can be simplified and solved. For a particular low-pass ladder network with unit elements, analytical solutions up to five elements complexity are given and the application of the results in real frequency matching is indicated.

REFERENCES

P.L.D. Abrie, 1999, *Design of RF and Microwave Amplifiers and Oscillators.* Artech House, London.

A. Aksen, 1994, *Design of lossless two-ports with mixed lumped and distributed elements for broadband matching.* PhD thesis, Lehrstuhl Nachrichtentechnik, Ruhr Universität Bochum.

A. Aksen and B. S. Yarman, 1994, A semi-analytical procedure to describe lossless two-ports with mixed lumped and distributed elements. *IEEE Int. Symp. Circuits and Systems*, 5:205–208.

S. Basu and A. Fettweis, 1988, On synthesizable multidimensional lossless two-ports. *IEEE Trans. Circuits and Systems*, 35:1478–1486.

V. Belevitch, 1968, *Classical Network Theory.* Holden Day, San Francisco.

N. K. Bose, 1982, *Applied Multidimensional Systems Theory.* Van Nostrand Reinhold, New York.

O. Brune, 1931. Synthesis of a finite two-terminal network whose driving-point impedance is a prescribed function of frequency. *J. Math. Phys.* 10:191–236.

W. K. Chen, 1988, *Broadband Matching, Theory and Implementations.* World Scientific, Singapore, 2. Edt.

S. Darlington, 1939, Synthesis of rectance 4-poles. *J. Math. Phys.*, 18:257–353.

A. Fettweis, 1970, Factorization of transfer matrices of lossless two-ports. *IEEE Trans. Circuit Theory*, 17:86–94.

A. Fettweis, 1972, Cascade synthesis of lossless two ports by transfer matrix factorization. In *Network Theory* (ed. R. Boite), Gordon & Breach, pages 43–103.

A. Fettweis, 1982, On the scattering matrix and the scattering transfer matrix of multidimensional lossless two-ports. *Archiv. Elektr. Ubertragung*, 36:374–381.

A. Kummert, 1989, Synthesis of two-dimensional lossless m-ports with prescribed scattering matrix. *Circuits Systems and Signal Proc.*, 8:97–119.

G.L. Matthaei, L. Young and E.M.T. Jones, 1964, *Microwave Filters, Impedance Matching Networks, and Coupling Structures*. McGraw-Hill, New York.

P.I. Richards, 1948, Resistor-transmission-line circuits. *Proc. IRE*, 36:217–220.

S. O. Scanlan and H. Baher, 1979, Driving point synthesis of a resistor terminated cascade composed of lumped lossless 2-ports and commensurate stubs. *IEEE Trans. Circuits and Systems*, 26:947–955.

A. Sertbas, A. Aksen and B.S. Yarman, 1998. Construction of some classes of two-variable lossless ladder networks with simple lumped elements and uniform transmission lines. *IEEE Asia Pacific Conf. Circuits and Systems*, pages 24–27.

M. N. S. Swamy and H. C. Reddy, 1986, Two-variable analog ladders with applications. In S.G. Tzafestas, editor, *Multidimensional Systems*, pages 267–315. Marcel Dekker, New York.

B. S. Yarman, 1985, Modern approaches to broadband matching problems. *Proc. IEE*, 132:87–92.

B. S. Yarman and A. Aksen, 1992, An integrated design tool to construct lossless matching networks with mixed lumped and distributed elements. *IEEE Trans. Circuits and Systems*, 39:713–723.

B. S. Yarman and H. J. Carlin, 1982, A simplified real frequency techniqe applied to broadband multi-stage microwave amplifiers. *IEEE Trans. Microwave Theory and Tech.*, 30:2216–2222.

B. S. Yarman and A. Fettweis, 1990, Computer-aided double matching via parametric representation of brune functions. *IEEE Trans. Circuits and Systems*, 37:212–222.

D. C. Youla, J. D. Rhodes, and P. C. Marston, 1972, Driving point synthesis of resistor terminated cascades composed of lumped lossless passive 2-ports and commensurate tem lines. *IEEE Trans. Circut Theory*, 19:648–664.

CHAPTER THIRTEEN

Reconstruction of Positron Emission Tomography Images by using MAP Estimation

F. Boschen[†], A. Kummert[†], H. Herzog[‡]

[†]   Laboratory for Communication Theory
Department of Electrical Engineering
University of Wuppertal, Germany
boschen/kummert@uni-wuppertal.de

[‡]   Institute of Medicine
Research Center Jülich KFA
Jülich, Germany

Abstract

Positron emission tomography (PET) is a technique that has been developed to study the metabolic activity of the human body (Herman 1980) (Deans 1983) (Barrett 1984). In the last years many algorithms have been developed for reconstructing tomography images. The maximum likelihood expectation maximization algorithm (ML-EM) (Vardi & Shepp 1982) is a very stable nonlinear method and was developed by Shepp and Vardi in 1982. For the first time, one was able to model the reconstruction process by taking into account stochastic properties of the underlying physical model.

However, the ML-EM algorithm causes some serious problems in the context of the application considered. It is an iterative procedure and seems to converge rapidly to a stationary point, however, the reconstructed image is distorted by superimposed high frequency noise. This poor performance motivated different modifications of the algorithm. These can be divided into two classes.

1. Stopping the algorithm at a step where the reconstructed image seems to have an acceptable quality (Llacer & Veklerov 1989). Obviously, it is a problem to determine a reasonable stop criteria and to explain the gap between this subjective best reconstruction and the optimal one in the maximum likelihood sense.

2. Modification of the nonlinear algorithm by using a priori information in order to improve the algorithm with Bayesian methods (Levitan & Herman 1987).

In this chapter the second method is used, based on an analysis of the ML-EM method.

13.1   INTRODUCTION

Positron emission tomography (PET) is a special form of Computer Tomography (CT) with the following properties. The most important feature of PET is the use of the emission of radioactive nuclide in contrast to illuminating the patient by X-rays in classical tomographs. The mathematical description of X-ray based CT and PET is the same. The measurements (projections) $p(l, \theta)$ and the underlying image $g(x, y)$ are related via the Radon-Transform

(Radon 1987)

$$p(l,\theta) = \int\limits_{-\infty}^{\infty} \int\limits_{-\infty}^{\infty} g(x,y)\,\delta\left(l - x\cos\theta - y\sin\theta\right) dx dy, \tag{13.1}$$

where l is the line-coordinate for the projection under the angle θ and x, y are the cartesian coordinates of the image (Fig. 13.1). The measured projection is the integral of the emitted energy (PET) or the attenuation (CT), respectively, along a line. This is illustrated by Fig. 13.1.

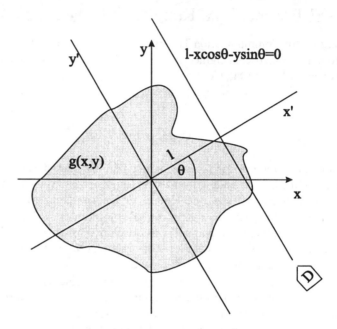

Figure 13.1: Principles of Tomography

Measurements are made under different angles θ. With this data it is possible to reconstruct the image of one slice (plane) of the inspected object. The analytical solution of (13.1) is given by

$$g(x,y) = \frac{1}{2\pi} \int\limits_{0}^{\pi} V.p. \int\limits_{-\infty}^{\infty} \frac{p'(l - l',\theta)}{\pi l'} dl'\, d\theta, \tag{13.2}$$

with

$$l = x\cos\theta + y\sin\theta, \tag{13.3}$$

where $V.p.$ denotes the principal value of the Cauchy integral and $p'(l,\theta)$ is the first derivative of $p(l,\theta)$ with respect to l. However, the numerical solution of the above integral is very delicate due to the pole of the kernel at $l' = 0$. Hence, alternative methods for the reconstruction of images had to be developed. The most familiar algorithm is the filtered backprojection (Herman 1980) (Deans 1983) (Barrett 1984), which can be characterized as follows

$$g(x, y) = \int_0^\pi s(x\cos\theta + y\sin\theta, \theta)\, d\theta, \tag{13.4}$$

where $s(l, \theta)$ is the filtered (with respect to l) version of $p(l, \theta)$, and the transfer function of the filter is described by $G(j\omega) = |\omega|$. In other words, the Fourier transforms $S(j\omega, \theta)$ and $P(j\omega, \theta)$ of the signals $s(l, \theta)$ and $p(l, \theta)$ are related by

$$S(j\omega, \theta) = P(j\omega, \theta)\, G(j\omega) = P(j\omega, \theta)\, |\omega|. \tag{13.5}$$

Although this method is numerically stable, the reconstruction, however, is marked with radial distortions caused by interpolation errors. Another method is based on the attempt to solve the problem by discretization and is known as the algebraic method. More precisely, the image $g(x, y)$ is interpreted as a two-dimensional discrete signal of finite size. Its samples (pixels) can be arranged in vector form $\underline{g} = [g_1, ..., g_B]^T$, where underlined letters represent vectors or matrices. The projection signal is discretized in a natural way since measurements are performed by an array of equispaced sensors. Each sensor signal is interpreted as a sample of the discretized projection. These samples are summarized to a vector $\underline{p} = [p_1, ..., p_D]^T$ which is related to $\underline{g}$ via

$$\begin{bmatrix} p_1 \\ p_2 \\ \cdot \\ \cdot \\ p_D \end{bmatrix} = \begin{bmatrix} a_{11} & a_{12} & \cdot & \cdot & a_{1B} \\ a_{21} & a_{22} & \cdot & \cdot & a_{2B} \\ \cdot & & \cdot & & \cdot \\ \cdot & & & \cdot & \cdot \\ a_{D1} & a_{D2} & \cdot & \cdot & a_{DB} \end{bmatrix} \begin{bmatrix} g_1 \\ g_2 \\ \cdot \\ \cdot \\ g_B \end{bmatrix}, \tag{13.6}$$

with

$$\sum_{d=1}^{D} a_{db} = 1, \quad b = 1, ..., B, \tag{13.7}$$

where $\underline{a} = (a_{db})$ is a constant coefficient matrix that describes the system. The coefficient matrix is sparse and badly conditioned. The number of equations is often different from the number of unknowns in the system above. Consequently, a direct inversion of the system matrix $\underline{a}$ is numerically critical and thus, iterative procedures for solving this system of equations appear to be more promising. One of the most severe problems associated with PET is the statistical fluctuation of the radioactive emission processes which causes noisy projection data. In order to reduce the influence of these effects on the reconstructed image, the so called ML-EM algorithm has been introduced by Vardi & Shepp (1982), where the samples of the image are modelled as independent Poisson distributed random variables.

13.2 ML-EM ALGORITHM

The ML-EM algorithm has been introduced by Vardi & Shepp (1982). In order to be able to judge the performance of this algorithm with respect to its statistical behaviour, we give a short introduction which is somewhat different to that in (Vardi & Shepp 1982). In particular we have to distinguish explicitly between random variables and their realizations (outcomes of experiments, measured data). Since this aspect is of fundamental importance for the correct interpretation of our results, we represent random variables by capital letters and their respective realizations by the corresponding small letters. As just mentioned, the generation of photons in the body of the patient can be modelled as a Poisson process. Consequently, the image samples will be considered as Poisson distributed random variables G_b, $b = 1, ..., B$, with mean value

$$\lambda_b = E\{G_b\}, \tag{13.8}$$

where E is the expectation operator. The random variable G_b itself can be considered (Moon 1996) as a sum of independent Poisson distributed random variables W_{db}, where W_{db} models the number of photons detected in sensor number d and emitted from image point b, i.e.

$$G_b = \sum_{d=1}^{D} W_{db} \tag{13.9}$$

and for the respective realizations we have

$$g_b = \sum_{d=1}^{D} w_{db}. \tag{13.10}$$

Furthermore, it can be shown (Moon 1996) that the mean values $\lambda_{db} = E\{W_{db}\}$ are associated with λ_b via

$$\lambda_{db} = a_{db}\lambda_b, \tag{13.11}$$

where the a_{db} are defined by (13.6) and can be determined from the geometry of the tomograph. Due to the independence of the random variables W_{db} we can define the likelihood function

$$l(\underline{\lambda}) = \prod_{b=1}^{B} \prod_{d=1}^{D} e^{-a_{db}\lambda_b} \frac{(a_{db}\lambda_b)^{w_{db}}}{w_{db}!}. \tag{13.12}$$

However, in order to obtain parameter estimators with small variances, large sets of measured data are required, which, however are usually not available in the application considered.

In the next step, the log-likelihood function is considered where products in (13.12) are transformed into sums

$$L(\underline{\lambda}) = \ln l(\underline{\lambda}) = \sum_{b=1}^{B} \sum_{d=1}^{D} (-a_{db}\lambda_b + w_{db} \ln \lambda_b + w_{db} \ln a_{db} - \ln(w_{db}!)), \tag{13.13}$$

where w_{db} is a realization of W_{db}. In this equation the quantities w_{db} are unknown and have to be estimated in the so called expectation step of the algorithm. This is done in an iterative procedure where the conditional expectation

$$\widehat{w}_{db}^{[k+1]} = E\left\{ W_{db} \middle| p_d, \widehat{\underline{\lambda}}^{[k]} \right\} \tag{13.14}$$

is used and $\widehat{w}_{db}^{[k]}$ represents the estimate of w_{db} in the kth iteration step, p_d is the measured projection value and $\widehat{\underline{\lambda}}^{[k]}$ is the estimate of $\underline{\lambda}$ in the kth iteration step. As outlined in

(Moon 1996), this procedure leads to

$$\widehat{w}_{db}^{[k+1]} = \frac{p_d a_{db} \widehat{\lambda}_b^{[k]}}{\sum\limits_{b'=1}^{B} a_{db'} \widehat{\lambda}_{b'}^{[k]}}. \qquad (13.15)$$

Next we consider the so called maximization step of the ML-EM algorithm. In order to maximize the log-likelihood function one has to set its partial derivatives with respect to the unknown parameters λ_b to zero

$$\frac{\partial}{\partial \lambda_b} \sum_{b=1}^{B} \sum_{d=1}^{D} \left(a_{db}\lambda_b + \widehat{w}_{db}^{[k+1]} \ln \lambda_b + \widehat{w}_{db}^{[k+1]} \ln a_{db} - \ln \left(\widehat{w}_{db}^{[k+1]}! \right) \right) = 0, \qquad (13.16)$$

which leads to

$$\widehat{\lambda}_b^{[k+1]} = \sum_{d=1}^{D} \widehat{w}_{db}^{[k+1]}. \qquad (13.17)$$

On the other hand, Equation (13.10) implies that the sum of realizations of w_{db} (belonging to the same experiment) over $d = 1, ..., D$, represents the realization (of the same experiment) g_b of the random variable G_b. Hence, a corresponding sum over estimations $\widehat{w}_{db}^{[k+1]}$ of the realizations w_{db} can be interpreted as an estimate $\widehat{g}_b^{[k+1]}$ of g_b, i.e.

$$\widehat{\lambda}_b^{[k+1]} = \widehat{g}_b^{[k+1]}. \qquad (13.18)$$

Obviously, the 'best' estimate $\widehat{\lambda}_b$ of the expected value λ_b of the random variable G_b is the current realization g_b of G_b, if we apply the ML-EM algorithm. This astonishing result gives deep insight into the mechanism of this algorithm. Obviously, the algorithm is not able to deliver a reliable estimate of λ_b, but simply tries to reconstruct the current radio-active activities, which, due to the stochastic nature of these processes, can be interpreted as the λ_b's superimposed by 'noise'. In other words, the algorithm is not able to reduce statistical fluctuations by means of averaging over independent measurements which would be the only possible mechanism to improve the SNR (signal to noise ratio) of the reconstructed image. Experiments with real data confirm this result, that the reconstructed image is distorted by superimposed high frequency noise (Fig. 13.2).

However, the stochastic nature of the radioactive processes is not the only reason for noisy effects in reconstructed images.

One has to interpret simulation results carefully, since, additionally, the convergence behaviour of the algorithm itself amplifies noisy artifacts during a long time of the iteration circle. This aspect will be discussed in the next section.

13.3　CONVERGENCE BEHAVIOUR

The convergence behaviour of the algorithm is analyzed by means of artificially constructed projection data. This is done by projecting an artificially created image g (which is deterministic) of an ideal disc via matrix $\underline{a}$, i.e. the projections

$$\underline{p} = \underline{a}\,\underline{g} \qquad (13.19)$$

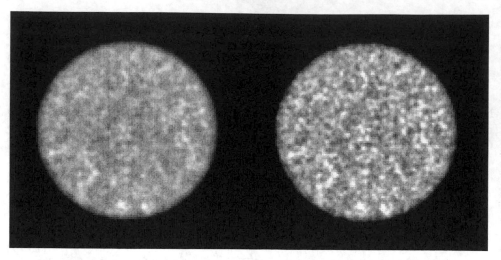

Figure 13.2: Reconstructed image of a cylinder phantom after 20 iterations (left) and 50 iterations (right)

are not distorted by noisy (statistical) effects. In other words, a good reconstruction algorithm should be able to determine $\underline{g}$ on basis of the given projections $\underline{p}$. Figure 13.3 shows a profile of this disc.

The Euclidean distance f between reconstruction $\widehat{\underline{g}}$ and original image $\underline{g}$ represents the reconstruction error and serves as a convergence criterion

$$f = \sum_{b=1}^{B} (g_b - \widehat{g}_b)^2 . \tag{13.20}$$

In a computer simulation with 19 000 iteration steps, this deviation has been measured. The algorithm converges slowly, but monotonically. Figure 13.4 shows the results of the first 3500 iteration steps.

In spite of the ideal data used in our experiments, the well known artifacts occurring during the iteration procedure had been also observed. These artifacts appear as superimposed noisy texture in the reconstructed images, whose granularity seem to become finer during the iteration process. Since fine structured noise is more disturbing for the visual perception of humans, many people believed to observe a decline of performance of the ML-EM algorithm after approximately 20 iterations. The high frequency noise often has been interpreted as an error caused by the ML-EM algorithm and not as a noise component of the measured signal. This subjective interpretation can be proved to be incorrect by analyzing the mathematically based quality measure f. The latter indeed was monotonically decreasing during all of our simulations. In order to explain this discrepancy between subjective and objective (mathematically based) quality judgment one has to investigate the spectral properties of the reconstruction error. Respective investigations have been performed on basis of the already described ideal disc image. The magnitude of the difference between the spectra of the reconstructed and the original profile after 19 000 iterations is shown in Figure 13.5.

The results of our computer simulations can be interpreted as follows. At the beginning of the iteration process, the reconstruction error signal has a relatively high energy, which

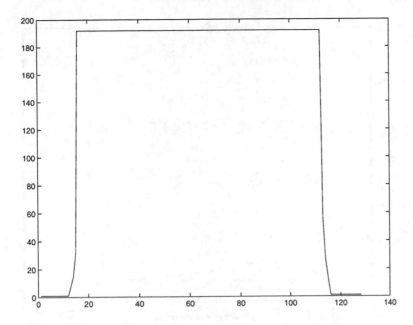

Figure 13.3: Profile of an artificial disc

is nearly uniformly distributed over the whole spatial frequency range (Fig. 13.6). With progressing iteration, the total error signal energy declines, however, it is more and more concentrated in the high spatial frequency band. In other words, after some iterations, the low frequency components of the original image are nearly perfectly reconstructed whereas the reconstruction of higher frequency components needs a large number of iteration steps. In particular, the latter statement is of special interest. Most people working with the ML-EM algorithm have observed a 'convergence' of the algorithm after approximately 20 iterations (Llacer & Veklerov 1989) resulting in a poor reconstruction. However, in the light of the above discussion, the algorithm is still far away from its equilibrium point. Thus, improvements are still achievable. However, due the extremely slow convergence of the algorithm with respect to the reconstruction of high frequency components, many thousands of iteration steps would be needed for significantly improving the results, which would be impossible in practice. In order to verify the last statements we tested the ML-EM algorithm with an ideal disc image of lower resolution. Indeed, after a sufficiently long iteration time, even the higher frequency components of the reconstruction error signal had been so small that they lay below the visual perception level.

In summary, differences between the low frequency components of reconstructed and original disc in the kth iteration step lead to a large correction signal. In contrast to this, the algorithm is very insensitive with respect to high spatial frequency components of the error signal.

13.4   CONJUGATE GRADIENT ALGORITHM

The expectation step of the ML-EM algorithm represents an iterative procedure to solve the system of Equations (13.6). The convergence is very slow and is influenced by the

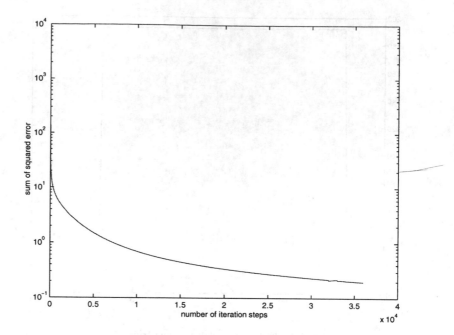

Figure 13.4: Sum of squared error as a function of the number of iteration steps

precise determination of the system coefficients a_{db}. Consequently, we replaced the ML-EM algorithm by the conjugate gradient (CG) algorithm which shows superior convergence behaviour.

The CG algorithm is a well known method for solving systems of equations with a sparse symmetric positive definite coefficient matrix. In order to meet these conditions, we solve the unregularized normal equations

$$\underline{a}^T \underline{a} \, \underline{q} = \underline{a}^T \underline{p}. \tag{13.21}$$

The CG algorithm is a regularization process, where the regularization parameter is given by the number of iteration steps. The algorithm itself is represented by the following recursions

$$
\begin{aligned}
\underline{q}^{[k]} &\leftarrow \underline{s}^{[k-1]} + \frac{\underline{s}^{T[k-1]}\underline{s}^{[k-1]}}{\underline{s}^{T[k-2]}\underline{s}^{[k-2]}} \underline{q}^{[k-1]}, \\
\underline{g}^{[k]} &\leftarrow \underline{g}^{[k-1]} + \frac{\underline{s}^{T[k-1]}\underline{s}^{[k-1]}}{\left(\underline{a}\,\underline{q}^{[k]}\right)^T\left(\underline{a}\,\underline{q}^{[k]}\right)} \underline{q}^{[k]}, \\
\underline{s}^{[k]} &\leftarrow \underline{s}^{[k-1]} - \frac{\underline{s}^{T[k-1]}\underline{s}^{[k-1]}}{\left(\underline{a}\,\underline{q}^{[k]}\right)^T\left(\underline{a}\,\underline{q}^{[k]}\right)} \underline{a}^T \underline{a}\,\underline{q}^{[k]},
\end{aligned} \tag{13.22}
$$

where the computation of step $k = 1$ is based on the initial values

$$
\begin{aligned}
\underline{g}^{[0]} &= \underline{0}, \\
\underline{q}^{[0]} &= \underline{a}^T \underline{p}, \\
\underline{s}^{[-1]} &= \underline{q}^{[0]}, \\
\underline{s}^{[0]} &\leftarrow \underline{s}^{[-1]} - \frac{\underline{s}^{T[-1]}\underline{s}^{[-1]}}{\left(\underline{a}\,\underline{q}^{[0]}\right)^T\left(\underline{a}\,\underline{q}^{[0]}\right)} \underline{a}^T \underline{a}\,\underline{q}^{[0]}.
\end{aligned} \tag{13.23}
$$

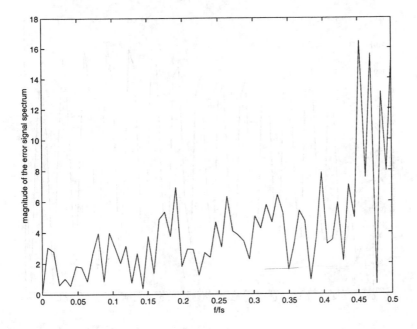

Figure 13.5: Magnitude of the difference of spectra between reconstructed and original profile after 19 000 iteration steps. Fs=sampling frequency

The vectors $\underline{q}$ and $\underline{s}$ represent auxiliary quantities which have the same size as the image vector $\underline{g}$. After a sufficiently large number of steps, the resulting vector $\underline{g}^{[k]}$ can be interpreted as an approximation of the underlying image vector $\underline{g}$.

The CG algorithm shows better convergence properties than the expectation step of the ML-EM algorithm. Hence, the number of iteration steps can be reduced and the approximation of image vector $\underline{g}$ is improved, especially in the higher frequency band.

13.5 MAP ESTIMATION

The 'best' estimate of λ_b produced by the ML-EM algorithm is the realization g_b itself (13.18). In view of this it is obvious that we need more information about the process in order to improve the estimation of λ_b. For doing this, Bayes theory is a helpful tool. First we define random variables $\widehat{\Lambda}_b$ with realizations $\widehat{\lambda}_b$. The $\widehat{\lambda}_b$ represent the possible values of λ_b and we try to calculate that value $\widehat{\lambda}_b$ with the highest probability. The Bayes theorem implies

$$f\left(\widehat{\lambda}_b \,|g_b\right) = \frac{f\left(g_b \,\Big|\widehat{\lambda}_b\right) f\left(\widehat{\lambda}_b\right)}{f\left(g_b\right)} \tag{13.24}$$

where the a posteriori probability distribution $f\left(\widehat{\lambda}_b \,|g_b\right)$ is expressed in terms of the conditional distribution $f\left(g_b \,\Big|\widehat{\lambda}_b\right)$ and the prior probability distribution $f\left(\widehat{\lambda}_b\right)$. Due to our

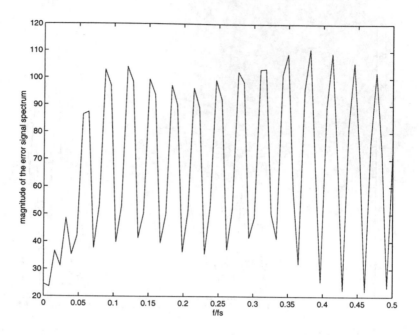

Figure 13.6: Magnitude of the difference of spectra between reconstructed and original profile after 20 iteration steps. Fs=sampling frequency.

assumption stated in section 13.2, the probability distribution $f\left(g_b \middle| \widehat{\lambda}_b\right)$ is Poisson distributed, with parameter $\widehat{\lambda}_b$, i.e.

$$f\left(g_b \middle| \widehat{\lambda}_b\right) = e^{-\widehat{\lambda}_b} \frac{\left(\widehat{\lambda}_b\right)^{g_b}}{g_b!}. \tag{13.25}$$

Furthermore, the random variable G_b is Poisson distributed with parameter λ_b, i.e.

$$f\left(g_b\right) = e^{-\lambda_b} \frac{\left(\lambda_b\right)^{g_b}}{g_b!}. \tag{13.26}$$

Obviously, $f\left(g_b\right)$ is independent of $\widehat{\lambda}_b$ and can therefore be omitted in our further considerations. To find the best estimate $\widehat{\lambda}_b$ of λ_b we have to maximize the a posteriori probability distribution $f\left(\widehat{\lambda}_b \middle| g_b\right)$. Similar to the ML algorithm, we assume the random variables $\widehat{\Lambda}_b$ to be independent and form the modified likelihood function

$$l\left(\underline{\widehat{\lambda}}\right) = \prod_{b=1}^{B} e^{-\widehat{\lambda}_b} \frac{\left(\widehat{\lambda}_b\right)^{g_b}}{g_b!} f\left(\widehat{\lambda}_b\right), \tag{13.27}$$

where the distributions $f\left(g_b\right)$ are omitted. The choice of the prior probability is a fundamental problem in Bayes theory. We use a prior distribution of Gibbsian form (Winkler

1995), so we get

$$f\left(\widehat{\lambda}_b\right) = \frac{1}{z}e^{-H\left(\widehat{\lambda}_b\right)} \tag{13.28}$$

where $H\left(\widehat{\lambda}_b\right)$ is the so called energy function and z the normalization factor. Next we transform the products into sums by building the loglikelihood function

$$L\left(\widehat{\underline{\lambda}}\right) = \ln l\left(\widehat{\underline{\lambda}}\right) = \sum_{b=1}^{B}\left(-\widehat{\lambda}_b + g_b \ln \widehat{\lambda}_b - \ln g_b! - \ln z - H\left(\widehat{\lambda}_b\right)\right). \tag{13.29}$$

In order to maximize this expression we set its partial derivatives with respect to $\widehat{\lambda}_b$ to zero and obtain as the result the system of equations

$$1 = g_b \frac{1}{\widehat{\lambda}_b} - \frac{\partial}{\partial \widehat{\lambda}_b} H\left(\widehat{\lambda}_b\right), \quad b = 1, ..., B \tag{13.30}$$

The energy function $H\left(\widehat{\lambda}_b\right)$ can be defined in various ways. Good numerical results have been achieved by using the expression

$$H\left(\widehat{\lambda}_b\right) = \beta \sum_{b' \in \Omega_1}\left(\widehat{\lambda}_b - g_{b'}\right)^2 + \frac{\beta}{\sqrt{2}} \sum_{b' \in \Omega_2}\left(\widehat{\lambda}_b - g_{b'}\right)^2 \tag{13.31}$$

where $\beta > 0$ is a coupling constant. Ω_1 contains the indices of the four nearest neighbours of pixel g_b in the vertical and horizontal directions, and, similarly, Ω_2 contains the indices of the four nearest neighbours of pixel g_b on the diagonals (which explains the factor $\sqrt{2}$). In fact, $H\left(\widehat{\lambda}_b\right)$ is minimal for constant configurations and maximal for configurations with maximal grey value differences between neighbours. If we introduce into (13.31) instead of the image points g_b its approximations $g_b^{[k]}$ computed by the CG algorithm we are able to solve (13.31) with respect to the optimal estimates $\widehat{\lambda}_{b,opt}$ of the unknown mean values λ_b. The MAP algorithm acts as a nonlinear low pass operator on $g_b^{[k]}$. In other words, $\widehat{\lambda}_{b,opt}$ is a smoothed version of $g_b^{[k]}$. On the one hand, the statistical reliability of the estimates of λ_b is improved, on the other, spatial resolution decreases.

Figure 13.7 shows a first result of the improved method. The reconstructions of the image are nearly the same with ML-EM algorithm and CGA algorithm, but the CGA is much faster. It is clearly seen, that the MAP filtering decreases the noise in the reconstruction without disturbing the steepness of the flanks.

13.6 CONCLUSIONS

It has been shown that the ML-EM algorithm is of weak statistical significance. The algorithm is not able to equalize the statistical fluctuations of the underlying physical process. Hence the ML-EM algorithm may be replaced by a CG algorithm without loss of quality. In other words, the quality of the reconstructed images is the same in both cases, however the convergence behaviour is much better for the CG method. To improve the statistical properties of the reconstructed images, more information is needed for a better estimation of λ_b. The Bayes theory is helpful in this context. Nevertheless a good approximation of g_b is required as a basis for a good estimation of λ_b for any method.

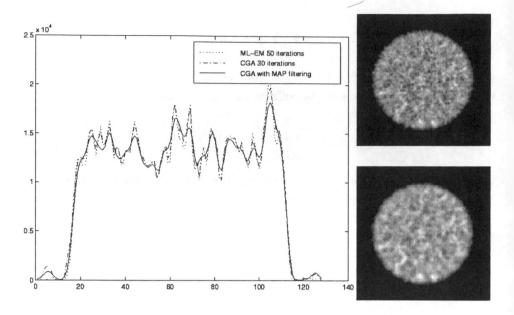

Figure 13.7: Profile of a reconstructed cylinder phantom (left-hand side) and the reconstructed disc computed by means of the CG algorithm without (top) and consecutive MAP filtering (bottom).

The estimation of λ_b depends strongly on the choice of prior information. A first attempt in modifying the algorithm has been presented, however, further investigations are necessary to find improved solutions. Essentially the MAP estimation is a modified ML algorithm.

An alternative way to take into account prior information is the use of anatomical magnetic resonance information (Lipinski *et al.* 1997).

Finally, the reconstructed images can be enhanced by applying standard linear and nonlinear techniques like edge enhancement, filtering etc. Nevertheless, these operations cannot remove errors which have been introduced by a reconstruction method of low performance. In other words, the improvement of existing reconstruction algorithms is a still challenging task.

REFERENCES

H. H. Barrett, 1984, *Progress in Optics*, volume The Radon Transform and its Applications. North Holland Physics.

S. R. Deans, 1983, *The Radon Transform and Some of Its Applications*. John Wiley & Sons.

G. T. Herman, 1980, *Image Reconstructions from Projections: The Fundamentals of Computerized Tomography*. Academic Press.

E. Levitan; G.T. Herman, 1987, A maximum a posteriori probalitity expectation maximization algorithm for image reconstruction in emission tomography. *IEEE Transactions on Medical Imaging*, MI-6(3).

B. Lipinski; H. Herzog; E. Rota Kops; W. Oberschelp; H.W. Müller-Gärtner, 1997, Expectation maximization reconstruction of positron emission tomography images using anatomical magnetic resonance information. *IEEE Transactions on Medical Imaging*, MI-16(2).

J. Llacer; E. Veklerov, 1989, Feasible images and practical stopping rules in emmision tomography. *IEEE Transactions on Medical Imaging*, 8(2).

T.K. Moon, 1996, The expectation maximization algorithm. *IEEE Signal Processing Magazine*.

J. Radon, 1987, *Gesammelte Abhandlungen*. Birkhäuser Verlag.

Y. Vardi; L.A. Shepp, 1982, Maximum likelihood reconstruction for emission tomography. *IEEE Transactions on Medical Imaging*, MI-1(2).

G. Winkler, 1995, *Image Analysis, Random Fields and Dynamic Monte Carlo Methods*. Springer Verlag Berlin-Heidelberg.

CHAPTER FOURTEEN

Inspection of Fixing Devices of Railroad Lines by Using Image Processing Algorithms

Anton Kummert

Laboratory for Communication Theory,
Department of Electrical Engineering,
University of Wuppertal, Germany
kummert@uni-wuppertal.de

Abstract

Railroad lines have to be inspected from time to time which is currently done by humans. In future, this task will have to be automated since security aspects in the context of new high speed tracks require shorter inspection intervals. For this purpose, an online analysis system has been developed, which is based on the automatic analysis of video images by means of signal processing and classification methods.

One of the inspection tasks is to verify the conditions of rail fastenings. In this chapter, principles are introduced which make the automatic recognition of railway clamps and their components possible.

The complexity of the problem described in this chapter is conflicting with very small frame rates of the on-line analysis unit and with requirements for a robust, reliable, and commercially acceptable signal processing system. The proposed solutions are designed to meet these requirements in an effective way.

14.1 INTRODUCTION

Optical and digital image processing can be used for the automation of railroad system inspection. This leads to the reduction of maintenance expenses and to the relief of technical personnel from wearisome tasks. To achieve this goal, a video sensor unit (cf. Fig. 14.1), which consists of a high speed line camera and a light source, is mounted on an inspection vehicle. The latter can be operated at speeds of up to 100 km/h during data acquisition. The on-board signal processing unit consisting of image processing hardware and a host computer performs all operations in real time. The results are displayed on a monitor (cf. Fig. 14.2). Besides the analysis of rail surfaces the system has to locate fixing devices in the images and to verify its conditions. The latter task is topic of this chapter whereas rail surfaces are not considered here. A broad spectrum of image processing and pattern recognition methods are discussed for locating and verifying the condition of fixing devices and its components.

a   b

Figure 14.1:   a) Sensor unit mounted on an inspection vehicle   b) Inspection vehicle

One of the most challenging problems of this application is the detection of screws which have to be distinguished from ballast (stones) and other arbitrarily scattered waste. In other words, three-dimensional objects have to be recognized from its two-dimensional projection where the projection axes are not exactly perpendicular to the rail surface. Furthermore, deviations with respect to form, degree of corrosion, noise, fluctuating illumination conditions, and a varying background are severe obstacles. This problem complexity is conflicting with the requirements for small frame rates and a robust, reliable, computationally fast, and commercially acceptable online signal processing system.

14.2   REGIONS OF INTEREST

An important step in any image processing application is the localization of regions of interest (ROI). In other words, this preprocessing procedure has to be performed as one part of the comprehensive analysis of video information presented through the captured images.

To begin with, segmentation of the large image regions corresponding to ballast, ties, and the rail has been performed, providing further analysis steps with expected positions or regions of interest. This segmentation has been done by using the Marr-Hildreth operator for edge detection, image pyramids for global image perception, morphological operations and a certain amount of additional analysis for the final exact determination of region boundaries (cf. (Khandogin *et al.* 1997, Velten *et al.* 1998)). The applicability of such an approach is illustrated by Fig. 14.3.

Rail and ties can be separated by the application of a specific edge detection procedure. In the output signal (cf. Fig. 14.3b) rail and ties correspond to distinctive regions and can be effectively separated from ballast.

To be more specific, horizontal projection of the binary edge image and subsequent me-

Figure 14.2: Regions of interest marked in an original video image: rail head, rail foot, cross bar, fixing device, screw.

dian filtering allows the detection of ties by using an appropriate threshold (cf. Fig. 14.4, where this algorithm has been applied to the image from Fig. 14.3).

A lot of computation time is saved by using the a priori knowledge that clamps are mounted on ties at the left- and right-hand sides next to the rail foot.

14.3 DETECTION OF CLAMPS

The geometric form of clamps is very distinct from that of the surrounding, it can be anticipated that the classification problem where the clamps have to be distinguished from their surroundings can be solved by a linear approach. Matched-filtering in combination with a suitable kind of image preprocessing represents a very effective and inexpensive solution.

Properties of the classification have to be analyzed in order to determine appropriate preprocessing steps. A matched filter determines the correlation between a pre-defined template $t\,(m,n)$ and the current signal $x\,(m,n)$. This operation can be realized effectively by using FFT algorithms. Template and signal can be interpreted as elements (vectors) of a Euclidean vector space. For this purpose, all signal values of $t\,(m,n)$ and $x\,(m,n)$ are rearranged forming the column vectors T and X. For example, all columns of an

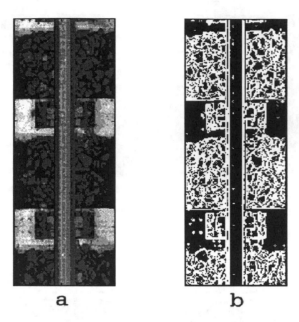

Figure 14.3:   a) Original video image sequence   b) Binary edge contour of (a)

$M \times N$ rectangular image can be stacked behind each other forming a column vector of length MN. This concept allows a geometric interpretation of the correlation operation $p\left(x\left(m,n\right);t\left(m,n\right)\right)$ as a scalar product

$$p\left(x\left(m,n\right);t\left(m,n\right)\right) = X^{t}T = \|X\|\,\|T\|\cos\left(\widehat{X,T}\right)$$

where $\|\cdot\|$ denotes the vector norm and $\widehat{X,T}$ represents the angle between the two vectors. Thus, correlation can be considered as a projection of the vector X onto the vector T.

For classification, the correlation function is usually used along with the subsequent threshold operation dividing the feature space into two halves by means of a plane. This kind of decision surface does not permit an effective separation. If the vector lengths $\|T\|$ and $\|X\|$, and thus their squared values (representing the signal energies) are normalized to a constant value, both the template and the vector X are projected on a sphere, and the threshold plane turns into a threshold circle on this sphere, providing a better separation property. The relation of the correlation function to the squared Euclidean distance often used to describe signal similarity is given by

$$\|X - T\|^{2} = \|X\|^{2} + \|T\|^{2} - 2X^{t}T$$

From this equation, it can also be inferred that the correlation function is an effective measure of signal similarity only if the signal energies of the template T and the signal X to be classified are normalized in the proposed way. With regard to the matched-filtering of an image, this condition necessitates the normalization of the local signal energies.

The term 'local' denotes the calculation of signal energy in a limited area of the template size around every pixel of ROI.

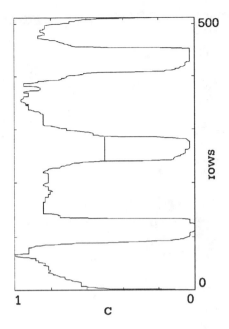

Figure 14.4: Horizontal projection of Fig. 14.2 processed by median-filtering

Explicit signal energy normalization at every image point is, however, unacceptable due to the increasing computation time. However, the equalization of histograms and the high-pass filtering carried out with respect to the whole image effectively contribute to the normalization of local signal energies. The first operation leads to a more homogeneous distribution of local signal variances. Relatively large image regions with low variance values correspond to high histogram values and lead to a better spreading of gray levels in this domain. Suitable high-pass filtering nearly eliminates fluctuations in the local mean value. In order to suppress noise, the adoption of a band-pass filter is necessary. Thus, the Laplacian of Gaussian (LoG) filter whose advantages are introduced in [5] has been applied for image preprocessing.

Preprocessing by filtering does not increase the total computation time because the pre-filtering of ROI can be replaced by the second pre-filtering of the template.

Some samples of clamps are shown in Fig. 14.5.

The typical shape of the two-dimensional correlation function achieved through the proposed preprocessing can be visualized by its horizontal and vertical 'shadow' (cf. Fig. 14.6). Shadow means that the maximal value of each line or column, respectively, is taken. All line maxima and column maxima, respectively, form the plotted one-dimensional curves.

The correlation function shows a very distinct and sharp peak. This behavior has proved to be very stable in a large set of test images, even when some clamps were heavily covered by ballast (cf. Fig. 14.7).

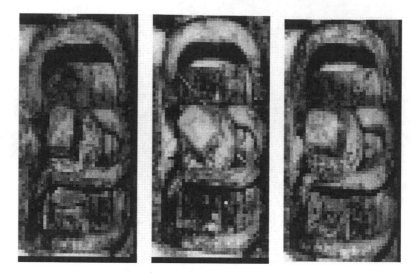

Figure 14.5: Some samples of clamps

14.4   SCREW DETECTION

After having detected a clamp, the condition of its fixing screw has to be checked. This task implies the well known recognition problem of three-dimensional objects by their two-dimensional projections under object rotations around an axis slanting to the image plane (cf. Fig. 14.8). Additionally, in this application, screws show considerable form deviations, are covered with some dirt and surrounded by a strong varying background, relatively similar to the screws themselves. In contrast to clamp recognition, the separation of screws from ballast constitutes a nonlinear problem, invoking the use of a neural network or a solution based fuzzy-logic.

The enormous variety in the appearance of the given background, ballast and garbage, has made the classificator design for screw recognition difficult. So, assembling a representative set of background samples has proved to be practically impossible. However, the screw cluster has been described quite well by prepared samples. Therefore, to build the classificator, a special strategy has been pursued along with the best possible selection of learning data. This strategy is based on the maximum generalization of the screw class and the best possible rejection of everything else. The mean value of the screw cluster has been added to the learning set and used as a start point of cluster mapping with very aggressive generalization. The RCE neural network (cf. (Cooper *et al.* 1982)) which provides a well-working scheme to learn only one class and to reject other input vectors has been chosen for classification. To improve the generalization given by the RCE network, the whitening-transformation (cf. (Fukunaga 1990)) calculated only for the screw class has been used.

This transformation is based on a principal component analysis of some type of correlation matrix

$$\mathbf{R} = [\mathbf{X}_1, \mathbf{X}_2 \cdots \mathbf{X}_n][\mathbf{X}_1, \mathbf{X}_2 \cdots \mathbf{X}_n]^t,$$

where $\mathbf{X}_1, \cdots, \mathbf{X}_n$ are signals (measured images) written in form of column vectors. The

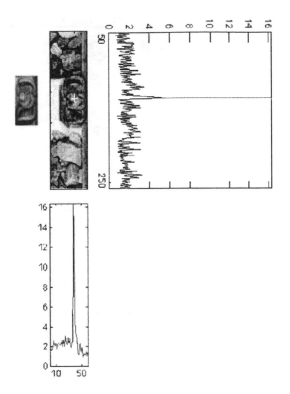

Figure 14.6: Visualization of the correlation function by means of two shadow curves. Template (average clamp image) and signal under test are shown also.

transformation itself can be written as

$$\mathbf{Z} = \Lambda^{-\frac{1}{2}} \mathbf{U}^t \mathbf{X},$$

where $\mathbf{U}$ is the matrix of eigenvectors and $\Lambda = diag\,(\lambda_1, \cdots, \lambda_d)$ consists of the eigenvalues of the correlation matrix $\mathbf{R}$, i. e.

$$\mathbf{R} = \mathbf{U}\Lambda\mathbf{U}^t.$$

Another serious problem in this application results from the large dimensionality of the feature space amounting to 750 if the pixel gray values are used as features. This affects the implicated stochastic modeling and the clustering of feature space. Generally speaking, the proper feature selection involves stochastic estimation itself. But, when pursuing this strategy, the problem of background representation through a suitable stochastic model arises because one is confronted with the task of screw separation from the given background. This makes, for example, feature extraction on the basis of principal component analysis inefficient. An appropriate feature set can be achieved on the basis of a priori knowledge about the given separation problem. The experiments with data and the considerations described in the preceding chapter have demonstrated that the geometric form detection

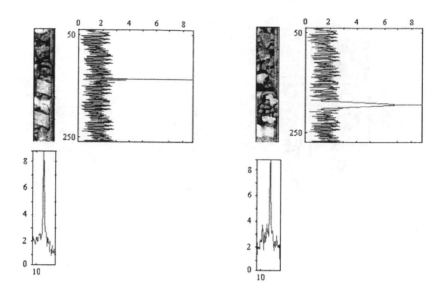

Figure 14.7: Two examples where clamps are covered by stones.

shows promising separation results. Consequently, both the stones and the screws can be equally well described by the set of the largest Fourier coefficients taken after the proposed normalization. Since the Fourier coefficients occur as pairs of complex conjugated numbers, only one half of them is sufficient for further processing.

In our application, only the 128 most significant FFT coefficients from 750 have been used for classification. To be more specific, the whole feature extraction and classification scheme for screws is organized as follows:

1. Equalization of histograms

2. FFT transform = 750 coefficients

3. LoG-filtering in frequency domain

4. Normalization of signal energy

5. Reduction to the 128 most significant values

6. Splitting of Fourier coefficients in absolute value and phase

7. Whitening transform with respect to absolute values and phase separately

8. Classification by means of neural network

Step 6 of this feature extraction algorithm performs a decomposition of an originally complex signal with respect to absolute value and phase in order to have real input signals for the neural network. Alternatively, recent work done by Miller & Bose (1998) imply the

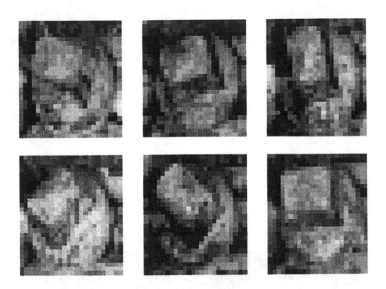

Figure 14.8: Screw samples

direct use of complex input signals, weights, and thresholds for neural nets using a generalized complex backpropagation algorithm for the training of coefficients. The very satisfactory results reported in (Miller & Bose 1998) encourage the use of a similar approach in future work.

The above procedure is performed for 25 positions around the maximum of the correlation function of a preceding pre-classification by means of matched filtering. In other words, linear filtering is used only for restricting the search area in order to save computation time, whereas exact localization is done by the above algorithm.

The last analysis step, namely classification by means of a restricted Coulomb energy (RCE) neural network deserves closer consideration. As already mentioned, separation surfaces of matched filtering are planes, circles, balls, whereas neural networks are able to realize very complicated separation surfaces (cf. Fig. 14.9).

The coefficients of the net have been determined by using a learning algorithm applied to a large data set.

14.5 SIMULATION RESULTS

The algorithms for the detection of railway clamps and fixing screws introduced above have been simulated and tested on a large amount of recorded images. They have proved to be efficient and reliable. In Fig. 14.10 three examples of visualized inspection results are shown. The first image represents the normal situation, whereas in the second image, the whole fixing device is missing. In the third example, a stone has been put onto the place of a missing screw.

Most of the included processing steps like filtering, FFT, matrix operations, and RCE neural network are designed for massive parallel computing. Special purpose chips and

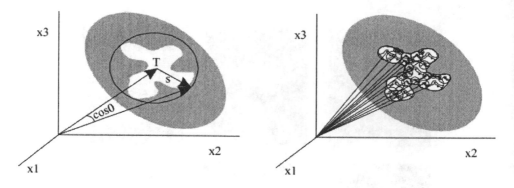

Figure 14.9: Different forms of separation surfaces for matched filtering and neural networks in the case of a 3-dimensional feature space

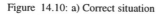

Figure 14.10: a) Correct situation   b) Missing fixing device   c) Screw replaced by stone

hardware modules are commercially available and make the implementation of the proposed real-time system possible. Thus, this chapter shows another example of a challenging applied problem being successfully solved by means of modern digital image processing.

14.6   CONCLUSIONS

The consequent use of principles of human vision and the exploitation of a priori knowledge leads to computationally fast and robust fault detection algorithms for the inspection of fixing devices. The efficiency and reliability of the methods described above have been verified by the analysis of large real data image sequences The direct use of complex input signals, weights, and thresholds for the neural network seems to be a promising approach for future work.

REFERENCES

L.N. Cooper, C. Elbaum, and D.L. Reilly, 1982, Self-organizing general pattern class separator and identifier, *U.S. Patent*, (4,326,259).

K. Fukunaga, 1990, *Introduction to Statistical Pattern Recognition*, Second ed., Academic Press, San Diego.

S. Haykin, 1994, *Neural Networks*, Prentice Hall, New Jersey 07458.

I. Khandogin, A. Kummert and D. Maiwald, 1997, Automatic damage detection for railroad tracks by analysis of video images, *in Proc. ICSPAT'97*, San Diego, CA, pp. 1130-1134.

J.S. Lim, 1990, *Two-Dimensional Signal and Image Processing*, Prentice-Hall, Englewood Cliffs, New Jersey 07632.

D. Marr, 1982, *Vision*, Freeman, San Francisco.

K. W. Miller and N. K. Bose, 1998, Mine detection using complex-valued artificial neural networks, to be published.

STN ATLAS Elektronik GmbH, 1996, benntec Videokontrolltechnik GmbH, Bremen, *RAIL CHECK Automated Inspection of Rail Networks*, Company Prospect.

J. Velten, A. Kummert and D. Maiwald, 1998, Multidimensional filters and algorithms for automatic realtime detection and classification of railroad sleepers in video images, in *Recent Advances in Information Science and Technology* (N. E. Mastorakis ed.), World Scientific Publishing.

CHAPTER FIFTEEN

Increase of Frame Rate in Virtual Environments by Using 2D Digital Image Warping

Wilfried Zeise and Anton Kummert

Laboratory for Communication Theory,
Department of Electrical Engineering,
University of Wuppertal, Germany
zeise/kummert@uni-wuppertal.de

Abstract

An image generator (IG) consists of three primary functional stages namely *database traversal, geometric transformation and rasterization* (Clay 1996, Silicon Graphics Inc. 1995). The image generation algorithms, which are used today for virtual environments, require special graphics hardware for the computation of all pixels of an image. They do not take into account, that successive images in a sequence are related to each other. These relations lead to a high degree of redundancy, since such image sequences mainly contain non-moving ore barely moving objects. Obviously, the computational load of the graphics hardware is proportional to the frame rate. Frame rate doubling, e.g. from 30 Hz to 60 Hz, causes nearly twice the hardware expense and therefore enormous costs. To avoid this increase of graphics hardware costs, image interpolation methods are of interest for achieving higher frame rates. Simple methods, like image repetition or linear interpolation with respect to time, lead to a considerable jerkiness and double contours (Bonse 1996, Girod 1993).

This paper presents a new interpolation method based on the knowledge that the human visual perception is characterized by cognitive interpretation, which structures the seen image into semantic objects (Schröder 1997). Hence, for a good modeling of the human visual system, the concept of objects should be integrated into image interpolation algorithms. In virtual environments the objects are usually described by polygons (in general triangles) (Foley *et al.* 1990, Rauber 1993).

15.1 INTRODUCTION

The field of computer-based image generation for visual, interactive simulation environments (virtual reality) is applied to architecture, town planning, entertainment, or training with driving simulators. The algorithms which are used today for image generation, require special graphics hardware for the computation of all pixels of an image. An image generator (IG) consists of three primary functional stages namely *database traversal, geometric transformation* and *rasterization* (Clay 1996, Silicon Graphics Inc. 1995).

Obviously, the computational load of the graphics hardware is proportional to the frame rate. The algorithms used today do not take into account that successive images in a sequence are related to each other what leads to a high degree of redundancy, since such image sequences mainly contain non-moving or barely moving objects.

A high frame rate is desired to avoid flickering. An increase of the frame rate, e.g. from 30 Hz to 60 Hz, i.e. frame rate doubling, leads to nearly twice the hardware expense and thus to enormous costs. Image repetition or linear interpolation is often used to obtain a higher frame rate, but it leads to a considerable jerkiness and double contours (Bonse 1996, Girod 1993).

To avoid the enormous increase of graphics hardware costs, new methods of image interpolation are of interest for achieving higher frame rates (Fig. 15.1).

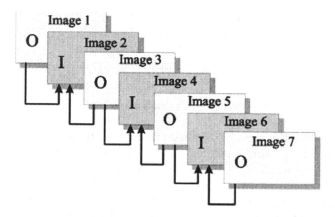

Figure 15.1: Image interpolation methods can be used to increase the frame rate.

15.2 PRINCIPLES OF REAL-TIME COMPUTER GRAPHICS

Graphics architectures can be divided into three different classes (Clay 1996, Zeise & Kummert 1998) (Fig. 15.2):

- high-end image generators

- personal computers

- graphics workstations.

In the case of high-end image generators the main application runs on the remote host. Special graphics hardware, which has a narrow band network connection to the application running on the main CPU, is used to compute database traversal and geometric transformations. The graphics database is resident in the graphics hardware.

Until recently, personal computers performed almost all of the graphics processing on their main CPU, because only marginal or no dedicated graphics hardware had been available. In this area a considerable innovation process took place, and today some graphics boards consist of geometry processors, texture memory and even memory for resident databases.

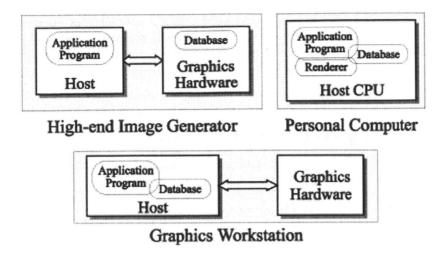

High-end Image Generator Personal Computer

Graphics Workstation

Figure 15.2: Three different classes of graphics architectures (Clay 1996).

A hybrid of these two different concepts are graphics workstations. They can have multiple host CPUs and several special processors, which make up the dedicated graphics hardware. Sometimes the host CPUs and the graphics hardware are connected via system software, compilers and libraries.

The process of displaying a three-dimensional database on a two-dimensional screen, dependent on the point of view, lighting etc., is called *rendering*. Its implementation in software and / or hardware is named a *rendering pipeline*. The latter consists of three primary functional stages (Clay 1996, Foley *et al.* 1990) (Fig. 15.3):

1. *Database Traversal:* This stage itself can be separated into three major parts: *application, traversal/culling* and *draw*. The main application process comprises the simulation process, which includes reading input from control devices, simulating the vehicle dynamics of moving objects, updating the visual database, and determining the current viewpoint.[1] This process is also responsible for supervising a possible interaction with other network simulation stations. The traversal/culling stage traverses the database and determines, which objects are visible. For each object a level of detail will be selected and a display list for the draw function will be generated. The last stage traverses the display list and sends graphics library commands (e.g. texture mapping, shadows and spot lights etc.) to the next pipeline stage.

2. *Geometric Transformation:* Here, per-vertex operations on the geometric primitives (surfaces, polygons, lines, points) are done. Geometric transformation includes modeling transformations of vertices and normals from eye coordinates to world coordinates, lighting calculations on a per-vertex basis, clipping of all objects outside the viewing frustum, and the projection of the scene onto the two-dimensional screen coordinates. From these computations, the lighting calculations are the most complex ones (Clay 1996). For every additional global light source a re-computation has to be done, and significant effort is added by distance attenuation and local lights.

---

[1] Viewpoint: position and orientation of the viewer.

3. *Rasterization:* The last stage of the rendering pipeline embodies rasterization of polygons in individual pixels, fill operations, depth comparison, gouraud shading, color blending, logical operations, texture mapping, possibly antialiasing, and also the video scan-out.

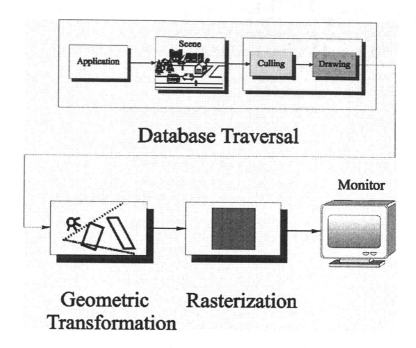

Figure 15.3: The three primary functional stages of the rendering pipeline.

Obviously, the rendering of three-dimensional graphics primitives uses memory accesses, integer, and floating-point calculations intensively. Hence, the use of 2D-transforms would be desirable to interpolate intermediate images. This concept helps to unburden the rendering pipeline and to increase the frame rate.

15.3 AFFINE TRANSFORMATIONS AND IMAGE WARPING

The human visual perception is characterized by cognitive interpretation, which structures the seen image into semantic objects (Schröder 1997). Especially, the timely visual-cognitive prediction (Bonse 1996) is realized on the basis of objects. This leads to a sharp perception of moving objects, since the eye traces the object movement. Hence, for a good modeling of the human visual system, the concept of objects should be integrated into image interpolation algorithms. To be in accordance with the human visual perception, each image in a sequence has to be separated into objects. The movement and the deformation of an object in an intermediate image has to be interpolated independently from each other object in the scene. In 3D computer graphics each object and the edges of its two-dimensional representation are known to the image generation algorithm. Therefore, no segmentation algorithm has to be used. The shape of a three-dimensional object is described by a wireframe-model, which consists of polygons (in general triangles) (Foley *et al.* 1990, Rauber 1993). Each triangle can have a special color or texture. By projecting this wireframe-model onto the image plane, we obtain a two-dimensional representation of the object, which can be used for image interpolation. The objects of computer-generated image sequences move only slightly during two successive images. Thus, the object model is assumed to be limited to two dimensions where the luminance variance is small with respect to time sampling. This concept is also realized in many modules for object-based image coding (Hötter 1992, Schröder 1997) and in the forthcoming MPEG-4 standard (Haskell *et al.* 1997). However, in this application a segmentation algorithm has to be used and each object must be triangulated, e.g. with the Delaunay triangulation algorithm (Schröder 1997). With this assumption the object movement can be approximated by the deformation of it's triangles, e.g. by an affine transformation.

Digital image warping is a class of image processing techniques that deal with the geometric transformation of digital images (Wolberg 1990). Geometric transformations describe the spatial relationship between two corresponding points in two images. We present an interpolation method that uses an image warping technique which is based on affine transformations and where the motion vectors of the triangle's vertices are linearly interpolated. The terms 'image warping' and 'affine transformation' are used as synonyms in this text.

An affine transformation comprises six degrees of freedom: translation into x-direction, translation into y-direction, scaling, stretching, shearing and rotation (Fig. 15.4). It is in general described by (Wolberg 1990)

$$[x, y, 1] = [u, v, 1] \begin{bmatrix} a_{11} & a_{12} & 0 \\ a_{21} & a_{22} & 0 \\ a_{31} & a_{32} & 1 \end{bmatrix}.$$

The transformation is done by using homogeneous coordinates. In homogeneous coordinates any 2D position vector $\mathbf{p} = [x, y]$ is represented by a 3D vector $\mathbf{p}_h = [x', y', w'] = [xw', yw', w']$. For obtaining $\mathbf{p}$ from $\mathbf{p}_h$, simply divide $\mathbf{p}_h$ by it's homogeneous coordinate w' (third component). This means $\mathbf{p} = [x, y] = [x'/w', y'/w']$. The use of homogeneous coordinates was introduced in the area of computer graphics to represent the translation of a position vector by a matrix multiplication. In affine transformations the division by the homogeneous coordinate w' is avoided by selecting $w' = 1$. Hence, the affine transformation matrix is characterized by it's last column $[0, 0, 1]^T$. It performs an orthographic or parallel plane projection from an input image vector $\mathbf{p}_i = [u, v]$ to an output image vector $\mathbf{p}_o = [x, y]$ and maps triangles into triangles. Parallel lines and equispaced points are preserved. The combination of different affine transformations by using the product of the associate matrices results in a new affine transformation matrix. Generally, this is not a commutative operation.

A transformation of a triangle with the vertices $[u_1, v_1]$, $[u_2, v_2]$, $[u_3, v_3]$ to a triangle with the vertices $[x_1, y_1]$, $[x_2, y_2]$, $[x_3, y_3]$ (Fig. 15.5) can be done by (Wolberg 1990)

$$\mathbf{X} = \mathbf{U}\mathbf{A}$$

where

$$\mathbf{X} = \begin{bmatrix} x_1 & y_1 & 1 \\ x_2 & y_2 & 1 \\ x_3 & y_3 & 1 \end{bmatrix}, \quad \mathbf{U} = \begin{bmatrix} u_1 & v_1 & 1 \\ u_2 & v_2 & 1 \\ u_3 & v_3 & 1 \end{bmatrix}, \quad \mathbf{A} = \begin{bmatrix} a_{11} & a_{12} & 0 \\ a_{21} & a_{22} & 0 \\ a_{31} & a_{32} & 1 \end{bmatrix}.$$

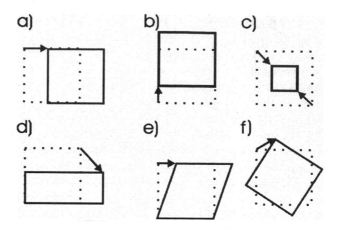

Figure 15.4: The six degrees of freedom of an affine transformation: a) translation into x-direction, b) translation into y-direction, c) scaling, d) stretching, e) shearing and f) rotation.

Hence, the transformation matrix $\mathbf{A}$ is given by

$$\mathbf{A} = \mathbf{U}^{-1}\mathbf{X} \tag{15.1}$$

or

$$
\begin{bmatrix}
a_{11} & a_{12} & 0 \\
a_{21} & a_{22} & 0 \\
a_{31} & a_{32} & 1
\end{bmatrix}
$$

$$
= \frac{1}{\det(\mathbf{U})}
\begin{bmatrix}
v_2 - v_3 & v_3 - v_1 & v_1 - v_2 \\
u_3 - u_2 & u_1 - u_3 & u_2 - u_1 \\
u_2 v_3 - u_3 v_2 & u_3 v_1 - u_1 v_3 & u_1 v_2 - u_2 v_1
\end{bmatrix}
\begin{bmatrix}
x_1 & y_1 & 1 \\
x_2 & y_2 & 1 \\
x_3 & y_3 & 1
\end{bmatrix}
$$

where

$$\det(\mathbf{U}) = u_1 (v_2 - v_3) - v_1 (u_2 - u_3) + (u_2 v_3 - u_3 v_2).$$

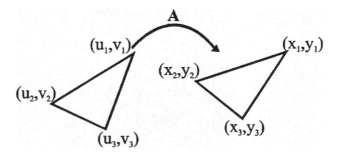

Figure 15.5: Deformation of a triangle by an affine transformation.

15.4 REALIZATION

For the computation of an interpolated image two successive images (previous image and present image), which are generated by the graphics hardware, are needed. The objects and the two-dimensional window coordinates of their vertices are known. Thus, no segmentation algorithms have to be used. An object list has to be defined for each image, which contains the two-dimensional window coordinates and the depth values of the vertices. Each image is assumed to consist of a non-moving background and a foreground with moving objects. The frame rate of the graphics hardware (e.g. 30 Hz) is selected in such a way that the motion of a vertex (linear or non-linear in time t) can be approximated by a linear motion. Thus, the deformation of a triangle can be described by an affine transformation.

For the interpolation of $N-1$ intermediate images, let the previous image be generated at time $t = 0$ and the present one at time $t = T$. Hence, the time interval T has to be divided into N equidistant subintervals. At time $t = k\Delta t$, where $k \in \{1, \ldots, N-1\}$ and $\Delta t = T/N$, we obtain the vertex coordinates $\mathbf{p}_k$ of an interpolated image by

$$\mathbf{p}_k = \mathbf{p}_0 + (\mathbf{p}_N - \mathbf{p}_0)\frac{k}{N}$$

where $\mathbf{p}_0$ and $\mathbf{p}_N$ are the corresponding vertex positions in the previous and in the present image, respectively (Fig. 15.6).

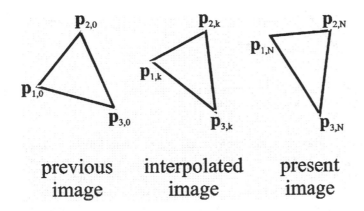

Figure 15.6: The motion of a vertex (linear or non-linear in time t) can be approximated by a linear motion.

The depth values $z(\mathbf{p}_k)$ of the vertices in the kth interpolated image are also obtained by linear interpolation:

$$z(\mathbf{p}_k) = z(\mathbf{p}_0) + (z(\mathbf{p}_N) - z(\mathbf{p}_0))\frac{k}{N}$$

where $z(\mathbf{p}_0)$ and $z(\mathbf{p}_N)$ are the depth values of the corresponding pixel positions $\mathbf{p}_0$ and $\mathbf{p}_N$, respectively. The depth values $z(x, y)$ of a new triangle in the interpolated image, which are needed for hidden-surface removal, can be obtained by interpolating the depth values of the triangle's vertices along each edge, and then across each scanline (Fig. 15.7) (Wolberg 1990):

$$
\begin{aligned}
z_0 &= \alpha z_A + (1 - \alpha) z_B, & 0 \le \alpha \le 1 \\
z_1 &= \beta z_C + (1 - \beta) z_B, & 0 \le \beta \le 1 \\
z_{x+1} &= z_x + \Delta z
\end{aligned}
$$

where

$$
\Delta z = \frac{(z_1 - z_0)}{(x_1 - x_0)}.
$$

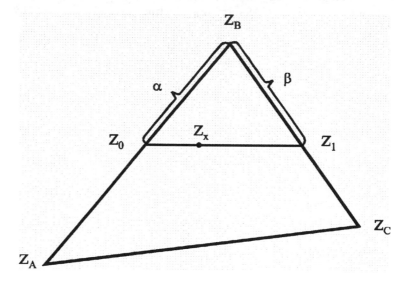

Figure 15.7: The depth values of the triangle's vertices are interpolated along each edge, and then across each scanline.

Now, for each triangle in the interpolated image a transformation matrix $\mathbf{A}$ has to be found by using Eq. 1 and the corresponding triangles in the interpolated image and the previous / present image. $\mathbf{A}$ is used to estimate the RGB values of the new triangle in the interpolated image. If the triangle is uncovered while moving from the previous to the present image, the relevant information has to be derived from the present image, since it contains texture values which cannot be obtained from the previous image (Fig. 15.8). If the triangle is covered, the previous image has to be used for deriving $\mathbf{A}$.

Each triangle in the interpolated image has to be rasterized. This means, every pixel in the new triangle has to be determined using a scanline method. After this, each pixel in the interpolated image has to be associated with the corresponding pixel in the previous / present image by computing

$$
\begin{aligned}
x &= a_{11}u + a_{21}v + a_{31} \\
y &= a_{12}u + a_{22}v + a_{32}
\end{aligned}
$$

where $[x, y]$ are the coordinates in the previous /present image and $[u, v]$ are the coordinates in the interpolated image.

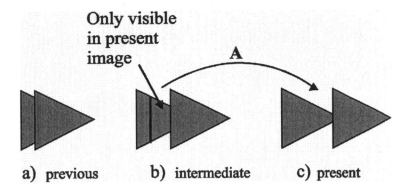

Figure 15.8: For uncovered triangles the present image has to be used for interpolation.

For simplification a scanline method for incrementing or decrementing the integer co-ordinates u and v is used. Set $\tilde{u} = u + 1$ and , $\tilde{v} = v$ then (Schröder 1997)

$$
\begin{aligned}
\tilde{x} &= a_{11}(u+1) + a_{21}v + a_{31} &= x + a_{11} \\
\tilde{y} &= a_{12}(u+1) + a_{22}v + a_{32} &= y + a_{12}
\end{aligned}
$$

where $\tilde{x}$ and $\tilde{y}$ are the pixel positions in the previous / present image corresponding to $\tilde{u}$ and $\tilde{v}$. A contains rational values and thus, $[x, y]$ will not always coincide with the given pixel grid (Fig. 15.9).

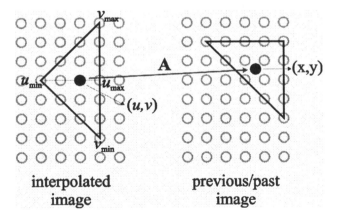

Figure 15.9: The coefficients of the transformation matrix A are rational and thus (x, y) will not always coincide with the given pixel raster.

We have to apply the so-called bilinear interpolation (Fig. 15.10), which takes the weighted mean of the four RGB values from the neighborhood. If C denotes any one of the three color components *R, G, B,* we have (Schröder 1997)

$$
\begin{aligned}
C_{bilin} &= & C(x, y_0) \\
&+ & \beta_y \left(C(x, y_0 + 1) - C(x, y_0) \right)
\end{aligned}
$$

where

$$C\left(x, y_0\right) = \begin{aligned} & C\left(x_0, y_0\right) \\ + \ & \beta_y\left(C\left(x_0 + 1, y_0\right) - C\left(x_0, y_0\right)\right) \end{aligned}$$

$$C\left(x, y_0 + 1\right) = \begin{aligned} & C\left(x_0, y_0 + 1\right) \\ + \ & \beta_x\left(C\left(x_0 + 1, y_0 + 1\right) - C\left(x_0, y_0 + 1\right)\right) \end{aligned}$$

$$\beta_x = x - x_0$$

and

$$\beta_y = y - y_0.$$

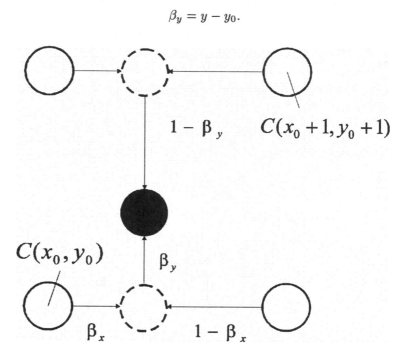

Figure 15.10: The principle of bilinear interpolation.

15.5 FIRST RESULTS

The method was tested on a sequence with resolution of 800 × 600 pixels. It describes the movement of a camera through a virtual landscape showing the front of two houses. The image sequence includes translation, rotation and scaling, and features covered and uncovered polygons (Fig.   15.11).[2] In our tests we computed one intermediate image between two successive images of the input sequence. A reference sequence has been generated with 60 Hz and was subsampled to 30 Hz. Therefore, we had $T = 1/30$ s,

---

[2]Objects in a scene are located in different distances to a viewer. Therefore, some parts of an object can be hidden by others in front of it. This can lead to covering or uncovering of triangles of an object by camera movement.

$N = 2$, $\Delta t = 1/60$ s and $t = nT$, where $n \in \mathbf{N}$. Each interpolated image had been compared with the corresponding 'correct' image from the original reference sequence (Fig. 15.12).

frame 10   frame 30   frame 50

Figure 15.11: Three images from the original image sequence.

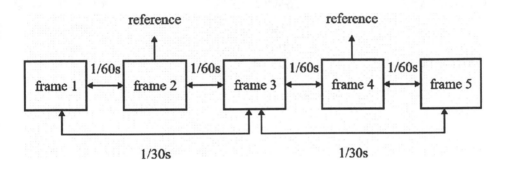

Figure 15.12: Subsampling of the original image sequence for obtaining reference images for the interpolated ones.

The quality of an interpolated image was measured by the PSNR, and the results were compared to image repetition and to linear interpolation. The simplest interpolation method with respect to the computational complexity is the image repetition. Here, the interpolated image is simply chosen equal to the preceding image. If $C_t(u,v)$ denotes any of the three color components $R_t(u,v)$, $G_t(u,v)$, $B_t(u,v)$ of an image at time t and at pixel position (u,v), and $C_{t+\Delta t}(u,v)$ denotes the color components for an intermediate image, we have

$$C_{t+\Delta t}(u,v) = C_t(u,v).$$

Linear interpolation with respect to time means that the pixels of the interpolated image are simply the mean values of the corresponding pixels of the preceding and succeeding image, respectively. In this case we have

$$C_{t+\Delta t}(u,v) = \frac{1}{2}C_t(u,v) + \frac{1}{2}C_{t+T}(u,v).$$

Figures 15.13, 15.14 and 15.15 show for three different interpolation methods the reference image, the interpolated image and the difference image.

In the field of image processing, the PSNR (**P**eak **S**ignal to **N**oise **R**atio) measures the

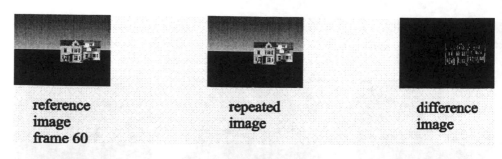

Figure 15.13: Reference image, interpolated image and difference image in the case of image repetition.

Figure 15.14: Reference image, interpolated image and difference image in the case of linear interpolation.

power of the error between the interpolated and reference images. It is described by

$$PSNR = 10 \log \left\{ \frac{255^2}{\frac{1}{MN} \sum\limits_{u=1}^{M} \sum\limits_{v=1}^{N} \left[\text{ref}\,(u,v) - \text{int}\,(u,v) \right]^2} \right\} dB$$

where M is the height of the image, N is the width, ref(u, v) is the luminance value of the reference image at pixel position (u, v), and int(u, v) is the luminance value of the interpolated image at pixel position (u, v). The quality of the interpolated image is growing with increasing values of PSNR. Fig. 15.16 shows simulation results for all three methods

Figure 15.15: Reference image, interpolated image and difference image in the case of image warping method.

and demonstrates the superiority of the new method compared to the other two.

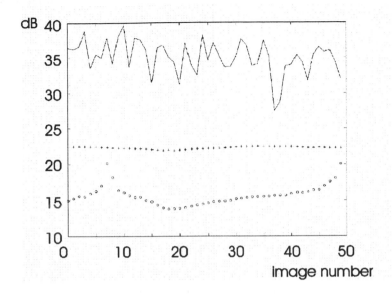

Figure 15.16: PSNR of the interpolated images for different interpolation methods (o image repetition, + linear interpolation, - image warping).

15.6 CONCLUSION

A new image interpolation method for computer-generated image sequences in virtual environments has been presented. A high frame rate is desired to avoid flickering. An increase of the frame rate, e.g. from 30 Hz to 60 Hz, i.e. frame rate doubling, leads to nearly twice the hardware expense and thus to enormous costs. The common image generation algorithms have to perform 3D geometric transformations, lighting computations, and perspective projections including perspective divisions. It is not taken into account that successive images in a sequence are related to each other which leads to a high degree of redundancy, since such image sequences mainly contain non-moving or barely moving objects. Since methods like image repetition or linear interpolation lead to considerable jerkiness and double contours, a new method has been presented which is based on the fact that the human visual perception is characterized by cognitive interpretation, which structures the seen image into semantic objects. The advantage of the method presented is its simplicity due to using 2D affine transformations exclusively. The superiority of the method compared to image repetition and linear interpolation is shown by measuring the PSNR of interpolated images.

REFERENCES

T. Bonse, 1996, Zur Konzeption einer visuell angepaßten Beschreibung und Darstellung von Bewegtbildern, *Ph.D. dissertation*, University of Dortmund, Germany.

S.R. Clay, 1996, *Optimization for Real-Time Graphics Application*, Silicon Graphics.

J. Foley, A. van Dam, S. Feiner, J. Hughes, 1990, *Computer Graphics*, Addison Wesley, Reading, USA.

B. Girod, 1993, Motion Compensation: Visual Aspects, Accuracy, and Fundamental Limits, in M. Sezan, R. Lagendijk (eds.): *Motion Analysis and Image Sequence Processing*, Kluwer Academic Publishers.

B.G. Haskell, A. Puri, A.N. Netravali, 1997, *Digital Video: An Introduction to MPEG-2*, Chapman & Hall, New York, USA.

M. Hötter, 1992, Objektorientierte Analyse-Synthese-Codierung basierend auf dem Modell bewegter, zweidimensionaler Objekte, *Ph.D. dissertation*, University of Hannover, Germany.

T. Rauber, 1993, *Algorithmen in der Computergraphik*, B.G. Teubner, Stuttgart, Germany.

K. Schröder, 1997, Objektbeschreibende Bewegtbildcodierung mit gittergestützter Prädiktion, *Ph.D. dissertation*, University of Dortmund, Germany.

Silicon Graphics Inc., 1995, *IRIS Performer Programmer's Guide*, Silicon Graphics, Mountain View, USA, Document No. 007-1680-030.

G. Wolberg, 1990, *Digital Image Warping*, IEEE Computer Society Press, Los Alamitos CA.

W. Zeise, A. Kummert, 1998, Digital interpolation in virtual environments, in *Proc. of International Conference on Signal Processing Applications & Technology*, Toronto, Canada, pp. 1005-1009.

Index